INTASC STANDARDS

D0077738

Source: Reprinted with permission of the Council of Chief State School Officers. (2010, July). Interstate Teacher Assessment and Support Consortium (InTASC). *Model Core Teaching Standards: A Resource for State Dialogue.* Washington, DC: Author.

16TH EDITION

FOUNDATIONS of AMERICAN EDUCATION

Becoming Effective Teachers in Challenging Times

James A. Johnson
Northern Illinois University

Diann Musial
Distinguished Teaching Professor Emerita, Northern Illinois University
Field Coordinator for Education, Great Basin College

Gene E. Hall
Professor, Urban Leadership
University of Nevada, Las Vegas

Donna M. Gollnick
Consultant, Council for the Accreditation of Educator Preparation

PEARSON

Boston   Columbus   Indianapolis   New York   San Francisco   Upper Saddle River
Amsterdam   Cape Town   Dubai   London   Madrid   Milan   Munich   Paris   Montreal   Toronto
Delhi   Mexico City   São Paulo   Sydney   Hong Kong   Seoul   Singapore   Taipei   Tokyo

Vice President and Editorial Director: Jeffery W. Johnston
Executive Editor: Ann Castel Davis
Editorial Assistant: Krista Slavicek
Senior Development Editor: Maxine Effenson Chuck
Vice President, Director of Marketing: Margaret Waples
Marketing Manager: Joanna Sabella
Senior Managing Editor: Pamela D. Bennett
Senior Project Manager: Sheryl Langner
Senior Operations Supervisor: Matthew Ottenweller
Senior Art Director: Diane C. Lorenzo

Text and Cover Designer: Candace Rowley
Cover Image: © Corbis Bridge/Alamy
Media Producer: Autumn Benson
Media Project Manager: Noelle Chun
Full-Service Project Management: Mary Tindle, S4Carlisle Publishing Services
Composition: S4Carlisle Publishing Services
Printer/Binder: Courier/Kendallville
Cover Printer: Lehigh-Phoenix Color
Text Font: 10.5/12, ITC Giovanni Std

Credits and acknowledgments for material borrowed from other sources and reproduced, with permission, in this textbook appear on the appropriate pages within the text.

Every effort has been made to provide accurate and current Internet information in this book. However, the Internet and information posted on it are constantly changing, so it is inevitable that some of the Internet addresses listed in this textbook will change.

Photo Credits: Photo credits are on page 417 and constitute a continuation of this copyright page.

Copyright © 2014, 2011, 2008, 2005 by Pearson Education, Inc. All rights reserved. Printed in the United States of America. This publication is protected by Copyright and permission should be obtained from the publisher prior to any prohibited reproduction, storage in a retrieval system, or transmission in any form or by any means, electronic, mechanical, photocopying, recording, or likewise. To obtain permission(s) to use material from this work, please submit a written request to Pearson Education, Inc., Permissions Department, One Lake Street, Upper Saddle River, New Jersey 07458 or you may fax your request to 201-236-3290.

Library of Congress Cataloging-in-Publication Data

Foundations of American education: becoming effective teachers in challenging times / James A. Johnson, Diann Musial, Gene E. Hall, Donna M. Gollnick.—Sixteenth edition
    pages cm
  ISBN 978-0-13-283672-2
  1. Education—Study and teaching—United States.   2. Education—United States.   3. Teaching—Vocational guidance—United States.   I. Johnson, James Allen, 1932-   II. Musial, Diann.   III. Hall, Gene E., 1941-
IV. Gollnick, Donna M.
  LB17.F67 2013
  370.973—dc23

                                                                        2012047004

10 9 8 7 6 5 4 3 2 1

ISBN 10:   0-13-283672-6
ISBN 13: 978-0-13-283672-2

We dedicate this, the 16th edition, to the many teacher educators who contribute so much to the development of the next generation of exceptional teachers. Without their professional expertise and dedication to teacher education, future teachers would be ill-prepared to succeed in these challenging times. As never before, the forthcoming generation of teachers is at the nexus of our rapidly changing society and the need to facilitate all students learning to the highest levels possible.

James A. Johnson, Diann Musial, Gene E. Hall, and Donna M. Gollnick

PREFACE

The sixteenth edition of *Foundations of American Education* provides updated, comprehensive coverage of the fast-paced world of information and underlying constructs that influence today's schools. In addition to being very current and thoughtful, this text, more than others in the market, clarifies and responds to the challenges that teachers are confronting head on and provides the foundational tools that will make the difference in their future success as teachers. Examination of critical topics related to the current social, political, and economic climate gives teachers a well grounded perspective and realistic approach to their developing teaching career. This emphasis on current practice is informed by serious, reflective philosophical and historical principles. This mixture of reflection on principles in the midst of pressures to change and remain current makes this edition especially significant.

The subtitle of this edition, *Becoming Effective Teachers in Challenging Times*, emphasizes that today's educators must confront the reality of educational challenges including increasing budget restraints, oversized classrooms, and students coming from families who are grappling with economic hardship. These challenges have always existed; however, over the last decade there has been an escalation. As a result, teachers must consider, reflect, and respond to divergent approaches to working with diverse classrooms with different types of learners. They must pull ideas drawn from different disciplines of study, different points of view, different experiences, different contexts, and different voices. This text helps students analyze these divergent perspectives through academic disciplines that include history, philosophy, politics, sociology, and the law. Students must recognize their impact on important issues such as diversity, reform, and their personal educational philosophy. Students need to understand these foundational concepts in the beginning of their learning so they can apply them to each step of their continuing development as professional educators.

WELCOME TO THE SIXTEENTH EDITION!

The fifteenth edition of *Foundations of American Education* has been updated to acknowledge the fast-paced world of information that influences today's students and schools and the other challenges that teachers face daily. A teacher's identity emerges and evolves in response to these challenges. This edition offers multiple opportunities for students to make sense of the changes in the world, to determine a reflective response to the present, and to adjust responses as new changes emerge. The sixteenth edition continues to prepare teachers for tomorrow's classrooms, today's diverse student population, and the emerging trends in education today.

NEW TO THIS EDITION!

- **Chapter 1, *Teaching in a Challenging World*—NEW!** Added to this chapter are two sections: "Teachers as Successful Entrepreneurs" and "The Challenge of Becoming a Great Teacher." New themes of meeting challenges, helping students learn, and meeting the Common Core Standards have been infused throughout the chapter.

- **Chapter 4, *Philosophy: Reflections on the Essence of Education*—NEW!** Two new sections to this chapter are "The Teacher as Philosopher" and "The Dynamic Relationship of Philosophy and Education."

- **Chapter 5, *Building an Educational Philosophy in a Changing World*** In this chapter, students are guided through a carefully scaffolded discussion, which helps them develop personal educational philosophies. New figures serve as a visual aid to help students envision how to assemble their philosophies.

- **Chapter 6, *The Place of Schools in Society* NEW!** A section on school choices presents innovative options to address the use of technology in schools. There are also expanded sections on types of public schools and on high schools that reflect current reform efforts.

- **Chapter 7,** *Diversity in Society and Schools* **NEW!** This chapter includes all new figures with updated data. Expanded sections include those on sexual orientation, sexual identity, and religion. Also featured is a revised and reorganized section on multicultural education.

- **Chapter 8,** *Students and Their Families* **NEW**! A section on parent involvement has been added to this chapter. This chapter also features a revised section on technology access, which now appears in the section on engagement in school.

- **Chapter 11,** *Standards, Assessment, and Accountability* **NEW!** Added to this chapter are new sections on Common Core State Standards, PARC, and SMARTER Balance. Common Core Standard integration is also reinforced by new tables that highlight Common Core Standards for Early Language Acquisition and Mathematics.

- **Chapter 12,** *Designing Programs for Learners in Challenging Times: Curriculum and Instruction* **NEW!** This chapter features a new section on progress monitoring. It also includes a discussion of integrating technology to enhance learning. The importance of data-driven instruction is highlighted in this chapter. Added to the Developmental Models (Comer) are the Models of Curriculum Reform.

- **Chapter 13,** *Becoming an Effective Teacher in a Challenging World* **NEW!** This final chapter provides practical information that helps the reader successfully pursue employment. It also summarizes some of the big ideas presented in the book, and provides strategies for networking and becoming part of educational associations.

- **Marginal URLs** In this edition, there are marginal links to useful websites that will provide teachers with useful tools that will enhance their instruction.

- **Revised Learning Outcomes** are aligned with the new InTASC standards.

FOCUS ON   PREPARING TEACHERS FOR TOMORROW'S CLASSROOMS

The sixteenth edition focuses on the importance of becoming an effective teacher in challenging times. Education constantly changes and teachers need to continue learning through professional development and the use of educational research to improve their teaching in tomorrow's classrooms. With many new references and a focus on the emerging trends that are impacting our schools, such as the emergence of Common Core Standards, the use of evidence-based practices, and social and global networking, this text invites students to embrace new methods of instruction. Explore this content that helps prepare teachers to succeed in tomorrow's classrooms:

- **Learning Outcomes**—Each topic of MyEducationLab™ connects intended learning outcomes to InTASC standards.

> **LEARNING OUTCOMES**
>
> After reading and studying this chapter, you should be able to:
>
> 1. Articulate the importance of educators in our society and our society's views of teachers. (InTASC Standard 10: Leadership and Collaboration)
> 2. Identify the characteristics of a profession and develop arguments for or against declaring teaching a profession. (InTASC Standards 9 and 10: Professional Responsibility)
> 3. Collect sources of evidence to show that you understand and are developing the knowledge, skills, and dispositions outlined in the InTASC standards. (InTASC Standards 1–10)
> 4. List many ways that you can improve your teaching. (InTASC Standards 1–10)
> 5. Research the basic requirements for the initial teaching license in the state where you plan to teach, including the types of tests and other assessments that are required. (InTASC Standards 1–10)
> 6. List and discuss the qualities of a great teacher. (InTASC Standards 1–10)

- **Journal for Reflection**—Found in every chapter, these activities give students the opportunity to pause and reflect on chapter content and how it relates to their own experiences in the classroom.

> **JOURNAL FOR REFLECTION 1.1**
>
> Record your thoughts at this stage of your professional development about:
> (1) the teaching profession,
> (2) its strengths and weaknesses,
> (3) your interest in teaching as a career, and
> (4) your excitement and doubts about working in the profession.

- **Teaching in Challenging Times**—Students are presented with a professional dilemma they could face and then asked to answer "What are my challenges?," allowing them to reflect on their responses to the dilemma.

> **TEACHING IN CHALLENGING TIMES**
>
> **Standardized Tests**
>
> Testing is pervasive in our educational system today. Many school districts and states require students to pass tests to move from one grade to another grade. They must pass tests to graduate from high school and to enter most colleges and universities. Teacher candidates, like you, are required to pass standardized tests to be licensed to teach.
>
> Not only are students and teacher candidates tested regularly and often, but also their schools and universities are held accountable for their performance on these tests. The aggregated results are published in newspapers and on websites. Schools and colleges are ranked within a state. Some are classified as low performing and lose part of their public funding. In some schools, teachers' and principals' jobs depend on how well their students perform on these standardized tests.
>
> The standardized tests that are being used in elementary and secondary education are supposed to test for evidence that students are meeting state standards. For the most part, they are paper-and-pencil tests of knowledge in a subject area. Although the state standards are advertised as being developed by teachers and experts, many educators argue that many of the standards expect knowledge and skills that are developmentally inappropriate at some grade levels. In areas such as social studies, recall of specific facts that cover spans of hundreds of years is not an uncommon requirement.
>
> It probably comes as no surprise that some teachers are teaching to the test, and even taking weeks out of the curriculum to coach students for the test. Some people believe that this constitutes a form of cheating. And due to pressure to do well on tests, some students find ways to cheat in an attempt to obtain higher scores.
>
> **WHAT ARE MY CHALLENGES?**
>
> 1. What are your perspectives on standardized tests at this point in your professional development?
> 2. What are some things that teachers can do to deal with the problems of standardized tests?
> 3. What are some of the factors that probably cause students to cheat?

SCHOOL-BASED OBSERVATIONS

1. Begin a list of the teaching challenges that you observe in schools. Reflect on the challenges that you had not expected when you initially thought about teaching as a career and how those challenges may influence your decision to become a teacher. How much have the teaching challenges you have observed met your initial expectations?

2. Ask several teachers what their major challenges and satisfactions are as educators. Analyze their answers and think about the major challenges and satisfactions you may experience as an educator.

PORTFOLIO DEVELOPMENT

1. Find and organize the many materials, artifacts, and records that you currently have. Examples may include term papers, transcripts, awards, letters of recognition, and observation journals. Organize these materials into logical categories.

At various points in the future, you will be drawing items out of the folio to develop a portfolio for completion of student teaching or to apply for a teaching position or national certification.

- **School-Based Observations activities**—This end-of-chapter activity invites students to apply chapter content through focused observations. Students have a chance to connect to the schools and classrooms in which they will teach.

- **Portfolio Development activities**—Students are encouraged to create artifacts for their teaching portfolio.

FOCUS ON   PREPARING TEACHERS FOR DIVERSE CLASSROOMS

The sixteenth edition introduces readers to diversity in every chapter with a new text feature and an integrated discussion of today's diverse classrooms. Explore the following content that will help prepare teachers for diverse classrooms:

- **Chapter 7—Diversity in Society and Schools**—Students are introduced to the social and educational issues faced by a diverse nation and are given opportunities to think critically and reflect on these issues.

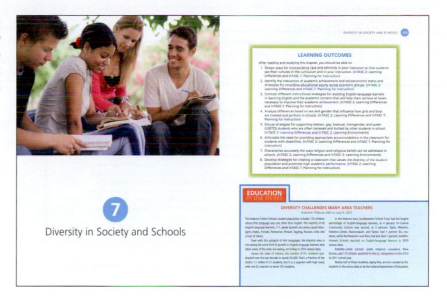

- **Perspectives on Diversity features**—Located in every chapter, these features allow students to read about real class situations that occur in diverse classrooms.

PERSPECTIVES on DIVERSITY

Thanksgiving

It's November—the time of the school year that many elementary teachers teach about American Indians and Thanksgiving, even though the traditional story does not match reality. Mrs. Starkes was no different. She was setting up her PowerPoint presentation to introduce the unit to her fourth graders in rural Texas.

"Are we going to talk about Indians today?" Joe asked excitedly.

"Yes," Mrs. Starkes replied.

"I am so excited," the petite blond girl in the first row squealed. "My great, great grandmother was Cherokee."

Mrs. Starkes was always surprised at how many of her students claimed to have American Indian ancestors, especially in November. She was determined to break the stereotypes that her students had of American Indians. She knew that some of the other teachers were teaching the Thanksgiving story with toothpick tipis, feathered headdresses, and paper-bag Indian vests. She wanted to break the Disney World view of American Indian princesses who saved early European settlers.

How could she break the myth that the Pilgrims provided a great feast for their American Indian neighbors to celebrate the harvest? It's the same story that the parents of most of her students learned when they were in school. The truth was difficult and depressing. Do her students have any idea that the Cherokees were driven from their homes in the Southeast and forced to walk the "Trail of Tears," which killed one in four of them, to their new government homes in Oklahoma?

"Do you know where Indians live today?" she began the lesson.

"In tipis," a number of students shouted. "In a longhouse," another student offered.

WHAT IS YOUR PERSPECTIVE?

1. How would you respond to the stereotypes the students have about American Indians and how would you help them develop a better understanding of the real history and current experiences of American Indians?

2. What is appropriate to teach fourth graders about the history of Thanksgiving?

3. Why do many myths and untruths about ethnic groups persist in our classrooms?

Source: Adapted from Starnes, B. A. (2009, February). Thoughts on teaching: Teaching the truth is not easy. *Phi Delta Kappan, 90*(6): 448–449. Copyright Phi Delta Kappa International, www.pdkintl.org, 2009. All rights reserved.

FOCUS ON CURRENT ISSUES IN EDUCATION TODAY

The sixteenth edition includes an integrated discussion of trends and current hot topics in education today.

EDUCATION in the NEWS

HISTORY OF THE FEDERAL ROLE IN EDUCATION

The original U.S. Department of Education was created in 1867 to collect information on schools and teaching that would help the states establish effective school systems. While the agency's name and location within the Executive Branch have changed during the past 145 or so years, this early emphasis on getting information on what works in education to teachers and education policy makers continues to the present day.

The passage of the Second Morrill Act in 1890 gave the then-named Office of Education responsibility for administering support for the original system of land-grant colleges and universities. Vocational education became the next major area of federal aid to schools, with the 1917 Smith-Hughes Act and the 1946 George-Barden Act focusing on agricultural, industrial, and home economics training for high school students.

World War II led to a significant expansion of federal support for education. The Lanham Act in 1941 and the Impact Aid laws of 1950 eased the burden on communities affected by the presence of military and other federal installations by making payments to school districts. And in 1944, the "GI Bill" authorized postsecondary education assistance that would ultimately send nearly 8 million World War II veterans to college.

The Cold War stimulated the first example of comprehensive federal education legislation, when in 1958 Congress passed the National Defense Education Act (NDEA) in response to the Soviet launch of the *Sputnik* satellite. To help ensure that highly trained individuals would be available to help America compete with the Soviet Union in scientific and technical fields, the NDEA included support for loans to college students; the improvement of science, mathematics, and foreign language instruction in elementary and secondary schools; graduate fellowships; foreign language studies; and vocational-technical training.

The antipoverty and civil rights laws of the 1960s and 1970s brought about the dramatic emergence of the Department of Education's equal-access mission. The passage of laws such as Title VI of the Civil Rights Act of 1964, Title IX of the Education Amendments of 1972, and Section 504 of the Rehabilitation Act of 1973, which prohibited discrimination based on race, sex, and disability, respectively, made civil rights enforcement a fundamental and long-lasting focus of the Department of Education. In 1965, the Elementary and Secondary Education Act launched a comprehensive set of programs, including the Title I program of federal aid to disadvantaged children, to address the problems of poor urban and rural areas. In that same year, the Higher Education Act authorized assistance for postsecondary education, including financial aid programs for needy college students.

• **Education in the News**—Every chapter begins with a real current news article from publications such as *NEA Today*, *Education Week*, and newspapers from across the country. The articles focus on educational issues and invite students to reflect on topics such as virtual schools, standardized testing, diverse classrooms, students and families, financing schools, and more.

WHO IS RIGHT?

SHOULD PARENTS HAVE A SAY IN PICKING THEIR CHILD'S TEACHER?

Yet another challenge for schools and for some teachers is the situation wherein a parent requests that her/his child be assigned to a certain teacher's class. The dilemma is debated by two contemporary teachers in the following article.

YES

Clyde Hodge teaches eighth-grade English in Stockton, California; is a chair of the SUSD Title VII/Johnson O'Malley Indian Education parent/student advisory committee; and is a member of both NEA's and CTA's American Indian/Alaska Native Caucuses (at the time this article was published.)

"I believe there are times when parents should have the right to request certain teachers under certain circumstances. I teach at a school district where the American Indian student population is approximately 8 percent, yet American Indian teachers represent only about 1 percent. I feel that American Indian students have a right to choose to attend the classes of American Indian teachers. If not, a large number of these students won't have an opportunity to be taught by demographically representative educational role models. Such modeling has proved to raise both academic testing outcomes and grades, as well as improving student quality of life.

While I believe that students should have the opportunity to achieve educational and intellectual multiculturalism, and that students need to interact with teachers of all demographic backgrounds, I believe parents should be able to request that their children have at least one teacher who represents their cultural or ethnic background. One of the best practices in teaching American Indian students is using native language and culture to promote success, which is often best achieved when at least one teacher shares the student's background."

NO

Daniel Fonder teaches fifth grade at Hillside Intermediate School in Bridgewater, New Jersey (at the time this article was published.)

"It's natural for parents to want to have input into who educates their child. Children are a parent's most prized possession, and every parent wants what's best for their child. That basic and understandable parental instinct is precisely the reason why parents should not have a say in who will be their child's teacher.

Teachers, guidance counselors, administrators, and other educators see the larger pictures. These professionals don't see what is best for one student without also seeing how it would impact the rest of the school community. Teachers who know the students and have experience creating successful classes in the previous years work very hard to make sure each student in the school is in an optimal learning environment.

To ensure the decisions being made in a school are made to benefit all students, there cannot be special interest voices for a particular student or group of students. Placing a student in the requested teacher's class in some cases, but not in others, leaves a school open to criticism by disenfranchised parents. Parental involvement should begin when the family receives notification of the student's teacher for the year—not before."

WHAT IS YOUR PERSPECTIVE ON THIS ISSUE?

Source: Adapted from "Should parents have a say in picking their child's teachers?" *NEA Today* (February, 2007), p. 43. Reprinted by permission of the National Education Association.

• **Who Is Right?**—Students read about the opposing sides of an educational issue by two educators and are directed to determine their stance on these important topics.

- **Web Solutions**—These features at the end of each chapter pose a dilemma that requires students to investigate one or more of the websites listed to help the students solve the dilemma.

WEB SOLUTIONS

You will eventually need to understand the teacher certification requirements for the state(s) In which you may wish to teach. It is never too early to begin that process; therefore, we highly recommend that you now decide in which state(s) may end up teaching, find the websites for their teacher certification offices, and search out the current requirement for a teaching credential in your field. The following websites may also be useful:

www.nasdtec.org Information on licensure requirements and state agencies that are responsible for teacher licensing are available on this website of the National Association of State Directors of Teacher Education and Certification.

www.ncate.org A list of institutions with teacher education programs accredited by NCATE and information about becoming a teacher are available on this website. It also includes links to state agencies and their licensure requirements.

- **Marginal URLs**—These URLs link out to current sites that help teachers enhance their teaching and student learning.

MyEducationLab™

MyEducationLab is an online homework, tutorial, and assessment product designed to improve results by helping students quickly master concepts, and by providing educators with a robust set of tools for easily gauging and addressing the performance of individuals and classrooms.

MyEducationLab engages students with high-quality multimedia learning experiences that help them build critical teaching skills and prepare them for real-world practice. In practice exercises, students receive immediate feedback so they see mistakes right away, learn precisely which concepts are holding them back, and master concepts through targeted practice.

For educators, MyEducationLab provides highly-visual data and performance analysis to help them quickly identify gaps in student learning and make a clear connection between coursework, concept mastery, and national teaching standards. And because MyEducationLab comes from Pearson, it's developed by an experienced partner committed to providing content, resources, and expertise for the best digital learning experiences.

In *Preparing Teachers for a Changing World,* Linda Darling-Hammond and her colleagues point out that grounding teacher education in real classrooms—among real teachers and students and among actual examples of students' and teachers' work—is an important, and perhaps even an essential, part of training teachers for the complexities of teaching in today's classrooms.

In the MyEducationLab for this course, educators will find the following features and resources.

ADVANCED DATA AND PERFORMANCE REPORTING ALIGNED TO NATIONAL STANDARDS

Advanced data and performance reporting helps educators quickly identify gaps in student learning and gauge and address individual and classroom performance. Educators easily see the connection between coursework, concept mastery, and national teaching standards with highly-visual views of performance reports. Data and assessments align directly to national teaching standards, including **InTASC and Common Core,** and support reporting for state and accreditation requirements

STUDY PLAN SPECIFIC TO YOUR TEXT

MyEducationLab gives students the opportunity to test themselves on key concepts and skills, track their own progress through the course, and access personalized Study Plan activities.

The customized Study Plan is generated based on students' pretest results. Incorrect questions from the pretest indicate specific textbook learning outcomes the student is struggling with. The customized Study Plan suggests specific enriching activities for particular learning outcomes, helping students focus. Personalized Study Plan activities may include eBook reading assignments, and review, practice, and enrichment activities.

After students complete the enrichment activities, they take a posttest to see the concepts they've mastered or areas where they still may need extra help.

MyEducationLab then reports the Study Plan results to the instructor. Based on these reports, the instructor can adapt course material to suit the needs of individual students or the entire class.

ASSIGNMENTS AND ACTIVITIES

Designed to enhance students' understanding of concepts covered in class, these assignable exercises show concepts in action (through videos, cases, and/or student and teacher artifacts). They help students deepen content knowledge and synthesize and apply concepts and strategies they have read about in the book. (Correct answers for these assignments are available to the instructor only.)

BUILDING TEACHING SKILLS AND DISPOSITIONS

These unique learning units help students practice and strengthen skills that are essential to effective teaching. After examining the steps involved in a core teaching process, students are given an opportunity to practice applying this skill via videos, student and teacher artifacts, and/or case studies of authentic classrooms. Providing multiple opportunities to practice a single teaching concept, each activity encourages a deeper understanding and application of concepts, as well as the use of critical thinking skills. After practice, students take a quiz that is reported to the instructor gradebook and performance reporting.

TEACHER TALK

This feature emphasizes the power of teaching through videos of master teachers, each speaker telling their own compelling stories of why they teach. Each of these featured teachers has been awarded the Council of Chief State School Officers Teachers of the Year award, the oldest and most prestigious award for teachers.

COURSE RESOURCES

The Course Resources section of MyEducationLab is designed to help students put together an effective lesson plan, prepare for and begin a career, navigate the first year of teaching, and understand key educational standards, policies, and laws.

It includes the following:

- The **Lesson Plan Builder** is an effective and easy-to-use tool that students can use to create, update, and share quality lesson plans. The software also makes it easy to integrate state content standards into any lesson plan.
- **The Certification and Licensure** section is designed to help students pass licensure exams by giving them access to state test requirements, overviews of what tests cover, and sample test items.

The Certification and Licensure section includes the following:

- **State Certification Test Requirements:** Here, students can click on a state and be taken to a list of state certification tests.
- Students can click on the **Licensure Exams** they need to take to find:
  - Basic information about each test
  - Descriptions of what is covered on each test
  - Sample test questions with explanations of correct answers
- **National Evaluation Series**™ by Pearson: Here, students can see the tests in the NES, learn what is covered on each exam, and access sample test items with descriptions and rationales of correct answers. Students can also purchase interactive online tutorials developed by Pearson Evaluation Systems and the Pearson Teacher Education and Development group.
- **ETS Online Praxis Tutorials:** Here students can purchase interactive online tutorials developed by ETS and by the Pearson Teacher Education and Development group. Tutorials are available for the Praxis I exams and for select Praxis II exams.
- The **Licensure and Standards** section provides access to current state and national standards.

The **Preparing a Portfolio** section provides guidelines for creating a high-quality teaching portfolio.

- **Beginning Your Career** offers tips, advice, and other valuable information on:
  - *Resume Writing and Interviewing:* Includes expert advice on how to write impressive resumes and prepare for job interviews.
  - *Your First Year of Teaching:* Provides practical tips to set up a first classroom, manage student behavior, and more easily organize for instruction and assessment.
  - *Law and Public Policies:* Details specific directives and requirements needed to understand under the No Child Left Behind Act and the Individuals with Disabilities Education Improvement Act of 2004.
- The **Multimedia Index** aggregates resources in MyEducationLab by asset type (for example, video or artifact) for easy location and retrieval.

Visit www.myeducationlab.com for a demonstration of this exciting new online teaching resource.

SUPPORT MATERIALS FOR INSTRUCTORS

The following resources are available for instructors to download on www.pearsonhighered.com/educators. Instructors enter the author or title of this book, select this particular edition of the book, and then click on the "Resources" tab to log in and download textbook supplements.

Instructor's Resource Manual and Test Bank (0-13-283682-3)

The Instructor's Resource Manual and Test Bank includes suggestions for learning activities, additional Experiencing Firsthand exercises, supplementary lectures, case study analyses, discussion topics, group activities, and a robust collection of test items. Some items (lower-level questions) simply ask students to identify or explain concepts and principles they have learned. But many others (higher-level questions) ask students to apply those same concepts and principles to specific classroom situations—that is, to actual student behaviors and teaching strategies.

PowerPoint Slides (0-13-283686-6)

The PowerPoint slides include key concept summarizations, diagrams, and other graphic aids to enhance learning. They are designed to help students understand, organize, and remember core concepts and theories.

MyEducationLab Correlation Guide (0-13-294350-6)

This guide connects chapter sections with appropriate assignable exercises on MyEducationLab.

TestGen (0-13-283681-5)

TestGen is a powerful test generator that instructors install on a computer and use in conjunction with the TestGen testbank file for the text. Assessments, including equations, graphs, and scientific notation, may be created for both print or testing online.

TestGen is available exclusively from Pearson Education publishers. Instructors install TestGen on a personal computer (Windows or Macintosh) and create tests for classroom testing and for other specialized delivery options, such as over a local area network or on the web. A test bank, which is also called a Test Item File (TIF), typically contains a large set of test items, organized by chapter and ready for use in creating a test, based on the associated textbook material.

The tests can be downloaded in the following formats:

TestGen Testbank file—PC
TestGen Testbank file—MAC
TestGen Testbank—Blackboard 9 TIF
TestGen Testbank—Blackboard CE/Vista (WebCT) TIF
Angel Test Bank (zip)
D2L Test Bank (zip)
Moodle Test Bank
Sakai Test Bank (zip)

ACKNOWLEDGMENTS

We are sincerely grateful to the many colleagues, reviewers, and editors who have helped us over the years to make this text the most popular and widely used book in the field. We thank our publisher, Pearson, for its support and for enabling us to deliver the message that we as professional educators deem crucial for the preparation of teachers. In particular, we thank Max Effenson Chuck, our outstanding development editor, as well as Ann Davis, for her work as our acquisitions editor.

We also thank our colleagues and other members of the academic community for their assistance. We sincerely thank our current reviewers for their help and guidance: Alan A. Block, University of Wisconsin—Stout; Juanita H. Brandford, Barry University; Samuel Cotton, Ball State University; Veronica L. Estrada, University of Texas-Pan American; Thuy Dao Jensen, University of Southern Indiana; Erwin V. Johanningmeier, University of South Florida; Thomas A. Kessinger, Xavier University; Linda A. Kraemer, Molloy College; Andrea Lewis, Spelman College; Lillian B. Poats, Texas Southern University; Carol Scateva, Lewis University; Heidi Schnackenberg, State University of New York, Plattsburgh; Vykuntapathi Thota, Virginia State University; and Ray Tucker, Kansas Wesleyan University.

Finally, we thank our families and friends for supporting us throughout the revision process and appreciate the comments and recommendations from the faculty and students who have used previous editions of this book. Their suggestions have led to a number of changes in the current edition. We encourage all our readers to provide feedback for improving future editions.

JAMES A. JOHNSON, professor of education at Northern Illinois University, has been an educator for more than thirty-five years, serving as a public school teacher, teacher educator, university administrator, researcher, national/international consultant and speaker, and strong education advocate. He is a lifelong member of, and active participant in, many professional associations, has been the lead author of all editions of this *Foundations of American Education* textbook, as well as the author or co-author of a dozen other college textbooks and scores of professional articles in various professional journals.

DIANN MUSIAL is a professor emerita in Foundations of Education and Northern Illinois University Distinguished Teaching professor. Currently, she is field coordinator for educational internships with Great Basin College and a member of Research and Doctoral Processes with Capella University. Diann has taught middle school science and mathematics in Chicago, Illinois; served as principal of an Individually Guided Education elementary school; and worked in industry as director of training. She has directed more than twenty state and federally funded staff development grants, developed countless performance assessments and test item banks, and co-authored *Integrating Science with Mathematics and Literacy: New Visions for Learning and Assessment* and *Foundations for Meaningful Educational Assessment*.

GENE E. HALL began his academic career as a faculty team member at the national R&D Center for Teacher Education, The University of Texas at Austin. The faculty team was charged with developing an experimental teacher education program, called the Personalized Teacher Education Program. Following more than a decade at UTA he became a faculty member at the University of Florida, then the University of Northern Colorado, and currently UNLV. He has twice served as the Dean of a College of Education. His research has always centered on studies of the change process in schools and business settings. He is the lead architect of the Concerns Based Adoption Model (CBAM), which is one of the major perspectives for understanding, facilitating, and evaluating change initiatives. He also has a continuing role nationally in regard to national accreditation of teacher education.

Publications include:

Hall, G.E., & Hord, S.M. (2011). *Implementing Change: Patterns, Principles and Potholes (3rd edition)*. Upper Saddle River, NJ: Pearson.

Hall, G.E., Quinn, L.F., & Gollnick, D.M. (2014). *Introduction to Teaching: Making a Difference in Student Learning*. Thousand Oaks, CA: Sage.

Hord, S.M., Roussin, J.L., & Hall, G.E. (2014). *Implementing Change Through Learning: Concepts, Conditions and Challenges*. Thousand Oaks, CA: Corwin Press.

DONNA M. GOLLNICK is an education consultant to the Council for the Accreditation of Educator Preparation. She previously served as Consultant and Senior Vice President for the National Council for Accreditation in Teacher Education (NCATE). She has been writing about multicultural education for the past thirty-five years. She is the co-author with Philip Chinn of the textbook, *Multicultural Education in a Pluralistic Society* (Pearson, 9th edition, 2013). She is a co-author of *Joy of Teaching,* an introductory textbook for students preparing to teach that was first published in 2007. She contributed to the 1995 *Handbook on Research in Multicultural Education,* which was co-edited by James A. Banks and Cherry A. M. Banks. She has contributed chapters and articles on cultural diversity and teacher education to numerous publications. Donna is a past president of the National Association for Multicultural Education (NAME) and has received Distinguished Alumni Awards from Purdue University and the University of Southern California. She was also honored by the American Association of Colleges for Teacher Education (AACTE) as an "Advocate for Justice."

BRIEF CONTENTS

CONTENTS

3 Historical Perspectives of Education   52

PART III Philosophical Foundations of Education

4 Philosophy: Reflections on the Essence of Education   74

PART IV Sociological Foundations of Education

SPECIAL FEATURES

1

Teaching in a Challenging World

LEARNING OUTCOMES

After reading and studying this chapter, you should be able to:

1. Articulate the importance of educators in our society and our society's views of teachers. (InTASC Standard 10: Leadership and Collaboration)

2. Identify the characteristics of a profession and develop arguments for or against declaring teaching a profession. (InTASC Standards 9 and 10: Professional Responsibility)

3. Collect sources of evidence to show that you understand and are developing the knowledge, skills, and dispositions outlined in the InTASC standards. (InTASC Standards 1–10)

4. List many ways that you can improve your teaching. (InTASC Standards 1–10)

5. Research the basic requirements for the initial teaching license in the state where you plan to teach, including the types of tests and other assessments that are required. (InTASC Standards 1–10)

6. List and discuss the qualities of a great teacher. (InTASC Standards 1–10)

EDUCATION
in the NEWS

HEROES EVERY ONE

By REG WEAVER

NEA Past President

We read about them every month in the pages of this magazine. We rub shoulders with them in our schools. We team up with them to make our communities better places.

Heroes.

The single mom who, after working hard all day as a high school custodian, trudges off to the local elementary school to meet with her child's teacher, instead of staying home and putting her feet up.

The retired music teacher who spends his mornings using music to teach language to preschool children with special needs. His students often learn to sing first and then to speak.

The middle school math teacher who stays late four days a week to tutor students in geometry and algebra so someday they will be able to attend college.

The cafeteria worker who, while dishing out the food she's cooked, keeps a vigilant eye on her diabetic students so they don't eat too much sugar and starch.

The elementary school teacher who goes to school at nights to learn Spanish so she can communicate with her students' parents.

The special education assistant who helps the special education teacher with children with the most severe disabilities—changing their diapers when they need changing.

The science teacher whose enthusiasm and preparation makes the subject come alive in her students' minds, lighting a fire that will glow for a lifetime.

The high school teacher who starts a chess club as an outlet for his most restless, high energy students—and then hauls them off to every chess tournament in the state.

The school bus driver who every year organizes a skiing weekend for inner city kids who otherwise would never get to ski or play in the snow.

The community college instructor who teaches English as a second language to immigrants at four different campuses and spends so much time in her car that her colleagues have dubbed her "the road scholar."

Heroes every one.

It is easy to take these folks for granted, though, because they don't toot their own horn. They're everyday people, not celebrities. I like to call them "unsung heroes." In fact, they don't think of themselves as heroes at all, and when someone like me sings their praises, it kind of embarrasses them. But that doesn't stop me.

Our unsung heroes are the exception to the rule that when all is said and done, more is said than done. Their actions speak louder than words. And in a society that rewards getting rather than giving, they give of themselves for the good of others, and then they give some more.

Yes, it is easy to take our unsung heroes for granted, but we must not. For they are the heart and soul of our Association. These are the folks who, when you come to them with a problem, always say: "What are we going to do about it?" They think in terms of possibilities rather than impossibilities, solutions rather than setbacks, and dos rather than don'ts.

Of course I am aware that a hero is often defined as somebody who does something dangerous to help somebody else. The firefighter who rushes into a burning building to save a child is definitely a hero. For me, however, the burn unit nurse who tenderly and skillfully cares for that firefighter's wounds through his long and agonizing recovery also qualifies as a hero. And so, too, do the many public school and college employees and retired and student educators I have had the privilege of meeting and knowing as president of NEA.

As educators and Association members, we are in the hope business, and these unsung heroes of ours, above all else, give us hope even during the times when hope seems ready to freeze over.

Unsung heroes of NEA, I am your number one fan!

QUESTIONS FOR REFLECTION

1. What is your perspective on the ideas about heroes suggested in this news item? Why?
2. What heroes would you add to those mentioned? Why?
3. What are some of the heroes that parents might have? Students? The general public?
4. What educational heroes would you expect to find mentioned in this chapter dealing with the education profession? Why?

Source: "Heroes Every One" by Reg Weaver, *NEA Today*, May 2005. See also "Classroom Superheroes" www.classroomsuperheroes.com. Reprinted by permission of the National Education Association.

MyEducationLab™

Visit the MyEducationLab for *Foundations of American Education* to enhance your understanding of chapter concepts with a personalized *Study Plan*. You'll also have the opportunity to hone your teaching skills through video- and case-based *Assignments and Activities* and *Building Teaching Skills and Dispositions* lessons.

We live in a very challenging and rapidly changing world in which there are many differing perspectives on education. These realities will greatly affect your work as an educator, and are therefore developed in various ways and used as themes throughout this book. Each chapter approaches these topics by sharing pertinent information and posing thought-provoking questions regarding the challenges educators face, the countless perspectives on education, and our constantly changing world. Our goal in this book is to help you learn more about these important realities, to enable you to make informed progress toward developing your own professional perspectives on education, to better understand our changing world, and to develop effective ways to meet the challenges you will face as an educator.

We also hope to remind you throughout this book that the major job of all educators is to help students learn. In fact, teachers, school support personnel, school administrators, school boards, educational policy makers, and all others involved in educational endeavors ultimately exist only to help students learn.

TODAY'S TEACHERS

Teaching is a profession that generally attracts the best and brightest college students into its ranks. Today's new teachers must meet rigorous national and state standards that did not exist a decade ago for entering the profession. Requirements for entering teacher education programs in colleges and universities are now more stringent than admission requirements for most other professions. Grade point averages of 3.0 and higher are becoming common requirements for admission; tests and other assessments must be passed before admission, at the completion of a program, and for state licensure. Clearly, not everyone can teach—only the best and the brightest.

Teacher candidates today are diverse in age and work experience. Some of you are eighteen to twenty-two years old, the traditional age of college students, but others of you are nontraditional students who are older and have worked for a number of years in other jobs or professions. Some of you may have worked as teachers' aides in classrooms. Others may be switching careers from, for instance, the armed forces, engineering, retail management, or public relations. Some of you may even be enrolled in non-traditional teacher preparation programs.

Whatever your particular background, we want to welcome you to this exciting profession in which new teachers represent such wonderfully diverse work experiences as well as varying educational, cultural, and economic backgrounds.

The Importance of Teachers to Society

Society has great expectations for its teachers. In addition to guiding students' academic achievement, teachers have some responsibility for students' social and physical development. They are expected to prepare an educated citizenry that is informed about the many issues critical to maintaining a democracy and to improving our world. They help students learn to work together and they try to instill the values that are critical to a just and caring society. Teachers are also asked to prepare children and youth with the knowledge and skills necessary to work in the **information age**; information and its management are critical to education and society.

Given these challenging and rapidly changing responsibilities, teaching is one of the most important careers in all societies, and especially in a democratic society. Although critics of our education system sometimes give the impression that there is a lack of public support for schools and teachers, most people believe that teachers play a very important role in our society.

This public trust should be encouraging and perhaps a bit frightening to you as a future educator—encouraging because you will be entering a highly regarded and trusted professional group, and frightening because you will be responsible for helping to uphold this public trust.

The Public View of Teachers and Schools

Teachers and parents agree that the quality of the teaching staff is of primary importance in selecting a school. Parents, guardians, and families generally know who the effective teachers are in a school and will do everything possible to ensure that their children are in those teachers' classes. At the same time, they know the teachers who are not as effective, and they steer their children into other classes if possible. They know the value of an effective teacher to the potential academic success of their children.

The extent to which parents should even have a say in picking their child's teachers is debated by two educators in the accompanying "Who Is Right?" feature.

The annual Phi Delta Kappa/Gallup Poll survey on the public's attitudes toward public schools asks respondents to grade schools in both their local area and the nation as a whole. Table 1.1 shows the results of the 2011 survey, which indicates that parents generally give high grades to the school their oldest child attends.

information age The current age in which information and its management are critical to education and societal advancement.

TABLE 1.1

The Public's Opinion of Public Schools

NATIONAL TOTALS

	'11 %	'10 %	'09 %	'08 %	'07 %
A & B	79	77	74	72	67
A	37	36	31	30	19
B	42	41	43	42	48
C	17	18	17	14	24
D	3	4	6	5	5
Fail	1	1	2	4	3
Don't know/refused	1	0	1	5	1

Source: From William J. Bushaw and Alec M. Gallup, "The 40th Annual Phi Delta Kappa/Gallup Poll of the Public's Attitudes toward the Public Schools," *Phi Delta Kappan* (September 2008), p. 12. Reprinted by permission of PDK International. www.pdkintl.org. All rights reserved.

WHO IS RIGHT?

SHOULD PARENTS HAVE A SAY IN PICKING THEIR CHILD'S TEACHER?

Yet another challenge for schools and for some teachers is the situation wherein a parent requests that her/his child be assigned to a certain teacher's class. The dilemma is debated by two contemporary teachers in the following article.

YES

Clyde Hodge teaches eighth-grade English in Stockton, California; is a chair of the SUSD Title VII/Johnson O'Malley Indian Education parent/student advisory committee; and is a member of both NEA's and CTA's American Indian/Alaska Native Caucuses (at the time this article was published.)

"I believe there are times when parents should have the right to request certain teachers under certain circumstances. I teach at a school district where the American Indian student population is approximately 8 percent, yet American Indian teachers represent only about 1 percent. I feel that American Indian students have a right to choose to attend the classes of American Indian teachers. If not, a large number of these students won't have an opportunity to be taught by demographically representative educational role models. Such modeling has proved to raise both academic testing outcomes and grades, as well as improving student quality of life.

While I believe that students should have the opportunity to achieve educational and intellectual multiculturalism, and that students need to interact with teachers of all demographic backgrounds, I believe parents should be able to request that their children have at least one teacher who represents their cultural or ethnic background. One of the best practices in teaching American Indian students is using native language and culture to promote success, which is often best achieved when at least one teacher shares the student's background."

NO

Daniel Fonder teaches fifth grade at Hillside Intermediate School in Bridgewater, New Jersey (at the time this article was published.)

"It's natural for parents to want to have input into who educates their child. Children are a parent's most prized possession, and every parent wants what's best for their child. That basic and understandable parental instinct is precisely the reason why parents should not have a say in who will be their child's teacher.

Teachers, guidance counselors, administrators, and other educators see the larger pictures. These professionals don't see what is best for one student without also seeing how it would impact the rest of the school community. Teachers who know the students and have experience creating successful classes in the previous years work very hard to make sure each student in the school is in an optimal learning environment.

To ensure the decisions being made in a school are made to benefit all students, there cannot be special interest voices for a particular student or group of students. Placing a student in the requested teacher's class in some cases, but not in others, leaves a school open to criticism by disenfranchised parents. Parental involvement should begin when the family receives notification of the student's teacher for the year—not before."

WHAT IS YOUR PERSPECTIVE ON THIS ISSUE?

Source: Adapted from "Should parents have a say in picking their child's teachers?" *NEA Today* (February, 2007), p. 43. Reprinted by permission of the National Education Association.

This same survey also asks citizens to indicate the most serious problems facing our schools. The results are shown in Table 1.2. Public school parents in their combined opinions overwhelmingly view "lack of financial support" as the major school problem.

Who Teaches in These Challenging Times?

Teachers come from varied backgrounds and hold a wide variety of perspectives. Some are Democrats, some Republicans, and some members of the Reform and other parties. Some belong to unions, but others don't. Teachers hold a variety of religious views. Because of these many differences, it is difficult to generalize about educators in the United States. However, taking a look at some of the similarities and differences among teachers may help you to understand the current teaching profession.

PROFILE OF U.S. TEACHERS. Although demographic data are elusive and constantly changing, the following snapshot of educators in the United States should help you get an idea of the profile of U.S. teachers. According to the U.S. Department of Education (U.S. Department of Education, 1999–2011), the United States has about 3.2 million public school teachers, about 400,000 private school teachers, and about 932,000 college and university

TABLE 1.2

The Public's View of Problems in Schools

	NATIONAL TOTALS		
	'11 %	'06 %	'01 %
Lack of financial support/funding/money	36	24	15
Overcrowded schools	6	13	10
Lack of discipline/more control	6	11	15
Fighting/violence/gangs	3	5	10
Use of drugs/dope	2	8	9

Source: From William J. Bushaw and Alec M. Gallup, "The 40th Annual Phi Delta Kappa/Gallup Poll of the Public's Attitudes toward the Public Schools," *Phi Delta Kappan* (September 2008), p. 12. Reprinted by permission of PDK International, www.pdkintl.org. All rights reserved.

faculty members. More than 60 percent of the teachers work at the elementary school level. In addition to teachers, our schools have about 411,000 administrative and education professionals.

Teachers should represent the diversity of the nation. However, white females are overrepresented in the teaching force, particularly in early childhood and elementary schools. Approximately 1.25 million teachers' aides, clerks, secretaries, and service workers staff the nation's public schools. There are another roughly one million education-related jobs, including education specialists in industry, instructional technologists in the military, museum educators, and training consultants in the business world. So

In addition to being passionate about helping learners, teachers must be good managers and take time to collaborate with their colleagues.

altogether, there are roughly six million people working in education-related positions in the United States, making education one of the largest professions in the country.

TEACHERS LEAVING THE PROFESSION. Although many teachers make careers out of teaching, unfortunately, some classroom teachers eventually decide that teaching is not the profession they wish to pursue. Figure 1.1 sheds light on the percentage of teachers who leave teaching.

Teachers leave the classroom for a number of reasons. Some leave to raise children and some decide to return to school full-time for an advanced degree. Others decide to pursue another career that might be more satisfying or pays a higher salary. Other reasons for leaving teaching are related to poor working conditions in schools, including lack of administrative support, student behavior problems, and little chance for upward mobility.

Teacher Supply and Demand

Many factors influence the number of teachers that a school district needs—and can afford—each year. These include the school budget, the number of students in schools, the ratio of teachers

FIGURE 1.1   Teachers leaving the profession.

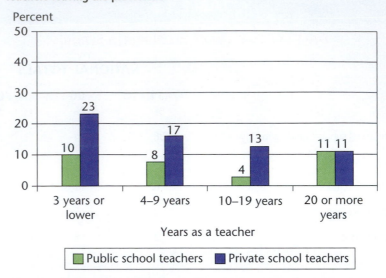

Source: U.S. Department of Education, National Center for Education Statistics, Teacher Follow-up Survey (TFS), "Current Teacher Data File," and "Former Data File," 2008–09.

Most teachers enter and remain in their profession because of a desire to work with young people.

to students in classrooms, immigration patterns, and migration from one school district to another. The supply of teachers depends on the numbers of new teachers licensed, teachers who retired or left the previous year, and teachers returning to the workforce.

Sometimes the supply is greater than the demand, but various estimates for the next decade indicate a relatively steady demand for new teachers beyond the number being prepared in colleges and universities. At this time, however, the United States does not seem to have a general teacher shortage. Instead, the problem is the distribution of teachers. School districts with good teaching conditions and high salaries do not face teacher shortages. However, inner-city and rural schools often do not have adequate numbers of qualified and licensed teachers, in part because of lower salaries. There also are greater shortages of teachers in those parts of the country with increasing populations, such as states in the Southwest.

AVAILABLE TEACHERS. The supply of new teachers in a given year consists primarily of two groups: new teacher graduates and former teacher graduates who were not employed as teachers during the previous year. Not all college graduates who prepared to teach actually begin teaching right after graduating. Generally, only about half the college graduates who have completed teacher education programs actually take teaching positions in the first few years after graduation.

It is estimated that nearly half the teachers hired by the typical school district are first-time teachers. A third are experienced teachers who have moved from other school districts or from other jobs within the district. Experienced teachers reentering the field make up the remainder of the new hires.

New Teachers. A number of new teachers are not recent college graduates. They are typically people who are changing careers or retirees from the military or business. These older new teachers with years of work experience often have completed alternative pathways into teaching through school-based graduate programs that build on their prior experiences. These teachers bring a valuable different perspective on education to their teaching positions.

GO TO ··›
More information on rural and urban schools can be found in Chapters 7, 8, and 9.

Unfortunately, still other new teachers have no formal preparation to teach; some do not even have a college degree. More often they have a degree in an academic area such as chemistry or history, but have not studied teaching and learning or participated in clinical practices in schools. Some states and school districts allow these individuals to teach with only a few weeks of training in the summer.

Returning Teachers. A number of licensed teachers drop out of the profession for a time but return later in life. We estimate that these teachers constitute about 20 percent of the new hires each year. Therefore, when you finish your teacher education program, you will be competing for teaching positions not only with other new graduates, but also with experienced teachers who are returning to the classroom or moving from one school district to another.

TEACHER DEMAND. The demand for teachers in the United States varies considerably from time to time, from place to place, from subject to subject, and from grade level to grade level. One of the major factors related to the demand for teachers is the number of school-age children, which can be projected into the future on the basis of birthrates. The projected percentage change in K–12 enrollment, by state, through 2019, is shown in Figure 1.2.

Many teachers will be retiring during the next decade, raising even higher the number of new and reentering teachers needed to staff the nation's schools. As you plan your teaching career, you will want to consider a number of factors such as salary, benefits, cost of living, workload, location, and other forces that influence the demand for teachers.

Student-to-Teacher Ratios. Obviously, one measure of a teacher's workload is class size. The number of students taught by a teacher varies considerably from school to school and from state to state. Elementary teachers sometimes may have more students in a class than secondary teachers, but secondary teachers may have five to seven classes each day.

The demand for teachers has gradually increased over time, in part, because some states and school districts are limiting the student-to-teacher ratio, especially in the primary grades. In large school districts, lowering the student-to-teacher ratio by even one student creates a demand

FIGURE 1.2   Projected percentage change in enrollment in public elementary and secondary schools through 2019.

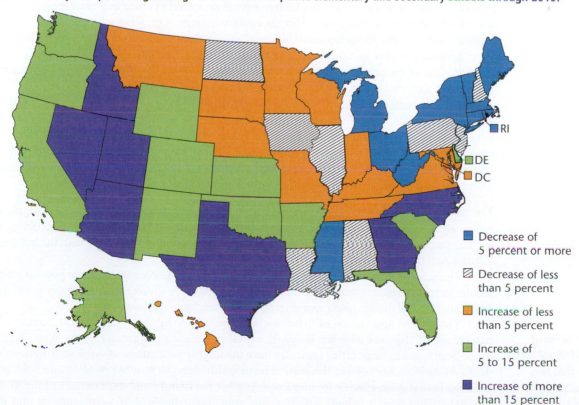

Source: U.S. Department of Education, National Center for Education Statistics, Common Core of Data (CCD), "State Nonfiscal Survey of Public Elementary and Secondary Education," 2007–2008; and State Elementary and Secondary Enrollment Model, 1980–2007.

The number of school-aged children in the United States is expected to increase during the next 10 years, increasing the need for teachers.

for many more teachers. Statewide initiatives to reduce the ratio have an even greater impact on the number of teachers needed.

Location of the School District. Within a given area because of, for example, new housing developments, population shifts may cause one school district to grow rapidly, build new schools, and hire new teachers, while a neighboring school district closes schools and reduces its number of teachers. Nevertheless, the greatest shortages are usually in urban schools with large proportions of low-income and culturally and linguistically diverse populations. Some teachers do not want to teach in large urban school districts because of poorer working conditions in some schools and relatively low salaries compared to schools in the wealthier suburbs. Other teachers believe that teaching in a large city is both challenging and fulfilling. We recommend that you explore the advantages and disadvantages of teaching in districts of different sizes and locations.

Teaching Field Shortages. Teacher shortages are more pronounced in some fields than others. For instance, as a percentage of total public school enrollment, the number of students requiring special education has risen considerably in recent years. Consequently, many school districts report the need for more special education teachers, especially in the case of certain exceptionalities.

There is also a general shortage of bilingual teachers, especially in certain geographical areas. The need for bilingual teachers is no longer limited to large urban areas and the southwestern states. Immigrant families with children have now settled in cities and rural areas across the nation. The projected demographics for the country indicate a growing number of students with limited English skills, requiring more bilingual and English-as-a-second-language teachers.

Licensed, highly qualified mathematics and science teachers are needed in many school districts. One of the problems especially in secondary schools is that teachers may have a state license, but too often it is not in the academic area they are assigned to teach.

Teachers often receive out-of-field assignments when teachers with the appropriate academic credentials are not available. Sometimes the assignments are made to retain teachers whose jobs have been eliminated as enrollments shift and schools are closed. The tragedy is that students suffer as a result—it is difficult to teach what you do not know. The federal legislation commonly referred to as the **No Child Left Behind Act (NCLB)** is designed to significantly reduce this out-of-field teacher assignment problem in the near future.

Teachers from Diverse Backgrounds. Although the student population is rapidly changing and becoming more racially, ethnically, and linguistically diverse, the teaching pool is becoming less so. The number of Latino students is rapidly increasing, pulling almost even with the number of African American students.

The school population is becoming more diverse at a faster rate than the population as a whole, in part because women of childbearing age are more diverse than the older population. The student population is also more diverse than its teachers, as shown in Figure 1.3.

No Child Left Behind Act (NCLB) A federal law passed in 2001 that sets goals for achievement for all students and requires that teachers meet certain qualifications.

The degree and nature of diversity in schools vary by the region of the country. The percentage of students who are Hispanic or Asian American is greater in the West. Schools in the South and in large cities typically have the largest percentage of African American students. Midwest schools have the least diversity, although the number of Hispanic students is growing in that area. Having greater knowledge of the history and experiences of the diverse groups attending your school will improve your understanding of your students and their families. It also sends a message to families and communities that you care about them and their experiences.

FIGURE 1.3   Race, ethnicity, and gender of students and teachers.

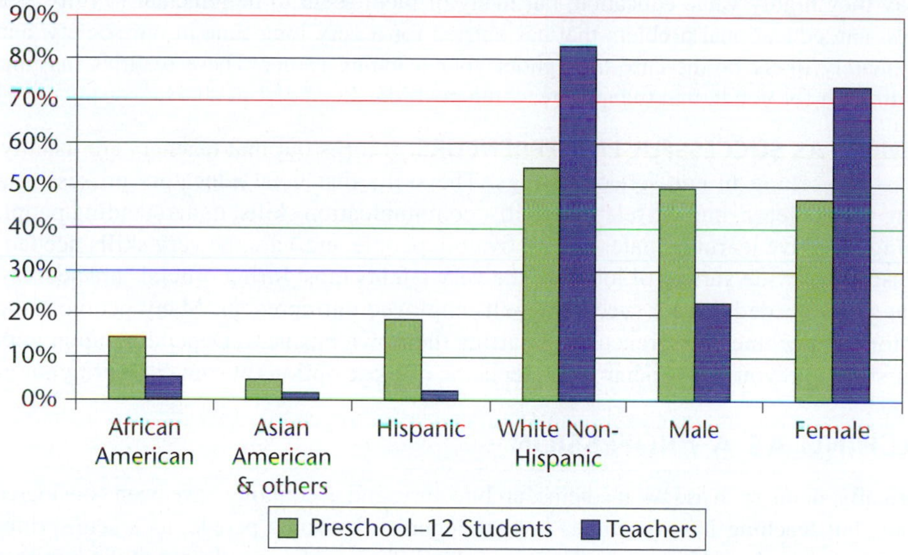

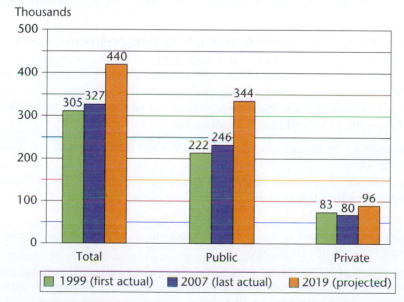

Source: U.S. Census Bureau. *Statistical Abstract of the United States: 2009* (128th ed., Tables 241 and 254). Washington, DC: U.S. Government Printing Office.

Having teachers from different ethnic and cultural backgrounds is extrememly important. Most schools are actively seeking culturally diverse faculties. Another implication of the demographics of increasing student diversity is that all teachers need to become skilled at understanding and teaching in diverse schools and classrooms.

By way of summary, Figure 1.4 shows the overall projected number of all kinds of K-12 teachers needed in the United States through 2019. However, keep in mind that the need for teachers varies greatly from state to state and district to district. When you eventually begin your search for a teaching position, you will need to more carefully check on the need for teachers in your field and in the geographical area of your interest.

SHORTAGE OF SCHOOL FUNDS. Our schools need more teachers than they can afford. This fact will be substantiated by any school hiring official that you may ask. The problem is not that there is a shortage of teachers, but rather that there is a shortage of school funds that limits the

GO TO ··⟶
Additional information on diversity may be found throughout this book, especially in Part IV.

FIGURE 1.4   New teacher hires.

Source: U.S. Department of Education, National Center for Education Statistics, Common Core Data (CCD), "State Nonfiscal Survey of Public Elementary/Secondary Education," 1999–2000 and 2007–08, etc.

number of teachers schools can afford to hire. It is perhaps a bit ironic that our citizens generally say they highly value education, but many of them seem to be reluctant to fully fund our schools—an educational problem that has existed for a very long time in our society, and will unfortunately likely be the case throughout your teaching career. These realities may make it more difficult for you to find the ideal teaching position.

TEACHERS AS SUCCESSFUL ENTREPRENEURS. It turns out that teachers are usually very successful working in non-school settings. The skills that most educators possess (such as helping people learn, human-relations skills, communication skills, understanding people, developing effective learning materials, motivating people, etc.) are the very skills needed to be successful in a wide variety of jobs, are the very talents most hiring officials are seeking, and are the skills needed to be a successful self-employed entrepreneur. Many people trained as educators do become entrepreneurs by starting their own business. Depending upon your particular situation, you may wish to consider some of these options at some point in your career.

TEACHING AS A PROFESSION

Historically, fields such as law, medicine, architecture, and accounting have been considered professions, but teaching has sometimes been thought of, by some people, as a semi-profession. This distinction is based in part on the prestige of different jobs as reflected in the remuneration received by members of a particular profession. Although teaching salaries remain lower than those of most other professionals in most parts of the country, educators consider themselves professionals. The good news is that during the past decade the prestige of teaching has risen. Most teachers have master's degrees and continue to participate in professional development activities throughout their careers. They manage their professional work, designing and delivering a curriculum during a school year. They develop their own unique teaching styles and methods for helping students learn. In this section, we explore the factors that characterize a profession and demonstrate that teaching itself is a full-fledged profession.

Professional Responsibilities

▶ Watch a 7th-grade Language Arts teacher employ many different roles of the profession— highlighting her professional knowledge and skills—in this **video.**

Being a professional carries many responsibilities. Professionals in most fields regulate licensure and practice through a professional standards board controlled by members of the profession rather than the government. Professional standards boards for teaching currently exist in about one fourth of the states; other agencies have this responsibility in the remaining states. These boards have a variety of titles and typically include many practicing educators. Not only do these boards set standards for licensure, but they also have standards and processes for monitoring the practice of teachers. They usually have the authority to remove a teacher's license.

DEVELOPING PROFESSIONAL COMMITMENTS AND DISPOSITIONS. Successful teachers exhibit **dispositions** (beliefs, attitudes, and values) that facilitate their work with students and parents. Teachers' values, commitments, and professional ethics influence interactions with students, families, colleagues, and communities. They affect student learning, motivation, and development. They influence a teacher's own professional growth as well. Dispositions held by teachers who are able to help all students learn include the following:

1. Enthusiasm for the discipline(s) she or he teaches and the ability to see its connections to everyday life
2. A commitment to continuous learning and engagement in professional discourse about subject matter knowledge and children's learning of the disciplines
3. The belief that all children can learn at high levels
4. Valuing the many ways in which people communicate and encouraging many modes of communication in the classroom
5. Development of respectful and productive relationships with parents and guardians from diverse home and community situations, seeking to develop cooperative partnerships in support of student learning and well-being.

dispositions The values, commitments, and professional ethics that influence beliefs, attitudes, and behaviors.

LEARNING TO USE AND CONDUCT EDUCATIONAL RESEARCH. Another important professional responsibility of all educators is to be able to understand, evaluate, and use educational research results. Parents rightly expect teachers to utilize the best of educational research in their classrooms, just as we patients rightly expect our physicians to utilize the most recent medical research results when they provide us with medical treatment.

Teachers can begin to better understand and use good educational research by enrolling in courses dealing with educational research, attending meetings on the subject, reading educational research journals, and doing Web searches on the topic. Teachers can also participate in research studies and, with the proper background, even design and carry out their own action research to help solve problems they face in their classrooms.

Professional Knowledge

Professionals provide services to their clients, and their work is based on unique knowledge and skills grounded in research and practice in the field. Professions require their members to have completed higher education, usually at the advanced level. The competence of most professionals is determined in training by **authentic assessments** in real-life settings. Traditionally, professionals have had control of their work with little direct supervision.

Yet another characteristic of a profession is that its members have some generally agreed-on knowledge base for their work. This professional knowledge has evolved from research and practice in the field. Teachers who have formally prepared to teach are usually more successful in classrooms than those who have no formal teacher training. Competent and qualified teachers are key to student learning.

To be a professional, teachers must also know the subjects they will be teaching. For example, secondary teachers should major in the academic area that they later will teach so that they learn the structure, skills, core concepts, ideas, values, facts, and methods of inquiry that undergird the discipline. They must understand the discipline well enough to help young people learn it and apply it to the world in which they live. As students learn about a concept or skill, teachers must be able to relate the content to the experiences of students in order to provide meaning and purpose.

Professional Skills

One of the cornerstones of the field of teaching is knowledge about teaching and learning and the development of skills and dispositions that help students learn. Therefore, teacher candidates study theories and research on how students learn at different ages. They must understand the influence of culture, language, and socioeconomic conditions on learning. They also have to know how to manage classrooms, motivate students, work with parents and colleagues, assess learning, and develop lesson plans. Teaching is a complex field. There are seldom right answers that fit every situation. Teachers must make multiple decisions throughout a day as they respond to individual student needs and events in the school and community, all while keeping in mind the professional ethics required by the education profession. Incidentally, by taking this course, you are taking an important step toward developing the professional skills needed to be an effective educator.

Qualified teachers have also had the opportunity to develop their knowledge, skills, and dispositions with students in schools. These field experiences and clinical practices such as student teaching and internships should be accompanied by feedback and mentoring from experienced teachers who know the subject they teach and how to help students learn. Work in schools is becoming more extensive in many teacher education programs. Some teacher candidates participate in yearlong internships in schools, ending in a master's degree. Others work in professional development schools in which higher education faculty, teachers, and teacher candidates collaborate in teaching and inquiry. In both of these cases, most, if not all, of the program is offered in the school setting.

Parents, and society in general, expect teachers to be competent professionals who demonstrate all of the skills just discussed. This is an expectation that all teachers must meet, even while meeting the many difficult challenges that they will inevitably face.

GO TO ⋯›
More helpful information on educational research can be found in every chapter.

This **video** showcases several teachers at different grade levels using their professional knowledge.

authentic assessment
An assessment that measures one's ability to perform a task in a real-life situation.

PERSPECTIVES on DIVERSITY

Understanding and Working with Students from Diverse Backgrounds

Jim is a first-year teacher. He grew up not having many opportunities to know or work with people from cultural backgrounds other than his own. He now works with students, colleagues, and parents who come from different socioeconomic, ethnic, and religious backgrounds. There are even a couple of students who have recently immigrated to the United States in his classroom. The only language Jim knows is English. He is worried that, due to his inexperience, he may have difficulty understanding and working with this vast array of students/colleagues/parents from diverse backgrounds.

WHAT IS YOUR PERSPECTIVE?

1. What suggestions might you have for Jim?
2. What cautions, if any, might you have for him?
3. What would you suggest that his school and colleagues do to help him?

An example of the many kinds of challenges that teachers face can be found in the above "Perspectives on Diversity" feature dealing with understanding and working with people of diverse backgrounds.

QUALITY ASSURANCE

Different professions have different means of providing quality control over those who enter and remain in their profession. Most other professions, such as law, medicine, and dentistry, require candidates to graduate from an accredited professional school before they are eligible to take a licensing examination to test the knowledge and skills necessary to practice responsibly. Some professions also offer examinations for certification of advanced skills, such as the CPA exam for public accountants, or for practice in specialized fields such as pediatrics, obstetrics, or surgery. The same quality assurance continuum now exists for teaching.

Accreditation

Both public schools and teacher education programs are subject to **accreditation programs**, which are standards established by accreditation agencies, some of which are mandated and some of which are voluntary. Accreditation provides assurance to the public that graduates of programs are qualified and competent to practice. The proportion of accredited schools, colleges, and departments of education in a state has been found to be the best predictor of the proportion of well-qualified teachers in a state. Because well-qualified teachers are the strongest predictor of student achievement on national achievement tests, accreditation is an important first step of a quality assurance system for the education field.

REGIONAL ACCREDITATION. The general concept of accreditation is related to an internal attempt on the part of a professional training system to examine and improve the quality of the profession that it serves. Six regional accreditation bodies offer accreditation to all K–12 schools and to colleges and universities. One of these six agencies, all of which are named by the general region in which they function, is functioning in your state right now. For instance, the North Central Association of Colleges and Schools (NCA) covers a large number of states in the upper central part of the nation. You might want to inquire whether your own institution is accredited by one of these six regional accrediting agencies. There is a good chance that the schools in which you will eventually teach will also be involved in some type of regional accreditation.

NCATE. Do you know whether the teacher education program you are now in has NCATE accreditation? Your college or university is probably accredited by one of the six regional accrediting bodies just discussed that applies standards to the university as a whole by reviewing its financial status, student services, and the general studies curriculum. However, professional accreditation in teacher education is granted to the school, college, or department of education that

accreditation programs
Recognition given to educational institutions that have met accepted standards applied by an outside agency.

is responsible for preparing teachers and other educators. Fewer than half of the roughly 1,300 institutions that prepare teachers in the United States are accredited by the profession's major accrediting agency, the National Council for Accreditation of Teacher Education (NCATE). However, the NCATE-accredited institutions graduate a majority of our new teachers. To learn more about the accreditation status of institutions, visit NCATE's website.

TEAC. Yet another somewhat smaller organization that offers accreditation to teacher education programs is the Teacher Education Accreditation Council (TEAC). This accrediting body, which was founded in 1997, is newer than NCATE and is also dedicated to helping improve degree programs for professional educators.

Licensure

When you graduate, you will be required to obtain a teaching license for the state in which you wish to teach. The requirements for your license are determined by the state in which you teach.

STATE TEACHER CERTIFICATION. State licensure is a major component of a quality-assurance system for professionals. To practice as a teacher, you must be granted a license from a state agency. A license to teach usually requires completion of a state-approved teacher education program and passing of a standardized test of knowledge. In addition, student teaching or an internship must be completed successfully.

States traditionally required candidates to take specific college courses, complete student teaching, and successfully pass a licensure examination for a license. Most states either already have developed, or are in the process of developing, **performance-based licensing** systems.

These systems will not specify courses to be completed; instead, they will indicate the knowledge, skills, and sometimes dispositions that candidates should possess. Future decisions about granting a license will depend on the results of state assessments based primarily on licensure test scores.

As already mentioned, requirements for teacher licensure differ from state to state. For this reason, if you plan to teach in a state different from the one in which you are going to school, you may want to contact that state directly for licensure information. The teacher certification officer at your institution should be able to provide you with licensure information and details about seeking a license in any particular state.

An initial teaching license allows a new teacher to practice for a specified period, usually three to five years, which is also known as the induction period. On completion of successful teaching during that period, and sometimes a master's degree, a professional license can be granted. Most states require continuing professional development throughout a teacher's career and periodic renewal of the license, typically every five years.

InTASC. The ten standards of the **Interstate New Teacher Assessment and Support Consortium (InTASC)** have been adopted or adapted for teacher licensure by many states. Figure 1.5 lists these ten standards, which describe what teachers should know and be able to do in their first few years of practice. You should learn the details of this important set of standards. You can do so by going to their website.

Before granting a professional license, some states are requiring teachers to submit **portfolios**, which are scored by experienced teachers, as evidence of teaching effectiveness. The portfolios that you begin to compile during your teacher education program could evolve into the documentation you will later need to submit for your first professional license. Portfolios are discussed more fully elsewhere in this book and at the end of each chapter.

PRAXIS. The Educational Testing Service (ETS) has developed a series of examinations, commonly called the *Praxis Series™*, that are designed to assess the knowledge and skills required to be an effective educator at various stages of a beginning teacher's career. Praxis I assesses academic skills, Praxis II assesses the subjects to be taught, and Praxis III assesses classroom performance. Some teacher education programs and most states make use of these tests as part of their admission, retention, graduation, and certification requirements. Perhaps you are familiar with these Praxis tests; you may even have taken some of them. In any case, you should become familiar with them. You can learn more about the *Praxis Series* by visiting its website.

performance-based licensing A system of professional licensing based on the use of multiple assessments that measure the candidate's knowledge, skills, and dispositions to determine whether he or she can perform effectively in that profession.

Interstate New Teacher Assessment and Support Consortium (InTASC) An organization that created a set of principles that describe what teachers should know and be able to do.

portfolio A compilation of works, records, and accomplishments that teacher candidates prepare for a specific purpose to demonstrate their learning, performance, and contributions.

FIGURE 1.5   InTASC Core Teaching Standards

The Learner and Learning

Standard #1: Learner Development. The teacher understands how learners grow and develop, recognizing that patterns of learning and development vary individually within and across the cognitive, linguistic, social, emotional, and physical areas, and designs and implements developmentally appropriate and challenging learning experiences.

Standard #2: Learning Differences. The teacher uses understanding of individual differences and diverse cultures and communities to ensure inclusive learning environments that enable each learner to meet high standards.

Standard #3: Learning Environments. The teacher works with others to create environments that support individual and collaborative learning, and that encourage positive social interaction, active engagement in learning, and self motivation.

Content

Standard #4: Content Knowledge. The teacher understands the central concepts, tools of inquiry, and structures of the discipline(s) he or she teaches and creates learning experiences that make the discipline accessible and meaningful for learners to assure mastery of the content.

Standard #5: Application of Content. The teacher understands how to connect concepts and use differing perspectives to engage learners in critical thinking, creativity, and collaborative problem solving related to authentic local and global issues.

Instructional Practice

Standard #6: Assessment. The teacher understands and uses multiple methods of assessment to engage learners in their own growth, to monitor learner progress, and to guide the teacher's and learner's decision making.

Standard #7: Planning for Instruction. The teacher plans instruction that supports every student in meeting rigorous learning goals by drawing upon knowledge of content areas, curriculum, cross-disciplinary skills, and pedagogy, as well as knowledge of learners and the community context.

Standard #8: Instructional Strategies. The teacher understands and uses a variety of instructional strategies to encourage learners to develop deep understanding of content areas and their connections, and to build skills to apply knowledge in meaningful ways.

Professional Responsibility

Standard #9: Professional Learning and Ethical Practice. The teacher engages in ongoing professional learning and uses evidence to continually evaluate his/her practice, particularly the effects of his/her choices and actions on others (learners, families, other professionals, and the community), and adapts practice to meet the needs of each learner.

Standard #10: Leadership and Collaboration. The teacher seeks appropriate leadership roles and opportunities to take responsibility for student learning, to collaborate with learners, families, colleagues, other school professionals, and community members to ensure learner growth, and to advance the profession.

Source: Council of Chief State School Officers. (2011, April). Interstate Teacher Assessment and Support Consortium (InTASC) Model Core Teaching Standards: A Resource for State Dialogue. Reprinted by permission of CCSSO.

Advanced Certification

Advanced certification has long been an option in many professions but is relatively new for teaching. Requiring advanced certification, like all issues related to education, is not supported by everyone.

Many states now have an advanced certification option for educators. Some states actually require teachers to progress through a series of certification levels, whereas other states have either optional levels of certification that are made available to teachers or only one certification level. You should inquire about the certification levels required or available in your state. You should also eventually understand the certification requirements and options in any school district in which you might consider working.

NBPTS. The **National Board for Professional Teaching Standards (NBPTS)** was established in 1987 to develop a system for certifying accomplished teachers. The first teachers were certified by NBPTS in 1995, and the number of teachers seeking national certification continues to increase.

The NBPTS standards outline what teachers should know and be able to do as accomplished teachers. These standards state that nationally certified teachers:

1. Are committed to students and their learning.

National Board for Professional Teaching Standards (NBPTS) A national association that creates and publishes standards and offers certification to accomplished teachers.

2. Know the subjects they teach and how to teach those subjects to students.

3. Are responsible for managing and monitoring student learning.

4. Think systematically about their practice and learn from experience.

5. Are members of learning communities.[1]

Why do teachers seek national certification? For one thing, recognition of accomplishment by one's peers is fulfilling. Nationally certified teachers are also aggressively being recruited by some school districts. Nationally certified teachers may also be paid an extra salary stipend of several thousand dollars. Your current teacher education program should be providing you with the basic foundation for future national certification.

To become eligible for national certification, you must teach for at least three years. The process for becoming nationally certified requires at least a year. The certification process requires the submission of portfolios with samples of student work and videotapes of the applicant teaching. In addition, teachers desiring NBPTS certification must complete a number of activities at an assessment center, where experienced teachers score the various assessment activities. Many teachers do not meet the national requirements on the first try but report that the process is the best professional development activity in which they have ever participated. Overwhelmingly, teachers report that they have become better teachers as a result. More and more parents in the future will likely desire nationally certified teachers in their children's classrooms.

Standards

Standards and standards-based education are prevalent at all levels of education today. To finish your teacher education program, you will have to meet professional, state, and institutional standards that outline what you should know and be able to do as a novice teacher. When you begin teaching, you will be expected to prepare students to meet state or district standards. Assessments are designed to determine whether students meet the preschool–grade 12 standards at the levels expected. Most states require teacher candidates to pass standardized tests at a predetermined level before granting the first license to teach. Some states require beginning teachers to pass **performance assessments** based on standards in the first three years of practice in order to receive a professional license.

Standards developed by the profession can be levers for raising the quality of practice. When used appropriately, they can protect students, including the least advantaged students, from incompetent practice (Darling-Hammond, 2000). Some educators view standards as a threat, especially when a government agency or other group holds individuals or schools to the standards, making summative judgments about licensure or approval. Others see standards as powerful tools for positive change in a profession or in school practices.

Standards are now used in many ways and at many educational levels throughout the nation. For instance, states have now created standards for public schools that apply to student learning. Standards usually lead to standardized testing, which can now be found in all public schools. And, as is the case with most public school activity, there are varied perspectives on the pros and cons of standardized testing in the public schools. The following "Teaching in Challenging Times" feature illustrates one of the challenges that teachers may face concerning standardized tests.

Given the trend to include students with disabilities in general education classrooms, it is likely that some of your students will have special needs, no matter what grades or subjects you teach.

 To hear a principal describe her views on standards and accountability, click on the video *A Principal's View on Standards.*

GO TO ···▸
Standards and assessment are discussed in more detail in Chapter 11.

performance assessments A comprehensive assessment system through which candidates demonstrate proficiencies in the area being measured.

[1]Based on National Board for Professional Teaching Standards (NBPTS) ©1987. All rights reserved.

TEACHING IN CHALLENGING TIMES

Standardized Tests

Testing is pervasive in our educational system today. Many school districts and states require students to pass tests to move from one grade to another grade. They must pass tests to graduate from high school and to enter most colleges and universities. Teacher candidates, like you, are required to pass standardized tests to be licensed to teach.

Not only are students and teacher candidates tested regularly and often, but also their schools and universities are held accountable for their performance on these tests. The aggregated results are published in newspapers and on websites. Schools and colleges are ranked within a state. Some are classified as low performing and lose part of their public funding. In some schools, teachers' and principals' jobs depend on how well their students perform on these standardized tests.

The standardized tests that are being used in elementary and secondary education are supposed to test for evidence that students are meeting state standards. For the most part, they are paper-and-pencil tests of knowledge in a subject area. Although the state standards are advertised as being developed by teachers and experts, many educators argue that many of the standards expect knowledge and skills that are developmentally inappropriate at some grade levels. In areas such as social studies, recall of specific facts that cover spans of hundreds of years is not an uncommon requirement.

It probably comes as no surprise that some teachers are teaching to the test, and even taking weeks out of the curriculum to coach students for the test. Some people believe that this constitutes a form of cheating. And due to pressure to do well on tests, some students find ways to cheat in an attempt to obtain higher scores.

WHAT ARE MY CHALLENGES?

1. What are your perspectives on standardized tests at this point in your professional development?
2. What are some things that teachers can do to deal with the problems of standardized tests?
3. What are some of the factors that probably cause students to cheat?

GO TO ⋯›
More information on the use of technology in education can be found throughout this book.

USING TECHNOLOGY TO BETTER UNDERSTAND STANDARDS. Just about all national and state educational standards can be rather easily found on the Web. Standards created by professional organizations can also be accessed by checking the websites of those organizations. We highly recommend that you find and carefully examine any standards that apply to your major(s) and to the teaching areas that are of interest to you. You should also become familiar with the educational standards that apply to the state(s) in which you intend to teach. Such standards should be useful in guiding you through your remaining teacher education preparation.

No Child Left Behind

The No Child Left Behind Act (NCLB) was signed into law by President George W. Bush on January 8, 2002. This act, which is actually a reauthorized version of the earlier Elementary and Secondary Education Act (ESEA), is built around four national education reform goals: stronger accountability for student learning results, increased educational flexibility and local control, expanded educational options for parents, and an emphasis on using teaching methods that have been proven to work. The act, which must be reauthorized occasionally, is likely to guide much of our public education for at least the next decade. This far-reaching law requires the tracking of all students' progress from grades 3 to 8 and also requires every student to pass the state proficiency test(s) by the end of the 2013–2014 school year.

GO TO ⋯›
No Child Left Behind: You will learn more about NCLB in various places throughout this book.

Perhaps of importance to you at this time as a future teacher, the No Child Left Behind Act requires that every classroom have a highly qualified, competent teacher who is fully certified and licensed in the areas being taught in every classroom. Like all sweeping pieces of legislation, the NCLB act is controversial, has many critics, and is subject to change. Because it will have a considerable impact on your future as an educator and citizen, we highly recommend that you review it more closely. Some educators, parents, and others feel that local, federal, and state requirements—such as NCLB and other various requirements and standards—place undue pressure on schools, teachers, and students to perform especially well on standardized tests.

IMPROVING BY REFLECTING

It is interesting, and perhaps useful to educators, to note that physicians proudly claim to "practice" medicine throughout their careers. Many people have suggested that teachers should borrow this concept and also proudly undertake to "practice" teaching throughout their careers. This interpretation of the word *practice* implies that teachers, like physicians, should constantly strive to improve their performance—something that all good teachers do. This section provides you with a few practical suggestions as you prepare to "practice" your profession as a teacher.

Systematic Observation

As you proceed through your teacher education program, you should seize every opportunity to observe a wide variety of activities related to the world of education. For instance, in addition to the observation and participation assignments you will have as part of the formal teacher education program, you should volunteer to visit and observe a wide variety of classrooms. You should also attempt to find summer employment that allows you to work with young people. The more time you spend with children, the better you will understand them and be able to work with them.

Informal Note-Taking

As you observe teachers and classrooms, write down your observations. This type of note-taking can be done in a variety of ways. For instance, when you enter a classroom, write a brief description of the setting, such as the physical appearance of the room, the number of students, the teaching devices available, and so on. Then systematically describe each thing you observe. The more detail you can record, the more you will learn from your observations.

Create a list of questions that interest you before you begin any given observation. If you are interested in how a teacher motivates students during a particular lesson, write down the question "What techniques does the teacher use to help motivate students?" Then record your observations under that question. The "School-Based Observations" feature, located at the end of each chapter, will help you get an idea of the types of observations you can make.

Analysis of Practice and Reflection

Once you have collected observations of teaching, children, classrooms, and schools, take time to think about what you have seen. Several techniques exist for systematically analyzing your observations, but equally important is taking time to reflect on these analyses. In our rush to get everything done, we frequently fail to take time to examine our experiences and impressions. However, being serious about finding time for thoughtful reflection is an important part of becoming an excellent teacher. The following processes can be helpful.

Reflective Journaling

Educators at all levels have come to realize that learners profit greatly from thinking reflectively about, and then writing down, what they learn in school. This process is called *reflective journaling*. If you are not now required to keep a journal in your teacher education program, we strongly recommend that you start doing so by completing the following "Journal for Reflection" feature.

JOURNAL FOR REFLECTION 1.1
Record your thoughts at this stage of your professional development about:
(1) the teaching profession,
(2) its strengths and weaknesses,
(3) your interest in teaching as a career, and
(4) your excitement and doubts about working in the profession.

You can go about keeping a journal in many ways. All you need is something to write on and the will to write. A spiral notebook, a three-ring binder, or a computer works fine. Preferably at the end of each day (at the very least once each week), briefly summarize your thoughts about and reactions to the major events and concepts you have experienced and learned. Spend more time thinking and reflecting, and write down only a brief summary. We believe that your journal should be brief, reflective, candid, personal, and preferably private, something like a personal diary. Try to be perfectly honest in your journal and not worry about someone evaluating your opinions.

When you start to work in schools, you will discover (if you have not already done so) that teachers in elementary and secondary schools use journaling with their students. Something about thinking and then writing down our thoughts about what we have learned helps us to internalize, better understand, and remember what we have learned.

Within each chapter in this book, we offer several suggestions for entries in your journal. We sincerely believe that reflective journaling throughout your teacher education program will enrich your learning and better prepare you for teaching.

Folio/Portfolio Development

As you move through your teacher education program and into your career as a teacher, you will find that you have been collecting stacks, boxes, and files of information and "stuff" related to you, your teaching, and the accomplishments of the students you have taught.

COLLECTING AND ORGANIZING MATERIAL. If you are like most teachers, you will not know for sure what to do with all of the teaching materials that you accumulate, yet you will be reluctant to throw any of it away. Be very careful about discarding material until you have organized a folio and anticipated the needs of various portfolios that you might have to prepare. A *folio* is an organized compilation of all the products, records, accomplishments, and testimonies of a teacher and his or her students. Imagine the folio as a large file drawer with different compartments and file folders. Some of the material included is related directly to you and your background. Other items or artifacts reflect what others have said about you. Other materials may include examples of projects that your students have completed.

A *portfolio* is a special compilation assembled from the folio for a specific occasion or purpose, such as a job interview or an application for an outstanding teacher award. The portfolio might also be used by you and your professors throughout your teacher education program to document your performance in meeting state, professional, and institutional standards. Portfolios are required in some states as evidence that you should be granted a professional teaching license after the first few years of actual work in classrooms. Portfolios will also be required for NBPTS certification later in your career. A folio or portfolio can be organized in any way you think will be most useful.

The occasions on which other people recognize your contributions and achievements are called *attestations*. Awards, letters of commendation, newspaper articles, and information on elected positions and committee memberships are examples of attestation items to keep in your folio.

Through your efforts as a teacher candidate and teacher, students complete assignments, assemble projects, achieve on examinations, and receive awards. Compile the works and successes of the people you have worked with, along with photographs and video records of your classroom and student projects. You may want to include videotapes of your teaching with a description of your classroom context and a written analysis of your teaching. Also include copies of your best lesson plans, committee reports, grant proposals, and other products that have resulted from your efforts as a leader.

PORTFOLIO DEVELOPMENT TASKS. To help you with your folio, we have included at the end of each chapter several suggestions in the Portfolio Development section. We have selected topics and tasks that are important to you at this early point in your teacher education program; in fact, these suggestions anticipate some of the items you may need to include in future portfolio presentations.

BEGINNING AND DEVELOPING YOUR CAREER

The following information will hopefully help you to learn more about becoming a certified educator in your field and in the state(s) where you hope to teach, to learn more about teacher salaries and benefits, to apply for teaching positions, and to eventually locate a teaching position.

Becoming Licensed

All teachers must obtain a license before they can legally teach in public schools. Many private schools also require their teachers to be licensed. Each state determines its own teacher licensure requirements.

LICENSURE TESTS. Most states require teacher candidates to pass one or more standardized tests at a specified level to be eligible for their first license to teach. Written assessments are required in many states, and many states require basic skills tests; in fact, many institutions require candidates to pass these tests before they are admitted into teacher education programs. More than half the states require candidates to pass tests in both professional pedagogical and content or subject-area knowledge. The cutoff scores that determine passing are set by states and vary greatly. Teacher candidates who do not pass the test in one state may be able to pass in another state that has a lower cutoff score.

An increasing number of states are requiring future teachers to major in an academic area rather than only in "education." Students complete courses in education, field experiences, and student teaching or an internship along with courses in a chosen academic major to become eligible for a license when the program is completed. You should clearly understand the requirements for a license in the state in which you are attending school and in any states in which you may wish to teach.

Searching for a Teaching Position

Teacher education candidates should begin thinking about employment early in their college careers. A helpful annual resource, which may be available in your college's job placement office, is the *Job Search Handbook for Educators* from the American Association for Employment in Education. This handbook contains suggestions for preparing your résumé, cover letters, and letters of inquiry; it also provides excellent practical suggestions for improving your interviewing techniques. Information on teacher supply and demand in different fields is included in the handbook as well.

School districts typically would like applicants to present evidence that responds to the following questions (along with portfolios containing illustrations of performance, which are very helpful in this process):

1. Can the candidate do the job? Does the candidate have the necessary academic background? Can the candidate provide evidence that his or her students learned something? Does he or she know how to assess learning? Is he or she sensitive to the needs of diverse children? Can the candidate respond well to individual differences? How strong is he or she with regard to community activities?

2. Will the candidate do the job? What interview evidence does the candidate provide that communicates a professional commitment to getting the job done?

3. Will the candidate fit in? Is this candidate a good match for the needs of the district and the student needs as identified? How will the candidate work with other teachers and staff?

4. Will the candidate express well what he or she wants in a professional assignment? Does the candidate have personal and professional standards of his or her own?

5. Does the district's vision match the candidate's vision?

Understanding the expectations of both the district and the candidate is critical if the candidate is to be successful.

You may also find that using *social media* can be helpful in your eventual search for a teaching position. You will undoubtedly need to be creative in doing so, but this rapidly developing, amazing network can greatly and rather easily expand your network of potentially useful connections.

Salaries in a Changing World

Teaching salaries vary considerably from state to state and from school district to school district. One reason for the higher salaries in some districts is the difference in the cost of living from one area to another. However, cost of living alone does not explain the differences. Some states and some school districts view teachers as professionals, have high expectations for them, support them through mentoring and professional development, use multiple assessments to determine teacher effectiveness, and pay salaries commensurate with those of other professionals.

SALARY DIFFERENCES. Each state's board of education is an agent of the state and is therefore empowered to set salary levels for employees of the school districts it governs. Each school system typically has a **salary schedule** that outlines the minimum and maximum salary for several levels of study beyond the bachelor's degree and for each year of teaching experience. For example, a

 To hear one superintendent's views about performance pay, click on the video *Performance Pay: A Superintendent's Perspective.*

salary schedule A printed negotiated schedule that lists salary levels based on years of experience and education.

beginning teacher with a bachelor's degree might be paid $35,000, and one with a master's degree might be paid $42,000. Teachers with twenty years of experience might be paid $50,000 to $76,000, depending on the school district in which they are employed. Schools also typically pay extra for additional duties such as coaching or working with extracurricular activities.

ADDITIONAL BENEFITS. All full-time teachers receive additional benefits that, when added to their basic salary, constitute their total compensation package. When you pursue your first teaching position, you will want to inquire about these benefits as well as the salary. Although the salary is usually of first concern to a teacher, additional benefits are equally important over the long term. Additional benefits vary from school to school but frequently include some type of health insurance benefits—hospitalization insurance, medical/surgical coverage, and major medical insurance. Somewhat less frequently, a teacher's medical insurance also includes dental care and prescription drugs; it may include coverage of eyeglasses and other types of less common medical services. Benefits often include a group life insurance policy as well.

Retirement Benefits

Full-time public school teachers are usually eligible for retirement benefits as part of their total compensation package. These benefits also vary from state to state. In some states, teachers receive a combination of state teacher retirement and Social Security retirement. In other states, a teacher's retirement may depend totally on a state program and be divorced entirely from the federal Social Security retirement system. It is sometimes possible for teachers who move from state to state to transfer their retirement benefits to the state in which they ultimately retire. A teacher's retirement package is an extremely important part of the total compensation package and needs to be well understood by everyone entering the profession.

Working Conditions

Almost everyone feels better about his or her work when the environment is supportive and conducive to high-quality output. The same is true for teachers and students. Like other factors in education, working conditions differ greatly from school to school. Within a single school district, the conditions can change dramatically across neighborhoods. Some schools are beautiful sprawling campuses with the latest technology. Unfortunately, in at least some other schools, toilets are backed up, paint is peeling off the walls, classes are held in storage rooms, or administrators are repressive. Most teachers who begin their careers in the second type of setting either aggressively seek assignments in other schools as soon as possible or leave the profession.

Teachers work under very different conditions from those of most other professionals. Secondary and middle school teachers usually work with students in forty-five- to fifty-five-minute time periods with brief breaks between classes. Elementary and early childhood teachers are usually in self-contained classrooms in which they have few breaks, and they even have to supervise students during recesses and lunch periods. They have little time during the school day to work with colleagues or to plan for the next lesson or the next day. In many schools, teachers still have limited access to telephones or computers for support in their work.

Improving Through Experience

Like all other professionals, teachers become more accomplished through experience. As mentioned before, most states do not grant a professional license to teachers until they have taught for at least three years. Teachers cannot seek national certification from the National Board for Professional Teaching Standards until they have taught for three years. When teachers leave the profession in their first few years of practice, schools lose an important developing resource. Good professional development programs for teachers such as **induction** programs, which provide special help for new teachers during their first few years, also help to retain new teachers.

Many schools now have a system that provides **mentoring** among teachers. This peer mentoring system is designed to facilitate teachers helping one another. As part of a new teacher induction program, many of these schools assign an experienced master teacher to mentor beginning teachers. When you search for your first teaching job, find out whether the school district provides induction programs, mentors, and professional development, especially for

induction Years one to three of full-time teaching.

mentoring An experienced professional helping a less experienced colleague.

beginning teachers. These are services hopefully offered by your school district that help you improve your skills as an educator.

Developing as a Teacher

Most educators feel that teaching improves dramatically during the first five years of practice. Often teachers hone their skills alone as they practice in their own classrooms and take advantage of available professional development activities. A more promising practice is the assignment of mentors to new teachers to assist them in developing their skills during the early years of practice.

Experienced teachers see teaching as a public endeavor. They welcome parents and others to the classroom. As cooperating teachers and mentors, they become actively engaged with higher education faculty in preparing new teachers. They become researchers as they critically examine their own practice, testing various strategies to help students learn and sharing their findings with colleagues in faculty and professional meetings.

RENEWAL OF LICENSE. Most states require teaching licenses to be renewed periodically. A professional license is usually not granted until after several years of successful practice. Some states require a master's degree; a few require the successful completion of a portfolio with videotapes of teaching that are judged by experienced teachers. To retain a license throughout one's career, continuing professional development activities will probably be required.

THE CHALLENGES OF BECOMING A GREAT EDUCATOR

We all live in a challenging and rapidly changing world, especially the professional world in which educators live. Many—if not most—of the topics discussed in this chapter will change over time; and you will need to keep up on current educational trends throughout your career as an educator.

Continuing professional development is one of the ongoing activities of career teachers. Often teachers return to college for a master's degree that may help to increase their knowledge and skills related to teaching and learning and the subjects they teach. They learn new skills such as the use of the Internet to help students learn. They learn more about the subjects they teach through formal courses, reading on their own and exploring the Internet, work in related businesses in the summers, or travel as time and resources permit. Teachers ask colleagues to observe their teaching and provide feedback for improving their work. They seek advice from other teachers and professionals with whom they work. They join and become active in professional organizations, attend and participate in professional meetings, read educational journals, explore and participate in educational research, keep up on world events, and so forth. Doing as many of these things as possible will improve your work as an educator and will even make your work more enjoyable.

Participants at a *2008 Phi Delta Kappa Summit on High-Performing Educators* developed a list of the qualities of a great teacher, which are shown in Figure 1.6. This list is a wonderful set of goals for you to keep in mind as you look ahead to your career as a "great educator."

> To hear two principals' views on what it means to be a professional, click on the video *Teachers as Professionals: Two Principals' Views.*

FIGURE 1.6	A Great Teacher

- Has the ability to be flexible, optimistic, self-reflective, progressive, and innovative;
- Must possess the ability to build relationships with students and teachers and have a passion for teaching;
- Excites a passion for learning in his or her students through skillful facilitation, using twenty-first century tools;
- Goes beyond the classroom as a collaborator with colleagues;
- Wants to improve himself or herself by learning good instructional skills;
- Is someone who knows the curriculum and works well as part of a team;
- Builds relationships and facilitates lifelong learning;

- Collaborates with families, peers, and the community;
- Shows appreciation and enthusiasm for cultural differences;
- Inspires others to achieve their potential;
- Understands the complexities of the teaching and learning environment;
- Has consistently high expectations for all students;
- Recognizes and adapts when he or she isn't getting through to students;
- Addresses the needs of the whole child;
- Uses assessment to inform instructional decision making; and
- Gives back through mentoring.

Source: Erin Young, "What Makes a Great Teacher?" *Phi Delta Kappan* (February 2009), p. 439. Reprinted by permission of *PDK International*, www.pdkintl.org. All rights reserved.

SUMMARY

TODAY'S TEACHERS

- There are about four million public and private school teachers—who are generally highly regarded and respected—in the United States today.
- Parents feel that adequate funding is the major problem in our public schools.
- Educators must constantly be attuned to the many different perspectives on education that are held by policy makers, parents, students, fellow educators, and society in general.
- Teacher supply and demand and teacher salaries vary greatly from place to place.

TEACHING AS A PROFESSION

- Educators must develop many professional skills, commitments, and dispositions to be effective teachers, and their major professional responsibility is to help students learn.
- The dispositions needed by teachers include enthusiasm for the subjects they teach, a commitment to continuing education, a belief that all children can learn, valuing communication with everyone, and valuing productive relationships.
- Teachers must have a keen understanding of teaching and learning, and possess the dispositions that help students learn.
- Successful teachers are reflective about their work, as shown in their ability to gather, analyze, and use data to improve their teaching.
- These teachers have a natural curiosity about their work and are continually searching for better answers to the challenges they face, and work to refine their professional skills throughout their entire career.

QUALITY ASSURANCE

- Each state determines its own teaching requirements and issues its own teaching certificates.
- A variety of agencies are attempting to improve the education profession through accreditation programs.
- InTASC has created a list of ten standards that describe what teachers should know and be able to do.

- PRAXIS examinations are designed to assess the knowledge and skills required to be an effective teacher.
- The NBPTS is a system for granting certification for accomplished teachers.
- Standards and standards-based education are prevalent at all levels of education today.

IMPROVING BY REFLECTING

- You can learn a good deal about teaching through systematic observation and reflective journaling.
- Beginning in their teacher education programs, teachers should write in reflective journals, collect and organize information and data, and compile information from their folios into portfolios for specific purposes such as performance assessments and job applications.
- Collecting, organizing, and saving material you produce during your teacher preparation program can help you learn and be useful to you in the future.

BEGINNING AND DEVELOPING YOUR CAREER

- People are typically required to take a variety of tests to become certified as teachers.
- School district employing officials typically want candidates to respond to the questions listed in this chapter.
- Many schools now have induction programs for new teachers that often involve mentoring by experienced master teachers.
- You should begin your job search process early with the help of your school's job placement office, and the annual *Job Search Handbook for Educators* can be very helpful.

THE CHALLENGES OF BECOMING A GREAT EDUCATOR

- The field of education will continue to present challenges to educators, and will change rapidly in the future.
- There will also continue to be a great variety of perspectives on education.

DISCUSSION STARTERS

1. What are the characteristics of a profession? What are your arguments for or against recognizing teaching as a profession?
2. Why do shortages of teachers probably exist in some subjects and not in others?
3. What should national accreditation tell you about your teacher education program?
4. What are some ways you can focus on improving by being reflective?
5. Of what potential value are journals, folios, and portfolios in preparing to teach?
6. What support should school districts provide to teachers in the induction years to encourage retention in the profession beyond three years?

SCHOOL-BASED OBSERVATIONS

1. Begin a list of the teaching challenges that you observe in schools. Reflect on the challenges that you had not expected when you initially thought about teaching as a career and how those challenges may influence your decision to become a teacher. How much have the teaching challenges you have observed met your initial expectations?

2. Ask several teachers what their major challenges and satisfactions are as educators. Analyze their answers and think about the major challenges and satisfactions you may experience as an educator.

PORTFOLIO DEVELOPMENT

1. Find and organize the many materials, artifacts, and records that you currently have. Examples may include term papers, transcripts, awards, letters of recognition, and observation journals. Organize these materials into logical categories.

At various points in the future, you will be drawing items out of the folio to develop a portfolio for completion of student teaching or to apply for a teaching position or national certification.

WEB SOLUTIONS

You will eventually need to understand the teacher certification requirements for the state(s) in which you may wish to teach. It is never too early to begin that process; therefore, we highly recommend that you now decide in which state(s) may end up teaching, find the websites for their teacher certification offices, and search out the current requirement for a teaching credential in your field. The following websites may also be useful:

www.nasdtec.org Information on licensure requirements and state agencies that are responsible for teacher licensing are available on this website of the National Association of State Directors of Teacher Education and Certification.

www.ncate.org A list of institutions with teacher education programs accredited by NCATE and information about becoming a teacher are available on this website. It also includes links to state agencies and their licensure requirements.

MyEducationLab™ Go to the topic **The Teaching Profession** in the MyEducationLab (**www.myeducationlab.com**) for *Foundations of American Education: Becoming Effective Teachers in Challenging Times, 16e* where you can:

- Find learning outcomes for **The Teaching Profession**, along with the national standards that connect to these outcomes.
- Complete Assignments and Activities that can help you more deeply understand the chapter content.
- Apply and practice your understanding of the core teaching skills identified in the chapter with the Building Teaching Skills and Dispositions learning units.
- Access video clips of CCSSO National Teachers of the Year award winners responding to the question, "Why Do I Teach?" in the Teacher Talk section.
- Create, update, and share quality lesson plans with the Lesson Plan Builder.

- Access state licensure test requirements, overviews of what tests cover, and sample test items in the Certification and Licensure section.
- Access current state and national standards in the Licensure and Standards section.
- Learn how to create a high-quality teaching portfolio in the Preparing a Portfolio section.
- Access tips, advice, and other information on resume writing and interviewing, your first year of teaching, and law and public policies in the Beginning Your Career section.
- Check your comprehension of the content covered in the chapter with the Study Plan. Here you will be able to take a chapter pretest, receive feedback on your answers, and then access personalized Review, Practice, and Enrichment exercises to enhance your understanding of chapter content. After you complete the exercises, take a posttest to confirm your comprehension.

2

The Early History of Education in a Changing World

LEARNING OUTCOMES

After reading and studying this chapter, you should be able to:

1. Detail the major educational accomplishments of the ancient Greeks; the ancient Romans; and the Europeans of the Middle Ages, Renaissance, Reformation, and Age of Reason. (InTASC 1–10)

2. List some of the most important early educators in the world and explain their contributions to education. (InTASC 9: Professional Learning and Ethical Practice)

3. Discuss the educational activity of the "Age of Reason." (InTASC 4: Content Knowledge)

4. Analyze what life was like for the colonial school teacher, student, and parent. (InTASC 9: Professional Learning and Ethical Practice)

5. Articulate the historical development of education of minority groups and females. (InTASC 1 and 2: The Learner and Learning)

6. Summarize the historical contributions of private schools in the United States. (InTASC 4 and 5: Content)

7. Analyze how an understanding of early U.S. educational history might be used to improve teaching today. (InTASC 1–10)

EDUCATION in the NEWS

TEACHING PATRIOTISM—WITH CONVICTION

By CHESTER E. FINN, JR.

Americans will debate for many years to come the causes and implications of the September 11 attacks on New York City and Washington, D.C., as well as the foiled attack that led to the crash of United Airlines Flight 93 in a Pennsylvania field. Between the first and second "anniversaries" of 9/11, another development deepened our awareness of the dangerous world we inhabit and of America's role therein—the successful war to liberate Iraq from its dictator and his murderous regime. Of course, the consequences—and contentiousness—of that conflict continue to resonate daily in newspaper headlines and on the evening news. In these challenging times, educators rightly wonder about their proper role. What should they teach young Americans? How should they prepare tomorrow's citizenry? What is most important for students to learn?

These are weighty questions, and there is every reason to expect them to linger. But it is now clearer than ever that, if we wish to prepare our children for unforeseen future threats and conflicts, we must arm them with lessons from history and civics that help them learn from the victories and setbacks of their predecessors, lessons that, in Jefferson's words, "enable every man to judge for himself what will secure or endanger his freedom."

Jefferson was right when he laid upon education the grave assignment of equipping tomorrow's adults with the knowledge, values, judgment, and critical faculties to determine for themselves what "will secure or endanger" their freedom and their country's well-being. The U.S. Supreme Court was right, half a century ago, when, in the epoch-shaping *Brown* decision, it declared education to be "the very foundation of good citizenship."

Teachers know this better than anyone, and many need no help or advice in fulfilling their responsibility. They're knowledgeable, savvy, creative, caring, and—may I say it?—patriotic, as many fine teachers have always been. They love our country and the ideals for which it stands. Teachers must communicate to their students the crucial lessons from history and civics that our children most need to learn. The events of 9/11 and the war on terrorism that has followed create a powerful opportunity to teach our daughters and sons about heroes and villains, freedom and repression, hatred and compassion, democracy and theocracy, civic virtue and vice.

On 10 April 2003, David McCullough told a Senate committee, "We are raising a generation of people who are historically illiterate. . . . We can't function in a society," he continued, "if we don't know who we are and where we came from." The solemn duty of all educators is to make certain that all our children know who they are. Part of that can be accomplished by teaching them about America's founders, about their ideals, and about the character, courage, vision, and tenacity with which they acted. From that inspiring history, true patriotism cannot help but grow.

QUESTIONS FOR REFLECTION

1. What is your perspective on the need for schools to teach patriotism?
2. What are some of the ways teachers could do so if they wished?
3. What are some of the potential disadvantages to teaching patriotism in our schools?

Source: "Teaching Patriotism—With Conviction" by Chester E. Finn, Jr., *Phi Delta Kappan*, April 2006. Reprinted with permission from PDK International, www.pdkintl.org. All rights reserved.

MyEducationLab™

Visit the MyEducationLab for *Foundations of American Education* to enhance your understanding of chapter concepts with a personalized *Study Plan*. You'll also have the opportunity to hone your teaching skills through video- and case-based *Assignments and Activities* and *Building Teaching Skills and Dispositions* lessons.

This part of the book briefly surveys the history of education. As you read this chapter, remember that historians see past events from various perspectives. *Celebrationist* historians, for instance, tend to see the brighter side of historical events and may tend, for example, to praise schools for past accomplishments. By contrast, *liberal* historians tend to study educational history through perspectives that focus on conflict, stress, and inconsistencies. *Revisionist* historians use yet another perspective, seeing celebrationist history as fundamentally flawed and concluding that we often learn more by studying what has been wrong with education than by rehearsing what has been right. *Postmodernist* historians believe that a person sees the history of education through the unique perspectives of her or his social class, race, ethnicity, gender, age, and so on. We challenge you to think critically as you read this and the next chapter and to formulate your own perspective through which to view educational history.

THE EVOLUTION OF SCHOOLING (TO 476 CE)

Informal education has been provided for children down through the ages by aboriginal people throughout the world. All people, regardless of their time and place in history, have cared for their young and attempted to prepare them for life's challenges. This was even true of the very earliest humans, who fed and protected their children and informally taught them—probably by example and admonition—the skills they needed to survive as adults. For instance, Native Americans, who lived and flourished in North America for thousands of years before the first Europeans arrived and established formal schools, educated generations of their children. Many other early societies, including those in China, Africa, and South America, for example, also successfully provided education that their children needed to help build their flourishing cultures. Unfortunately, records do not exist that would help us better understand these earliest informal educational systems. If such records did exist, we would probably be quite impressed with the educational efforts of our aboriginal ancestors.

As written language came into use, humans felt the need for a more formal education. As societies became more complex and the body of knowledge increased, people recognized a need for schools. What they had learned constituted the subject matter; the written language allowed them to record this knowledge and pass it from generation to generation.

Non-Western Education

It is impossible to determine when schools first came into existence. However, the discovery of cuneiform mathematics textbooks dated to 2000 BCE suggests that some form of school probably existed in Sumer (now part of Iraq) at that time. There is also evidence to suggest that formal schools existed in China during the Hsia and Shang dynasties, perhaps as early as 2000 BCE.

Western Education

It was not until about 500 BCE that a Western society advanced sufficiently to generate an organized concern for formal education. This happened in Greece during the **Age of Pericles**, 455–431 BCE.

Greece consisted of many city-states, one of which was Sparta, a militaristic state whose educational system was geared to support military ambitions. The aims of Spartan education

Age of Pericles
A period (455–431 BCE) of Greek history in which sufficiently great strides were made in human achievement to generate an organized concern for formal education.

centered on developing such ideals as courage, patriotism, obedience, cunning, and physical strength. Plutarch (46–120 CE), a writer of later times, said that the education of the Spartans "was calculated to make them subject to command, to endure labor, to fight, and to conquer." There was relatively little intellectual content in Spartan education.

In sharp contrast to Sparta was Athens, another Greek city-state, which developed an educational program that heavily stressed intellectual and aesthetic objectives. Between the ages of eight and sixteen, some Athenian boys attended a series of public schools. These schools included a kind of grammar school, which taught reading, writing, and counting; a gymnastics school, which taught sports and games; and a music school, which taught history, drama, poetry, speaking, and science as well as music. Because all city-states had to defend themselves against aggressors, Athenian boys received citizenship and military training between the ages of sixteen and twenty. Athenian girls were educated in the home. Athenian education stressed individual development, aesthetics, and culture.

The Western world's first great philosophers came from Athens. Of the many philosophers that Greece produced, three stand out: Socrates (470–399 BCE), Plato (427–347 BCE), and Aristotle (384–322 BCE).

SOCRATES. Socrates left no writings, but we know much about him from the writings of Xenophon and Plato. He is famous for creating the **Socratic method** of teaching, in which a teacher asks a series of questions that leads the student to a certain conclusion. This method is still commonly used by teachers today.

Socrates traveled around Athens teaching the students who gathered about him. He was dedicated to the search for truth and at times was very critical of the existing government. In fact, Socrates was eventually brought to trial for inciting the people against the government by his ceaseless questioning. He was found guilty and given a choice between ending his teaching or being put to death. Socrates chose death, thereby becoming a martyr for the cause of education. Socrates' fundamental principle, "Knowledge is virtue," has been adopted by countless educators and philosophers throughout the ages. Incidentally, some historians speculate that Socrates might not have really existed, but rather might have been a mythical character created by other writers—something that many writers did at that time, as evidenced by the rich Greek mythology we now treasure.

The aboriginal ancestors of today's Native Americans, like other aboriginal peoples, probably taught their children by admonition and example.

PLATO. Plato was a student and disciple of Socrates. In his *Republic,* Plato set forth his recommendations for the ideal society. He suggested that society should contain three classes of people: artisans, to do the manual work; soldiers, to defend the society; and philosophers, to advance knowledge and to rule the society. Plato's educational aim was to discover and develop each individual's abilities. He believed that each person's abilities should be used to serve society. Plato wrote, "I call education the virtue which is shown by children when the feelings of joy or of sorrow, of love or of hate, which arise in their souls, are made conformable to order."

ARISTOTLE. Like Plato, Aristotle believed that a person's most important purpose in life was to serve and improve humankind. Aristotle's educational method, however, was scientific, practical, and objective, in contrast to the philosophical methods of Socrates and Plato. Aristotle believed that the quality of a society was determined by the quality of education found in that society. His writings were destined to exert greater influence on humankind throughout the Middle Ages than the writings of any other person.

The early Greek philosophers, including Plato and Aristotle, articulated the idea that females and slaves did not possess the intelligence to be leaders and therefore should not be educated. Unfortunately, our world's current struggle with racism and sexism, deeply rooted in Western civilization, is traceable to the ancient world.

ROMAN SCHOOLS. In 146 BCE, the Romans conquered Greece, and Greek teachers and their educational system were quickly absorbed into the Roman Empire. Many of the educational and

GO TO ···>
More information on important educational philosophy pioneers can be found in Chapters 4 and 5.

Socratic method A way of teaching that centers on the use of questions by the teacher to lead students to a certain conclusion.

philosophical advances made by the Roman Empire after that time were actually inspired by enslaved Greeks.

Before 146 BCE, Roman children were educated primarily in the home, though some children attended schools known as *ludi,* where the rudiments of reading and writing were taught. The Greek influence on Roman education became pronounced between 50 BCE and 200 CE, when an entire system of schools was developed. Some children, after learning to read and write, attended a *grammaticus* school to study Latin, literature, history, mathematics, music, and dialectics. These **Latin grammar schools** were somewhat like twentieth-century secondary schools in function. Students who were preparing for a career of political service received their training in schools of rhetoric, which offered courses in grammar, rhetoric, dialectics, music, arithmetic, geometry, and astronomy.

QUINTILIAN. One of the most influential Roman educators was Quintilian (35–95 CE). In a set of twelve books, *The Institutes of Oratory,* he described current educational practices, recommended the type of educational system needed in Rome, and listed the great books that were in existence at that time.

Regarding the motivation of students, Quintilian stated,

> Let study be made a child's diversion; let him be soothed and caressed into it, and let him sometimes test himself upon his proficiency. Sometimes enter a contest of wits with him, and let him imagine that he comes off the conqueror. Let him even be encouraged by giving him such rewards that are most appropriate to his age. (Quintilian, trans. 1905, p. 12)

These comments apply as well today as they did when Quintilian wrote them nearly 2,000 years ago. Quintilian's writings were rediscovered in the 1400s and became influential in the humanistic movement in education.

The Romans had a genius for organization and for getting the job done. They made lasting contributions to architecture, and many of their roads, aqueducts, and buildings remain today. This genius for organization enabled Rome to unite much of the ancient world with a common language, a religion, and a political bond—a condition that favored the spread of education and knowledge throughout the ancient world.

EDUCATION IN THE MIDDLE AGES (476–1300)

By 476 CE (the fall of the Roman Empire), the Roman Catholic Church was well on the way to becoming the greatest power in government and education in the Western world. In fact, the rise of the church to power is often cited as a main cause of the Western world's plunge into the Dark Ages. As the church stressed the importance of gaining entrance to heaven, life on earth became less important. Many people viewed earthly life as nothing more than a way to a better life in the hereafter. You can see that a society in which this attitude prevailed would be less likely to make intellectual advances, except perhaps in areas tangential to religion.

The Dark Ages (400–1000)

As the name implies, the Dark Ages was a period when, in much of the Western world, human learning and knowledge didn't just stand still but actually regressed. This regression was due to a variety of conditions, including political and religious oppression of the common people. However, there were some examples of human progress during this time. In fact, some historians believe this historical period was not "dark" at all but rather an era of considerable human progress—another example of the differing perspectives with which historians view the past.

CHARLEMAGNE. During the Dark Ages, one of the bright periods for education was the reign of Charlemagne (742–814). Charlemagne realized the value of education, and as ruler of a large part of Europe, he was in a position to establish schools and encourage scholarly activity. In 768, when Charlemagne came into power, educational activity was at an extremely low ebb. The church conducted the little educating that was carried on, mainly to induct people into the faith and to train religious leaders. The schools where this religious teaching took place included *catechumenal schools,* which taught church doctrine to new converts; *catechetical schools,* which at first taught the catechism but later became schools for training church leaders; and *cathedral* (or *monastic*) *schools,* which trained clergy.

Latin grammar schools
An early type of school that emphasized the study of Latin, literature, history, mathematics, music, and dialectics.

ALCUIN. Charlemagne sought far and wide for a talented educator who could improve education in the kingdom, finally selecting Alcuin (735–804), formerly a teacher in England. While Alcuin served as Charlemagne's chief educational adviser, he became the most famous educator of his day. It is reported that Charlemagne himself often sat in the Palace School with the children, trying to further his own meager education.

Roughly during Alcuin's time, the phrase **seven liberal arts** came into common usage to describe the curriculum that was then taught in some schools. The seven liberal arts consisted of the *trivium* (grammar, rhetoric, and logic) and the *quadrivium* (arithmetic, geometry, music, and astronomy). Each of these seven subjects was defined broadly; collectively they constituted a more comprehensive study than today's usage of the term suggests. The phrase *liberal arts* has survived and is commonly used now as a reference to general education as opposed to vocational education.

The Revival of Learning

Despite the efforts of men such as Charlemagne and Alcuin, little educational progress was made during the Dark Ages. However, between 1000 and 1300—a period frequently referred to as the "age of the revival of learning"—humankind slowly regained a thirst for education. This revival of interest in learning was supported by the rediscovery of the writings of some of the ancient philosophers (mainly Aristotle) and renewed interest in them and in the reconciliation of religion and philosophy.

THOMAS AQUINAS. Thomas Aquinas (1225–1274), more than any other person, helped to change the church's views on learning. This change led to the creation of new learning institutions, among them the medieval universities. The harmonization of the doctrines of the church with the doctrines of philosophy and education was rooted in the ideas of Aristotle. Himself a theologian, Aquinas formalized **scholasticism**, the logical and philosophical study of the beliefs of the church. His most important writing was *Summa Theologica,* which became the doctrinal authority of the Roman Catholic Church. The educational and philosophical views of Thomas Aquinas were formalized in Thomism—a philosophy that has remained important in Roman Catholic parochial education.

MEDIEVAL UNIVERSITIES. The revival of learning brought about a general increase in educational activity and the growth of educational institutions, including the establishment of universities. These medieval universities, the true forerunners of our modern universities, included the University of Bologna (1158), which specialized in law; the University of Paris (1180), which specialized in theology; Oxford University (1214); and the University of Salerno (1224). By the time Columbus sailed to North America in 1492, approximately eighty universities already existed in Europe.

Although the Middle Ages produced a few educational advances in the Western world, we must remember that much of the Eastern world did not experience the Dark Ages. Mohammed (569–632) led a group of Arabs who later captured northern Africa and southern Spain. The Eastern learning that the Arabs brought to Spain spread slowly throughout Europe over the next few centuries through the writings of such scholars as Avicenna (980–1037) and Averroës (1126–1198). These Eastern contributions to Western knowledge included significant advances in science and mathematics, including the Arabic numbering system.

EDUCATION IN TRANSITION (1300–1700)

Two very important movements took place during the educational transition period of 1300 to 1700: the Renaissance and the Reformation. The Renaissance represented the protest of individuals against the dogmatic authority the church exerted over their social and intellectual life. The Renaissance started in Italy (around 1300) when people reacquired the spirit of free inquiry that had prevailed in ancient Greece. The Renaissance slowly spread through Europe, resulting in a general revival of classical learning, called *humanism.*

The second movement, the Reformation, represented a reaction against certain beliefs of the Roman Catholic Church, particularly those that discouraged learning and that, in consequence, kept lay people in ignorance.

seven liberal arts
A medieval curriculum that consisted of the trivium (grammar, rhetoric, logic) and the quadrivium (arithmetic, geometry, music, astronomy).

scholasticism The logical and philosophical study of the beliefs of the church.

The Renaissance

The common people were generally oppressed by wealthy landowners and royalty during the eleventh and twelfth centuries. In fact, the common people were thought to be unworthy of education and to exist primarily to serve landed gentry and royalty. The Renaissance represented a rebellion on the part of the common people against the suppression they experienced from both the church and the wealthy, who controlled their lives.

VITTORINO DA FELTRE. An important and influential educator during the Renaissance was Vittorino da Feltre (c. 1378–1446), a man from the eastern Alps region. Da Feltre studied at the University of Florence, where he developed an interest in teaching. He also developed a keen interest in classical literature and, along with other educators of that time, began to believe that people could be educated and also be Christians at the same time—a belief that the Roman Catholic Church generally did not share at that time.

Da Feltre established several schools, taught in a variety of others, and generally helped to advance the development of education during his lifetime. He believed that education was an important end in itself and thereby helped to rekindle an interest in the value of human knowledge during the Renaissance (Smith & Smith, 1984, pp. 84–88).

ERASMUS. One of the most famous humanist educators was Erasmus (1466–1536), and two of his books, *The Right Method of Instruction* and *The Liberal Education of Boys,* formed a humanistic theory of education. Erasmus had considerable educational insight for that period of time. Concerning the aims of education, he wrote:

> The duty of instructing the young includes several elements, the first and also the chief of which is that the tender mind of the child should be instructed in piety; the second, that he love and learn the liberal arts; the third, that he be taught tact in the conduct of social life; and the fourth, that from his earliest age he accustom himself to good behavior, based on moral principles. (Compayré, trans. 1888, pp. 12–13, 88–89)

The Reformation

It is difficult for people today to imagine the extent to which the Roman Catholic Church dominated the lives of the common people through most of what is now Europe during the fifteenth and sixteenth centuries. The church and the pope had enormous influence over European royalty during this time. In fact, some historians suggest that the pope and other church officials were in some ways more powerful than many individual kings and queens. After all, the Roman Catholic Church could and frequently did claim that unless members of royalty abided by its rules, they were destined to spend eternity in hell—an extremely frightening prospect for any human being. Consequently, it is understandable that the church wielded great influence throughout most of Europe.

LUTHER. The Protestant Reformation had its formal beginning in 1517. In that year, Martin Luther (1483–1546), who was a priest, published his ninety-five theses, which stated his disagreements with the Roman Catholic Church. One of these disagreements held great implications for the importance of formal education. The church believed that it was not necessary for each person to read and interpret the Bible; rather, the church would pass on the "correct" interpretation to the laity. Luther felt not only that the church had itself misinterpreted the Bible, but also that people were intended to read and interpret the Bible for themselves. If one accepted the church's position on this matter, formal education remained relatively unimportant for the masses. If one accepted Luther's position, however, education became important for all people so that they might read and interpret the Bible for themselves. In a sense, education became important as a way of obtaining salvation.

IGNATIUS OF LOYOLA. To combat the Reformation movement, Ignatius of Loyola (1491–1556) organized the Society of Jesus (Jesuits) in 1540. The Jesuits worked to establish schools to further the cause of the Roman Catholic Church, and they tried to stem the flow of converts to the cause of the Reformation. Although the Jesuits' main interest was religious, they soon grew into a great teaching order and were very successful in training their own teachers. The rules by which the Jesuits conducted their schools were stated in the *Ratio Studiorum*; a revised edition still guides Jesuit schools today. The improvement of teacher training was one of the Jesuits' main contributions to education.

COMENIUS. Among many other outstanding educators during this transition period was Johann Amos Comenius (1592–1670). Comenius is perhaps best remembered for his many textbooks, including *Orbis Pictus*. His books were among the first to contain illustrations. The invention and improvement of printing during the 1400s made it possible to produce books, such as those of Comenius, more rapidly and economically—a development that was essential to the growth of education. Much of the writing of Comenius reflected the increasing interest that was then developing in science.

LOCKE. John Locke (1632–1704) was an influential English educator during the late seventeenth century. He wrote many important educational works, including *Some Thoughts on Education* and *Essay Concerning Human Understanding*. He viewed a young child's mind as a blank slate (*tabula rasa*) on which an education could be imprinted. He believed that teachers needed to create a nonthreatening learning environment—a rather revolutionary idea at that time.

EDUCATIONAL AWAKENING (1700)

As we have suggested, educational progress in the world was slow and developed in only a few places through the seventeenth century. This section demonstrates why many of our current educational ideas can be traced to the early 1700s.

The Age of Reason

A revolt of the intellectuals against the superstition and ignorance that dominated people's lives at the time influenced education in this early modern period. This movement became the keynote of the period known as the **Age of Reason**; and François-Marie Arouet (1694–1778), a French writer who used the pen name "Voltaire," was one of its leaders.

Those who joined this movement became known as *rationalists* because of the faith they placed in human rational power. The implication for education in the rationalist movement is obvious: If one places greater emphasis on the human ability to reason, then education takes on new importance as the way in which humans can develop this power.

DESCARTES AND VOLTAIRE. The work of René Descartes (1596–1650) laid the foundations for rationalism. This philosophy evolved three axioms that gradually became well accepted by thinking people. These axioms were (1) that reason was supreme, (2) that the laws of nature were invariable, and (3) that truth could be verified empirically—that is, verified by exact methods of testing. These ideas became the basis for disputing some of the traditional teachings of the church and for resisting the bonds that royalty had traditionally placed on the common people. These axioms also influenced the thinking of Voltaire. Voltaire was an articulate writer who was also brilliant, clever, witty, and vain—qualities that probably helped him become extremely influential.

FREDERICK THE GREAT. One of the influential leaders during the Age of Reason was Frederick the Great (1712–1786). Frederick was a friend of Voltaire's and supported the notion that education was of value. He was a liberal thinker for his time and one of the few leaders who did not attempt to force the common people into a particular form of religion. Frederick also permitted an unusual amount of free speech for his era and generally allowed the common people a degree of liberty that most rulers considered dangerous.

As a consequence, education had an opportunity to develop, if not flourish, during his reign as leader of Prussia. During Frederick's reign, Prussia passed laws regarding education and required teachers to obtain special training as well as licenses to teach.

Morality and Education

Early educational efforts attempted to instill in students the morals and beliefs of the society in which they existed. These efforts have continued right down through history to our present schools. An example can be found in the accompanying "Who Is Right?" feature, in which two contemporary educators debate a sex education question.

Age of Reason The beginning of the modern period of education, a period in which European thinkers emphasized the importance of reason. The writing of Voltaire strongly influenced the rationalist movement.

WHO IS RIGHT?

IS "ABSTINENCE-ONLY" THE BEST SEX EDUCATION POLICY FOR SCHOOLS TO IMPLEMENT?

Early school curricula were historically driven by a desire to help children read the Bible and develop strict moral standards. The debate about how to best help students develop socially acceptable sexual behavior carries on today, as shown in this debate.

YES

Elizabeth Bradley teaches math at Lewiston High School in Lewiston, Maine, and won a Presidential Award in 2000 for her work. She has taught for fifteen years, interrupted by eight years as a business applications programmer.

Consider this:

"Good morning, class. Today we're going to learn how to have safe sex (now referred to as 'safer sex' because safe sex doesn't really exist).

"We'll show you how to put a condom on a banana, and some other things you can do to minimize your risk of contracting an incurable disease, which may make you sterile (chlamydia), be a precursor to cervical cancer (HPV), or cause death (HIV).

"Oh, and you might end up pregnant. Then your choices are abortion ("one dead, one wounded," to quote a recent bumper sticker), adoption (a lifelong hole in your heart), or parenthood (a 24/7 commitment that will make school, college, work, independence, and emotional stability very difficult)."

Why can't we take the drinking and driving approach of "Just don't do it"? Statistics show that kids do care about what the adults in their lives have to say. . . .

Let's raise the standard and tell kids, unequivocally, what is in their best interest. Why is it that we want so much to protect their sexual activity, but not their very lives?

NO

Eileen Toledo has taught English in middle schools for fourteen years, currently at the Pablo Avila Junior High School in Camuy, Puerto Rico. She runs the "Baby, Think It Over" program one period a week and wrote a master's thesis on it.

The reality is that more students are becoming sexually active at earlier ages. As an educator, I had to get involved. I have been using "Baby, Think It Over" at my junior high school for five years. . . .

At school, we talk about child abuse, how to place babies to sleep correctly, and more. Students budget the weekly costs of caring for a baby. They inquire about jobs available to them at their age (13–16). Students realize how hard raising a baby can be for them. . . .

We also discuss STDs, and we talk about how making love is different from sex, which is what teens are having. Making love is a beautiful experience in a true relationship between adults ready and able to take on responsibilities, not teens who got pregnant by mistake. . . .

Yet I cannot be so naive as not to see that most teens become sexually active at an early age. So I must also talk about birth control. . . .

Students who have complete information about disease transmission and contraceptive use are the most likely to remain abstinent and will protect themselves if they choose to be sexually active. We have worked with over 400 students, and only three became pregnant in high school.

WHAT IS YOUR PERSPECTIVE ON THIS ISSUE?

Source: Adapted from "Is 'Abstinence-Only' the Best Sex Education Policy for Schools to Implement?" *NEA Today* (February 2003), p. 23. Reprinted by permission of the National Education Association.

The Emergence of Common Man

The second pivotal trend of the early modern period that affected education was the concept sometimes called the **Emergence of Common Man**. Whereas the Age of Reason was sparked by a revolt of the learned for intellectual freedom, the thinkers who promoted the emergence of common man argued that common people deserved a better life—politically, economically, socially, and educationally.

ROUSSEAU. One of the leaders in this movement was Jean-Jacques Rousseau (1712–1778), whose *Social Contract* (1762) became an influential book during the French Revolution. Rousseau was a philosopher, not an educator, but he wrote a good deal on the subject of education. His most important educational work was *Émile* (1762), in which he states his views concerning the ideal education for youth. Rousseau felt that the aim of education should be to return human beings to their "natural state." His view on the subject is well summed up by the opening sentence of *Émile*: "Everything is good as it comes from the hand of the author of nature: but everything degenerates in the hands of man." Rousseau's educational views came to be known as *naturalism*.

Emergence of Common Man A period during which the idea developed that common people should receive at least a basic education as a means to a better life.

Rousseau's most important contributions to education were his belief that education must be a natural process, not an artificial one, and his compassionate, positive view of the child. Rousseau believed that children were inherently good—a belief in opposition to the prevailing religiously inspired belief that children were born full of sin.

PESTALOZZI. Johann Heinrich Pestalozzi (1746–1827) was a Swiss educator who put Rousseau's theory into practice. Pestalozzi established two schools for boys, one at Burgdorf (1800–1804) and the other at Yverdun (1805–1825). Educators came from all over the world to view Pestalozzi's schools and to study his teaching methods. Pestalozzi enumerated his educational views in a book entitled *Leonard and Gertrude.* Unlike most educators of his time, Pestalozzi believed that a teacher should treat students with love and kindness.

Swiss educator Johann Heinrich Pestalozzi (1746–1827) put Rousseau's theory into practice.

Key concepts in the Pestalozzian method included the expression of love, understanding, and patience for children; compassion for the poor; and the use of objects and sense perception as the basis for acquiring knowledge.

HERBART. Johann Friedrich Herbart (1776–1841) was an educator who studied under Pestalozzi and was influenced by him. Whereas Pestalozzi had successfully put into practice and further developed Rousseau's educational ideas, it remained for Herbart to organize these educational views into a formal psychology of education. Herbart stressed apperception (learning by association). The **Herbartian teaching method** developed into the following five formal steps:

1. *Preparation:* Preparing the student to receive a new idea
2. *Presentation:* Presenting the student with the new idea
3. *Association:* Assimilating the new idea with old ideas
4. *Generalization:* Generalizing the new idea derived from combination of old and new ideas
5. *Application:* Applying the new knowledge

Herbart's educational ideas are contained in his *Science of Education* (1806) and *Outlines of Educational Doctrine* (1835).

FROEBEL. Friedrich Froebel (1782–1852) was another European educator influenced by Rousseau and Pestalozzi who made a significant contribution to education. Froebel's contributions include the establishment of the first kindergarten (or *Kleinkinderbeschaftigungsanstalt*), an emphasis on social development, a concern for the cultivation of creativity, and the concept of learning by doing. He originated the idea that women are best suited to teach young children.

JOURNAL FOR REFLECTION 2.1

Select a person mentioned in this chapter (or another individual from the history of education who is of interest to you) and learn more about that person and her or his influence on today's schools. Make journal entry notes about what you learn.

EVOLVING PERSPECTIVES OF EDUCATION IN OUR RAPIDLY DEVELOPING NATION

The earliest settlers to America from Europe brought with them a sincere interest in providing at least rudimentary education for their children. Naturally, they brought their European ideas about education with them and, soon after arrival, created educational programs throughout colonial America. This section will briefly examine these early colonial school programs.

Herbartian teaching method An organized teaching method, based on the principles of Pestolozzi, that stresses learning by association and consists of five steps: preparation, presentation, association, generalization, and application.

Colonial Education

The early settlements on the East Coast were composed of groups of colonies: the Southern Colonies, centered in Virginia; the Middle Colonies, centered in New York; and the Northern Colonies, centered in New England. Each of these groups developed a somewhat unique educational system.

SOUTHERN COLONIES. The Southern Colonies soon were made up of large tobacco plantations. There was an immediate need for cheap labor to work on the plantations; in 1619, only twelve years after Jamestown was settled, the colony imported the first slaves from Africa. Other sources of labor for the Southern Colonies included Europeans from a variety of backgrounds who had purchased passage to the New World by agreeing to serve a lengthy period of indentured servitude on arrival in the colonies. There soon came to be two very distinct classes of people in the South—a few wealthy landowners and a large mass of laborers, most of whom were slaves.

The educational provisions that evolved from this set of conditions were precisely what one would expect. Few were interested in providing education for the slaves, with the exception of missionary groups such as the English Society for the Propagation of the Gospel in Foreign Parts. Such missionary groups tried to provide some education for slaves, primarily so that they could read the Bible. The wealthy landowners hired tutors to teach their children at home. Distances between homes and slow transportation precluded the establishment of centralized schools. When upper-class children grew old enough to attend college, they were usually sent to well-established universities in Europe.

MIDDLE COLONIES. The people who settled the Middle Colonies came from various national (Dutch, Swedish) and religious (Puritan, Mennonite, Catholic) backgrounds. This is why the Middle Colonies have often been called the melting pot of the nation. This diversity of backgrounds made it impossible for the inhabitants of the Middle Colonies to agree on a common public school system. Consequently, the respective groups established their own religious schools. Many children received their education through an apprenticeship while learning a trade from a master already in that line of work. Some people even learned the art of teaching school through apprenticeships with experienced teachers.

NORTHERN COLONIES. The Northern Colonies were settled mainly by the Puritans, a religious group from Europe. In 1630 approximately one thousand Puritans settled near Boston. Unlike people in the Southern Colonies, people in New England lived close to one another. Towns sprang up and soon became centers of political and social life. Shipping ports were established, and an industrial economy developed that demanded numerous skilled and semiskilled workers—a condition that eventually created a growing middle class and common schools.

EARLY SCHOOL LAWS. These conditions of common religious views, town life, and a large middle class made it possible for the people to agree on common public schools and led to very early educational activity in the Northern Colonies. In 1642 the General Court of Massachusetts enacted a law that stated:

> This Co^t [Court], taking into consideration the great neglect of many parents & masters in training up their children in learning do hereupon order and decree, that in every towne y chosen men take account from time to time of all parents and masters, and of their children, concerning their ability to read & understand the principles of religion & the capitall lawes of this country. (Shurtleff, 1853)

This law did nothing more than encourage citizens to look after the education of children. However, five years later in 1647 another law was enacted in Massachusetts that required towns to provide education for their youth. This law, which was often referred to as the **Old Deluder Satan Act** because of its religious motive, stated:

Old Deluder Satan Act
An early colonial education law (1647) that required colonial towns of at least fifty households to provide education for youth.

> It being one chiefe proiect of y ould deluder, Satan, to keepe men from the knowledge of y Scriptures It is therefore orded [ordered], ye evy [every] towneship in this jurisdiction, aft y Lord hath increased y number to 50 household, shall then forthw appoint one w [with] in their towne to teach all such children as shall resort to him to write & reade & it is furth ordered y where any towne shall increase to y numb [number] of 100 families or househould, they shall set up a grammar schoole, y m [aim] thereof being able to instruct youth so farr as they shall be fited for y university [Harvard]. (Shurtleff, 1853)

PERSPECTIVES on DIVERSITY

Religious Perspectives in the Classroom

Kevin, a secondary school student, had been worrying for a week about the next unit in his biology class. It was supposed to introduce the concept of evolution which, he had learned from his family and at church, was not the way the world developed. He liked science, but believed that science was wrong on this one. Ever since he was a baby he had been learning about creationism and how God created the world. His minister recently had told the congregation about the theory of intelligent design that countered the explanations of evolution. Kevin knew that Mr. Jenkins, his biology teacher, didn't attend Kevin's church. He didn't know his religious beliefs, but if Mr. Jenkins was going to teach evolution, he must not be very religious. He wondered what he should do when Mr. Jenkins began the discussion of evolution next week.

After Mr. Jenkins introduced the section on evolution on Monday, he called on Kevin, who had raised his hand. Kevin confidently stood and said, "Mr. Jenkins, are we also going to talk about intelligent design as part of this lesson?"

Somewhat surprised, Mr. Jenkins responded, "Son, intelligent design is not science. It is a non-scientific theory and does not help explain the development of species in our world. It has no place in my biology class."

Embarrassed, Kevin slid back into his seat. But he was going to talk with his parents and minister about Mr. Jenkins's brusque response to his question. He thought, "It isn't fair that other explanations of the world are totally dismissed. Other students in the class should know that research supports intelligent design as well."

WHAT IS YOUR PERSPECTIVE?

1. Why do you think Kevin is so adamant that other perspectives on the development of the world should be explored in his biology class? Why might Mr. Jenkins think otherwise?

2. How would you have responded to Kevin's request to include intelligent design in this biology unit? Why?

3. What do you think might have been taught about this topic in a science class during the Colonial period?

These Massachusetts school laws of 1642 and 1647 served as models for similar laws that were soon created in other colonies.

RELIGION IN THE CLASSROOM. Colonial schools almost always were religious in nature. In fact, the Bible was often the only book used, and religious prayers were routinely used in the Colonial classroom. The concept of "separation of church and state" did not exist at that time like it does now in our public schools. The above "Perspectives on Diversity" feature relates a possible dilemma for contemporary teachers.

TYPES OF COLONIAL SCHOOLS. Several different kinds of elementary schools sprang up in the colonies, such as the **dame school**, which was conducted by a housewife in her home; the writing school, which taught the child to write; a variety of church schools; and charity, or pauper, schools taught by missionary groups.

In 1635 the Latin Grammar School was established in Boston—the first permanent school of this type in what is now the United States. The grammar school was a secondary school. Its function was college preparatory, and the idea spread quickly to other towns. Charlestown opened its first grammar school one year later, in 1636, by contracting William Witherell "to keep a school for a twelve month." Within sixteen years after the Massachusetts Bay Colony had been founded, seven or eight towns had Latin grammar schools in operation. Transplanted from Europe, where similar schools had existed for a long time, these schools were aimed at preparing boys for college and "for the service of God, in church and commonwealth."

EARLY AMERICAN COLLEGES. Harvard, the first colonial college, was established in 1636 for preparing ministers. Other early American colleges included William and Mary (1693), Yale (1701), Princeton (1746), King's College (1754), College of Philadelphia (1755), Brown (1764), Dartmouth (1769), and Queen's College (1770). The curriculum in these early colleges was traditional, with heavy emphasis on theology and the classics. An example of the extent to which the religious motive dominated colonial colleges can be found in one of the 1642 rules governing Harvard College, which stated: "Let every Student be plainly instructed, and earnestly pressed to consider well, the maine end of his life and studies is, to know God and Jesus Christ."

dame school A low-level primary school in the colonial and other early periods, usually conducted by an untrained woman (a dame) in her own home.

MONITORIAL SCHOOLS. In 1805, New York City established the first *monitorial school* in the United States. The monitorial school, which originated in England, represented an attempt to provide economical mass elementary education for large numbers of children. Typically, the teacher would teach hundreds of pupils, using the better students as helpers. By 1840, however, nearly all monitorial schools had been closed; the children had not learned enough to justify continuance of this type of school.

HORACE MANN. Between 1820 and 1860, an educational awakening took place in the United States. This movement was strongly influenced by Horace Mann (1796–1859). As secretary of the state board of education, Mann helped to establish **common elementary schools** in Massachusetts. These common schools were designed to provide a basic elementary education for all children. Among Mann's many impressive educational achievements was the publication of one of the very early professional journals in this country, *The Common School Journal*. Through this journal, Mann kept educational issues before the public.

In 1852, Massachusetts passed a compulsory elementary school attendance law, the first of its kind in the country, requiring all children to attend school. By 1900, thirty-two other states had passed similar **compulsory education** laws.

Financing public education has always been a challenge in America. As early as 1795, Connecticut legislators decided to sell public land and create a permanent school fund to help finance public schools. As more and more children attended school, other states soon took action to establish school funding plans as well.

GO TO ⋯⟩
More detailed information on current school finances can be found in Chapter 9.

HENRY BARNARD. The first U.S. commissioner of education was a prominent educator named Henry Barnard (1811–1900). He was a longtime supporter of providing common elementary schools for all children and wrote enthusiastically about the value of education in the *Connecticut Common School Journal* and in the *American Journal of Education,* which he founded. He had also served as the Rhode Island commissioner of public schools and as the chancellor of the University of Wisconsin before holding the prestigious position of commissioner of education for the entire United States. Barnard also strongly supported kindergarten programs for very young children as well as high school programs for older students.

REFLECTIONS ON EARLY U.S. ELEMENTARY EDUCATION. If we look back at the historical development of U.S. elementary education, we can make the following generalizations:

1. Until the late 1800s, the motive, curriculum, and administration of elementary education were primarily religious. The point at which elementary education began to be more secular than religious was the point at which states began to pass compulsory school attendance laws.

2. Discipline was traditionally harsh in elementary schools. The classical picture of a colonial schoolmaster equipped with a frown, dunce cap, stick, whip, and a variety of abusive phrases is more accurate than one might expect. It is no wonder that children historically viewed school as an unpleasant place. Pestalozzi had much to do with bringing about a gradual change in discipline when he advocated that love, not severe punishment, should be used to motivate students.

3. Elementary education was traditionally formal and impersonal. The ideas of Rousseau, Pestalozzi, Herbart, and Froebel helped to change this condition gradually and make elementary education more student centered; this was becoming apparent by 1900.

4. Early elementary schools were traditionally taught by poorly prepared teachers.

5. Although the aims and methodology varied considerably from time to time, the basic content of colonial elementary education was reading, writing, and arithmetic (commonly referred to as the "3-Rs.")

common elementary schools Schools that originated in the mid-nineteenth century designed to provide a basic elementary education for all children.

compulsory education School attendance that is required by law on the theory that it is of benefit to the state or commonwealth to educate all people.

The Need for Secondary Schools

Contemporary U.S. high schools have a long and proud tradition. They have evolved from a series of earlier forms of secondary schools that were created to serve the needs of society at various points in the nation's history.

AMERICAN ACADEMY. By the middle of the eighteenth century, there was a need for more and better trained skilled workers. Benjamin Franklin (1706–1790), recognizing this need, proposed a new kind of secondary school in Pennsylvania. This proposal brought about the establishment, in Philadelphia in 1751, of the first truly American educational institution—the *American Academy*. Franklin established this school because he thought the existing Latin grammar schools were not providing the practical secondary education that youth needed. The philosophy, curriculum, and methodology of Franklin's academy were all geared to prepare young people for employment. Eventually, similar academies were established throughout America, and these institutions eventually replaced the Latin grammar school as the predominant secondary educational institution. They were usually private schools, and many of them admitted girls as well as boys. Later on, some academies even tried to train elementary school teachers.

HIGH SCHOOL. In 1821 the *English Classical School* (which three years later changed its name to *English High School*) opened in Boston, and another distinctively American educational institution was launched. This first high school, under the direction of George B. Emerson, consisted of a three-year course in English, mathematics, science, and history. The school later added to its curriculum the philosophy of history, chemistry, intellectual philosophy, linear drawing, logic, trigonometry, French, and the U.S. Constitution. The school enrolled about one hundred boys during its first year.

The high school was established because of a belief that the existing grammar schools were inadequate for the day and because most people could not afford to send their children to the private academies. The high school soon replaced both the Latin grammar school and the private academy, and it has been with us ever since.

JUNIOR HIGH/MIDDLE SCHOOL. About 1910 the first *junior high schools* were established in the United States, which typically consisted of grades 7, 8 and 9. A survey in 1916 showed 54 junior high schools in 36 states. One year later a survey indicated that the number had increased to about 270. More recently, some school systems have abandoned the junior high school in favor of what is called the *middle school,* which usually consists of grades 6, 7, and 8.

The Evolution of Teaching Materials

As one might expect, the first schools in colonial America were poorly equipped. The only teaching materials, if any, likely to be found then were hornbooks, maybe a Bible, perhaps one or two other religious books, slates and slate pencils, and later on a small amount of scarce paper and a few quill pens.

THE HORNBOOK. The **hornbook** was the most common teaching device in early colonial schools (see Figure 2.1). Hornbooks differed widely but typically consisted of a sheet of paper showing the alphabet that was covered with a thin transparent sheet of cow's horn and tacked to a paddle-shaped piece of wood. A leather thong was often looped through a hole in the paddle so that students could hang the hornbooks around their necks. Hornbooks provided students with their first reading instructions. Records indicate that hornbooks were used in Europe in the Middle Ages and were common there until the mid-1700s.

As paper became more available, the hornbook evolved into a several-page "book" called a *battledore*. The battledore, printed on heavy paper, often resembled an envelope. Like the hornbook, it typically contained the alphabet and various religious prayers and/or admonitions.

THE *NEW ENGLAND PRIMER*. Very few textbooks were available for use in colonial Latin grammar schools, academies, and colleges, although various religious books, including the Bible, were often used. A few books dealing with history, geography, arithmetic, Latin, Greek, and certain classics were available for use in colonial secondary schools and colleges during the eighteenth century.

The first real textbook to be used in colonial elementary schools was the *New England Primer*. Records show that the first copies of this book were printed in England in the 1600s. Copies of the *New England Primer* were also printed as early as 1690 in the American colonies. An advertisement for the book appeared in the *News from the Stars Almanac*, published in 1690 in Boston. The oldest extant copy of the *New England Primer* is a 1727 edition, now in the Lenox Collection of the New York Public Library.

The *New England Primer* was a small book, usually about 2 by 4 inches, with thin sheets of wood covered with paper or leather. It contained fifty to one hundred pages, depending on how

GO TO ···›
More information about historical and current school organizations can be found in Chapters 6 and 9.

hornbook A single page typically containing the alphabet, syllables, a prayer, or other simple words, tacked to a wooden paddle and covered with a thin transparent layer of cow's horn; used in colonial times as a beginner's first book or preprimer.

FIGURE 2.1   The hornbook was the most common teaching device in colonial American schools.

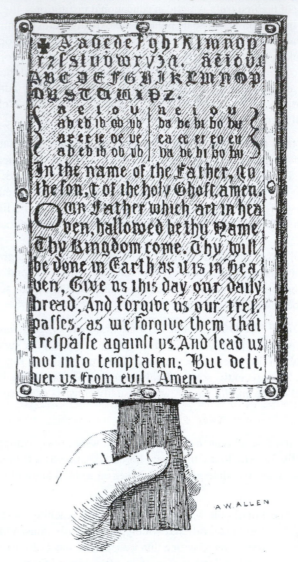

HORN-BOOK IN THE BRITISH MUSEUM.

many extra sections were added to each edition. The first pages displayed the alphabet, vowels, and capital letters. Next came lists of words arranged from two to six syllables, followed by verses and tiny woodcut pictures for each letter in the alphabet. Figure 2.2 shows a sampling of these pictures and verses. The contents of the *New England Primer* reflect the heavily religious motive in colonial education.

BLUE-BACKED SPELLER. The primer was virtually the only reading book used in colonial schools until about 1800, when Noah Webster published *The American Spelling Book*. This book became known as the *Blue-Backed Speller* because of its blue cover. It eventually replaced the *New England Primer* as the most common elementary textbook. Figure 2.3 shows a page from a *Blue-Backed Speller* printed about 1800.

The *Blue-Backed Speller* was approximately 4 by 6 inches; its cover was made of thin sheets of wood usually covered with light blue paper. The first part of the book contained rules and instructions for using the book; next came the alphabet, syllables, and consonants. The bulk of the book was taken up with lists of words arranged according to syllables and sounds. It also contained rules for reading and speaking, moral advice, and stories of various sorts.

TEACHING MATERIALS IN AN EARLY SCHOOL. By 1800, nearly two hundred years after the colonies had been established, school buildings and teaching materials were still very crude and meager. You can understand something of the physical features and equipment of

FIGURE 2.2   Page from the *New England Primer.* How does this page from the *New England Primer* reveal the religious motive in colonial American education?

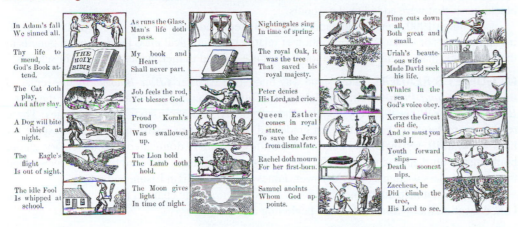

an 1810 New England school by reading the following description written by a teacher of that school:

> The size of the building was 22 × 20 feet. From the floor to the ceiling it was 7 feet. The chimney and entry took up about four feet at one end, leaving the schoolroom itself 18 × 20 feet. Around three sides of the room were connected desks, arranged so that when the pupils were sitting at them their faces were toward the instructor and their backs toward the wall. Attached to the sides of the desks nearest to the instructor were benches for small pupils. The instructor's desk and chair occupied the center. On this desk were stationed a rod, or ferule; sometimes both. These, with books, writings, inkstands, rules, and plummets, with a fire shovel, and a pair of tongs (often broken), were the principal furniture. (Monroe, 1905, p. 282)

SLATES. About 1820 a new instructional device—the *slate*—was introduced in American schools. These school slates were thin, flat pieces of slate stone framed with wood. The pencils used were also made of slate and produced a light but legible line that was easily erased with a

FIGURE 2.3   Cover from the *Blue-Backed Speller.* Noah Webster's *Blue-Backed Speller* came to replace primers around 1800. In addition to the alphabet, syllables, consonants, lists of words, and rules for reading and speaking, the *Speller* contained stories like the one shown here.

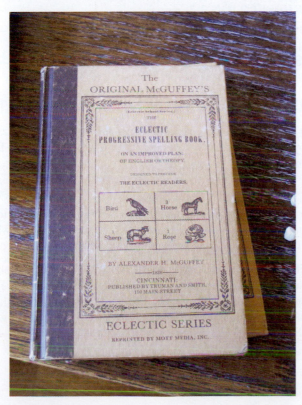

rag. The wooden frames of some of the slates were covered with cloth so that noise would be minimized as students placed the slates on the desk. Later on, large pieces of slate made up the blackboards that were added to classrooms.

By about 1900, pencils and paper had largely replaced the slate and slate pencil as the writing implements of students. The invention of relatively economical mass production of pencils in the late 1800s made them affordable for student use and led to their widespread use in schools.

MCGUFFEY'S *READERS*. In the same way that Noah Webster's *Blue-Backed Speller* replaced the *New England Primer,* William Holmes McGuffey's *Reader* eventually replaced the *Blue-Backed Speller.* It became very popular and eventually sold about sixty million copies. These readers were carefully geared to each grade and were meant to instill in children a respect for hard work, thrift, self-help, and honesty. McGuffey's *Readers* dominated the elementary school book market until approximately 1900, when they were gradually replaced by various newer and improved readers written by David Tower, James Fassett, William Elson, and others.

One cannot help but be awed by the contrast and dramatic changes that have taken place in U.S. education today from its humble beginning centuries ago.

Using Technology to Help Understand History

A case could probably be made for the claim that teachers have always used some form of technology to help students learn. This would require a broad definition of the term "technology" to include any form of visual or audio materials, such as the printed word, anything the learner could see, hornbooks, slates, and so on. While this might make for interesting historical debate, it is probably not very important to you at this point.

However, it is very important at this point that you realize that there is a wealth of wonderful technology now available to help you learn about history in general and the history of education more specifically. For instance, doing a word search on just about any important person who impacted the history of education will yield a wealth of information about that person. The same is true if you do a word search on just about any historical topic or object that may be of interest to you. For instance, searching on any of the teaching materials just mentioned (such as, for example "hornbooks") will provide you with not only written information, but also pictures of hornbooks. Searching for "education museums" will also provide you with a great deal of interesting educational history information from various sites.

JOURNAL FOR REFLECTION 2.2

1. Try to learn more about the historical development of education in the particular grade or subjects you are thinking of teaching.
2. Record in your journal any especially pertinent things you learn.

MEAGER EARLY EDUCATION FOR DIVERSE POPULATIONS

It is sad but true that students of color, girls, and students with disabilities have been historically badly underserved by our educational system and, until relatively recently, have often not even been allowed to attend school.

Education of African Americans

Unfortunately, general efforts have been made only recently in this country to provide an education for African Americans. In the following subsections, we briefly explore why this was the case and discuss some of the early African American educators who struggled to correct this injustice.[1]

EARLY CHURCH EFFORTS TO EDUCATE AFRICAN AMERICANS. Probably the first organized attempts to educate African Americans in colonial America were by French and Spanish missionaries. These early missionary efforts set an example that influenced the education of both African Americans and their children. Educating slaves posed an interesting moral problem for the church. The English colonists had to find a way to overcome the idea that converting enslaved

---

[1] We wish to thank Dr. Jack Davis for his contribution to this section.

people to Christianity might logically lead to their freedom. The problem they faced was how to eliminate an unwritten law that a Christian should not be a slave. The church's governing bodies and the bishop of London settled the matter by decreeing that conversion to Christianity did not lead to formal emancipation.

The organized church nevertheless provided the setting where a few African Americans were allowed to develop skills in reading, leadership, and educating their brethren. Often African Americans and whites attended church together.

Eventually, some preachers who were former slaves demonstrated exceptional skill in "spreading the gospel." The Baptists in particular, by encouraging a form of self-government, allowed African Americans to become active in the church. This move fostered the growth of African American congregations; thus, Baptist congregations gave enslaved as well as free African Americans an opportunity for education and development that was not provided by many other denominations.

EARLY SCHOOLS FOR AFRICAN AMERICAN CHILDREN. One of the first northern schools established for African Americans appears to have been that of Elias Neau in New York City in 1704. Neau was an agent of the Society for the Propagation of the Gospel in Foreign Parts.

In 1807 several free African Americans, including George Bell, Nicholas Franklin, and Moses Liverpool, built the first schoolhouse for African Americans in the District of Columbia. Not until 1824, however, was there an African American teacher in that district—John Adams. In 1851, Washington citizens attempted to discourage Myrtilla Miner from establishing an academy for African American girls. However, after much turmoil and harassment, the white schoolmistress from New York did found her academy; it is still functioning today as the School of Education at the University of the District of Columbia.

Boston, the seat of northern liberalism, established a separate school for African American children in 1798. Elisha Sylvester, a white man, was in charge. The school was founded in the home of Primus Hall, a "Negro in good standing." Two years later, sixty-six free African Americans petitioned the school committee for a separate school and were refused. Undaunted, the patrons of Hall's house employed two instructors from Harvard; thirty-five years later, the school was allowed to move to a separate building. The city of Boston opened its first primary school for the education of African American children in 1820—one more small milestone in the history of African American education.

FREDERICK DOUGLASS. Born in slavery in Maryland in 1817, Frederick Douglass (ca. 1817–1895) ran away and began talking to abolitionist groups about his experiences in slavery. He attributed his fluent speech to listening to his master talk. Douglass firmly believed that if he devoted all his efforts to improving vocational education, he could greatly improve the plight of African Americans. He thought that previous attempts by educators to combine liberal and vocational education had failed, so he emphasized vocational education solely.

JOHN CHAVIS. African Americans' individual successes in acquiring education, as well as their group efforts to establish schools, were greatly enhanced by sympathetic and humanitarian white friends. One African American who was helped by whites was John Chavis (1763–1838), a free man born in Oxford, North Carolina. Chavis became a successful teacher of aristocratic whites, and his white neighbors sent him to Princeton "to see if a Negro would take a college education." His rapid advancement under Dr. Witherspoon soon indicated that the venture was a success. He returned to Virginia and later went to North Carolina, where he preached among his own people. The success of John Chavis, even under experimental conditions, represented another small step forward in the education of African Americans.

Early efforts to provide formal education for African American children were few. The African American Children's school was one example.

PRUDENCE CRANDALL. A young Quaker, Prudence Crandall (1803–1890), established an early boarding school in Canterbury, Connecticut. The problems she ran into dramatize some of the Northern animosity to educating African Americans. Trouble arose when Sarah Harris, a "colored girl," asked to be admitted to the institution. After much deliberation, Miss Crandall finally consented, but white parents objected to the African American girl's attending the school and withdrew their children. To keep the school open, Miss Crandall recruited African American children. The pupils were threatened with violence; local stores would not trade with her; and the school building was vandalized. The citizens of Canterbury petitioned the state legislature to enact a law that would make it illegal to educate African Americans from out of state. Miss Crandall was jailed and tried before the state supreme court in July 1834. The court never gave a final decision because defects were found in the information prepared by the attorney for the state; the indictment was eventually dropped. Miss Crandall continued to work for the abolition of slavery, for women's rights, and for African American education. Prudence Crandall became well known, and she deserves considerable credit for the advances made by minorities and women in the United States.

BOOKER T. WASHINGTON. Booker T. Washington (1856–1915) was one of the early African American educators who contributed immensely to the development of education in the United States. He realized that African American children desperately needed an education to compete in society, and he founded the Tuskegee Institute in 1880. This Alabama institution provided basic and industrial education in its early years and gradually expanded to provide a wider ranging college curriculum. It stands today as a proud monument to Booker T. Washington's vision and determination concerning the education of African American youth.

EARLY AFRICAN AMERICAN COLLEGES. Unfortunately, despite these efforts, African Americans received pathetically little formal education even after the Emancipation Proclamation, issued by President Abraham Lincoln on January 1, 1863. At that time, the literacy rate among African Americans was estimated at 5 percent. In the late 1700s and early 1800s, some communities did set up separate schools for African Americans; however, only a very small percentage ever had a chance to attend the schools. A few colleges such as Oberlin, Bowdoin, Franklin, Rutland, and Harvard admitted African American students, but, again, very few had the opportunity to attend college then. There were even a few African American colleges such as Lincoln University in Pennsylvania (1854) and Wilberforce University in Ohio (1856); however, the efforts and opportunities for the education of African Americans were few relative to the size of the African American population.

Although there was no great rush to educate African Americans, the abolition of slavery in 1865 signaled the beginning of a slow but steady effort to improve their education. By 1890, African American literacy had risen to 40 percent; by 1910 it was estimated that 70 percent of African Americans had learned to read and write. These statistics showing the rapid increase in African American literacy are impressive; however, they are compromised by a report of the U.S. commissioner of education showing that by 1900, fewer than seventy of every one thousand public high schools in the South were providing for African Americans. Even worse, while educational opportunities for African Americans were meager, for other minority groups such as Native Americans and Hispanic Americans they were practically nonexistent.

Education of Asian Americans

The Second World War brought about discrimination against Japanese Americans when the U.S. government placed more than 100,000 Japanese American citizens in internment camps and in some cases confiscated their property. Not until 1990 did the government officially apologize and pay restitution for having done so. In hindsight, many believe that this treatment of U.S. citizens of Japanese background constituted a form of discrimination.

In the decades following the Korean and Vietnam wars, the number of Asian immigrants to the United States has increased dramatically. Large numbers of Vietnamese, Cambodians, Laotians, and Thais have been included in this recent migration. Although many of these Asian immigrants have experienced considerable success, the majority have struggled to receive an education and find suitable jobs. Many feel that they have been discriminated against and have not received equal educational and employment opportunities. Yet many of the highest achieving high school students are Asian Americans, proof of the fact that their families typically place a high value on education.

Education of Hispanic Americans

The number of Hispanic American students in U.S. schools has increased dramatically in recent years. But the historical background of this increase can actually be traced to the very first formal schools in North America. The earliest formal schools on this continent were started and conducted in the sixteenth century by Spanish missionaries in Mexico and the southwestern part of what is now the United States. Some historians even assert that the Spanish had established several "colleges" in North America before Harvard was founded in 1636. This assertion is probably true if one defines a mission school as a college, because some of them prepared boys for the ministry. As with the other early schools in the Americas, the missionaries established these early Spanish schools primarily for religious purposes—to help people read the Bible and thus gain salvation. Students at early mission schools in what is now Mexico and in Florida, California, Arizona, New Mexico, Cuba, and elsewhere were taught by Catholic priests in the Spanish language. After the United States won its independence and grew to include what we now think of as the Southwest, these early Spanish schools gradually became part of the larger English-speaking U.S. school system.

Unfortunately, Hispanic American education did not develop as quickly or as well as that of the majority population. This discrepancy is due at least in part to the facts that many Hispanic Americans are in the lower income brackets, that many immigrated to the United States without well-developed English language skills, and that many suffered discrimination. Like other minority groups in the United States, Hispanic Americans have not historically been afforded equal educational opportunities.

GO TO ⋯>
Multicultural education is presented in more detail in Chapters 6, 7, and 8.

Education of Women

Historically, women have not been afforded equal educational opportunities in the United States. Furthermore, many authorities claim that U.S. schools have traditionally been sexist institutions. Although there is much evidence to support both of these assertions, it is also true that an impressive number of women have made significant contributions to educational progress.

Colonial schools did not provide education for girls in any significant way. In some instances girls were taught to read, but females could not attend Latin grammar schools, academies, or colleges. We will look briefly at a few of the many outstanding female educators who helped to develop our country's educational system, in spite of their own limited educational opportunities.

EMMA WILLARD. Whereas well-to-do parents hired private tutors or sent their daughters away to a girls' seminary, girls from poor families were only taught to read and write at home (provided someone in the family had these skills). Emma Willard (1787–1870) was a pioneer and champion of education for females during a time when there were relatively few educational opportunities for them. She opened one of the first female seminaries in 1821 in Troy, New York, and this school offered an educational program equal to that of a boys' school. In a speech designed to raise funds for her school, she proposed the following benefits of seminaries for girls:

1. Females, by having their understandings cultivated, their reasoning power developed and strengthened, may be expected to act more from the dictates of reason and less from those of fashion and caprice.

2. With minds thus strengthened, they would be taught systems of morality, enforced by the sanctions of religion; and they might be expected to acquire juster and more enlarged views of their duty, and stronger and higher motives to its performance.

3. This plan of education offers all that can be done to preserve female youth from contempt of useful labor. The pupils would become accustomed to it, in conjunction with the high objects of literature and the elegant pursuits of the fine arts; and it is to be hoped that both from habit and association they might in future life regard it as respectable.

4. The pupils might be expected to acquire a taste for moral and intellectual pleasures which would buoy them above a passion for show and parade, and which would make them seek

to gratify the natural love of superiority by endeavoring to excel others in intrinsic merit rather than in the extrinsic frivolities of dress, furniture, and equipage.

5. By being enlightened in moral philosophy, and in that which teaches the operations of the mind, females would be enabled to perceive the nature and extent of that influence which they possess over their children, and the obligation which this lays them under to watch the formation of their characters with unceasing vigilance, to become their instructors, to devise plans for their improvement, to weed out the vices of their minds, and to implant and foster the virtues. And surely there is that in the maternal bosom which, when its pleadings shall be aided by education, will overcome the seductions of wealth and fashion, and will lead the mother to seek her happiness in communing with her children, and promoting their welfare. (Willard, 1893, pp. 12–14)

Many other female institutions were established and became prominent during the mid- and late 1800s, including Mary Lyon's Mount Holyoke Female Seminary; Jane Ingersoll's seminary in Cortland, New York; and Julia and Elias Mark's Southern Carolina Collegiate Institute at Barhamville, to name just a few. Unfortunately, not until well into the twentieth century were women generally afforded access to higher education.

MARIA MONTESSORI. Maria Montessori (1870–1952), born in Italy, first became a successful physician and later a prominent educational philosopher. She developed her own theory and methods of educating young children. Her methods utilized child-size school furniture and specially designed learning materials. She emphasized independent work by children under the guidance of a trained teacher. Private Montessori schools still thrive in the United States today.

ELLA FLAGG YOUNG. Yet another example of an outstanding early female educator is Ella Flagg Young (ca. 1845–1918). Overcoming immense obstacles, she earned a doctorate at the age of fifty under John Dewey, was appointed head of the Cook County Normal School in Illinois, and became superintendent of the gigantic Chicago public school system in 1909—all achievements that were unheard of for a female at that time. She was also elected the first female president of the male-dominated National Education Association.

MARY MCLEOD BETHUNE. Mary McLeod Bethune (1875–1955) was one of seventeen children born to African American parents in Mayesville, South Carolina, and the first family member not born in slavery. She received her first formal schooling at age nine in a free school for African American children. It is reported that she would come home from school and teach her brothers and sisters what she had learned each day. She came to believe that education was the key to helping African American children move into the mainstream of American life, and she devoted her life to improving educational opportunities for young African American women. She eventually started the Daytona Normal and Industrial School for Negro Young Women and later Bethune-Cookman College, where she served as president until 1942. She also believed that education helps everyone to respect the dignity of all people, regardless of color or creed, and that it is needed equally by Caucasian Americans, African Americans, and all other Americans. Bethune went on to serve as founder and head of the National Council of Negro Women; director of the Division of Negro Affairs of the National Youth Administration, President Franklin D. Roosevelt's special adviser on minority affairs; and special consultant for drafting the charter of the United Nations. Bethune was an effective, energetic human rights activist throughout her life and also a dedicated and professional career educator.

THE NINETEENTH AMENDMENT. Various groups first took interest in advancing the cause of females in the United States in the mid-1800s. The women's rights convention held at that time passed twelve resolutions that attempted to spur interest in providing females more equal participation and rights in U.S. society. The Civil War also furthered interest in the rights of women throughout the country, very likely, in part, as a spin-off of the abolition of slavery. It is interesting to note that not all the people in favor of doing away with slavery supported improved rights for women. For instance, not until 1920, when the Nineteenth Amendment passed, did women have the right to vote.

Unfortunately, the right to vote did not necessarily do much to improve the status of women; females continued to be denied equal educational and employment opportunities. The civil rights movement after World War II served as another impetus to the women's movement and gave rise to an additional round of improvements for females in U.S. society. Some authorities would trace the emergence of the current feminist movement to the 1960s, when a variety of activist groups coalesced to work against discrimination of all kinds in U.S. society. Some groups and individuals feel that adequate educational provisions and opportunities for females, minorities, and those with disabilities are still lacking in our school systems today at all levels.

PRIVATE EDUCATION IN AMERICA

Private education has been extremely important in the development of the United States. In fact, private schools carried on nearly all of the education in colonial times. The first colonial colleges such as Harvard, William and Mary, Yale, and Princeton were all private institutions. Many of the other early colonial schools, which can be thought of as **religion-affiliated schools**, were operated by churches, missionary societies, and private individuals.

The Right of Private Schools to Exist

In 1816 the state of New Hampshire attempted to take over Dartmouth College, which was a private institution. A lawsuit growing out of this effort ultimately resulted in the U.S. Supreme Court's first decision involving the legal rights of a private school. The Supreme Court decided that a private school's charter must be viewed as a contract and cannot be broken arbitrarily by a state. In other words, the Court decided that a private school could not be forced against its will to become a public school.

GO TO ··>
Additional information on legal aspects of education can be found in Chapter 10.

Subsequent court decisions have reconfirmed the rights of private education in a variety of ways. Generally speaking, for instance, courts have reconfirmed that private schools have a right to exist and in some cases even to share public funds, as long as these funds are not used for religious purposes. Examples of such actions include the use of state funds to purchase secular textbooks and to provide transportation for students to and from private schools.

THE IMPORTANT ROLE OF PRIVATE EDUCATION IN AMERICA. Not until after the Revolution, when there was a strong sense of nationalism, did certain educators advocate a strong public school system for the new nation. However, such recommendations were not acted on for many years. In the meantime, some Protestant churches continued to expand their schools during the colonial period. For instance, the Congregational, Quaker, Episcopal, Baptist, Methodist, Presbyterian, and Reformed churches all, at various times and in varying degrees, established and operated schools for their youth. It was the Roman Catholics and Lutherans, however, who eventually developed elaborate **parochial school** systems operated by their respective denominations.

Parochial Schools

As early as 1820 there were 240 Lutheran parochial schools in Pennsylvania. Although the number of Lutheran schools in that particular state eventually dwindled, Henry Muhlenberg and other Lutheran leaders continued to establish parochial schools until the public school system became well established. The Missouri Synod Lutheran Church has continued to maintain a well-developed parochial school system. Currently in the United States there are approximately 1,700 Lutheran elementary and secondary schools, which enroll about 200,000 pupils, and most of these schools are operated by the Missouri Synod Lutheran Church.

The Roman Catholic parochial school system grew rapidly after its beginnings in the 1800s. Enrollment in Catholic schools mushroomed between 1900 and 1960 from about 855,000 to more than five million students. The Roman Catholic parochial school system in the United States is now the largest private school system in the world.

A number of other religious groups have developed and operated their own parochial schools from time to time, and some of them still do today. Examples of such religious groups include the Mormons, Mennonites, Quakers, Wisconsin Synod Lutheran Churches, and various other religious groups.

religion-affiliated school A private school over which, in most cases, a parent church group exercises some control or to which the church provides a subsidy.

parochial school An educational institution operated and controlled by a religious denomination.

TEACHING IN CHALLENGING TIMES

How Can the Busy Teacher Keep Up with Historical and Contemporary Research?

Ask any teacher what her or his major problems are and "not having enough time" will likely be near the top of the list. So it is perhaps not surprising that many teachers find it difficult to keep up with current research that may help educators do a better job. And yet one of the important hallmarks of a professional is finding, evaluating, and implementing the results of valid and reliable research. For instance, when a person goes to a medical doctor, he or she expects that physician to be using knowledge based on the most recent medical research. By the same token, parents have a right to expect, when they send their children to school, that teachers will be using the most recent educational research in their educational practice. Thus, the professional dilemma is this: How do busy teachers locate, read, evaluate, and implement the best research results into their teaching? This task is made even more difficult by the fact that although a great volume of education research is constantly being conducted, a fair amount of it is not necessarily valid or reliable.

Teachers who are determined to put good research results into practice must first be able to read, understand, and evaluate educational research. To learn how to do this, you may need to take some basic research courses at a nearby college or university. You may also need to read research reports found in a variety of professional journals in your specialty fields. This may mean subscribing to such journals or getting your school to make them available. You may also wish to attend a variety of professional meetings where research is presented and discussed. And after you locate good research findings, you will need to do careful planning when you implement these research results in your classroom.

Unfortunately, there is no simple solution to this professional dilemma. We know that because we, too, struggle with this problem. However, we are convinced that the first step to solving this dilemma is becoming determined to offer your clients (your students and their parents) the very best education possible. We also are convinced that to do so requires knowledge of the best and most recent educational research.

WHAT ARE MY CHALLENGES?

1. What are your feelings about this professional dilemma at this point in your career development?
2. What might you be able to do at this time to help you prepare to deal with this dilemma?
3. To what degree do you feel your current teachers are keeping up with, and using, research in their teaching?

LEARNING FROM EDUCATIONAL HISTORY

Some educators do not yet realize that having an understanding of historical educational research can help them be a more effective educator. Knowing about our educational past can help you take advantage of past educational successes and avoid repeating some past educational failures. When you face a problem or need to make a decision concerning your teaching, you should take into consideration what educational research, past and present, might help you make wise decisions that will improve your work with students.

An understanding of our educational past will also help you better realize how very, very important the work of educators has been in our society and throughout the world.

Keeping Up on Historical and Current Research

By this time you realize that there is a great deal of information that you will need to be an effective teacher. This presents another dilemma for already busy educators like the one you will be. The accompanying "Teaching in Challenging Times" feature deals with one aspect of this challenge.

This chapter illustrates that there have been many different perspectives on education throughout the ages, and that a number of big historical ideas have grown out of the more detailed history of education discussed in the chapter. These include the ideas that adults in early societies provided the informal education that they felt necessary for children to succeed in their society; that more formal schools likely came into existence only as people developed written languages; that all societies around the world have developed their own forms of education, down through the ages, designed to fulfill their unique needs; and that human progress has, in large part, depended on education.

Perspectives on education in a challenging and changing world is a major theme throughout the book. Differing perspectives and change also apply to educational history. As pointed out earlier in this chapter, historians approach the understanding of history from differing perspectives and will certainly continue to do so in the future. The world of education will also certainly continue to change in the future, and this change will likely take place even more rapidly. And understand history is also a challenge. So each of our individual attempts to understand educational history will undoubtedly vary from person to person and will undoubtedly evolve over time.

JOURNAL FOR REFLECTION 2.3

1. Record in your journal some of the most important things you learned from this chapter.
2. Which, if any, of the items you listed will likely have practical value for you as a future educator? In what ways will it be helpful?

SUMMARY

THE EVOLUTION OF SCHOOLING (TO 476 CE)

- Any study of the beginnings of formal education should start with the fact that parents have always attempted to provide, in one way or another, the informal education their children needed to survive in their society.
- Formal schools very likely did not come into existence until four or five thousand years ago, as humans developed written languages.
- Current evidence suggests that one of the first well-organized educational systems was that evolved by the Greeks during what is commonly called the Age of Pericles.
- Greek knowledge and schools eventually blended into Roman schools and libraries.
- Examples of important educators from this early period included Socrates, Plato, Aristotle, and Quintilian.

EDUCATION IN THE MIDDLE AGES (476–1300)

- The period from 400 until 1000 is often called the Dark Ages because of the lack of educational activity in much of the Western world.
- Alcuin was an example of one of the few educators to make important contributions during the Dark Ages.
- During the latter part of the Middle Ages, there was a revived interest in learning, as exemplified by the work of Thomas Aquinas and the establishment of medieval universities.

EDUCATION IN TRANSITION (1300–1700)

- This period of educational history is commonly marked by two historical movements: the Renaissance and the Reformation.

- The Renaissance represented a rebellion on the part of the common people against their economic, educational, and religious suppression under the church, royalty, and landed gentry.
- These common people gradually demanded a better life and developed a spirit of inquiry, which created an interest in education and schooling.
- The fourteenth through eighteenth centuries saw the sometimes erratic, but nevertheless fairly continuous, progression of educational development and advancement throughout much of the world.
- The Protestant Reformation, led by Martin Luther, and the work of Ignatius of Loyola did much to improve education during this time.

EDUCATIONAL AWAKENING (1700)

- In the Western world, this period is often divided into the Age of Reason, which emphasized people's rational and scientific abilities, and the Emergence of Common Man, which sought to create a better education and life for all people.
- Examples of people who contributed to educational advancement in various ways during this period were Descartes, Voltaire, Rousseau, Pestalozzi, Herbart, and Froebel.

EVOLVING PERSPECTIVES OF EDUCATION IN OUR RAPIDLY DEVELOPING NATION

- Our earliest colonists brought their educational ideas and expectations with them from Europe and, soon after arriving in the New World, set about creating schools that fulfilled their needs.
- These efforts varied widely, from private tutorial education for plantation owners' children in the South, to religious

schools in the Middle Colonies, to public schools in the North.

- Most education was driven by religious motives, and much of the formal education beyond that needed to read the Bible was provided only for boys from the more well-to-do families.
- Elementary and secondary education for all children developed slowly.
- Schools and teaching materials were humble and meager in colonial America.
- Early colonial schools were poorly equipped.
- The hornbook was the most commonly used teaching device in colonial schools.
- Other somewhat later colonial textbooks included the *New England Primer* and the *Blue-Backed Speller*.
- The slate was an early device that students could write on.

MEAGER EARLY EDUCATION FOR DIVERSE POPULATIONS

- Early efforts to provide education for the poor, people of color, and women were very meager or nonexistent.

- Examples of early pioneers of African American education include Frederick Douglass, John Chavis, Prudence Crandall, and Booker T. Washington.
- Examples of female educational pioneers include Emma Willard, Maria Montessori, Ella Flagg Young, and Mary McLeod Bethune.

PRIVATE EDUCATION IN AMERICA

- The earliest education was provided by private schools, which have remained a very important part of our educational system.
- Parochial schools, conducted by religious groups, still prevail and make important contributions to education today.

LEARNING FROM EDUCATIONAL HISTORY

- This chapter illustrates that an understanding and appreciation of the history of education can help teachers be more effective.
- The "Teaching in Challenging Times" feature challenges you to find a way to keep up on historical and contemporary educational research during your educational career.

DISCUSSION STARTERS

1. What were the major contributions of several ancient societies to the development of education?
2. What factors contributed to the decline of education during the Dark Ages?
3. What were the strengths and weaknesses of Jean-Jacques Rousseau's ideas about children and education?
4. Discuss the evolution of elementary schools.

5. What historical conditions led to that uniquely U.S. institution, the comprehensive high school?
6. What are the highlights of the history of education of African Americans?
7. Discuss the roles that private schools have played in U.S. education.

SCHOOL-BASED OBSERVATIONS

1. More than two hundred years ago, Jean-Jacques Rousseau advocated that children be taught with love, patience, understanding, and kindness. As you work in the school, experiment with this basic approach to see whether it is effective for you. You might also wish to observe experienced teachers to see to what extent they teach children with love, patience, understanding, and kindness. We suggest that you experiment with other constructive ideas in this chapter as you observe and participate in the classroom.

2. As you work in schools, observe how they have changed relative to schools of the past. How are schools today similar to those of the past? How much and in what ways are students today similar to their historical counterparts? In what ways are they different?
3. While you are in the schools, visit with experienced teachers and administrators to discuss the ways that schools have changed over the years. Also ask how students, teaching methods, and parents have changed.

PORTFOLIO DEVELOPMENT

1. Make a list of the historical educational ideas mentioned in this chapter that are still valid and useful for educators today.

2. Summarize the evolution of the goals of public schools in colonial America and the United States. Develop a chart that creatively portrays this evolution.

3. Write an essay on the importance of education in the historical development of the United States.

WEB SOLUTIONS

Your instructor believes that understanding the past will help inform your future as a teacher. She asks you to write a paper about how the history of education will help you develop your perspective on education. To learn more about resources that were used and the environment in which they were used, go to the following websites:

www.cedu.niu.edu/blackwell The Blackwell History of Education Museum and Research Collection is one of the largest collections of its kind in the world. Much of the collection is listed on this website.

The Blackwell Museum has developed a variety of instructional materials (also listed on its website) designed to help you learn more about the antecedents of early American and U.S. education.

www.historyofeducation.org.uk The *History of Education* journal of the History of Education Society, located in England, is a useful general source of educational history.

www.countryschoolassociation.org A wonderful site for information on early one-room country schools.

MyEducationLab™

Go to the topic **History and Philosophy of Education** in the MyEducationLab (**www.myeducationlab.com**) for *Foundations of American Education: Becoming Effective Teachers in Challenging Times, 16e* where you can:

- Find learning outcomes for **History and Philosophy of Education**, along with the national standards that connect to these outcomes.
- Complete Assignments and Activities that can help you more deeply understand the chapter content.
- Apply and practice your understanding of the core teaching skills identified in the chapter with the Building Teaching Skills and Dispositions learning units.
- Access video clips of CCSSO National Teachers of the Year award winners responding to the question, "Why Do I Teach?" in the Teacher Talk section.
- Create, update, and share quality lesson plans with the Lesson Plan Builder.

- Access state licensure test requirements, overviews of what tests cover, and sample test items in the Certification and Licensure section.
- Access current state and national standards in the Licensure and Standards section.
- Learn how to create a high-quality teaching portfolio in the Preparing a Portfolio section.
- Access tips, advice, and other information on resume writing and interviewing, your first year of teaching, and law and public policies in the Beginning Your Career section.
- Check your comprehension of the content covered in the chapter with the Study Plan. Here you will be able to take a chapter pretest, receive feedback on your answers, and then access personalized Review, Practice, and Enrichment exercises to enhance your understanding of chapter content. After you complete the exercises, take a posttest to confirm your comprehension.

Historical Perspectives of Education

LEARNING OUTCOMES

After reading and studying this chapter, you should be able to:

1. List and detail several of the most important changes that have been made in the U.S. educational system during the past half century. (InTASC 1–10)

2. Explain the major changes in the evolution of the teaching profession. (InTASC 9 and 10: Professional Responsibility)

3. Discuss the development of the major aims of American education. (InTASC 1–10)

4. Explain the evolution of teacher training in colonial America and the United States. (InTASC 9 and10: Professional Responsibility)

5. Name some of the important major historical trends in American education. (InTASC 1–10)

6. Decide, explain, and defend the degree to which you believe it is possible to know, understand, and profit from the history of education. (InTASC 1–10)

EDUCATION in the NEWS

HISTORY OF THE FEDERAL ROLE IN EDUCATION

The original U.S. Department of Education was created in 1867 to collect information on schools and teaching that would help the states establish effective school systems. While the agency's name and location within the Executive Branch have changed during the past 145 or so years, this early emphasis on getting information on what works in education to teachers and education policy makers continues to the present day.

The passage of the Second Morrill Act in 1890 gave the then-named Office of Education responsibility for administering support for the original system of land-grant colleges and universities. Vocational education became the next major area of federal aid to schools, with the 1917 Smith-Hughes Act and the 1946 George-Barden Act focusing on agricultural, industrial, and home economics training for high school students.

World War II led to a significant expansion of federal support for education. The Lanham Act in 1941 and the Impact Aid laws of 1950 eased the burden on communities affected by the presence of military and other federal installations by making payments to school districts. And in 1944, the "GI Bill" authorized postsecondary education assistance that would ultimately send nearly 8 million World War II veterans to college.

The Cold War stimulated the first example of comprehensive federal education legislation, when in 1958 Congress passed the National Defense Education Act (NDEA) in response to the Soviet launch of the *Sputnik* satellite. To help ensure that highly trained individuals would be available to help America compete with the Soviet Union in scientific and technical fields, the NDEA included support for loans to college students; the improvement of science, mathematics, and foreign language instruction in elementary and secondary schools; graduate fellowships; foreign language studies; and vocational-technical training.

The antipoverty and civil rights laws of the 1960s and 1970s brought about the dramatic emergence of the Department of Education's equal-access mission. The passage of laws such as Title VI of the Civil Rights Act of 1964, Title IX of the Education Amendments of 1972, and Section 504 of the Rehabilitation Act of 1973, which prohibited discrimination based on race, sex, and disability, respectively, made civil rights enforcement a fundamental and long-lasting focus of the Department of Education. In 1965, the Elementary and Secondary Education Act launched a comprehensive set of programs, including the Title I program of federal aid to disadvantaged children, to address the problems of poor urban and rural areas. In that same year, the Higher Education Act authorized assistance for postsecondary education, including financial aid programs for needy college students.

In 1980, Congress established the Department of Education as a cabinet-level agency. Today, the Department of Education operates programs that touch on every area and level of education. The department's elementary and secondary programs annually serve more than roughly 14,000 school districts and some 56 million students attending more than about 97,000 public schools and roughly 28,000 private schools. Department programs also provide grant, loan, and work-study assistance to nearly 11 million postsecondary students.

QUESTIONS FOR REFLECTION

1. What is your reaction to, and evaluation of, the evolution of the role of our federal government in education?
2. What do you believe were some of the reasons our federal government became involved in education matters?
3. How would you evaluate the current federal government's involvement in education?

Source: Adapted from *The Federal Role in Education,* Washington, DC: U.S. Department of Education. Retrieved January 30, 2009, from www.ed.gov?about/overview/fed/role.html.

MyEducationLab™

Visit the MyEducationLab for *Foundations of American Education* to enhance your understanding of chapter concepts with a personalized *Study Plan.* You'll also have the opportunity to hone your teaching skills through video- and case-based *Assignments and Activities* and *Building Teaching Skills and Dispositions* lessons.

MORE STUDENTS AND BIGGER SCHOOLS

Many dramatic changes have occurred in education in the United States during the past half century. Examples of these rapid and often controversial changes that represent various perspectives will be briefly discussed in this chapter. The big historical ideas presented in this chapter are:

1. The phenomenal change and growth in both the size and complexity of U.S. educational establishments
2. The tremendous new demands and expectations being placed on our schools and teachers by the current information age
3. The major, as-yet-unsolved challenge to our society and to our schools to provide excellent equal educational opportunities to all students
4. An understanding that the history of education is of very practical value in helping contemporary educators improve education.

Enrollment Growth

Perhaps the single most dramatic change that has occurred in education during the past half-century is the sheer expansion in size of the educational enterprise. The total number of public school students in the United States has about doubled during this time. Although part of this rapid growth in school enrollment was attributable to overall population growth, a good part was due to the fact that greater percentages of people were going to school. Furthermore, people were staying in school much longer, as shown by the almost doubled enrollment in higher education.

Need for More Schools

As school enrollment dramatically increased, the need for new classrooms and buildings to house these students also increased. This need for new schools was generally concentrated in cities and suburbs. In fact, because of increased busing, school district consolidation, and shifting populations, some smaller rural schools were no longer needed, whereas more densely populated areas saw a drastic shortage of classrooms. Many schools had to resort to temporary mobile classrooms. Other strategies for coping with classroom shortages included larger classes; split scheduling that started some classes very early in the day and others very late; and classes held in a variety of makeshift areas such as gymnasiums, hallways, and storage closets. Many schools also rented additional space in nearby buildings. Fortunately, over time taxpayers were generally willing to approve the necessary bond referenda to provide the needed additional schools during this period of rapid growth in student enrollment.

Need for More Teachers

Naturally, this surge in student enrollment required many additional teachers, and at times colleges simply could not produce enough. To alleviate this situation, states lowered teacher certification requirements—sometimes to the point at which no professional education training was required at all. Over time, however, the nation managed to meet the demand for more teachers.

As one would expect, dealing with the increased numbers of students and teachers required a great deal more money. More buses had to be purchased, more books and other instructional materials had to be obtained, more school personnel had to be hired—more of everything was required to provide education to the burgeoning school population.

School District Consolidation

The consolidation of school districts is another notable administrative trend during the past seventy-five years. The number of separate school districts was reduced from 117,000 in 1940 to about 14,000 today. There was a corresponding decline in the number of one-teacher schools over this same period.

This is one of thousands of one-room schools established to educate rural children during the westward movement in America.

Growth of Busing

Both the number and the percentage of students who are bused to school have increased considerably during the past seventy-five years, as have the total cost and per-pupil cost of busing. In addition to the general busing of students necessitated by school district consolidation, integration efforts have often involved busing students away from their neighborhood schools. Busing students to school is still a big operation for the U.S. educational enterprise. It is estimated that about 60 percent of all students are bused to school by about 450,000 school buses.

Bigger School Budgets

Educational growth has driven the nation's public education costs to record heights. This rapid historical increase is illustrated by noting that the approximate cost of public education was $2 billion in 1940, $5 billion in 1950, $15 billion in 1960, $40 billion in 1970, $97 billion in 1980, and $208 billion in 1990. Even if the figures are corrected for inflation, public education has become considerably more expensive: The percentage of the gross domestic product spent on education had risen from 3.5 percent in 1940 to 7 percent by 1980 (U.S. Department of Commerce, 1982, p. 23).

GO TO ⋯▸
See Chapter 9 for more information on the current cost of education.

Rapid Curricular Growth and Changes

As enrollments have increased and schools have grown larger, more diverse curricula and programs have been developed in U.S. schools. This rapid growth of programs places a great deal of work and pressure on teachers, school administrators, and school boards.

Curricular growth, like most change, was the result of an accumulation of many smaller events. One such event was the publication in 1942 of the report of the Progressive Education Association's Eight-Year Study (1932–1940) of thirty high schools. The study showed that students attending "progressive" schools achieved as well as students at traditional schools. This report helped to create a climate that was more hospitable to experimentation with school curricula and teaching methodologies. The publication of a series of statements on the goals of U.S. education (the "Purposes of Education in American Democracy" [Educational Policies Commission (EPC), 1938], the "Education for All American Youth" [EPC, 1944], and the "Imperative Needs of Youth" [EPC, 1952]) helped broaden our schools' curricular offerings.

In 1958, shortly after the Soviet Union launched *Sputnik,* the world's first artificial satellite, Congress passed the National Defense Education Act (NDEA). This act provided a massive infusion of federal dollars to improve schools' science, mathematics, engineering, and foreign language programs. Eventually, innovative curricula such as SMSG mathematics, BSCS biology, and PSCS physics grew out of these programs. Other school programs, such as guidance, were later funded through the NDEA. Note that in the case of the NDEA, the federal government called on the schools to help solve what was perceived to be a national defense problem. Regardless of the motive, the NDEA represented another milestone that contributed significantly to the growth of the U.S. educational enterprise.

If one were to compare today's school curriculum with that of any school seventy-five years ago, one would find impressive changes. The 1940 curriculum was narrow and designed primarily for college-bound students, whereas today's curriculum is broader and designed for students of all abilities. This growth in the school curriculum has come about through the dedicated work of many people and represents one of the truly significant accomplishments in U.S. education.

Growth of Special Education Programs

GO TO ··➔
See the index for more information about education for students with exceptionalities.

Perhaps curriculum growth is best illustrated in the area of special education. Public schools historically did not provide special education programs for children with disabilities; rather, they simply accommodated such children as best they could, usually by placing them in regular classrooms. Teachers had little or no training to help them understand and assist the special child. In fact, relatively little was known about common disabilities.

Not until the federal government passed a series of laws during the later twentieth century—including Public Law 94-142, the Education for All Handicapped Children Act—did schools begin to develop well-designed programs for students with disabilities. These new special education programs required teachers who had been trained to work with students with visual or hearing impairments, students with behavior disorders, and students with a range of other exceptionalities. States and colleges then developed a wide variety of teacher-training programs for special educators.

JOURNAL FOR REFLECTION 3.1

1. Interview a retired teacher about the educational changes she or he has observed over a lifetime, and about the use of technology.
2. Ask what advice this retired educator has for beginning teachers today and record the answers.

MORE CHANGES, CHALLENGES, AND PERSPECTIVES

In the following pages, we will briefly explore the increasing complexities of educational systems in the United States and then look at some of the recent developments that have contributed to the professionalization of the field of education.

Increasing Federal Involvement

As shown in the "Education in the News" feature at the beginning of this chapter, our federal government has played an increasingly important role in education over the years. Policy makers at the federal level have provided funds for specific education programs and have passed many laws and regulations pertaining to schools. Presidents have created programs and regulations affecting schools; and federal courts have handed down decisions that have had great ramifications for our schools. And a variety of federal agencies have created programs and regulations for our schools.

The 1940s saw the nation at war, which provided the impetus for the federal government to pass a number of laws that affected education. The Vocational Education for National Defense Act was a crash program to prepare workers needed in industry to produce goods for national defense. The program operated through state educational agencies and trained more than seven million workers. In 1941 the Lanham Act provided funds for building, maintaining, and operating community facilities in areas where local communities had unusual burdens because of defense and war initiatives.

GI BILL. The federal government recognized a need to help young people whose careers had been interrupted by military service. The GI Bill of 1944 provided for the education of veterans of World War II. Later, similar bills assisted veterans of the Korean conflict. These federal acts afforded education to more than ten million veterans at a cost of almost $20 billion. Payments were made directly to veterans and to the colleges and schools the veterans attended. In 1966 another GI Bill was passed for veterans of the war in Vietnam. The initial cost of these acts amounted to a wonderful national investment because the government was repaid many times over by the increased taxes eventually paid by veterans who received this financial aid and later were employed.

NATIONAL SCIENCE FOUNDATION. The National Science Foundation, established in 1950, emphasized the need for continued support of basic scientific research. It was created to "promote the progress of science; to advance the national health, prosperity, and welfare; to secure the national defense; and for other purposes." The Cooperative Research Program of 1954 authorized the U.S. commissioner of education to enter into contracts with universities, colleges, and state education agencies to carry on educational research.

CATEGORICAL FEDERAL AID. Beginning in 1957, when the first Soviet space vehicle was launched, the federal government further increased its participation in education. The NDEA, the Vocational Education Act of 1963, the Manpower Development and Training Act of 1962, the Elementary and Secondary Education Act of 1965, and the International Education Act of 1966 are examples of increased federal participation in educational affairs. Federally supported educational programs such as Project Head Start, the National Teacher Corps, and Upward Bound are further indications of such participation.

All of these acts and programs have involved categorical federal aid to education—that is, aid for specific uses. Some people believe that the federal influence on education has recently been greater than either state or local influence. There can be no denying that through federal legislation, U.S. Supreme Court decisions, and federal administrative influence, the total federal effect on education is indeed great. Indications are that this effect will be even more pronounced in the future. It will remain for historians to determine whether this trend in U.S. education is a beneficial one.

THE STRUGGLE FOR EQUAL EDUCATIONAL OPPORTUNITY. The past half century has also been characterized by an increasing struggle for **equal educational opportunity** for all children, regardless of race, creed, religion, or gender.

This struggle was initiated by the African American activism movement, given additional momentum by the women's rights movement, and eventually joined by many other groups such as Hispanic Americans, Native Americans, and Asian Americans. Other chapters of this book will discuss the details of this relatively recent quest for equal educational opportunity. We mention it briefly at this point simply to emphasize that the struggle for equal educational opportunity represents an important but underrecognized recent historical movement in education. Today, many observers are pointing out that with the accelerated growth of minority subcultures within this nation, our economic and political survival depends to a great degree on educational opportunities and achievement for all segments of U.S. society.

NO CHILD LEFT BEHIND. One of the federal government's recent major efforts to improve education and to help children—especially disadvantaged children—learn is the sweeping legislation commonly referred to as No Child Left Behind (NCLB). While the goal of this law is admirable, it has been widely criticized, especially by the education profession. Examples of this criticism are that (1) sufficient funds have not been made available to effectively implement the law, (2) the mandated testing required by the law is not sufficiently valid or reliable and is too time-consuming, and (3) the law and testing do not take into account the extremely varied abilities of students. Recent changes in this law have allowed states to opt out of its requirements; and, as of this printing, twenty-nine states have chosen to do so. This law will be discussed in more detail throughout this book, but it is mentioned here as yet another example of increasing federal involvement in education. The accompanying "Perspectives on Diversity" feature, pertaining to NCLB, presents a thought-provoking challenge for a hypothetical teacher.

The Professionalization of Teaching

Formal teacher training is a relatively recent phenomenon. Teacher-training programs were developed during the late nineteenth century and the first half of the twentieth century. By the midpoint of the twentieth century, each state had established teacher certification requirements. Since then, teacher training and certification have been characterized by a "refinement" or "professionalization" movement.

GO TO ···>
Chapters 9 and 10 present more information on the administrative and financial aspects of federal involvement in education.

GO TO ···>
More information on NCLB can be found throughout the book. See index for locations.

equal educational opportunity Access to a similar education for all students, regardless of their cultural background or family circumstances.

PERSPECTIVES on DIVERSITY

Testing Students for NCLB

Because Dwayne has a learning disability, he is eligible for a special accommodation for the state tests that are conducted annually during the spring as part of No Child Left Behind (NCLB). Annette Beckett, a new teacher, has agreed to serve as the writer for the fourth grader during the next round of state assessments. She feels comfortable with this assignment because she had a dual elementary and special education major even though she is currently teaching in a second-grade classroom that does not have any students with disabilities. She also participated in an online training program for faculty who would be serving in this role for English-language learners and students with disabilities. She felt ready for the assignment.

During the test, Ms. Beckett sat next to Dwayne so that she could read to him from his test booklet. The process was working well. When they reached the section on comprehension, she read the passage, followed by the questions and possible answers from which Dwayne would have to choose. She paused to provide him time to respond. Dwayne, however, says, "Ms. Beckett, I didn't understand it. Please read it again."

Ms. Beckett thinks, "Does he really want me to read the whole passage again? He probably only needs to hear the middle section to respond to the question."

WHAT IS YOUR PERSPECTIVE?

1. If you were in Annette's position, what would you do? What are you required to do as the teacher providing the accommodation that Dwayne needs?
2. Could teachers or test prompters guide students to the correct answers? What could happen to a teacher who provided inappropriate assistance to a student?
3. What is the purpose of the annual testing of student achievement that is one of the key elements of NCLB?
4. Why are many teachers and parents concerned about the annual testing requirements of NCLB?

In addition to teacher education, this professionalization movement has touched just about all facets of education: curriculum; teaching methodology; training of school service personnel (administrators, counselors, librarians, and media and other specialists); in-service teacher training; teacher organizations; and even school-building construction. To understand clearly this professionalization movement, one need only compare pictures of an old one-room country school with a modern school building, read both a 1940 and a current publication of the American Federation of Teachers or National Education Association, contrast a mid-twentieth-century high school curriculum with one from today, or compile a list of the teaching materials found in a 1940 school and a similar list for a typical contemporary school.

Continued Importance of Private Schools

Nearly all early schools in colonial America were private and religion was the main purpose of education. Children were taught to read primarily so that they could study the Bible, and most early colleges were private, established primarily to train ministers.

As the public school system developed, however, the religious nature of education gradually diminished to the point that relatively few U.S. children attended religious schools. There have always been certain religious groups, however, who have labored to create and maintain their own private schools so that religious instruction could permeate all areas of the curriculum. The most notable of these religious groups has long been the Roman Catholic Church. During the past twenty-five years, though, enrollment in non-Catholic religious schools has grown dramatically, whereas Catholic school enrollment has declined.

Despite this recent trend, some Roman Catholic dioceses operate extremely large school systems, sometimes larger than the public school system in the same geographical area. One example is the Chicago archdiocese, which operates one of the largest Roman Catholic school systems in the United States.

With rare exceptions, private and parochial schools struggle to raise the funds they need to exist. They typically must charge a tuition fee, rely on private contributions, and conduct various fund-raising activities. In recent years, some school districts have made tuition vouchers available to parents who choose not to send their children to public schools.

Home Schooling

Many years ago, with few exceptions, the only parents who taught their children at home were those who lived so far from a school that it was impossible for their children to attend. In the past several decades, however, a growing number of parents have been choosing to educate their children at home—at least through the elementary grades and sometimes even through high school. The motivation for **home schooling** varies, but often it stems from a concern that children in the public schools may be exposed to problems such as drugs, alcohol, smoking, or gangs.

Other parents have religious motives, wanting their children to be taught in a particular religious context. Still other parents, who may have had bad experiences with public schools, simply feel they can provide a better education for their children at home. Recent laws and court cases have generally upheld the right, within certain parameters, of parents to educate their children if they choose to do so. The number of parents providing home schooling has grown each year in the last decade. A recent development among a minority of those who home school is a philosophy sometimes referred to as *unschooling*, in which parents provide no instruction but allow their children to learn through whatever they naturally do. As one would expect, there are many different perspectives on the value of home schooling in our society.

Continuing/Adult Education

Many forms of education for adults have existed for at least two centuries in this country. Shortly after the United States became a nation, a need to help new immigrants learn English caused schools, churches, and various groups to offer English language instruction; factories found a need to offer job and safety training; churches taught adult religious instruction; and so forth. The New York public schools, as well as many other large school systems, developed extensive English-language programs as well as adult vocational programs for people who were unemployed. Adult education took a great variety of forms and quickly grew into a vast network of programs dealing with nearly all aspects of life in the United States.

An example of a large early adult education development can be found in the Chautauqua movement at Lake Chautauqua, New York. Started in 1874 by the Methodist Sunday school, this adult education effort expanded to include correspondence courses, lecture classes, music education, and literary study on a wide variety of subjects throughout the eastern part of the nation.

Public schools increasingly offered adult education classes during the nineteenth century. Some of the larger public school systems, such as in Gary, Indiana, developed adult educational programs with an emphasis on vocational and technical training. Gradually, nearly all schools serving rural areas developed adult agricultural education programs to improve farming methods.

In 1964 the Economic Opportunity Act provided adult basic education funding to help adults learn to read and write. Since that time there has been a proliferation of continuing/adult education programs of all types throughout the United States. These programs serve an increasingly important purpose in our rapidly changing society, helping adults meet the challenges they face. They help new immigrants learn the English language, provide job training for people who are unemployed, update job skills, teach parenting skills, enable people to move to higher level employment, help people explore new hobbies, provide enrichment programs for retired folks, and generally make the world of education available to nearly all citizens regardless of age. The exploding popularity of the Elderhostel programs and other activities now offered for senior citizens, and the crowded evening parking lots at high schools and colleges throughout the country, attest to the popularity and success of continuing/adult education programs. In the future, as the world becomes increasingly complex and as more people remain active and healthy in old age, we predict that such adult/continuing education programs will continue to grow.

Evolution of Educational Testing

Educators have undoubtedly attempted to measure and assess student learning from the very beginning of formal education. However, it is only in the last sixty years that educational assessment has taken on vastly more importance, to the point in contemporary education that many feel assessment has become the proverbial "tail that wags the dog" in education decision-making. Let's briefly review this recent evolution of educational assessment.

home schooling Teaching children at home rather than in formal schools.

Many historians suggest that the increased attention given to educational testing in the past sixty years was sparked by James Conant, who had become president of Harvard University in 1933. Conant and his colleagues were influenced by the developments in mental ability testing done by Alfred Binet in France and by Lewis Terman in the United States, which were used extensively by the U.S. Army to test recruits.

Conant seized on a relatively new test called the Scholastic Aptitude Test (SAT), developed by Carl Bright at Princeton University, as a way to assess a student's potential for success at Harvard. He also helped to create a new organization, called the Educational Testing Service (ETS), which became—and remains—the major power in the educational assessment area. By the 1960s, more than a million high school students were taking the SAT, which most colleges used as one criterion for admission.

Many so-called standardized tests have been developed during the past sixty years in an attempt to measure different kinds of aptitude, learning, motivation, and virtually every aspect of education. These standardized tests have come under much criticism from many educators, parents, and others, who question their fairness and accuracy. Even so, they continue to be heavily used today.

GO TO ··⟩

See Chapter 11 for more information on educational assessment.

Educators have faced increasing pressure in recent years to develop improved ways to assess student learning. Much of this pressure has come from taxpayers, government, and the industrial world, often in the form of a demand for greater accountability. Most states have implemented a required system of achievement testing. The results of these achievement tests are commonly used to evaluate and compare schools—a controversial and unfair practice, according to many educators.

In fact, while agreeing that accurate educational assessment is absolutely essential to the educational enterprise, a growing number of educators are questioning many aspects of the increasing emphasis on educational assessment. This important topic will be discussed in various places throughout the text. Suffice it to point out here that educational assessment has grown rapidly and taken on increasing importance, for better or worse, in the past sixty years.

CHANGING AIMS OF EDUCATION

The aims of education in the United States have reflected changing perspectives on education over the years. During colonial times, the overriding aim of education at all levels was to enable students to read and understand the Bible, to gain salvation, and to spread the gospel.

After the colonies won independence from England, educational objectives—such as providing U.S. citizens with a common language, attempting to instill a sense of patriotism, developing a national feeling of unity and common purpose, and providing the technical and agricultural training the developing nation needed—became important tasks for the schools.

Committee of Ten

In 1892 a committee was established by the National Education Association (NEA) to study the function of the U.S. high school. This committee, known as the **Committee of Ten**, made an effort to set down the purposes of the high school at that time and made the following recommendations: (1) High school should consist of grades 7 through 12; (2) courses should be arranged sequentially; (3) students should be given very few electives in high school; and (4) one unit, called a Carnegie unit, should be awarded for each separate course that a student takes each year, provided that the course meets four or five times each week all year long.

The Committee of Ten also recommended trying to graduate high school students earlier to permit them to attend college sooner. At that time, the recommendation implied that high schools had a college preparatory function. These recommendations became powerful influences in shaping secondary education.

Committee of Ten
A historic National Education Association (NEA) committee that studied secondary education in 1892.

Seven Cardinal Principles

Before 1900, teachers had relatively little direction in their work because most educational goals were not precisely stated. This problem was partly overcome in 1918 when the Commission on Reorganization of Secondary Education published the report *Cardinal Principles of Secondary Education,* usually referred to as the Seven Cardinal Principles. In reality, the Seven Cardinal

Principles constitute only one section of the basic principles discussed in the original text, but that is the part that has become famous. These principles stated that the student should receive an education in the following seven fields: health, command of fundamental processes, worthy home membership, vocation, civic education, worthy use of leisure, and ethical character.

The Eight-Year Study

The following goals of education, or "needs of youth," were listed by the Progressive Education Association in 1938 and grew out of the Eight-Year Study of thirty high schools conducted by the association from 1932 to 1940:

1. Physical and mental health
2. Self-assurance
3. Assurance of growth toward adult status
4. Philosophy of life
5. Wide range of personal interests
6. Aesthetic appreciations
7. Intelligent self-direction
8. Progress toward maturity in social relations with age-mates and adults
9. Wise use of goods and services
10. Vocational orientation
11. Vocational competence.

"Purposes of Education in American Democracy"

Also in 1938, the Educational Policies Commission of the National Education Association set forth the "Purposes of Education in American Democracy." These objectives stated that students should receive an education in the four broad areas of self-realization, human relations, economic efficiency, and civic responsibility.

"Education for All American Youth"

In 1944 this same commission of the NEA published another statement of educational objectives, entitled "Education for All American Youth":

> Schools should be dedicated to the proposition that every youth in these United States—regardless of sex, economic status, geographic location, or race—should experience a broad and balanced education which will
>
> 1. equip him to enter an occupation suited to his abilities and offering reasonable opportunity for personal growth and social usefulness;
> 2. prepare him to assume full responsibilities of American citizenship;
> 3. give him a fair chance to exercise his right to the pursuit of happiness through the attainment and preservation of mental and physical health;
> 4. stimulate intellectual curiosity, engender satisfaction in intellectual achievement, and cultivate the ability to think rationally; and
> 5. help to develop an appreciation of the ethical values which should undergird all life in a democratic society.[1]

"Imperative Needs of Youth"

In 1952 the Educational Policies Commission made yet another statement of educational objectives, entitled "Imperative Needs of Youth":

1. All youth need to develop salable skills and those understandings and attitudes that make the worker an intelligent productive participant in economic life. To this end most youth need supervised work experience as well as education in the skills and knowledge of their occupations.
2. All youth need to develop and maintain good health and physical fitness.

---

[1]1944 NEA statement. Reprinted by permission of the National Education Association.

3. All youth need to understand the rights and duties of the citizen of a democratic society, and to be diligent and competent in the performance of their obligations as members of the community and citizens of the state and nation.

4. All youth need to understand the significance of the family for the individual and society and the conditions conducive to successful family life.

5. All youth need to know how to purchase and use goods and services intelligently, understanding both the values received by the consumer and the economic consequences of their acts.

6. All youth need to understand the methods of science, the influence of science on human life, and the main scientific facts concerning the nature of the world and of man.

7. All youth need opportunities to develop their capacities to appreciate beauty in literature, art, music, and nature.

8. All youth need to be able to use their leisure time well and budget it wisely, balancing activities that yield satisfactions to the individual with those that are socially useful.

9. All youth need to develop respect for other persons, to grow in their insight into ethical values and principles, and to be able to live and work cooperatively with others.

10. All youth need to grow in their ability to think rationally, to express their thoughts clearly, and to read and listen with understanding.[2]

These various statements concerning educational objectives, made during the last century, sum up fairly well the historical aims of U.S. public education. These changing aims also show how perspectives on the purposes of education have evolved over time.

The following "Who Is Right?" feature shows that differing perspectives on the aims of education still exist today.

PREPARATION OF TEACHERS

Because most present-day teachers have excellent preparation including at least four—and often five to eight—years of college education, it is difficult to believe that teachers have historically had little or no training.

European Beginnings of Teacher Training

The first formal teacher-training school in the Western world of which we have any record was mentioned in a request to the king of England, written by William Byngham in 1438, requesting that "he may yeve withouten fyn or fee (the) mansion ycalled Goddeshous the which he hath made and edified in your towne of Cambridge for the free herbigage of poure scolers of Gramer" (Armytage, 1951).

Byngham was granted his request and established Goddeshous College as a teacher-training institution on June 13, 1439. Students at this college gave demonstration lectures to fellow students to gain practice teaching. Classes were even conducted during vacations so that country schoolmasters could also attend. Byngham's college still exists today as Christ's College of Cambridge University. At that early date of 1439, Byngham made provision for two features that are still considered important in teacher education today: scheduling classes so that teachers in service can attend and providing some kind of student teaching experience. Many present-day educators would probably be surprised to learn that these ideas are nearly 600 years old.

Teachers in the various kinds of colonial elementary schools typically had only an elementary education themselves, but a few had attended a Latin grammar school or a private academy. It was commonly believed that to be a teacher required only that the instructor know something about the subject matter to be taught; therefore, no teacher, regardless of the level taught, received training in the methodology of teaching.

Because many colonial schools were conducted in connection with a church, the teacher was often considered an assistant to the minister. Besides teaching, other duties of some early colonial teachers were "to act as court messenger, to serve summonses, to conduct certain ceremonial services of the church, to lead the Sunday choir, to ring the bell for public worship, to dig the graves, and to perform other occasional duties."

---

[2]Educational Policies Commission 1952. Reprinted by permission of the National Education Association.

WHO IS RIGHT?

IS TEACHING MANNERS A GOOD USE OF CLASSROOM TIME?

Historically, schools emphasized the teaching of manners, but schools today have tended to place less emphasis on this subject, a trend that some believe to be unfortunate.

YES

Kirk Hollinbeck teaches fourth grade at Procter Elementary in Independence, Missouri.

When children aren't taught manners at home, I believe the responsibility falls to the school. Teaching students how to respond when greeted, to say please and thank you, and to make eye contact are skills that last a lifetime. In recent years, mounting expectations, additional responsibilities, and dwindling resources have made teaching more stressful. How can we find time to teach manners and courtesy? I incorporate them into my student behavior expectations. I teach the importance of good manners and courtesy the first day and model positive behaviors all year. I teach "please" and "thank you" when I pass out pretzels or cereal for snack time. Students have two choices when I offer a snack: they can say "thank you" or "no thank you." Mouths drop when I take the snack back because a student forgot to say "thank you." I model courtesy through my interactions with students, colleagues, and parents. We practice how to make eye contact and discuss ways to respond when greeted.

I was surprised that many students have never been taught what to do when someone says "good morning." When I talk with a student or another adult, my students have learned that they must wait until our conversation has finished before I will talk to them. Is teaching manners and courtesy a good use of classroom time? Do you prefer adults who are polite or rude?

NO

Carolyn Cowgill is a retired teacher from the Central Bucks School District in Doylestown, Pennsylvania.

School is a social experience, and teachers will always spend some time each day dealing with manners. However, with so many academic subjects to thoroughly introduce, discuss, and lock in (especially with testing requirements), it should not be the teacher's responsibility to teach basic manners as part of the formal curriculum. Manners should be taught at home from the time a parent begins the dialogue while feeding and diapering the baby!

Before a child enters school, caretakers, parents, or relatives need to define traditional boundaries and reward courteous interactions with others. Before starting school, children must learn patience, to consider others' space and feelings, how to communicate their needs politely, and to treat each other with kindness. If parents have done their job, teachers only need to reinforce manners in the classroom and on the playground. Most children will accept the rules at school because they have already heard them at home, and having sets of rules makes children feel safe.

Further, because children pick up somewhat different cues for manners in each unique culture, families are the best teachers of manners. When children begin school, they then have a basis for observing their classmates and teachers and adapting to appropriate classroom manners.

WHAT IS YOUR PERSPECTIVE ON THIS ISSUE?

Source: "Is Teaching Good Manners a Good Use of Classroom Time?" *NEA Today* (November 2006), p. 43. Reprinted by permission of the National Education Association.

Colonial Teachers

Elementary school teachers in colonial America were very poorly prepared; in fact, more often than not, they had received no special training at all. The single qualification of most teachers was that they themselves had been students. On the other hand, most colonial college teachers, private tutors, Latin grammar school teachers, and academy teachers had received some kind of college education, usually at one of the well-established colleges or universities in Europe. As time passed, however, a few received their education at an American colonial college.

Teachers as Indentured Servants

One of the first forms of teacher training grew out of the medieval guild system, in which a young man who wished to enter a certain field of work served a lengthy period of apprenticeship with a master in the field. Some young men became teachers by serving as apprentices to master teachers, sometimes for as long as seven years.

Sometimes the colonies used white indentured servants as teachers. Many people who came to the United States bought passage by agreeing to work for some years as indentured

FIGURE 3.1 1786 advertisement for indentured servants.

> Men and Women Servants
>
> ## JUST ARRIVED
>
> In the ship Paca, Robert Caulifield, Master in five weeks from Belfast and Cork, a number of healthy Men and Women SERVANTS.
> Among them are several valuable trademan, viz.
> Carpenters, Shoemakers, Coopers, Blacksmiths, Staymakers, Bookbinders, Clothiers, Diers, Butchers, Schoolmasters, Millrights, and Labourers.
> Their indentures are to be disposed of by the Subscribers,
>
> Brown, and Maris
> William Wilson

servants. The ship's captain would then sell the indentured servant's services, more often than not by placing an ad in a newspaper. Such an ad, shown in Figure 3.1, appeared in a May 1786 edition of the *Maryland Gazette*.

Records reveal that among early immigrants who were advertised and sold as teachers, there were many indentured servants and convicted felons. In fact, it has been estimated that at least one-half of all the teachers in colonial America may have come from these sources. This is not necessarily a derogatory description of these early teachers when we consider that many poor people bought their passage to the colonies by agreeing to serve as indentured servants for a period of years, and that in England at that time hungry and desperate people could be convicted as felons and deported for simply stealing a loaf of bread.

Teaching Apprenticeships

Some colonial teachers learned their trade by serving as apprentices to schoolmasters. Court records reveal numerous such indentures of apprenticeship; the following was recorded in New York City in 1772:

> This Indenture witnesseth that John Campbel Son of Robert Campbel of the City of New York with the Consent of his father and mother hath put himself and by these presents doth Voluntarily put and bind himself Apprentice to George Brownell of the Same City Schoolmaster to learn the Art Trade or Mastery—for and during the term of ten years And the said George Brownell Doth hereby Covenant and Promise to teach and instruct or Cause the said Apprentice to be taught and instructed in the Art Trade or Calling of a Schoolmaster by the best way or means he or his wife may or can.[3]

Teacher Training in Academies

One of Benjamin Franklin's justifications for proposing an academy in Philadelphia was that some of the graduates would make good teachers. Speculating on the need for such graduates, Franklin wrote,

> A number of the poorer sort [of academy graduates] will be hereby qualified to act as Schoolmasters in the Country, to teach children Reading, Writing, Arithmetic, and the Grammar of their Mother Tongue, and being of good morals and known character, may be recommended from the Academy to Country Schools for that purpose; the Country suffering at present very much for want of good Schoolmasters, and obliged frequently to employ in their schools, vicious imported servants, or concealed Papists, who by their bad Examples and Instructions often deprave the Morals and corrupt the Principles of the children under their Care.[4]

The fact that Franklin said some of the "poorer" graduates would make suitable teachers reflects the low regard for teachers typical of the time. The academy that Franklin proposed was established in 1751 in Philadelphia, and many graduates of academies after that time did indeed become teachers.

---

[3]Court records New York City 1772.

[4]Benjamin Franklin, "Paper on the Academy," July 31, 1750.

Normal Schools

Many early educators recognized this country's need for better-qualified teachers; however, it was not until 1823 that the first teacher-training institution was established in the United States. This private school, called a **normal school** after its European prototype, which had existed since the late seventeenth century, was established by the Reverend Mr. Samuel Hall in Concord, Vermont. Hall's school did not produce many teachers, but it did signal the beginning of formal teacher training in the United States.

The early normal school program usually consisted of a two-year course. Students typically entered the normal school right after finishing elementary school; most normal schools did not require high school graduation for entrance until about 1900. The nineteenth-century curriculum was much like the curriculum of the high schools of that time. Students reviewed subjects studied in elementary school, studied high school subjects, had a course in teaching (or "pedagogy" as it was then called), and did some student teaching in a model school, usually operated in conjunction with the normal school. The subjects offered by a normal school in Albany, New York, in 1845 included English grammar, English composition, history, geography, reading, writing, orthography, arithmetic, algebra, geometry, trigonometry, human physiology, surveying, natural philosophy, chemistry, intellectual philosophy, moral philosophy, government, rhetoric, theory and practice of teaching, drawing, music, astronomy, and practice teaching.

Horace Mann was instrumental in establishing the first state-supported normal school, which opened in 1839 in Lexington, Massachusetts. Other public normal schools, established shortly afterward, typically offered a two-year teacher-training program. Some of the students came directly from elementary school; others had completed secondary school. Some states did not establish state-supported normal schools until the early 1900s.

First State Normal School was adopted from European teacher training schools and is still standing in Lexington, Massachusetts.

State Teachers' Colleges

During the early part of the twentieth century, several factors caused a significant change in normal schools. For one thing, as the population of the United States increased, so did the enrollment in elementary schools, thereby creating an ever-increasing demand for elementary school teachers. Likewise, as more people attended high school, more high school teachers were needed. To meet this demand, normal schools eventually expanded their curriculum to include secondary teacher education. The growth of high schools also created a need for teachers who were highly specialized in particular academic subjects, so normal schools gradually established subject matter departments and developed more diversified programs. The length of the teacher education program was expanded to two, three, and finally four years; this longer duration fostered development and diversification of the normal school curriculum. The demand for teachers increased from about 20,000 in 1900 to more than 200,000 in 1930, only thirty years later.

The United States gradually advanced technologically to the point at which more college-educated citizens were needed. The normal schools assumed a responsibility to help meet this need by establishing many other academic programs in addition to teacher training. As normal schools extended their programs to four years and began granting baccalaureate degrees, they also began to call themselves *state teachers' colleges*. For most institutions, the change in name took place during the 1930s.

Changes in Mid-Twentieth-Century Teacher Education

Universities entered the teacher preparation business on a large scale around 1900. Before then, some graduates of universities had become high school teachers or college teachers, but not until about 1900 did universities begin to establish departments of education and add a full range of teacher education programs to the curriculum.

normal school The first type of American institution devoted exclusively to teacher training.

FIGURE 3.2 Evolution of teacher preparation institutions.

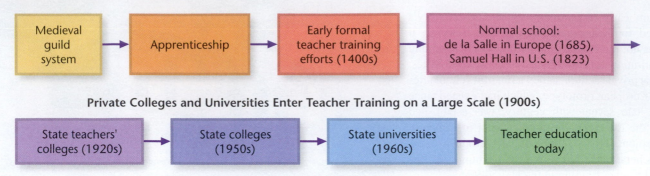

Just as the normal schools expanded in size, scope, and function until they became state teachers' colleges, so the state teachers' colleges expanded to become *state colleges*. This change in name and scope took place for most institutions around 1950. The elimination of the word *teacher* really explains the story behind this transition. The new state colleges gradually expanded their programs beyond teacher education and became multipurpose institutions. One of the main reasons for this transition was that a growing number of students coming to the colleges demanded a more varied education. The state teachers' colleges developed diversified programs to try to meet their demands.

Many of these state colleges later became state universities, offering doctoral degrees in a wide range of fields. Some of our largest and most highly regarded universities evolved from normal schools. Figure 3.2 diagrams the evolution of U.S. teacher preparation institutions.

Obviously, establishing the teaching profession has been a long and difficult task. Preparation of teachers has greatly improved over the years from colonial times—when anyone could be a teacher—to the present, when people (only the best and the brightest) such as you must meet rigorous requirements for permanent teacher certification.

JOURNAL FOR REFLECTION 3.2

1. Describe and evaluate a learning experience you remember from your own school days.
2. What made the experience memorable, and what role did the teacher play in the learning process?

RECENT TRENDS IN EDUCATION

Education experienced major changes and a wide variety of perspectives following World War II as John Dewey, George Counts, William Bagley, W. W. Charters, Lewis Terman, and other intellectuals who had held sway during the first half of the twentieth century yielded to a somewhat less philosophically oriented breed of researchers represented by Abraham Maslow, Robert Havighurst, Benjamin Bloom, J. P. Guilford, Lee Cronbach, Jerome Bruner, Marshall McLuhan, Noam Chomsky, and Jean Piaget.[5] The Progressive Education Association closed its doors, and a series of White House conferences on children, youth, and education were inaugurated in an attempt to improve education.

No school system on earth has been scrutinized, analyzed, and dissected as profoundly and as mercilessly as that in the United States. From the late 1940s to the mid-1950s, educational institutions at all levels were not only flooded with unprecedented numbers of students but also censored and flailed unmercifully by self-ordained critics (Hyman Rickover, Arthur Bestor, and Rudolph Flesch). In retrospect this frantic rush to simultaneously patronize and criticize the institution seems a curious contradiction. The public schools were characterized as godless, soft, undisciplined, uncultured, wasteful, and disorganized. Critics who remembered the high failure rates on tests given to World War II draftees were determined to raise the public's levels of physical fitness and literacy; others who detected a weakening of moral and spiritual values were eager to initiate citizenship and character education programs. The enrollment in nonpublic schools doubled, correspondence schools of all kinds sprang into existence, and the popular press carried

---

[5]We thank Dr. Donald Barnes for many of the ideas presented in this section.

articles and programs designed to help parents augment the basic skills taught within the school program. In 1955 there were an estimated 450 correspondence schools serving 700,000 students throughout the country.

New Emphases in Education

Fortunately, although some people were highly critical of the schools, not everybody panicked. There were physical fitness programs, character education projects, a general tightening of educational standards, and much more. J. P. Guilford, E. Paul Torrence, Jacob Getzels, and others explored the boundaries of creativity; Alfred Barr and D. G. Ryans carried out exhaustive studies of teacher characteristics; and just about everybody experimented with new patterns of organization. There were primary block programs, interage groupings, plans devised by and named for George Stoddard and J. Lloyd Trump, core programs, and a host of other patterns or combinations of plans structured around subject areas, broad groupings of subjects, or pupil characteristics. There were programs for the gifted and the not-so-gifted, and there was a new concern for foreign language instruction as well as the functional use of English. There was also a limited resurgence of Montessori schools and several one-of-a-kind experimental schools such as Amidon and Summerhill. While all this was taking place within the schools, the school systems themselves were consolidating; by 1960 there were only about one-third as many school districts as had existed twenty years earlier.

ANALYSIS OF TEACHING. Another emphasis found expression in the **analysis of teaching**. For half a century, researchers had been attempting to identify the characteristics and teaching styles that were most closely associated with effective instruction. Hundreds of studies had been initiated, and correlations had been done among them. During the 1950s, the focus began changing from identification of what ought to occur in teaching to scrutiny of what actually does occur. Ned Flanders and other researchers developed observational scales for assessing verbal communications between and among teachers and students. The scales permitted observers to categorize and summarize specific actions by teachers and students. These analyses were followed by studies of nonverbal classroom behaviors.

Another series of investigations involving the wider range of instructional protocols was patterned after the time-and-motion studies used earlier for industrial processes. Dwight Allen and several other educators attempted to analyze teacher behaviors, delineate the components of effective teaching, and introduce teacher candidates to the elements judged most important to good teaching. The change in focus from studies of teacher characteristics to analyses of what actually occurs in classrooms has offered educators highly fruitful insights into teaching and learning and has provided usable instruments for further investigations of classroom behavior. It is now possible to assess the logical, verbal, nonverbal, affective, and attitudinal dimensions of instruction, as well as the intricate aspects of cognition and concept development.

TEACHER EFFECTIVENESS. During the past fifty years, research has focused even more closely on the instructional patterns of effective teachers. The **effective teaching** movement that is based on this research offers today's teachers important skills. In common with the schoolteachers of sixty years ago, today's teachers learn to be strong leaders who direct classroom activities, maximize the use of instructional time, and teach in a clear, businesslike manner.

Effective teachers now employ structured, carefully delineated lessons. They break larger topics into smaller, more easily grasped components, and they focus on one thought, point, or direction at a time. They check prerequisite skills before introducing new skills or concepts. They accompany step-by-step presentations with many probing questions. Teachers offer detailed explanations of difficult points and test students on one point before moving on to the next. They provide corrective feedback where needed and stay with the topic under study until students comprehend the major points or issues. Effective teachers use prompts and cues to assist students through the initial stages of acquisition.

This recent emphasis on demonstration, prompting, and practice is a far cry from the relatively unstructured classroom activities of the recent past. We now emphasize carefully created learning goals and lesson sequences. It will be interesting to see whether the educational pendulum swings back to a new focus on student concerns and initiatives at some time in the future.

GO TO ⋯>
More information on effective teaching can be found in Chapters 12 and 13.

analysis of teaching
Procedures used to enable teachers to critique their own performance in the classroom.

effective teaching
A movement to improve teaching performance based on the outcomes of educational research.

THE EVOLUTION OF EDUCATIONAL TECHNOLOGY. In some sense, even very early educators made use of what might be considered forms of basic educational technology. For instance, if a caveman or cavewoman used a stick or a finger to draw a symbol of something in the dirt or sand in an effort to teach a child something, that might be considered a rudimentary form of educational technology. Printed words are a form of educational technology, and hornbooks used as early as the Middle Ages contained printed words. The use of pictures, such as those included in the form of woodcuts in early books, are also forms of early educational technology.

Needless to say, technology has evolved over time to the advanced forms that we are familiar with today—technological advancements that early educators undoubtedly never dreamed of. One wonders what forms of educational technology—that we, during this age, cannot even imagine—might be developed at some point in the future. What do you think?

STUDY OF THE LEARNING PROCESS. Several leading educational researchers in the United States and Europe have sought to analyze and describe how children learn. All of these investigators have stressed the importance of successful early learning patterns and the problems associated with serious learning deficits. They also believe that important elements within the environment may be changed or modified to promote learning. Lev Vygotsky, a Russian, developed a social development theory in the late 1800s that suggested social interaction among children plays a major role in cognitive development. His work contributed significantly to the founding of constructionist psychology.

Robert Havighurst, a University of Chicago professor, identified specific developmental tasks that he believes children must master if they are to develop normally. He even suggests there may be periods during which certain tasks must be mastered if they are to become an integral part of children's repertoire of responses. There may also be "teachable moments" (periods of peak efficiency for the acquisition of specific concepts/skills) during which receptivity is particularly high. Havighurst has caused educators to look carefully at the motivations and needs of children (Havighurst & Neugarten, 1962).

Jean Piaget. A Swiss psychologist, Jean Piaget (1896–1980) was educated at the University of Paris. Through his work with Alfred Binet, who developed one of the first intelligence tests, Piaget became interested in how children learn. He spent long hours observing children of different ages and eventually created a theory of mental or **cognitive development**.

Piaget believed that children learn facts, concepts, and principles in four major stages.

cognitive development
A learner's acquisition of facts, concepts, and principles through mental activity.

Jean Piaget, French child psychologist.

- Stage 1: Up until about age two, he suggested, a child is at the *sensorimotor stage* and learns mainly through the hands, mouth, and eyes.
- Stage 2: From about two to seven years of age, a child is at the *preoperational stage* and learns primarily through language and concepts.
- Stage 3: Between ages seven and eleven, a child's learning is characterized by *concrete operations*, which involve the use of more complex concepts such as numbers.
- Stage 4: The final learning stage identified by Piaget is called the *formal operations* stage. This stage typically begins between ages eleven and fifteen and continues throughout adulthood. During this final stage, the learner employs the most sophisticated and abstract learning processes. Although children do not all fit neatly into these categories, Piaget's work has contributed much to educators' understanding of the learning process and has helped teachers develop more appropriate teaching strategies for students at different developmental stages.

Many important educators were concerned about providing education for all children, including those of different ethnic and cultural backgrounds. The authors of this textbook believe that knowledge of educational history can help contemporary educators better serve students in general and, for example, can help them improve multicultural education, which is especially challenging to educators today. The accompanying "Teaching in Challenging Times" feature explores this possibility.

A contemporary of Havighurst, Jerome Bruner of Harvard, has also postulated a series of developmental steps or stages that he believes children encounter as they mature. These involve action, imagery, and symbolism. Bruner's cognitive views have stressed student inquiry and the breaking down of larger tasks into components.

TEACHING IN CHALLENGING TIMES

Can a Knowledge of History Help to Improve Multicultural Education?

When you become a teacher, you will be expected to provide multicultural education for your students, regardless of the age level or subjects you teach. Most teachers today face the dilemma of wanting to provide their students with a high-quality multicultural program, but being frustrated by the lack of time and support for doing so.

As you will learn, racial and ethnic prejudice and injustice have been present throughout U.S. educational history. Unfortunately, there is still considerable racial and ethnic strife in the United States today, and much of this strife has filtered into the halls of education. Debates rage about how schools should meet the educational demands of a complex multicultural society. As a teacher, you will be expected to join in this debate and help search for answers.

James Banks, a leading researcher in multicultural education at the University of Washington, feels past efforts have been too superficial. He asserts that "additive approaches" treat multicultural material as "an appendage to the main story of the development of the nation and to the core curriculum." Instead, multicultural education should integrate multicultural perspectives throughout the curriculum, on an equal footing with white European perspectives.

Despite the lack of both time and adequate school district encouragement and support, there are many things that a determined and creative teacher can do to integrate multicultural education throughout the curriculum. Teachers can also encourage the school district to develop and support comprehensive programs for multicultural education and then participate in developing those plans.

WHAT ARE MY CHALLENGES?

1. What are the historical antecedents that have contributed to the lack of racial and ethnic understanding in U.S. society?
2. Should education programs seek to eliminate cultural differences among individuals or to preserve and perhaps celebrate them?
3. What can you do in your classroom to improve multicultural education? Why and how?
4. What additional information would you like about multicultural education, and where might you find such information?

Benjamin Bloom, author of *Taxonomy of Educational Objectives* and distinguished service professor at the University of Chicago, has attempted to identify and weigh the factors that control learning. He believes that one can predict learning outcomes by assessing three factors: (1) the cognitive entry behaviors of a student (the extent to which the pupil has mastered prerequisite skills), (2) the affective entry characteristics (the student's interest in learning the material), and (3) the quality of instruction (the degree to which the instruction offered is appropriate for the learner). Bloom's research is reflected in models of direct instruction, particularly mastery learning, in which teachers carefully explain, illustrate, and demonstrate skills and provide practice, reinforcement, corrective feedback, and remediation.

B. F. SKINNER. Burrhus Frederic (B. F.) Skinner (1904–1990) became one of the foremost early educational psychologists in U.S. education. He developed **behavioral theory**, which was a theory focusing on outward behavior that suggested students could be successfully trained and conditioned to learn just about anything a teacher desired.

This required the teacher to break down the learning into small sequential steps. Skinner even experimented with teaching machines that presented the learner with small sequential bits of information—an idea that has been revived today in the form of computer-assisted instruction. Skinner published many works, including *The Technology of Teaching, Beyond Freedom and Dignity*, and *Walden Two*. He contributed much to our present-day understanding of human learning and helped to advance the technology of teaching.

Educational Critics

Another change in education was pointed out by a phalanx of critics—all holding differing perspectives but all focusing on low educational standards—including Edgar Friedenberg (*Coming of Age in America*), Charles Silberman (*Crisis in the Classroom*), Jonathan Kozol (*Death at an Early Age*), Ivan Illich (*Deschooling Society*), John Holt (*How Children Fail*), and even the federal government (*A Nation at Risk*, 1983). Some critics, such as Silberman, urged schools to refurbish what they already have; others, including Illich, wanted to abandon the

behavioral theory
A theory that considers the outward behavior of students to be the main target for change.

schools altogether. These critics have not gone unnoticed: Friedenberg's call for alternatives to traditional education, Silberman's endorsement of open education, and Kozol's plea for equal opportunity are all reflected to some degree in innovative programs currently being used from coast to coast.

You, and all educators, need to learn much about multicultural programming, as Kozol and others remind us. We believe that a good understanding of educational history can help you do that.

JOURNAL FOR REFLECTION 3.3

What are your perspectives on some of the relatively recent trends in education that you have observed or experienced? Record your responses in your journal.

Major Educational Events of the Past Century

As we moved into the twenty-first century, many people reflected on educational accomplishments in the United States during the past hundred years. As would be expected, perspectives differ considerably on this subject. Ben Brodinsky, an education journalist, has suggested that the GI Bill of Rights should perhaps be considered the single most important educational event of the past century. He lists the desegregation of schools as the second most important and the federal Education for All Handicapped Children Act as the third most important educational event of the twentieth century.

Undoubtedly, many important educational events and accomplishments occurred during the twentieth century—the list could go on and on. One example of significant progress made by the U.S. educational system in the past seventy-five years is reflected in the increased percentage of students completing high school—from about 50 percent in 1940 to about 70 percent in 1990. What would you put on your list of the most important educational changes, events, and/or accomplishments of the last century?

Figure 3.3 shows a timeline of yet other efforts that have influenced education over the past half-century.

It is difficult to draw meaningful inferences from recent events that have not yet stood the test of time. The implications of recent educational events will eventually be found in the answers to questions such as these: What should be the role of the federal government in education? How can equal educational opportunity be achieved in the United States? How professionalized should teachers and the school system be? To what degree should educational policy and practice be influenced by litigation? How will school reform movements change the practice of education? What will be the expanding and evolving future role of technology in our schools? The answers to these questions—and other questions you may have in mind—will be colored by the perspectives through which people view the world, children, and schools. We believe that viewing all educational questions through well-informed historical perspectives yields more valid answers.

LOOKING BACK TO HELP US LOOK AHEAD!

As we have pointed out a number of times, perspectives on education have changed throughout history and are now changing ever more rapidly. This makes predicting the future of education very difficult—perhaps even impossible, and somewhat foolhardy. Rather than attempting to do so, our best advice to you is that you should expect to experience many changes, challenges, and ever diverse perspectives on education during your career as an educator. Of course, you will need to try to understand and adapt to these rapid changes and the challenges they present to you as an educator. Knowing and understanding educational history will help you do this better.

FIGURE 3.3 Timeline of selective efforts to improve schools.

	1953–61	1961–69	1969–74	1974–77	1977–81	1981–89	1989–93	1993–2001	2000s	2008–
Presidents	Eisenhower	Kennedy, Johnson	Nixon	Ford	Carter	Reagan	G. H. W. Bush	Clinton	G. W. Bush	Obama
Crisis	*Sputnik*	Civil rights	Viet Nam			Ending the Cold War			Two wars and declining economy	Stimulating economic recovery
Federal Office for Education	U.S. Office of Education	U.S. Office of Education	U.S. Office of Education, National Institute of Education	U.S. Office of Education	U.S. Department of Education	U.S. Department of Education	U.S. Department of Education	U.S. Department of Education	U.S. Department of Education	U.S. Department of Education
Policies	Build state and local capacity to educate people with disabilities	Elementary and Secondary Education Act (ESEA)	Reauthorization of ESEA linking federal aid to student achievement	Education for All Handicapped Children Act (P.L. 94-142)	Reauthorization of ESEA with federal aid dependent on rising test scores	Education summit; first meeting of president and governors	Reauthorization of ESEA, with high-stakes testing	Reauthorization of ESEA; now called No Child Left Behind (NCLB), response to intervention (RTI)		American Recovery and Reinvestment Act
Related Reports and Publications						*A Nation at Risk*		*Goals 2000*	Public posting of test scores for all public schools	
Change Initiatives Based on Research		Major curriculum development projects: science and math	Effective teachers: direct instruction and classroom management			Effective schools: whole school and principals		School reform programs, school improvement, and value added	Standards, data-driven decision making, professional learning communities (PLCs)	Early childhood, reform and investment in K–12, restore leadership in higher education
Teacher Challenge					Effectively Help Students Learn					

SUMMARY

MORE STUDENTS AND BIGGER SCHOOLS

- During the past seventy-five years the U.S. education system has experienced unprecedented changes and growth in both size and complexity.

- The great increase in numbers of students over these years has created a challenging need for more school buildings and many more teachers.

- Population increases and shifts from rural settings to cities required bigger schools and large, elaborate school busing systems.

- There has also been an amazing expansion of educational curricula and program diversification for different types of students at all levels during the past sixty years.

- All of this growth in size and programs has resulted in a tremendous increase in school budgets.

- Programs for students with special needs have increased tremendously in recent history.

- There has also been notable growth in other educational programs designed to better serve the needs of the increasingly diverse student populations now found in our schools.

MORE CHANGES, CHALLENGES, AND PERSPECTIVES

- There have been many changes and improvements in the teaching profession during the past seventy-five years, as U.S. educational systems have grown in complexity, especially in funding and control.

- The federal government has increased its involvement in public education through legislation and agencies such as the GI Bill, the National Science Foundation, the National Defense Education Act, the Elementary and Secondary Education Act, Project Head Start, Upward Bound, and the National Teacher Corps, to name just a few.

- Each of these federal acts, while providing funds for specific school programs, has also placed new demands and regulations on our schools.

CHANGING AIMS OF EDUCATION

- An impressive series of important statements have been made over the years in an attempt to determine and articulate the essential aims of education in the United States.

- These statements clearly show how perspectives on education have changed over time.

PREPARATION OF TEACHERS

- The history of teacher preparation shows an evolution from very meager and humble beginnings centuries ago to a complex and professional state today.

- Educators should be proud of the history of advancement in the preparation of educators and be mindful and proud of the current rigorous professional training they receive.

RECENT TRENDS IN EDUCATION

- Many recent trends in education include professional advancements such as analysis of the teaching act, teacher effectiveness research, sociological studies, the development of new learning theories, and other research efforts designed to help us better understand and improve student learning.

- Widely read critics of our schools during the past sixty years include Friedenberg, Silberman, Kozol, Illich, and Holt.

- Various governmental agencies at the state and national levels have also been critical of our schools in recent years, resulting in many reports and calls for school reforms.

LOOKING BACK TO HELP US LOOK AHEAD!

- We live in a rapidly changing world that challenges teachers to "keep up-to-date."

- Even our understanding of the history of education changes.

- Every current educational challenge can be informed by educational history.

DISCUSSION STARTERS

1. Other than those mentioned in this chapter, what additional recent educational developments seem particularly important to you? Why are they important?

2. Has the increased federal involvement in education been good or bad for schools? How so?

3. In your opinion, in what respect, if any, has education become professionalized?

4. In your opinion, how much progress has the United States really made in providing equal educational opportunity? Defend your answer.

5. What is happening in education at this very moment that is likely to be written about in future history of education books?

SCHOOL-BASED OBSERVATIONS

1. As you work in the schools, look to see how the continuing struggle for equal educational opportunity is progressing. Also, analyze what you observe in order to determine the degree to which teaching has been professionalized—a movement that has gained impetus during the last sixty years. Finally, as you participate in classrooms, look for evidence that the work of the educational pioneers discussed in this chapter (such as Bloom, Skinner, and Piaget) has made an impact in U.S. classrooms.

2. Discuss with experienced educators the changes they have observed during their careers. Visit with veteran educational administrators to discuss changes they have seen in education over the years.

PORTFOLIO DEVELOPMENT

1. Prepare a creative educational history project (using a poster, videotape, audio recording, slide presentation, or some other creative medium) dealing with a topic, person, or idea that is of interest to you. Design your project so that it can be used as part of your job placement credentials.

2. Create a list of the most useful outcomes of U.S. education during the past sixty years. What can you as a beginning teacher learn, if anything, from your list?

WEB SOLUTIONS

You are doing a PowerPoint presentation to a group of faculty in order to show how best practices have evolved throughout the years. You want to be able to show the classroom environment, organization, and materials that teachers have used in order to show that education is dynamic and adapts to changes over time. However, there are still contentious issues that remain; they are reflected in school curricula, lesson plans, and policies throughout the country. Go to the following websites to help develop your presentation:

www.scholastic.com/Instructor The Scholastic Instructor site contains a variety of educational materials such as articles, contests, free materials for teachers, and chats with other educators on many subjects, including the history of education.

www.si.edu This site provides links to each museum of the Smithsonian Institution in Washington, D.C., and includes much historical information.

www.cdickens.com/articles/dickjane.htm Information about the Dick and Jane readers that were used in many schools.

www.insight-media.com A wonderful source of information about history of education media.

MyEducationLab™ Go to the topic **History and Philosophy of Education** in the MyEducationLab (**www.myeducationlab.com**) for *Foundations of American Education: Becoming Effective Teachers in Challenging Times, 16e* where you can:

- Find learning outcomes for **History and Philosophy of Education**, along with the national standards that connect to these outcomes.
- Complete Assignments and Activities that can help you more deeply understand the chapter content.
- Apply and practice your understanding of the core teaching skills identified in the chapter with the Building Teaching Skills and Dispositions learning units.
- Access video clips of CCSSO National Teachers of the Year award winners responding to the question, "Why Do I Teach?" in the Teacher Talk section.
- Create, update, and share quality lesson plans with the Lesson Plan Builder.
- Access state licensure test requirements, overviews of what tests cover, and sample test items in the Certification and Licensure section.
- Learn how to create a high-quality teaching portfolio in the Preparing a Portfolio section.
- Access tips, advice, and other information on resume writing and interviewing, your first year of teaching, and law and public policies in the Beginning Your Career section.
- Check your comprehension of the content covered in the chapter with the Study Plan. Here you will be able to take a chapter pretest, receive feedback on your answers, and then access personalized Review, Practice, and Enrichment exercises to enhance your understanding of chapter content. After you complete the exercises, take a posttest to confirm your comprehension.

4

Philosophy: Reflections on the Essence of Education

LEARNING OUTCOMES

After reading and studying this chapter, you should be able to:

1. List major philosophical questions associated with the three major branches of philosophy: metaphysics, epistemology, and axiology. (InTASC 4: Content Knowledge)

2. Define philosophy and describe methods of inquiry used by philosophers. (InTASC 4: Content Knowledge)

3. Elaborate on the major tenets of idealism, realism, pragmatism, and existentialism and compare writers from different schools of philosophy. (InTASC 4: Content Knowledge)

4. Relate philosophical concepts to teaching and learning and explain why idealism and realism are teacher centered while pragmatism and existentialism are student centered. (InTASC 1: Learner Development; InTASC 3: Learning Environments; InTASC 8: Instructional Strategies)

5. Describe the characteristics of Eastern and Native North American ways of knowing. (InTASC 2: Learning Differences; InTASC 9: Professional Learning and Ethical Practice)

EDUCATION in the NEWS

AMONG MANY TEENS, CHEATING IS PART OF SCHOOL

By SHARON NOGUCHI

Excerpt from *San Diego Mercury News,* March 31, 2012

The honest truth about cheating in high school lurks just below the veneer of virtue: A whole lot of students do it, regularly and with impunity.

The Leland High School students disciplined last week in a test-stealing scandal differ from their high school peers around the Bay Area in one important respect: They got caught.

At least eight seniors and one junior at Leland High in San Jose copied from stolen tests, school officials say, and have been suspended. One faces expulsion.

Cheating is as old as testing, but among youths it is evolving in its ubiquity and apparent acceptance. These days, the Internet makes cheating easy. Indifferent teachers make it possible. And students at competitive schools like Leland say the workload and expectations often make the practice necessary.

"It's pretty much normal that kids are cheating on tests," senior Amanda Cendejas said about students in her upper-level classes at Leigh High School in San Jose. And, students around the Bay Area said, they openly share exam and homework answers online and don't fear

repercussions. "They don't care if they post on Facebook because the teacher is not on it," Cendejas said. "Not many of us would rat anybody out."

A survey conducted last year in a Midwest school district found that 53 percent of high school students admitted to cheating on tests, 62 percent turned in work done by others and 72 percent admitted working with classmates on homework when collaboration was not permitted.

Such numbers have remained high over time, said Don McCabe, the Rutgers Business School professor who conducted the survey of 4,800 students. A nationwide survey in 2010 indicated that two-thirds of high school students admit to cheating in some form.

Local schools have found similar results: At Amador Valley High in Pleasanton, 83 percent of students said homework is copied often or even very often, Principal Jim Hansen said.

"Students have a different view of what's OK," McCabe said. With many opportunities to draw on classmates and the Internet for answers, "students say to me: Why shouldn't I use it?"

McCabe, who has studied cheating for twenty years, said the number of self-reported cheaters is decreasing at the college level, but he thinks that merely reflects the increasing number of students who think there's nothing wrong with borrowing work. "They honestly feel they're not cheating. The student definition is changing."

A PILE OF EXCUSES

Students give various rationalizations for cheating—lack of time, dislike of busywork, high stakes for success, clueless or unreasonable teachers, and simply an opportunity to be seized.

At San Jose's Lynbrook High, the workload is hard and heavy, students say. And one freshman, who didn't want her name used, said teachers expect A's. "Therefore, we're compelled to cheat."

In the school's online magazine, Aletheia, another student wrote anonymously, "Honestly, who hasn't cheated before? I've done it so much that I don't feel bad about it anymore. I don't feel good, but I no longer hate myself for cheating."

For teachers, the challenge is to outsmart bright minds adept at outfoxing the system. "For me, it becomes a game to create an assignment that can't be easily copied online," said Leigh High School English teacher Beth Nakamura.

But discerning literary symbolism or mastering the Krebs cycle isn't always important to students; they're looking at the endgame: college.

"Going to school is just about getting good grades," a Leigh junior said. "I'm filling my brain with meaningless stuff just to get into college."

A fellow student, a junior, agreed about the drive for a high grade-point average. "If you don't go to a good college, you are not going to do anything in life," she said. "I cheat, and I don't feel bad about it."

RESPECT COUNTS

Some teachers say there are ways to prevent cheating.

Mt. Diablo High teacher Dan Reynolds said he sees few problems in his English classes. "If I put expectations in place, about classroom and testing behavior, students will meet those expectations." But he doesn't invite temptation either: During tests, all electronics are left in a box at the door or in backpacks.

Students also acknowledged that when kids respect the teacher, there is less cheating.

Other schools are taking broader action. At Palo Alto High, Principal Phil Winston has formed a committee to examine a two-decade-old academic honesty policy. At Amador Valley, the school is engaging in a Stanford University-based program, "Challenge Success," to look at issues related to stress, including cheating, and come up with plans to remedy them.

Meanwhile, the rate of high school cheating nationwide is marginally increasing, said Richard Jarc, executive director of the Los Angeles-based Josephson Institute, which seeks to improve the ethical quality of society.

"No one seems to be saying, 'Oh my god, we have to do something about it,' " Jarc said. "It's pretty scary. These kids are going to school to become doctors, lawyers, and bridge builders.

"I don't want one of them to be my bridge builder or my doctor."

QUESTIONS FOR REFLECTION

1. Do you think that cheating in school is OK if teachers ignore it? Why? Why not?
2. If you were a committee member at Palo Alto High, what remedies would you recommend to reduce cheating? How would your remedies also reduce stress?
3. Philosophers study ethical behavior in light of big ideas such as the nature of goodness, justice, and human nature. Explain your personal view about cheating in school in light of these big ideas.
4. Instead of concentrating on ways to lessen stress, how could schools help students develop and clarify their own ethical stance with regard to cheating?

Source: Excerpt from "Among Many Teens, Cheating Is Part of School" by Sharon Noguchi, *San Diego Mercury News,* March 31, 2012. Reprinted by permission of The YGS Group.

MyEducationLab™

Visit the MyEducationLab for *Foundations of American Education* to enhance your understanding of chapter concepts with a personalized *Study Plan.* You'll also have the opportunity to hone your teaching skills through video- and case-based *Assignments and Activities* and *Building Teaching Skills and Dispositions* lessons.

STRUCTURE AND METHODOLOGY OF PHILOSOPHY

Philosophy provides a way to examine and interpret the world—to ask basic questions about human nature, beauty, principles of right and wrong, and how knowledge and reality are defined. Philosophical thinking helps to uncover the essentials—the basic principles that undergird teaching and learning.

The philosophical perspective is especially important because our personal philosophy of life is seldom explicit. Rather, philosophy resides in people's minds and hearts and is seldom expressed in words or specific ideas. Our personal philosophy becomes evident in the manner in which we respond to everyday problems and questions. The perspective of philosophy helps us to focus on the underlying issues and assumptions and beliefs that are not always evident to us in the hectic pace of contemporary life.

Because philosophy deals with underlying values and beliefs, it naturally pervades all aspects of education. The perspective of philosophy presents opposing views about human nature, knowledge, and the world in which we live. By examining these different, often opposing views, you will be able to identify your own philosophical position and state it in clearer language and concepts.

Although philosophy can be defined in many different ways, it is best thought of as a passion to uncover and reflect on the underlying meaning of things. Derived from the Greek *philos*, which means "love," and *sophos*, which means "wisdom," the word *philosophy* means "love of wisdom." Early philosophers did not claim to be wise; rather, they viewed themselves as reflective thinkers in search of wisdom. To many contemporary philosophers, conveying information or wisdom is not as important as helping others in their own search for wisdom.

Education presupposes ideas and questions about the world in which we live, human nature, knowledge and how we know things, and ethics. Questions that focus on these big ideas are ultimately of a philosophical character. Teachers must constantly confront the underlying assumptions that guide conduct, determine values, and ultimately explain that which influences the direction of all existence. Philosophy reminds teachers to continue the search for truth and not be satisfied with pat answers, even answers that are provided by so-called experts. To a philosopher, an expert is not one who professes truth; an expert is one who searches, questions, and reflects. Hence, the study of philosophy is at the heart of education.

The Branches of Philosophy

Philosophy includes branches that investigate large and difficult questions—questions about reality or being, about knowledge, and about goodness and beauty and living a good life. Throughout the centuries, entire branches of philosophy have evolved that specialize in and center on major questions. For example, questions about the nature of reality or existence are examined in metaphysics, questions about knowledge and truth are considered in epistemology, and questions about values and goodness are central to axiology.

METAPHYSICS. Metaphysics is a branch of philosophy that is concerned with questions about the nature of reality and the world in which we live. Literally, metaphysics means "beyond the physical." It deals with such questions as "What is reality?" "What is existence?" and "Is the universe rationally designed or ultimately meaningless?" Metaphysics is a search for order and wholeness—a search applied not to particular items or experiences but to all reality and to all existence.

The questions in metaphysics, especially those about humanity and the universe, are extremely relevant to teachers and students of education. Theories about how the universe came to be and about what causes events in the universe are crucial if scholars are to interpret the physical sciences properly.

A teacher's classroom approach will be linked to the teacher's metaphysical beliefs. If, for example, the teacher believes that very specific basic knowledge is crucial to the child's intellectual development, it is likely that this teacher will focus on the subject matter. If, on the other hand, the teacher holds that the child is more important than any specific subject matter, it is likely that this teacher will focus on the child and allow the child to provide clues as to how he or she should be instructed.

EPISTEMOLOGY. Epistemology is a branch of philosophy that examines questions about how and what we know. What knowledge is true, and how does knowledge take place? The epistemologist attempts to discover what is involved in the process of knowing: Is knowing a special sort of mental act? Is there a difference between knowledge and belief? Can people know anything beyond the objects with which their senses acquaint them? Does knowing make any difference to the object that is known?

Because epistemological questions deal with the essence of knowledge, they are central to education. Teachers must be able to assess what is knowledge to determine whether a particular piece of information should be included in the curriculum. How people know is of paramount importance to teachers because their beliefs about learning influence their classroom methods. Should teachers train students in scientific methods, deductive reasoning, or both? Should students study logic and fallacies or follow intuition? Teachers' knowledge of how students learn influences how they will teach.

AXIOLOGY. Axiology is a branch of philosophy that deals with the nature of values. It includes such questions as "What is good?" and "What is beautiful?" Questions about what should be or what values we hold are highlighted in axiology. This study of values is divided into ethics (moral

metaphysics An area of philosophy that deals with questions about the nature of ultimate reality.

epistemology An area of philosophy that deals with questions about the nature of understanding and how we know things.

axiology An area of philosophy that deals with the nature of values. It includes questions such as "What is good?" and "What is beautiful?"

values and conduct) and aesthetics (values in the realm of beauty and art). Ethics deals with such questions as "What is the good life?" and "How should we behave?" One major question to be examined is "When does the end justify any means of achieving it?" Aesthetics deals with the theory of beauty and examines such questions as "Is art public and representative, or is it the product of private creative imagination?" Good citizenship, honesty, and correct human relations are all learned in schools. Sometimes these concepts are taught explicitly, but often students learn ethics from *who* the teacher is as well as from *what* the teacher says.

Both ethics and aesthetics are important issues in education. Should a system of ethics be taught in the public schools? If so, which system of ethics should be taught? Aesthetics questions in education involve deciding which artistic works should or should not be included in the curriculum and what kind of subject matter should be allowed or encouraged in a writing, drawing, or painting class. Should teachers compromise their own attitudes toward a piece of artwork if their opinion differs from that of a parent or a school board? Take a moment to consider the "Teaching in Challenging Times" feature regarding the complexities that surround teaching morals and values in public schools.

Thinking as a Philosopher

Philosophy provides the tools people need to think clearly. As with any discipline, philosophy has a style of thinking as well as a set of terms and methodologies that distinguish it from other disciplines. Philosophers spend much of their energy developing symbols or terms that are both abstract (apply to many individual cases) and precise (distinguish clearly). Developing ideas that embrace more and more instances (abstraction) while at the same time maintaining a clear and accurate meaning (precision) is difficult, but this tension is at the heart of the philosopher's task. The entire process is what is meant by *understanding*: uncovering the underlying, the foundational, and the essential principles of reality.

There is great variety in the ways philosophers think. Hence it is difficult to set forth a simple set of rules or thinking steps that can accurately be labeled philosophical thinking. To give you a

TEACHING IN CHALLENGING TIMES

Teaching Morals and Values in Public School

So often we consider schools as a place where students learn to be good citizens. Even though this is a common assumption held by many, it is difficult to determine what values are the important ones. Living in a society that encourages diversity and free speech, the question of what values should be taught in public schools can be difficult to answer. Even more difficult is the question of how one would teach these values in a classroom setting.

One school of thought, influenced by the work of Lawrence Kohlberg (1981), suggests that there is a body of morals that spans all cultures. These morals can be taught through the use of dilemmas that children are asked to first consider and then discuss the reasoning behind their thinking. By so doing, students may develop increasingly more sophisticated understandings about the moral component of everyday dilemmas.

For example, a teacher could ask students to consider an incident on the playground where they witnessed her/his best friend laugh at another child because that child was obese. The teacher would then provide various responses to this event including, for example, reporting the incident to the teacher, talking directly to your friend, or ignoring the event. After students selected what action they would take, the teacher would ask students to discuss why they chose their different responses. One reason that there is continued interest in having schools focus on developing morals is that children are faced with an increasingly more complex society and cannot be expected to simply absorb and develop values on their own.

In contrast to this emphasis on teaching values, there is another school of thought that rejects direct instruction of values on the grounds that democracy demands that its citizens be free to clarify their own sets of values. This school of thought, influenced by the ideas of Syd Simon's text *Values Clarification*, encourages teachers to refrain from direct instruction of morals and asks teachers to help students define their own sets of individually selected values. The teacher's role is to simply assist students in the clarification of the consequences of selecting any one set of morals or values.

WHAT ARE MY CHALLENGES?

1. What values could you defend as worthy for all students to acquire across different cultures, religions, and so on?
2. How would you approach the teaching of values if required to do so by your school district?

sense of philosophical thinking, it is easier (and more accurate) to describe two different thinking styles that philosophers use interchangeably as they wrestle with large, unstructured questions. The first way of thinking can be labeled **analytic thinking**. Philosophers employ this style when they attempt to examine questions of the "what seems to be" type. A second philosophical style of thinking is called prophetic thinking. This style focuses on questions of the "what ought to be" type.

ANALYTIC WAYS OF THINKING IN PHILOSOPHY. When philosophers encounter a contemporary problem, they often spend time analyzing it in an attempt to clarify or find the "real" problem, not just the surface issues. To do so, philosophers use abstraction, imagination, generalization, and logic. These analytic thinking processes help focus the problem clearly and precisely.

Abstraction. The notion of **abstraction** covers a multitude of meanings. The word *abstract* is derived from the Latin verb *abstrahere*, meaning to "draw away." Abstraction, then, involves drawing away from a concrete level of experience to a conceptual plane of principles or ideas. The process of abstraction can be thought of as a three-step process that moves thinking from singular concrete instances to more general, universal ideas. The three steps involve (1) focusing attention on some feature within one's experience, (2) examining the precise characteristics of the feature, and (3) remembering the feature and its characteristics later so as to apply them to other instances or combine them with other ideas.

When teachers are asked to examine a new textbook series, for example, they will often be presented with promotional material about the important subject matter and learning tools that the series contains. The process of abstraction helps teachers pull away from the "bells and whistles" or the concrete examples in the text. Abstraction enables teachers to consider the underlying themes that are implicit and that provide a cohesive structure to the entire text series. Abstraction helps teachers uncover hidden messages.

Imagination and Generalization. According to Herbert G. Alexander (1987) the second step of analytic thinking is the use of imagination. Imagination can be thought of as the altering of abstractions. In philosophy, the use of imagination assists the process of abstraction by filling in the details of an idea, selecting details, and relating ideas to one another.

Imaginative explorations occur in many different ways. Usually, they occur when a person first focuses on some abstraction or idea. Ideas come when one makes observations, reflects about past experiences, reads, views a dramatic work or piece of art, or converses with others. Once ideas are selected, imaginative explorations can be made about them. Basic assumptions about things can be examined, arguments can be justified or clarified, and ideas can be distinguished from or related to other ideas. Experiential evidence, logical consistency, and a host of other criteria can be employed. The outcome of the whole imaginative process is the development of a system of ideas that has greater clarity and more interrelationships to other ideas or sets of propositions. This last step of the imaginative exploration process is sometimes referred to as generalization, because it ultimately results in the development of a comprehensive set of ideas.

Generalization sets ranges and limits to the abstractions that have been altered by imagination. As one's imagination relates more and more ideas to one another, the process of generalization determines which relationships should be emphasized or de-emphasized.

When teachers consider new ways to support student motivation, they can use these same processes. For example, teachers often imagine different types of mathematics contests or science Olympiads that might spur students' interests. As they imaginatively apply these contests to the classroom setting, teachers might abstract the competitiveness component as a necessary aspect of contests and Olympiads. Teachers might then wonder about the hidden messages of winning at the expense of others' losses. Teachers might generalize that the competitive approach could bring about knowledge wars; knowledge contests might make students less willing to share what they know with others. To complete this inquiry, teachers need to use logic.

Logic. Philosophy deals with the nature of reasoning and has designated a set of principles called logic. Logic examines the principles that allow us to move from one argument to the next. There are many types of logic, but the two most commonly studied are deductive and inductive logic. **Deduction** is a type of reasoning that moves from a general statement to a specific conclusion. **Induction** is a type of reasoning that moves in the opposite direction, from the particular instance to a general conclusion.

analytic thinking
A thinking strategy that focuses on questions of the "what seems to be" type; includes abstractions, imagination, generalization, and logic.

abstraction A thought process that involves drawing away from experiences to a conceptual plane.

deduction A type of reasoning that moves from a general statement to a specific conclusion.

induction A type of reasoning that moves from the particular instance to a general conclusion, in the opposite direction from deduction.

FIGURE 4.1 Analytic ways of thinking: Focus and solve problems clearly and precisely.

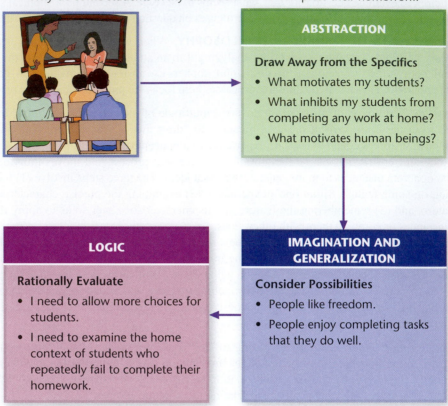

Specific Problem Confronts a Teacher
"Why do some students in my classroom fail to complete their homework?"

ABSTRACTION

Draw Away from the Specifics
- What motivates my students?
- What inhibits my students from completing any work at home?
- What motivates human beings?

LOGIC

Rationally Evaluate
- I need to allow more choices for students.
- I need to examine the home context of students who repeatedly fail to complete their homework.

IMAGINATION AND GENERALIZATION

Consider Possibilities
- People like freedom.
- People enjoy completing tasks that they do well.

Philosophy provides tools that help people think clearly. It is important for educators to have a philosophy, both as a means of developing their ability to think clearly about what they do on a day-to-day basis and as a means of seeing how their workaday principles and values extend beyond the classroom to the whole of humanity and society. Figure 4.1 describes how analytic ways of thinking help teachers solve a classroom problem. Studying philosophy enables you to recognize the underlying assumptions and principles of things so you can determine what is significant.

PROPHETIC WAYS OF THINKING IN PHILOSOPHY. In contrast to the search for underlying universal principles that is the focus of an analytic way of thinking, **prophetic thinking** seeks to uncover multiple, even divergent realities or principles. Prophetic thinking has emerged as a counterpoint to the highly successful—but rigid—analytic thinking style. According to Cornel West (1993), a prophetic thinker is one who goes beyond abstraction. A prophetic thinker lives in multiple realities, feeling and touching these realities to such a degree that understanding is ultimately achieved. And a prophetic thinker understands multiple realities so well that bridges can be built between and among the multiple worlds. In his book *Prophetic Thought in Postmodern Times*, West (1993) identifies four basic components of prophetic thinking: discernment, connection, tracking hypocrisy, and hope.

1. *Discernment.* Discernment is the capacity to develop a vision of "what should be" out of a sophisticated understanding of what has been and is. This first component of prophetic thought is quite different from the abstract approach of the analytic thinker. The prophetic thinker is more concerned with the concrete, specific aspects of reality. To discern a situation is to take the entire situation into account to get beyond abstract principles. A discerning teacher is one who sees beyond mere test scores, beyond simple classroom rules. A discerning teacher examines the total content of a child's life and makes decisions based on this content. An outsider could criticize a discerning teacher for bending rules or being inconsistent. Yet a prophetic thinker would applaud the teacher for being wise. The prophetic thinker is a bit of a historian, building the future on the best of the past and present.

prophetic thinking
A thinking strategy that focuses on questions of the "what ought to be" type; includes discernment, connection, tracking hypocrisy, and hope.

2. *Connection.* A prophetic thinker must relate to or connect with others. Rather than considering humankind in the abstract, prophetic thinkers value and have empathy for other human beings. They show empathy, the capacity to get in contact with the anxieties and frustrations of others. Many teachers really do care and work hard to help students. However, they are often unable to make the connection that would complete caring relations with their students. Teachers' willingness to empathize with students is often thwarted by society's desire to establish teaching on a firm scientific footing. But to students, the failure to connect means that teachers sometimes look as though they simply do not care. According to Nel Noddings (1993, 2005) both teachers and students have become victims in the search for the one best method of instruction.

3. *Tracking Hypocrisy.* Although the relationship between empathy and teaching is important, it is equally important for the prophetic teacher to identify and make known "the gap between principles and practice, between promise and performance, between rhetoric and reality" (West, 1993, p. 5).

Teachers not only teach content, but also find ways to help students seek connections to the world around them and apply ideas to their daily lives.

Tracking hypocrisy ought to be done in a self-critical rather than in a self-righteous manner. It takes boldness as well as courage to point out inconsistencies between school policies and practices, but when doing so a prophetic teacher remains open to others' points of view. New evidence might reveal that one's position is no longer valid, or it might enhance one's original thinking. Figure 4.2 describes how prophetic ways of thinking help teachers solve a classroom problem.

FIGURE 4.2   Prophetic ways of thinking: Uncover multiple realities or principles.

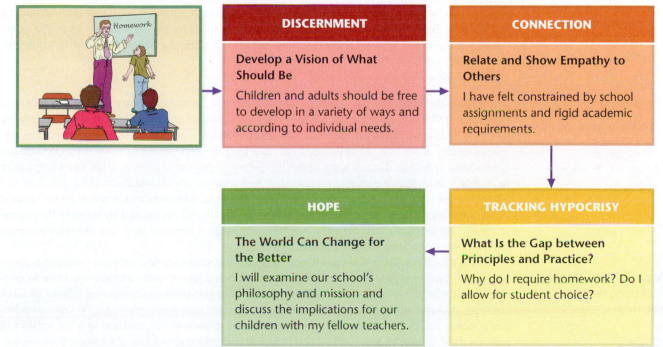

4. *Hope.* The fourth and perhaps most important component of prophetic thought is simply hope. West admits that given the numerous and horrific examples of people's inhumanity to one another, it is hard to take hope seriously. Still, without it, all thought is meaningless. West says:

> To talk about human hope is to engage in an audacious attempt to galvanize and energize, to inspire and to invigorate world-weary people. Because that is what we are. We are world-weary; we are tired. For some of us there are misanthropic skeletons hanging in our closet. And by misanthropic I mean the notion that we have given up on the capacity to do anything right; the capacity of human communities to solve any problem. (West, 1993, p. 6)

GO TO ···>
Chapters 12 and 13 describe ways to integrate technology into instruction and assessment.

West challenges educators to see "skeletons" as challenges, not as conclusions. Even when confronted with educators' failures at creating a better community of scholars, the prophetic teacher must remember that the world is unfinished, that the future is open ended, and that what teachers think and do can make a difference.

Technology and Philosophy

Most of the time we think of technology as a tool that helps us work efficiently or improve the quality of a product. Philosophers of technology take a broader look at technology by asking questions about the consequences that technology has on the physical and human condition. For example, the philosopher Martin Heidegger (1993) believed technology provided the greatest danger, yet the greatest possibility for humankind. Heidegger was concerned about technology because it has the power to present information by emphasizing the worth of an object while de-emphasizing its dangers. He called this power of technology *enframing,* and he was concerned that humans' ability to present things in a specific way could hide the actual essence of a thing.

With the release of new technologies increasing exponentially, other philosophers struggle to determine whether any one technology enhances or detracts from the essence of life and the natural order. Some philosophers contend that technology is developing so quickly that mankind no longer controls its direction. They contend that technology now has the power to develop autonomously because humans have become so dependent on it.

John Dewey considered technology a natural component of the changing world. Because change is natural, then technology is natural. The key is to use our rational minds and inquiry to determine the effects of a technology and use it in ways that enhance but do not detract from the needs of all members in society.

No matter what you may think about technology, it is here to stay. Using the analytic and prophetic tools of philosophy can help direct the use of technology in ways that nourish society and schools. By constantly asking broader questions and encouraging students to do the same, schools can provide a forum for controlling and encouraging the development of technology.

The Teacher as Philosopher

Philosophic thinking can look daunting and out of reach. In our ever-expanding world, who has the time to reflect on such big ideas? Yet, when you consider that teachers are charged with the task of preparing students for life in this complex world, it would seem that they, more than any other member of society, are obligated to assume the role of philosopher. Even if teachers do not consciously reflect or discuss ideas about the nature of human existence, what knowledge is of most worth, how learning should be provided, and what values should direct behavior, they live out their answers to these big questions. They answer these questions by the way they set up their classrooms, by the way they teach students, by the rules they impose, and by the way they relate to others. No teacher can escape the role of a philosopher because they live out their personal philosophies every time they enter the classroom.

GO TO ···>
Chapter 12 provides ways of reflecting based on data-driven instruction.

So, which is better? You can choose to ignore the need to reflect on your own views about the world, human nature, knowledge, and ethical behavior, or you can take the time to constantly examine these large questions and clarify your personal understanding. To do so takes courage, because thinking about these bigger questions can sometimes clarify your own imperfections. Yet, is this not what learning is all about, constantly reconsidering what we do and how we do it in light of new information? Clearly the reflective teacher is a natural philosopher.

JOURNAL FOR REFLECTION 4.1
Classroom activities that deal with what is good (right) or evil (wrong) are in the realm of axiology. Prepare lists of the goods and the evils of the U.S. educational system. Then, propose recommendations for change that might counteract as many of the evils as possible.

SCHOOLS OF PHILOSOPHY AND THEIR INFLUENCE ON EDUCATION

As philosophers attempt to answer questions, they develop answers that are clustered into different schools of thought. These schools of philosophical thought are somewhat contrived; they are merely labels developed by others who have attempted to show the similarities and differences among the many answers philosophers develop. As you examine the schools of thought described in this section, keep in mind that the individual philosophers who represent these schools are individual thinkers, like yourself, who do not limit their thinking to the characteristics of any one label or school of thought. The four well-known schools of thought that we discuss next are idealism, realism, pragmatism, and existentialism. In addition to these, we will touch on Eastern thought and Native North American thought. Technically, these two final clusters of thought are not termed schools because they encompass greater diversity and often extend beyond the limits of philosophy into beliefs, customs, and group values.

Idealism

Idealism's roots are found in the writings of Plato. **Idealism** is a school of philosophy that holds that ideas or concepts are the essence of all that is worth knowing. The physical world we know through our senses is only a manifestation or imperfect representation of the spiritual world. The spiritual world is everlasting and is not subject to change because it is perfect (metaphysics).

Idealists believe in the power of reasoning but de-emphasize both the scientific method and sense perception, which they hold suspect. Rather, idealists contend that the rational mind has the ability to reason its way to the underlying ideas that support the physical world. All that is necessary is for the individual, through introspection, to search for these universal ideas that are lodged deep in our minds (epistemology).

Idealists search and value universal or absolute truths or ideas that remain constant throughout the centuries. Idealists contend that truth, goodness, and beauty transcend and connect all other ideas and, hence, they are important to all cultures and peoples. Idealists contend that values are unchanging because they underlie all aspects of existence and are perfect (axiology).

EDUCATIONAL IMPLICATIONS OF IDEALISM. The educational philosophy of the idealist is idea centered rather than subject centered or child centered because the ideal, or the idea, is the foundation of all things. Knowledge is directed toward self-consciousness and self-direction and is centered in the growth of rational processes about big ideas. Some idealists note that the individual, who is created in God's image, has free will and that it is this free will that makes learning possible. The idealist believes that learning comes from within the individual rather than from without. Hence, real mental growth and spiritual growth do not occur until they are self-initiated.

What Should We Teach? Idealists' educational beliefs include an emphasis on the study of ideas or great works that persist throughout the ages. They also emphasize the importance of great leaders as examples for us to imitate. For idealists the teacher is the ideal model or example for the student. Teachers pass on the cultural heritage and the unchanging content of education, such as knowledge about great figures of the past, the humanities, and a rigorous curriculum.

How Should We Teach? Idealists emphasize the methods of lecture, discussion, and imitation. They believe that thinking clearly and accurately is critical to uncovering the big ideas that

GO TO ··⇢
Chapter 2 describes the historical context in which early philosophers developed their thinking.

idealism A school of philosophy that considers ideas to be the only true reality.

account for the universe. So, there is an emphasis on asking questions that spark thought. No one philosopher is an idealist. Rather, philosophers answer questions, and some of their answers are similar. These similarities are what make up the different schools of philosophy. To describe adequately any one school of philosophy, such as idealism, one needs to go beyond these general similarities to examine the subtle differences posed by individual thinkers. Plato and Socrates, Immanuel Kant, and Jane Roland Martin represent different aspects of the idealist tradition.

Matching Ideas from Philosophical Schools to Your Own. Studying the schools of philosophy can guide you in the development of your own philosophy of education. Throughout this chapter, simply jot down any ideas presented by a philosophical school (like idealism) that match your own. Then write down why these ideas make sense to you.

You will probably find that ideas from different philosophical schools match your own thinking. So keep track of the school that relates to each idea you select. Because you have just reviewed the ideas of idealism concerning what and how to teach, it would be wise to start recording your personal list based on these questions:

- What important knowledge and skills do I think should be taught?
- How should I teach these ideas and skills?

PLATO AND SOCRATES. According to Plato (427–347 BCE), truth is the central reality. Truth is perfect; it cannot, therefore, be found in the world of matter because the material world is both imperfect and constantly changing. Plato did not think that people create knowledge; rather, they discover it. In one of his dialogues, he conjectures that humanity once had true knowledge but lost it by being placed in a material body that distorts and corrupts that knowledge. Thus, humans have the arduous task of trying to remember what they once knew.

The modern world knows the philosophy of Socrates only through Plato, who wrote about him in a series of texts called *dialogues*. Socrates (470–399 BCE) spoke of himself as a midwife who found humans pregnant with knowledge—knowledge that had not been born or realized. This Socratic "Doctrine of Reminiscence" speaks directly to the role of the educator. Teachers need to question students in such a way as to help them remember what they have forgotten. In the dialogue *Meno*, Plato describes Socrates' meeting a slave boy and through skillful questions leading the boy to realize that he knows the Pythagorean theorem, even though he does not know that he knows it. This emphasis on bringing forth knowledge from students through artful questioning is sometimes called the Socratic method.

IMMANUEL KANT. The German philosopher Immanuel Kant (1724–1804), in the *Metaphysics of Morals and the Critique of Practical Reason*, spelled out his idealistic philosophy. Kant believed in freedom, the immortality of the soul, and the existence of God. He wrote extensively on human reason and noted that the only way humankind can know things is through the process of reason. Hence, reality is not a thing unto itself but the interaction of reason and external sensations. Reason fits perceived objects into classes or categories according to similarities and differences. It is only through reason that we acquire knowledge of the world. Once again, it is the idea or the way that the mind works that precedes the understanding of reality.

JANE ROLAND MARTIN. Often labeled a feminist scholar, Jane Roland Martin (1929–) is a contemporary disciple of Plato's dialogues. In *Reclaiming a Conversation*, Jane Roland Martin (1985) describes how women have historically been excluded from the "conversation" that constitutes Western educational thought. Martin advocates a return to Plato's approach. Dialogues such as the *Apology*, the *Crito*, and the *Phaedo* illustrate educated persons— well-meaning people of good faith, people who trust and like one another, people who might even be called friends—getting together and trying to talk ideas through to a reasonable conclusion. They engage in conversation, learning something from one another and from the conversation itself.

For Martin, to be educated is to engage in a conversation that stretches back in time. Education is not simply something that occurs in a specific building at a specific time. Nor is it simply training or preparation for the next stage in life. Education is the development of the intellectual and moral habits, through the give-and-take of the conversation, that ultimately give "place and character to every human activity and utterance." Education—the conversation—is the place where one comes to learn what it is to be a person.

SOCRATIC DIALOGUE TO ENHANCE REFLECTIVE LEARNING. The ancient philosophers Socrates and Plato believed that learning is best achieved through dialogue. When using Socratic dialogue, the teacher does not teach a subject by direct exposition. Instead, learners' beliefs are challenged by the teacher through a series of questions that lead learners to reflect on their beliefs, induce general principles, and discover gaps and contradictions in their beliefs. Using this type of questioning strategy is difficult when attempting to teach precise mathematical, scientific relationships, so researchers set up a study in a science class to see if Socratic dialogue was effective in teaching science concepts (Kor, Self, & Tait, 2001).

In the Kor et al. (2001) study, students were asked to investigate a spring balance system on their own. The spring balance system models an experimental apparatus that verifies Archimedes' principle in a physics laboratory. One group of students investigated the spring balance system with the help of a teacher who assumed the role of a Socratic tutor and who prescribed immediate and intelligent feedback based on the Socratic questioning method. A second group of students investigated the spring balance system with the help of a Socratic tutor as well as the assistance of an articulation tool that provided direct instruction about problems similar to the spring balance system problem. After both groups of students investigated the spring balance system, students were post-tested. Results showed that all students improved their understanding of Archimedes' principle. However, students who received only the help of Socratic dialogue improved their understanding on a surface level and did not achieve a more abstract understanding of critical attributes. In contrast, students who were assisted by both Socratic dialogue and carefully structured problems significantly improved both surface level and abstract understanding concerning Archimedes' principle.

This research shows that Socratic dialogue is an effective teaching tool even in science. When teachers guide the development of students' understandings, learning occurs. However, when teachers wish to help students understand technical, abstract principles, Socratic dialogue needs to be enhanced by carefully structured, supporting problems that are designed to make explicit to the learner underlying critical entities that might be missed.

Realism

Realism's roots lie in the thinking of Aristotle. **Realism** is a school of philosophy that holds that reality, knowledge, and value exist independent of the human mind. In other words, realists reject the idealist notion that ideas are the ultimate reality. Figure 4.3 illustrates the dualistic positions of idealism and realism.

Every piece of the physical world is composed of matter. Matter takes on many forms or structures and this is what accounts for the different components that compose the world. The reason things look different from one another is due to the form that structures their matter (metaphysics).

Realists endorse the use of the senses and scientific investigation (reason) to find truth in the physical world. Knowing involves both sensation (taking in information through the senses) and abstraction (pulling out the underlying principles). By pulling out these underlying characteristics or principles, one can then classify things into different groups. Aristotle claims that the art of thinking well is to be able to distinguish things based on essential differences (epistemology).

realism A school of philosophy that holds that reality, knowledge, and value exist independent of the human mind. In contrast to the idealist, the realist contends that physical entities exist in their own right.

FIGURE 4.3 Dualistic positions of idealism and realism.

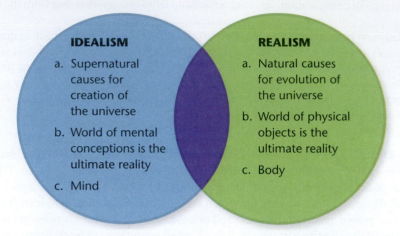

IDEALISM

a. Supernatural causes for creation of the universe

b. World of mental conceptions is the ultimate reality

c. Mind

REALISM

a. Natural causes for evolution of the universe

b. World of physical objects is the ultimate reality

c. Body

Values and norms come from rights and responsibilities that derive from rational thinking. Because human beings have the ability to reason, their values and norms are those that are logical and consistent with the physical nature of the world. By studying the world logically, natural laws can be uncovered and values are derived from these natural laws (axiology).

EDUCATIONAL IMPLICATIONS OF REALISM. Contemporary realists emphasize the importance of scientific research and development. Curriculum has reflected the impact of these realist thinkers through the appearance of standardized tests, serialized textbooks, and a specialized curriculum in which the disciplines are seen as separate areas of investigation.

What Should We Teach? Realists contend that the ultimate goal of education is advancement of human rationality. Schools can promote rationality by requiring students to study organized bodies of knowledge, by teaching methods of arriving at this knowledge, and by assisting students to reason critically through observation and experimentation. Teachers must have specific knowledge about a subject so that they can order it in such a way as to teach it rationally. They must also have a broad background to show relationships that exist among all fields of knowledge. Thus, the realist curriculum would be a subject-centered curriculum and would include natural science, social science, humanities, and instrumental subjects such as logic and inductive reasoning.

How Should We Teach? Realists place considerable importance on the role of the teacher in the educational process. The teacher should be a person who presents content in a systematic and organized way and should promote the idea that there are clearly defined criteria one can use in making judgments (axiology). Realist teachers would emphasize the importance of teaching students to use experimental and observational techniques. In the school setting, they would teach logical, clear content and clarify how things differ from one another by classifying them. Realists would support careful testing of students' knowledge.

Matching Ideas from Realism to Your Own. As noted earlier in this chapter, studying the schools of philosophy can guide you in the development of your own philosophy of education. As you review the educational implications for realism, you will see that there are similarities between what realists say is important and what idealists also say is important. What differs is that realists recognize that ideas change, whereas idealists contend that ideas remain the same. Therefore, when it comes to teaching thinking skills, realists value experimental and observational thinking more than idealists would. Take time to reflect on realism and select from it what you think is worth teaching and how it should be taught.

Keep in mind that although we have described a number of general characteristics of realism, they can never fully capture the thinking of the individual philosophers who compose the school. It is important to examine the ideas of individual realist thinkers: Aristotle, Locke, and Whitehead.

ARISTOTLE. Aristotle (384–322 BCE) thought that ideas (forms) are found through the study of the world of matter. He believed that one could acquire knowledge of ideas or forms by investigating matter. To understand an object, one must understand its absolute form, which is unchanging. To the realist, the trees of the forest exist whether or not there is a human mind to perceive them. This is an example of an independent reality. Although the idea of a flower can exist without matter, matter cannot exist without form. Hence, each tulip shares universal properties with every other tulip and every other flower. However, the particular properties of a tulip differentiate it from all other flowers. Aristotle's writings are known for their analytic approach. In contrast to Plato, whose writings are in the form of a conversation, Aristotle took great care to write with precision.

JOHN LOCKE. John Locke (1632–1704) believed in the *tabula rasa* (blank tablet) view of the mind. Locke stated that the mind of a person is blank at birth and that the person's sensory experiences make impressions on this blank tablet. Locke distinguished between sense data and the objects they represent. The objects, or things people know, are independent of the mind or the knower insofar as thought refers to them and not merely to sense data. Ideas (round, square, tall) represent objects. Locke claimed that primary qualities (such as shapes) represent the world, whereas secondary qualities (such as colors) have a basis in the world but do not represent it.

> The little or almost insensible impressions on our tender infancies have very important and lasting consequences: and there it is, as in the fountains of some rivers, where a gentle application of the hand turns the flexible waters into channels, that make them at first, in the source, they receive different tendencies, and arrive at last at very remote and distant places.
>
> I imagine the minds of children as easily turned, this or that way, as water itself; and though this be the principal part and our main care should be about the inside yet the clay cottage is not to be neglected. (Locke, 1812)

ALFRED NORTH WHITEHEAD. Alfred North Whitehead (1861–1947), a philosopher and mathematician, attempted to reconcile some conflicting tenets of idealism and realism. He proposed "process" to be the central aspect of realism. Unlike Locke, Whitehead did not see objective reality and subjective mind as separate. He saw them as an organic unity that operates by its own principles. The universe is characterized by patterns, and these patterns can be verified and analyzed through mathematics.

> Culture is activity of thought and receptiveness to beauty and humane feelings. Scraps of information have nothing to do with it. . . . In training a child to activity of thought, above all things we must beware of what I will call "inert ideas"—that is to say, ideas that are merely received into the mind without being used, or tested, or thrown into fresh combinations.
>
> In the history of education, the most striking phenomenon is the schools of learning, which at one epoch are alive with a ferment of genius, in a succeeding generation exhibit merely pedantry and routine. The reason is that they are overladen with inert ideas. Education with inert ideas is not only useless: it is, above all things, harmful—Corruptio optimi, pessima. (Whitehead, 1929, pp. 1–2.)

Pragmatism

Pragmatism's roots come from the thinking of a number of nineteenth-century American philosophers including Charles S. Peirce (1839–1914), William James (1842–1910), and John Dewey (1859–1952). **Pragmatism** is a process philosophy that stresses evolving and change rather than being. It differs from most forms of idealism and realism by a belief in an open universe that is dynamic, evolving, and in a state of becoming. There are no unchanging ideas (idealism) nor are there universal laws (realism). Because the underlying principle that explains the universe is change, many pragmatists claim that a metaphysical foundation for their thinking is unverifiable.

Because change is so important, pragmatists place a great deal of emphasis on the importance of understanding what it means to know. To the pragmatist, knowing is a transaction

pragmatism A late-nineteenth-century U.S. school of philosophy that stresses becoming rather than being.

or a conversation between the learner and the environment. This transaction or conversation between learner and environment alters or changes both the learner and the world. Like the realist, the pragmatist believes that we learn best through experience, but pragmatists believe that the experience changes both the knower and the world. Whereas realists are concerned with passing organized bodies of knowledge from one generation to the next, pragmatists stress applying knowledge—that is, using ideas as instruments for problem solving (epistemology).

Wedded as they are to change and adaptation, pragmatists do not believe in absolute and unchanging truth or values. Because we live in a constantly changing universe, values change too. What contributes to personal and social growth is the only underlying principle. We can clarify values by testing them and reconstructing them as needed. Values that work at one time or in one place or in one society might not work in another (axiology).

EDUCATIONAL IMPLICATIONS OF PRAGMATISM. Pragmatists stress the changing nature of reality. There are no absolutes and hence the teacher needs to help students learn to question what is and solve problems as they naturally occur. Realists and idealists call for a curriculum centered on academic disciplines, but pragmatists prefer a curriculum that draws the disciplines together to solve problems—an interdisciplinary approach. Pragmatists emphasize that truth is found in the real world, which is always changing. So, it is critical to present concepts as they relate to contemporary problems and questions. Figure 4.4 illustrates the relationships among realism, idealism, and pragmatism.

What Should We Teach? Because the world is always in flux, knowledge is subject to revision, so it is more important to know how to construct, use, and test knowledge claims. For pragmatists the most important thing to know is how to question what we know and how to reconstruct what we know to match the changing world. Therefore, pragmatists are less interested in transmitting large bodies of information; rather, they favor solving problems through interacting with the environment in an intelligent and reflective manner. Teaching students to use methods of scientific inquiry is a high priority.

How Should We Teach? Pragmatists view the school as a community of learners. Cultural diversity enriches society just as physical diversity enriches the universe. So, schools should use integrated and democratic teaching and learning approaches. Because the process of problem solving is more important than teaching specific subject matter, pragmatists prefer the use of learner-centered problems as a teaching focus. Facilitating student investigations and activities, providing technology and other resources, and encouraging

FIGURE 4.4   Relationship of realism, idealism, and pragmatism.

IDEALISM	PRAGMATISM	REALISM
a. Idea	a. Experience	a. Nature
b. Mind	b. Problem solving with reason	b. Body

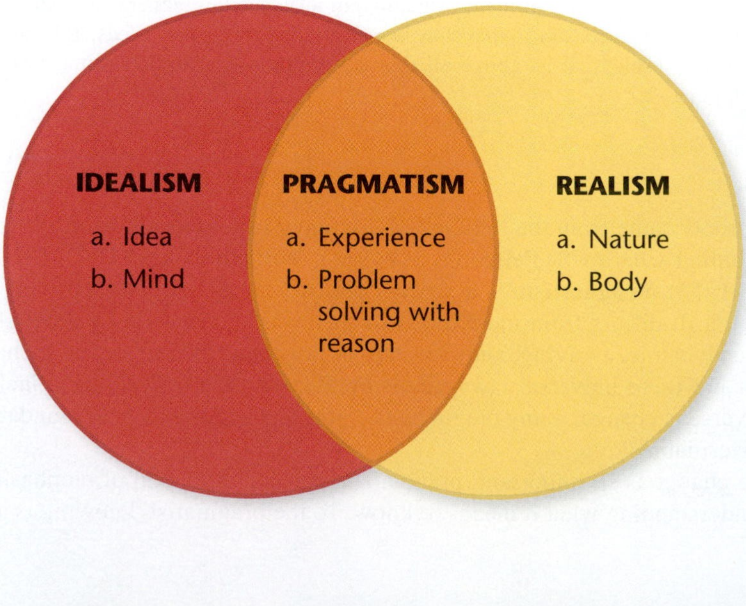

students to collaborate as a learning community are the key characteristics of a worthy teaching approach.

Matching Ideas from Pragmatism to Your Own. Now take a moment to record the key ideas from pragmatism that match your own. You will find that pragmatism has components of both idealism and realism. For example, pragmatists value the development of theories or ideas (like idealism); they also note that ideas change and are subject to experimental and observational techniques (like realism). However, pragmatists contend that there are no underlying principles that account for the world other than the concept of change. This notion is not held by either realists or idealists.

CHARLES SANDERS PEIRCE. Charles Sanders Peirce (1839–1914) is one of the earliest pragmatist thinkers. He introduced the principle that belief is a habit of action undertaken to overcome indecisiveness. He believed that the purpose of thought is to produce action and that the meaning of a thought is the collection of results of actions. For example, to say that steel is "hard" is to mean that when the operation of scratch testing is performed on steel, it will not be scratched by most substances. The aims of Peirce's pragmatic method are to supply a procedure for constructing and clarifying meanings and to facilitate communication.

JOHN DEWEY. Early in his philosophical development, John Dewey (1859–1952) related pragmatism to evolution by explaining that human beings are creatures who have to adapt to one another and to their environments. Dewey viewed life as a series of overlapping and interpenetrating experiences and situations, each of which has its own complete identity. The primary unit of life is the individual experience.

Dewey wrote the following passage early in his career. In it he shows his zeal for education as a social force in human affairs.

> I believe that all education proceeds by the participation of the individual in the social consciousness of the race. This process begins unconsciously almost at birth, and is continually shaping the individual's powers, saturating his consciousness, forming his habits, training his ideas, and arousing his feelings and emotions.
>
> In sum, I believe that the individual is a social individual and that society is an organic union of individuals. If we eliminate the social factor from the child we are left only with an abstraction; if we eliminate the individual factor from society, we are left only with an inert and lifeless mass. (Dewey, 1897)

RICHARD RORTY. Richard Rorty (1931–2007) was a contemporary pragmatist philosopher who spent much of his life reinventing the work of John Dewey in light of the chaotic, everchanging nature of the world. Rorty contended that reality is not fixed, and it is the task of thinkers to come up with a procedure for correctly describing the nature of reality. He argued that reality is the outcome of inquiry, and as human inquiry shifts so too will the nature of what we call *real*. Rorty contended that different disciplines have different avenues for studying the world and therefore these avenues of inquiry create different realities. The way an artist looks at the world and creates a work of art and the way a chemist looks at the world and develops a new way of looking at molecules both affect the very nature of what *is*. Essential to this point of view is the understanding that disciplines such as science, mathematics, art, and history are not rooted in a fixed reality but are constructed by groups of people who are trying to make sense of the world. Hence, disciplines are arbitrary contrivances and one discipline is as good as another. Also, because disciplines are created by persons, they are subject to all the foibles, limitations, and prejudices of any human convention.

Although Rorty did not speak directly to the field of education, his work provides a significant challenge to teachers. No longer can teachers represent expert knowledge as accurate or as true. Rather, expert knowledge is the current agreement of scholars at this point in time. Expert knowledge is simply a set of ideas and procedures that have been found to be useful. Rorty contended that a thinker should no longer be represented as a discoverer; rather, a thinker is more of a maker or cobbler who crafts meaning. People come together, agree on certain things, and then try to talk or reason their way to a sensible conclusion. Expertise is more a matter of "usefulness" than truth.

Existentialism

One way of understanding the heart of existentialism is to ponder a quote from Jean-Paul Sartre: "Existence precedes essence." **Existentialism** contends that reality is nothing more than lived existence, and the final reality resides within each individual. There is nothing absolute, not even change. There is no ultimate principle or meaning.

Existentialists believe that we live an alien, meaningless existence on a small planet in an unimportant galaxy in an indifferent universe. Each individual is the creator of her or his essence; each individual is the creator of her or his meaning. Whereas some people might be paralyzed by this view, existentialists are energized by their quest to clarify their identity and create meaning. You might say that the very meaninglessness of life compels us to instill life with meaning (metaphysics).

To existentialists, knowing is a personal reflective process. Existentialists accept the usefulness of scientific knowledge about the physical and psychological world, but they contend that this knowledge is limited. The most significant knowledge is personal and nonscientific. Knowledge is about the human condition and the personal choices that each human makes (epistemology).

The key value for the existentialist is that human beings are free to make choices. However, this freedom is wrapped up in a search for meaning. We define ourselves; that is, we make meaning in our world by the choices we make. In effect, we are what we choose. We can choose to give up our freedom and allow others to define us or we can choose to be inner directed and authentic (axiology).

EDUCATIONAL IMPLICATIONS OF EXISTENTIALISM. The existentialist believes that most schools, like other corporate symbols, de-emphasize the individual and the relationship between the teacher and the student. Existentialists claim that when educators attempt to predict the behavior of students, they turn individuals into objects to be measured, quantified, and processed. Existentialists tend to feel that tracking, measurement, and standardization militate against the creation of opportunities for self-direction and personal choice.

What Should We Teach? According to the existentialist, education ought to be a process of developing a free, self-actualizing person—a process centered on the feelings of the student. Therefore, proper education does not start with the nature of the world and with humankind, but with the human individual or self. At school, students should be encouraged to discuss their lives and the choices they are making. Because we all live in the same meaningless predicament, we can learn by asking questions of one another, suggesting answers to concerns, and engaging in dialogue.

How Should We Teach? The existentialist educator would be a free personality engaged in projects that treat students as free personalities. The highest educational goal is to search for oneself. Teachers and students experience existential crises; each such crisis involves an examination of oneself and one's life purposes. Education helps to fill in the gaps with understanding that the student needs in order to fulfill those purposes; it is not a mold to which the student must be fitted. Students define themselves by their choices.

The existentialist student would have a questioning attitude and would be involved in a continuing search for self and for the reasons for existence. The existentialist teacher would help students become what they themselves want to become, not what outside forces such as society, other teachers, or parents want them to become.

Matching Ideas from Existentialism to Your Own. The ideas of existentialism are more difficult to apply to education in that they focus so much on the individual development of a person rather than on the transmittal of ideas and concepts about the world. However, existentialism does provide a perspective about the importance of responding to individual ways of thinking and understanding that is not evident in realism, idealism, or pragmatism. So, take a moment to consider the ideas of existentialism and those that match your own. Then write down why these ideas make sense to you. Remember to organize your personal list based on these questions:

- What important knowledge and skills do I think should be taught?
- How should I teach these ideas and skills?

existentialism A school of philosophy that focuses on the importance of the individual rather than on external standards.

Existentialist thinkers are as varied as the notions of individual thought and self-defined meaning would suggest. There are atheistic existentialists as represented by Jean-Paul Sartre, critical existentialists as exemplified by Friedrich Nietzsche, and humanistic existentialists such as Maxine Greene.

JEAN-PAUL SARTRE. Modern existentialism was born amidst the pain and disillusionment of World War II. Jean-Paul Sartre (1905–1980) broke with previous philosophers and asserted that existence (being) comes before essence (meaning).

Sartre saw no difference between being free and being human. This view opens great possibilities, yet it also creates feelings of dread and nausea as one recognizes the reality of nonbeing and death as well as the great responsibilities that accompany such radical freedom to shape oneself out of one's choices. The process of answering the question "Who are we?" begins at a crucial event in the lives of young people called the existential moment—that point somewhere toward the end of youth when individuals realize for the first time that they exist as independent agents.

FRIEDRICH NIETZSCHE. Friedrich Nietzsche[1] (1844–1900) was an existential philosopher who stressed the importance of the individuality of persons. Throughout his writings, Nietzsche indicts the supremacy of herd values in modern democratic social systems. He criticizes the way social systems such as modern educational institutions foster a spirit of capitalistic greed. When Nietzsche turns his attention primarily to social systems, human beings are portrayed much more as victims of social dynamics than as inferior or superior beings.

In Nietzsche's texts there is a strategy to liberate people from the oppression of feeling inferior within themselves, a teaching of how not to judge what one is in relation to what one should be. Although Nietzsche did not author a comprehensive teaching methodology, he teaches how to cultivate a healthy love of self-care, a taste for solitude, literacy as a vital capacity, and an overall gratitude for one's existence (Sassone, 2002). Nietzsche observed that most teachers and parents

> . . . hammer even into children that what matters is something quite different: the salvation of the soul, the service of the state, the advancement of science, or the accumulation of reputation and possessions, all as the means of doing service to mankind as a whole; while the requirements of the individual, his great and small needs within the twenty-four hours of the day, are to be regarded as something contemptible or a matter of indifference. (Nietzsche, trans. 1986)

MAXINE GREENE. A theme that permeates most of Maxine Greene's work is her unyielding faith in human beings' willingness to build and transcend their lived worlds. To Greene (1917–) philosophy is a deeply personal and aesthetic experience. Her writing blurs the distinction between philosophy and literature. This is appropriate because Greene contends that living is philosophy. Greene (1988) asserts that schools must be places that offer "an authentic public space where diverse human beings can appear before one another as best they know to be."

The existentialist philosophy is one that supports the importance of humans developing their personal identities and determining what is and is not significant and worthy. In the above quote, Maxine Green states that schools are a place where diverse human beings can appear before others as they authentically see themselves.

Many schools have policies about personal attire. The "Who Is Right?" feature explores the issue of requiring teachers to wear business attire in the classroom. Given that schools should be a place where diverse human beings can appear as they authentically see themselves, what is your perspective on this issue?

The Dynamic Relationship of Philosophy and Education

We have carefully discussed four different schools of philosophy and shown how they influence teaching and learning. Educational philosophy develops from the application of philosophy to classroom life. The way curriculum is organized, the manner in which instruction is delivered,

---

[1]This section on the writings of Nietzsche was developed in 2008 by Dr. Leslie Sassone from the Foundations of Education at Northern Illinois University, DeKalb Illinois.

WHO IS RIGHT?

SHOULD TEACHERS WEAR BUSINESS ATTIRE TO SCHOOL?

School districts differ in their policies regarding what type of attire teachers must wear. Because clothing is often considered a symbol of one's identity, the issue of wearing business attire is controversial.

YES

Ray Waters teaches English at Gulf Breeze High School in Gulf Breeze, Florida.

If educators want to be paid and treated as professionals, we should carry ourselves as professionals. An already tarnished image of public education is further sullied by teachers who choose to enter a classroom dressed for a day at the beach or for yard work.

Business attire in the classroom portrays an image of an educator who is proud of the work he or she does. What degree of respect can teachers expect to receive if they don't dress like adult role models intent on providing the very best education for their students? Would a doctor see patients in shorts and a T-shirt? Would an attorney enter a courtroom with flip-flops and Capri pants? Would a businessperson attend a corporate board meeting in a warm-up suit?

Our school, as with most high schools, has theme days—pep rally Fridays and homecoming week—when casual, or even bizarre, dress is encouraged. However, when the "fun" is over, school administrators should ensure that the faculty dress appropriately for the classroom. The job of an administrator is to create a culture at a school that accepts nothing short of the most professional behavior. Appropriate dress is not the only quality of professionalism, but it is the most conspicuous.

Evaluation instruments should include sections on professional dress. Warm-up suits, jeans, Birkenstocks, T-shirts, and Hawaiian print shirts are the daily attire of a few members of our faculty. High school students are mature enough to see hypocrisy. If students are required to meet an appropriate standard of dress, why aren't educators?

If educators are ever to enjoy the respect of the public and the compensation we deserve, let's start with something we can control. Let's outwardly show our pride in our profession by implementing dress codes for teachers.

NO

Eileen Elrod is a guidance counselor for Grayson County Schools in Virginia.

Form follows function and never is that more true than in defining "professional attire" in a school setting. Our duties are as varied as our job descriptions and attire must follow accordingly.

I will not forget the day I smugly walked down the hall after breakfast duty, proudly wearing my new dress pants and blouse, only to look down to see the label from a student's breakfast syrup container stuck to my pants. I've also learned that the red paint used in lower grades bonds permanently to better clothing.

My vest of bright green fabric depicting construction tractors might not portray the most professional air, but it stimulates children to talk. The merits of each tractor and brand have been described at length by even the quietest child. These were students who had been shy and uncertain of themselves. The vest got them talking.

Weaving dog and cat buttons into my shoelaces would not make a favorable impression in the corporate world, but it entertains young children who sit on the rug for a story.

My winter coat must lie either on a chair or on the floor because no closet or coat rack is available. Even those fortunate enough to have closets find them so full the doors won't close. Therefore, we wear washable work jackets.

I allow school spirit to override stereotyped professionalism when I wear the sweatshirts that are gifts from the wrestling team and coach. The gift of popular clothing is priceless and wearing these items tells team members, "You are important."

When choosing how we will dress our primary thought must be for our children and the tasks we do. We should not select clothing to make a fashion statement. Clothing is part of our curriculum.

WHAT IS YOUR PERSPECTIVE ON THIS ISSUE?

Source: "Should Teachers Wear Business Attire to School?" *NEA Today* (February 2006), p. 45. Reprinted by permission of the National Education Association.

the character of school environments, and the processes used in testing and grading are informed by the philosophical views held by educators, parents, and legislators. Such views vary greatly among school districts and states.

Table 4.1 compares the answers that idealism, realism, pragmatism, and existentialism provide when you use the concepts that underlie each of these philosophies and apply them to educational questions. As you examine this table, you will notice that two of the philosophies are categorized as teacher centered. The reason for this is that as one applies realism and idealism to educational questions, the answers they provide tend to be teacher centered. In this context, *teacher centered* means that the responsibility for learning weighs heavily on the teacher rather than the student. The student is more of a receiver of knowledge and the teacher is the provider.

GO TO ··➤

Chapter 12 describes how curriculum and instruction differ based on diverse points of view.

TABLE 4.1

Educational Implications of Philosophy

EDUCATIONAL QUESTIONS	TEACHER-CENTERED PHILOSOPHIES		STUDENT-CENTERED PHILOSOPHIES	
	IDEALISM	REALISM	PRAGMATISM	EXISTENTIALISM
What should students learn? (Metaphysics)	Big ideas that remain important throughout time: intellectual history, literature, philosophy, mathematics	Ideas that result from careful investigations about the physical world: science, technology, engineering, mathematics	Change is constant and what we know is learned through inquiry that involves human interaction in society	Existence is the only constant and what is learned is determined by the unique needs of individuals
What is the proper curriculum goal? (Human Nature)	The same big ideas should be understood and appreciated by all	Mastery of the laws of the universe	Ongoing creation of new ideas about the physical and social world based on the unending process of change	Personal freedom and development for each individual
What is the proper teaching approach? (Epistemology)	Teaching for understanding of key ideas: lecture, discussion, questioning	Teaching for mastery of information and skills: demonstration, inquiry, critical thinking	Teaching for problem solving through inquiry projects, hands-on learning, product development	Teaching for meaning: Individual exploration, discovery methods, and authentic pedagogy
How should character development occur? (Axiology)	Imitation of exemplars, heroes	Training in rules of conduct that relate to ethical inquiry	Group decision making in light of consequences	Development of individual responsibility for decisions and preferences

On the other hand, the answers provided by pragmatism and existentialism are categorized as student centered. The reason for this is that as one applies the idea of pragmatism and existentialism to education, the responsibility for learning falls on the learner's shoulders. The learner is more active in creating the learned knowledge and the teacher is more of a coach or mentor who helps the learner create her/his knowledge and skills.

Take a moment to consider how a classroom would look if it were guided by the ideas of a single philosophical school. You will find that by doing this for each of the four philosophies, your image of classroom life will look and feel quite different.

JOURNAL FOR REFLECTION 4.2

Now that you have developed a list of those ideas from each of the classical philosophical schools that match your own, develop a paragraph that analyzes which philosophies tend to include the most similarities and the fewest to your own thinking.

EASTERN AND NATIVE NORTH AMERICAN WAYS OF KNOWING

Most studies of Western philosophy typically begin with the Greek philosophers. Yet there is evidence that Platonic philosophy owed much of its development to Eastern thinkers who emphasized the illusory quality of the physical world. In addition, native peoples from many lands have developed a way of thinking about life and education that extends and reorganizes the writing of Western thinkers. To ignore such ways of knowing would violate the very nature of philosophy, which, as noted at the beginning of this chapter, is a search for truth.

Eastern Ways of Knowing

Although there are differences among the writings of the Far Eastern and Near Eastern philosophers, **Eastern ways of knowing**, as a group, stress inner peace, tranquility, attitudinal development, and mysticism. In general, Eastern ways of knowing emphasize order, regularity, and patience that are both proportional to and in harmony with the laws of nature.

Western philosophy tends to emphasize logic and materialism; Eastern ways of knowing, on the other hand, stress the inner rather than the outer world, intuition rather than sense, and mysticism rather than scientific discoveries. Western philosophers tend to begin with the outer, material world and abstract to concepts and underlying principles; Eastern ways of knowing begin with the inner world and then reach to the outer world of phenomena.

It is sometimes charged that Eastern ways of knowing are not philosophies but religions. Because the Eastern ways of knowing have such early beginnings and maintain a strong bent toward the spiritual side of nature, their stories maintain a language of gods and goddesses, much like Greek mythology. Unlike the Greeks, who tried to separate philosophy from religion, Eastern thinkers intertwined religious doctrines with philosophical views about the nature of the world and humans' interactions with it.

Eastern thinkers have always concerned themselves with education, which they view as a way of achieving wisdom, maintaining family structure, establishing law, and providing for social and economic concerns. Instruction includes the things that one must do to achieve the good life, and education is viewed as necessary not only for this life but also for achievement of the good life hereafter.

One good reason to study Eastern ways of knowing is that they offer vantage points from which to examine Western thought. Eastern ideas encourage one to seriously question the Western world's most basic commitments to science, materialism, and reason. Although we could analyze many more different types of Eastern thinking, we focus here on the ideas of the Far East or Eastern Asia, including India, China, and Japan because of their long, relatively stable traditions, enormous land area, and immense population. Consider the implications that Eastern ways of knowing have for curriculum in the "Perspectives on Diversity" feature.

Eastern ways of knowing A varied set of ideas, beliefs, and values from the Far and Near East that stress inner peace, tranquility, attitudinal development, and mysticism.

PERSPECTIVES on DIVERSITY

Curriculum and Eastern Ways of Knowing

Chi Mae Lin was thrilled to find out that she had been selected to participate in the curriculum committee at her rural high school in southern Nevada. She had been working as a Junior–Senior English teacher for only two years, and she knew that this appointment was a sign that her teaching and professional conduct were making a difference in the minds of her colleagues. At the first meeting, committee members were asked to develop required reading lists for specific courses in an effort to keep the curriculum current and compatible with academic standards. Chi Mae was asked to prepare the reading list for Junior English.

After reviewing the current required reading list, Chi Mae noticed that all of the readings were written by American and European authors. So, she selected two new readings, one written by an author from Japan and another written by an author from Tibet. Her rationale for this change was based on the importance of expanding the students' perspectives about the nature of the world and humans' relationship to it.

On the day that Chi Mae made this proposal to the curriculum committee, she was surprised to find that the committee members were unimpressed with her selection—in fact, the committee's response to her proposal seemed to generate hostility rather than debate. One committee member, with a rising voice, shouted at her: "Why did you select two authors from the Middle East? Don't you know you are working with rural students living in the United States? The original documents are translations and were not even written in English."

WHAT IS YOUR PERSPECTIVE?

1. Why do you think Chi Mae thought that the Japanese and Tibetan authors might expand students' perspectives about the nature of the world?

2. What did the committee member mean by reminding Chi Mae that she was working with rural students in the United States?

3. In what way would ideas from a piece of literature written in a different language offer students a new perspective?

4. Would it have been better if Chi Mae had suggested writings that were originally written in English by an American author with a Japanese or Tibetan background? Why or why not?

INDIAN THOUGHT. Far Eastern Indian thought has a long, complex history and is permeated by opposites. To Western philosophers, opposites need to be reconciled, but to the Eastern mind, this need for consistency is unimportant. For example, great emphasis is placed on a search for wisdom, but this does not mean a rejection of worldly pleasures. Though speculation is emphasized, it has a practical character. Far Eastern Indian thinkers insist that knowledge be used to improve both social and communal life and that people should live according to their ideals. In Far Eastern Indian thought, there is a prevailing sense of universal moral justice, according to which individuals are responsible for what they are and what they become (Ozman & Craver, 2008).

CHINESE THOUGHT. The emphasis of Far Eastern Chinese philosophy is on harmony; correct thinking should help one achieve harmony with life. This harmony of government, business, and family should then lead toward a higher synthesis. Confucianism and Taoism provide two major contexts for Chinese thought.

For more than two thousand years, Confucian thought has influenced education, government, and culture in China. Confucius (551–479 BCE) believed that people need standards for all of life, so rules were developed for a wide range of activities. Confucian thought gives education a high place, but stresses building moral character more than merely teaching skills or imparting information. This moral approach has a practical component. Children should obey and defer to parents and respect the wisdom adults have gained in their journey through life. Following these principles enables children to become *chun-tzu*, persons distinguished by faithfulness, diligence, and modesty.

The central concept of Taoism is that of the *Tao*, meaning "the Way" or "the Path." The Tao is the way the universe moves, the way of perfection and harmony. It is conformity with nature. Perhaps the most significant aspect of the Tao is letting things alone, not forcing personal desires onto the natural course of events. It is a noncompetitive approach to life. Taoists believe that conflict and war represent basic failures in society, for they bring ruin to states and disrespect for life.

JAPANESE THOUGHT. Japanese thought is rooted in Shinto, a way of thinking that recognizes the significance of the natural world. This respect for all nature permeates Japanese thought and life. Shinto accepts the phenomenal world (the world people apprehend through their senses) as absolute; this acceptance leads to a disposition to place greater emphasis on intuitive, sensible, concrete events rather than on universal ideas. On the social level, the Japanese express this focus on the natural world through many artifacts, including the patterns of traditional kimonos. Within the house, flowers are arranged in vases and dwarf trees placed in alcoves, flowers and birds are engraved on lintels, and nature scenes are painted on sliding screens.

EDUCATIONAL IMPLICATIONS OF EASTERN WAYS OF KNOWING. Eastern educational thought places great emphasis on the teacher–student relationship. Change springs from this relationship; that is, the student is changed as a result of contact with the guru, master, or prophet. Eastern educational thought emphasizes transformation: The individual must be transformed to face life. Attitude shaping is important because the attitude a person holds toward life will determine the individual's levels of goodness and wisdom.

A recurring educational aim in Eastern ways of knowing is to put humanity in tune with nature. There is great emphasis on observing nature and learning through wanderings and pilgrimages. The importance of achieving wisdom, *satori,* enlightenment, or nirvana is supreme. All paths must lead to this, and from this wisdom spring virtue, right living, and correct behavior.

Native North American Ways of Knowing

Just as the rich past and diverse cultures make it difficult to summarize Eastern thought, Native North American ways of knowing are equally difficult to synthesize. **Native North American ways of knowing** include a varied set of beliefs, positions, and customs that span the different tribes in North America. These beliefs, positions, and customs center on the relationship of humans to all of nature, including the earth, the sun, the sky, and beyond. Because Native North American ways of knowing center on the relationship of humans to all of nature, it is sometimes

GO TO ···>
Chapters 6 and 7 describe how teachers' understanding of diverse ways of knowing is a component of teaching and learning.

Native North American ways of knowing
A varied set of beliefs, philosophical positions, and customs that span the different tribes in North America.

Native North American ways of knowing provide a perspective that connects knowledge to the earth that surrounds us and of which we are a part.

difficult to separate knowing from a way of life. In fact, to understand is to live and to develop an ever closer, more profound human-to-nature relationship. The types of relationships and the symbols that inform these human-to-nature relationships differ widely among tribes.

Although Native North American ways of knowing differ across the four hundred–plus tribes in North America, these ways of knowing do have similar elements. They all include traditional stories and beliefs that dictate a way of knowing and living. All include a reverence for nature and a sense of humans' responsibility to nature. And all groups make reference to a supreme being—although the names are different, the relationships vary, and the expectations of some supreme beings are interpreted through natural elements. Thus, the Black Hills are sacred to the Lakota, the turtle is revered as Mother Earth by the Ojibwa, and so on. Native North American ways of knowing are orally developed rather than written. Hence, they change slightly from age to age. Additionally, the ways of knowing are subject to interpretation by the shaman, or holy one.

NAVAJO THOUGHT: HARMONY AND INNER FORMS. The Navajo nation is the largest tribe in the United States. The Navajos' early history was nomadic, and their thoughts and customs are known for their unique ability to assimilate with and adapt to the thought and customs of other tribes. As with most Native North American cultures, the Navajo universe is an all-inclusive unity viewed as an orderly system of interrelated elements. At the basis of Navajo teachings and traditions is the value of a life lived in harmony with the natural world. Such a view enables one to "walk in beauty." To understand the Navajo worldview, one must note the teachings of the "inner forms" of things. These inner forms were set in place by First Man and First Woman. The concept of inner form is similar to the concept of a spirit or soul; without it, the Navajos say, the outer forms would be dead (Wilson, 1994a).

LAKOTA THOUGHT: ONENESS WITH THE ENVIRONMENT. The Native American culture of the Great Plains, of which the Lakota form a part, is based on mystical participation with the environment. All aspects of this ecosystem, including earth, sky, night, day, sun, and moon, are elements of the oneness within which life was undertaken. The Lakota celebrate the "sacred hoop of life" and observe seven sacred rites toward the goal of ultimate communion with Wakan-Tanka, the Great Spirit (Wilson, 1994b).

HOPI THOUGHT: PATH OF PEACE. The Hopi follow the path of peace, which they believe is a pure and perfect pattern of humankind's evolutionary journey. The Road of Life of the Hopi is represented as a journey through seven universes created at the beginning. At death the conduct of a person in accordance with the Creator's plan determines when and where the next step on the road will be taken. Each of the Hopi clans has a unique role to play, and each role is an essential part of the whole. Hopis must live in harmony with one another, with nature, and with the plan. Out of this complex interplay, then, the plan is both created and allowed to unfold.

> We feel that the world is good. We are grateful to be alive. We are conscious that all men are brothers. We sense that we are related to other creatures. . . . When you go out of your house in the morning and see the sun rising, pause a moment to think about it. When you take water from a spring, be aware that it is a gift of nature. (Albert Yava, Big Falling Snow, Hopi). (Wilson, 1994c)

EDUCATIONAL IMPLICATIONS OF NATIVE NORTH AMERICAN WAYS OF KNOWING. Native North American educational thought emphasizes the importance of nature. The pursuit of knowledge and happiness must be subordinate to a respect for the whole universe. To know is to understand one's place in the natural order of things. To be is to celebrate through ritual and stories the spirit that informs all reality. These principles encourage educators to study the physical and social world by examining the natural relationships that exist among things, animals, and humans. Studying ideas in the abstract or as independent entities is not as important as understanding the relationships among ideas and the physical reality. Native American thought supports the use of hands-on learning, making connections, holding discussions, and celebrating the moment. In fact, these very educational approaches are supported by many best practice educational research studies (Bransford, Brown, & Cocking, 2000; Donovan & Bransford, 2005).

Matching Ideas from Eastern and Native North American Ways of Knowing to Your Own

The ideas of Eastern and Native North American ways of knowing share a number of similarities. They both show a reverence for the world in which we live and value the importance of harmony with nature and each other. However, there are many different nuances to this theme based on the geographical location of writers (India, China, and Japan) as well as the tribe to which Native writers belong (Cherokee, Lakota, and Hopi).

So, take a moment to consider the ideas of Eastern and Native American thinkers and determine which ones match your own. Then, write down why these ideas make sense to you. Remember to organize your personal list based on these questions:

- What important knowledge and skills do I think should be taught?
- How should I teach these ideas and skills?

JOURNAL FOR REFLECTION 4.3

Consider the four components of analytic and prophetic thinking as described in the first part of this chapter. Then, describe which aspects of these types of Western thinking fit Eastern and Native North American ways of knowing.

SUMMARY

STRUCTURE AND METHODOLOGY OF PHILOSOPHY

- The study of philosophy permeates every aspect of the teacher's role and provides the underpinning for every decision. Teachers are natural philosophers in that they live out their personal answers to the big questions of philosophy by the way they set up their classrooms, by the way they teach students, by the rules they impose, and by the way they relate to others.

- Philosophy revolves around three major types of questions: those that deal with the nature of reality (metaphysics), those that deal with knowledge and truth (epistemology), and those that deal with values (axiology).

- Decisions about the subject matter emphasized in a curriculum are metaphysical in that they deal with the nature of reality or what is worth knowing — Questions related to what is true and how we know are epistemological. Classroom methods are practices that aim to assist learners in acquiring knowledge and truth in the subject area. Classroom activities that deal with ethics (what is right or wrong), beauty, and character are in the realm of axiology (values).

- Analytic and prophetic thinking provide two approaches to the process of philosophy. Analytic thinking provides clarity and precision, whereas prophetic thinking fosters breadth and sensitivity.

SCHOOLS OF PHILOSOPHY AND THEIR INFLUENCE ON EDUCATION

- Idealism is a school of philosophy that holds that ideas or concepts are the essence of all that is worth knowing. The physical world we know through our senses is only a manifestation or imperfect representation of the spiritual world.

- Realism is a school of philosophy that holds that reality, knowledge, and value exist independent of the human mind. In other words, realists reject the idealist notion that ideas are the ultimate reality.

- Pragmatism is a process philosophy that stresses evolving and change rather than being. It differs from most forms of idealism and realism by a belief in an open universe that is dynamic, evolving, and in a state of becoming.

- Existentialism contends that reality is nothing more than lived existence, and the final reality resides within each individual. There is nothing absolute, not even change. There is no ultimate principle or meaning.

- The way the curriculum is organized, the manner in which instruction is delivered, the character of school environments, and the processes used in testing and grading are informed by the philosophical views held by educators, parents, and legislators.

- Idealism and realism reflect a teacher-centered approach to education because they place greater responsibility on teachers to teach specific content and thinking skills. Pragmatism and existentialism reflect a student-centered approach to education because they provide greater opportunity for students to create their own meaning.

EASTERN AND NATIVE AMERICAN WAYS OF KNOWING

- Eastern ways of knowing stress the inner rather than the outer world, intuition rather than sense, and mysticism rather than scientific discoveries. Order, regularity, and patience that are proportional to and in harmony with the laws of nature are key to a good life.

- Native North American ways of knowing include a varied set of beliefs, positions, and customs that span more than four hundred different tribes in North America. Beliefs, positions, and customs center on the relationship of humans to all of nature, including the earth, the sun, the sky, and beyond. To understand is to live and to develop an ever closer, more profound human-to-nature relationship.

- Both Eastern and Native North American ways of knowing share an underlying sensitivity to nature and an emphasis on wisdom, virtue, spirituality, and harmony within the larger universe.

- The educational implications of these ways of knowing include the importance of teaching respect for the earth and awareness of the interrelationships among all things.

DISCUSSION STARTERS

1. How would you describe philosophy to a young child?
2. In your opinion, which is the most important aspect of a given philosophy (for the teacher): the metaphysical component, the epistemological component, or the axiological component? State the rationale for your choice.
3. Early Greek philosophers suggest that all knowledge is based on experience. Discuss the implications of this statement for teaching methodology.
4. Describe the ways that Eastern and Native North American ways of knowing might influence what and how you teach.

SCHOOL-BASED OBSERVATIONS

1. As you visit schools and classrooms, be alert for indications of philosophical concepts and different philosophical views. Examine the lesson plans that teachers have developed and consider whether their focus is on subject matter acquisition, the development of character, or the development of skills. These emphases can be a clue to the type of philosophy that a teacher endorses. You might wish to talk with teachers about their educational ideas.
2. Many schools have written statements describing their philosophy of education. Ask several schools to send you a copy of their philosophy of education. When you receive them, look for similarities and differences among the philosophical statements.
3. As you visit schools and classrooms, focus on the approaches to discipline that teachers employ. What do these approaches imply about teachers' views of human nature?

PORTFOLIO DEVELOPMENT

1. According to idealistic philosophy, character education can be enhanced through study and imitation of exemplars/heroes in the historical record. Identify an exemplary educator from history and describe how you could teach character through that person's example. Place your essay in your folio as an example of your teaching methodology.

2. Assist a student as a mentor or tutor. Before beginning, gather samples of the student's thinking and schoolwork. Try to think like the student and by so doing uncover areas in which the student needs help. Develop a diagnosis that details what changes will be beneficial. Place these ideas in your folio as an example of your diagnostic and metacognitive skills.

WEB SOLUTIONS

You have been invited to make a presentation to the school board about the professional responsibilities of public school teachers that extend beyond classroom teaching. As part of your presentation, you want to include the idea that teachers are committed to ask difficult questions about the justice and equity within educational trends and practices. The following websites provide insights about some of these critical questions and reflective practices:

www.philosophyofeducation.org The Philosophy of Education Society (PES) comprises educators who are committed to the critical normative and interpretive aspects of education. The mission of PES is to encourage scholarship in the field of philosophy of education; to discuss curricular, methodological, and institutional issues in the field; and to offer educators at large a forum for the philosophical analysis of educational issues. The site provides Internet resources, papers, and discussions that help teachers understand questions and concerns that flow from a philosophical perspective on education.

www.pdcnet.org The Philosophy Documentation Center (PDC) is a nonprofit organization dedicated to providing affordable access to the widest possible range of philosophical materials. Established in 1966, the PDC provides access to scholarly journals, reference materials, conference proceedings, and instructional software. This site provides easy access to the ideas and writings of a wide variety of philosophers of education.

www.indigenous.ku.edu This is the website at the University of Kansas for the Global Indigenous Nations Studies Program. This program fosters and promotes scholarships focused on understanding the experiences and improving the lives of indigenous peoples around the world. It promotes and reports new knowledge concerning issues such as globalization, decolonization, empowerment, tribal sovereignty, ethnic and legal identity, social injustice, traditional beliefs, languages, public health, environmental resource management, and human rights.

MyEducationLab™ Go to the topic **History and Philosophy of Education** in the MyEducationLab (**www.myeducationlab.com**) for *Foundations of American Education: Becoming Effective Teachers in Challenging Times, 16e*, where you can:

- Find learning outcomes for **History and Philosophy of Education**, along with the national standards that connect to these outcomes.
- Complete Assignments and Activities that can help you more deeply understand the chapter content.
- Apply and practice your understanding of the core teaching skills identified in the chapter with the Building Teaching Skills and Dispositions learning units.
- Access video clips of CCSSO National Teachers of the Year award winners responding to the question, "Why Do I Teach?" in the Teacher Talk section.
- Create, update, and share quality lesson plans with the Lesson Plan Builder.

- Access state licensure test requirements, overviews of what tests cover, and sample test items in the Certification and Licensure section.
- Access current state and national standards in the Licensure and Standards section.
- Learn how to create a high-quality teaching portfolio in the Preparing a Portfolio section.
- Access tips, advice, and other information on resume writing and interviewing, your first year of teaching, and law and public policies in the Beginning Your Career section.
- Check your comprehension of the content covered in the chapter with the Study Plan. Here you will be able to take a chapter pretest, receive feedback on your answers, and then access personalized Review, Practice, and Enrichment exercises to enhance your understanding of chapter content. After you complete the exercises, take a posttest to confirm your comprehension.

5

Building an Educational Philosophy in a Changing World

LEARNING OUTCOMES

After reading and studying this chapter, you should be able to:

1. Identify philosophy, psychology, and sociology concepts that influence the development of an educational philosophy. (InTASC 4: Content Knowledge)

2. Identify the major tenets of the teacher-centered educational philosophies of essentialism, behaviorism, and positivism. (InTASC 4: Content Knowledge)

3. Identify the major tenets of the student-centered educational philosophies of progressivism, humanism, and constructivism. (InTASC 4: Content Knowledge)

4. State the components of your personal philosophy of education in light of classroom organization, discipline practices, motivation, and classroom climate. (InTASC 1: Learner Development; InTASC 4: Content Knowledge; InTASC 9: Professional Learning and Ethical Practice)

5. List the characteristics of teachers as change agents. (InTASC 9: Professional Learning and Ethical Practice; InTASC 10: Leadership and Collaboration)

EDUCATION in the NEWS

GIRL WHO FOUGHT BULLIES NOW LABELED ONE BY SCHOOL

Published: Saturday, May 26, 2012

UMATILLA

By THERESA CAMPBELL, Staff Writer

theresacampbell@dailycommercial.com

"Caution: This campus is 100 percent against bullying. Speak out," reads a sign outside Umatilla High School, and one senior said she did speak out and has been punished for doing so.

Stormy Rich, 18, thought she was doing the right thing in reporting bullying incidents she witnessed against a mentally-challenged middle school girl by a group of girls on morning bus rides to school.

"I'm a very outspoken person," Rich said. "I stick up for what I feel is right. In the school code of conduct handbook, it is clearly stated that bullying is a non-tolerable offense."

Rich was riding that middle school bus because she earned enough credits to avoid having to take a first-period high school class and an earlier high school bus. The two schools are only a few blocks away.

Rich—who said she felt compelled to speak out because the girl couldn't even comprehend she was being picked on—first complained to the bus driver but the bullying continued. She then complained to a high school official, who said he would contact the middle school, but nothing changed.

"I would sit on the bus every single day and see the bullying was still going on and nothing was being done," Rich said. "It was aggravating."

The senior demanded the bullies stop, which worked for a while. She said they then began threatening her, even though she complained about this to school personnel on almost a daily basis for about two weeks. The mother and daughter even contacted police.

"Enough is enough," Rich said in her written complaint. "Something should be done."

That something was a letter sent to Rich's mother, Brenda, on May 4, saying her daughter was kicked off the middle school bus. A district school official said Rich displayed bullying behavior in her comments.

"She said what I did made me the bully, with me telling the kids that if they didn't stop, and if the school didn't do anything, that I would have to handle it," Rich said. "To me, it was just going too far."

According to Christopher Patton, communications officer for Lake County Schools, a courtesy had been extended to Rich to ride the middle school bus.

"Due to circumstances on the bus, the privileges were revoked," he said.

Patton said he could not discuss the bullying complaints filed by Rich or her mother. He also could not say if any action was taken about those complaints.

"I can't comment about student discipline, unfortunately," Patton said. "I think you're heading down a dangerous path because you've got one side of the story. . . . There are other parents that are involved in this."

Asked if the district had additional complaints on the issue, Patton replied: "Just this one parent."

"My daughter was punished incorrectly," said Brenda Rich. "Stormy was standing up for a child with emotionally challenged disabilities that should not have been bullied. The district's policy clearly states that anybody [who] in good faith files a report on bullying will not face any repercussions and she is."

Brenda Rich said she has met the bullied student and the young girl does not comprehend sarcasm or even understand what "hate" means. She views everybody as her "friend."

"Just because she doesn't understand what people are doing to her is wrong, it doesn't mean it's OK," said Brenda Rich, who questions if the schools' anti-bullying policies are really working.

". . . This child doesn't have the ability to stand up for herself, she has no voice. Stormy was her voice, even more so than the girl herself."

Her daughter won't have school transportation issues much longer.

Stormy Rich will graduate next week with a 3.67 GPA and has been awarded scholarships. She strives to continue to help others and plans to start nursing studies at Daytona State College.

QUESTIONS FOR REFLECTION

1. In this article, Stormy is faced with moral dilemmas focused on her concern for a student with special needs. If Stormy was one of your students and shared her thinking with you about this situation, what might you say to her? How might your own philosophy of education guide your response to her questions?

2. Think about ethical issues that you have faced in the past. Select one incident that you would have liked to share with your teachers or school administrators. In what ways could they have helped you? What stopped you from seeking their help?

3. Students often face ethical challenges regarding moral conduct; yet these sorts of issues are seldom discussed openly in the classroom. Why do schools tend to shy away from including ethical issues or controversial topics in the classroom setting? What are some ways that you think schools could incorporate issues of moral conduct and ethical dilemmas in the curriculum?

Source: "Girl Who Fought Bullies Now Labeled One By School" by Theresa Campbell. Copyright 2012 by *The Daily Commercial.* Reprinted with permission.

MyEducationLab™

Visit the MyEducationLab for *Foundations of American Education* to enhance your understanding of chapter concepts with a personalized *Study Plan.* You'll also have the opportunity to hone your teaching skills through video- and case-based *Assignments and Activities* and *Building Teaching Skills and Dispositions* lessons.

 Listen to several teachers talk about how they develop and nurture their philosophies of teaching and learning in this **video.**

THE DYNAMIC RELATIONSHIP BETWEEN PHILOSOPHY AND EDUCATION

Educational philosophy can be analyzed as the application of philosophy to the classroom. The way curriculum is organized, the manner in which instruction is delivered, the character of school environments, and the processes used in testing and grading are informed by the philosophical views held by educators, parents, and legislators. Such views vary greatly among school districts and states.

Educational philosophers attempt to develop cohesive ideas about teaching and learning by drawing on one or more compatible philosophies. They also attempt to clarify how these different philosophical approaches to curriculum, instruction, and assessment work or do not work together.

Educational philosophies are not pure philosophies in the classical sense; rather, educational philosophies also draw on psychological and sociological theories. This merger of different ideas and theories from different disciplines occurs because education itself is interdisciplinary. So, educational philosophies can be thought of as a mixture of philosophical ideas about existence, human nature, and truth and goodness along with psychological ideas about motivation, learning theory, and relationships, along with sociological ideas about society, norms, and equality.

Developing a Philosophy of Education

A philosophy of education is not just a set of written words; it is a reflective platform on which decisions about teaching and learning are made in an effort to develop learners. A teacher's practices in the classroom provide the clearest indicators of her or his personal philosophy. A worthy goal for beginning educators is to become comfortable with a variety of classroom practices that address the needs of learners. It is not a matter of selecting one methodology over another, but rather of understanding different methodologies and using them responsibly. Your philosophy of education develops gradually over time; it is a living platform that is never complete. Your educational philosophy emerges based on your experiences with learners in and out of the classroom, your use of different teaching and assessment methods, and your interactions with parents and other teachers.

Building on the Philosophies of Others

One strategy that can help you develop your own personal philosophy of education is to build on the educational philosophies of others. In the first part of this chapter we describe six major educational philosophies to show you how different classical philosophies give rise to divergent educational philosophies. We believe that this examination of different educational philosophies will prepare you, in the second part of the chapter, to develop your own philosophy of education.

The six educational philosophies presented in this chapter are organized according to the degree to which they focus on external (teacher-based) versus internal (student-based) authority. For example, a behaviorist educational philosopher primarily employs teacher-based authority. It would be inappropriate for the behaviorist to focus on personal choice because behaviorism essentially aims to control human behavior through teacher-directed reinforcement. On the other hand, a constructivist educational philosopher tends to emphasize student-based authority. Constructivist philosophers of education focus on developing students' individual meaning and hence they provide greater opportunity for students to decide what classroom rules should be followed.

Educational philosophy is more than a set of words. It is embodied in the way teachers relate to students, other teachers, principals, and parents.

This same distinction (between teacher-centered versus student-centered authority) can be used to group the classical schools of philosophy that undergird all educational philosophies. For example, the ideas and principles that surround idealism and realism imply that external (teacher-centered) authority is important to the attainment of truth and goodness, whereas pragmatism and existentialism focus more on the innate worth of the individual (student-centered authority).

Figure 5.1 helps you get started examining the six different educational philosophies that have developed over time. It provides a broad overview of these educational philosophies by clustering those that are teacher centered and those that are student centered. The three teacher-centered educational philosophies are essentialism, behaviorism, and positivism. Each of them tends to organize the classroom environment, instruction, and assessment approaches in a similar manner in that the teacher makes most of the decision about the components of the classroom. You will find that many of these ideas are drawn from the classical philosophies of idealism and realism.

GO TO ··›
See Chapter 4 for more information about teacher-based and student-based schools of philosophy.

You will also notice that the three student-centered educational philosophies of progressivism, humanism, and constructivism differ in the way that they organize the classroom environment, instruction, and assessment approaches. Each of them tends to permit greater freedom and student choice and they draw primarily from the classical philosophies of pragmatism and existentialism.

To varying degrees, these educational philosophies are used by classroom teachers and are applied to the way they organize their classrooms, their instruction, and their assessments. As you study these different educational philosophies, you will find that one or more of them clearly meshes with your own views. Start an educational philosophy journal. Make a note in your journal when you find a match between your own thinking and a specific aspect of an educational philosophy.

FIGURE 5.1   Teacher-centered versus student-centered classroom approaches.

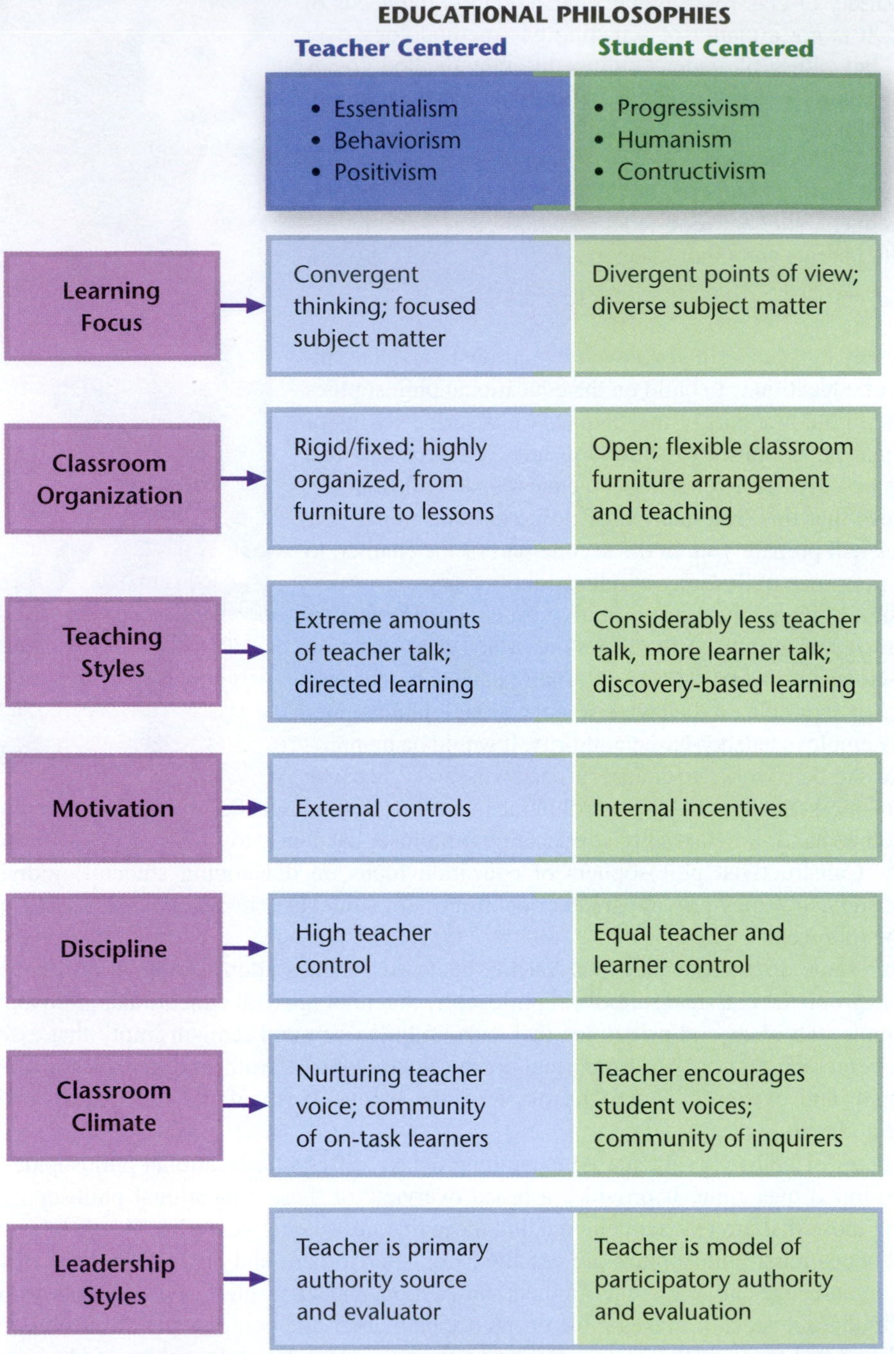

EDUCATIONAL PHILOSOPHIES

	Teacher Centered	Student Centered
	• Essentialism • Behaviorism • Positivism	• Progressivism • Humanism • Contructivism
Learning Focus	Convergent thinking; focused subject matter	Divergent points of view; diverse subject matter
Classroom Organization	Rigid/fixed; highly organized, from furniture to lessons	Open; flexible classroom furniture arrangement and teaching
Teaching Styles	Extreme amounts of teacher talk; directed learning	Considerably less teacher talk, more learner talk; discovery-based learning
Motivation	External controls	Internal incentives
Discipline	High teacher control	Equal teacher and learner control
Classroom Climate	Nurturing teacher voice; community of on-task learners	Teacher encourages student voices; community of inquirers
Leadership Styles	Teacher is primary authority source and evaluator	Teacher is model of participatory authority and evaluation

TEACHER-CENTERED EDUCATIONAL PHILOSOPHIES

Essentialism, behaviorism, and positivism are educational philosophies that espouse a teacher-centered approach to teaching and learning. Each of these teacher-centered educational philosophies' approach to subject matter, classroom organization, teaching methods, and assessment places most of the responsibility on the teacher, whose job it is to enable students to learn what is important. Although each of these educational philosophies forms a distinct cohesive whole, all three are rooted in an authoritarian principle—that is, that truth and goodness are entities best understood by the person with expertise who is in authority. The students' role, then, is to attempt to master and follow the directions of those in power.

This chapter presents each educational philosophy's perspectives on curriculum, teaching, and learning. In addition, for each educational philosophy, we describe an illustrative classroom activity that is consistent with the educational philosophy. The classroom activity is further analyzed according to the nature of the learner (active or passive); the nature of the subject matter; the use of the subject matter; and the type of thinking that is emphasized (convergent—focused on right answers, or divergent—focused on developing multiple perspectives).

Essentialism

Essentialism holds that an educated person in a given culture must have a common core of information and skills. Schools should be organized to transmit this core of essential material as effectively as possible. The three basic principles of essentialism are (1) a core of information, (2) hard work and mental discipline, and (3) teacher-centered instruction. The back-to-the-basics movement is a truncated form of essentialism because it focuses primarily on the three Rs and discipline. Essentialism draws equally from the philosophies of both idealism and realism.

Essentialist teaching methods require formal discipline through emphasis on required reading, lectures, memorization, repetition, and examination.

Essentialism has a close relative called **perennialism**. Like essentialism, perennialism holds that an educated person must have a common core of information and practice mental discipline. However, perennialism has a different definition of the common core. The term *perennial* means "ongoing or long lasting," so perennialists define a common core as time-honored ideas, the great works of past and present thinkers, and the ability to reason. To know reality, perennialists maintain that we must examine individual things and objects around us to find their essence. Instead of focusing on primarily current events, perennialists would have students focus on the big ideas and concepts that remain constant.

Essentialists are not so intent on transmitting underlying, basic truths; rather, they advocate the teaching of a basic core of information that will help a person live a productive life today. Hence, this core of information can and will change. Essentialism stresses the disciplined development of basic skills rather uncovering essences or underlying principles. The following educational implications are provided from the essentialist point of view.

ESSENTIALIST LEARNING FOCUS. Essentialism's goals are to transmit the cultural heritage and develop good citizens. The role of the student is that of a learner. School is a place where children come to learn what they need to know, and the teacher is the person who can best instruct students in essential matters. (See the Essentialist Class Activity.)

ESSENTIALIST CLASS ACTIVITY

Mr. Jackson's second graders had just learned to count money. He decided to let them play several games of "musical envelopes." Each student was given one envelope, with each envelope containing a different amount of paper "nickels," "dimes," "quarters," and "pennies." Students were told to open their envelopes and count the money inside and write the total amount on the front of their envelopes. When the music stopped, students were told to state their totals when called on by the teacher. The student with the most money for each game got a special prize (Duck, 1981, p. 40).

In this essentialist class activity, the nature of the learner is *passive* because students are given very clear and direct instructions that do not permit individual approaches. The nature of the subject matter is *structured* in that students are required to approach the task in a singular, specific, organized way. The use of the subject matter is *cognitive*, and the thinking approach is *convergent* because there is little room for emotional involvement and there is only one correct answer for each envelope.

essentialism An educational philosophy that holds that there is a common core of information and skills that an educated person must have; schools should be organized to transmit this core of essential material.

perennialism An educational philosophy that holds that there is a core of long-lasting ideas that an educated person must understand.

ESSENTIALIST CURRICULUM. The essentialist curriculum focuses on subject matter that includes literature, history, foreign languages, and religion. Teaching methods require formal discipline and feature required reading, lectures, memorization, repetition, and examinations. Essentialists generally agree about teaching the laws of nature and the accompanying universal truths of the physical world. Mathematics and the natural sciences are examples of subjects that contribute to the learners' knowledge of natural law. Activities that require mastering facts and information about the physical world are significant aspects of essentialist methodology. With truth defined as observable fact, instruction often includes field trips, laboratories, audiovisual materials, and nature study. Habits of intellectual discipline are considered ends in themselves.

Essentialism envisions subject matter as the core of education. Severe criticism has been leveled at U.S. education by essentialists who advocate an emphasis on basic education. Essentialism assigns to the schools the task of conserving the heritage and transmitting knowledge of the physical world. In a sense, the school is a curator of knowledge.

With the burgeoning of new knowledge in contemporary society, essentialism may be contributing to the slowness of educational change. In this context, essentialism has been criticized as obsolete in its authoritarian tendencies. Such criticism implies that essentialism does not satisfy the twenty-first-century needs of U.S. youth. Essentialist educators deny this criticism and claim to have incorporated modern influences in the system while maintaining academic standards.

ESSENTIAL SCHOOLS REFORM MOVEMENT. The Essential Schools movement is a contemporary school reform effort developed by Dr. Theodore Sizer that has many characteristics of essentialism. Sizer (2004; Sizer et al., 2009) contends that students need to master a common core of information and skills, and he encourages schools to strip away the nonessentials and focus on having students "use their minds well." The Essential Schools movement does not specify what content is essential in a given culture at a given time. Rather, "essential schools" are required to analyze clearly what this core of information should be and to change the curriculum to emphasize this core.

The Coalition of Essential Schools promotes a vision of schooling in which students engage in in-depth and rigorous learning. Essential schools select a small number of core skills and areas of knowledge that they expect all students to demonstrate and exercise broadly across content areas. Ten common principles have been developed by Dr. Sizer in collaboration with Essential School participants to guide the efforts of the coalition. These principles include the following:

- Using the mind well with a focus on clear, essential learning goals
- An attempt to apply these goals to all students
- Personalized teaching and learning
- Emphasis on student-as-worker
- Student performance on real tasks with multiple forms of evidence
- Principal and teachers as generalists first and specialists second
- Budgets that do not exceed those of traditional schools by more than 10 percent
- Nondiscriminatory policies and practices.

Now that you have had a chance to consider the ideas of essentialism, use Figure 5.2 to examine how these ideas specify the learning focus, classroom organization, teaching styles, discipline, motivation, and classroom climate. As you examine the bullets within this figure, consider which ones match your own way of thinking and jot them down in your journal.

Behaviorism

behaviorism A psychological theory and educational philosophy that asserts that behaviors represent the essence of a person and that all behaviors can be explained as responses to stimuli.

B. F. Skinner (1904–1990), the Harvard experimental psychologist and philosopher, is the recognized leader of the movement known as behaviorism. **Behaviorism** is a psychological theory and educational philosophy that holds that one's behavior is determined by environment, not heredity. Skinner verified Pavlov's stimulus–response theory with animals and, from his research, suggested that human behavior could also be explained as responses to external stimuli. Because of its focus on the careful examination of environment, behaviors, and responses, behaviorism is closely linked to realism. Other behaviorists' research expanded on Skinner's work in illustrating the effect of the environment, particularly the interpersonal environment, on shaping individual behavior.

FIGURE 5.2   Essentialism educational implications.

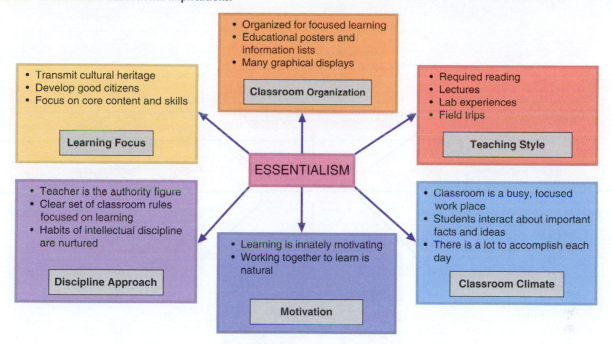

BEHAVIORIST LEARNING FOCUS. Behaviorists hold that one's behavior is determined by environment, not heredity. This suggests that by carefully controlling the stimuli in the classroom, the teacher can significantly influence student behavior. Behaviorists believe that the school environment must be highly organized and the curriculum based on carefully developed behavioral objectives, and they hold that knowledge is best described as behaviors that are observable. They contend that empirical evidence is essential if students are to learn and that students must employ the scientific method to arrive at knowledge. The primary task of educators is to develop learning environments that lead to desired behaviors in students. (See the Behaviorist Class Activity.)

BEHAVIORIST CLASS ACTIVITY

Students in Mr. Drucker's civics class were given merit tokens for coming into the room quietly, sitting at their desks, preparing notebooks and pencils for the day's lesson, and being ready to begin answering comprehension questions in their workbooks. On Fridays students were allowed to use their tokens at an auction to buy items that Mr. Drucker knew they wanted. Sometimes, however, students had to save tokens for more than two weeks to buy what they liked best (Duck, 1981, pp. 50–51).

In this behaviorist class activity, the nature of the learner is *passive*, in that students are carefully manipulated by providing responses to their behaviors that make students do what the teacher wants. The nature of the subject matter is *structured* in that the workbooks and comprehension questions are carefully focused and lead students step by step. The use of the subject matter is *affective* (having to do with feelings) because the teacher attempts to provide merit tokens that relate to what students desire. The thinking approach is *convergent* in that the comprehension questions require one correct answer.

BEHAVIORIST CURRICULUM: REINFORCEMENT. The concept of reinforcement is critical to teacher practices in behaviorism. The behaviorist teacher endeavors to foster desired behaviors by using both positive reinforcers (things students like, such as praise, privileges, and good grades) and negative reinforcers (things students wish to avoid, such as reprimands, extra homework, and lower grades). The theory is that behavior that is not reinforced (whether positively or negatively) will eventually be "extinguished"—that is, it will cease to occur. In general, behaviorists contend that learning takes place when approved behavior is observed and then positively reinforced.

FIGURE 5.3   Behaviorism educational implications.

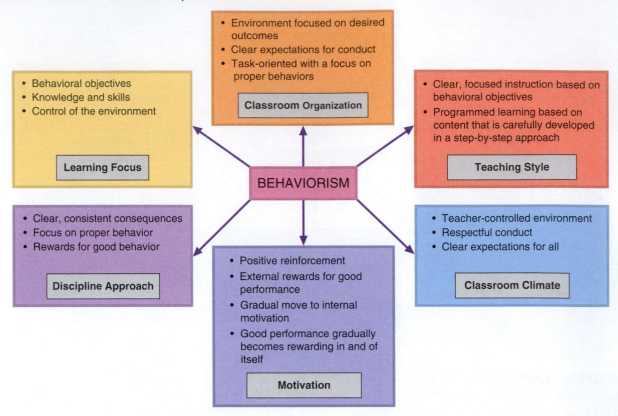

A teacher may provide nonverbal positive reinforcement (smiling, nodding approval) or negative reinforcement (frowning, shaking the head in disapproval). Similarly, nondirective statements, questions, and directive statements may be positive or negative. Both children and adults respond to the models other people (peers, adults, heroes) represent to them by imitating the model behavior. Behaviorists contend that students tend to emulate behaviors that are rewarded.

Behaviorists have supplied a wealth of empirical research that bears on the problems of attaining self-control, resisting temptation, and showing concern for others. Behaviorists do not attempt to learn about the causes of students' earlier problems. Rather, the behaviorist teacher focuses on the here-and-now environment and must ascertain what is happening in the classroom to perpetuate or extinguish students' behavior. For example, if a student shouts out whenever she wishes and disturbs others in the class, the behaviorist teacher focuses on what response can be provided consistently to make this behavior cease. It does not matter what (in the past) may account for this unwanted behavior; the key is changing the current environment.

Now that you have had a chance to consider the ideas of behaviorism, use Figure 5.3 to examine how these ideas specify the learning focus, classroom organization, teaching styles, discipline, motivation, and classroom climate. As you examine the bullets within this figure, consider which ones match your own way of thinking and jot them down in your journal.

Positivism

The educational philosophy of positivism stems from what the social scientist Auguste Comte (1798–1857) described as "positive knowledge." Comte divided the thinking of humankind into three historical periods, each of which was characterized by a distinct way of thinking. The first was the theological era, in which people explained things by reference to spirits and gods. The second was the metaphysical era, in which people explained phenomena in terms of causes, essences, and inner principles. The third was the positive period, in which thinkers did not attempt to go beyond observable, measurable fact.

The positivist position rejects essences, intuition, and inner causes that cannot be measured. Empirical verification is central to all proper thinking. This educational philosophy rejects beliefs about mind, spirit, and consciousness and holds that all reality can be explained by laws of matter and motion. In sum, **positivism** limits knowledge to statements of observable fact based on sense perceptions and the investigation of objective reality. In the 1920s positivism became a rallying point for a group of scholars in Vienna. Because the group consisted largely of scientists, mathematicians, and symbolic logicians, positivism became known as logical positivism.

Because positivist teachers are highly focused on teaching statements based on observable facts, they can sometimes overlook student engagement. It is difficult to balance the need to provide students with exact and precise information while also allowing students an opportunity to explore and make sense of ideas on their own. Consider the "Teaching in Challenging Times" feature about the challenges related to student boredom and a lack of interest in learning.

POSITIVIST LEARNING FOCUS. Direct instruction is a teaching and learning approach that requires teachers to clearly and precisely identify and state what a student needs to learn and master, as well as to restate this expectation through different media and assignments. It is a teaching and learning approach that places the responsibility for clear, precise expectations on the teacher. Once a teacher has identified precisely what students should know and be able to do, the teacher is expected to clearly describe to students exactly what they should know and

Positivism focuses learning on acquisition of facts based on careful, empirical observation and measurement of the world.

positivism A social theory and educational philosophy that limits truth and knowledge to what is observable and measurable.

TEACHING IN CHALLENGING TIMES

Adjusting the Attitude of Learners

Teachers in today's schools meet face-to-face with an increasing number of attitude problems from some learners. These problems are manifested in a lack of respect for teachers, visual boredom in learning, and a lack of a career work ethic. The lack of respect may come from a societal image of teachers embodied in the saying "Those who can't, teach!" Additionally, whatever is wrong in society tends to be blamed on the teacher and the school program. Teacher authority is usurped by parents and society, both challenging the teacher's right to discipline students, even the unruly ones. Some students call into question the worthiness of professional teachers, who are considered to have lower status when compared with other professions. The fact that teachers tend to be grossly underpaid for the type of workload they face may bolster such questions.

Some students exhibit boredom and are not motivated to learn because they do not see the relevance of what they are studying. To them, much of what they study seems to be important only for the tests they take and thus has no relevance to their lives. They yearn for assurance that teachers not only are competent but also care. The lack of a work ethic may be attributable to an environment that provides everything

material they need and want. This student problem may be related to the "good life" quality of a society that tends to have everything it needs. Many students have economically secure homes, are provided with an overabundance of goods and services, and are not held accountable for responsible activities within their families.

This dilemma does not paint a glowing picture of what is waiting for the teacher when she or he enters the classroom. If this picture is accurate, and if it is to be altered, then the teacher needs to actively develop with the students a common ground for the establishment of respect for each other.

WHAT ARE MY CHALLENGES?

1. How can you (as a teacher) show respect for your students and how can you teach your students to show respect for each other?

2. How can you prepare a learning environment that has meaning for the everyday life of the learner?

3. In what ways can you work with the home and community in providing a learning atmosphere in which students develop a work ethic and recognize its value?

be able to do. Teachers are encouraged to use repetition and have students practice and practice again, recite and recite again, whatever is to be learned. Teachers are further encouraged to have students repeat the main ideas of the instruction by using different media: oral recitation, writing, restating, drawing, and so forth. The key ingredient for this approach is the use of clear, uncluttered statements and restatements about the focus of learning.

This approach to teaching and learning fits the positivist educational theory, because in such an educational approach knowledge is considered something that is clear and precise. If all knowledge is clear, precise, and the same for all, then teachers can be expected to require all students to learn the same knowledge. Direct instruction is possible because all knowledge that is worthy is also clear and precise. (See the Positivist Class Activity.)

POSITIVIST CLASS ACTIVITY

Humberto Diaz introduced the meaning of surface tension to his junior high science students. He then told students that they could observe surface tension by watching water drops come together as they were placed on the surface of a penny. During class he then distributed eyedroppers, water, and pennies to the students. He directed the students to determine how many drops of water could fit on the surface of the penny before spilling over. Students were to collect data and develop a data table and corresponding charts. At the end of the class, Mr. Diaz asked the students to discuss their findings and draw a conclusion about the surface tension of water.

In this positivist class activity, the nature of the learner is *active*, because students are asked to investigate and collect data on their own. The nature of the subject matter is *structured*, because students are provided carefully developed directions concerning what they are to do. The use of the subject matter is *cognitive* because students are provided questions that are focused on a single, important concept. The thinking approach is *divergent* because students are encouraged to think about how they will determine the number of drops that fit on a penny and why the numbers may differ across groups.

POSITIVIST CURRICULUM. Practiced as an educational philosophy, positivism focuses the curriculum on the acquisition of facts based on careful empirical observation and measurement of the world. Positivism requires schools to develop content standards that represent the best understandings of experts who have already uncovered important ideas based on their own observation and measurement. Students are encouraged both to master these expert understandings and to develop their own skills of observation, classification, and logical analysis.

Testing students' acquisition of content standards is a valued activity for the positivist educator. Creating objective tests that are free from bias is critical to education. Because empirical knowledge is proven by years of careful analysis, there is a set of truths that students should master and understand according to a clear set of criteria. The only way to ensure that such knowledge has been attained and understood is to test all students according to the same objective set of criteria.

Now that you have had a chance to consider the ideas of positivism, use Figure 5.4 to examine how these ideas specify the learning focus, classroom organization, teaching styles, discipline, motivation, and classroom climate. As you examine the bullets within this figure, consider which ones match your own way of thinking and jot them down in your journal.

JOURNAL FOR REFLECTION 5.1

Consider the different teacher-centered educational philosophies and recall a teacher you know who seems to follow one of these educational philosophies. Describe the ways in which the teacher's actions represent the teacher-centered educational philosophy.

STUDENT-CENTERED EDUCATIONAL PHILOSOPHIES

Progressivism, humanism, and constructivism espouse a student-centered approach to subject matter, classroom organization, teaching methods, and assessment. Although each of these educational philosophies forms a distinct cohesive whole, all three are rooted in a student-centered principle—that is, the belief that truth and goodness belong to all persons no matter what their station. Teachers are learners and learners are teachers, and education is the process through which individuals help one another to clarify personal meaning.

FIGURE 5.4   Positivism educational implications.

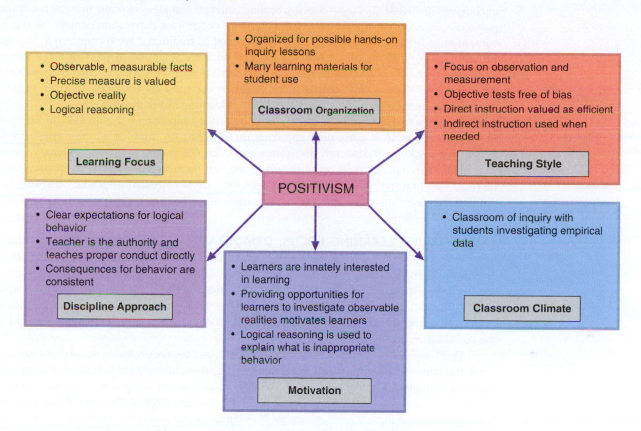

As with the teacher-centered positions, we will present each student-centered educational philosophy's ideas on curriculum, teaching, and learning. In addition, for each philosophy we will describe a representative program along with an illustrative class activity. The class activity is further analyzed according to the nature of the learner (active or passive); the nature of the subject matter; the use of the subject matter; and the type of thinking that is emphasized (convergent—focused on right answers, or divergent—focused on developing multiple perspectives).

Progressivism

In the late 1800s, with the rise of democracy, the expansion of modern science and technology, and the need for individuals to be able to adjust to change, people in Western societies had to have a new and different approach to acquiring knowledge in order to solve problems. As noted in Chapter 4, a U.S. philosopher, Charles S. Peirce (1839–1914), founded the philosophical system called *pragmatism*. This philosophy held that the meaning and value of ideas could be found only in the practical results of these ideas. Later, William James (1842–1910) extended Peirce's theory of meaning and asserted that if an idea works well it can be considered true. The satisfactory working of an idea constitutes its whole truth. Pragmatism was carried much further by John Dewey, who insisted that ideas must always be tested by experiment. His emphasis on experiment carried over into his educational philosophy, which became the basis for what was usually described as progressive education (Dewey, 1916). **Progressivism** is an educational theory that emphasizes that ideas should be tested by experimentation and that learning is rooted in questions developed by learners.

From its establishment in the mid-1920s through the mid-1950s, progressivism was the most influential educational view in the United States. Progressivists basically favor human experience as a basis for knowledge rather than authority. Progressivism favors the scientific method of teaching and learning, allows for the beliefs of individuals, and stresses programs of student involvement that help students learn how to think. Progressivists believe that the school should actively prepare its students for change. Progressive schools emphasize learning *how* to think rather than *what* to think. Flexibility is important in the curriculum design, and the emphasis is

progressivism An educational philosophy that emphasizes that ideas should be tested by experimentation and that learning is rooted in questions developed by the learner.

on *experimentation*, with no single body of content stressed more than any other. This approach encourages *divergent thinking*—moving beyond conventional ideas to come up with novel interpretations or solutions. And because life experience determines curriculum content, all types of content must be permitted. Certain subjects regarded as traditional are recognized as desirable for study as well. Progressivist educators would organize scientific method–oriented learning activities around the traditional subjects. Such a curriculum is called experience centered or student centered, whereas the essentialist and positivist curricula are considered subject centered. Experience-centered curricula stress the *process* of learning rather than the result.

Progressivism as a contemporary teaching style emphasizes the process of education in the classroom. It is a teaching approach that focuses on interdisciplinary problems that encompass a variety of academic disciplines and skills rather than a subject-centered approach to problem solving. It would be naive to suggest that memorization and rote practice should be ruled out. In progressive teaching, however, they are not stressed as primary learning techniques. The assertion is that interest in an intellectual activity will generate all of the practice needed for learning.

PROGRESSIVIST LEARNING FOCUS: DEMOCRACY. A tenet of progressivism is that, to become an important social institution, the school must take on the task of improving society. To this end, progressivism is deemed a working model of democracy. Freedom is explicit in a democracy, so it must be explicit in schools. But freedom, rather than being a haphazard expression of free will, must be organized to have meaning. Organized freedom permits each member of the school society to take part in decisions, and all must share their experiences to ensure that the decisions are meaningful.

Pupil–teacher planning is the key to democracy in classrooms and is the process that gives some freedom to students, as well as teachers, in decisions about what is studied. For example, the teacher might ask students to watch a film about an issue of interest and then have them list questions about the issue that were not answered by the film but that they would like to investigate. Students and the teacher can then analyze the questions and refine them for research. Such questions can become the basis for an inquiry and problem-solving unit of study.

Progressivism views the learner as an experiencing, thinking, exploring individual. Its goal is to expose the learner to the subject matter of social experiences, social studies, projects, problems, and experiments that, when studied by the scientific method, will result in functional knowledge from all subjects. Progressivists regard books as tools to be used in learning rather than as sources of indisputable knowledge. (See the Progressivist Class Activity.)

PROGRESSIVIST CLASS ACTIVITY

Mr. Brandese Powell asked his second graders to look at a cartoon that pictured a well-dressed man and woman in an automobile pulled by a team of two horses. The highway they were traveling along passed through rolling farmland with uncrowded meadows, trees, and clear skies in the background. He led a discussion based on the following questions:

1. What is happening in this picture?
2. Do you like what is happening in the picture? Why or why not?
3. What does it say about the way you may be living when you grow up?
4. Are you happy or unhappy about what you have described for your life as an adult?
5. How can we get people to use less gasoline now?
6. What if we could keep companies from making and selling cars that could not travel at least forty miles on one gallon of gasoline?

In this progressivist class activity, the nature of the learner is *active* because the teacher is asking open-ended questions that bring out the different ways that learners think about the picture. The nature of the subject matter is *ill structured*, because although there is an order to the questions, the direction that the discussion may take is open ended. The use of the subject matter is *cognitive* and *affective* because the concepts that underlie the picture are both rational and value laden. The thinking approach is *divergent* because there is no single, correct answer to the discussion questions.

PROGRESSIVIST CURRICULUM: CRITICAL PEDAGOGY. Many people believe that the socialization aspect of progressivism—the fact that it represents the leading edge of society and helps students learn how to manage change—is its most valuable aspect. However, progressivism is criticized for placing so much stress on the processes of education that the ends are neglected. Its severest critics contend that progressive educators have little personal commitment to anything, producing many graduates who are uncommitted and who are content to drift through life. Progressivists counter by stating that their educational view requires that students be taught to analyze world events, explore controversial issues, and develop a vision for a new and better world. Teachers would critically examine cultural heritages, explore controversial issues, provide a vision for a new and better world, and enlist students' efforts to promote programs of cultural renewal. Although teachers would attempt to convince students of the validity of such democratic goals, they would employ democratic procedures in doing so.

A contemporary version of progressivism is rooted in the work of Henry Giroux, who views schools as vehicles for social change. He calls on teachers to be transformative intellectuals and wants them to participate in creating a new society. Schools should practice "critical pedagogy," which unites theory and practice as it provides students with the critical thinking tools to be change agents (Giroux, 1985, 2001).

Now that you have had a chance to consider the ideas of progressivism, use Figure 5.5 to examine how these ideas specify the learning focus, classroom organization, teaching styles, discipline, motivation, and classroom climate. As you examine the bullets within this figure, consider which ones match your own way of thinking and jot them down in your journal.

Humanism

Humanism is an educational philosophy that is concerned with enhancing the innate goodness of the individual. It rejects a group-oriented educational system and seeks ways to enhance the individual development of the student. Humanism is rooted both in the writings of Jean-Jacques Rousseau and in the ideas of existentialism. Rousseau (1712–1778), the father of romanticism, believed that the child entered the world not as a blank slate but with certain innate qualities and tendencies. In the opening sentence of *Émile*, Rousseau's famous treatise on education, he

humanism An educational philosophy that contends that humans are innately good—that they are born free but become enslaved by institutions.

FIGURE 5.5   Progressivism educational implications.

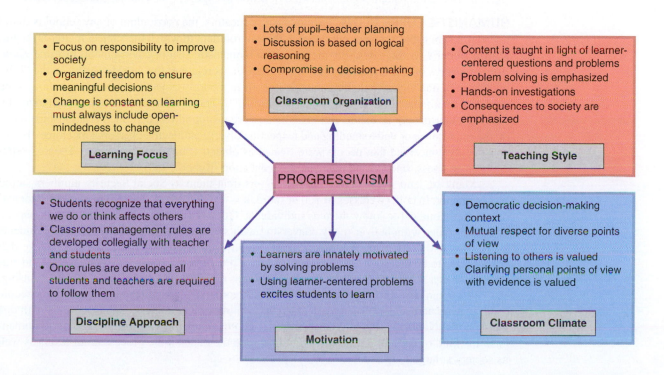

states that "God makes all things good; man meddles with them and they become evil" (Rousseau, trans. 1979). Thus, Rousseau believed in the basic goodness of all humans at birth. He also believed that humans are born free but become enslaved by institutions. Humanistic education mingles some of these ideas from Rousseau with the basic ideas of existentialism.

Humanists believe that most schools de-emphasize the individual and the relationship between the teacher and the student. Humanists claim that as educators attempt to predict the behavior of students, they turn individuals into objects to be measured. According to the humanist, education should be a process of developing a free, self-actualizing person—a process that is centered on the student's feelings. Therefore, education should not start with great ideas, the world, or humankind, but with the individual self.

Humanists believe that education should be without coercion or prescription and that students should be active learners and make their own choices.

HUMANISTIC LEARNING FOCUS. Because the goal of humanism is a completely autonomous person, education should be without coercion or prescription. Students should be active and should be encouraged to make their own choices. The teacher who follows humanistic theory emphasizes instruction and assessment based on student interests, abilities, and needs. Students determine the rules that will govern classroom life, and they make choices about the books to read or exercises to complete.

Humanists honor divergent thinking so completely that they delay giving their own personal opinions and do not attempt to persuade students to particular points of view. Even though they emphasize the affective and thereby may make students feel a certain urgency about issues, it is always left to the individual student to decide when to take a stand; what kind of stand to take; whether a cause merits action; and, if so, in what kind of action to engage. (See Humanistic Class Activity.)

HUMANISTIC CURRICULUM. To humanistic educators, the curriculum of any school is found not so much in subject matter, but rather in the environment in which the subject matter is taught. Martin Buber's writings describe the heart of a humanistic school environment. In *I and Thou*, Buber portrays two different ways in which individuals relate to the outside world. In the "I–It" relationship, one views something outside oneself in a purely objective manner, as a thing to be used and manipulated for selfish ends. In contrast, "I–Thou" relationships are characterized by viewing other people as sacred entities who deserve profound respect. Such relationships focus on the importance of understanding and respecting diverse, subjective, personal meanings. Buber was deeply concerned that people were treated as objects ("Its") rather than as "Thou's," especially in business, science, government, and education (Buber, 1958).

Many students today believe that educators treat them as Social Security numbers stored in a computer. In college classes of 100 or more, it is difficult for teachers to remember students' names, let alone get to know them as individuals. Often teachers assign material, mark papers, and give grades without ever really conversing with students. When the semester ends, students leave class and are replaced by other, equally anonymous students. Buber did not believe that schools had to be this way. He contended that in a proper relationship between teacher and student, there is a mutual sensibility of feeling. There is empathy, not a subject–object relationship.

A humanistic school environment (in other words, its curriculum) is one in which people (both teacher and student) share their thoughts, feelings, beliefs, fears, and aspirations with one another. Nel Noddings (2005, 2010) labels this an *environment of caring*. According to humanists, this kind of caring relationship should pervade the educational process at all levels as well as society at large.

HUMANISTIC CLASS ACTIVITY

Ms. Fenway wanted her ninth graders to really recognize the effectiveness (and manipulation) of television, radio, and Internet advertising. She asked students to write down any five slogans or jingles they could remember and the products advertised. Ms. Fenway selected from their items at random and tested the class. For each slogan, class members had to identify the product advertised. The test was corrected in class by the students and submitted to Ms. Fenway for a grade.

When the tests were graded and returned, students were very surprised because the grading scale was reversed. Those students who had all correct answers received Fs, and those who had only one correct answer received As. When students asked why she had reversed the grades, Ms. Fenway responded, "Because those of you who knew every product's slogan have been somewhat manipulated by advertising. On the other hand, those of you who knew very few products' slogans have avoided the influence of advertising." Ms. Fenway then told students the grades were not their actual grades; rather, they were simply an indicator of how strongly we all are influenced by contemporary advertising.

She then asked whether students resented some companies' selling tactics. Next, she and the class made a list of questions to ask themselves in order to avoid spending money in ways they might later regret. She also asked for specific examples of spending money for items they later wished they hadn't bought.

In this humanist class activity, the nature of the learner is *active* because the teacher asked students questions that were open ended and permitted the individual student to build on her or his own experiences. The thinking approach is *divergent* because there was no one correct answer or way of thinking about the answer. The nature of the subject matter is *structured* in that the teacher directed the questions and slowly unfolded each question to build on the prior one. The use of the subject matter is both *cognitive* and *affective*. It was cognitive because logic was required in the last question focused on avoiding spending money in ways that that students might regret. The activity was also affective because she built the activity around students' preferences for different products.

Inspired by humanism, many educators attempt to personalize education in less radical ways. Examples include individualizing instruction, open-access curriculum, nongraded instruction, and multiage grouping. Each of these approaches attends to the uniqueness of the learner. Block scheduling permits flexibility for students to arrange classes of their choice. Free schools, storefront schools, schools without walls, and area vocational centers provide humanistic alternatives to traditional school environments.

Educational programs that address the needs of the individual are usually more costly per pupil than traditional group-centered programs. Consequently, as taxpayer demands for accountability mount, humanistic individualized programs are often brought under unit-cost scrutiny. Nonetheless, growing numbers of educators are willing to defend increased expenditures to meet the needs of the individual learner within the instructional programs of the schools.

Now that you have had a chance to consider the ideas of humanism, use Figure 5.6 to examine how these ideas specify the learning focus, classroom organization, teaching styles, discipline, motivation, and classroom climate. As you examine the bullets within this figure, consider which ones match your own way of thinking and jot them down in your journal.

Constructivism

Constructivism is an educational philosophy that emphasizes developing personal meaning through hands-on, activity-based teaching and learning. Constructivism is closely associated with existentialism. The American Psychological Association (APA) has encouraged teachers to reconsider the manner in which they view teaching. The APA contends that students are active learners who should be given opportunities to construct their own frames of thought. Teaching techniques should include a variety of different learning activities during which students are free to infer and discover their own answers to important questions. Teachers need to spend time creating these learning situations rather than lecturing. Constructivist educators consider true learning to be the active framing of personal meaning (by the learner) rather than the framing of someone else's meaning (the teacher's).

constructivism An educational philosophy that emphasizes hands-on, activity-based teaching and learning during which students develop their own frames of thought.

FIGURE 5.6   **Humanism educational implications.**

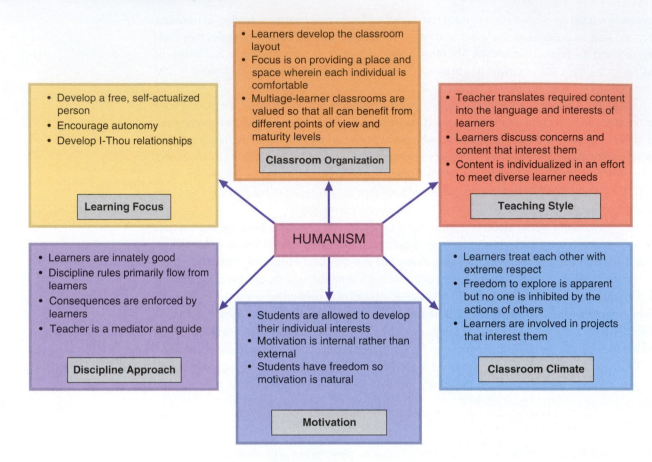

Such a view of teaching and learning has profound ramifications for the school curriculum. If students are to be encouraged to answer their own questions and develop their own thinking frame, the curriculum needs to be reconceptualized. Constructivist theorists encourage the development of critical thinking and the understanding of big ideas rather than the mastery of factual information. They contend that students who have a sound understanding of important principles that were developed through their own critical thinking will be better prepared for the complex, technological world.

CONSTRUCTIVIST LEARNING FOCUS: PROBLEM-BASED LEARNING. Problem-based learning has recently emerged as a student-centered teaching and learning approach that is in keeping with constructivist tenets. Based on Dewey's concept of teaching through student-centered problems, this educational methodology centers student activities on tackling authentic contemporary problems. Problem-based learning is a radical approach in that it challenges educators to focus curriculum on student interests and current societal problems and concerns rather than on disciplinary-content coverage.

In a problem-based experience, students are presented with a "hook." The hook might be a letter from a civic group, a request from an environmental agency, or any other motivating beginning. The hook describes a contemporary dilemma and requests students to take on some real-life role to solve the problem. Problem-based learning usually requires students to spend time finding the core problem, clarifying the problem, assessing what is and is not known about the problem, gathering needed data to complement what has been uncovered, and finally presenting a position statement and/or suggesting a solution. Throughout the process, teachers act as guides or coaches and give great latitude to student interest. Students learn content and skills within the problem context. Teachers spend time selecting problems that are compatible with student maturity levels and curricular needs. (See the Constructivist Class Activity.)

CONSTRUCTIVIST CLASS ACTIVITY

Reiko Nishioka's sophomore biology class had just completed reading Michael Crichton's novel *Jurassic Park* when a letter from movie producer Steven Spielberg arrived addressed to each student in the class. The letter requested each student's assistance in Spielberg's effort to determine which aspects of the novel were or were not scientifically accurate with regard to dinosaurs. The letter asked students to prepare a written summary and to send the summary, along with proper documentation, to Spielberg's production company. Because time was limited, Spielberg requested that the summaries be completed within three weeks. Reiko provided time for her students to think about the letter and then asked them to determine what they would do next.

In this constructivist class activity, the nature of the learner is *active* because students not only determine what it is they need to find out or learn but also how they will learn the material. The nature of the subject matter is *unstructured*, because students are free to tackle many different concepts based on their interests and they must figure out how they will learn the material. The use of the subject matter is *authentic* to real life because the content is embedded in a contemporary problem or concern. Finally, the thinking approach is *divergent* because there is no single correct answer to the problem.

CONSTRUCTIVIST CURRICULUM: PERSONALIZED LEARNING. Constructivist ideas about curriculum stand in sharp contrast to the authoritarian approaches we described earlier. Traditionally, learning has been thought of as a mimic activity, a process that involves students repeating newly presented information. Constructivism, on the other hand, focuses on the personalized way a learner internalizes, shapes, or transforms information. Learning occurs through the construction of new, personalized understanding that results from the emergence of new cognitive structures. Teachers and parents can invite such transformed understandings, but neither can mandate them.

Accepting this simple proposition—that students learn by shaping their own understandings about their world—makes the present structure of the school problematic. According to constructivist principles, educators should invite students to experience the world's richness and empower them to ask their own questions and seek their own answers. The constructivist teacher proposes situations that encourage students to think. Rather than leading students toward a particular answer, the constructivist teacher allows students to develop their own ideas and chart their own pathways. But schools infrequently operate in such a constructivist way. Typically, schools determine what students will learn and when they will learn it.

Now that you have reviewed the descriptions, learning foci, and curricular implications of progressivism, humanism, and constructivism, you can better understand why they are grouped as student-centered philosophies. All of these educational philosophies are focused on students' interests, ideas, and contemporary societal problems. These philosophies use cognitive and affective subject matter and open-ended learning tasks and encourage students to take control of their own learning. Direct instruction by the teacher is limited and emphasis is on helping students develop their own perspectives and ways of thinking. In the next section of this chapter, you will explore your own thinking about teaching and learning in light of both teacher-centered and student-centered educational philosophies. Ultimately, you are asked to develop your own educational philosophy and also provide a rationale for your thinking.

As you consider the ideas of constructivism, use Figure 5.7 to examine how these ideas specify the learning focus, classroom organization, teaching styles, discipline, motivation, and classroom climate. As you examine the bullets within this figure, consider which ones match your own way of thinking and jot them down in your journal.

JOURNAL FOR REFLECTION 5.2

Choose and write down a metaphor for each of the educational philosophies you have studied so far. For example, "constructivism is a shared voyage into new and uncharted territory." Then design a metaphor for your personal educational philosophy and clarify how it compares to the other metaphors.

FIGURE 5.7   **Constructivism educational implications.**

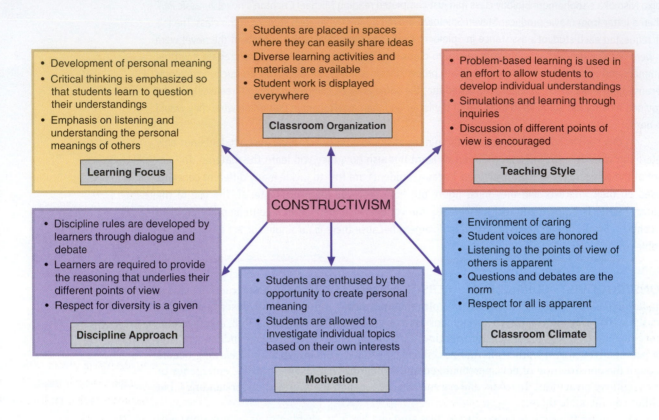

 To see how philosophy influences two teachers' instruction, click on the video *Examining Teaching Philosophies.*

DEVELOPING YOUR OWN PHILOSOPHY OF EDUCATION

This section helps you to clarify your role as a teacher in society and identify effective classroom practices. It offers a number of big ideas or key concepts that will challenge your image of what constitutes a good teacher. Ideas such as classroom environment or climate, voice and space, community of learners, and teacher as leader are presented to help you clarify your own approach to education. Which type of environment is best for today's students? How much teacher control is needed? Whose voices are predominant and whose voices are muted in today's classrooms? What teaching and learning methods will you use and how will you determine if these methods are working? These questions are examined and shown to be important to the development of a classroom climate that is either directed and didactic (like essentialism, behaviorism, and positivism) or open and authentic (like progressivism, humanism, and constructivism).

As you examine and refine your own philosophy of education, it is helpful to review how the six different educational philosophies relate to the contemporary classroom. Figure 5.1 summarizes how teacher-centered educational philosophies versus student-centered philosophies affect learning focus, classroom organization, teaching styles, motivation, discipline, classroom climate, and leadership styles. You may find that this chart quickly provides you a starting point for the clarification of your own personal philosophy of education. You may want to refer to this chart and the figures that relate to the individual educational philosophies as you read throughout the next section of this chapter.

What Does an Educational Philosophy Look Like?

Figure 5.8 provides an example of a philosophy of education that developed and changed over time based on decisions that a teacher made and evaluated along the way. You will notice that the sample educational philosophy is organized according to specific headings that relate to the different aspects that any philosophy of education should include: Learning Focus and Goals, Classroom Organization, Lesson Planning, Student Assessment and Evaluation, Motivation, Classroom Climate and Student Voice, and Personal Learning Focus.

Learning Focus and Goals

Throughout my entire teaching and learning career I have been fascinated by the diverse ways each of us makes sense of the world. Learning is inextricably intertwined with our identity; we know things as we know ourselves. Personal identity interacts with our knowledge of the world and this interaction is at the center of the act of teaching.

For me, learning is an artistic act; learners fashion their understanding by linking and structuring personal experiences into a whole. This new idea is framed and bounded momentarily so that learners can step back and view the idea internally. Then, they can share the idea and describe the unique way they know something much like an artist does when sharing a work of art.

Classroom Organization

My instructional methods and learning environment center on the development of learning situations that force a student to come to grips with her or his personal understanding. Hence, for me teaching is the designing of educational experiences that bring out students' thinking. On the practical level, this means that I employ simulations, case studies, problem-based learning events as well as readings, personal investigations and presentations. Rather than telling students things, I prefer to place students in learning situations that allow them to figure out their own meanings.

Teaching Style and Lesson Planning

As a teacher I must constantly assess what type of understandings might develop learners' personal frames of thought. I have come to value the beauty and the usefulness of rich ideas that tend to cross disciplines but also bring structure and focus to individual frames of thought. These ideas can be found in the work of great scientists, mathematicians, writers, poets, educators, artists, etc. Examples include equality, justice, power, individuality, place, environment, voice, community (drawn from the social sciences) and interaction, cycle, time and space, matter and energy, organism, equilibrium, field, force (drawn from the physical sciences) and symmetry, scale, validation, replication, quantification, probability (drawn from mathematical sciences) and form, function, line, color, hue, tone, mood (drawn from the arts). I find that by anchoring my teaching on the development of these larger ideas, students can better assess their own understandings and extend them through their exploration of these ideas.

Student Assessment and Evaluation

An instructional event is incomplete if it ends with a student simply clarifying a personal knowing. To complete a lesson, this knowing needs to always be challenged or at least submitted for review to other knowers. This final component of a learning event implies that to know is to frame a personal understanding, communicate it and allow the community of scholars (other knowers) to respond and perhaps modify that understanding. I do not simply conclude my courses of study with a final paper; rather I conclude it with a presentation based on a paper wherein students receive feedback and are challenged to develop new questions about their understanding. In fact, I explicitly state at the beginning of each new course that the epitome of a learner is the ability to frame a new question based on something he or she thinks they understand.

Motivation

I contend that sharing personal understanding with others is at the heart of learning. My classroom setting must convey this freedom for students to make sense of things on their own and to communicate their understandings even if they are not yet complete. In order to provide this freedom to express incomplete understandings, I need to make certain that learners feel comfortable seeking help from others and also that learners are taught to patiently listen to one another and provide helpful feedback.

Classroom Climate

I began my formal teaching career working with seventh and eighth grade students in an inner city, poor neighborhood of Chicago. It was there among these children that I began to understand how the context of children's and adults' lives influenced what they knew and how they knew it. I did not fully understand, then, that there is such an integral relationship between who we are and what we know. Fortunately, as teacher I remain a learner and through these early experiences, I began to understand the importance of providing a safe place for students to make sense of their lives in light of what others have discovered. Only by providing students a voice to clarify their own needs could the classroom function and learning occur. It was in Chicago that I began to view my teaching role no longer as a provider of truth, but as a prod or questioner who gently tries to extend and refine the personal understandings of my students.

Source: Copyright © 2012 by Diann Musial. Reprinted by permission.

We will keep referring to this sample philosophy of education throughout this part of the chapter in an effort to show how clarifying your responses to these different categories helps you build your own educational philosophy.

Learning Focus and Goals

One of the first components of an educational philosophy deals with the overall goal for learning. What is it that you believe are the most important outcomes for learners? Another way of asking this question is: What knowledge and skills are of the most worth?

Let's begin by looking at the way that the sample educational philosophy responds to these learning focus and goal questions.

Throughout my entire teaching and learning career I have been fascinated by the diverse ways each of us makes sense of the world. Learning is inextricably intertwined with our identity; we know things as we know ourselves. Personal identity interacts with our knowledge of the world and this interaction is at the center of the act of teaching.

This overall goal is centered on respect for the individual ways that learners understand concepts. The writer sees a strong connection between how learners know something and who they are, how they act, and what they like. So the learning focus of this educational philosophy centers on the development of each learner's unique way of knowing things. Immediately, you can see that this educational philosophy is one that is learner centered rather than teacher centered. Progressivism, humanism, and constructivism inform the learning focus of this educational philosophy.

Now, take a look at the next paragraph, which focuses on the nature of learning:

For me, learning is an artistic act; learners fashion their understanding by linking and structuring personal experiences into a whole. This new idea is framed and bounded momentarily so that learners can step back and view the idea internally. Then, they can share the idea and describe the unique way they know something much like an artist does when sharing a work of art.

This paragraph shows that the writer recognizes that all of us know things differently. Such a view of learning implies that the writer does not view teaching as the act of telling students what she knows. Direct instruction and multiple-choice examinations would not be viewed to be as important as having students form concepts in their own unique way. Assessments would tend to include more open-ended questions so that students could share their unique ways of stating ideas. This view of learning can cause dilemmas for the writer because performance on multiple-choice tests is currently very important.

Classroom Organization

Because the way you organize your classroom encompasses and affects all other aspects of teaching and learning, it is useful to begin thinking about this topic next. All teachers must be able to organize their classrooms in such a way that they are conducive to teaching and learning. In fact, many school principals are quick to assert that the easiest way to predict the success of a beginning teacher is to evaluate her or his ability to organize the classroom.

A common misconception is that good classroom organization means maintaining a controlled atmosphere and refusing to allow any behavior that even looks ungoverned or unplanned. Actually, **classroom organization** is a multifaceted dimension of teaching that includes the content, methods, and values that infuse the classroom environment. It is a dimension of teaching that requires analysis and selection similar to that used in the identification of a preferred teaching philosophy.

classroom organization
A multifaceted dimension of teaching that includes the content, method, and values that infuse the classroom environment, planning, and discipline practices.

The physical setting of the classroom tends to reflect whether the teacher follows a directive or nondirective theory of education.

THE PHYSICAL SETTING. The mere arrangement of classroom furniture and the use of classroom materials may be predicated on the teacher's perception of the learners as passive or active. Teacher-centered educational philosophies would support classrooms arranged in rows because this type of classroom arrangement has often been thought to be the best for classroom control and supervision. Also, this arrangement allows the teacher to capture the attention of students quickly and focus students on specific, important pieces of essential information.

Student-centered educational philosophies tend to support more open classrooms with small circles for special groupings in reading, mathematics, and other specific subjects. The teacher intends learning for the students to be divergent in nature, and the student is expected to be more active in the learning process. This is not to suggest that one type of classroom arrangement is better than another or that one theory is superior to another, but we do suggest that the teacher-in-training examine classroom theory as it relates to the physical environment for learning.

Let us return to the exemplar philosophy of education and consider what type of physical setting this teacher might use. One key to determining this is as follows:

 My instructional methods and learning environment center on the development of learning situations that force a student to come to grips with her or his personal understanding. Hence, for me teaching is the designing of educational experiences that bring out students' thinking. On the practical level, this means that I employ simulations, case studies, problem-based learning events as well as readings, personal investigations and presentations. Rather than telling students things, I prefer to place students in learning situations that allow them to figure out their own meanings.

Based on this quote the teacher would most likely set up a classroom with a variety of learning centers (readings, hands-on activities, computer stations, video and audio resources with headphones, etc.). Student seats would be arranged in small groups to permit discussions. Students would be free to roam around the room much of the time, working on all sorts of learning activities and personal investigations.

JOURNAL FOR REFLECTION 5.3

Think about the different student seating arrangements in various classrooms you encounter. Sketch each seating arrangement and describe the types of student interaction and the types of learning that each seating arrangement supports. Draw the seating arrangement that you prefer, and describe the types of student interaction and learning that it encourages.

TEACHING STYLE AND LESSON PLANNING. Careful lesson planning is mandatory if effective teaching and learning are to follow. If the learners are considered to be passive (teacher centered), the lesson plan might emphasize students' absorption of the factual content of the subject matter. Adherents of teaching styles that consider the learners to be active participants (student centered) would tend to emphasize thinking processes and skills and view the factual content of the subject matter as important but variable.

Regardless of the expectation for the learner, active or passive, all teachers need to plan sound lessons. Every lesson should be built from a basic set of general objectives that correspond to the overall goals of the school district. This is not to suggest that every third-grade classroom in a school district should have the same daily learning objectives for the students. Daily lesson objectives can vary from classroom to classroom depending on the particular needs of the students being served. However, if those daily teaching objectives are closely related to the overall objectives of the school district, then cross-district learning will reflect the school district's overall goals.

Lessons are often tied to some form of teaching units. These units should be planned in detail to include suggestions for teaching the lessons, types of materials to be used, and specific plans for evaluation. When it comes to designing teaching units, the differences between teacher-centered and student-centered styles become more pronounced. The reason is that the types of questions and learning content can differ greatly. For example, if a teacher is generally focused on teaching essential pieces of information and verifying that students understand this information in a very specific way, teaching units would tend to be shorter and focused on precise, specific learning outcomes. The unit would tend to have short, focused assignments based on some overall theme that students complete and submit for review by the teacher. On the other hand, if a teacher is focused on the development of big ideas that students learn and make sense of in their own unique way, learning units would tend to have a number of related investigations that students complete in an effort to make sense of the big ideas that underlie the teaching unit.

Initially, these are all decisions that must be made by the teacher based on the implications of her or his educational philosophy. Let us return to the educational philosophy example to determine what type of learning units this teacher would probably design:

As a teacher I must constantly assess what type of understandings might develop learners' personal frames of thought. I have come to value the beauty and the usefulness of rich ideas that tend to cross disciplines but also bring structure and focus to individual frames of thought. These ideas can be found in the work of great scientists, mathematicians, writers, poets, educators, artists, etc. Examples include equality, justice, power, individuality, place, environment, voice, community (drawn from the social sciences) and interaction, cycle, time and space, matter and energy, organism, equilibrium, field, force (drawn from the physical sciences) and symmetry, scale, validation, replication, quantification, probability (drawn from mathematical sciences) and form, function, line, color, hue, tone, mood (drawn from the arts). I find that by anchoring my teaching on the development of these larger ideas, students can better assess their own understandings and extend them through their exploration of these ideas.

Given that the teacher's educational philosophy is focused on large interdisciplinary ideas that students are to explore, the learning units would focus on one or more big ideas. The learning activities include a number of open-ended investigations during which students gather data and make sense of the information in their own words. Learning journals and a portfolio might be used to keep all of their information and insights organized. The teacher would coach each student along the way by asking probing questions in an effort to redirect each student and assist him or her by clarifying misconceptions.

STUDENT ASSESSMENT AND EVALUATION. In assessing student progress and assigning grades, most teacher-centered and student-centered teachers use a variety of techniques including examinations, term papers, project reports, group discussions, and performance assessments. If the subject matter is treated as a bundle of information, teacher-made tests will tend to seek certain facts and concepts as "right" answers, suggesting emphasis on convergent thinking. However, if the subject matter is treated as big ideas that are applicable to problem solving, and if students are expected to engage in processes and develop skills to arrive at several "right" answers, teacher-made tests will tend to allow for divergent thinking.

How you develop your classroom philosophy will also dictate the emphasis you place on a student's academic performance. You must decide whether a student is to be compared with his or her peers or with a set of expectations based on individual needs and differences. Generally, teachers who support student-centered classrooms look for divergence in learning and tend to place less emphasis on group norms. Teachers who favor teacher-centered authority for the classroom with a stress on convergence in learning are more apt to favor student evaluation strategies that are based on group norms.

Returning to our exemplar educational philosophy, we can use the following segment to infer what types of assessment this teacher might use.

GO TO ··›
For more information about student assessment and evaluation, see Chapter 11.

For me, a teacher is primarily a facilitator who helps students both clarify what it is they seem to know and also to question the limits of that knowing … An instructional event is incomplete if it ends with a student simply clarifying a personal knowing. To complete a lesson, this knowing needs to always be challenged or at least submitted for review to other knowers. This final component of a learning event implies that to know is to frame a personal understanding, communicate it and allow the community of scholars (other knowers) to respond and perhaps modify that understanding. I do not simply conclude my courses of study with a final paper; rather I conclude it with a presentation based on a paper wherein students receive feedback and are challenged to develop new questions about their understanding. In fact, I explicitly state at the beginning of each new course that the epitome of a learner is the ability to frame a new question based on something he or she thinks they understand.

Based on this, the teacher would probably use a wide variety of assessments so that students could receive all sorts of feedback about their understanding. However, such a teacher would emphasize open-ended questions that allow students to construct their own answers rather than pick them in a multiple-choice test format. The reason for this is that the teacher wants students to think about big ideas and then describe their understanding of these ideas. Forced-choice tests limit this exploration and hence essays, interviews, learning journals, and portfolios would be heavily employed.

Motivation

The concept of **motivation** is derived from the word *motive*, which means an emotion, desire, or impulse acting as an incitement to action. This definition of motive has two parts: First, the definition implies that motivation is internal because it relates to emotions, desires, or other internal drives; second, it implies that there is an accompanying external focus on action or behavior. Organizing a learning environment so that it relates to student needs and desires (internal) and also permits active participation in the learning process (external) is important to student motivation.

Teachers want students to be motivated to do many things: complete homework, be responsible, be lifelong learners, be on time, have fun, care about others, and become independent. However, it is not always clear how one sets up a classroom environment that ultimately promotes these desired outcomes. For example, in a teacher-centered orientation, control is primarily in the hands of the teacher. In such a setting, motivation tends to come in the form of rules and regulations. Students are given clear directions concerning their responsibilities, and they are expected to follow these directions because the teacher is in charge. For some students, this clarity of expectations and rules is comfortable. Students achieve because they must; in such a setting, the second half of motivation (external action) is achieved, but not the first (internal desire). The reason students' internal motivation may suffer is that they recognize that both the task of teaching and the responsibility for their learning belong primarily to the teacher.

In a learner-centered setting, the responsibility for learning is primarily borne by the students. The teacher attempts to produce a climate of warmth and mutual respect. Students are encouraged to achieve specific outcomes, but ultimately, they are free to select those that most interest them. In this type of setting, the first aspect of motivation (internal desire) is achieved, in that students select the learning outcomes and processes that interest them; however, the second aspect of motivation (external action) is not as clearly achieved, in that students act according to their personal desires and these desires do not always match those of the teacher.

Your task is to consider carefully the "sources of power" that best reflect your philosophy of education. Figure 5.9 illustrates five different power sources that relate to five different levels of motivation (Schmuck & Schmuck, 1983). Power can be coercive when the motivation is "to obey." Power can take the form of rewards when the motivation is "to get." Power can be seen

> Watch this **video** to see how a 5th-grade teacher motivates her students to learn about arthropods.

motivation Internal emotion, desire, or impulse acting as an incitement to action.

FIGURE 5.9   Sources of power and types of motivation responses.

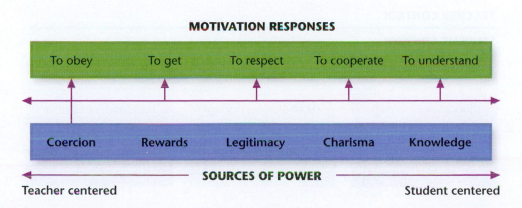

as legitimate when the motivation is "to respect." Power can be in the form of charisma when the motivation is "to cooperate." Finally, power can be knowledge when the motivation is "to understand." Your philosophy of teaching could include all of these sources of power. All of them might be necessary at one time or another. On the other hand, it is important to assess how you set up your classroom rules and environment and make certain that they match your personal understanding of where power should lie in the teaching and learning process.

As a teacher, you should arrange the classroom environment so that it matches your personal philosophy. Let's return to the educational philosophy exemplar and see what type of classroom environment and source of power would motivate her students to learn.

I contend that sharing personal understanding with others is at the heart of learning. My classroom setting must convey this freedom for students to make sense of things on their own and to communicate their understandings even if they are not yet complete. In order to provide this freedom to express incomplete understandings, I need to make certain that learners feel comfortable seeking help from others and also that learners are taught to patiently listen to one another and provide helpful feedback.

Clearly, this educational philosophy views the classroom as one in which students feel free to express themselves and make mistakes. After reading this approach to motivation, what type of power do you think the writer is emphasizing?

Classroom Management and Discipline

The attention given by the national media to disruptive behavior in the classroom has rekindled conflicting views regarding discipline. Polls of parents and teachers alike list discipline among the top issues confronting the schools. The main source of dissatisfaction for nearly two thirds of today's teachers is their inability to manage students effectively. Teachers also are concerned about the effect disruptive behavior has on learning. The discipline dilemma—how to achieve *more* teacher control in the classroom while adhering to a more open philosophy that advocates *less* teacher control—precludes the development of a school discipline policy that would satisfy both views. Depending on the school district's expectations, the teacher might be caught between conflicting demands.

Carl Glickman and Charles Wolfgang (1978) have identified three schools of thought along a teacher–student control continuum (Figure 5.10). Noninterventionists hold the view that teachers should not impose their own rules; students are inherently capable of solving their own problems. Interactionists suggest that students must learn that the solution to misbehavior is a reciprocal relation between student and teacher. Interventionists believe that teachers must set classroom standards for conduct and give little attention to input from the students.

As you prepare to be a teacher, you need to identify your own beliefs regarding control in the classroom. The goal is to keep disruptive behavior at a minimum, thus enhancing the

To see how one teacher uses the establishment of classroom rules as the basis for classroom management and discipline, click on the video **Establishing Rules and Procedures at the Beginning of the School Year.**

FIGURE 5.10   Teacher–student control continuum.

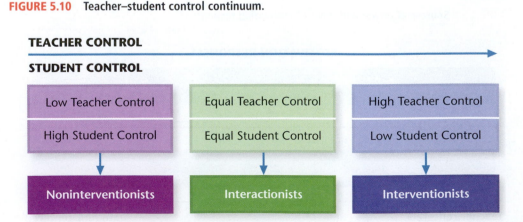

FIGURE 5.11   Teacher behaviors related to theories of classroom management.

Choice Theory		Conflict Resolution			Assertive Discipline	
Visually looking on	Nondirective statements	Probing questions	Modeling	Reinforcement	Directive statements	Physical intervention
NONINTERVENTIONISTS		**INTERACTIONISTS**			**INTERVENTIONISTS**	

students' potential for learning as well as your own job satisfaction. Where maintenance of discipline is the primary concern, one might choose from among the entire range of possibilities along the Glickman–Wolfgang continuum regardless of one's own teaching style preference.

Figure 5.11 illustrates how classroom management relates to different types of teacher behaviors. In the following section, we examine three types of discipline along the teacher–student control continuum; that way you, as a future classroom teacher, can understand how different kinds of teacher behaviors can be used to support your preferred teaching philosophy.

TYPES OF DISCIPLINE. Whatever the personal philosophy of the teacher, he or she must address the wishes of the district when establishing classroom management schemes. The division of views on classroom discipline has inspired numerous books to assist teachers with discipline problems, and many special courses and workshops have been developed to deal with classroom discipline strategies. But because very few beginning teachers are given extensive exposure to discipline strategies in teacher preparation programs, the vast range of alternatives makes the choice of strategies difficult for teachers who have yet to develop their own styles. The following discipline approaches are described because they offer a variety of alternatives in classroom management. Based on your own educational philosophy, you will find that one or more of them is compatible with your own thinking.

Choice Theory. The psychiatrist William Glasser (2000) has advanced **choice theory** as a way to determine classroom discipline practices. He suggests that a person's total behavior is composed of feelings, physiology, actions, and thoughts. How a person manages these aspects of behavior makes up an operational definition of control theory. Choice theory contends that we choose most of our behaviors in an effort to gain control of ourselves and other people.

According to Glasser, people are driven by six basic needs. All of our choices and behaviors are based on the urgency for survival, power, love, belonging, freedom, and fun. If there is an imbalance in any of these six basic needs, people act out. Choice theory encourages you to realize that it is somewhat natural and human for students not to take responsibility for disrupting class or deviating from classroom norms. As a matter of fact, even adults find it difficult to take responsibility for some of their own behaviors that deviate from the norm. Choice theory requires teachers to consider the many factors that can account for problem behaviors rather than responding immediately. Teachers are encouraged to seek the assistance of counselors, social workers, and parents to fully understand what is causing the problem behavior and only then to design an appropriate response.

Choice theory is one of the more difficult management approaches for a new teacher to implement. The first challenge to a new teacher is to evaluate the inappropriate behavior exhibited by the student, determine which need the student thinks is being met by that behavior, and think of appropriate replacement behaviors. The next step, according to choice theory, is to help the student identify the inappropriate behavior and the natural consequences of that behavior. This is done through a series of questions:

- What are you doing?
- What are you supposed to be doing?
- What is the rule?
- Are you making the best choices?

GO TO ·· >
For more information about classroom management, see Chapter 12.

choice theory A theory of discipline that contends that people choose most of their behaviors to gain control of other people or of themselves.

It is important for teachers not to impose artificial consequences for problem behaviors. The key to choice theory is to get students to design a plan on their own. This can be accomplished by follow-up questions such as these:

- What is your plan?
- What choices do you need to make?
- What are you going to do to bring your plan into action?

Take another look at Figure 5.11 and you will see that choice theory falls within the noninterventionist type of classroom control. As a prospective teacher, you will need to evaluate whether choice theory is compatible with your view of human nature. If you believe that problem behavior is a natural consequence of our need to balance and fulfill natural urges for survival, power, love, belonging, freedom, and fun, then choice theory will fit your philosophy of education. If, however, you believe that humans are blank tablets who simply need to be directly taught the proper ways of acting, this approach probably won't be for you. You may find the following discipline approach (an interventionist) more compatible with your beliefs.

Assertive Discipline. Assertive discipline is a teacher-in-charge, structured classroom management approach designed to encourage students to choose responsible behavior. Developed by Lee Canter (2010) this discipline approach is based on consistency, follow-through, and positive relationship building. The underlying tenet of this approach is that teachers have a right to teach and pupils have a right to learn.

Assertive discipline contends that the teacher has the right to determine what is best for students and to expect compliance. No pupil should prevent the teacher from teaching or keep another student from learning. Student compliance is imperative in creating and maintaining an effective and efficient learning environment. To accomplish this goal, teachers must react assertively, as opposed to reacting aggressively or nonassertively.

Assertive discipline requires teachers to develop a clear classroom discipline plan. The classroom plan must clarify behaviors that are expected of students and clarify what students can expect from the teacher in return. The aim of the plan is to have a fair and consistent way to establish a safe, orderly, positive classroom in which teachers teach and pupils learn. The plan consists of three parts:

- *Rules* that students must follow at all times
- *Positive recognition* that students will receive for following the rules
- *Consequences* that result when students choose not to follow the rules

According to assertive discipline, students cannot be expected to guess how a teacher wants them to behave in all situations. If students are to succeed in the classroom, they need to know, without doubt, what is expected of them. When students are not given the limits they need, they will act up in order to make the adults around them take notice. A student's disruptive behavior is often a plea for someone to care enough to make him or her stop.

Assertive discipline is not without critics. Some contend that assertive discipline is undemocratic. It conveys a message that only those with power have the right to make rules. Some teachers have responded to this criticism by allowing students to enter into the rule-making process. However, in the end, the assertive discipline teacher makes the final decision.

Other critics contend that children should obey rules because that is the right thing to do, not because there is some reward associated with obeying or some punishment for not obeying. The long-term implications of rewarding behavior as suggested by the assertive discipline model is that children obey because of positive feedback or because they are told to obey by an authority figure. Real discipline, according to the critics of assertive discipline, should be internal. Responsible behavior should be based on doing what is right.

Return to Figure 5.11 and revisit the behaviors that are associated with an interventionist theory of control. As a prospective teacher, you will need to assess to what degree assertive discipline and its related behaviors fit your philosophy of education. If your philosophy tends to be focused on the teacher's responsibility to control students, assertive discipline is compatible. If your philosophy is focused on students' authority, you would need to modify some of the assertive discipline tenets or not use this approach to discipline.

Conflict Resolution. As another approach to discipline, conflict resolution focuses on the process of teaching students how to recognize problems and then solve them constructively. Students are taught to be conflict managers and are trained to deal with difficulties on the playground, in the hallways, and in the classroom. The student "managers" learn specific skills that enable them, for example, to guide a discussion about a problem between two people who are fighting. There are a variety of ways to train the students, but the underlying benefit is that the students solve their own problems with minimal assistance from adults. Advocates of conflict resolution contend that permitting students to share in the structure and even the enforcement of discipline policies helps them learn to contribute to the school and to society as a whole.

Peer mediation programs are closely associated with conflict resolution approaches. The focus of peer mediation is not so much the resolution of conflict but rather the proactive cultivation of a climate of peace. In these programs, students receive training in empathy development, social skills, and bias awareness. The overall goal of peer mediation training is to help students develop a social perspective wherein joint benefit is considered over personal gain.

Revisit Figure 5.11 and review the types of control behaviors that relate to an interactionist approach to classroom control. These behaviors are compatible with conflict resolution and peer mediation.

Discipline Guidelines. There is no cookbook formula for classroom discipline rules and procedures. Some general guidelines, however, can help the beginning teacher to establish some operating rules that will be accepted and practiced by students:

1. Students and teachers need to learn the importance of considerate behavior and communication.
2. Students need to be treated with respect. Students who are treated with respect develop strong self-esteem.
3. Teachers need to apply critical thinking skills when creating disciplinary rules or analyzing needed disciplinary action.
4. Teachers need to examine how their actions of a social or instructional nature may have helped trigger misbehavior.

The way the teacher introduces and uses these general principles for establishing rules for discipline will set the tone for classroom interactions, creating an environment that is conducive to learning and that minimizes classroom interruptions.

Classroom discipline strongly reflects the teacher's operating classroom philosophy. As you examine the educational philosophy that wins your interest and support, search for its applications to discipline in your classroom. The "Perspectives on Diversity" feature discusses the choice of a classroom discipline approach.

Classroom Climate

John Goodlad, in his observation of more than one thousand classrooms, found that differences in the quality of schools have little to do with teaching practices. Differences come from what Goodlad (1984, 2004) called an overall **classroom climate**. Classroom climate is not a simple set of rules or ways of acting; it is a holistic concept, one that involves a set of underlying relationships and an underlying tone or sense of being and feeling.

Different types of classroom climate have been found to be successful. Goodlad's research showed that successful schools are ones with favorable conditions for learning, parent interest in and knowledge of the schools, and positive relationships between principals and teachers and teachers and students. S. M. Johnson (1990) identified school climate as one of the most important components contributing to effective learning and high levels of student motivation. Diane Ravitch (2001) defined a positive school climate as relaxed and tension free. Teachers and students alike know that they are in a good school, and this sense of being special contributes to high morale.

Vito Perrone (1991) set out to uncover the underlying characteristics of a classroom climate that could be linked to increased student achievement. After examining hundreds of studies, Perrone determined that a successful learning climate was one in which (1) students have time to wonder and find a direction that interests them; (2) topics have an "intriguing" quality, something

classroom climate
A holistic concept that involves a set of underlying relationships and a tone or sense of being and feeling in the classroom.

PERSPECTIVES on DIVERSITY

Classroom Management

Raja Manijue was concerned about his classroom management practices in his sixth-grade classroom. He had involved students in a discussion concerning his classroom discipline expectations at the beginning of the year and thought the students had agreed with his approach. Recently, however, Raja noticed that several of his students consistently challenged his authority when he called for silence and they often refused to stay seated during assignments.

After attending a professional development workshop on different classroom management approaches, Raja was impressed with an interactionist approach toward discipline that required students and teachers to negotiate classroom discipline rules and consequences. Raja notified students that he would hold a discussion on Monday to discuss new discipline rules and consequences; he asked all students to develop a list that they thought would be helpful and come prepared to share their ideas.

On Monday, Raja asked students to take out their list of ideas. He then went around the room and asked students to share one of their ideas. He was eager to hear what the students who were especially difficult to manage would suggest. Sadly, one after another refused to share her or his thinking. Raja explained that it was important to share ideas so that everyone's thinking was included in the new discipline approach. However, the disruptive students refused to offer anything.

Disappointed by the disruptive students' refusal to share their thinking, Raja decided to call each of the students' parents and ask them for support. When he called the first parent and asked for help, he was shocked to hear "Why are you bothering me with this? As the teacher you need to demand that my son obey you. In my native country, teachers are in charge and students must listen. Students have no place in developing classroom rules."

WHAT IS YOUR PERSPECTIVE?

1. Why do you think the parent thought that Raja should not require students to participate in developing classroom rules?
2. What does the parent's response imply about her view of authority?
3. Should Raja modify his interactionist approach toward discipline in an effort to take into account this parent's view of authority? Why or why not?

---

common seen in a new way; (3) teachers permit—even encourage—different forms of expression and respect students' views; (4) teachers are passionate about their work; (5) students create original or personal products; (6) students do something—they participate in activities that matter; and (7) students sense that the results of their work are not predetermined.

The problem with establishing a certain type of school climate is that climate is not something that can be developed artificially. Climate arises from the interactions of all of the things that teachers do in the classroom. There are two concepts, however, that can help you examine climate a little more closely: voice and space.

VOICE. *Voice* is a term brought to education by Henry Giroux. Giroux's (1981, 2001) concept of **voice** refers to the multifaceted and interlocking set of meanings through which students and teachers actively engage in dialogue with one another. Each individual voice is shaped by its owner's particular cultural history and prior experience. Voice, then, is the means that students have at their disposal to make themselves "heard" and to define themselves as active participants in the world. Voice is an important pedagogical concept because it alerts teachers to the fact that all learning is situated historically and mediated culturally and derives part of its meaning from interaction with others.

Teacher voice reflects the values, ideologies, and structuring principles teachers use to understand and mediate the histories, cultures, and subjectivities of their students. For instance, teachers often use the voice of common sense to frame their classroom instruction. It is often through the mediation of teacher voice that the very nature of the schooling process is either sustained or challenged. The power of teacher voice to shape schooling is inextricably related not only to a high degree of teacher self-understanding but also to the possibility for teachers to join together in a collective voice for social betterment. Thus, teacher voice is significant in terms of its own values as well as in relation to the ways it functions to shape and mediate school and student voices.

GO TO ⋯›
For more information about voice, see Chapter 7.

voice The multifaceted interlocking set of meanings through which students and teachers actively engage with one another.

Teachers need to be aware of the voices of their students as well as their own voice. Too often the teacher's voice is the only voice that counts in a classroom. Teachers must analyze the interests that different voices represent less as oppositional components and more as a medley that shapes the individual meanings of all participants in the learning process.

As a teacher you will find that small group discussions provide a key opportunity for students to share their thinking with others. However, it is important for the teacher to visit each of the discussion groups; listen to the conversation; and encourage students who are silent to speak and, vice versa, encourage students who are controlling the conversation to listen. Establishing a rubric that clearly details the characteristics of a good discussion can also help. Using this rubric, students can regularly evaluate their own discussion participation.

By creating an environment in which students listen to each other with respect and build on one another's ideas, a teacher helps students build a community of inquiry.

SPACE. "Authentic public space" is a concept developed by Maxine Greene (1975, p. 12). She contends that a climate consists of spaces between and among people. The manner in which this space is maintained and the type of space that is created determine the climate. Space that permits students to explore, take risks, make mistakes, and take corrective action is an authentic space—one in which people do not have to engage in pretense. Space that requires perfection, does not tolerate divergent responses, and is limited is a space that restricts freedom (Greene, 2000).

Another way of creating space is by developing a "community of inquiry." This phrase, coined by Charles Sanders Peirce (1955), has come to mean an environment in which students listen to one another with respect, build on one another's ideas, challenge one another to supply reasons for their opinions, assist one another in drawing inferences, and seek to identify one another's assumptions. Teachers ask questions and students answer them without either party feeling the least twinge of embarrassment, because the process of such thinking and rethinking is natural. An ongoing dialogue ensues and a community of inquiry forms.

Ultimately, classroom climate arises from the beliefs and values held by teachers and students. Your understanding of your own views and beliefs is critical to the climate that will ultimately emerge in your classroom. Your clarity about your most deeply held views on the nature of knowledge, the nature of reality, and the importance of teacher-led versus student-led actions will ensure that your classroom climate authentically represents you.

Returning to the sample educational philosophy in Figure 5.8, it is clear that providing an authentic space for all students' voices is critical. This is evident in the following quote.

I began my formal teaching career working with seventh and eighth grade students in an inner city, poor neighborhood of Chicago. It was there among these children that I began to understand how the context of children's and adults' lives influenced what they knew and how they knew it. I did not fully understand, then, that there is such an integral relationship between who we are and what we know. Fortunately, as teacher I remain a learner and through these early experiences, I began to understand the importance of providing a safe place for students to make sense of their lives in light of what others have discovered. Only by providing students a voice to clarify their own needs could the classroom function and learning occur. It was in Chicago that I began to view my teaching role no longer as a provider of truth, but as a prod or questioner who gently tries to extend and refine the personal understandings of my students.

To see how a teacher exposes his philosophy, using organization and effective teaching skills to minimize management problems, click on the video *Essential Teaching Skills in an Urban Classroom.*

Personal Teaching and Learning Vision

As you consider the components of your personal philosophy of education, you will face the question of student learning. What constitutes your vision for a learned person? Is learning about the acquisition of knowledge? Is it concerned with good thinking? Or is it concerned with good character? An easy answer, of course, is that learning includes all of these things: knowledge, thinking, and dispositions. However, as a teacher you will need to determine what the proper mix is: How much learning time should be spent on knowledge acquisition, how much time should be devoted to practicing skills, and how much time should be spent on the development of character traits or values? You will not find easy answers to these questions in your district's curriculum guide or textbooks. These tools provide only a set of opportunities for learning; your philosophy of education will be the force that guides you in determining which of all these things you wish to emphasize in your teaching.

JOURNAL FOR REFLECTION 5.4

Describe the teaching method and classroom environment that you believe have been most effective for you as a learner. Identify the educational philosophy or philosophies that would encourage the teaching method and environment you have selected. Create a graphic that visually represents your own theory of teaching and learning.

YOUR PHILOSOPHY OF EDUCATION BEYOND THE CLASSROOM

The way you manage your classroom and the content, teaching methods, and values you stress will be based on your personal view of the proper role of the teacher in society. A classroom philosophy must incorporate this larger societal view into other views that relate to student learning and behavior in the classroom.

Schools play a role within the larger society. This role is determined by a number of factors: the expectations of society's leaders, economic conditions, the ideologies of powerful lobbying groups, and the philosophies of teachers. It is especially important for educators to examine the role of the school in terms of the larger society—because if such reflection does not occur, schools will merely reflect the status quo or the needs and desires of a single powerful group.

Watch this **video** to listen to a teacher discuss the options for teachers to become agents of change, particularly as technology becomes more prevalent in classrooms.

change agent A person who actively endeavors to mobilize change in a group, institution, or society.

adaptation In the context of social change, an educational approach that favors the promotion of a stable climate in schools to enable students to obtain an unbiased picture of changes that are occurring in society and thus to adapt to those changes.

Teachers as Change Agents

An age-old question about the role of schools in a changing society concerns the proper role of the school and the teacher in relation to change. Should teachers be **change agents**, actively working for changes in the existing scheme of things? Or should they reemphasize eternal truths and cultural positions? This question of change versus transmission of ongoing values has been articulated in a variety of ways.

CHANGE AS ADAPTATION. Isaac L. Kandel (1881–1965) was a leader in the essentialist educational philosophy movement who advocated change as a process of **adaptation**. The adaptation approach emphasizes the importance of promoting stability in schools and enabling the individual to adapt to the larger environment (Kandel, 1938). The school should provide students with an unbiased picture of the changes that occur in society. But schools cannot educate for a new social order, nor should teachers use the classroom to promote doctrine. Change occurs first in society. Schools follow the lead.

If a teacher's educational philosophy is one in which the goal for teaching is the mastery of facts and skills so that students can enter society and get a job, that teacher would tend to look at change as the process of adaptation. Students would be taught to accept society as it is today and develop skills that make success in the world of work and daily life possible.

CHANGE AS RATIONAL PROCESS. John Dewey (1937) believed that schools have a part in social change. He contended that change continually occurs, often without a clearly defined direction. Schools need to assume a leadership role in this change because educators have the time to study newer scientific and cultural forces, estimate their direction and outcome, and determine which changes may or may not be beneficial. Schools need to provide an environment in which students can learn these analytic skills and participate in helping society determine the direction that is of most worth.

If a teacher determined that students needed to participate in an ever-changing society, that teacher would tend to provide students with many opportunities to wrestle with problems that characterize society. Students would also be asked to constantly question their own thinking and share their ideas with others.

CHANGE AS DIALECTIC. Samuel Bowles and Herbert Gintis (1975, 2006) call for a dialectical humanism through which teachers can help students explore the tension between the individual and society. They identify a conflict, or **dialectic**, between the reproductive needs of society and the self-actualizing needs of the individual. Bowles and Gintis claim that entities such as schools, churches, peer groups, and town meetings attempt to mediate this tension between individual freedom and responsibility for the community. The problem schools face is that they are often unaware that they are mediating this underlying tension, and teachers are often caught in the middle of the dilemma. Teachers are asked to respond to the unique needs of the individual while simultaneously answering to the conflicting needs of society.

Bowles and Gintis call on teachers to develop a participatory democracy in which all interested parties learn both to pursue their interests and to resolve conflicts rationally. As a teacher, you will become part of the educational system. As part of this system, you will be asked to make decisions about student outcomes, discipline procedures, instructional methodologies, and assessment methods. Your decisions regarding these educational issues will be greatly influenced by how you perceive teachers as change agents. You will make different decisions depending on whether you determine that teachers need to help schools adapt to the demands of society, rationally change the social order, reconstruct society, or participate in a dialectic. Your task is to consider carefully each of these change paradigms and select the one that matches your personal system of beliefs. Examine the "Who Is Right?" feature concerning the use of controversial topics in the classroom. It is a contemporary example of how communities' views about the proper role of schools can affect what is taught in the classroom.

Teaching can be looked at in a variety of ways, ranging from helping students create their own meaning to taking a deliberate stand and arguing for social change.

JOURNAL FOR REFLECTION 5.5

Develop a statement that depicts how you intend to function as a teacher/leader within the larger society. Describe one position you support that is related to a political action.

Teachers as Leaders

Teachers serve as leaders for their students. Evidence of this can be found in the testimonials that are offered by former students when they have become adults. Most students, whether they have achieved graduate degrees or have followed vocational pursuits immediately after high school, report remembering teachers who had a personal impact on their lives. These students will usually discuss the leadership and modeling behaviors of the teachers they remember.

The idea of teachers as leaders suggests that the new teacher should be aware of the need to develop a beginning repertoire of leadership qualities to which students can look for guidance during their developmental years. These leadership qualities—and the practice of them—are highly dependent on the classroom philosophy that the new teacher puts into practice. Some beginning concepts for teacher leadership are vision, modeling behaviors, and use of power.

dialectic A conflict between opposing forces or ideas; in change theory, this conflict is the one between individual needs and the needs of society.

WHO IS RIGHT?

SHOULD TEACHERS EXPRESS THEIR VIEWS ON CONTROVERSIAL TOPICS IN CLASS?

Communities differ in their perspectives about the use of controversial topics in the classroom. Should schools advocate for social change by encouraging students to debate controversial topics?

YES

Rachael Rice is an artist and activist who teaches fifth- to eighth-grade art at Barre City Elementary and Middle School in Barre, Vermont.

If those views support civil and human rights, of course they should!

I believe one cannot advocate for children anywhere without advocating for children everywhere. This means advocating for children in Iraq, Afghanistan, and Palestine as well as in Western and European countries.

Advocating for peace is now considered controversial in my district, as are rainbows and pink triangles ("pro-gay"). Here at Barre City School, I have had a "Safe Space Ally" sign illegally stolen off my door by a former school board member. Our administration forbade me to replace it, citing "controversy."

At one time, the abolition of slavery, desegregation, and women voting were considered controversial topics. But today, we as teachers are freely encouraged to support equal rights around Dr. Martin Luther King's birthday, and to examine the effects of prejudice as we study the Holocaust or slavery. We are encouraged to educate students for participation in the democratic process, which depends so much upon the freedom to express dissent.

So the truth is that teachers are supported when they express controversial views, as long as their opinions are aligned with those of the majority.

Of course, it is extremely important for teachers who express strong opinions to respect the fact that some students may feel intimidated. That's why I tell all my students on the first day of school not to believe anything I say just because I say it.

I urge them to turn a critical eye toward their teachers as well as toward their studies.

They trust me to help create a safe environment in which unpopular sentiments may be expressed and responded to in appropriate, kind ways.

The best teachers teach students to think for themselves.

NO

Lacey Pitts is an NEA student member in Americus, Georgia.

I do not believe teachers should share their opinions on controversial topics in the classroom. Too often teachers attempt to share their views to stimulate conversation, but only end up alienating students.

I am in college and still in a student's position, and I am not far removed from being a high school student. I was in a classroom where a teacher attacked my personal view and I remember how terrible it felt.

I was in tenth grade. The teacher opened a discussion of homosexuality in the classroom by stating that she felt homosexuality was wrong and a sin, implying that supporting such an alternative lifestyle was also wrong.

I was crushed, having family members and very close friends who were homosexual. I felt attacked for my love of these people and for accepting their lifestyle choices.

My teacher was supported by other students, but no one, not even I, advocated homosexuality. I was afraid of being told I was wrong and feared a personal attack by the teacher or other students. My voice was silenced in the classroom.

As educators, we must never allow this stifling to occur. Instead, we must strive to construct and foster environments that support differences in views and opinions by informing students of all arguments involved. We are in the classroom to guide, inform, and inspire our students.

When I become a teacher, I plan to play devil's advocate on controversial topics. I want my students to hear and consider all sides of an issue.

Impartiality is the key to allowing our students to think and decide their own stances on these topics individually.

Teachers must correct misstatements of facts, but a student's individual opinion should be allowed expression without fear of judgment.

WHAT IS YOUR PERSPECTIVE ON THIS ISSUE?

Source: "Should Teachers Express Their Views on Controversial Topics in Class?" *NEA Today* (October 2005), p. 40. Reprinted by permission of the National Education Association.

VISION. Classroom leadership behaviors begin when a teacher possesses both a vision and the intent to actualize that vision for the students. How a teacher actually puts his or her vision into practice depends wholly on the teacher's philosophical convictions. A **vision** is a mental construct that synthesizes and clarifies what you value or consider to be of highest worth. The clearer the vision or mental picture, the easier it is for a leader to make decisions or persuade or influence others. Formulating a vision requires reflection concerning what you believe about truth, beauty, justice, and equality. It is important to consider these issues and formulate a vision about how schools and classrooms should be organized and what ideas should be implemented.

Linda Sheive and Marian Schoenheit (1987) offer five steps to help leaders put their visions into action:

1. Value your vision.
2. Be reflective and plan a course of action.
3. Articulate the vision to colleagues.
4. Develop a planning stage and an action stage.
5. Have students become partners in the vision.[1]

If teachers reflect on their vision, they can plan the course of action they need to use with their learners. Articulation provides teachers with an opportunity to share their vision with colleagues. In-service or staff development sessions are excellent times to articulate a classroom vision. Visions require a planning stage and an action stage if they are to become reality. Planning and action stages should involve the students who are intended to be the receivers of this vision. For example, if a teacher wishes students to be reflective in their learning environment, then the teacher needs to help the students understand the benefits of reflectiveness and become partners in planning for it. The teacher might engage the students in free and open discussions of the vision and its importance to the learning environment in the classroom.

MODELING. If teachers hold certain expectations of learner behaviors in the classroom, it is imperative that they model those behaviors with the students. If the classroom teacher is rigid and fixed in his or her classroom practices and creates an authoritarian atmosphere, then the students will probably respond accordingly. On the other hand, if the teacher provides a more democratic classroom, the students will respond similarly in their classroom encounters. We would caution that a laissez-faire environment will probably produce a classroom where learners have little or no direction. Teachers should consider the modeling effect on the classroom environment and exhibit behaviors consistent with their philosophy of education.

EMPOWERMENT. The concept of power in the classroom should not be considered good or bad; power in itself has no value structure. The use of power, however, gives it a good, poor, or bad image. All leaders have power that is associated with their position, but the successful leader is judicious in its use. The nature of the teaching position entrusts a teacher with power both within and outside the classroom. How a teacher uses power in the classroom or in the school building is wholly determined by the classroom philosophy the teacher wants to project.

Teachers' use of power can be classified into two different styles: teacher centered and learner centered. A teacher-centered power style is based on an authoritarian construct for the classroom. Learners are not expected to be active verbally in the learning process but are generally expected to be receivers and practicing users of teacher-given information. Learning is very convergent. It is selected and given to the learner in the particular way in which the teacher wishes the student to acquire it.

A learner-centered power style views the learner as someone who is verbally active and who seeks divergence in learning. Learner-centered power styles encourage the active participation of the learner in exploring learning and helping to determine the extent to which he or she

vision A mental construction that synthesizes and clarifies what a person values or considers to be of highest worth.

---

[1]Based on Sheive. L. T. and Schoenbeit, M. B. (1987). Vision and the worklife of educational leaders. In *Leadership: Examining the Elusive*. Alexandria, VA: Association for Supervision and Curriculum Development, p. 99.

will engage in alternative approaches. Learning is very divergent. These power styles tend to recognize differences in learning, individual interests, and higher order learning.

Past and present practices in schools tend to lean heavily on the teacher-dominant style. Therefore, although many teachers in training study both categories of teaching styles, they tend to see only one major type in practice when they visit schools. We suggest that you continually study both major styles so that you can apply either one as needed on the basis of your classroom objectives for students and your classroom philosophy.

Teachers' use of power extends beyond the classroom. Teachers, by their very occupation, are empowered with both rights and responsibilities. They have a unique obligation to advocate for the needs of children, to remind society of its obligations to coming generations, to look beyond material wealth, and to consider the spiritual wealth of knowledge. Teachers, by virtue of their occupation, are given certain rights to speak and be heard.

SUMMARY

THE DYNAMIC RELATIONSHIP BETWEEN PHILOSOPHY AND EDUCATION

- Educational philosophy can be analyzed as the application of philosophy to the classroom.
- Humanism and existentialism reflect a student-centered approach to education because they place more emphasis on developing students' individual meaning.
- A philosophy of education is not a set of written words. It is a platform on which decisions are made and a teacher's professional life is led.
- One strategy that can help teachers develop their personal philosophy of education is to build on the educational philosophies of others.

TEACHER-CENTERED EDUCATIONAL PHILOSOPHIES

- Teacher-centered educational philosophies (essentialism, behaviorism, and positivism) emphasize the importance of controlling the subject-matter content, thinking processes, and discipline procedures within the classroom setting.
- Essentialism holds that there is a common core of information and skills that an educated person in a given culture must have.
- Behaviorism is a psychological theory and educational philosophy that holds that one's behavior is determined by environment, not heredity.
- Positivism is an educational philosophy that rejects beliefs about mind, spirit, and consciousness and holds that all reality can be explained by laws of matter and motion.

STUDENT-CENTERED EDUCATIONAL PHILOSOPHIES

- Student-centered educational philosophies (progressivism, humanism, and constructivism) place less emphasis on the external control of the teacher and more emphasis on developing students' personal meaning.
- Progressivism promotes individual student inquiry, humanism stresses student freedom, and constructivism emphasizes the importance of supporting personal meaning.
- The humanistic educational philosophy is concerned with enhancing the innate goodness of the individual. It rejects a group-oriented educational system and seeks ways to enhance the individual development of the student.
- Constructivism is an educational philosophy that emphasizes developing personal meaning through hands-on, activity-based teaching and learning.

DEVELOPING YOUR OWN PHILOSOPHY OF EDUCATION

- One way of clarifying your philosophy of education is to examine the different aspects of teaching and determine your own preferences for classroom organization, student motivation, your discipline approach, and classroom climate.
- Classroom organization includes the way you set up your classroom, the way you develop lesson plans and implement those plans, and the way you assess students.
- Motivation approaches include noninterventionist, interactionist, and interventionist.

- Classroom climate involves the type of voice you choose to encourage and how much space you provide for collaboration and discussion.
- Most teachers use various aspects of different educational philosophies as they determine the specific type of classroom organization, discipline, motivation, and classroom climates that they prefer. For this reason, we encourage an eclectic approach—an approach that draws on many different sets of ideas.

YOUR PHILOSOPHY OF EDUCATION BEYOND THE CLASSROOM

- In life, one must consider the implications of a philosophy of education for acting responsibly in society. What types of societal change match your philosophy of education, and what type of responsible leadership does your philosophy compel you to assume?
- Teachers can choose to be a change agent in society by helping students prepare to enter society (adaptation), by helping students deal with change in a rational way (rational process), or by directly working on specific change initiatives (change as dialectic).
- Teachers can lead by modeling and empowerment.
- The need to be clear about your personal approach to teaching and learning becomes especially important as calls for alternative approaches to teaching and learning increase.

DISCUSSION STARTERS

1. Your philosophy of education is more than a set of words; it is based on actions such as how you treat learners, how you set up your classroom, and what types of rules you enforce. Select one key idea that you would include in your educational philosophy and describe something you would do in your classroom that reflects this idea.

2. What were the characteristics and behaviors of one of your favorite teachers who had a teacher-centered educational philosophy? What about a favorite teacher who had a student-centered educational philosophy?

3. Constructivism rules out some of the conventional notions about educating youth. It emphasizes students' construction of personalized understandings of the world rather than an established curriculum. What implications does constructivism have for grouping students?

4. Teachers must be able to manage the classroom in such a way that the environment created is conducive to teaching and learning. How do you plan to organize your classroom to set up such an environment?

5. What is your vision of democracy in the classroom? To what degree should students be permitted to decide what they will study, when they will study, and how they will study? Why?

SCHOOL-BASED OBSERVATIONS

1. This chapter contains examples of classroom activities associated with various educational theories. As you work in the schools, take the class activity features placed throughout this chapter with you and see whether you can determine which educational philosophies you are observing. Then decide which educational philosophy you subscribe to and determine whether your own classroom activities are consistent with your personal educational philosophy.

2. Interview several teachers who organize their classrooms and teaching materials differently. Using probing questions, try to uncover the educational philosophy or philosophies that account for the differing teaching approaches.

3. Prepare a synopsis of your overall philosophy of education. Then interview a teacher who seems to teach and organize the classroom the way you would. Ask the teacher to review your synopsis.

PORTFOLIO DEVELOPMENT

1. Select one major concept from one of the national standards documents (available in your college library). Describe ways that you might help students learn a particular concept. You might consider methods that helped you learn a concept. Then, determine and explain which educational philosophy or philosophies match your description best. Include this description and explanation in your portfolio as an example of your ability to analyze lessons in terms of theories.

2. Prepare a synopsis of your overall philosophy of education perspective. Include your views about classroom organization, motivation, discipline, and climate. Try to develop a graphic that clearly shows how all of these components connect and are consistent with your overall perspective.

3. Develop a statement that depicts how you intend to function as a teacher/leader within the larger society. Describe one position you support related to political action.

WEB SOLUTIONS

You have been asked to participate in a review of your district's philosophy of education and mission statement. As a beginning exercise, each committee member has been asked to critique the school district's philosophy of education and mission statement in light of contemporary societal issues and demands. The following websites may assist you in preparing your critique:

education.illinois.edu/eps/educational-theory *Educational Theory* is a quarterly publication that fosters the continuing development of educational theory and encourages wide and effective discussion of theoretical problems within the education profession. You will find this journal filled with contemporary concerns that relate to teaching and learning.

www.funderstanding.com/content/constructivism Funderstanding contains a variety of theories on learning, instruction, assessment, influences, history of education, learning patterns, and educational reforms, as well as additional links.

http://pbln.imsa.edu The Illinois Mathematics and Science Academy (**www.imsa.edu**) has developed a network of problem-based-learning programs and ideas, examples of problem-based learning in classrooms, access to a problem-based-learning teachers' network, and other resources that relate to the use of problem-based learning in contemporary schools.

www.criticalthinking.org The Foundation for Critical Thinking is dedicated to providing educators, students, and the general public with access to information about critical thinking, theory and practice, concepts, techniques for learning and teaching, and classroom exercises.

www.theteachersguide.com The Teachers Guide is a Web-based company that provides information, professional articles, resources, books, virtual field trips, and educational software related to classroom management, educational psychology, special education, and so on. Click on Class Management for more information.

http://educationnorthwest.org Chartered in the Pacific Northwest in 1966 as Northwest Regional Educational Laboratory, Education Northwest now conducts more than 200 projects annually, working with schools, districts, and communities across the country on comprehensive, research-based solutions to the challenges they face.

MyEducationLab™   Go to the topic **History and Philosophy of Education** in the MyEducationLab (www.myeducationlab.com) for *Foundations of American Education: Becoming Effective Teachers in Challenging Times, 16e,* where you can:

- Find learning outcomes for **History and Philosophy of Education**, along with the national standards that connect to these outcomes.
- Complete Assignments and Activities that can help you more deeply understand the chapter content.
- Apply and practice your understanding of the core teaching skills identified in the chapter with the Building Teaching Skills and Dispositions learning units.
- Access video clips of CCSSO National Teachers of the Year award winners responding to the question, "Why Do I Teach?" in the Teacher Talk section.
- Create, update, and share quality lesson plans with the Lesson Plan Builder.

- Access state licensure test requirements, overviews of what tests cover, and sample test items in the Certification and Licensure section.
- Access current state and national standards in the Licensure and Standards section.
- Learn how to create a high-quality teaching portfolio in the Preparing a Portfolio section.
- Access tips, advice, and other information on resume writing and interviewing, your first year of teaching, and law and public policies in the Beginning Your Career section.
- Check your comprehension of the content covered in the chapter with the Study Plan. Here you will be able to take a chapter pretest, receive feedback on your answers, and then access personalized Review, Practice, and Enrichment exercises to enhance your understanding of chapter content. After you complete the exercises, take a posttest to confirm your comprehension.

6

The Place of Schools in Society

LEARNING OUTCOMES

After reading and studying this chapter, you should be able to:

1. Explore the roles of schools and how they contribute to the socialization of children and youth. (InTASC 3: Learning Environment)

2. Examine culture, its characteristics, and its impact in schools. (InTASC 2: Learning Differences)

3. Explain the school choices available to parents in a growing number of school districts. (InTASC 3: Learning Environment)

4. Understand why schools have evolved into different groupings of students by age and grades. (InTASC 1: Learner Development)

5. Characterize some of the differences between rural, suburban, and urban schools and their impact on students. (InTASC 2: Learning Differences)

EDUCATION in the NEWS

MORE VALLEY STUDENTS SIGNING UP FOR VIRTUAL SCHOOLS

By RAY PARKER

The Arizona Republic, May 24, 2009

An increasing number of Arizona's 62,000 high-school graduates have chosen a route suited to the MP3 generation: online classes.

At Primavera Online High School, one of Arizona's largest public high schools, about 9,000 students take classes in English literature, Spanish, and calculus. They join clubs, enter science fairs, and talk one-on-one with their teachers.

No one complains about the mystery meat at the school cafeteria, and no one ever gets asked to, or snubbed at, a school dance.

More than a decade after being created by state lawmakers, the 14 Internet-based schools in Arizona have become a quiet force in the state's education system. These full-time, tuition-free, virtual schools allow students to learn at any time and from any computer.

More than 26,000 students took online courses in 2008, and enrollment numbers are growing. An estimated 1,475 students in Arizona are graduating from virtual schools this year.

"We've experienced the growth because I believe kids want more flexibility in their high-school careers, and many because of the economic times, want to work . . . and our classes are available 24 hours a day," said Primavera Online Principal Dane Van Deinse.

Kayla Gibson, eighteen, who will graduate this week from Primavera Online, said it was easy for her to complete schoolwork online "even though it does take a lot of self-motivation to complete the work."

Some virtual-school students are enrolled in traditional middle and high schools but use the online courses as supplements. Others are home-school students who use virtual classes as a small or large part of their curriculum since online classes encompass grades K–12.

The Legislature in 1998 passed the Technology Assisted Project-Based Instruction (TAPBI) program to "improve pupil achievement and extend academic options beyond the four walls of the traditional classroom."

Two school districts, Deer Valley Unified and Mesa Public Schools, and two charter schools, Sequoia Choice and Arizona Virtual Academy, have participated since the beginning, while ten new providers have been added for a total of fourteen virtual schools.

Online schools received a total of $57.4 million from the state in 2008; their funding is based on student enrollment. TAPBI student enrollment increases each year: there were 10,800 students in 2005, 15,200 in 2006, and 24,100 in 2007.

Virtual schools set up shop in office buildings where administrators, technical workers, and customer-service staff work. When signing up for a class, the student gets an introductory phone call from the teacher. Students follow detailed lesson plans and communicate with the teacher by phone or by e-mail at least once a week.

Geoffrey Wall, seventeen, of Tempe, will graduate this week from Arizona Connections Academy. He will enter Arizona State University in the fall as an art major.

"What I liked was the freedom because I had the ability to use my time the way I wanted to use it," he said.

As a former ice skater, Wall spent a lot of time practicing in the rink. He said the virtual school helped him fulfill his Arizona education requirements and taught him a lot about working independently.

"If I was picking up on something really quickly, I could just keep going," Wall said.

Taking classes outside of classrooms requires some adjustments. Art students send drawings to teachers by mail or create them on computers. Some students enter "discussions" in virtual classes that are similar to chat rooms. Science students conduct experiments in their kitchens.

The schools have tried to create extracurricular activities by forming online clubs and other programs, such as science fairs with projects posted on school websites.

The system works for Shawntae Swartz, fifteen, of Tempe. Swartz takes online classes through Primavera while enrolled in the 3-D animation program at East Valley Institute of Technology in Mesa.

"In anything there's going to be ups and downs, but I can get credits faster and at my own pace," she said.

QUESTIONS FOR REFLECTION

1. Have you ever taken online courses? How did you like them? What were the advantages and disadvantages of this mode of delivery of instruction?

2. What are some of the limitations of virtual schools like Primavera Online High School?

3. Do you have any interest in teaching in a virtual school or online courses? Why or why not?

Source: "More Valley students signing up for virtual schools." May 24, 2009. © *The Arizona Republic.* Used with permission. Permission does not imply endorsement.

MyEducationLab™

Visit the MyEducationLab for *Foundations of American Education* to enhance your understanding of chapter concepts with a personalized *Study Plan.* You'll also have the opportunity to hone your teaching skills through video- and case-based *Assignments and Activities* and *Building Teaching Skills and Dispositions* lessons.

social efficiency A theory that the primary purpose of schools is to prepare students for their optimal role in society as determined by tests or other measures.

social mobility The movement of an individual or family up or down in social class, such as moving from the lower class to the middle class as one finishes college and earns a larger income.

PURPOSES OF SCHOOLS

Private schools and academies were first established in colonial days for the children of the elite. However, that did not mean that other children were not being educated as they worked with adults. When possible, low-income families were sending their children to the homes of neighbors where mothers or other women in the home would teach them how to read. It was not until the 1800s that public schools began to be built for the commoner. Even so, children were not required to attend schools for over another century. The focus of these early common schools was to teach children to read the Bible, develop high morals, and become a good citizen.

Today's schools play many roles in society beyond those for which the common schools were designed. They teach the basic skills of literacy and computation, but they also reflect society's high ideals such as universal education for all children. What should students be taught? Should we prepare students with the knowledge and skills they will need for their future jobs? Should they learn to think for themselves, even questioning some of what they are taught? Should we teach them the dispositions that will help them be good citizens, be respectful of others, and make sound decisions about their life? Should they learn to appreciate the arts, be healthy and active adults, and live effectively in a global, interdependent world?

Our own philosophical and political perspectives help determine how we view the roles of schools and what good education is. Should schools primarily support democratic equality, **social efficiency**, **social mobility**, or some other goal? Advocates of democratic equality view education as a public good through which all students should be exposed to a liberal arts education and learn to be productive citizens in a democracy. Proponents of social efficiency believe that schools should serve the private sector by preparing students for their optimal role in society as determined by testing or other measures. People who support social mobility view education as an asset that can be accumulated and used for social competition. Achieving these credentials provides us a competitive advantage in securing a desirable position in society as can be seen in the higher salaries and prestige that most college graduates receive.

School boards, educators, parents, and communities have their own beliefs and perspectives about the basic roles of schools. Their beliefs may draw on national reports calling for the reform of education. Through such reports as well as discussions and debates among educators, policy makers, and others, U.S. society continually refines and redefines its ideas about schools. The five roles described in the following section are a sample of those most often mentioned by educators and the public. Most schools address each of these roles, but in any given school or community, one goal may receive prominence over others. As you read the roles outlined below, think about your own views regarding the roles of schools in society.

JOURNAL FOR REFLECTION 6.1 —————————————————————

Which of the following ideals do you think schools should mirror? Why?

- Be a model of our best hopes for society and a mechanism for remaking society in the image of those hopes.
- Adapt students to the needs of society by preparing them for specific roles and jobs.
- Serve the individual hopes and ambitions of their students and parents.

Academic Achievement

The focus of accountability for academic achievement is performance on test scores. Parents and students know when testing days are scheduled. Teachers and principals know that their future employment could depend on how their students score on the state tests. Television stations and news reporters cover a school's preparation for the testing days. Teachers prepare students to take the tests, sometimes teaching to tests and neglecting subjects that are not being tested such as social studies, science, and the arts.

Media reports of student scores on achievement tests highlight a school's ability to offer students a strong academic background. Some school districts base their reputations on how well their students perform and how many are admitted to colleges. In some communities, parents camp out overnight to be first in line to enroll their children in a preschool that will hopefully provide the jump start needed for success on future tests to ensure later admission to prestigious colleges and universities.

State and national standards provide the framework for what students should know and be able to do to be academically proficient. Standards exist not only in academic areas, but also for the arts, health, and physical education. The Common Core Standards, which had been adopted by most states in spring 2012, identify the essential required levels of knowledge and skills in English language arts and literacy in history/social studies, science, and technical subjects as well as mathematics. The National Governors Association and the Council for Chief State School Officers (2010) have developed these standards to help students become successful in college and careers. National tests will assess students' attainment of those proficiencies. Schools have revised their curricula to be standards based, knowing that their students will be tested annually to determine if they are at grade level. School systems' reputations and their state funding are dependent on how well students perform on these tests.

GO TO ···>
A more detailed discussion of standards and accountability can be found in Chapter 11.

Workforce Readiness

Preparing students to contribute to the economic growth of the nation has been a major purpose of schools for over a century (Cuban, 2011). The current sense of crisis regarding students not being prepared to work effectively in the market-driven global economy has its roots in the U.S. Department of Education's release of the report *A Nation at Risk* in 1983. The education system has been blamed for students not performing at the top of international tests of knowledge and skills, for students not developing the critical thinking and problem-solving skills needed for a growing number of jobs, and for not enough students being prepared in the science, technology, engineering, and mathematics fields. In addition, workforce projections indicate that 62 percent of U.S. jobs will require postsecondary education by 2018 (Carnevale, Smith, & Strohl, 2010).

What should our youth know by the time they finish high school? Four hundred U.S. employers identified four sets of skills that new hires should have to be successful in their businesses:

1. Professionalism/Work Ethic skill set, which includes dispositions that are desirable in the workplace such as timeliness, appropriate dress, responsibility, and integrity.
2. Oral and Written Communications skill set, which requires clear articulation of thoughts and ideas as well as being able to write memos, letters, and reports.

3. Teamwork/Collaboration skill set, which requires being able to work effectively with diverse colleagues and customers.

4. Critical Thinking/Problem Solving skill set, which helps employees use knowledge, facts, and data to solve problems. (The Conference Board, Partnership for 21st Century Skills, Corporate Voices for Working Families, & Society for Human Resource Management, 2006).[1]

Three in four of these employers say that K–12 schools should be held responsible for preparing students with these skills. Employers complain that newly hired employees, especially high school graduates, too often do not have either the basic or **applied skills** to participate effectively in the workplace. Business owners want graduates with vocational skills appropriate to the job, but they also want them to have dispositions or values and attitudes such as punctuality and a good work ethic. Business owners and the nation's leaders also worry that not enough engineers, computer scientists, and other workers in the STEM (science, technology, engineering, and mathematics) professions are being produced by high schools and colleges to meet the needs of the country. The production of U.S. students in these areas has fallen behind that of other nations (Thomasian, 2011).

What should be the role of schools in preparing today's youth for the workforce? Is it to ensure that students have the knowledge and skills to keep the economy competitive in a changing world where new jobs continually emerge? Is it to help students learn a trade, learn how to learn, or learn how to take orders and follow the rules? These questions are particularly important when conditions are changing as rapidly as they are in today's society. The vocation for which one is prepared initially may become obsolete within a few years. The *Framework for 21st Century Learning* (Partnership for 21st Century Skills, 2011), which is supported by many business leaders, calls for today's students to master the basic core subjects and develop global awareness; civic literacy; health literacy; and financial, economic, business, and entrepreneurial literacy. They also must have information, media, and technology skills to work effectively in today's workforce. Employers in The Conference Board et al. (2006) report project that the emerging economy will require workers who are competent in more than one language, can make appropriate health and wellness choices, and are creative and innovative. Meeting all of these expectations will be a major challenge for schools.

GO TO ⋯>

The *21st Century Learning Knowledge and Skills* framework is discussed in more detail in Chapter 11.

Citizenship

Citizenship is much more than voting in elections and knowing facts about the nation's history, heroines, and heroes. "It requires citizens who are informed and thoughtful, participate in their communities, are involved in the political process, and possess moral and civic virtues" (Gould, 2011, p. 6). Preparing students to be active citizens requires them to be involved in the democratic process as part of their school experience. The Campaign for the Civic Mission of Schools has identified the following six proven practices for civic learning:

1. *Classroom instruction,* including courses in government, history, economics, law, and democracy that are not lectures, but which encourage the active engagement of students.

2. *Discussion of current events and controversial issues* that includes issues important and relevant to the lives of young people.

3. *Service learning* that provides students opportunities for community service linked to the formal curriculum and classroom instruction.

4. *Extracurricular activities* that allow students to be involved outside of the classroom in the school or community.

5. *School governance* to allow students to practice democracy.

6. *Simulations of democratic processes* such as voting during elections and participating in debates and trials. (Gould, 2011)

applied skills Use of basic skills such as English language arts, mathematics, science, and social studies in the workplace to perform one's job.

The involvement of large numbers of youth in the 2008 and 2012 national elections, even though in some cases they were not old enough to vote, is a positive sign of their engagement in the civic affairs of the nation. Research finds that effective civic learning contributes to a higher voting rate, discussion of politics at home, greater volunteering and involvement in community

---

[1] "Are They Really Ready to Work" *Partnership for 21st Century Skills*. © 2006 The Conference Board, Inc. Reprinted by permission.

activities, and the development of greater confidence in speaking publicly and communicating with elected officials (Gould, 2011). Teachers can also model civic behavior through their engagement in community and political activities locally, nationally, or internationally.

The standards of the National Council for the Social Studies (2010) include civic ideals and practices as one of the 10 themes that should be addressed in social studies programs. Students are expected

> to acquire a historical and contemporary understanding of the basic freedoms and rights of citizens in a democracy, and learn about the institutions and practices that support and protect these freedoms and rights, as well as the important historical documents that articulate them. Students also need to become familiar with civic ideals and practices in countries other than our democratic republic. (NCSS, 2010, p. 6)

Citizenship cannot be taught in a single course. Across courses and in school activities, school officials and teachers work to develop democratic citizens who respect others; believe in human dignity; are concerned about and care for others; and fight for justice, fairness, and tolerance. Students can learn through practice in the classroom how to be active, involved citizens.

Developing citizenship skills can begin in school when students practice democracy in the classroom or become involved in student government.

Social Development

Schooling also provides opportunities for students to develop their social skills by interacting with others. In this process, students should learn to respect others; they also learn a set of rules for working appropriately with peers and adults. Although schools usually do not provide a course that teaches skills in social development, appropriate behavior is constantly reinforced by teachers and other school professionals in the classroom and on the playground.

Teachers can give students opportunities to work with other students from diverse racial, gender, language, religious, and ability groups; one of the by-products of these interactions is that students learn more about their similarities and differences. Teachers can encourage interactions across groups through **cooperative learning** activities in which students from different groups are placed together. Other team projects allow students to work together who might not otherwise seek one another out. A part of teaching is helping students learn to work together positively.

Cultural Transmission

Schools around the world are expected to transmit the **culture** of their nation to young people so they can both maintain it and pass it on to the next generation. Schools have often approached this task by teaching history with an emphasis on important events and heroes. This emphasis helps children learn the importance of patriotism and loyalty. Formal and hidden curricula reflect and reinforce the **values** of the national culture—the principles, standards, and qualities the culture endorses.

These national values and rules are so embedded in most aspects of schooling that most teachers and students do not realize they exist. The only exceptions may be students who do not feel a part of the **common culture** or whose families have recently immigrated. In these cases, students and families quickly learn that schools might not reflect or support aspects of their culture that differ from the common culture. This dissonance between schools and families is most noticeable for students who are not European American or whose native language is not English. Students from religious backgrounds that have not evolved from Judeo-Christian roots may also question the culture that is being transmitted at school. The challenge for educators is to transmit the common culture while including the richness and contributions of many who are not yet accepted as an integral part of that culture. In this way, schools begin to change and expand the common culture.

cooperative learning An instructional strategy for grouping students from different groups and learning abilities to work collaboratively on projects and assignments.

culture Socially transmitted ways of thinking, believing, feeling, and acting within a group of people that are passed from one generation to the next.

values Principles, standards, and qualities that are considered worthwhile or desirable.

common culture The shared values, traditions, history, experiences, and behaviors that are common across groups in society.

THE ROLE OF CULTURE IN SCHOOLS

Culture provides a blueprint for how we think, feel, and behave in a society. It imposes rules and order to help us understand the subtleties of our shared language, nonverbal communications, and ways of thinking and knowing. We have the same biological and psychological needs no

▶ Listen to on educator talk about embracing student and family cultures to create a welcoming school environment in this **video.**

matter where we live in the world, but the ways we meet those needs are culturally determined. The location of the group, available resources, and traditions have a great influence on how and what we eat, how we groom and dress, how we teach and learn, and how we interact with each other.

Culture is learned, shared, adapted, and dynamic. We learn our culture through **enculturation**, which occurs when parents, grandparents, religious leaders, teachers, television shows, and our neighbors teach us the culture and its acceptable norms of behavior. We internalize cultural patterns so well and so early in life that we often have difficulty accepting different—but equally appropriate—ways of behaving and thinking by others, sometimes leading to miscommunications and misunderstandings in society and the classroom. When schools use a different language or linguistic pattern from that used at the home of students, or when students' behaviors have different meanings at home than at school, dissonance between schools and the home can occur (Gay, 2010). Understanding cultural differences and learning to recognize when students do not share our own cultural patterns are critical steps in the provision of an equitable learning environment.

Culture is not stagnant. It is dynamic, continually adapting to serve the needs of the group. We adapt our culture as we move from one section of the country to another or around the globe, as do some of our students who are new immigrants or whose families are in the armed services. Cultures differ, in part, because of the geographic region in which we live. For example, Eskimos who live with extreme cold, snow, and ice have developed different cultural patterns than groups in the South Pacific islands with limited land and an unlimited body of water. Technological changes in the world and society also transform cultures. For example, technology has allowed robots to perform routine jobs and has provided opportunities for more people to work remotely from home.

Common Culture

The legal system, democratic elections, and middle-class values of American society, which serve as the foundation for many of our institutions and traditions, were based on western and northern European traditions. As new immigrants assimilated into society over a few generations, a common culture evolved. It is reflected in the ways most middle-class families live. These commonalities make it fairly easy for people to identify us as "American" when we visit other countries.

The common culture had its beginnings in the cultures of the white, middle-class Protestants who began immigrating to the colonies from western and northern Europe five centuries ago. Until recently, the ancestors of these early settlers dominated the country's political system, holding the highest government and corporate positions. In this role, they had great influence over the institutional policies and practices that maintained their power. The Civil Rights struggles of the 1960s and 1970s opened the political and corporate worlds to a growing number of women and persons of color. During this period, the Civil Rights Act and the Voting Rights Act were passed to protect the rights of all people and to promote greater equality across groups in education, housing, and other areas. Our history as a nation of many diverse groups and our experiences in struggling for equality across groups has refined our common culture.

What are some of the characteristics of the common culture? Universal education and literacy for all citizens are valued. Our job or career is important in being recognized as successful. Fun is usually a relief from work. Technology in all of its forms, from cell phones to the computer, has a great impact on our lives, especially those of young people. Achievement and success are highly valued and demonstrated by the accumulation of material goods such as houses, cars, boats, clothes, and vacations. **Individualism** and **freedom** are core values that undergird the common culture of the United States. Independence and self-reliance are the major focus of individualism in which toughness and strength are admired. Freedom is a cornerstone of democracy but is generally defined as having control of our own destiny and success with little or no interference by others, especially by government. To some people freedom means being able to live where they want, do what they want, believe what they want, and improve their material conditions as they see fit. To others freedom has a more political tone: the freedom of speech, the freedom to protest, and the freedom to have one's rights respected. These two concepts often take precedence over an individual's responsibility for community and the common good (Bellah, Madsen, Sullivan, Swidler, & Tipton, 2008).

enculturation The process of learning the characteristics and behaviors of the culture of the group to which one belongs.

individualism Value based on independence and self-reliance in which toughness and strength are admired.

freedom Having control of one's own life with little or no interference by others, especially by government.

Cultures of Families

Although we share a common culture as we interact in school and at work, a family's unique culture will take precedence in the homes of your students, especially if they do not feel they are full-fledged members of the common culture. Students arrive at school with the traditions, language, and behaviors of their families' cultures. To some families, their **ethnicity** (for example, African American, Navajo, Serbian American, or Korean American) is their primary identification. They may speak a language other than English at home. Families also range along a continuum from poor to wealthy, which may affect students' health and well-being and their ability to engage effectively in school. Families may also be greatly influenced by the discrimination they face because of their race, ethnicity, immigration status, language, religion, or sexual orientation.

Knowing more about your students' cultural identity can help you make schooling and the curriculum more real or authentic for them. It also shows that you respect their families and communities. How can you know more about the cultures of the various communities and your students? You could participate in community activities and celebrations that will provide an understanding of students' cultural traditions. You could volunteer with community groups to coach, tutor, or serve food at a homeless shelter. You could actively participate in school activities in the evenings and on the weekends to interact more with other students in the school and their parents. Another approach to learning more about the cultures of your students is to take classes in ethnic studies, women's studies, religious studies, sociology, or anthropology to build your knowledge base. To help you think about the role of diversity training, two teachers' views are presented in the "Who Is Right?" feature.

When we meet our students for the first time, we usually identify them immediately by their gender and race, and maybe their ethnicity. We may not know their religion and its importance to their families unless they are wearing a garment or jewelry associated with a specific religion. We may not know the importance of their ethnicity or language. Therefore, we need to be very careful about stereotyping them based on factors that can be easily identified. Culture is far more complex and important in a student's own identity than we can know without much more information.

Cultural Values

Although schools are expected to transmit the culture of the United States to the younger generation, educators do not always agree on *whose* culture should be transmitted. Is it always the common culture even though diverse racial, ethnic, language, and religious groups have their own cultures with different traditions, experiences, and histories? How can schools begin to accommodate all of these differences?

Some conservative politicians and popular talk show hosts argue that schools should ignore diversity. They believe that all students should learn the common heritage and adopt the common culture as their own. Multicultural theorists and educators present another perspective. They argue that student diversity enriches the school community and society. They believe in a pluralistic approach in which cultural differences are valued and integrated throughout the curriculum and all activities of the school. In this approach, teachers draw on the cultural backgrounds and experiences of students to teach academic knowledge and skills.

Parents' choices of schools—including religious schools, home schooling, or **ethnocentric schools** that build the curriculum around the histories and experiences of the family's ethnic group—have been based in part on the values that they believe education can impart. Although schools usually do not offer a course in which values are explicitly presented and discussed, values implicitly influence the formal and **hidden curriculum**. Curricula usually support the common culture and the current ideological, political, and economic order of society. However, some families believe that public schools do not value their religion. Some parents do not want their children exposed to the secular values of a public school or what they perceive to be inappropriate language and disrespectful behavior by students. Although these values may not seem controversial to some readers, they can be the cause of extensive debate and emotional pleas at school board meetings and community forums.

The emphasis on individualism and competition prevalent in many schools is not compatible with the cooperative patterns practiced in many American Indian, Latino, and African

GO TO ···>
Groups in the United States are discussed in greater detail in Chapter 7.

GO TO ···>
Incorporating the cultures of students in the curriculum is discussed in Chapter 7.

ethnicity A shared national origin or the national origin of one's ancestors when they immigrated to the United States.

ethnocentric schools The curriculum is designed around the histories and experiences of an ethnic group. Afrocentric schools and tribal schools are the most common examples.

hidden curriculum The implicit values and expectations that teachers and schools convey about learning and behavior.

WHO IS RIGHT?

SHOULD TEACHERS BE REQUIRED TO TAKE DIVERSITY TRAINING?

How can you learn about cultures different than your own, especially those that are represented in the school in which you are teaching? Many teachers, as pointed out below, have taken a course on multicultural education when they were in college, but a number of experienced teachers have not had formal training related to diversity. These two teachers present their perspectives on whether such training is needed.

YES

Mary Cartier is a student member [of the National Education Association] at Michigan State University. She is a junior studying Secondary Spanish Education with a minor in Teaching Speakers of Other Languages.

Looking around my education classes at Michigan State University, I often see only White, female students. In fact, it's the highest demographic of teachers anywhere. Students need to know that their teachers respect and accept them, not only on an individual level, but also as members of society. If they don't see themselves in their teachers, students want to know that at least they're understood.

All educators will, no matter where they work, teach students from different backgrounds than their own, whether they are from a different social class, race, ethnicity, sexual orientation, or level of physical ability. Diversity training can help educators relate more effectively to students who are different from themselves.

In one of my very first classes at MSU, I was able to mentor a young kindergartner, whom I will call Jack. A young African-American student, Jack was unaware of the connotations of race, but he immediately noticed the difference between his own skin color and mine. I didn't ignore his comments, but rather chose to use the occasion as an opportunity to help him understand that there are many different types of people in the world. I feel this was important for me to do because as an African-American male, Jack will soon grow up to realize that race has many real consequences in life. Ignoring that fact would have been a disservice to both of us.

Children don't come into this world knowing how to discriminate—it's a learned behavior that can be stopped or prevented. Kids spend many hours in schools, and if they can be in an environment that breaks stereotypes and creates unity through diversity, it can continue the progress of social justice for our next generation of children.

NO

Suzanne Emery is a retired member who taught English and journalism in San Diego City Schools.

Of course, every September a faculty does need a "heads-up" session on the year's groups of kids, of their home life, their homeland, and needs. The same holds true when there is an influx of students in the middle of the year, as happened after Hurricane Katrina. These sessions are necessary tools, but quite different from required diversity trainings.

Too much in-service for employed teachers can be so demeaning, dumbed down, and even insulting, that required diversity training for all teachers would merely push the scale farther and infuriate the ones most needing some enlightenment. And it is a fallacy to assume that only the traditional "majority" members could use some enlightenment. Prejudice and downright ignorance is colorblind. We reflect our backgrounds, our families, our religions, and our communities.

Additionally, at least half of the people now teaching have entered the profession in the past five years, all earning credentials that have specified, in most states, at least one course or strand in meeting the needs of a culturally diverse student population. The experienced faculty have, for the most part, been "in-serviced" almost annually in various sensitivities of their community. For San Diego, that included everything from language variations for native African-American kids, to practices of Hmong families, to ways to involve differently-abled kids in field trips, to how it is that our Muslim girls can become track stars while wearing head coverings and workout sweats.

As futile as it is to teach ethics to politicians who already know right from wrong, it is folly to believe a few mandated diversity meetings can fundamentally change classroom behavior. Teachers already recognize that their students are very diverse, but must eventually achieve similar success.

WHAT IS YOUR PERSPECTIVE ON THIS ISSUE?

Source: "Should Teachers Be Required to Take Diversity Training?" *NEA Today* (May 2006), p. 41. Reprinted by permission of the National Education Association.

American communities. These differences can lead to conflict between parents and schools and among groups within a community. Families turn to the courts when they believe that schools have acted inappropriately. They may not believe that the schools use a democratic process in which they can be heard or that the community will support their petitions because they hold a minority position. School prayer, creationism, the banning of books, sex education, segregation, bullying, and discrimination are among the areas that have been tested in the courts.

Because parents and other groups in a community may vehemently disagree about the values to be reinforced in schools, teachers should be aware of their own cultural values. Knowing your own values as well as those of the families represented in the school should help you prevent potential conflicts. Expectations can vary greatly from one community or school to another. When a controversial topic, program, or book is being initiated in the classroom, good communications with families will be critical in making the transition smoothly.

JOURNAL FOR REFLECTION 6.2

- How does your family describe your cultural background?
- What characteristics about your culture, if any, were valued in school?
- What characteristics of students from ethnic, language, or religious backgrounds different from your own were valued in school?

Culture of Schools

A school also has a culture that generally reflects the nation's common culture and the community in which it is located. A school's culture, which is sometimes referred to as the school climate or ethos, provides meaning for its students, teachers, school officials, and parents. Schools have their own unwritten rules and norms for behavior, including how students interact with the teacher and each other. They develop their own traditions and rituals related to athletics, extracurricular clubs, graduation exercises, school social events, and the ways teachers interact with each other and parents. They have mascots, cheerleaders, school colors, and school songs that distinguish them from other schools. Over time, they have developed reputations for the academic achievement of their students or the prowess of their football, basketball, or other sports teams. They also develop reputations for the establishment of a safe or dangerous environment. Some schools are influenced greatly by the religions and cultures of the children's families, others by the presence of a university or large military base.

The cultural patterns that develop in a school can have a powerful impact on the academic performance of students and the ways that teachers feel about their work and students. The culture of some schools is very supportive of academic achievement with expectations that all students will attend postsecondary education. Educators in those schools work together to meet that goal, parental support is solicited, and the community celebrates academic performance. Other schools champion an inclusive culture that fosters equity, caring, collaboration, and academic growth for all of its students. Other schools develop cultures in which students and educators value and support the arts, character education, religious orientations, or the whole child's development. Unfortunately, some schools have toxic cultures that do not respect students or value parental and community cultures.

Competition in athletics and other extracurricular activities reflects the traditions of a school's culture.

Students and teachers are more likely to want to be in school and engaged in learning and teaching when the culture in positive and supportive. Characteristics of positive school cultures include high expectations for student learning, safe and caring environments, shared values and trust, powerful pedagogy and curriculum, high motivation and engagement, family and community partnerships, and a professional faculty community (Character Education Partnership, 2010). Teachers and school leaders are key in developing and maintaining the cultures that help students to learn and care about learning.

Schools develop histories and memories that are transferred from generation to generation. Some students become the school leaders, fitting easily into the school culture. Some thrive in a cultural environment where they are popular and have many friends. Other students never seem to fit into the school culture; some because the school culture is very different from their own family's culture and adapting to the school culture causes dissonance at home. Other students feel marginalized and alienated, which may lead to their leaving school before graduation. As a result, some graduates have very positive memories of their schools and retain lifelong feelings of pride about them. Others remember never fitting in and never being understood by their peers and teachers.

FIGURE 6.1 Enrollment in public and private schools.

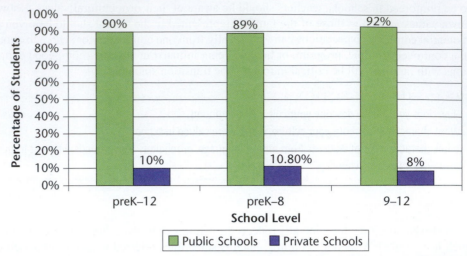

Source: Aud, S., Hussar, W., Kena, G., Bianco, K., Frohlich, L., Kemp, J., & Tahan, K. (2011). *The Condition of Education 2011* (NCES 2011-033). Washington, DC: U.S. Department of Education, National Center for Education Statistics.

GO TO ⋯>

The historical development of public schools is discussed in greater detail in Chapter 2.

charter schools Public schools established by teachers, parents, nonprofit organizations, and others under a contract with the state or local school district. They are exempt from many state and district regulations as they design and deliver programs for improving the academic performance of students.

virtual schools Education programs offered without the teacher and student being in the same room or location for instruction. Most programs are offered online via Web-based technologies.

magnet schools Public schools with a focused curriculum such as the arts or mathematics and science. These schools are designed to attract a diverse student population from across a school district or state.

voucher A check or credit granted by a school district or state to pay part or all of the tuition for children to attend a private school.

SCHOOL CHOICES

In the past, parents had no say in which public school their children would attend unless a private school was nearby and affordable. Children were assigned to a public school based on their home address. Today, increasing numbers and types of options to the traditional neighborhood public school are available. As shown in Figure 6.1, the parents of one in ten students have chosen a private school for the education of their children. Other parents are choosing non-traditional schools such as **charter** or **virtual schools**. The problem for many parents now is not whether they have a choice, but which school is best for their children. Most options are available within larger public school districts as well as in private schools.

Public Schools

The schools that were established after Europeans began to settle the British North American colonies were private and attended by the children of the elite owners of property. In 1674 Massachusetts began to require towns with at least fifty families to appoint a teacher and collect taxes to support schools. When the Land Ordinance was passed in 1785, it required the new territories north and west of the Ohio River to set aside a parcel of land for a public school in each township. By the 1830s, "common schools," which were designed, in part, to reduce the tensions across socioeconomic groups, were being attended by students from families of different social classes. During this period, most African American, Hispanic, and American Indian students attended segregated schools if they were in school at all. In many parts of the country low-income students did not attend school regularly and, when they did, it was often for only a few grades.

When immigrant Roman Catholic families expressed concerns about the Protestant Bible being taught in the common schools in 1842, riots erupted in Philadelphia and New York City. When the two sides could not reach agreement on the curricula, the Roman Catholic Church established its own private schools (Spring, 2011). Over time, the public school curriculum became more secular.

Children and youth today have the right to attend a public school; in fact, they are required to attend school until they are sixteen to eighteen years old, depending on the laws of the state in which they live. Approximately 50 million students are currently enrolled in public P–12 schools, but that number is projected to increase to more than 52 million by 2020 (Aud et al., 2011).

PUBLIC SCHOOL CHOICES. Discussions about providing parents a choice of schools that their children can attend were initiated in the 1980s when the federal government funded **magnet schools**. In 1990 the state of Wisconsin passed legislation to provide low-income families in Milwaukee the opportunity to use a **voucher** to send their children to a private school. With the passage of No Child Left Behind (NCLB) in 2001, parents were allowed more options for choosing a school.

Most public school options allow for parent and student involvement in school decision-making. All represent, in some way, a break with the traditional public school. The creation of choices also causes competition between schools, which some people believe will lead to more efficiency and effectiveness. However, the research to date, though limited, does not provide clear evidence of a trend toward higher student achievement in non-traditional schools (Ravitch, 2010).

MAGNET SCHOOLS. In the 1960s some parents were calling for school choice, in part, to counteract the racially segregated schools that existed across the country. Early alternative schools were opened in Tacoma, Washington in 1968, Boston in 1969, and Minneapolis in 1970. In the early 1970s Houston called its Performing and Visual Arts School a "magnet school" because it was attracting students from across the city.

Many school districts continued to be pressured by citizens and ordered by the courts to equalize the proportions of students from different racial groups in each school. A growing number of urban school districts developed special academic programs and custom-designed facilities to attract a racially diverse student body from across the city. Many of the magnet schools emphasized a theme such as the performing and visual arts, math and science, or the liberal arts. Whatever the theme, the faculty, curriculum, and students generally choose the magnet school because of their interest in the school's theme.

CHARTER SCHOOLS. Charter schools are the most popular option in the public school system. They have been created by academic institutions, nonprofit foundations, teachers, parents, and entrepreneurs for a variety of reasons. These schools include Montessori schools, Edison Schools, experiential learning schools, and KIPP (Knowledge Is Power Program) academies. Founders of other charter schools have designed curricula and climates that are centered in the ethnic heritages of the students and community. Others have created schools around a particular philosophy that teachers and parents support. Although all charter schools are supposed to provide students with a strong academic background that meets standards, some focus more directly on academics with the goal that most of their students will attend and complete college.

Charter schools are established through a contract with either a state agency (e.g., the state department of education) or a local school board for a specific time period, usually three to five years. The contract, or charter, lays out how the school will operate in exchange for receiving public funding. Charter schools have greater autonomy than traditional public schools and can be released from district and state regulations such as hiring licensed teachers, following the teachers' union contract, or using the district's textbooks. However, charter schools are still held accountable for student learning and, in most settings, having a diverse student body.

As of 2012, forty-two states and the District of Columbia had passed legislation to permit the establishment of charter schools (Center for Education Reform, 2012c). Arizona, the District of Columbia, Indiana, Michigan, and Minnesota are states with strong charter laws, as ranked by the Center for Education Reform (2012a). More than 5,700 charter schools, serving 1.9 million students, existed in 2011 (Center for Education Reform, 2012b). As you might expect with the majority of charter schools located in central cities, over half of the students in those schools are African American, Hispanic, or American Indian students (Center for Education Reform, 2010). As shown in Figure 6.2, charter schools are generally smaller than other public schools, and over half of them are located in cities. Three in four charter schools are either elementary or combined elementary schools (Aud et al., 2011).

VIRTUAL SCHOOLS. The opportunities for students to meet in a classroom online is quickly becoming commonplace. Virtual schools, or "cyberschools," and virtual courses exist across the span of schooling from preschool through college and into professional development for teachers and other workers. The number of students enrolled in online courses has increased from 45,000 in 2000 to more than 1.8 million in 2009–2010, with 70 percent of them being high school students. By the 2010–2011 school year, 250,000 students were enrolled full-time in virtual schools—a 25 percent increase over the previous year (International Association for K–12 Online Learning, 2012). At least one full-time virtual school operates in thirty states (Watson, Murin, Vashaw, Gemin, & Rapp, 2011).

The most common reason for a student to participate in an online school is that the course is not available in their school building (iNACOL, 2012). For example, students in rural areas have taken courses in foreign language and other subjects because teachers for those subjects do

GO TO ··›
The consequences of not meeting AYP are discussed in Chapters 8 and 11.

FIGURE 6.2 Enrollment in charter and traditional public schools: 2008–2009.

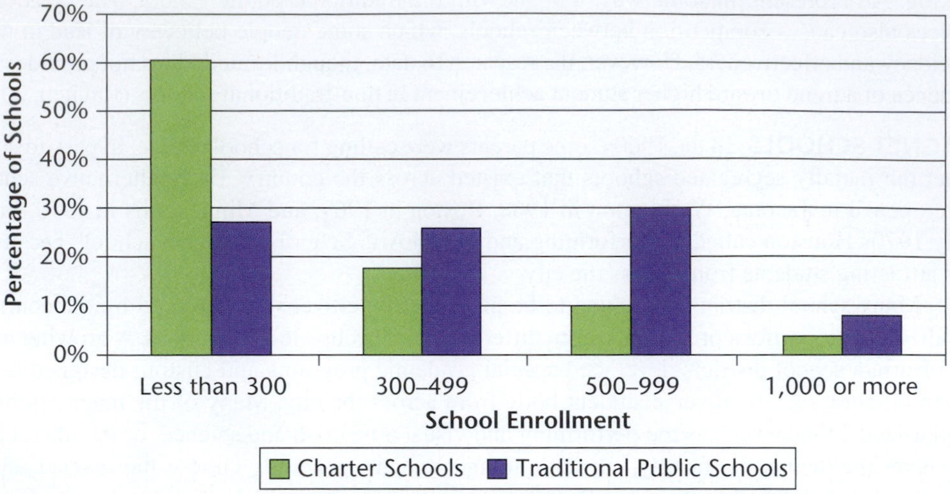

Source: Aud, S., Hussar, W., Kena, G., Bianco, K., Frohlich, L., Kemp, J., & Tahan, K. (2011). *The Condition of Education 2011* (NCES 2011-033). Washington, DC: U.S. Department of Education, National Center for Education Statistics.

not exist in their schools. Advanced placement (AP) courses via technology are also popular. The second most common reason to take an online course is for credit recovery when students have not completed core courses required for graduation (iNACOL, 2012). Online technologies also provide a valuable resource for students who are being home schooled.

Virtual schools are generally tuition-free public charter schools. Forty states operate virtual schools or manage state-led online initiatives for students in their states. The oldest and largest state-led school is the Florida Virtual School, which now offers online courses in forty-nine states and fifty-seven countries, serving over 122,000 students (Florida Virtual School, 2011). A for-profit company, K12 Inc. of Herndon, VA, is the largest provider of full-time public virtual schools (Miron, Urschel, Aguilar, & Dailey, 2012). Virtual schools will be recruiting an increasing number of teachers to deliver online instruction and coach students. Is this an option that you are interested in pursuing?

VOUCHERS. The most controversial school choice option is **school vouchers**. At its simplest, a voucher program issues a check or a credit that can be used by parents to send their child to a private school. Generally, the argument for vouchers is based on equalizing educational opportunity for students of color and students from low-income families whose children may be attending schools that are not meeting NCLB's **adequate yearly progress (AYP)** requirements. Advocates often argue that vouchers are a market-driven strategy that will force public schools to compete with private schools, leading to improvement in both. Proponents also argue that parents of private schools pay twice—the tuition for the private school plus tax dollars for public schools. Opponents worry that vouchers may encourage the most highly motivated students to abandon public schools (Harvey, 2011/2012).

Wisconsin adopted the first law that allowed low-income families in Milwaukee to move their children from a public to a private school with a voucher of public funds. Ohio adopted a similar voucher plan for Cleveland families in 1996. The most expansive use of vouchers is in the District of Columbia as a result of Congress enacting the Opportunity Scholarship Program for 1,700 students in 2004. Although Congress closed the D.C. voucher program to new students in 2009, it was back in President Obama's budget in 2011.

Most voucher programs are funded with state tax dollars. Legislation that supported early voucher programs limited them to low-income families. State legislation in 2011 expanded the availability of vouchers to middle class families in Indiana and Wisconsin and to any family in Douglas County, Colorado. Not all voucher programs are publicly funded. Some programs are funded by private foundations and occasionally by individuals. Typically, the amount of a voucher is equivalent to the amount the public school receives for each student.

The debates about vouchers center on the use of public dollars to support private schools. The most serious point of contention is when a voucher funded with state education money is used to pay for a child to attend religious-affiliated schools, which are the main beneficiaries of vouchers. Some opponents have claimed that vouchers raise constitutional questions about the

school vouchers A program offered by a school district that issues a check or a credit that can be used by parents to send their child to a private school.

adequate yearly progress (AYP) The annual progress report of how students in a school performed on the state's achievement tests as required by No Child Left Behind. Schools whose students are not performing at grade level are labeled by the state as "low performing."

separation of church and state, but the U.S. Supreme Court ruled that Cleveland's school voucher program was constitutional under the federal Establishment Clause of the First Amendment.

Research on voucher programs has found that students' academic achievement has not improved as a result of vouchers. Parents may be more satisfied because school conditions and safety in the private schools they have chosen are better than in the public schools their children would have attended. Graduation rates have been higher for students with a voucher than for their peers who remained in public schools, but researchers have not been able to determine whether this difference is due to the private school or to the motivation of their parents who moved their children to a private school (Center on Education Policy, 2011).

GO TO ··>
Legal issues related to the separation of church and state are presented in Chapter 10.

JOURNAL FOR REFLECTION 6.3

- How do you feel about allowing parents to choose a school for their children?
- Of the choices discussed in this section, in which type of school would you prefer to teach? Why?

Private Schools

Private schools have been an integral part of our nation's educational resources since colonial times. Because each private school is free to determine and practice its own philosophy of education, the spirit and environment vary from school to school, even though schools may display similar organizational structures and educational programs. They serve students from all racial, religious, economic, and language backgrounds. Some are progressive and innovative; some are conservative and traditional. They are large and small, day and boarding, single-sex and coeducational. They include Montessori, special education, vocational, technical, alternative, and preschools (Broughman, Swaim, & Hryczaniuk, 2011). They range from elite secondary schools (mainly in the Northeast), to alternative schools for high school dropouts, to faith-supported schools, to schools that are operated for profit.

The majority of private schools are at the elementary level with only 8 percent at the secondary level. More students are enrolled in private kindergartens than any other grade level. Private schools are more likely to be located in cities or their suburbs than in rural areas. Although enrollment in private schools had grown to 5.3 million by 2001, it had declined to 4.7 million by 2009 (Broughman et al., 2011).

PAROCHIAL SCHOOLS. Four in five private school students attend a school supported by a religious group. The culture of a parochial school may have a positive impact on student achievement. Some researchers have found that students at religious schools—especially African American and Hispanic students—perform better on standardized tests than their public school peers (Broughman, Swaim, & Keaton, 2008). Many religious groups sponsor schools, including the Amish, Muslims, Jews, Quakers, Catholics, and many Protestants, as shown in Figure 6.3. However, enrollment in

FIGURE 6.3 Percent of private schools and private school students by the school's religious orientation.

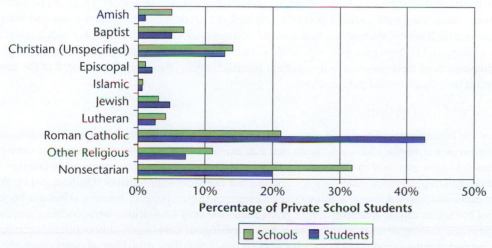

Source: Broughman, S. P., Swaim, N. L., & Hryczaniuk, C. A. (2011). *Characteristics of Private Schools in the United States: Results from the 2009–10 Private School Universe Survey* (NCES 2011-339). Washington, DC: National Center for Education Statistics, Institute of Education Sciences, U.S. Department of Education.

Parochial schools are parents' most popular choice if they choose to send their children to a private school.

different religious schools has shifted during the past twenty years. Although enrollment in Roman Catholic schools is higher than in any other private schools, it decreased from 45 percent of total enrollment in private schools in 1995–1996 to 39 percent in 2009–2010 (Aud et al., 2011).

SINGLE-SEX EDUCATION. Most single-sex schools and colleges today are private and share a goal of helping their students develop confidence, academic achievement, and leadership skills by building on their unique learning styles and cultural experiences. Schools or academies in some urban areas have been established for young African American men, with the goal of improving their opportunities for enrolling in and being successful in college and life. All-girls and all-boys schools are more likely to be at the secondary than any other level. In fact, 15 percent and 13 percent of all private secondary schools are all-boys or all-girls, respectively. They are more likely to be located in the Northeast and in cities than in other areas (Broughman et al., 2011).

Home Schooling

Home schooling requires no public support; instead, children learn at home with their parents serving as the teacher. An estimated 2 million students are being schooled at home (Ray, 2011), representing 3.9 percent of the K–12 population—up from 1.7 percent in 1999. Although the education program for 84 percent of homeschooled students is provided totally at home, other students attend a school for nine to twenty-five hours per week (Planty et al., 2009). Homeschooled students sometimes participate in sports and other extracurricular activities at the local public school.

Teaching a homeschooled student requires parents to know the subjects they are teaching, organize each day's instruction, and facilitate their children's learning. One of the advantages, as well as potential weaknesses, is that in most states the subjects taught are self-determined. This can work in favor of students' interests but may also contribute to gaps in their education. However, parents may use online education programs to supplement their curriculum.

Why do parents choose to homeschool their children? In a national survey of parents, three reasons were prominent: One in three parents indicated that they wanted to provide religious or moral instruction that was not available at a school. One in five parents was concerned about the school environment, and 17 percent of parents were dissatisfied with the academic instruction provided at a school (Planty et al., 2009). The evidence is clear that home schooling is a success for many students. Studies have found that homeschooled students score 15 to 30 percentile points above their public school peers on standardized academic achievement tests, and homeschooled high school students score above the average on SAT and ACT tests for college admission (Ray, 2011). However, research studies are not yet able to determine whether the higher achievement of these students is due to their homeschooling; they may have scored at the same level if they had attended public schools.

Innovative Options

online learning Education that occurs over the Internet with either synchronous instruction in which the teacher can interact with students in real time or non-synchronous instruction to which students have access at any time.

You are beginning your teaching career at a very exciting time in which teaching and learning may break out of the classroom mode that has existed in most schools over the past century. These changes may lead to eliminating seat-time requirements in a classroom and to changes in school funding, textbook requirements, and teacher licensure requirements (Quillen, 2011). You are quite likely to teach one or more courses electronically, especially because states are beginning to require **online learning** before graduation. You may be teaching and coaching students whom you seldom or never see; they may live in a different state or possibly a different country. Advocates for these and other innovative options argue that they will serve students more effectively than current teaching strategies and school structures.

ONLINE AND HYBRID LEARNING. Online learning, which occurs over the Internet with synchronous or non-synchronous instruction, is becoming common in P–12 settings and continuing through graduate education. Thirty percent of high school students and 19 percent of middle school students were taking online courses in 2010 (Project Tomorrow, 2011). Although 78 percent of these students access online courses from home, most students (92 percent) access their courses at school (iNACOL, 2012). Hybrid or blended programs combine online work with face-to-face instruction by and interactions with teachers in a school setting. The hybrid approach is the most common at this time, but full-time online programs in virtual schools are growing each year.

PERSONALIZING EDUCATION WITH TECHNOLOGY. Technology is allowing education to be customized for each student, a task that has been very difficult in classrooms with thirty students. In addition, technology is allowing students to work at their own pace at any time of the day. Although teachers may prepare and deliver online lessons and activities, their jobs have changed dramatically from being the authority at the front of the room delivering knowledge to students or managing the recitation of students. The work of students is becoming more hands-on, applying and testing knowledge in real-world situations that have meaning for them. Teachers serve as coaches to help students understand subjects while pushing them to higher levels of learning. One example is the online Khan Academies, which offers lessons at no cost on the core subjects of math, science, and the humanities. Each lesson is approximately ten minutes in length, and the system tracks the lessons with which students have been engaged. Students or adults can choose their own lessons or teachers can assign lessons to students. The website includes over 3,000 videos, interactive challenges, and assessments. The online system allows teachers to monitor the progress of their students and encourages them to serve as coaches to students as they participate in the academy.

SCHOOL LEVELS

By the mid-nineteenth century, many elementary-aged children attended common schools, but it was not until the end of that century that high schools began to be established. Schooling was not further divided into early childhood and middle level education until the twentieth century. Although some one-room schools still exist in rural areas, most school districts have schools designed for different age groups that will be described in this section. Not everyone agrees that it is appropriate to divide schools based on age. Some reformers suggest that age distinctions are no longer necessary as students use technology to progress at their own rates. Future schools could be designed for students to work on their own in computer labs, coming together for small groups or teamwork with each other and teachers as appropriate. At this point, however, your state will expect that you have been prepared to work with students at a specific grade level except for subjects such as physical education, special education, music, and art, which generally require a license to teach in grades K–12.

Early Childhood Education

At the end of the nineteenth century, G. Stanley Hall, a professor at Johns Hopkins University, defined childhood as the years between ages four and eight, which remains the age range for primary education in today's schools although early childhood education encompasses birth through age eight. Between 1930 and the 1950s, early childhood education programs had a behaviorist orientation, in which good habits were developed through exercise and drill. With a renewed interest in Piaget and the developmental stages of childhood, the field later took on a developmental approach. By the beginning of the twenty-first century, academics were being emphasized, and young children were being assessed. One of the resulting changes of the emphasis on academics is discussed in the "Teaching in Challenging Times" feature.

HEAD START. The most well-known early childhood program is the federally funded **Head Start program**, which was created as part of President Lyndon Johnson's War on Poverty in 1964 to help three- to five-year-old children from low-income families to be better prepared to enter school. It was created not only to provide educational services, but also emotional, social, health, nutritional, and psychological support for students. Parents are encouraged to be active volunteers in the program. When Head Start was reauthorized in 2007, the curriculum was

Head Start program
Federally funded program for three- to five-year-old children from low-income families to provide educational services and emotional, social, health, nutritional, and psychological support that will prepare them to enter kindergarten.

TEACHING IN CHALLENGING TIMES

What Has Happened to Play?

A new research study shows that "play is disappearing from kindergarten classrooms," reports Edward Miller of the Alliance for Childhood. Early childhood educators, researchers, and advocates decry the fact that the country's emphasis on academics and accountability has pushed play out of kindergarten classrooms. Perhaps the pendulum has swung too far to the side of cognitive development, to the demise of other skills that are identified in the *21st Century Learning Knowledge and Skills* framework: collaboration, critical thinking, creativity, and physical activity. Some advocates worry that the removal of play is contributing to mental health problems and obesity in young children. The amount of time now available for free play—games, make-believe, and artwork of their choice—has moved to the background, if it exists at all. Because recesses have been eliminated or limited in time in a number of schools, some states are considering legislation requiring recesses in pre- and elementary schools. Is it time for the pendulum to swing the other way, or can educators and policy makers reach a balance that includes both ends of the continuum to develop a whole, healthy child with the appropriate cognitive knowledge and skills?

WHAT ARE MY CHALLENGES?

1. Why does the elimination of play in early childhood programs concern some researchers and advocates for children? Do you agree with them? Why or why not?

2. What has led to the reduction of play time in so many schools? How have teachers lost control of their classrooms to outside forces?

3. Who should be involved in the development of a more balanced approach to teaching preschoolers and kindergartners?

Source: From Jacobson, L. "Children's lack of playtime seen as troubling health, school issue" as first appeared in *Education Week*, December 3, 2008. Reprinted with permission from Editorial Projects in Education.

---

aligned with states' early learning standards, and the qualifications for Head Start teachers were raised. Children generally attend Head Start programs for half a day, but some schools offer full-day programs. To participate in Head Start, the income of a child's family must be at the federal poverty level or below although schools can allow 10 percent of their Head Start students to be in families above the poverty level.

Montessori model An educational program originally designed for three- to six-year olds that is well organized into subject-based work centers where children interact with the classroom materials. It includes little or no large-group instruction.

MONTESSORI SCHOOLS. Some parents choose to send their children to a Montessori school in which the teacher is the facilitator of learning. The **Montessori model**, which was developed by medical doctor Maria Montessori, includes little or no large-group instruction, especially for three- to six-year-olds. The teacher works with one child at a time or with a small group of children. Built into every day at a Montessori school is one uninterrupted three-hour work period during which children are allowed to explore their environment without being required to attend any individual or small-group activities. The Montessori classroom must be well organized into subject-based work centers where children interact with the classroom materials. A typical classroom may have thirty to thirty-five students ranging in age from two and a half to six years old with one teacher and one nonteaching assistant. The same teacher remains with the same students as they move through this developmental stage. Older children help teach the skills they have already learned to the younger children, allowing the teacher to observe and record the skills mastered for the child's portfolio, which is the only form of assessment used. No grades are given, and no forms of punishment or rewards are used.

High Scope model An approach to early childhood education based on the belief that children are active learners and on the child development theories of Jean Piaget.

HIGH SCOPE MODEL. Another popular approach to early childhood education is the **High Scope model** that is based both on the belief that children are active learners and on the child development theories of Jean Piaget. Students explore materials within structured subject-based centers where items and shelves are clearly labeled with pictures and words so children can experience **environmental print** and categorize materials. High Scope classrooms have a fixed daily schedule and regular classroom routines with the goal of helping children who are economically disadvantaged achieve greater school success and develop social responsibility. It is designed to provide students with language and literacy, logic and mathematics, music and movement, and creative learning activities to contribute to their cognitive, physical, and affective development. The teacher creates a portfolio with examples of each child's work and completes developmental checklists to show growth throughout the year. High Scope teachers make regular home visits to help parents learn how to work with their children and to learn more about a student's home culture and language to ensure that they are reflected and respected in the classroom.

environmental print The words, signs, and symbols that children see in their daily lives on cereal boxes, television, and street signs as well as at fast food restaurants and other places they visit.

REGGIO EMELIA APPROACH. The Reggio Emelia approach to early childhood education was originated by a teacher, Loris Malaguzzi, after the end of World War II at the Diana School in the city of Reggio Emelia in Northern Italy. It was designed to meet the social, emotional, and educational needs of all children ranging in age from birth to six years old. Children are subdivided into an infancy group for children up to three years old and a school group for three- to six-year-olds. A group of up to twenty-four children grows together with the same two teachers, an assistant, and the support of parent volunteers for a three-year cycle. Teachers collaborate with each other, parents, children, and community members in meeting the individual needs of each student. The curriculum is project based, allowing teachers to build on known areas of interest, such as dinosaurs, shadows, and community- or family-inspired events and interests. While working on their projects, children are encouraged to collaborate with other children to explore information and materials. A sense of community is developed in the school by having some common areas where children from all age groups can mingle and interact. These common areas include a small-group room, a kitchen for children to have snacks, a multiage-appropriate physical development/tumble room, and other small play areas. The Reggio approach ensures that children, their families, their teachers, and the entire community take an active role in the education of each child.

Typical early childhood classrooms in the United States incorporate one or more of these approaches to instruction. A school district may have both the federally funded Head Start and prekindergarten classrooms in schools that use the same packaged curriculum, but also include elements of the Montessori, High Scope, and Reggio Emelia approaches. Some school districts offer specialized early childhood programs such as Montessori and language-immersion programs in addition to the regular Head Start or prekindergarten classes.

Elementary Schools

The first school based on grades was established in 1848 in Boston—the city that was on the leading edge of establishing the roots of our educational system. In the Quincy School, teachers worked in a classroom with fifty-six students who sat at desks that were bolted to the floor. This model was adopted across the country and changed little until progressiveness influenced the structure of the classroom in the twentieth century, turning the bolted desks into tables and movable desks that could be easily moved together for group activities. Over time, class sizes became smaller, averaging 15.6 students by 2007–2008 (Aud et al., 2010) with student/teacher ratios lower in smaller rural schools and higher in large urban schools.

GO TO ··→
For more information on the history of elementary schools, see Chapter 2.

Elementary schools often include the primary grades of PK–3 or K–3 plus the fourth, fifth, and/or sixth grades. In some states and districts they span grades K–8. State licensure or certification for teachers may cover only the primary or upper elementary grades or K–6 or K–8. If you are planning to teach in an elementary school, you should check the grade-level span for licensure in the state in which you plan to teach to ensure that you take the courses that will lead to the appropriate license.

Most elementary teachers work in self-contained classrooms with twenty to thirty or more students who move to the next grade with a different teacher at the end of a school year. In some schools, teachers team teach with specialists in mathematics, science, reading, language arts, and social studies. Some schools have **resource teachers** who work with classroom teachers to accommodate students with special needs related to reading, mathematics, English, or a disability. Some schools practice **looping**, in which teachers remain with the same students for two to three grades.

Elementary schools are more impacted by state testing than other levels because students in grades 3–8 are assessed annually. The elementary grades are also important in setting the standards and establishing behaviors for academic learning. Teachers who ensure that their students are learning are critical, especially in the early grades. Research finds that a student who has a good teacher for three to four years in a row will have a much better chance than other students of being academically successful throughout his or her school career (Bransford, Darling-Hammond, & LePage, 2005; Sanders & Rivers, 1996). The academic foundation established in elementary schools influences a student's future performance in school. For example, a study by the Annie E. Casey Foundation (2010) found that students who were reading at grade level at the end of the third grade were more likely to finish high school.

resource teachers Specialized teachers who work in a regular classroom with students who have special needs related to reading, mathematics, English, or a disability.

looping An educational practice in which teachers remain with the same students for two to three grades.

Middle Level Education

Schools for early adolescents were first established as junior high schools in Columbus, Ohio, and Berkeley, California, in 1909–1910 to better meet the needs of seventh, eighth, and ninth graders as they transitioned from childhood to adolescence. However, the growth of these schools across the United States was primarily due to the organizational needs of school districts, not the unique needs of early adolescent students. The large influx of immigrant children and the increasing number of students not passing to the next grade caused elementary schools to become overcrowded. They were often attached to high schools to relieve the overcrowded elementary schools. The number of junior high schools peaked at over 7,000 in the 1970s (Lutz, 2004). They had become miniature high schools that many believed were not effectively serving young adolescents.

Believing that significant physical, emotional, intellectual, and social changes occur between the ages of ten and fifteen, proponents for middle schools called for a more developmentally appropriate school organization. The ideal was to have teachers who were more affectionate and sensitive to young people. General education was promoted over an emphasis on mastery of subject matter (Lutz, 2004). Middle schools began to replace junior high schools, but their growth was again greatly influenced by the realities faced by school districts. As the baby boom generation of the 1950s overcrowded elementary schools, a wing was added to the high school for students in the fifth or sixth to ninth grades.

The middle school generally has at least three grades and not more than five grades and includes at least grades 6 and 7. As the number of junior high schools declined, the number of middle schools grew to more than 13,000. The most successful middle schools maintain their roots for providing developmentally responsive programs and practices such as collaborative and cooperative learning strategies. They generally have adopted interdisciplinary team teaching and block scheduling (McEwin & Greene, 2011).

High Schools

After the first high school was established in Boston in 1821, their numbers grew slowly until the end of that century. They grew even more during the Great Depression of the 1930s when children were pushed out of the workforce and into the high schools. By 2010–2011 nearly 15 million students were enrolled in grades 9–12 (Aud et al., 2011). Almost all students begin high school today, with 92 percent finishing high school or a general educational development GED certificate by age twenty-five (Aud et al., 2011). However, fewer students are completing high school within four years, with more than 50 percent of African American and Hispanic male students in a number of urban areas dropping out of school (Swanson, 2009). Only three in five students with disabilities earned a regular school diploma in 2009 (Alliance for Excellent Education, 2011), which has increased over the past fifteen years (Agus, 2010). As projections suggest that postsecondary education will be necessary for an increasing number of jobs, the number of students who finish high school and enter college immediately after high school has increased over time to 70 percent. However, fewer students from low-income, African American, and Hispanic families begin college at that point or later (Aud et al., 2011), limiting their future job and income opportunities.

TRADITIONAL HIGH SCHOOLS. Secondary schools are generally larger than elementary and middle schools, with an average of over 700 students per school. Twelve percent of them were identified as in need of improvement under NCLB in 2005–06 (Agus, 2010). Because only 58 percent of secondary schools offer at least one advanced placement (AP) course (Agus, 2010), a number of students do not have access to higher level English language arts, mathematics, and science courses that may better prepare them for college work.

High schools today are being attacked as wastelands for young people. The curriculum and structure appear to have changed little over the past fifty years (Foundation for Excellence in Education, 2010). They are condemned for not integrating technology, critical thinking, and problem solving into the curriculum to prepare graduates for a changing workforce in which they will have to adapt to new jobs throughout their careers. Too many graduates are not proficient in mathematics and reading and are not competitive on international tests with their peers in Canada, Japan, South Korea, and a number of European countries. As a result, governors, businesses, and organizations have established committees to reform high schools with the goal of changing the school culture to improve student achievement and increase graduation rates.

FIGURE 6.4   Twelfth grade students at proficient level or above by race and ethnicity.

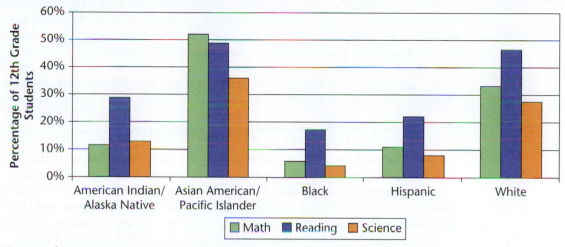

Source: National Assessments for Educational Progress (NAEP). (2009). *The nation's report card: Grade 12 national results.* Washington: DC: Author, National Center for Education Statistics, Institute of Education Sciences, U.S. Department of Education. Retrieved on March 18, 2012, from http://nationsreportcard.gov/.

Students in approximately 2,000 of the lowest performing high schools account for the highest dropout rate. In these schools, 60 percent or less of the freshman class finishes high school in four years. Many of the dropouts are lost in the ninth grade as students learn that they have not been prepared for the academic work of high school. As many as 40 percent of these ninth graders repeated the ninth grade and only 10 to 15 percent of these repeaters end up graduating from high school. Low attendance rates and failing grades in middle school have been found to be predictors of dropping out before graduation (Alliance for Excellent Education, 2010). African American, American Indian, and Hispanic students are being hurt the most by these conditions because they are six times more likely than white students to attend these low-performing schools (Alliance for Excellent Education, 2012), which do not help them develop the basic academic proficiencies required for postsecondary education and many jobs. Performance of twelfth graders on selected National Assessments for Educational Progress (NAEP) tests are shown in Figure 6.4.

HIGH SCHOOL REFORMS. Among the proposed high school reforms was the creation of small high schools to promote stronger relationships among students and teachers with the goals of increasing student engagement and improving student achievement. These small schools were sometimes stand-alone schools and at other times, schools within larger high schools (Bloom & Unterman, 2012). Both the development of small high schools and research about small high schools have been supported by private funding such as the Bill and Melinda Gates Foundation. Research has found mixed results about the effectiveness of this effort. One of the success stories has been in New York City, where twenty-three large failing high schools were replaced by 216 small high schools. They were able to reduce the risk of dropping out of school for ninth graders and increase graduation rates (Bloom & Unterman, 2012).

HIGH SCHOOL INNOVATIONS. Other innovative projects are integrating technology and hands-on learning throughout the high school curriculum. One example is the acclaimed High Tech High (HTH), which in 2011 was operating eleven charter schools (five high schools, four middle schools, and two elementary schools) with diverse student bodies in San Diego, Chula Vista, San Marcos, and other California communities. They integrate technical and academic education in a hands-on approach to prepare students for both high tech and liberal arts fields with a goal of increasing the number of low-income students and students of color who study math and engineering. Students also participate in internships in local businesses and agencies. How successful are the High Tech High schools? All of their graduates since the first graduating class in 2003 have been admitted to postsecondary colleges—80 percent of them four-year institutions, including our most prestigious universities. They are among the highest achieving schools in California, and 30 percent of their graduates enter math or science fields (High Tech High, 2012). HTH also offers credentialing programs and a Master of Education program for teachers.

Another innovative approach is the New Tech Network, which was founded in Napa, California, in 1996. Faculty at its eighty-six public high schools in sixteen states use a project-based approach to engage students and faculty in real world problems (New Tech Network, n.d.). Students actively engage with technology as a primary tool in the learning process. New Tech is now a subsidiary of KnowledgeWorks, an Ohio-based organization that is one of the leaders in high school reform. One commonality across High Tech High, New Tech Network, Knowledge-Works, and similar reform efforts is the involvement of business leaders in the design and support of their schools.

THE SENSE OF PLACE: SCHOOL LOCATIONS

The people who share our space and place have a great influence on our culture and lives. We become comfortable with the place where we live, understanding what is expected of us and others. When we move from one area of the country to another, we may suffer some cultural shock, having to learn the culture of the new area. The same is true for students and families as they move from one district to another, especially if they have moved to a new region of the country.

Rural Communities

Nineteen percent of the population lives in rural areas or towns with fewer than 2,500 residents (U.S. Census Bureau, 2011). By urban and suburban standards, rural families live long distances from one another, and children may travel long distances to school. To the rural family, however, the distances are not great, and a feeling of neighborliness exists. The social structure is less stratified than in more populous geographical areas, and everyone may appear to know everyone else. Values tend to be somewhat conservative as compared to other areas.

Although 32 percent of the nation's schools are located in rural areas and another 14 percent in towns, only 24 percent of public school students attend these schools (Aud et al., 2011). These schools have a larger percentage of white and American Indian students than other areas of the country, but the Hispanic population is growing in a number of rural areas. Rural schools are generally smaller than ones in cities, and the student-to-teacher ratio is lower. Rural students generally perform better on national achievement tests than their town and city peers but less well than students in most suburban schools (Aud et al., 2011).

Despite the pivotal role of schools in rural life, these schools face real difficulties. In some school districts, teacher shortages may result in the staffing of schools by teachers with a limited academic background in the subjects they teach. Not all courses (for example, art and foreign languages) can be offered because of the limited number of teachers. Principals may be assigned to several schools, and support services may be limited because of the lack of funds. Teachers in rural areas sometimes feel isolated, especially if they are not from the area. As ethnic diversity increases in these areas, teachers will be confronted with cultures and languages to which they may have had little or no exposure.

Children in farming communities experience aspects of life that are foreign to most city and suburban students.

Rural communities cherish their small schools—where students know each other, their teachers, and most community members. They usually fight proposals for consolidating schools because of the long historical traditions associated with their particular schools. In addition, they worry about consolidated schools being so far away that they cannot actively participate in their children's and grandchildren's education. Some students end up riding a bus for one or more hours daily to reach a consolidated school.

Suburban Communities

Nearly half of the U.S. population lives in the suburbs, which have become diverse as families of color have moved into them from the city. The suburbs are becoming even more economically,

racially, ethnically, linguistically, and religiously diverse as new immigrants settle in them (Frey, Berube, Singer, & Wilson, 2009). Some communities actively solicit and celebrate diversity. In others, it is discouraged. Breaking past patterns of immigrants settling in their own enclaves in cities, some of today's immigrants from Central America, South America, Asia, and the Middle East are bypassing cities and moving directly into the suburbs or rural areas. After years of population growth in the suburbs, population is declining as retirees and young singles choose urban living over living in the exurbs—the country's outer suburbs.

High-tech companies have found the suburbs ideal for their research and development on software, electronics, and biotechnologies. Entrepreneurs and professionals are attracted to suburban research parks, often moving into elite housing developments near their jobs. However, poverty now exists in the suburbs as well as in cities and rural areas. Forty percent of suburban public school students were eligible for free or reduced-price lunches in the 2009–2010 school year (National Center for Education Statistics, 2011).

Families may move from cities to the suburbs to ensure that their children receive a better education. Funding for schools has traditionally been higher in the suburbs than other areas. Wealthy suburbs boast beautiful school buildings, sometimes on sprawling campuses, with the latest in technology, qualified teachers, advanced placement courses, gifted and talented programs, and numerous extracurricular activities. However, not all suburban schools are of this high quality. Students who are English-language learners, who are from low-income families, or who are from backgrounds other than European are more likely to attend the older schools in the region.

Although the overall racial and ethnic diversity of suburban school districts has increased, the diversity of individual schools has been limited. The typical white suburban student will attend a school with a 75 percent white student population. The school that a typical African American, Asian American, or Hispanic suburban student attends will have a 34 percent, 31 percent, or 48 percent white population, respectively. Hispanic students are increasingly attending suburban schools in which half or more of the students are Hispanic (Fry, 2009).

Enrollments in suburban schools are, on the average, larger than those of urban and rural schools (National Center for Education Statistics, 2011). The student-to-teacher ratio is also slightly higher in suburban schools at 16.1 students per teacher compared to 15 in rural schools and 15.9 in urban schools (Aud et al., 2011). Suburban students outperform their rural and urban counterparts on achievement tests (Aud et al., 2011), and more suburban students than students from other areas attend college. Safety is generally less of a concern for students, parents, and teachers.

Urban Communities

Urban areas are usually rich in educational and entertainment resources such as libraries, museums, theaters, professional sports, colleges, and universities. People from different economic and cultural backgrounds intermingle in many parts of a city. An expensive restaurant can be on one block with a soup kitchen on the next block. Homeless people and families are more visible in urban areas as affordable housing becomes scarcer and the number of public housing units does not meet the needs of the population. Cities provide creative energy for many of their inhabitants, but they are oppressive and dangerous for others. Many families live in safe environments with good schools, parks, and recreational facilities. Others live in toxic environments that contribute to high incidences of asthma and other diseases. Some sections of the city are scarred by gunshots and graffiti. Ambulances, police raids, and funerals for young people in these parts of the city are common occurrences.

Because many high schools, especially in urban areas, are not serving students well, a number of reforms have been proposed for them by groups as diverse as the Bill and Melinda Gates Foundation and the National Governors Association.

FIGURE 6.5   Student diversity in the largest one hundred school districts.

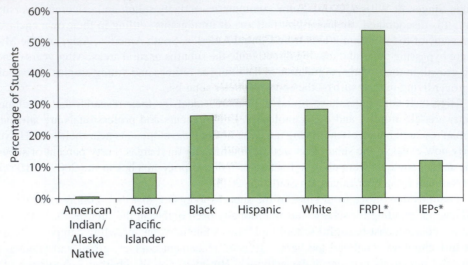

FRPL* = Free or reduced price lunch for students from low-income families
IEPs* = Individualized educational plan for students with disabilities

Source: Sable, J., Plotts, C., & Mitchell, L. (2010). *Characteristics of the 100 Largest Public Elementary and Secondary School Districts in the United States: 2008–09* (NCES 2011-301). Washington, DC: U.S. Department of Education, National Center for Education Statistics.

The largest one hundred public school districts represented less than 1 percent of all school districts, but were responsible for 22 percent of all public school students (Sable, Plotts, & Mitchell, 2010). Students in these largest districts are very diverse, as shown in Figure 6.5.

Schools across a city look different and serve their students differently. Upper middle class parents are more able to donate funds to assist their schools when teachers of art and music have been cut from the district's budget. When their children are not learning at the expected level, they can hire tutors. Although many low-income parents are actively engaged in their children's education, the proportion of upper middle class parents involved is higher. They talk with teachers; they ensure that their children have the best teachers; they encourage their children to study and participate in extracurricular activities; and they monitor their children's performance. Low-income parents lack the same **cultural capital**. Their income does not permit them to support school activities in the same way.

A school may serve as a refuge for some urban students. However, some students have less than desirable classrooms and schools that do not provide maximum conditions for learning. Teachers in urban schools generally have less experience than suburban teachers and are not as likely to have majored in the subjects they are teaching (Darling-Hammond, 2010). When students are in overcrowded classrooms with teachers who do not know the content well and who have trouble managing the class, students may become less engaged in their academic work and drop out of school at higher rates than their peers in suburban and rural schools. Urban schools can be difficult for both students and teachers, as described in the "Perspectives on Diversity" feature.

Urban schools can be highly centralized, authoritative, and bureaucratic. However, communities are electing their own school boards in a number of urban school districts. Those with reform-minded leaders are reducing the bureaucracy, becoming more decentralized, and allowing parents more choice in their schools. However, in a few cities such as New York City and Washington, DC, mayors have taken over the management of their schools with the goal of reforming schools and improving student learning.

Magnet schools are popular in urban areas. Seven percent of the schools in the one hundred largest school districts are magnet schools or have magnet programs within a school, enrolling 11 percent of the students. Five percent of urban schools are charter schools, with the largest percentage in Albuquerque (21 percent), Milwaukee (21 percent), and large cities in Florida and California (Sable et al., 2010). Although research suggests that small class size is critical to improving learning in areas with students who are socially and economically disadvantaged (Leithwood & Jantzi, 2009), the average student-to-teacher ratio in urban schools is higher than in rural schools (Aud et al., 2011).

cultural capital The knowledge and ideas required to maintain or gain status and power in society.

PERSPECTIVES on DIVERSITY

Make Me Learn

Mr. Huang starts his Algebra I class even though only half of the students have arrived. When Jamal walks in ten minutes late, he sits at the back of the room and begins talking about last night's basketball game.

"Jamal, where's your homework?" says Mr. Huang.

"Ain't got it," he says as he turns back to his friends.

"How do you think you can pass this class without turning in your homework?" Mr. Huang returns to the problem on the blackboard. "Who can solve this equation?" he asks the few students who are listening.

Around the room, students are tuned into their iPods or talking to their neighbors. In the back of the room, they are arguing about whether LeBron James or Kobe Bryant is the best NBA player. Only two students hand in their homework, and most will be lucky to get a "D" at the end of the grading period.

Jamal walks over to the wall to check his average. It is under thirty. On his way back to his desk, he tells a friend, "No way he's gone to fail me. He knows I'll come after him. He's not keeping me from graduating."

Mr. Huang walks over to Jamal's desk to remind him that his mother asked Mr. Huang to tutor him after school. "Why haven't you met me after school? There's no way you can pass this class without some extra help. Let's start by putting away that iPod."

"No way, man. You can't tell me what to do. When I feel like it, I will meet you for tutoring. I don't have the feeling yet."

Another student in the back of the room jumps up, saying, "I'm tired of this. Anybody going with me," and starts out of the classroom.

"I'm with you," Jamal retorts as he leaves his seat and departs the room.

WHAT IS YOUR PERSPECTIVE?

1. Very little learning appears to be happening in this classroom. Why is Mr. Huang having such a difficult time handling the students in his classroom?

2. What strategies would you use to engage these eleventh graders in Algebra I?

3. The National Governors Association, the Gates Foundation, and others are calling for a major reform of high schools. What changes need to occur in urban schools like this one to develop an academic environment that promotes learning?

Source: Adapted from "Will Jonathan Graduate?" by L. O. Parker, November 11, 2007, *The Washington Post 130*(341), pp. A1, A16–A18.

SUMMARY

PURPOSES OF SCHOOLS

- Schools serve many purposes, including a student's development of knowledge and skills for academic proficiency, workforce involvement, citizenship, social development, and cultural transmission.

THE ROLE OF CULTURE IN SCHOOLS

- Culture determines the way we behave and think within society.
- People who live in the same country generally share a common culture that is incorporated into the policies and institutions of society, including schools.
- Families have their own unique cultural backgrounds based on their ethnicity, native language, and religion that may differ from the common culture.
- Schools have their own cultures with histories and traditions that affect the way students and teachers behave.

SCHOOL CHOICES

- Parents have the option to place their children in public or private schools or to homeschool them.

- Parents have a growing number of options within the public schools as the number of magnet, charter, and virtual schools increases.
- A few school districts allow qualified families to receive a voucher to enroll their children in private schools at public expense.

SCHOOL LEVELS

- Schools have been divided into four levels based on the age of students—prekindergarten, elementary, middle level, or high school—to meet the needs of children and youth.

THE SENSE OF PLACE: SCHOOL LOCATIONS

- The place in which we live affects our cultural identity and life experiences.
- Poverty is greater in central city and urban areas, but is growing in suburban areas.
- Schools in suburban areas—except those closest to urban areas—have greater financial support, and students perform at higher levels on achievement tests.

DISCUSSION STARTERS

1. Since the release of *A Nation at Risk* in 1983, the school curricula for early childhood education through high school have become standards based and the performance of students is assessed regularly. How did these changes contribute to the different roles of schools discussed in this chapter?

2. Students and families bring their cultures into the classroom. Teachers also bring to school their cultures, which may be different than that of their students. What problems can arise if teachers establish their own culture as the norm to be followed in the classroom? What cultural norms should guide a classroom in which students are culturally diverse?

3. Charter school advocates often indicate that state and district regulations are obstacles to good schools that help students learn. What regulations are they talking about?

How might those regulations prevent a school from being as effective as it could be?

4. Most states match the licenses that teachers receive to a specific subject or age level of students, which in turn matches the school levels discussed in this chapter. Why are teachers not generally granted a single license to teach students across the P–12 grades? What teachers can receive a license that crosses all of the grade levels?

5. The income status of students' families in central cities and rural areas are somewhat equal, but their schools are different in size, diversity, and culture. What obstacles to a good education may students face in these two different settings? What are the positive elements of their school locations that could contribute to a more effective education for students in those two areas?

SCHOOL-BASED OBSERVATIONS

1. Select a charter school in your area to visit. During your observations, identify characteristics of the school culture, students, teachers, and instruction that are similar to and different from the neighborhood schools that you have attended or observed. Record your observations in your journal or portfolio.

2. Visit two schools located in different communities (i.e., rural, suburban, or urban) and systematically record

characteristics such as the ethnic and racial composition of the students, the income level of families, the size of the student population and teaching force, the student-to-teacher ratios, the general school climate, and other observable characteristics. What appears to be working well at the schools? What appears to be problematic at the schools?

PORTFOLIO DEVELOPMENT

1. To develop an understanding of school culture and its role in the establishment of effective schools, record the characteristics of schools by using one of the following two approaches:

   a. When you visit a school, record the condition of the school, the characteristics of documents on the walls of the building, the type of instruction observed in classrooms, the reflection of students' cultures in the school, the mission of the school, and generally how students and teachers feel about the school. Also record the diversity of the school population, which is usually

available on the school's website, and how students are performing on state-required standardized tests, which is also available on the website. As you look at your observations and data, write a paper or newspaper article about how the school culture supports (or does not support) student learning.

   b. Review a selected number of the U.S. Department of Education's Blue Ribbon schools (**http://www2.ed.gov/programs/nclbbrs/index.html**) or the effective schools identified by the Education Trust (**http://www.edtrust.org/dc/resources/success-stories**). Write a report, newspaper article, or a blog about the school cultures of some of the schools that appear to be serving their students well, at least in terms of improving their academic achievement.

2. Some critics of charter schools worry that the establishment of charter schools will harm public schools. Write a paper on or blog about the strengths and disadvantages of charter schools. Include in your paper an analysis of the contributions charter schools could make to public schools and how you think their establishment is supporting or harming public schools.

WEB SOLUTIONS

To learn more about the schools and culture of the innovative schools in High Tech High and New Tech Network, visit their websites at **http://www.hightechhigh.org/** and **http://www.newtechnetwork.org/**. You will be able to tour schools, listen to students describe their experiences, and consider whether these are the types of schools in which you would like to teach.

How is your state reforming its education system through technology? Check your state's performance against the Foundation for Excellence in Education's ten elements of high quality digital learning at **http://digitallearningnow.com/nations-report-card/#VA**.

Check out the promoting power of your high school and the ones you are observing at **http://www.all4ed.org/promotingpower**.

MyEducationLab™ Go to the topic **Schools and Society** in the MyEducationLab (**www.myeducationlab.com**) for *Foundations of American Education: Becoming Effective Teachers in Challenging Times, 16e*, where you can:

- Find learning outcomes for **Schools and Society**, along with the national standards that connect to these outcomes.

- Complete Assignments and Activities that can help you more deeply understand the chapter content.

- Apply and practice your understanding of the core teaching skills identified in the chapter with the Building Teaching Skills and Dispositions learning units.

- Access video clips of CCSSO National Teachers of the Year award winners responding to the question, "Why Do I Teach?" in the Teacher Talk section.

- Create, update, and share quality lesson plans with the Lesson Plan Builder.

- Access state licensure test requirements, overviews of what tests cover, and sample test items in the Certification and Licensure section.

- Access current state and national standards in the Licensure and Standards section.

- Learn how to create a high-quality teaching portfolio in the Preparing a Portfolio section.

- Access tips, advice, and other information on resume writing and interviewing, your first year of teaching, and law and public policies in the Beginning Your Career section.

- Check your comprehension of the content covered in the chapter with the Study Plan. Here you will be able to take a chapter pretest, receive feedback on your answers, and then access personalized Review, Practice, and Enrichment exercises to enhance your understanding of chapter content. After you complete the exercises, take a posttest to confirm your comprehension.

Diversity in Society and Schools

LEARNING OUTCOMES

After reading and studying this chapter, you should be able to:

1. Design ways for incorporating race and ethnicity in your classroom so that students see their cultures in the curriculum and in your instruction. (InTASC 2: Learning Differences and InTASC 7: Planning for Instruction)

2. Identify the interaction of academic achievement and socioeconomic status and strategies for providing educational equity across economic groups. (InTASC 2: Learning Differences and InTASC 7: Planning for Instruction)

3. Contrast different instructional strategies for assisting English-language learners in learning English and the academic content that will help them achieve at levels necessary to improve their academic achievement. (InTASC 2: Learning Differences and InTASC 7: Planning for Instruction)

4. Analyze differences based on sex and gender that influence how girls and boys are treated and perform in schools. (InTASC 2: Learning Differences and InTASC 7: Planning for Instruction)

5. Discuss strategies for supporting lesbian, gay, bisexual, transgender, and queer (LGBTQ) students who are often harassed and bullied by other students in school. (InTASC 2: Learning Differences and InTASC 3: Learning Environments)

6. Articulate the need for providing appropriate accommodations in the classroom for students with disabilities. (InTASC 2: Learning Differences and InTASC 7: Planning for Instruction)

7. Characterize accurately the ways religion and religious beliefs can be addressed in schools. (InTASC 2: Learning Differences and InTASC 3: Learning Environments)

8. Develop strategies for creating a classroom that values the diversity of the student population and promotes high academic performance. (InTASC 2: Learning Differences and InTASC 7: Planning for Instruction)

EDUCATION in the NEWS

DIVERSITY CHALLENGES MANY AREA TEACHERS

Kokomo Tribune (IN) on July 5, 2011

The Kokomo-Center Schools student population includes 174 children whose first language was one other than English. The majority of its English-language learners, 111, speak Spanish, but others speak Mandarin, Arabic, Punjabi, Romanian, Persian, Tagalog, Russian, Urdu and a host of others.

Even with this polyglot of first languages, the Kokomo area is not seeing the same kind of growth in English-language learners that other areas of the state are seeing, according to 2010 census data.

Across the state of Indiana, the number of ELL students quadrupled over the last decade to nearly 50,000. That's a fraction of the state's 1.1 million K-12 students, but it is a segment with high need, with one ELL teacher to every 150 students.

In the Kokomo area, Southeastern School Corp. had the largest percentage of English-language learners, at 4 percent. Tri-Central Community Schools was second, at 3 percent. Taylor, Western, Kokomo-Center, Maconaquah, and Tipton had 1 percent ELL students, while Northwestern and Peru had less than 1 percent. Eastern-Howard Schools reported no English-language learners in 2010 census data.

Kokomo-Center Schools' public relations consultant, Dave Barnes, said 174 children qualified for the ELL designation in the 2010 to 2011 school year.

Nearly half of those students, eighty-five, are not counted as ELL students in the census data or by the Indiana Department of Education, however, because they are fluent in English and don't receive any special services with language.

Students must pass a fluency test two years consecutively to be considered fluent, and 85 of the 174 English-language learners have met that standard.

An additional sixty-two are in mainstream classrooms and receive some special instruction in English. About twenty-seven qualify for extensive language assistance.

Barnes said the number of English-language learners has been stable in the last five years, and the Kokomo-Center Schools have not experienced the growth in that population that the state has had.

Barnes said teachers do have to be aware of students who are in the regular classrooms but may have some difficulties with academic English.

"You just have to be aware, and especially when you have a written assignment, you may need to help them a little more with their grammar."

As an English teacher, he's provided a Spanish language copy of a novel he was teaching to a student who was fluent in English, but might miss the nuances because it wasn't his native language.

He had other students who carried a Mandarin/English translator, and when they would read a word they did not know, they could enter it into the translator for a definition.

"They were very intelligent kids. They would see it in Mandarin and say, 'Oh yeah, I understand,' and they could use it in a sentence in English once they understood."

For Spanish-speaking students, the school often tries to pair them up with an English-language native who also speaks Spanish, he said, and community members who speak Mandarin have also come in to help in translation, particularly for parent meetings.

Barnes said English-language learners must pass state assessments like native speakers, but can have some accommodations.

He added, though, that the students' parents can decline any language assistance, and those students still have to pass the assessments.

"The parents can decline any English language development, and there's not a thing we can do," he said.

QUESTIONS FOR REFLECTION

1. How different is the diversity in Kokomo, Indiana, from where you grew up? Why do you think those differences exist?
2. What are the challenges for teachers when immigrant students in their schools have a number of different native languages?
3. How would you categorize the instructional strategies that Mr. Barnes recommends to teachers for working with English-language learners?

Source: From *Kokomo Tribune* (IN), 2011. Reprinted with permission.

---

multicultural education An educational strategy that values diversity, promotes social justice, and provides equality to all students regardless of their race, ethnicity, socioeconomic status, gender, language, sexual orientation, religion, or ability.

race Classification of people by their skin color (e.g., black or white), other phenotypic characteristics, and ancestry.

gender The behavioral, cultural, and psychological traits typically associated with one sex.

ethnic groups Groups based on the national origin (that is, a country or area of the world) of one's family or ancestors in which members share a culture and sense of common destiny.

Multicultural education holds educators morally and ethically responsible to help all students learn, regardless of their socioeconomic status, ethnicity, **race**, language, **gender**, religion, sexual orientation, or ability. In multicultural education, teachers and administrators view all aspects of education—the curriculum, teacher and student interactions, staffing patterns, discipline, and extracurricular activities—through a multicultural lens to ensure that the needs of students from diverse groups are an integral part of the education process.

In multicultural education, diverse groups and multiple perspectives are integrated throughout the curriculum and school activities. The history and experiences of groups are studied throughout the school year. Multicultural education is not simply periodically adding information about diverse groups into a lesson because it is Black History or Women's History Month. It is more than being reminded of the experiences of others in highlighted sections of textbooks that discuss, for example, the internment of Japanese Americans during World War II, the struggles of labor unions in the coal mines of West Virginia, or an outstanding mathematician of color. In some schools, multicultural education begins and ends with sampling ethnic foods and participating in ethnic festivals. Although these activities contribute to a superficial understanding of differences, they do not help students understand the multicultural world in which they live.

This chapter will explore the groups to which your students and their families belong. Each section also discusses how a student's group memberships generally impact on the student's educational experiences. At the end of the chapter, we will examine ways to make your classrooms and schools multicultural.

RACE AND ETHNICITY

American Indian tribes and Alaska Natives are the only indigenous **ethnic groups** in the United States. Therefore, more than 99 percent of the U.S. population, or their ancestors, came from somewhere else at some time during the past five hundred years. The families of your students may identify with a country of origin, although the geographical boundaries may have changed since their ancestors emigrated. A growing number of people have mixed heritage, with ancestors from different parts of the world.

Although many people now identify themselves by their **panethnic membership** (for example, as African American or Asian American), race remains a political reality in U.S. society. It has become integrally interwoven into the nation's policies, practices, and institutions, including the educational, economic, and judicial systems. As a result, whites have advantages that are reflected in higher achievement on tests and higher incomes in adulthood. The issue of race encompasses personal and national discussions of affirmative action, immigration, desegregation, and a color-blind society. Race and ethnicity may be linked, but they are not the same. Both influence our cultural identity and status in society.

Having greater knowledge of the history and experiences of the diverse groups attending your school will improve your understanding of your students and their families. It also sends a message to families and communities that you care about them and their experiences.

Race

Race and gender are among the first physical characteristics we notice when we meet another person. However, race does not explain differences among people's behaviors, languages, socioeconomic standing, and academic achievements. Although race is no longer accepted as a scientific concept for classifying people, it has become a social construction for identifying differences.

Our ideas about race are created from experiences in our own racial group and with other groups. They are also informed by reflections of racial differences in the media. Race has become politicized and institutionalized in the policies and actions of judges, teachers, legislators, police, employers, and others who are in charge of institutions that affect people's lives. Our stereotyped views of race usually bestow positive attributes and high status on our own race and negative attributes or lower status on others.

Skin color is a signifier of race but does not capture its meaning. Many people have mixed racial backgrounds that place them along a continuum of skin color; they might not be obviously white, black, brown, or otherwise easily identifiable as one race or another. At one time, state laws declared a person's official race as nonwhite if a small percentage of his or her racial heritage was other than white. The official message was, and continues to be, that white is the ideal and that anything else, even small percentages of a race other than white, is less than ideal. This example is one of many ways in which race affects our everyday lives and becomes an integral part of our identity. Whether we like it or not, race continues to be used to sort people in society.

Persons of color usually identify themselves by their race or ethnic group and are usually identified as such by others. They are confronted with their race almost daily in encounters with employers, salespeople, and colleagues or as they watch the evening news. Whites, on the other hand, are seldom confronted with their race; in fact, many see themselves as raceless. White has become the norm against which persons of color are classified as *other*. As a result, many whites are unable to see how their race has privileged them in society. When you are unable to recognize racist policies and practices in the school or do not confront them, you may lose the trust and confidence of students of color. Being fearful to address race and racial disparities in your classroom and school will not serve your students well.

Ethnicity

The national origin of our family is the primary determinant of our ethnicity. We share a common history, language, traditions, and experiences with other members of our ethnic group that help sustain and enhance the culture of the group within the United States. Identity with our ethnic group is strongest when we maintain a high degree of interpersonal associations with other members of our group and share common neighborhoods.

Ethnic cohesiveness and solidarity are strengthened as members organize to support and advance the group, fight discrimination, and influence political and economic decisions that affect the group as a whole. In the 1960s, civil rights struggles led to calls for changes in schools, colleges, government programs, and employment to support equality across ethnic groups. During this period, African Americans, Hispanic Americans, Asian Americans, and American Indians called for recognition of their ethnic roots in the school curriculum. By the 1970s, southern and

MyEducationLab™
Visit the MyEducationLab for *Foundations of American Education* to enhance your understanding of chapter concepts with a personalized *Study Plan*. You'll also have the opportunity to hone your teaching skills through video- and case-based *Assignments and Activities* and *Building Teaching Skills and Dispositions* lessons.

panethnic membership
Ethnic membership based on national origin from a continent such as Africa, Asia, or Europe.

FIGURE 7.1   Panethnic and racial composition of the U.S. population in 2009.

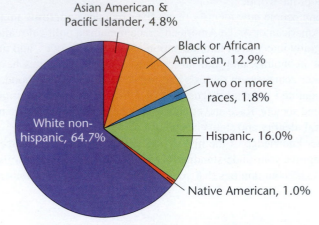

Asian American &
Pacific Islander, 4.8%

Black or African
American, 12.9%

Two or more
races, 1.8%

White non-
hispanic, 64.7%

Hispanic, 16.0%

Native American, 1.0%

Source: U.S. Census Bureau. (2011). *Statistical Abstract of the United States: 2012* (131st ed.). Washington, DC: Author.

eastern European groups had also joined this movement. Ethnic studies programs were established in colleges and universities and some high schools to study the history, contributions, and experiences of groups that had traditionally been excluded.

The U.S. Census Bureau reports population data on the racial and ethnic groups shown in Figure 7.1, but these broad classifications do not accurately describe the ethnic diversity of the country. For example, there are more than 500 American Indian tribes. Today, 2.4 million citizens identify themselves as American Indian or Alaska Native only. Another 2.6 million indicate they are partially Native American or Alaska Native (U.S. Census Bureau, 2011). The American Indian population identifies with one or more of the 565 tribal governments recognized by the federal government (Bureau of Indian Affairs, 2011). Some identify with a tribe that is not recognized. The Cherokee, Navajo, Choctaw, Sioux (that is, Dakota, Lakota, and Nakota peoples), and Chippewa have over 100,000 members each.

Most panethnic classifications include numerous ethnic groups with identities and loyalties linked to specific countries. Asian Americans include recent immigrants and people whose ancestors emigrated from countries as diverse as Afghanistan, India, Korea, Japan, and the Philippines. Hispanics include people from Mexico, Central America, Puerto Rico, Cuba, Spain, and South America. Although Africans continue to immigrate to the United States, most African Americans have long historical roots in this country; many have ancestors not only from Africa but also from Europe and American Indian tribes. European Americans range from western Europeans whose families may have lived in the United States for several hundred years, to those from eastern Europe whose families immigrated in large numbers during the first half of the twentieth century, to recent immigrants from Russia and other former Soviet countries. The largest number of European Americans identifies their ancestry as German (17 percent), Irish (12 percent), English (9 percent), Italian (6 percent), and Polish (3 percent) (U.S. Census Bureau, 2011). By 2050, European Americans will comprise less than half of the U.S. population (U.S. Census Bureau, Population Division, 2008).

JOURNAL FOR REFLECTION 7.1

- How do you characterize your ethnic and racial heritage?
- What has been the nature of your interactions with other groups?
- Have your experiences been positive or negative?
- How could you become more knowledgeable of individuals from ethnic and racial groups different from your own?

Immigration

The United States is often referred to as a land of immigrants who left their original homelands because of economic hardship or political repression. However, this picture is only partially true. The groups that have suffered most from discrimination are those who are indigenous or whose ancestors entered the country involuntarily. American Indians were here long before Europeans and others appeared. They suffered greatly as the foreign intruders took over the land and almost annihilated the indigenous population. Not until the year 2000 did the U.S. government admit to the near genocide of native peoples when the head of the Bureau of Indian Affairs apologized for "the agency's legacy of racism and inhumanity that included massacres, forced relocations of tribes and attempts to wipe out Indian languages and cultures" (Kelley, 2000).

The ancestors of most African Americans were brought involuntarily to America by slave traders as a commodity to be sold. They were not allowed to be citizens until 1868, and males were not granted the right to vote until 1870. Although some Africans had voluntarily immigrated before the Revolutionary War, the number of Africans who voluntarily immigrated was small until the last half of the twentieth century.

Latinos have a long history in North and South America and the Caribbean islands as a result of their ancestors being among the early European explorers. When the United States won the Mexican-American War in 1848, Mexican citizens were inhabitants of the southwestern lands that were annexed by the government. Today, more Mexicans immigrate legally to this country than any other group. Other Hispanics who have crossed the border to obtain jobs and have better opportunities for economic stability have been **unauthorized**, not possessing the appropriate papers to be in the United States. The number of unauthorized workers in the country has decreased since its high in 2007 as the inflow from Mexico has decreased and deportations have more than doubled (Passell & Cohn, 2011). Unauthorized workers and their families constantly face possible deportation, loss of everything they have gained in this country, and separation from their families. You may know students whose parents were arrested and deported while their children were in school. Children of unauthorized immigrants may worry that this scenario will happen to their families, which could lead to inattention and stress that affects their concentration and academic performance. Due in large part to the movement of families from Mexico into the United States, 13 percent of Latino students are foreign-born, and 62 percent of Hispanic students have at least one foreign-born parent (U.S. Census Bureau, 2011).

Chinese, Japanese, and Filipinos first came to the United States in the nineteenth century to provide labor needed on the West Coast for mining gold and building railroads. Early Asian immigrants were often seen as a threat to the dominant population, leading to severe restrictions on their immigration. The Chinese Exclusion Act of 1882 eliminated immigration from China for decades. During World War II, immigration from Japan was stopped, and Japanese American families were interned. Not until the Immigration Act of 1965 were Asian Americans allowed again to immigrate in any significant numbers.

Chinese Americans are the largest Asian ethnic group in the United States today with 3.3 million, followed by Asian Indians with 2.8 million. Other Asian ethnic groups in the United States today with more than a million people include Koreans and Vietnamese (U.S. Census Bureau, 2011). Asian American students are more likely to be foreign born (25 percent) and have one or more foreign-born parents (88 percent) than any other panethnic group (U.S. Census Bureau, 2011). The majority (64 percent) of Asian American students speak their native language at home, with Vietnamese, Korean, and Chinese being the most common languages (Aud et al., 2011).

Europeans from northern and western European countries comprised the major portion of immigrants to the United States in the first three centuries after Columbus arrived in the Americas. This pattern began to change in the 1800s. Between 1815 and 1920, 5.5 million Irish came to the United States. Later in the century, Jews came from Russia and Eastern Europe (Takaki, 1993). With the growing need for labor at the beginning of the twentieth century, companies recruited workers from southern and eastern Europe. More recently, the largest numbers of immigrants have come from the eastern European countries that were part of the former Soviet Union. Although most of the nation's white non-Hispanic students are not foreign-born, one in fifteen has at least one foreign-born parent (U.S. Census Bureau, 2011).

Schools are early recipients of new immigrants. More than one in five students has at least one parent who was born outside the United States (U.S. Census Bureau, 2011). Immigrants today are settling beyond the traditional urban areas in California, Florida, Illinois, New Jersey, New York, and Texas. States that have had limited ethnic diversity in the past are becoming home to students from other countries as immigrant families are sponsored by persons in these communities or settle in rural areas and towns of small-to-medium size because of jobs and values that are similar to their own. As a result, the school population is becoming more diverse at a faster rate than the population as a whole, as shown in Figure 7.2.

unauthorized Not holding legal papers for admission into countries of which you are not a citizen.

FIGURE 7.2   Race, ethnicity, and gender of students compared to the population in 2008.

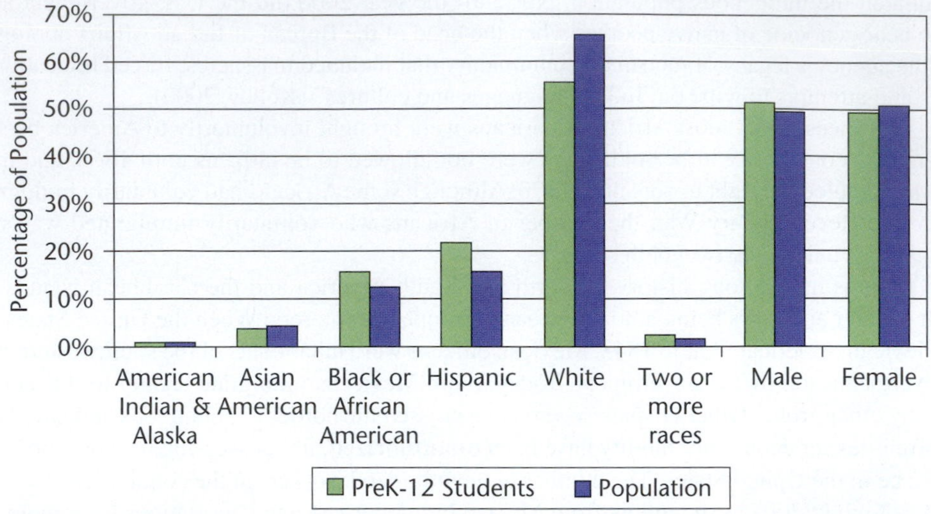

Source: (1) Aud, S., Hussar, W., Planty, M., Snyder, T., Bianco, K., Fox, M., Frohlich, L., Kemp, J., & Drake, L. (2010). *The Condition of Education 2010* (NCES 2010-028). Washington, DC: National Center for Education Statistics, Institute of Education Sciences, U.S. Department of Education. (2) U.S. Census Bureau. (2011). *Statistical Abstract of the United States: 2012* (131st ed.). Washington, DC: Author.

Racial and Ethnic Disparities in Education

Students of color who have a long history of inequitable treatment in society and the education system have closed the **achievement gap** with white students since the 1970s, but have not eliminated it (Barton & Coley, 2010). Although today's schools place a greater emphasis on academics for all students regardless of their race, ethnicity, gender, or socioeconomic status, students of color except for Asian Americans are not yet participating at the same levels as white students in higher level courses and programs, nor scoring at the same level on achievement tests. For example, African American student participation in advanced placement (AP) courses and performance on AP exams is far below that of other groups. Hispanic students are more likely to be in mathematics classes taught by teachers who have not majored in mathematics. The classes in which students of color sit generally have more students than other schools. They change schools more frequently than white students and have greater fear for their safety in schools. All of these factors have an effect on cognitive development and academic achievement (Barton & Coley, 2009).

The pattern of academic achievement for most students of color is similar to that of low-income students. The percent of white fourth-grade students scoring at the proficient level or above on National Assessment of Educational Progress (NAEP) tests of reading is more than twice that of Hispanic and African American students. The gap grows wider by the eighth grade and even wider by the twelfth grade. Although all students today are performing at higher levels on NAEP's mathematics test, the gap between whites and students of color is increasing (Barton & Coley, 2009).

SOCIOECONOMIC STATUS

Most people want "the good life," which in the United States includes a decent job, affordable housing, good health, a good education for their family members, and periodic vacations. **Socioeconomic status (SES)** is one measure for identifying a family's standard of living. Our family's SES also has a great impact on our chances of attending college and attaining a job that ensures material comfort throughout life. It is determined by one's occupation, income, and educational attainment. Wealth and power are other important factors that affect the way one is able to live, but these data are difficult to measure. We may be able to guess a family's socioeconomic status if we know such things as where they live, their jobs, the type of car they drive, the schools their children attend, and the types of vacations they take.

achievement gap The differences in academic achievement, especially as measured on standardized tests, among groups of students based on their race, ethnicity, socioeconomic status, native languages, sex, and exceptionalities.

socioeconomic status (SES) The economic condition of individuals based on their own or their family's income, occupation, and educational attainment.

Social Stratification

Most societies are characterized by **social stratification**, in which individuals occupy different levels of the social structure. Wealth, income, occupation, and education help define these social positions. However, high or low rankings are not based solely on SES criteria. Race, age, gender, religion, and **disability** can contribute to higher or lower rankings as well. Although members of most ethnic groups can be found at all levels of the socioeconomic scale in the United States, those from northern and western European backgrounds historically have been overly represented at the highest levels.

Social mobility remains one of the core values of the U.S. culture. We are told that hard work will lead to better jobs, higher income, and a better chance to participate in the good life. We read stories of individuals who were born in poverty but through hard work became wealthy as corporate presidents, successful writers, athletes, or entertainers. Although upward mobility continues to occur, the chances of moving from poverty to riches, no matter how hard one works, are low without interventions such as a college education and lots of good luck. Individuals who are born into wealthy families are likely to attend good schools, finish college, and find high-paying jobs (Hacker & Pierson, 2010; Page & Jacobs, 2009). They are raised with high expectations, have the economic resources to assist them in meeting these expectations, and usually end up meeting them.

Class Structure

Families are sometimes divided into distinct classes based on the economic level of their families. Individuals who do manual work for a living are sometimes described as "working class" or "blue-collar" workers. When farm laborers and service workers are included in the working class, this group represents 37 percent of the employed population (U.S. Census Bureau, 2011). Most members of this class have little control over their work. Some of the jobs are routine, mechanical, and not mentally challenging. Work sometimes is sporadic and affected by an economy in which employees face layoffs, replacement by computerized equipment and other advances in technology, part-time work, and unemployment as jobs move to locations with cheaper labor. Benefits such as vacation time and health plans are often limited. The education required for working-class jobs is usually less than that required for many middle-class positions, except for skilled and crafts workers who have had specialized training and may have served apprenticeships.

Most people who don't perceive themselves as poor or rich identify themselves as middle class. If we define middle-class families as those whose incomes fall in the third or fourth quintile of income earners in the United States, which would be 40 percent of the population, salaries can range from $38,551 to $100,000 (U.S. Census Bureau, 2011). It includes both blue-collar and professional or managerial workers. Families in this class have very different lifestyles at opposite ends of the income continuum. A $100,000 salary in a neighborhood where most families earn more than $250,000 seems low; in another neighborhood, a family making $100,000 would be considered well off.

The professionals, managers, and administrators in this group expect to move into the more affluent upper middle class as they progress in their careers with the goal of becoming one of the 11 percent of U.S. families earning more than $150,000 annually (U.S. Census Bureau, 2011). Professionals are men and women who have usually obtained professional or advanced degrees. They include teachers, lawyers, physicians, college professors, scientists, and psychologists. Excluding teachers, most of these families earn far above the median income of $60,088 (U.S. Census Bureau, 2011). Successful executives and businesspeople are the managers and administrators in this group. These workers usually have more autonomy over their jobs and working conditions than working- and lower-middle-class workers.

The upper class consists of wealthy and socially prominent families. The income and wealth of members of this class are far higher than those of the other classes, and the gap is growing. Protests such as Occupy Wall Street in 2011 brought attention to the high salaries earned by the top 1 percent that included corporate chief executive officers and Wall Street executives. The incomes of corporate chief executive officers have grown dramatically over the past thirty years. In 1980 they earned forty-two times as much as their employees; by 1990 they earned eighty-five times as much; and by 2010 the multiple had grown to 325 (Anderson, Collins, Klinger, & Pizzigati, 2011).

social stratification Levels of social class ranking based on income, education, occupation, wealth, and power in society.

disability An ongoing physical, mental, or emotional condition that can make it difficult for a person to perform activities such as walking, climbing stairs, dressing, bathing, learning, or remembering.

These great differences contribute to limited interactions with members of other classes. Children in this class rarely attend public schools, isolating them from peers of other social classes. The greatest assimilation of lifestyles and values probably occurs among members of ethnically and culturally diverse groups in the upper class.

Poverty

The U.S. government established a poverty index in the 1960s that indicated the income that would be used to determine poverty regardless of where the family lived, with the exception of Hawaii and Alaska. The 2012 federal guidelines set the threshold at an annual income of $23,050 for a family of four (U.S. Department of Health & Human Services, 2012). These poverty thresholds are set at about half the income needed to meet basic needs for housing, food, child care, and transportation (Fass, 2009). As a result, many families are above the poverty level, but still do not have an adequate income to purchase their basic needs. Many members of these low-income families work in full- or part-time jobs that pay such low wages they cannot pull their families out of poverty.

In 2009, 43.6 million persons (14.3 percent of the population) and 8 million families (10.5 percent of all families) earned incomes below the poverty-level threshold. The percent of blacks and Hispanics in poverty is double that of whites, which is at 12 percent (U.S. Census Bureau, 2011). The differences in poverty levels among groups are due to disparate education, incomes, and unemployment, which are affected by a history of discrimination against some groups. The median income of white families was $62,545 in 2009; African American and Hispanic families earned 61 percent and 64 percent of the income of white families, respectively (U.S. Census Bureau, 2011). Although this income disparity among groups decreases with two-income families with the same level of education, it does not disappear. Women who worked full-time in 2009 continued to earn less than men at about 80 percent of men's wages or salaries (U.S. Bureau of Labor Statistics, 2010).

Children, the elderly, and most persons of color suffer disproportionately from poverty. Over one in five U.S. children were in poverty in 2010 (Addy & Wight, 2012). The percent of U.S. children in poverty is almost double that of most other major industrialized nations, with only Chile, Turkey, Romania, Mexico, and Israel having a higher child-poverty rate (Organisation for Economic Co-operation and Development, 2011). Another 22 percent of the nation's children lived in low-income families above the federal poverty level. Thus, 44 percent percent of our children lived in low-income families, often making them eligible for free or reduced-price lunches in schools and special academic programs (Addy & Wight, 2012). As with adults, Hispanic, American Indian, and African American children are more likely than other children to live in poverty, as shown in Figure 7.3.

Children under the age of six are more likely to live in low-income families than older children (Addy & Wight, 2012). High-quality educational experiences can contribute to their

FIGURE 7.3 Children (birth to age eighteen) in low-income families by racial and ethnic group in 2010.

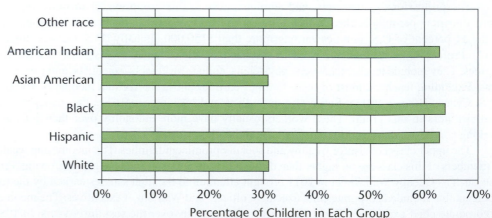

Percentage of Children in Each Group

Source: Addy, S., & Wight, V. R. (2012, February). *Basic Facts about Low-Income Children, 2010: Children under Age 18.* New York City: National Center for Children in Poverty. Retrieved April 12, 2012, from http://nccp.org/publications/pdf/text_1049.pdf. Reprinted by permission.

cognitive and social development in very positive ways. Programs that help parents develop their parenting skills have also been found to improve the academic achievement of students who are suffering from the harsh economic conditions in which their families live. Education programs—including Early Head Start, Head Start, and preschools for three- and four-year-olds—are being offered by a growing number of schools with low-income students.

Socioeconomic Status and Academic Achievement

Students whose parents have not finished high school do not perform as well on standardized tests as students whose parents have finished high school and college—factors that generally correlate with higher incomes (National Center for Education Statistics, 2009). Low-income students also do not perform as well on the National Assessment of Education Progress (NAEP) tests that are given annually to samples of fourth, eighth, and twelfth graders, as shown in Figure 7.4.

Factors outside of school contribute to the performance of students in school (Noguera, 2011). Students of color and students from low-income families are more likely to be exposed to environmental hazards such as lead and mercury. The chances of these students being hungry and eating nonnutritious foods are greater than for their more affluent peers. School factors that contribute to their lower academic performance include less access to certified and experienced teachers. They are more likely to have substitute teachers because teachers are absent more than in schools where the students are from higher income families. The turnover of teachers from year to year is also greater. These students also have less access to technology in their schools. During the summer, low-income students and students of color do not participate in education enrichment programs at the same rate as their classmates, limiting their chances to grow academically at the same rate (Barton & Coley, 2009).

Receiving a quality education is critical for low-income students to improve their chances of entering college and earning a middle-class income or above as adults. As a teacher, you should hold high expectations for the academic performance of these students (Torff, 2011) and ensure that they are learning the subjects that you are teaching. In your teacher education program, you should learn how to assess student learning and make adjustments to your instruction when students are not getting it. Understanding what students know when they enter your classroom and being able to draw on real-world experiences that are meaningful to your students will contribute to your being successful with low-income students.

GO TO ⋯›
More information about parenting and early childhood education programs can be found in Chapter 8.

FIGURE 7.4 **Performance on NAEP reading tests by family income*.**

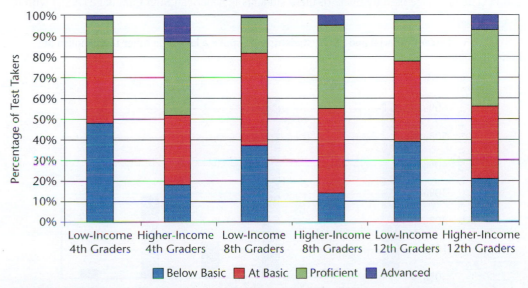

*Low income is defined as students eligible for free or reduced-price lunches.

Note: The data for 4th and 8th graders is from the 2011 administration of the NAEP tests whereas 12th graders last took the test in 2009.

Source: National Center for Education Statistics. (2011). *NAEP Data Explorer*. Washington, DC: Institute of Education Sciences, U.S. Department of Education. Retrieved on April 23, 2012, from http://nces.ed.gov/nationsreportcard/naepdata/dataset.aspx.

LANGUAGE

Language interacts with our ethnic and socioeconomic background to socialize us into linguistic and cultural communities. Children learn their native or heritage language by imitating adults and their peers. By age five, they have learned the syntax of their language and know the meanings of thousands of words. When cultural similarities exist between the speaker and listener, spoken messages are decoded accurately. But when the speaker and listener differ in ethnicity or class, miscommunication can occur. Even within English, a word, phrase, or nonverbal gesture takes on different meanings in different cultural groups and settings. The miscommunications between you and your students may be due to inaccurate decoding rather than the lack of linguistic ability.

Language Diversity

More than 57 million U.S. residents speak a language other than English at home (U.S. Census Bureau, 2011). Spanish is the language used most often, followed by Chinese, Tagalog, French, Vietnamese, German, Korean, Russian, and Arabic (U.S. Census Bureau, 2011). The native language is used in the homes of over half of the Hispanic and Asian American students, as shown in Figure 7.5. Depending on the community in which you teach, you also may find students who speak Haitian, Creole, Urdu, Swahili, or one of the hundreds of other native languages used by families in the United States. While the majority of the population whose native language is not English is fluent in English, you may have in your classroom new immigrant students who know little or no English and have very limited school experiences in their home countries. Only 5 percent of the nation's children have difficulty speaking English (Aud et al., 2011).

As immigrants assimilate into the common culture of the United States, their native language is often replaced by English within a few generations. The native language is more likely to be retained when schools and the community value bilingualism. As commerce and trade have become more global, professionals and administrators have realized the advantages of knowing a competitor's culture and language. They are encouraging their children to learn a second language at the same time that many of our educational policies are discouraging native speakers from maintaining their native language while learning English. The movement in some states for English-only usage in schools, in daily commerce, on street signs, and on official government documents highlights the dominance of English desired by some citizens. Ballot initiatives in Arizona, California, and Massachusetts have banned the use of students' native languages for instruction.

In addition to **English as a second language (ESL)**, your classroom may include a student with a hearing disability. Hearing disabilities affect 0.2 percent of the population (Aud et al., 2011). The language used by many of these students is American Sign Language (ASL) with its

English as a second language (ESL) An educational program for teaching English to speakers of other languages without the use of the native language for instruction.

FIGURE 7.5 Percent of racial and ethnic students who spoke a language other than English at home in 2009.

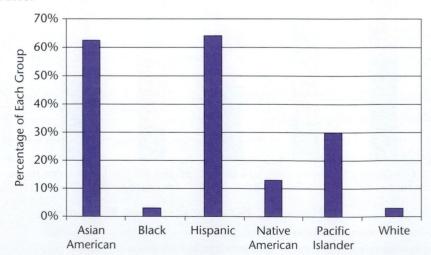

Source: Aud, S., Hussar, W., Kena, G., Bianco, K., Frohlich, L., Kemp, J., & Tahan, K. (2011). *The Condition of education 2011* (NCES 2011-033). Washington, DC: U.S. Department of Education, National Center for Education Statistics.

own complex grammar and well-regulated syntax. As with oral languages, children learn ASL very early by imitating others who use the language. To communicate with people without hearing disabilities, many individuals with hearing disabilities also use signed English, in which the oral or written word is translated into a sign. ASL is a critical element in the identity of people with hearing disabilities. The language can be more important to their identity than their membership in a particular ethnic, socioeconomic, or religious group.

Dialect Diversity

The majority of the population uses Standard English for official and formal communications. However, numerous regional, local, ethnic, and class (or SES) dialects are identifiable across the country. Each has its own set of grammatical rules that are known to its users. Although each dialect serves its users well, Standard English is usually viewed as more credible in schools and the work world. Although teachers may be bidialectal, they are expected to use Standard English as the example that should be emulated by students.

Many Americans are bidialectal or multidialectal in that they speak Standard English at work but speak their native or local dialect at home or when they are socializing with friends. Social factors have an influence on which dialect is appropriate in a specific situation. At one time, students were not allowed to use a dialect other than Standard English in the classroom. Some schools have proposed using the dialect of the community as a teaching tool, but such proposals usually have limited public support. Today, students are generally allowed to speak their dialects in schools but are encouraged to learn Standard English to provide them an advantage when they later seek employment.

Education for Language Diversity

The growing number of ELLs in U.S. schools calls for educators to understand language learning and how to help students learn English while they are learning mathematics, science, and other subjects. Differences between the languages used at home and at school can lead to dissonance among students, their families, and school officials. Many students who enter school with limited English skills are not only trying to learn a second language but also adjusting to a new culture.

Members of Congress, state legislators, and school board members regularly debate strategies for teaching English-language learners. The debate centers on whether to use students' native languages in instruction. One instructional program is **bilingual education**, which uses both English and the native language. Another program immerses English-language learners in English-only classrooms. Other programs bridge the two. Many school districts and some states require bilingual education if a specific number of students who speak the same native language are enrolled in a school. This approach requires teachers or teacher assistants who are fluent in both English and the native language.

No Child Left Behind (NCLB) called for ELLs to become English proficient and meet standards as measured by standardized tests. Voters in some states have passed state initiatives that limit language assistance to ELLs to one year. The problem with this approach is that research shows that one year of English instruction is generally not enough time to develop proficiency for academic success in classes taught only in English. The amount of time required for English proficiency depends on multiple factors such as age, prior schooling experiences, parents' education level, instruction provided, exposure to English, and teacher quality. For most ELLs, at least five years is required to develop language skills and academic achievement equal to that of native English speakers (Civil Rights Project, 2002). The result is that these students may fall further behind their classmates in conceptual understanding of the subjects being taught while they learn English.

FOUR POPULAR APPROACHES TO LANGUAGE INSTRUCTION. The four most popular approaches to language instruction funded under Title III of NCLB use English for instruction. They include (1) content-based English as a second language (ESL), (2) pull-out ESL, (3) sheltered English instruction, and (4) structured English immersion (Viadero, 2009).

Content-Based ESL and Sheltered Instruction. In content-based ESL and sheltered instruction, teachers teach the academic subjects at the same time they are teaching English to a group of

GO TO ⋯›
The impact of No Child Left Behind (NCLB) on other educational components is discussed in Chapters 1, 9, and 11.

bilingual education An educational program that uses English and the native language of students in classroom instruction.

students who could be from various language and cultural backgrounds. Sheltered instruction traditionally meant that only ELLs were in classes. Today, sheltered programs include classes for newcomers (that is, new immigrant students) as well as classes with both ELLs and English-speaking students.

Structured English Immersion. This approach is similar to the sheltered instruction approach, but all of the students in the classroom are **English-language learners (ELLs).**

Pull-Out Programs. These programs remove ELLs from their regular classroom to teach English. Teachers using these approaches should have knowledge and skills in teaching ESL (National Clearinghouse for English Language Acquisition, n.d.).

GO TO ··→
For a curricular perspective on teaching English-language learners, see Chapter 12.

English-language learners (ELLs) Students whose first language is not English and who are learning English at the same time they are learning the content specified in the curriculum standards.

Bilingual education uses both the native languages of students and English in classrooms to ensure that students learn the academic concepts being taught.

BILINGUAL AND TWO-WAY IMMERSION PROGRAMS. Language instruction programs that use students' native languages and English are used less often in the nation's schools. Between fifteen and thirty-one states report the use of dual language, transitional bilingual, two-way immersion, heritage language, or developmental bilingual programs (Viadero, 2009). The dual language or two-way immersion programs are the most popular. These classes, in which students develop proficiency in both the home language and English, are usually available at the elementary level and include an equal number of English speakers and speakers of the second language.

In transitional bilingual education, academic subjects are taught in the native language as students learn English. Gradually, more and more of the instruction is conducted in English. Developmental bilingual education, by contrast, supports bilingualism and literacy in both English and the native language. Both languages have equal status, and both are used for instructional purposes. The goal of heritage language programs, which are sometimes called Indigenous Language Programs, is literacy in English and the home language, especially for endangered languages (National Clearinghouse for English Language Acquisition, n.d.). In all of these programs, teachers should be fluent in both English and the second language.

Another type of immersion program uses a second language for instruction and helps students understand and appreciate a second culture while maintaining their own native culture and language. World languages immersion is designed for English speakers who want to learn a second language in a classroom that uses Spanish, French, Japanese, Farsi, or another language for instruction. Issues around students becoming competent in two languages are debated in the "Who Is Right?" feature. Two-way immersion is used to develop bilingualism in all students as language training is integrated with academic instruction. Classes usually have an equal number of English speakers and speakers of another language.

NEWCOMER PROGRAMS. Newcomer programs are designed to help immigrant students develop basic English skills, study core content areas, learn the common culture, and develop or strengthen their native literacy skills (Short & Boyson, 2012). These programs are designed for large numbers of new immigrants who have limited or no experience with English and often have limited literacy skills in their native language. They are sometimes found within a school, but some large school districts have one or more schools specifically for new immigrants.

WHO IS RIGHT?

SHOULD ALL STUDENTS BE BILINGUAL?

Many immigrant students enter school using a language other than English. The role of schools in teaching them English and encouraging the maintenance of their own native language has long been debated. Another side of the coin is the importance of native English speakers learning a second language so that they are fluent in at least two languages. This debate illustrates two teachers' perspectives on these issues.

YES

Douglas Ward is a bilingual learning disabilities resource teacher at William Nashold Elementary school in Rockford, Illinois. He is in his third year of teaching and is certified in bilingual special education and several other fields.

Yes, all students should be bilingual. Unfortunately, in the United States very few students become truly proficient in a foreign language. That is one reason for the shortage of foreign language and bilingual teachers.

Before the world wars, many immigrants in the United States used their native languages daily while they learned English. But the world wars and isolationist policies created a climate in which it was unpopular to speak anything but English. In some cities, fines were imposed on anyone caught speaking a foreign language in public business.

Many descendants of immigrants never learned their parents' or grandparents' native languages—in my case, Polish and German—because of these attitudes. My grandparents and parents, pressured by society, did not understand the importance of passing on their languages to me.

Learning a foreign language involves more than learning how to read, write, and speak. More important, it teaches students about a culture. Lack of understanding of cultural differences causes intolerance and war.

The people of the United States and the world need to be, not just tolerant, but accepting of other cultures. We need to embrace and celebrate our many cultures. Studying a foreign language and becoming bilingual opens one's mind to new thinking and creates new opportunities to communicate with other people.

Language can be the key to a lasting peace between enemies. Learning another language is the best way to make friends.

Students in many other countries learn at least one foreign language in their public schools. In the United States, few schools even offer a foreign language in elementary school.

As global businesses and trade expand, the need to know a second language is growing tremendously. Many businesses in other countries want to do business with us. Their salespeople speak English and know our customs. We need people who know other languages and cultures so that our exports will increase and our economy will become stronger.

Learning another language may also spill over into other areas. Research shows that bilingualism leads to cognitive advantages that may raise scores on some intelligence tests.

Studies also show a correlation between knowing two languages and linguistic abilities that may facilitate early reading acquisition. That, in turn, could boost academic achievement.

NO

Suzanne Emery retired last year after thirty-five years of teaching English and journalism, the last twenty-five at San Diego's Mira Mesa High School. She reviews questions for California's high school exit exam and edits the San Diego Education Association newsletter.

American education cannot be all things for all people.

We've agreed generally on the need to improve achievement in the basic curriculum. Bilingualism should not be added to the mix. Nor should it join all the other mandates that politically correct states and school districts impose: cultural holidays, parenting classes, good health activities, well-rounded social growth, adequate physical activities, proper nutrition, and suicide prevention.

A second language is always a luxury. It is needed only for the college bound and then only in certain majors.

We're told that European countries require two languages. But many European countries are very small, so bilingualism is a survival skill. And few other countries try to educate 100 percent of their children, as we do. In Europe, education is at the top of parents' priorities. Need we talk about the distractions here?

And what is the second language of bilingual children around the world? It is English. We need to educate our own kids for success in that universal language. Our schools can barely gather materials and teachers for the standard curriculum, let alone for another language.

If schools required a second language, what would it be? Spanish, Japanese, or French? How should we decide? What about all our students who speak Hmong, Farsi, or Tagalog? Would we mandate a third language for them?

Comfort in two languages is valuable in many venues and often desired for reasons of tradition. But families that want another language can do what they've always done: Saturday school, magnet schools, and temple classes.

(continued)

(continued)

If a district is so insular that it lacks the diverse quilt of contemporary America, its sterility and guilt should not be visited on the rest of the country.

So many American schools are like mine in San Diego where students regularly exchange videos with relatives in Vietnam, make the annual family pilgrimage to Mexico, edit the Islamic Center's youth newsletter, and produce pamphlets in graphic arts class for the Buddhist temple.

Here in California, with the nation's largest enrollment of newcomers, the challenge is to prepare all students for world-class competition, culminating with a high school exit exam in English, because English communication is key to success in academics and in adult life. That also applies to the rest of the country.

We cannot afford another diversion added to the overflowing plate of public education.

WHAT IS YOUR PERSPECTIVE ON THIS ISSUE?

Source: "Should All Students Be Bilingual?" *NEA Today* (May 2002), p. 11. Reprinted by permission of the National Education Association.

PARENT INVOLVEMENT. As a school decides the appropriate approach for teaching English-language learners, parents should be involved in the discussions and decisions. Together, educators and parents will have to decide whether they want to promote bilingualism among all students or only among the English-language learners. Is the goal for English-language learners to become competent in both English and their native language or to move into English-only instruction as soon as possible? Each approach has learning implications for students and cost implications for school systems.

GENDER

We are culturally different because of our biological sex and our gender, which is our feminine and masculine traits, even when we are members of the same socioeconomic, ethnic, and religious group. These differences are not just physical appearance. We segregate ourselves by gender at social gatherings, seek different types of jobs, and are expected to take on different family roles. We think and act differently in a number of settings and situations. We treat boys and girls and young women and young men differently in our classrooms. What is the cause of these differences? Some of them may be the result of biology, but others are based on the expectations of our culture and society. In this section we will explore these differences and similarities and their impact on student behavior and learning.

Differences Between Females and Males

Learning the gender of a baby is one of the important rites of parenthood. However, the major difference between infant boys and girls is the way adults respond to them. There are few actual physical differences, particularly before puberty. By age two, children realize they are a girl or a boy; by five or six, they have learned their gender and stereotypical behavior. In most cultures, boys are generally socialized toward achievement and self-reliance, girls toward nurturance and responsibility. Differences in the expectations and behaviors of the two genders may be rooted in their groups' ethnicity, religion, and socioeconomic status.

In schools, girls and boys perform differently in academic subjects and behave differently in the classroom. For years, boys outperformed girls in mathematics, and girls had higher scores than boys on reading achievement tests. However, these gaps between the two sexes are decreasing. For example, women are now majoring in mathematics in college at a higher rate than in the past, earning over 40 percent of the math degrees (National Center for Education Statistics, 2011). Differences in performance on achievement tests continue to narrow, although girls generally outperform boys on reading and writing achievement tests while boys score higher than girls on national assessments of mathematics (Aud et al., 2011). On tests for college admission, males perform at higher levels than females on both the critical reading and mathematics sections of the SAT although the gap on the verbal portion is small (U.S. Census Bureau, 2011).

FIGURE 7.6   Mean earnings of males and females working full time year-round in 2009.

Source: U.S. Census Bureau. (2011, September). *Income, poverty and health insurance coverage in the United States: 2009,* Current Population Reports, series P60-238, and Detailed Tables—Table PINC-04. Washington, DC: Author. Retrieved on April 23, 2012, from http://www.census.gov/hhes/www/cpstables/032010/perinc/new04_000.htm.

Some researchers attribute these gender differences to the development of specific hemispheres at the top of the brain. Females tend to have a well-developed left side of the brain, which is associated with verbal skills such as reading, speaking, and writing. The right side, which boys use more often, is associated with spatial skills of measuring and working with blocks or other objects (Eliot, 2009). Other researchers dispute the claim that differences are based primarily on biology (Eliot, 2009; Jordan-Young, 2010).

A major difference between males and females is how they are treated in society. Men are generally found in positions of superiority as evidenced by their disproportionate employment in the highest status and highest paying jobs, leading to inequitable earnings by women across their life span, as shown in Figure 7.6. Sometimes this relationship extends into the home, where the father and husband may both protect the family and rule over it. At times this relationship leads to physical and mental abuse of women and children.

Gender Equity in Education

Gender-specific behavior is sometimes stereotypically reinforced in classrooms. Girls are more likely than boys to be quiet, follow the rules, and help the teacher. Boys and young men tend to be rowdier and less attentive. Researchers who claim that sex differences are biologically determined find that classrooms are girl-friendly, ignoring the ways that boys learn (Cleveland, 2011). However, teachers may reinforce or counteract these stereotypical behaviors in appropriate ways to support learning for the two sexes.

The number of single-sex classes and schools has increased significantly since 1992 when the U.S. Department of Education allowed public funds to be used to support single-sex education. Some educators have found that academic achievement has improved for both girls and boys when they are in classrooms with students of the same sex. These schools may focus on developing the confidence, academic achievement, and leadership skills of young women or men by using the learning styles and cultural experiences central to their gender. Schools in some urban areas have been designed for African American young men to validate their culture and develop their self-esteem, academic achievement, and leadership capacities in order to confront the hostile environments they sometimes face in society. Although parents and educators may be encouraged by the classroom environment and performance of some students in single-sex classrooms, the research has not yet shown that they improve academic performance (Sadker, Sadker, & Zittleman, 2009).

Schools can play an important role in helping young women and men realize their potential. If gender **equity** existed, females and males would be expected to participate at nearly the same rates in academic courses. Let's look at some of today's realities. Girls are more likely to participate in AP courses and take AP tests (Handwerk, Tognatta, Coley, & Gitomer, 2008). They are

equity The state of fairness and justice across individuals and groups; it does not require the same educational strategies across groups but does expect equal results.

Title IX prevents discrimination in education programs based on gender. Schools must make provisions for girls and young women to participate in intramural, club, and interscholastic sports.

enrolling in mathematics courses, including higher-level courses, at about the same rate as boys (National Center for Education Statistics, 2007). Although girls are taking high school physics courses at the same rate as boys, only two in five of the college graduates in physical sciences are female (Aud et al., 2011). Females earn 17 percent of the bachelor's degrees in engineering and engineering technologies and 18 percent of the bachelor's degrees in computer science (Aud et al., 2011). On the other hand, girls are more likely to complete three or more years of foreign language than boys (National Center for Education Statistics, 2007). They take biology courses at a slightly higher rate than boys, earn about the same number of doctorates in biological sciences, and are almost 80 percent of new veterinarians (Aud et al., 2011). To promote gender equity, females should be encouraged to become involved in mathematics, science, and computer science. Males should be encouraged to participate in areas in which they are underrepresented: the fine arts, foreign languages, advanced English, and the humanities.

A gender-equitable education does not mean that all students are always treated the same. Different instructional strategies may be needed for the two groups to ensure participation and learning. Understanding cultural differences among females and males is important in developing appropriate teaching strategies. Not all girls and young women respond to instruction in the same way. Their other group memberships intersect with their gender in determining their interactions with teachers and effective instructional strategies. Multicultural teaching affirms students' gender and experiences in ways that promote learning for both males and females.

Teachers in gender-sensitive classrooms monitor interactions among girls and boys as well as their own interactions with the two genders. They intervene when necessary to equalize opportunities between them. If boys are not performing as well as girls in language arts or if girls are not performing as well in mathematics, the challenge is to develop approaches that will improve all students' performance.

Title IX

Title IX of the 1972 Higher Education Amendments is the major legislation that addresses the civil rights of girls and women in the education system. It requires federally funded colleges and schools to provide **equal educational opportunity** to girls and women. Title IX has been credited for increasing the number of girls and young women participating in college preparatory courses, completing professional degrees in college, and participating in sports. In the year that Title IX passed only 7 percent of law degrees were earned by females as compared to 46 percent in 2009. Eight percent of the medical degrees and 13 percent of the doctorates were awarded to females in 1970, but by 2009, women received 49 percent of all medical degrees and 52 percent of all doctorates (Aud et al., 2011).

Participation in sports is associated with higher levels of family satisfaction. However, many families report that their daughters do not have the same opportunities to participate in organized sports at school as their sons (Sabo & Veliz, 2008). Although Title IX has led to a dramatic increase in the number of females involved in sports, providing them equal opportunities has been the most controversial part of Title IX. It requires the percentage of male and female athletes to be substantially proportionate to the percentage of males and females in the student population. In addition, the school must have a history and continuing practice of expanding opportunities for the underrepresented gender to participate in sports. Even if a school is not meeting the proportionate expectation, the school must be fully and effectively meeting the interests and abilities of the underrepresented gender (Staurowsky, Hogshead-Makar, Kane, Wughalter, Yiamouyiannis, & Lerner, 2007).

equal educational opportunity Access to similar education for all students regardless of their gender, cultural background, or family circumstances.

The number of girls and women participating in sports has increased dramatically since Title IX was passed. Fewer than 300,000 girls participated in high school sports in 1972 compared to more than 3 million high school girls now participating (National Federation of State High School Associations, 2011). The number of women participating in college sports has increased from 32,000 to more than 184,000 (Zgonc, 2010). Although access to school sports is similar for girls and boys in many communities, a gap exists in low-income and urban schools where fewer girls participate in athletics and physical education (Staurowsky et al., 2007).

SEXUAL ORIENTATION

Although the common understanding among the research community is that sexual orientation is not chosen (Ost & Gates, 2004), some cultural and religious groups believe that homosexuality is a choice of lifestyles. These groups place high value on heterosexuality and denigrate or outlaw homosexuality as part of their religious doctrine or community mores. Heterosexuality has long been the norm against which sexual identity is measured, and, to many people, the only acceptable sexual orientation. These different perspectives about sexual orientation are reflected in state and national discussions about civil unions and marriage among gays and lesbians. They are also reflected in schools that may ban holding hands or attending proms with a same sex partner. Lesbian, gay, bisexual, transgender, and queer students are harassed in their schools and communities. How will you handle issues related to sexual orientation when they arise in your classroom or school?

Sexual Identity

Unless teachers or students are **LGBTQ**, they may have limited knowledge about sexual identities other than heterosexual. They know they are expected to date a person of the opposite sex, get married, and have children. To do otherwise would disappoint their families. To be LGBTQ could be devastating to a family who thinks sexual orientation is a choice made by their child or that any orientation other than heterosexuality is wrong. A number of groups—such as the Gay, Lesbian and Straight Education Network (GLSEN) and Parents, Families, and Friends of Lesbians and Gays (PFLAG)—help families and teachers to be supportive of LGBTQ family members and friends. However, many LGBTQ students do not have supportive families or friends and sometimes are either thrown out of their homes or harassed to a level that leads them to choose to leave home. As a result, they comprise the largest number of homeless youth on the nation's streets.

Based on the study of the sexual behavior of the adult population by Alfred Kinsey in the 1940s and 1950s, 90 percent of the population was projected to be exclusively heterosexual. More recent data indicate that 3.5 percent of the population identifies themselves as LGBT (Keen, 2011). What terms describe the sexual orientations of the population? Heterosexual refers to being sexually attracted to members of the opposite sex. Lesbians are women who are sexually attracted to other women; gay men are sexually attracted to other men; and bisexuals are sexually attracted to both sexes. Transgender refers to people whose biological sex (i.e., male or female) does not match their psychological view of themselves. It is a biological male who feels like a female or a girl who identifies herself as a boy. Some transgender people cross-dress to look and behave like the opposite sex; others have surgery to alter their physical gender characteristics.

The "Q" in LGBTQ refers to questioning or queer. "Queer" is a political term that challenges the status quo and rejects assimilation into the dominant society. Some members of the LGBTQ community remember queer as a derogatory term used against them in the past and do not use the term to identify themselves. Questioning individuals are unsure about their sexuality or are not ready to accept a predetermined label (Savage & Harley, 2009). Many youth do not accept the current labels for their sexual orientation and continue in blogs and other forums to identify themselves differently.

Supporting LGBTQ Students

Harassment of LGBTQ students at school is far too common. GLSEN's National School Climate Survey found that two in five LGBT twelve- to twenty-one-year-old students had been pushed or shoved at school. Nine in ten of these students hear "that's so gay" or other negatives uses of

LGBTQ Term used to refer to lesbian, gay, bisexual, transgender, and queer individuals or issues.

GO TO ⋯

See Chapter 8 for more discussion of sexual harassment.

the word "gay" by their peers. Three in four report being called a faggot or dyke. Harassment is not always face-to-face—over half of the students in this study were harassed or threatened by classmates through text messages and postings on the Internet (Kosciw, Greytak, Diaz, & Bartkiewicz, 2010). It is not only LGBTQ students who are victims of this harassment; students who are perceived as gay, whether or not they are, are also targets of these comments. The suicides of a number of students who have been harassed have received media attention, which has helped bring the seriousness of the harassment to the attention of the public.

LGBTQ students also experience invisibility and isolation in school (Savage & Harley, 2009). They do not generally see positive images of themselves—if they are discussed at all—in textbooks or the curriculum. The school and public library may have been stripped of books and other information on LGBTQ issues. They do not learn that different sexual orientations are normal in a society (American Psychological Association, 2008). They have no place to turn for information on their sexuality other than the Internet.

Educators must be aware of students' safety. A number of court cases have reinforced the need for schools to become intolerant of the harassment of LGBTQ students. Such a strategy will require teachers to intervene when students are verbally or physically harassing each other. A growing number of states and schools are developing policies for treating all students with equal respect and dignity that explicitly indicate the **inclusion** of LGBTQ students.

The link between student engagement and academic success applies to all students. When LGBTQ students do not attend school in order to avoid the expected harassment, they are not engaged. Their grades drop, and they are more susceptible to dropping out of school. They are more likely than their heterosexual peers to engage in high-risk sexual behaviors or drug and alcohol abuse (Meyer, 2010). Educators could more proactively include LGBTQ people in the curriculum and be open about acknowledging the contributions of LGBTQs to society. Educators can also provide an environment that promotes the healthy development of LGBTQ students. Students report that they feel safer in schools with a student-initiated Gay-Straight Alliance club (Kosciw et al., 2010).

EXCEPTIONALITIES

More than 54 million people, or nearly 20 percent of the population over six years old, have a disability; 12 percent of the population has a severe disability (Brault, 2008). Some people are born with a disability. Others develop a disability as they age or have an accident or illness that leads to a disability. Older people are more likely to have disabilities, with half of the population over age sixty-five having a disability (Brault, 2008). The 13 percent of the public school population who receive special education services have the disabilities listed in Figure 7.7. In addition, approximately 7 percent of the student population is classified as gifted and talented (Gollnick & Chinn, 2013).

FIGURE 7.7   **Public school students served under the Individuals with Disabilities Education Act (IDEA) by disability in 2008–09.**

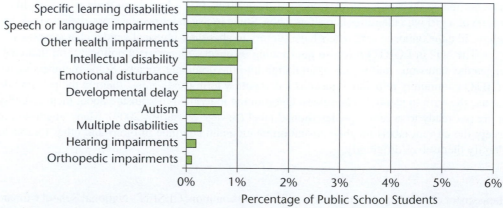

Source: Aud, S., Hussar, W., Kena, G., Bianco, K., Frohlich, L., Kemp, J., & Tahan, K. (2011). *The Condition of Education 2011* (NCES 2011-033). Washington, DC: U.S. Department of Education, National Center for Education Statistics.

inclusion The integration of all students, regardless of their background or abilities, in all aspects of the educational process.

Some educators make a determination about the potential of students with disabilities as early as kindergarten, which can lead to low academic expectations for students who could perform at high levels if appropriate accommodations were made for their disability. At this point their academic performance lags behind their peers. Only 57 percent of the students with disabilities are earning a high school diploma, although another 15 percent of them receive a certification of attendance (Planty et al., 2008). Students with disabilities are 11 percent of the undergraduate population and 8 percent of the enrollment in graduate and first professional degree programs (U.S. Census Bureau, 2011). Dropout rates for this population are relatively high. Persons with disabilities are disproportionately underrepresented in the labor force—sometimes because they are unable to go to work, but more often because the workplace has not made the accommodations that would make it possible for them to work productively.

Persons without a disability may react with disdain toward individuals with disabilities, viewing them as inferior. But like all other individuals, people with disabilities want to be recognized as persons in their own right. They have the same needs for love and the same desire to be as successful as persons without disabilities. However, society has historically not accepted them as equals. Some individuals with severe disabilities are placed in institutions out of the sight of the public. Others are segregated in separate schools or classes. Too often they are rejected and made to feel inept and limited in their abilities. As educators, we should be helping students with disabilities develop their academic potential and skills for college and employment. This goal will require overcoming the prejudice and discrimination that many of these students face in school and in their communities.

Inclusion

Historically, inclusion referred primarily to the integration of students with disabilities in general education classrooms. Today it is used more broadly to define the practice of fully integrating all students into the educational process, regardless of their race, ethnicity, gender, socioeconomic status, religion, physical or mental ability, language, or sexual orientation. Ideally, all students see themselves represented in the curriculum as well as in classes for the gifted.

As students with disabilities or giftedness are integrated into classrooms, collaboration is required among the adults, including parents, who work with these students. You should not be expected to serve as both the teacher and special education specialist. Ideally, teachers of general education collaborate with a special education resource teacher, a teacher's aide when needed, and appropriate specialists such as a speech/language pathologist, occupational therapist, physical therapist, vision specialist, adaptive physical education teacher, school psychologist, or school nurse. As a member of the team, you are expected to individualize instruction by following each student's **individualized educational plan (IEP)**. At times, students with disabilities may be pulled out of the classroom for special services, but these special sessions should be limited and should be used only to meet complex individual needs.

Following Congress's passage in 1975 of Public Law 94-142, which later became the Individuals with Disabilities Education Act (IDEA), the number of students with disabilities in regular classrooms grew dramatically. By 2008-09, 95 percent of children and youth with disabilities were in those classrooms for part or all of the school day. Five percent of them were in separate special education schools, in residential facilities, at home, or in a hospital. Many teachers have not been prepared to work effectively with students with disabilities and often do not know the accommodations that should be provided to support their learning. An example of the challenges you may face in an inclusive classroom is described in the "Teaching in Challenging Times" feature. It is quite likely that you will have a number of students with disabilities in your classroom during your career. How could you prepare yourself to provide them the equitable education they deserve?

One of the goals of inclusion is to provide students with disabilities the same opportunities for learning academic content to which others are exposed. Most students with disabilities can achieve at the same levels as their peers without disabilities, but they may require accommodations that allow them to access the content, the instruction, and the tools for learning. These accommodations may require physical changes in the classroom, such as increasing the height of a desk so that students in wheelchairs have a work space. It may require the provision of computers for students who cannot hold or control a pencil. It may require books in Braille or the use of sign language and taped books.

GO TO ⋯›
Dropouts are discussed in greater detail in Chapter 8.

To see how an IEP helps guide instructional planning for one student, click on the video *Reviewing an IEP.*

individualized education plan (IEP) A program designed to meet the needs of a child eligible for special education services. The plan helps educators understand the child's disability and provides directions for the services to be provided by teachers and other school professionals.

TEACHING IN CHALLENGING TIMES

Inclusion of Students with Disabilities

Over time, classroom teachers have been given increased responsibility for making sure the needs of a child with an IEP are met in their classroom. Although a child may enter the classroom with an IEP requiring support from special educators, ultimately and legally it is the teacher's responsibility to make sure the IEP is implemented in the classroom. It is also the teacher's responsibility to handle any behavior or social difficulties that may occur in the classroom. Furthermore, the teacher must work with special educators to adapt lessons and assignments to the ability level of all students. Teachers must promote success for all learners rather than expecting failure.

Picture yourself as a teacher in an inner-city second-grade classroom. You have twenty-five students from low-income homes and several children for whom English is their second language. Among these students are three children with IEPs and four learners who are making limited academic progress but do not qualify for special education services.

The three children with IEPs have varied needs. One child is a girl in a wheelchair with physical needs requiring a nurse to accompany her in the classroom. Another child is an eight-year-old boy who was born with Down syndrome. He too has multiple needs, including speech/language therapy, occupational therapy to work on his fine-motor skills, and a behavior plan monitored by the school psychologist. The third child has attention deficit/hyperactivity disorder (ADHD). His academic skills lag behind by a full year below grade level, and his attention span is minimal during periods of instruction.

In addition to these three children with IEPs, four children are reading at the first-grade level. Although these children are obviously having difficulties with reading, writing, and spelling, they do not currently qualify for special education services because their performance level is not two standard deviations below their intelligence quotient–derived ability level.

Unfortunately, there is no reading specialist in your school to help teach the learners performing below grade level. Furthermore, the special education teacher is only required to provide direct services to the students with IEPs for two hours a week. A special education assistant has been assigned to assist with the children with IEPs in your classroom, but her time is split between all six first- and second-grade classes in your school building, so you are lucky to have her assistance on a daily basis. If the special educator or assistant is out for any reason, a substitute is rarely provided.

WHAT ARE MY CHALLENGES?

1. What would you do to include the student in the wheelchair in as many classroom activities as possible and to encourage social interactions with her peers?

2. What would you do to make sure the child with Down syndrome is accepted and included by his peers?

3. What would you do to differentiate instruction to meet the needs of the children who aren't reading at grade level but do not receive special education services?

Researchers are finding improved student outcomes for students with disabilities who are in inclusive classrooms. Students without disabilities also receive positive benefits. Inclusion helps them become more tolerant of others, appreciate diversity, and be more responsive to the needs of others (Lipsky & Gartner, 1996).

Disproportionate Placements

GO TO ··>
A curriculum perspective on teaching students with disabilities can be found in Chapter 12.

The Individuals with Disabilities Education Act (IDEA) requires that students with disabilities be provided a free and appropriate public school education. African American students, English-language learners, and students from low-income families are more likely than their peers to be in special education classes. Students labeled intellectually disabled or emotionally disabled are disproportionately from low-income families. This pattern is also found in the placement of males and students of color in special education and gifted classes: African American and American Indian students, like males in general, are overrepresented in these disability categories (Gollnick & Chinn, 2013). At the same time, Hispanic, African American, and American Indian students are underrepresented in gifted and talented programs. You will need to monitor the reasons for your referrals of students to be tested for placement in these classes to ensure that you are providing equity in the delivery of education services.

Disproportionate placements of students in special education and gifted education programs may be due to a number of factors. Tests used for placement may be biased against low-income students, English-language learners, and students who have not assimilated into the common culture. Some educators who recommend students for special programs are intolerant of cultural differences and do not want students in their classes who they believe will disrupt the classroom. Schools should monitor recommendations and placements to find out if students from some groups are being disproportionately placed in these special programs and take corrective action if needed.

Response to Intervention

The regulations for the IDEA, which was reauthorized by Congress in 2004, promote the Response to Intervention (RTI) instructional model for identifying special education students. A growing number of early childhood and elementary teachers link lessons with frequent monitoring to identify students who may need special education services. RTI is a multitiered screening system that allows teachers to determine whether students are learning, using interventions as necessary. The first two tiers are instruction for all students in general education. The next tier is generally small-group instruction for students who are having difficulty learning. The final tier is individualized instruction for students who need a more intensive level of instruction. Students in the last tier may be eligible for special education services (Council for Exceptional Children, n.d.). The RTI screening process is replacing other procedures that have been used in the past to identify special education students.

RELIGION

Religion can have a great influence on the values and lifestyles of families and can play an important role in the socialization of children and young people. Religious doctrines and practices often guide beliefs about the roles of males and females. They also provide guidance regarding birth control, marriage, child-rearing, friendships, and political attitudes.

By age five, children are generally able to identify their family's religious affiliation. Although 64 percent of the population reports that religion is an important part of their daily life, less than half attend a religious service on a weekly basis (Newport, 2009). However, strong religious perspectives are reflected in the daily lives of many families.

Religious Identity

Religious pluralism flourishes in this country. With the influx of immigrants from Asia, Africa, and the Middle East during the past few decades, religious diversity among the population has increased further as greater numbers of families practice non-Western religions such as Islam, Hinduism, and Buddhism. Other families declare themselves atheists or simply do not participate in an organized religion. Some individuals and families live in religious cults that are established to promote and maintain a religious calling. Some religious groups believe that their religion is the only correct and legitimate view of the world. Other groups recognize that religious diversity has grown out of different historical experiences and accept the validity of diverse groups. At the same time, every major religion endorses justice, love, and

 To see how classrooms can accommodate students' religious identity, watch this **video.**

Public schools cannot advance a religion, but neither can religion be ignored in the curriculum. Diverse religious beliefs should be acknowledged and respected in classrooms and schools.

FIGURE 7.8   **Self-described religious diversity of the adult U.S. population in 2008.**

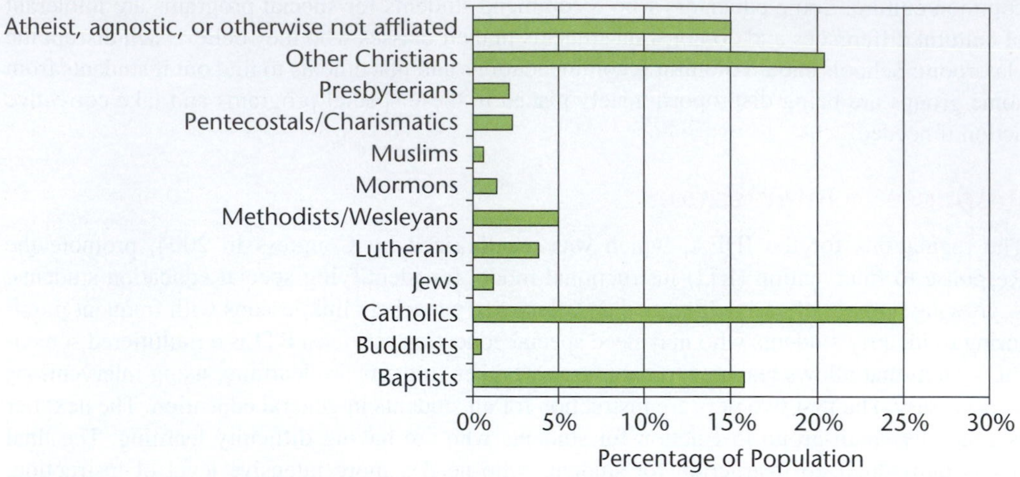

Source: U.S. Census Bureau. (2011). *Statistical Abstract of the United States: 2012* (131st ed.). Washington, DC: Author.

compassion as virtues that most individuals and nations should try to achieve. Most Western religions are compatible with the values of the common culture; they also usually promote patriotism and emphasize individual control of life.

Three in four adults in the United States identify themselves as Christian; 4 percent identify themselves as Jews, Buddhists, Muslims, or members of other world religions; and 16 percent are atheists, antagonists, or otherwise unaffiliated with a religious faith (U.S. Census Bureau, 2011). Although they are not as dominant as earlier in U.S. history, Protestants comprise over half of the population and Catholics 25 percent of the population. Within each of the major religious groups, distinct denominations and sects have the same general history but may differ greatly in their beliefs and perspectives on the correct way to live. The churches that serve the largest percentages of the Christian community are shown in Figure 7.8 along with the other world religions with the largest memberships in the United States.

For many people, religion is essential in determining their cultural identity. Some religious groups, such as the Amish and Hutterites, establish their own communities and schools to maintain their religion, foster mutual support, and develop group cohesiveness. Members of religious groups promote primary relationships and interactions with other members of the same faith. Most social activities are linked to religion, and institutions have been developed to reflect and support their religious beliefs. In many rural areas, the church is the center of social and community activities.

Religion in Schools

Learning to read the Bible and applying its moral lessons were the foundation of early public schools. Gradually the Bible was removed from public schools as the curriculum became more **secular**. However, Bible verses were still being read or prayers being said to open school days in some public schools well into the twenty-first century.

The First Amendment indicates that "Congress shall make no law respecting an establishment of religion, or prohibiting the free exercise thereof." Many court cases during the past century have helped to sort out the application of this section of the amendment to schools. Families are generally satisfied with schools when the schools reflect the values that are important in their religion. But they may attack schools when the curriculum, assigned readings, holidays, school convocations, and graduation exercises are perceived to be in conflict with their religious values. Court cases have addressed the teaching of evolution, religious clubs in schools, the Pledge of Allegiance, citing of the Bible, religious holidays, school prayer, and teaching about religion. Other cases address teachers' religious-liberty rights when teachers have been released from their jobs because they have been promoting their own religious ideas in their classrooms or because students think that a teacher is denigrating their religion while teaching.

secular Not based on nor related to religion.

There are many misperceptions about how religion can be addressed in public schools. Educators cannot say prayers or require students to pray in public schools. However, students can pray in school as long as it is not disruptive and doesn't infringe on the rights of others. Teachers can teach about religion, but they cannot privilege a religion, promote their religious faith, nor denigrate the beliefs of religious groups or non-believers. The Equal Access Act of 1984 allows students to establish religious clubs in secondary schools if other clubs exist at the school.

The Pew Forum on Religion & Public Life (2010) reports that we have little knowledge about religions other than our own. This religious illiteracy may contribute to the growing intolerance among groups, including **anti-Semitic** and **Islamophobia** hate crimes (Haynes, 2012). The teaching of religions may be helpful in improving our tolerance of our neighbors from religious and faith traditions different from our own. Religions are included in national and state standards for social studies as well as textbooks. Public schools can offer courses on world religions or other religious studies.

GO TO ···>
Legal issues about religion in schools are discussed in Chapter 10.

JOURNAL FOR REFLECTION 7.2

- How has your religious background had an influence on your perceptions of persons with other religious beliefs?
- How will you respond if the school district in which you teach asks you to teach something that is against your religious beliefs?

MULTICULTURAL EDUCATION

Diversity, **social justice**, and equality provide the foundations for multicultural education. However, multicultural education does not have universal acceptance. It has been the subject of public and academic discussion during the past fifty years. Editorials, national news programs, radio talk shows, and debates among college students and faculty periodically focus on the importance of diversity in society and the school curriculum. Campaigns for political office include debates about immigration, provision of services to unauthorized workers and their children, English-only policies, affirmative action, women's health, and gay rights. Simply put, the perspective of one side is that the recognition and promotion of diversity will strengthen the nation. The other perspective views the promotion of diversity as dividing the nation and leading to greater conflict among groups. This second perspective also argues that the Western tradition is denigrated when diversity and multiple perspectives are highlighted.

Multiculturalists argue that multicultural education will help unify a nation comprised of numerous ethnic groups who have long faced discrimination. They believe that individuals should have the opportunity to learn more about one another and to interact on an equal basis in schools and society. They also believe that members of diverse groups can maintain their diverse history, traditions, and cultures while developing together a common civic culture. An outgrowth of these debates has been the establishment of general education requirements for ethnic, women's, and global studies in colleges and universities. Most states also expect teacher education candidates to study diversity and to be able to incorporate it into their teaching. Most of the developing state and national standards for preschool through college curricula include references to diversity.

Students in some schools are from the same racial, ethnic, and socioeconomic group. They have little exposure to the racial, language, and religious diversity or the multicultural reality of the country as a whole. Even with limited ethnic and racial diversity, most schools have males and females with different sexual identities and from different religious and socioeconomic backgrounds. The ethic of social justice is just as important in these settings as in those with greater ethnic and language diversity. To provide a well-rounded and balanced curriculum for these students, you may need to work harder at bringing different perspectives to presentations and discussions. You probably will need to develop innovative strategies for providing direct exposure to diversity and issues of equality. Technology could be used to connect your students to students in other parts of the country or world. They can explore other groups and perspectives on the Internet or social networking outlets.

Listen to the way two different teachers discuss the importance of multicultural education to student learning as well as self-esteem in this **video.**

anti-Semitic Prejudice or discrimination against Jews.

Islamophobia Hatred of persons who practice or identify with the Islam religion or who live in or have immigrated from countries that are primarily Muslim countries.

social justice Concept of society in which justice for all people is valued and society's benefits are shared equally.

Classrooms and schools that are multicultural are models of democracy and equity. This effort requires educators to:

1. Place the student at the center of the teaching and learning process.
2. Promote human rights and respect for cultural differences.
3. Believe that all students can learn.
4. Acknowledge and build on the life histories and experiences of students' group memberships.
5. Critically analyze oppression and power relationships to help students understand racism, sexism, classism, and discrimination against persons with disabilities, gays, lesbians, the young, and the aged.
6. Critique society in the interest of social justice and equality.
7. Participate in collective social action to ensure a democratic society. (Gollnick & Chinn, 2013)

Although you should begin to grapple with these issues now, the process of learning about others and reflecting on one's attitudes and actions in these areas is a lifelong activity.

Incorporating Diversity

For centuries, women, people with low incomes, and members of oppressed ethnic and religious groups have fought for an education equal to that available to persons with power. Courageous educators established schools to educate students of color when they were not allowed to attend school. Early in the twentieth century, Carter G. Woodson established the Association for the Study of Negro Life and History to study and write about the history and culture of African Americans. Along with Woodson, W. E. B. DuBois, Charles C. Wesley, and other scholars provided the foundation for the study of racial and ethnic groups. By the 1920s, the Intercultural Service Bureau in New York City was promoting the incorporation of intercultural education into the curriculum to increase knowledge about new immigrants, improve tolerance among groups, and reduce prejudice against them. In 1954 the Supreme Court declared illegal separate-but-equal education for black and white students in *Brown v. Board of Education*. The civil rights struggles of the 1960s laid the groundwork for new curriculum content about African Americans, Hispanics, American Indians, and Asian Americans. Attention to equity for women, individuals with disabilities, and English-language learners soon followed. These events led to the development of multicultural education.

CULTURALLY RESPONSIVE TEACHING. Teaching is complex. You cannot determine the learning styles, prior knowledge, or cultural experiences of students by simply knowing that they are from a specific ethnic group or SES level. You will need to observe and listen to students and their parents as well as assess student performance to develop the most effective teaching strategies. When teachers validate the cultures of students and communities, students begin to feel that teachers care about them, which is a first step in building a foundation for trust between teachers and students who are from different racial and ethnic groups. A part of building trust is to teach the history of a group truthfully, not to gloss over the contributions of men and women of color or the discrimination faced by groups throughout history.

An inclusive curriculum begins to reflect the reality of our multicultural world rather than only the piece of it that belongs to the culture of the teacher. For example, learning science and mathematics would be enhanced for American Indian and other students if the knowledge and traditions of various tribes and nations were incorporated into the curriculum. In addition, the presentation and discussion of topics from **multiple perspectives** allow students to see that there are many ways to view a topic based on one's own perspective, experiences, and interpretations. For example, a study of pioneers moving westward would look different from the perspectives of pioneers, Congress, and American Indians. Viewing many academic and controversial topics in today's news from the multiple perspectives of different groups discussed in this chapter, researchers, policy makers, and others can help students learn to listen to others as well as analyze their perspectives and weigh them in determining their own views. The "Perspectives on Diversity" feature shows the dilemma that an elementary teacher faces in teaching about Thanksgiving.

multiple perspectives Views from people or groups of people whose histories and experiences provide different ways of looking at a current or past event, policies, research, and practices in the world.

Many students will be more willing to learn if they find their cultures in the curriculum and feel that their cultures are valued in their interactions with teachers and administrators. Adding a course on ethnic studies or women's studies to the curriculum is an easy way to introduce students to the culture, history, and experiences of others, but it is not enough. The history, contributions, and experiences of racial, ethnic, socioeconomic, and religious groups can be integrated in most social studies courses. The struggles for equality faced by these groups, women, English-language learners, LGBTQs, and persons with disabilities should be included in the curriculum. Issues such as racism, sexism, classism, ableism, and discrimination against other groups should be confronted in the classroom as they arise. The stories, books, and songs used by students should reflect diverse cultures and be written by authors from diverse groups. The word problems used in mathematics and science can be pulled from diverse cultures. You may have to think about groups or perspectives that have been omitted from the curriculum or book you are using and develop supplementary materials to ensure that the curriculum is multicultural.

To demonstrate respect for students' backgrounds and experiences, you should help students see the relationship between subject matter and the world in which they live. Students should see themselves in the representations (that is, books, examples, word problems, and films) that are used in a classroom. An effective teacher teaches the same concept by explaining it in different ways, relating it to something meaningful in students' lives, and demonstrating it in multiple ways. For most beginning teachers, these various explanations may be limited; with experience, however, you should be able to draw on many different strategies to take advantage of each student's learning style and cultural patterns.

VALIDATING STUDENT VOICES. In multicultural education, all participants have **voice**. Teachers do not dominate the dialogue. Students, especially low-income students, students of color, students with disabilities, and English-language learners, may think that teachers are not

voice The right and opportunity to speak and be heard as an equal.

PERSPECTIVES on DIVERSITY

Thanksgiving

It's November—the time of the school year that many elementary teachers teach about American Indians and Thanksgiving, even though the traditional story does not match reality. Mrs. Starkes was no different. She was setting up her PowerPoint presentation to introduce the unit to her fourth graders in rural Texas.

"Are we going to talk about Indians today?" Joe asked excitedly.

"Yes," Mrs. Starkes replied.

"I am so excited," the petite blond girl in the first row squealed. "My great, great grandmother was Cherokee."

Mrs. Starkes was always surprised at how many of her students claimed to have American Indian ancestors, especially in November. She was determined to break the stereotypes that her students had of American Indians. She knew that some of the other teachers were teaching the Thanksgiving story with toothpick tipis, feathered headdresses, and paper-bag Indian vests. She wanted to break the Disney World view of American Indian princesses who saved early European settlers.

How could she break the myth that the Pilgrims provided a great feast for their American Indian neighbors to celebrate the harvest? It's the same story that the parents of most of her students learned when they were in school. The truth was difficult and depressing. Do her students have any idea that the Cherokees were driven from their homes in the Southeast and forced to walk the "Trail of Tears," which killed one in four of them, to their new government homes in Oklahoma?

"Do you know where Indians live today?" she began the lesson.

"In tipis," a number of students shouted. "In a longhouse," another student offered.

WHAT IS YOUR PERSPECTIVE?

1. How would you respond to the stereotypes the students have about American Indians and how would you help them develop a better understanding of the real history and current experiences of American Indians?

2. What is appropriate to teach fourth graders about the history of Thanksgiving?

3. Why do many myths and untruths about ethnic groups persist in our classrooms?

Source: Adapted from Starnes, B. A. (2009, February). Thoughts on teaching: Teaching the truth is not easy. *Phi Delta Kappan, 90*(6): 448–449. Copyright Phi Delta Kappa International, www.pdkintl.org, 2009. All rights reserved.

interested in them, their cultures, or their perspectives when they are seldom asked to respond in class, their opinions are never requested, and they are never assigned to lead a group.

Including student voices in the classroom dialogue is not always easy. Many students have limited experience with active participation in their own learning. When the classroom climate begins to include student voices, students may express anger and be confrontational; they may test the limits of the language that can be used and the subjects that can be broached. Allowing student voices to be an integral part of classroom discourse may test your patience as you and your students figure out how to listen and contribute to the learning process. At the same time, tolerance, patience with one another, and the willingness to listen will develop as student voices contribute to the exploration of the subject matter.

Respect for differences is key in affirming student voices. For many educators, this affirmation requires relinquishing the power they have traditionally had as the voice of authority with the right answers. Class time no longer is monopolized by teacher talk. The meaningful incorporation of student voices requires the development of listening skills and the validation of multiple perspectives, languages, and dialects. It should allow students to participate in the dialogue and the learning process through speaking, writing, and artistic expression. It should allow them to use the modes of communicating with which they feel most comfortable while teaching them other modes.

The affirmation of student voices requires that educators listen to the voices of *all* students. The stories or narratives of others will increase student knowledge and tolerance of differences. Many students will learn to value both their own culture and those of others. In the process, teachers and students will also learn that they have much in common.

Ensuring Equality

Schools and educators should question whether their policies and practices are equitable. One step in this investigation might be an examination of how accessible gifted, talented, and honors programs are to students from diverse groups. A truly egalitarian society ensures not only that their schools are safe, adequately staffed, and supportive of learning but also that the schools of other people's children have the same amenities. Such a society works toward the elimination of racism, sexism, and other forms of discrimination in education.

JOURNAL FOR REFLECTION 7.3
- How has your own education reflected diversity, social justice, and equality?
- Why do you think multicultural education should be integrated into the school curriculum and environment?
- What role do you think multicultural education will play in your own teaching?

Schools reflect the inequities of the broader society. As you consider some of these inequities, ask yourself the following questions:

- How fair is it for some students to attend school in dilapidated, foul-smelling, crowded buildings while others attend classes in beautiful buildings with future-oriented technology and well-groomed grounds?
- How fair is it that wealthier students are exposed to an intellectually challenging curriculum and experiences while many low-income students have only a limited number of advanced placement classes offered in their schools?
- How accurate are curricula and pedagogy that do not reflect the rich plurality of the people, histories, experiences, and perspectives of the groups that make up the United States and the world?

EQUAL EDUCATIONAL OPPORTUNITY. One way to address equality in the educational system is to offer equal educational opportunity, which should provide all students, regardless of their backgrounds, with similar opportunities to learn and benefit from schooling. Neither educators nor policy makers agree on what constitutes equal educational opportunity. On the surface, it would seem that all students should have access to high-quality teaching, small classes, up-to-date technology, college preparatory courses, buildings that support learning, and safe environments.

In reality, most equal educational opportunity programs have been designed to overcome educational deficiencies of underserved students by providing compensatory or remedial programs to reduce the educational gaps that have given advantaged students a head start.

Even when a school has the latest technology, is clean and well maintained, and is staffed by qualified professionals, equal opportunity is not automatically guaranteed. Many other factors need to be considered. What percentages of students in advanced mathematics and science classes are female or students of color? Which students make up the college preparatory and advanced placement classes? Who is assigned to or chooses a general or vocational track? Who is referred to special education classes? Who has access to the best teachers? Who participates in which extracurricular activities? Who is suspended? If the percentages of students from diverse groups in these various school settings are somewhat proportional to their representation in the school population as a whole, equal educational opportunity may be approaching the goal of its supporters.

EQUALITY OF RESULTS. Schools today are expected to provide all students with the opportunity to learn the skills outlined in national standards for mathematics, science, English, the arts, foreign languages, history, geography, civics, and economics. Policy makers not only expect U.S. students to meet minimal standards, they expect them to achieve higher scores on international tests than students in other countries. If educators actually believed that all students could learn, they would ensure that all students have access to higher level knowledge. Students would not be tracked into low-ability and boring classes. They would promote critical thinking and the ability to view the world and academic subjects from multiple perspectives.

When the goal is to ensure equality of results, students who are not performing well academically or in other ways could become intellectual challenges for a team of teachers and other support personnel. The focus would be on ensuring learning rather than simply moving students from one grade to another.

PRACTICING EQUITY IN THE CLASSROOM. Caring and fairness are two qualities that students praise when describing successful teachers. Students know whether teachers view them as special or as incompetent or worthless. Teacher perceptions may be based on a student's personal characteristics; sometimes they are based on group membership. A teacher may feel that homeless children who arrive in dirty clothes and smelling badly have little chance of success. Teachers may pity children from one-parent homes and blame their lack of academic achievement on not having two parents. Teachers may ignore English-language learners until they learn English. Are these fair practices?

A school that provides multicultural education will not tolerate such unjust practices by teachers. Both the classroom and the school will be models of democracy in which all students are treated equitably and fairly. In such a school, teachers and instructional leaders confront their own biases and develop strategies for overcoming them in their own interactions with students and colleagues. They learn to depend on one another for assistance, both in developing a multicultural curriculum and in ensuring that students are not subject to discrimination. As a result, students learn to respect differences and to interact within and across ethnic and cultural groups as they struggle for social justice in the school and in the community.

Teachers sometimes give more help to some students than to others. They might praise some students while correcting and disciplining others. Their expectations for academic success may differ depending on students' family income or ethnic group. Most teachers do not deliberately set out to discriminate against students, especially in any harmful way. The problem is that we have been raised in a racist, sexist, and classist society in which biases are so embedded that it is sometimes difficult for us to recognize anything other than the very overt signs. We often need others to point out our discriminatory practices so that we can correct them.

A good pattern to begin to develop even now, early in your teacher education program, is to reflect on your own practice. A key to ensuring that interactions with students are equitable is the ability to recognize our own biases and make appropriate adjustments. We must be able to admit that we sometimes make mistakes. An ability to reflect on our mistakes and why they occurred should lead to better teaching.

Teachers must be able to transcend their own cultural backgrounds to develop learning experiences that build on the cultural backgrounds of all of their students.

Teaching for Social Justice

Social justice focuses on how we help others who are less advantaged than we are. Most religions measure the quality of a society by the justice and care it gives to those in the greatest need—the homeless, the sick, the powerless, and the uneducated. The ethic of social justice, especially as it relates to teacher–student relationships, is essential in the teaching profession, along with other moral commitments. Social justice in education requires schools to provide all students equal access to a high-quality education. Practices that perpetuate current inequities are confronted and strategies for eliminating them are employed. Social justice, democracy, power, and equity become more than concepts to be discussed in class; they serve as guides for action in the classroom, school, and community. Social justice educators become advocates not only for their own empowerment but also for that of students and other powerless groups.

A theory of social justice suggests that school systems give those students with the fewest advantages the most advantages in their education and schooling to begin to ensure an equal and fair playing field. The goal might be to use the best-funded and most successful schools as the norm for all schools, with the least advantaged receiving the greatest resources for education. Practices today are usually the reverse, with the most economically advantaged students attending attractive and safe schools with the greatest resources and most qualified teachers. Resources for education are not shared equally across groups.

Multicultural teaching helps students struggle in class with social problems and issues that many students face daily in their lives both within and outside of school. Racism, sexism, classism, prejudice, and discrimination are felt differently by students of color than by other students. Anger, denial, guilt, and affirmation of identity are critical elements of learning about and struggling with the inequities of society. Although it is sometimes difficult to discuss these issues in the classroom, doing so can lead to a more diverse and equitable classroom.

In teaching for social justice, teachers help students understand the inequities, oppression, and power struggles that are realities in society. But this kind of teaching does not stop there. It provides hope for a world that is more equitable and socially just. Students and teachers become engaged in confronting injustice and working to remove the obstacles that prevent equality.

reconstructionism A philosophy that contends that educators can analyze societal issues and problems and redesign schools to overcome problems such as racism and sexism.

Students learn to apply the knowledge and skills they are learning to a local, regional, or global issue. The learning becomes authentic because it is related to the world that students care about. Students can take on community projects that examine pollution in their neighborhoods, political stances in their regional area, or the cost of food in their neighborhood versus another part of town. Students and teachers who tackle social justice as an integral part of their classroom work are providing multicultural education and **reconstructionism**. They are doing more than learning about the world; they are also working toward making it better for those who are least advantaged.

SUMMARY

RACE AND ETHNICITY

- Although race is not accepted as a scientific concept for classifying people, it is a social construct that continues to be used to sort people in the United States.
- Ethnicity is determined by the national origin of one's ancestors.
- As a result of immigration from Asia, Mexico, Central America, and the Middle East after immigration laws changed in 1965, the United States has become more racially and ethnically diverse.
- Disparities exist in the academic achievement of students from different racial and ethnic groups.

SOCIOECONOMIC STATUS

- The way students and their families live is greatly affected by their socioeconomic status, which is determined by income, wealth, occupation, and educational attainment.
- The population is socially stratified, providing some groups more advantage and prestige than others in society and schools.
- Students from higher income families almost always score higher on achievement tests than middle- and low-income peers.

LANGUAGE

- Nearly one in five residents of the United States speaks a language other than English at home, contributing to a growing number of English-language learners in schools.
- A number of students use a dialect that is not Standard English in their home environments.
- A number of educational programs are used in schools to help ELLs learn English.

GENDER

- Some theorists and researchers credit differences between males and females to biology; others have found that culture and society determine them.

- Educators can help reduce the differences between girls and boys in their participation and achievement in academic areas.
- Title IX has contributed to equalizing the participation of males and females in courses and sports.

SEXUAL ORIENTATION

- Students struggle with their sexual identity, in part, because of societal discrimination against people who are not heterosexual.
- More than half of LGBTQ students report verbal, physical, or sexual harassment by other students while they are in school.

EXCEPTIONALITIES

- Today's teachers are likely to have one or more students with disabilities in their classrooms.
- Like members of other underserved groups in society, students with disabilities are often labeled and stereotyped in ways not conducive to learning.
- Response to Intervention (RTI) is a popular approach to identifying students with disabilities.

RELIGION

- Religious diversity in the United States is increasing beyond Protestants, Catholics, and Jews.
- Families who are not Christian do not always see their traditions and values reflected in the public schools and often feel discriminated against because of their religion.

MULTICULTURAL EDUCATION

- Multicultural education is based on the principles of democracy, social justice, and equality.
- Educators who value the diversity of students strive to provide educational equality in which all students are provided challenging and stimulating learning experiences that help them learn at high levels.
- Social justice education promotes equity for all students, abandoning practices that sort students and give privilege to those from advantaged backgrounds.

DISCUSSION STARTERS

1. Racial and ethnic groups are not always integrated throughout the school curriculum. What are some ways in which you can integrate the racial and ethnic background of your students into the curriculum? How can you learn more about the ethnic and racial groups that may be represented in your future classroom?

2. Over 40 percent of the nation's children live in families that fall below the official poverty level or are low-income, lacking the resources that more affluent students have to be academically successful in school. What could you do as a teacher to increase the chances of students from low-income families being at the proficient levels on the assessments used at your school?

3. Policy makers and politicians disagree on the importance of helping English-language learners maintain their native languages. What is your position on this issue? What programs would schools provide to ELLs if your position became policy in a school district? What results would you expect if your position became policy?

4. Research shows that some students perform better academically and socially when they are segregated in single-sex classrooms. In which cases do you think such segregation is appropriate?

5. Most LGBTQ students report that there are few teachers with whom they can talk or report harassment related to their sexual orientation. How do you see your role in supporting LGBTQ students in your school? In what ways could you support them?

6. Most classrooms today include one or more students with disabilities. Where will you turn for assistance in providing the necessary accommodations to help those students learn at the levels they are capable of learning?

7. You may be assigned to a school in which the community includes families who are Christian, Muslim, and Jewish. How will you ensure that you are respecting their perspectives on how their children should be treated in school? When will their perspectives impact school practices?

8. Diversity, social justice, and equality are concepts that support multicultural education. What conditions and practices in schools suggest that these concepts are undergirding the education system as you know it? What are signs that these concepts are being addressed and implemented in schools?

SCHOOL-BASED OBSERVATIONS

1. Examine the curriculum, textbooks, bulletin boards, and other materials used in a classroom that you are observing to determine which groups studied in this chapter are included and which never appear.

2. In a school with English-language learners, interview two or more teachers about the programs they use to ensure that students do not fall behind academically because their native language is not English. How do the teachers rate the effectiveness of these programs?

PORTFOLIO DEVELOPMENT

1. Identify one cultural group with which you have limited or no experience and write a paper on the group's historical and current experience in the United States. What other information will be helpful to you if students from this group are in your classroom when you begin teaching? How will you work effectively with the families from this group?

2. Select two schools in different parts of your state and analyze the student achievement data in one of the subject areas tested in your state. How are students in the grade that you plan to teach (or closest to the grade you plan to teach) performing on the test? What differences exist among groups of students in the school? What should teachers consider in improving their students' test scores in the next testing cycle?

WEB SOLUTIONS

As the number of English-language learners (ELLs) increases in schools across the country, teachers need to have the knowledge and skills to help students learn both English and the subject being taught. What are your state's policies on the use of bilingual education in classrooms? What strategies for teaching ELLs are recommended by the state? What are the state's requirements for becoming certified in English as a second language (ESL)? For information on state policies and requirements, check the website of your state department of education.

MyEducationLab™ Go to the topic **Student Diversity** in the MyEducationLab (**www.myeducationlab.com**) for *Foundations of American Education: Becoming Effective Teachers in Challenging Times, 16e,* where you can:

- Find learning outcomes for **Student Diversity**, along with the national standards that connect to these outcomes.
- Complete Assignments and Activities that can help you more deeply understand the chapter content.
- Apply and practice your understanding of the core teaching skills identified in the chapter with the Building Teaching Skills and Dispositions learning units.
- Access video clips of CCSSO National Teachers of the Year award winners responding to the question, "Why Do I Teach?" in the Teacher Talk section.
- Create, update, and share quality lesson plans with the Lesson Plan Builder.

- Access state licensure test requirements, overviews of what tests cover, and sample test items in the Certification and Licensure section.
- Access current state and national standards in the Licensure and Standards section.
- Learn how to create a high-quality teaching portfolio in the Preparing a Portfolio section.
- Access tips, advice, and other information on resume writing and interviewing, your first year of teaching, and law and public policies in the Beginning Your Career section.
- Check your comprehension of the content covered in the chapter with the Study Plan. Here you will be able to take a chapter pretest, receive feedback on your answers, and then access personalized Review, Practice, and Enrichment exercises to enhance your understanding of chapter content. After you complete the exercises, take a posttest to confirm your comprehension.

8

Students and Their Families

LEARNING OUTCOMES

After reading and studying this chapter, you should be able to:

1. Respect the different family backgrounds from which students come and understand the importance of not stereotyping student behavior or academic potential on the basis of the type of students' families. (InTASC 2: Learning Differences)

2. Provide appropriate support to children and young people who need caring adults to help them maneuver through the tribulations and challenges of the childhood and the teenage years. (InTASC 1: Learner Development)

3. Support young people as they face the challenges of discovering their sexuality and availability of alcohol and drugs. (InTASC 2: Learning Differences)

4. Analyze the role that prejudice and discrimination play in marginalizing students. (InTASC 2: Learning Differences)

5. Probe the reasons that some students leave school early and the importance of making school meaningful and important to those students. (InTASC 1: Learner Development; InTASC 2: Learning Differences; InTASC 7: Planning for Instruction)

6. Develop strategies for engaging parents in schools and in their children's learning. (InTASC 10: Leadership and Collaboration)

EDUCATION in the NEWS

SCHOOLS, COMMUNITY GROUPS PARTNER FOR SUMMER PROGRAMS IN SACRAMENTO AREA

By DIANA LAMBERT

dlambert@sacbee.com

Sacramento Bee June 5, 2012 (Page 1B)

Published: Tuesday, Jun. 5, 2012 – 12:00 am | Page 1B   Last Modified: Thursday, Jun. 7, 2012 – 3:00 pm

Sharpening math skills during summer recess, learning to play an instrument, or taking a painting class had become a thing of the past for most Sacramento-area students in recent years.

State budget cuts had left schools with little money to fund summer classes beyond those for teens in need of credits to graduate.

But some local school districts are leveraging partnerships with community groups and national nonprofits to bring enrichment programs to thousands of students this summer.

Sacramento City Unified funds about half of its summer school program through partnerships with "a multitude" of foundations and community organizations, said Zenae Scott, district summer school coordinator.

"I think partnerships have increased," Scott said. "More importantly, they are much more strategic and intentional."

The district uses grants from the David and Lucile Packard Foundation, the California Endowment, and numerous other nonprofits, as well as state and federal grants, to keep summer school open at ten sites for about 3,500 students.

It also is partnering with the Magic Johnson Foundation and Best Buy for the second year to offer the Geek Squad Summer Academy for fourth- through sixth-graders.

Elk Grove Unified is in its second year of a middle school summer program in partnership with Think Together and the National Summer Learning Association. The three-year program, with staff and curriculum from Think Together—a nonprofit provider of extended learning time programs—serves 1,800 students who are unlikely to be able to afford summer learning programs on their own, according to officials at the National Summer Learning Association.

Most of the cost of the summer school program comes from a $900,000 Smarter Summers grant from the Walmart Foundation.

Twin Rivers Unified has opted for a grass-roots approach, bringing together multiple community partners this summer to start a district-wide enrichment program for 500 first- through ninth-grade students.

The community partners, which include the Center for Fathers and Families, the Mutual Assistance Network, Sacramento Start, and the Boys and Girls Club of Greater Sacramento and the Stanford Settlement, held their own summer programs in previous years.

This year they come together to offer Summer Fun and Exploration at six sites in the school district. The seven-week program includes sports, arts, and mentoring programs, as well as a focus on science, technology, engineering, and math. Older students take part in a community service project and an anti-bullying class.

"This year we are all working together," said Rashid Sidqe, deputy executive director of the Center for Fathers and Families. "The kids wear the same shirt with the same logo. We hold professional development classes together."

He said the collaboration has meant at least 200 more students will be able to attend summer school this year.

Gary Huggins, CEO of the National Summer Learning Association, said partnerships between schools and nonprofit organizations are critical to operating summer school programs. He said the number of these partnerships is on the upswing.

The Sacramento City Unified, Twin Rivers Unified, and Elk Grove Unified programs all focus on schools in high-need areas.

"When we look at summer learning loss, the people affected the most are low-income and students of color," Scott said. "The gap widens when they don't take summer programs. They don't have the opportunities to have the same experiences as kids from more affluent families."

Huggins said that thinking of summer school as an "extra," instead of a necessity, is unwise considering that schools are on the hook for reaching achievement targets and must ramp up achievement to meet new national standards.

But even with outside help, districts aren't able to accommodate all the children who need or want to attend summer school.

"Obviously, in the past—if you look back at what we offered during the summer—we served a lot more students, and there were acceleration activities," said Elk Grove Unified spokeswoman Elizabeth Graswich.

"Nationally there are 14 million kids in summer learning programs," Huggins said. "There are 24 million more on the outside looking in, who would be interested in taking part in those programs."

Those kids lose on average about two months of math skills and low-income or disadvantaged kids lose two months of reading skills over the summer, he said.

The learning loss is cumulative and has a big impact on the achievement gap, as it disproportionately affects low-income students, according to education experts.

"Two-thirds of the ninth-grade achievement gap can be attributed to summer learning loss in reading," Huggins said.

Dee Nishimoto, director of Student Learning Assistance at San Juan Unified, understands how important reading is during school breaks. She said much summer learning loss can be attributed to limited access to books.

San Juan Unified, which stopped offering its four-day-a-week elementary summer enrichment program because of budget cuts, is combating learning loss with a limited summer reading program. The four-hour program is held every Monday at elementary and K-8 schools mostly in the district's neediest areas.

Elk Grove Unified doesn't have funds for elementary school summer enrichment programs, so some of its school sites are using federal funds to pay for summer classes. The Title I and Title III money is for schools in low-income areas or for English-language learners.

Folsom Cordova Unified hasn't offered summer learning programs for most elementary students for about five or six years, said Janie DeArcos, assistant superintendent. The district holds two camps for middle school girls interested in engineering and a four-day camp for third- through sixth-grade students in the district's gifted program.

QUESTIONS FOR REFLECTION

1. In what way can summer programs contribute to reducing the achievement gap among groups of students?
2. Why have many school districts had to reduce the number of or eliminate summer school programs?
3. How are community organizations in the Twin Rivers Unified school district contributing to student learning during the summer?

Source: From the *Sacramento Bee*, 2012. © Copyright *The Sacramento Bee.* All rights reserved.

TODAY'S FAMILIES

Families in the United States have changed dramatically during the past sixty years. In the 1950s, the norm was a working father and a mother at home with two or more school-aged children. Today few mothers remain at home until their children finish high school. Families today include mothers working while fathers stay at home with the children, single-parent families, families with two working parents, remarried parents, childless marriages, families with adopted children, gay and lesbian parents, extended families, grandparents raising grandchildren, and unmarried couples with children. As pointed out in the "Teaching in Challenging Times" feature, we must learn to value and respect the diversity of the families in our schools as we work with parents and other caregivers to help students learn.

TEACHING IN CHALLENGING TIMES

Family Diversity

For decades schools have been populated with students whose families do not fit the 1950s model of families with both a mother and a father. More and more students have been raised by single mothers and now by a growing number of single fathers. Some students do not live with either parent but stay instead with relatives or in a foster home. As adults become more open about their sexual orientation, teachers will also be introduced to lesbian and gay parents who may be living with a partner or separated from a partner.

The curriculum and instructional materials seldom mirror the diversity of families, which may include parents with special needs, interracial parents, single parents, gay and lesbian parents, and foster parents. The dilemma for teachers extends beyond the curriculum. They must figure out how to value and respect the diversity of families. Otherwise, both students and parents will feel ignored, isolated, and discriminated against by educators. Teachers may also have to help other students develop an understanding of this diversity. Sometimes students respond to family differences in negative and hurtful ways.

WHAT ARE MY CHALLENGES?

1. How do you characterize families headed by a mother who has never been married? How do you expect her children to behave in school?

2. How will you respond when two men meet with you to discuss the academic progress of their child?

3. How can a school develop a climate of acceptance of all students regardless of the structure and nature of the families in which they live?

Parents are generally older than in the past, in part, because they marry later. Only one in four of today's young people under thirty years of age has been married (U.S. Census Bureau, 2011). Most men and women work for a number of years before marrying. However, they do not always stay married to the same person, which leads to children who are being raised by a single parent; parents who live in separate households, but have joint custody; a stepparent; other family members; or a nonrelated family.

Seven in ten children under eighteen years old live with two parents, even though one of them may be a stepmother or stepfather. Almost one in four U.S. children lives with his or her mother only; 3 percent live with only their father. African American children are more likely than children from other groups to live with a single mother (U.S. Census Bureau, 2011). Ideally, it would be advantageous for children to have two caring and loving parents to nurture them. However, children from all types of families are academically successful in school and become well-adjusted adults. It is not the type of family that disadvantages students or makes it difficult for them to adjust appropriately and achieve well in school. The factor that is most correlated with such disadvantage is the economic well-being of families. Those in poverty are more likely than their more affluent peers to have problems in school.

As a teacher, you should monitor your interactions with students and their families to avoid labeling a child as dysfunctional because he or she lives in a family structure different from your own. Too often, teachers develop a self-fulfilling prophecy about students in nontraditional families not being able to achieve academically. Instead, we should have high expectations for the academic success of all students and do everything possible to help them meet our expectations.

Parenting

Most parents want what's best for their children, but there is no simple guidebook for steering children through the complex terrain they will have to navigate as they grow up. Often parents draw from their own experiences as children and adults. However, the world is different than when they grew up. For example, they did not have access to the technology that is an integral part of the lives of their children. The Internet was not used broadly by the population until the 1990s. Cell phones, texting, avatars, chat rooms, MySpace, Facebook, YouTube, wikis, and tweeting did not exist when most of the parents of your students were born.

Parents and caretakers are critical in setting the stage for future learning during the early years before children begin school. Reading to young children and limiting the amount of time children spend watching TV have a strong relationship to reading scores. By age four, the

MyEducationLab™

Visit the MyEducationLab for *Foundations of American Education* to enhance your understanding of chapter concepts with a personalized *Study Plan.* You'll also have the opportunity to hone your teaching skills through video- and case-based *Assignments and Activities* and *Building Teaching Skills and Dispositions* lessons.

Three in ten children under eighteen years of age live in nontraditional families without both a mother and a father, but those nontraditional families provide the love and support necessary to raise children.

children of professional parents have a much larger vocabulary than do other children. Access to resources such as books, computers, and the Internet also contributes to academic success. Parental involvement in school activities and ensuring that homework is done also are correlated with good grades (Barton & Coley, 2009).

To increase students' chances of making it safely through childhood and adolescence, teachers and parents need to work together, setting high standards and helping young people meet them. Some schools have hired a school–parent coordinator or liaison to help bridge the gap between the two. They encourage parents to participate in their children's education and try to improve their communications with parents, which will be discussed later in this chapter.

Economic Stress

Families continue to suffer from the recent recession. A number of them may have lost their jobs or worry about losing their jobs as well as their homes. Teachers report that more students are coming to school hungry. Seven in ten parents and 65 percent of the students worry about their family having enough money to cover basic needs (MetLife, 2012). In addition, schools have had to cut services and teachers. Almost two in three teachers report that the number of students and families needing health and social support has increased over the past year, but school districts have reduced or eliminated those services along with after-school programs as part of their budget-cutting (MetLife, 2012). In this section, we examine how limited family incomes affect families and the schooling of their children.

HOMELESSNESS. Individuals and families with low incomes often temporarily lose the ability to pay their rent or maintain mortgages, ending up homeless on the streets of small and large cities. During economic crises such as the one that occurred in 2008–2009, newly homeless people set up tents in and near cities or began living in their cars. The National Law Center on Homelessness and Poverty (NLCHP) (2012) estimates that more than three million people in the United States are without shelter at some point during a year. Many more families are just a paycheck, illness, or emergency away from being homeless. Many low-income families spend 50 percent of their income on rent, rather than the recommended 30 percent (NLCHP, 2012). The homeless

Poverty and the lack of affordable housing are the major reasons for the growing number of homeless adults, children, and families in both rural and urban areas.

includes families, youth, children, people with disabilities, veterans, people using illegal drugs, people with mental health problems, and working people who do not earn enough to rent housing. Life is very rough when living on the streets. Homeless people are physically attacked and suffer disproportionately from health and mental problems.

Causes of Homelessness. The U.S. Conference of Mayors (2011) reports that unemployment is the major cause of homelessness in the twenty-nine cities surveyed. A consistent reason for homelessness is a shortage of affordable rental housing. A reason is the growing number of people and families in poverty. A job does not always guarantee housing; three in ten members of the homeless population have jobs (National Center on Family Homelessness [NCFH], 2011), but employment is part time or sporadic or adults are earning wages too low to purchase necessary food, clothing, and housing. A full-time minimum-wage job often does not provide enough income for a family to rent a one-bedroom unit at fair market prices. The decreasing government supports and domestic violence have also contributed to the growing number of homeless families (NCFH, 2011).

Homeless families comprise around one-third of the homeless population. As shown in Figure 8.1, they disproportionately are headed by women. The mother of a homeless family is generally in her late twenties with two young children (NCFH, 2011). Over nine in ten of them already have been the victims of violent incidents. Homeless mothers are more likely than other mothers to have lived in foster care earlier in their lives (NCFH, 2011). They and their children suffer from chronic health problems such as asthma, anxiety, and depression (NCFH, 2011). Homelessness is devastating to families who are sometimes separated from partners and their children. Only 65 percent of homeless mothers live with at least one of their children; of the homeless men, only 7 percent of them live with at least one of their own children (NCFH, 2011). Homeless children may be placed in foster care or left with relatives or friends while their families are experiencing homelessness.

Homeless Children. In the United States more than 1.6 million children, or one in forty-five, are homeless at some time during a year. Every night more than 200,000 children have no home; many are staying in shelters at night or doubling up in the homes of friends or relatives (NCFH, 2011). Nearly half of the homeless children are under six years old. Children who live in shelters and on the streets often suffer from inadequate health care. They may be surrounded by diseases such as whooping cough and tuberculosis. They are not always inoculated against common childhood diseases, making them more susceptible to illness than most other children. They suffer from asthma and ear infections at disproportionately high rates. Children in homeless shelters also face hypothermia, hunger, and abuse by their parents or other adults. These illnesses may prevent homeless children from attending school on a regular basis. Their lack of regular medical and dental services can cause treatable problems to interfere with their ability to concentrate in classrooms and focus effectively on academic lessons. Completing homework on the street or in a homeless shelter may be difficult if not impossible without supportive adults.

Homeless Youth. Unaccompanied young people are most often homeless because they have run away from home or been released from foster care or some other institutional setting. Nearly half of them report that family conflict and violence were the primary reason for their homelessness (National Coalition for the Homeless [NCH], 2008). They are disproportionately gay, lesbian, bisexual, or transgendered (NCH, 2009). For many of these children, the negative experiences and conditions of their childhood may become the foundation for mental health problems and delinquent behaviors later in life.

Few homeless youth stay in emergency shelters because of admissions policies and other obstacles (NCH, 2008). Instead they sleep in abandoned buildings and on the street. Because

FIGURE 8.1   Characteristics of the homeless.

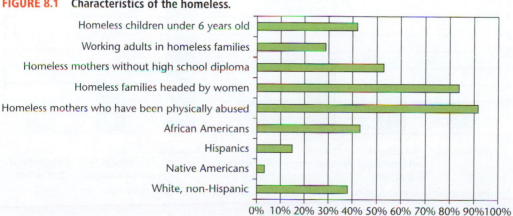

Source: National Center on Family Homelessness. (2011, December). The characteristics and needs of families experiencing homelessness. Reprinted by permission.

they have difficulty finding jobs to earn money for their basic needs, they may end up exchanging sex for money, increasing their chances of contracting AIDS or HIV-related illnesses. Homeless teenagers who are not with their families find it challenging to attend school on a regular basis.

Homeless Students in School. Survival alone can be all encompassing for families who are homeless as they worry about where they will sleep, what they will eat, and how to remain safe. Homeless children usually do not want their school peers or teachers to know they are homeless. The school environment may not be welcoming because these children cannot participate at the same level as other students.

Homeless students do not fare as well as their classmates in life or in schools, as shown in Figure 8.2. However, some homeless students are very **resilient** and able to succeed in school against all odds. Many homeless youth who are living on their own and know the value of an education are enrolled in high school. As a teacher, you may have to be creative in ensuring that these students participate equally in class work and have time to complete homework assignments. Finishing high school and college can provide these students the skills needed for a path to economic stability in the future.

Moving frequently is a characteristic of low-income families, with many of them moving to different housing annually. Such residential instability can temporarily lead to homelessness (Cunningham, Harwood, & Hall, 2010). As a result, low-income and homeless students are also changing schools. They face barriers to regularly attending school such as the lack of transportation, lack of school supplies, lack of clothing, and often poor health (National Association for the Education of Homeless Children and Youth [NAEHCY], 2007–2011). Although the McKinney-Vento Homeless Assistance Act, which was passed in 1987, eliminated the residency requirement for students, homeless children sometimes are not allowed to attend the school that would best serve their needs. Provision of transportation back to the student's school of origin is not always deemed feasible by school systems. Homeless students are sometimes forced to wait to enroll in a school while personal records are collected. However, access to schools is less of a problem than it was in the past. Almost nine in ten of the nation's homeless students are enrolled in school although less than four in five attend school regularly.

resilient The ability to overcome overwhelming obstacles to achieve and be successful in school and life.

Today's advocates focus on students' classroom success. A high-quality education offers homeless children a chance for academic and economic success. To ignore them because they do not have a home or are not well groomed deprives them of the opportunity to rise above their current circumstances. They need more, not less, of our attention. Your support can be the difference in whether they continue to come to school. Your advocacy for their learning and belief that they can learn can help them through a rough economic period for their families.

FIGURE 8.2 **Rates at which homeless children are more traumatized than their classmates.**

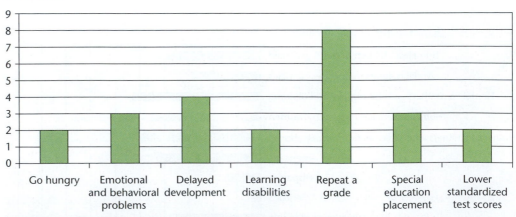

Note: The numbers of the vertical axis are the number of times the rate of nonhomeless children (e.g., 1 time, 2 times, etc.).

Sources: Bassuk, E. L., Murphy, C., Coupe, N. L., Kenney, R. R., & Beach, C. A. (2010). *America's Youngest Outcasts 2010.* National Center on Family Homelessness. Reprinted by permission.

SCHOOL PROGRAMS FOR STUDENTS FROM LOW-INCOME FAMILIES. Federal legislation in the 1960s provided an influx of financial support to schools to support students from low-income families with the goal of making up for some of the educational disadvantages with which many of them entered school. The programs are available for low-income students at all levels of the educational system. African American, Hispanic, and American Indian students are more likely than white and Asian American students to attend high-poverty schools, which would make them eligible for these federal funds. Urban areas have twice as many high-poverty schools as suburban areas. This section summarizes some of the programs that you are likely to encounter in the schools in which you will work in the future.

Title I. **Title I** is the cornerstone of the programs for students from low-income families. It has been part of the Elementary and Secondary Education Act since it was first passed in 1965, most recently as part of No Child Left Behind. The assistance is provided to public schools with large numbers of students whose families meet the federal poverty level or are close to the poverty level to help these students meet state academic standards. The school district must also provide services to eligible private schools. Current Title I provisions require the involvement of parents as advisers to school leaders.

Title I serves more than 21 million students. Of all the students who receive Title I services, over three in five are enrolled in preschool through the fifth grade, one in five in grades 6–8, and nearly one in five in grades 9–12 (U.S. Department of Education, 2011). In the largest school districts, more than half of the students attend schools eligible for Title I funds (Sable, Plotts, & Mitchell, 2010).

The federal legislation for No Child Left Behind requires that all teachers in Title I schools be highly qualified teachers who have a bachelor's degree, are fully licensed by the state, and demonstrate competence in the subjects they are teaching, usually by passing a state licensure test. Title I schools that do not meet adequate yearly progress (AYP) for two consecutive years must offer families the option to transfer their children to another school. After a school does not meet AYP for three years, low-income students must be offered supplemental education services, which include free tutoring to students to help them raise their academic achievement. After five years of not meeting AYP, the school district must begin planning the restructuring of the school.

Head Start. **Head Start** is a federally funded program designed to serve children from low-income families by addressing the needs of the whole child. In addition to educating three- to five-year-old children, teachers work with social workers, nurses, other health professionals, and directly with parents. Teachers and social workers make periodic home visits to work with the parents, providing them parenting/teaching skills to use when they work with their children. Head Start children receive breakfast and lunch daily at school. Along with working on academic skills, Head Start teachers also teach social skills, play skills, healthy habits, and table manners. Head Start was expanded in 1995 to include Early Head Start programs to serve the needs of two-year-olds and their families.

Free or Reduced-Price Lunch. Many of the nation's children face food insecurity—they are not sure they will always have a meal, let alone a nutritious one. The National School Lunch Program helps to bridge this gap by providing nutritionally balanced **free or reduced-price lunches** daily in schools. Students eligible for this program live in families with an annual income that is 185 percent or less of the federal poverty level or $42,643 for a family of four in 2012–2013 (U.S. Department of Agriculture, 2012). Most of the schools that serve free or reduced-price lunches also serve breakfast through the School Breakfast Program. These breakfasts provide more fruits and milk than most of these students would normally consume. In addition, breakfast contributes to greater attention in class, improved academic achievement, and fewer discipline problems. To continue providing food throughout the summer, the Summer Food Service Programs provide free meals at local summer education and enrichment programs in areas where children are eligible for free or reduced-price school meals. Nearly half of all elementary and secondary students are eligible for free or reduced-price lunches (National Center for Education Statistics, 2012). A larger proportion of students in the largest school districts are eligible for free or reduced-price lunches with all students in some schools being eligible (Sable et al., 2010).

GO TO ⋯›
Other aspects of No Child Left Behind are discussed in greater detail in Chapters 1, 9, and 11.

Title I A federal program, first passed by Congress in 1965, that provides financial assistance to schools with large numbers of low-income students to help students meet state standards.

Head Start A federally funded early childhood education program for three- to five-year-olds from low-income families that is designed to close the academic gap between them and more advantaged students before kindergarten.

free or reduced-price lunch The provision of school lunches to students who live in families with an annual income of 185 percent or less of the federal poverty level.

FIGURE 8.3   Before- and after-school care received by U.S. children.

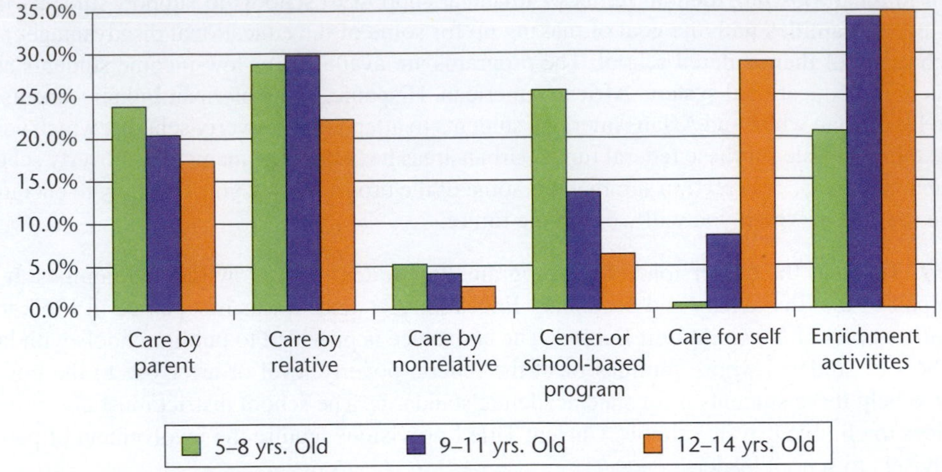

Source: U.S. Census Bureau. (2010). Who's minding the kids? Child care arrangements: Spring 2010 – Detailed tables. Washington, DC: Author. Retrieved on June 2, 2012, from http://www.census.gov/hhes/childcare/data/sipp/2010/tables.html.

Children Left Alone After School

Most single parents work outside the home and in many two-parent families both parents work. Unless working parents have been lucky enough to have a job that supports a flexible schedule that allows them to be home when their children are not in school, they are not available to care for their children during the period immediately after school. The result is children of all ages being left alone or in the care of others. Parents worry about the safety of their children after school, more so in urban than in suburban and rural areas (MetLife, 2012).

Parents or relatives provide supervision after school for half of the students in grades K–5. Older students are more likely to care for themselves after school, as shown in Figure 8.3. Other children stay with adults other than their parents, attend center-based programs, or participate in extracurricular activities such as sports, arts, or clubs. Most parents have to pay a fee for child care, especially if persons other than relatives are caring for their children. Some families cannot afford the cost of such care, which averages $138 per week (U.S. Census Bureau, 2011). As a result their children are left with other family members or left to fend for themselves.

Children who are responsible for their own care after school experience more accidents and injuries. They also are at risk of behavior problems, lower social competence, and poorer academic performance. Adolescents left on their own are more likely to engage in risky activities such as smoking, drinking alcohol, and using drugs. Self-care is more prevalent among children over age ten than younger ones. It is also more prevalent when mothers work full time or when there is a single parent. Families make choices about whether to leave children alone after school based, in part, on the safety of their neighborhoods and the health and maturity of their children.

Educators should be sensitive to the realities faced by children left alone after school. They are sometimes frightened to be at home alone, especially when they have no siblings. The process of traveling from school to home can be dangerous and scary in neighborhoods where drugs are being sold and peers are tempting one another to misbehave. Adolescents may be tempted to experiment with drugs and sex while adults are not around. Television may become the babysitter, providing children with the opportunity to learn from educational programs—or from inappropriate programs. In most cases, children are thankful for caring adults who can provide supervision and assistance.

DANGERS CHILDREN AND YOUTH FACE

The love and care of adults help children and young people pass safely through childhood and adolescence. Unfortunately, some children face danger at home, in the streets of their neighborhood, and at school that is difficult for most of us to imagine. As an educator, you should be able to recognize signs of the violence that can greatly affect children's well-being and future lives. You should know when to intervene and provide support that can make a difference in their lives as well as their academic performance at school. In this section, we examine some of the immediate dangers faced by today's students.

Child Abuse

Most children have probably been faced with angry parents who raise their voices or even spank them on occasion. However, some family members seriously hurt children. Child abuse is reported annually for more than three million children for the abuses identified in Figure 8.4. More than eighty-four children per hour are treated in emergency rooms as a victim of abuse (Centers for Disease Control and Prevention [CDC], 2012). One in every 109 children is the victim of abuse, with almost four in five victims of abuse suffering from **neglect**, which means the child is not being provided with his or her basic needs by parents, caretakers, or relatives. Females are slightly more likely to be the victims. Children under age four are the most vulnerable, as shown in Figure 8.5, representing more than one in three of all of the victims under eighteen years old (U.S. Department of Health and Human Services, 2011). High school girls (11 percent) are more likely than boys (5 percent) to be sexually abused (CDC, 2010). Sensational news stories report sexual abuse of children by strangers, but the abusers usually are family members, intimate partners, friends, or acquaintances.

Children and young people who are abused or neglected may arrive at school hungry, bruised, and depressed. They may arrive early at school and seem to have little desire to leave the safety of the school. These children, like all others, need teachers who are caring, retain high expectations for them, and can provide hope for the future. School and other social service professionals may be the only adults available to support youngsters who have been abused.

Bruises, burns, broken bones, depression, withdrawal, extreme thinness, and nervousness that appear more often than one should expect may be signs of abuse. Educators should not investigate cases that they think may be abuse; they should instead report them as required by law. Not reporting could lead to fines and/or prison terms. Most school districts have procedures

neglect The lack of providing basic needs of housing, food, clothing, education, or medical care to children.

FIGURE 8.4   Types of child abuse.

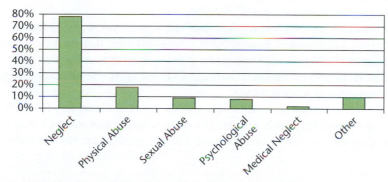

Source: U.S. Department of Health and Human Services, Administration for Children and Families, Administration on Children, Youth and Families, Children's Bureau. (2011). *Child Maltreatment 2010.* Washington, DC: Author.

FIGURE 8.5   Age of the victims of child abuse.

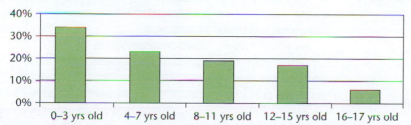

Source: U.S. Department of Health and Human Services, Administration for Children and Families, Administration on Children, Youth and Families, Children's Bureau. (2011). *Child Maltreatment 2010.* Washington, DC: Author.

for reporting suspected abuse, including to whom the abuse should be reported. Even though a teacher has told his or her supervisor about possible abuse, the teacher should check to ensure that the appropriate agency was notified.

What might educators do to help eliminate, or at least reduce, the number of students who suffer from abuse? Parents are critical to making necessary changes. Some schools and family services organizations are working with parents to help them develop better parenting skills and to be able to more effectively manage their children's behavior through time-outs and interacting positively with them. As you interact with the parents of your students, you may be able to encourage them to participate in such sessions to improve their ability to interact effectively with their children with the goal of improving children's learning and academic achievement.

Sexual Harassment

GO TO ···>
Sexual orientation is also discussed in Chapter 7.

Harassment is not rare in schools; it is a common occurrence for many students. Nearly half of the middle school and high school students in a national survey indicated that they had been sexually harassed at school, with the majority reporting that it had a negative effect on them (Hill & Kearl, 2011). The harassment of both girls and boys occurs electronically via text, e-mail, or social networking as well as in person in the hallways, classrooms, and cafeterias of schools. The harassment ranges from unwelcome comments to touching and, in some cases, physical intimidation or rape. Girls are more likely than boys to be sexually abused (Hill & Kearl, 2011). LGBT students suffer disproportionately; they report verbal, sexual, and physical harassment that ends in physical assault for one in five LGBT students (Kosciw, Greytak, Diaz, & Bartkiewicz, 2010).

The most common harassment experienced by students is verbal abuse, which includes unwanted comments, jokes, or gestures. Significant differences in the victims of sexual harassment do not appear to be based on race, ethnicity, or socioeconomic status except in one case. Low-income students report being touched in unwelcome ways more often than their more affluent peers. Harassers are more likely to be a male student or group of male students than a female (Hill & Kearl, 2011).

Sexual harassment is experienced less often via cyber-harassment than in person, with one in five students receiving unwelcome sexual comments or photos in a text message, e-mail, or post on social networking sites. Rumors can spread quickly through these sources, embarrassing students, accusing them of sexual promiscuity, or labeling them as a lesbian or gay. Many of these students are also harassed in person (Hill & Kearl, 2011).

Why do students sexually harass other students? Perhaps not realizing how much their actions can hurt their victims, most harassers don't think it is a big deal or they were trying to be funny. Some harassers (34 percent) show some remorse when they report that they "were being stupid" (Hill & Kearl, 2011). Teachers can help students know the inappropriateness of such behavior by confronting it when it occurs.

Harassment affects students in different ways, as shown in Figure 8.6. Girls are more likely than boys to report being negatively impacted by being sexually harassed by a boy. Low-income students and students who have been harassed both in person and electronically were most

FIGURE 8.6   **Impact of sexual harassment on students.**

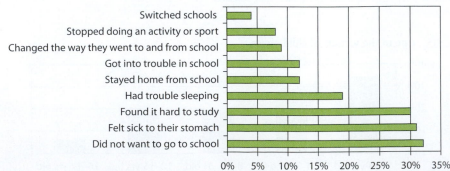

Source: Hill, C., & Kearl, H. (2011, November). *Crossing the Line: Sexual harassment at school.* Washington, DC: American Association of University Women (AAUW). Reprinted by permission.

negatively affected by the harassment (Hill & Kearl, 2011). A biennial study of school climate found that academic success is negatively affected when students feel unsafe or uncomfortable in school. LGBT students are more likely than other students to skip a class or miss a day of school because of the harassment. When they have been verbally or physically attacked, LGBT students miss school even more often (Kosciw et al., 2010). The patterns were more likely to occur for LGBT students of color (Diaz & Kosciw, 2009). Not attending classes makes it even more difficult to maintain good grades and think about attending college.

About half of the harassed students in the American Association of University Women (AAUW) study ignored the harasser (Hill & Kearl, 2011). Girls were more likely than boys to tell the harasser to stop or try to defend themselves. Boys were more likely to turn it into a joke. Few students report incidents of sexual harassment to school officials or another adult. They were more likely to talk to a parent, other family member, or friend. Half of them do nothing (Hill & Kearl, 2011). They don't think reporting an incident will make a difference, and, in some cases, believe that it could make matters worse (Kosciw et al., 2010).

What can a teacher and school do to prevent sexual harassment? Students suggest that the school designate a person to whom they can talk and who can provide online resources. They encourage teachers to have classroom discussions about sexual harassment. The strongest recommendation from students is that they be allowed to anonymously report an incident as a victim or bystander (Hill & Kearl, 2011). Research has also found that harassment is reduced when a school enforces its sexual harassment policies and punishes harassers (Kosciw et al., 2010).

Bullying

You probably hear or read national and local news stories about **bullying** in schools where bigger, stronger, or more aggressive students establish dominance over their victims. Twenty-eight percent of students between twelve and eighteen years old reported being bullied at school in 2008–2009 (NCES, 2011). Middle schools report the largest percentage of bullying incidents (CDC, 2011b). For younger students, the bully may be the student who pushes them out of the cafeteria line. The bully may be the student who forces others to turn over their money or do his or her homework. The bully is usually the perpetrator of sexual harassment against female and LGBT students described in a previous section. Such behavior cannot be excused as just "boys being boys." Bullying takes the form of belittling weaker students, calling them names, and harassing or threatening them. Sometimes the outcome of bullying is assault or murder.

Three in ten adolescents report being a bully, being the victim of bullying, or both (Hamburger, Basile, & Vivolo, 2011). Bullies are at increased risk for substance abuse, poor academic performance, and violence in later life. Victims are at increased risk of experiencing anxiety, depression, headaches, and poor school adjustment (CDC, 2011b).

Bullying also occurs electronically via the Internet and cell phones. The attacks occur on social networking websites, in chat rooms, and in instant messages. The types of technology that make electronic bullying possible will probably grow as young people engage with new, easily accessible technologies. Six percent of young people report that they have been cyber-bullied during a school year (CDC, 2011b). Making rude or nasty comments is the most common electronic aggression, followed by rumor spreading and threatening or aggressive comments (Hertz & David-Ferdon, 2008). In **cyber-bullying** the victim does not always know the aggressor as he or she would with bullying on the school grounds.

Educators cannot afford to ignore the bullying that occurs in schools. It can lead to serious future problems for the bullies and their victims (Hertz & David-Ferdon, 2008). Research shows

bullying Behavior of students who establish dominance over another student through physical or verbal harassment that is perpetuated over time on the victim.

cyber-bullying Harassment from a distance rather than face-to-face through the use of technologies such as texting, social networking, and e-mail to share embarrassing photos, spread rumors, and attack victims.

Many schools are combating bullying through conflict resolution and other programs that help students learn to respect others, stop harassment, and effectively handle interpersonal problems.

that bullying can be prevented by working with students and parents. States and schools are developing safe school laws and policies that promote changing the behaviors of bullies. They include procedures for reporting and investigating incidences.

School should be a safe haven for children and youth. You can assist in the elimination of harassment, bullying, and other youth violence. Modeling appropriate behavior with students by avoiding sexual references, innuendos, and jokes is an important step. Teachers should not be passive bystanders. You should intervene when you directly witness harassment and bullying and report it to the appropriate school official (Hill & Kearl, 2011). School districts are being sued by families when school authorities do not intervene to stop the harassment of their children.

Suicide

Suicide is the third leading cause of adolescent death behind automobile accidents and homicide. Fourteen percent of high schoolers report seriously considering suicide in the previous year; 11 percent made a suicide plan, and 6 percent actually attempted it (CDC, 2010). Hispanic youth are more likely than their peers to commit suicide. Male adolescents are more likely to commit suicide, but females are more likely to think about it and make nonlethal attempts (CDC, 2009). Gay teens are at particular risk, being two to three times more likely to attempt suicide than their peers (Gay, Lesbian & Straight Education Network, 2011).

Suicide attempts are often calls for help. As a teacher, you should be alert for signs that may suggest the need for a referral to other professionals. Warning signs include changes in a person's mood, changes in sleeping patterns, anxiety, and withdrawing from friends and family (American Association of Suicidology, n.d.). Suicide attempts are often precipitated by interpersonal conflicts or severe stress. Being aware of these signs could help you know to alert a health professional or principal in your school. Providing support for gay students could also lead to a reduction in teen suicide rates.

CHALLENGES OF THE TEEN YEARS

Most U.S. teenagers are not the dangerous, drug-using, sexually promiscuous, nonproductive adolescents of the stereotypes in the media. Young people might not always agree with the adults with whom they interact, and sometimes they even break the rules, but most finish high school and attend postsecondary education. In many other respects, today's teens are more like their counterparts of past generations than different from them.

Nevertheless, young people face numerous challenges as they mature to adulthood. Increased pressures to grow up quickly, peer pressures, and the media provide conflicting messages that contribute to the difficulty of this period. Many students are able to draw on the support of friends, family, religion, and their own inner strength to resist being drawn into negative responses. Others find their own ways of countering circumstances over which they may have no control.

Teenagers are trying to figure out who they are and how they fit into the family, neighborhood, school, and larger world. They are searching for answers, but in their own ways. One of the challenges for parents, caretakers, educators, and youth workers is to encourage young people to make sound choices among the unlimited possibilities while avoiding excessive interference. You can provide the guidance they are seeking by listening to them if they decide to share their concerns and providing positive suggestions as they try to sort out their options. Believe it or not, many teenagers want adults to recognize them and help them through difficult periods and important decision-making points such as whether to go to college or participate in a project.

Adults usually regard teenagers as too young to deserve the benefits of adulthood. They expect teenagers to enjoy youth, begin dating, develop friendships, plan their future, and learn how to behave like responsible adults. Other adults see adolescents as teenage mothers, gang members, drug abusers, and troublemakers. Young people are bombarded by messages about themselves in music, movies, books, and television. Other potent influences are the circumstances in which teenagers live, which may include drugs, violence, and the lack of adult support. Young people must sort through all of these influences as well as the messages given by significant peers and adults in their lives.

Many teens, especially inner-city youths, report that the messages they receive about themselves in the media and schools are usually negative. They feel that adults and communities do not care about them. This feeling is validated by cuts in funding for the schools, parks, and community centers needed to assist youths in many communities. They have learned to feel that schools have rejected them and do not expect much of them.

Respect from adults is critical in helping youth develop self-esteem. Teenagers don't always have appropriate adult support at home; their parents may be too tired or too busy or have too many problems themselves to care adequately for their children. For many teens, schools and neighborhood organizations are their primary sources of adult supervision and guidance. A caring adult can help teenagers develop their self-esteem by serving as a mentor, a gentle but firm critic, and a coach or advocate. Young people who believe in themselves and think they can be academically successful usually are. You can help your students develop positive self-esteem and see themselves as academically capable by giving them positive feedback and support as you push them to produce at high levels. In this section we examine some of the societal challenges that our children and youth face on the way to adulthood.

Sexuality and Pregnancy

The defining of our sexuality—our nature as sexual beings—begins in the early teens and continues throughout life. Coming to terms with our sexuality often involves turmoil both within ourselves and with our parents and caretakers during the teen years. The development of a healthy sexual self is a complicated process.

Many teenagers associate sex with the freedom and sophistication of adulthood. The decision to have sex is one that causes much consternation among young people. Their uncertainty is fueled by the mixed messages they receive from parents, teenage friends, religious doctrines, the media, and older friends. At the same time that one medium glamorizes sex, other voices tell teenagers that abstinence before marriage is the only moral option. Teenagers' apprehensions and activities related to sex may affect their school behavior and their ability to perform satisfactorily in school.

Girls and women often connect sex with being accepted, being attractive, and being loved. Boys and men, by contrast, sometimes link sex with status, power, domination, and violence—a far cry from the loving relationship that many females have envisioned. Thus, ideal sexuality for men and women may differ.

Teenage sex is not as prevalent as some believe. The percentage of young people who have ever had sexual intercourse has decreased during the past twenty-five years from more than 50 percent to 46 percent of high school students, with males being slightly more sexually active than females. Approximately one in three high schoolers is sexually active (that is, had had sex in the past three months) with the majority of them using contraceptives (CDC, 2010). One of the results of early sexual activity is teenage pregnancy. Although the number of teenage pregnancies and births has been declining, the rate in the United States remains one of the highest among industrialized nations (Hamilton & Ventura, 2012).

Poverty appears to be the most important factor in determining teenage mothers. It is a key risk factor for teen pregnancy, but its damaging impact can be buffered through strong social networks and supportive institutions (CDC, 2011a). Most unmarried teenage mothers continue to live with their parents, but their families are disproportionately low-income. Reducing family poverty may also reduce teenage pregnancy. Many teenage parents, especially mothers, are forced to take on adult responsibilities much earlier than society expects of its youth. Teenage mothers are sometimes forced to fend for themselves in impoverished conditions. Their own parents can provide little or no support, and the fathers of their children are often absent and either not contributing or unable to contribute financially. Poverty also contributes to the births of babies with low birth weights and babies who are more likely than other children to experience health problems, developmental delays, abuse, neglect, and poor academic performance (Annie E. Casey Foundation, 2009).

Staying involved in school is very important to the welfare of both the mother and her child. Statistics show that "a child born to an unmarried, teenage, high school dropout is ten times as likely to be living in poverty as a child born to a mother with none of these three characteristics" (Annie E. Casey Foundation, 2003, p. 44). Encouraging teenage mothers to complete their high school and college education can contribute greatly to their future economic well-being.

Overall, teenagers are becoming more responsible about their sexual activity and are using contraception to reduce the risk of pregnancy and the transmission of AIDS and other sexually transmitted diseases. School programs such as sex education and health clinics are helpful, but they are not always supported by families and communities. However, the programs that have proven most effective are ones that convince teenagers that they should either practice abstinence or use contraceptives consistently and carefully (National Campaign to Prevent Teen and Unplanned Pregnancy, 2009). As many young people struggle with the development of their sexuality, they may seek guidance from teachers and other adults whom they respect.

Substance Abuse

Another perplexing question with which many teenagers struggle is whether to experiment with cigarettes, alcohol, or drugs. Although not as glamorized in films and advertisements as in the past, drinking and smoking are still associated with independence and adult behavior. Teens use drugs for different reasons. Sometimes biological predispositions or psychological problems trigger drug use. In other cases, social pressures, family problems, or self-hate lead young people to test drugs.

The public worries about drugs in schools. In the 2011 Phi Delta Kappa/Gallup Poll of the public's attitudes toward public schools, respondents ranked drugs as the fifth greatest problem that public schools face behind funding, discipline, overcrowding, and fighting (Bushaw & Lopez, 2011). Parents worry about drug use interfering with their child's ability to function effectively. Drug use may lead to cutting school, hanging out with the wrong crowd, being arrested, and **chemical dependency** that may require professional treatment to break.

A large percentage of teenagers do try one or more drugs, but alcohol is their favorite, being used more than twice as often as other drugs. Half of our high school seniors at some time have tried an illicit drug—usually marijuana—but most are not regular users. Younger students are experimenting with drugs, but the rate of illicit drug use by eighth graders has been declining since its peak in 1996. One in sixteen eighth graders is already smoking cigarettes. Although the rate of usage is higher than the public may find acceptable, current usage by all teenagers—except for marijuana—is at the lowest level in thirty-three years, as shown in Figure 8.7. The bad news is the high rates of nonmedical use of prescription painkillers such as Vicodin and OxyContin as well as sedatives and barbiturates (Johnston, O'Malley, Bachman, & Schulenberg, 2012).

Drug use varies by group membership. Students who plan to attend college are less likely to use drugs. Male teenagers are more likely than females to use illicit drugs. Differences in the overall use of illicit drugs in urban, suburban, and rural areas are small. They are also small across socioeconomic groups. White students are more likely to use licit and illicit drugs than Hispanic and African American students (Johnston et al., 2012).

chemical dependency
The habitual use, for either psychological or physical needs, of a substance such as drugs, alcohol, or tobacco.

FIGURE 8.7   Students in grades 8, 10, and 12 using selected substances in the past month.

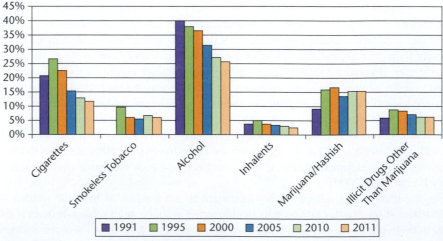

Source: Drawn from Table 3 in Johnston, L. D., O'Malley, P. M., Bachman, J. G., and Schulenberg, J. E. (2012). Monitoring the future: National results on adolescent drug use: Overview of key findings, 2011. Institute for Social Research, The University of Michigan. Reprinted by permission.

Economic Realities

Young people may be worried and somewhat pessimistic about their future economic conditions. However, they continue to seek out post-secondary education to improve their job and career opportunities. Sixty-eight percent of high school graduates go to college immediately after high school although African American (66 percent) and Hispanic (60 percent) students enroll immediately after high school at lower rates than whites (70 percent). Differences also exist in the immediate enrollment in college by a family's socioeconomic status; 52 percent of low-income students go to college immediately after high school as compared to 67 percent of middle-income and 82 percent of high-income students. Females make up 57 percent of the students enrolled in college (Aud et al., 2012).

Fewer high school students than in the past are working after school and in the summer.

The percentage of high schoolers working today is 20 percentage points less than two decades ago. In 2010, 16 percent of high schoolers aged sixteen years and older worked while attending school, with more females than males holding jobs (Aud et al., 2012). Although the rates increased to 31 percent during the summer for sixteen to nineteen year olds, the employment rate was at a historic low. Part of this difference could be attributed to nearly half of these students attending summer school. Another contributor to the low employment rates for young people is the weak economy (U.S. Bureau of Labor Statistics, 2011).

After-school jobs are particularly beneficial to students from low-income families who do not have family or school connections to help them find employment. Unfortunately, many students who could derive long-term benefits from working while in high school—especially those in inner-city areas—have limited access to jobs. The lack of employment opportunities contributes to low self-esteem and pessimism about the future and the value of school. In addition, in communities experiencing high unemployment, many young people do not have opportunities to learn how to work either through their own experiences or through the modeling of working adults.

JOURNAL FOR REFLECTION 8.1

- Thinking back on your childhood and youth, which of the challenges discussed in these last two sections did you face?
- How were you able to manage the challenge in positive ways?
- How did your family or educators provide support to you during this period?

PREJUDICE AND DISCRIMINATION

A democratic society is built on the principles of social equality and respect for individuals within society. However, many persons of color; limited-English speakers; women; persons with disabilities; people with low incomes; people affiliated with religions other than Christianity; and lesbians, gays, bisexuals, transgenders, and queers (LGBTQs) do not experience the equality that other members of society enjoy.

Power relationships among groups influence young people's perceptions of themselves and the members of other groups. Schools are one example of institutions in which power relationships exist. Students' work and class rules are determined by teachers. Teachers are evaluated and disciplined when necessary by principals who report to a superintendent of schools. The rules and procedures for managing schools traditionally have been established by authorities who are not directly involved with the school and who may not even live in the community served by the school. Parents, especially in economically disadvantaged areas, often feel powerless in the education of their children.

Power allows access to societal benefits such as good housing, tax deductions, the best schools, and social services. A more equitable sharing of resources for schools would guarantee that all students, regardless of family income or ethnic background, would have qualified teachers, sufficient books and other instructional resources, well-maintained buildings and playgrounds, and access to high-level academic knowledge. Unfortunately, such equality does not exist in all of our schools.

Prejudice

One of the struggles of youth is the construction of self, including identification and affiliation with one's gender and a racial or ethnic group. This process appears to be integrally tied to identifying **otherness**, which involves assigning characteristics and behaviors to members of other groups to distinguish oneself from them. The construction of "others" places us either in a dominating or submissive role relative to others. Some young men identify themselves in relation to young women. They exert their masculinity as power over their female counterparts in academics, sports, and sometimes relationships. Believing that they are the ones who should wield power over others, white males in some communities build their identity in opposition to males of color.

Our perceptions of others not only affect how we see ourselves in relationship to them, but also influence how society treats members of different groups. **Prejudice** is a preconceived negative attitude toward members of specific ethnic, racial, religious, or socioeconomic groups. This prejudice sometimes extends to people with disabilities or people of a different sexual orientation or gender. Such negative attitudes are based on numerous factors, including information about members of a specific group that is stereotypical and many times not true. Prejudiced individuals may have had little or no direct social contact with members of other groups that would have presented them with experiences that counteract such stereotypes.

An individual's prejudice may have a limited negative impact on members of the other group. However, these attitudes are often passed on to children through the **socialization** process. Also, prejudiced attitudes can be transformed into discriminatory behavior that prevents members of a group from being interviewed for jobs, joining social clubs, or being treated like other professionals. Prejudices are often reinforced by schools in which a disproportionate number of students in low-achieving or special education tracks are males, English-language learners, students of color, or students from low-income families. Observing that these students are not enrolled in academically challenging courses, some other students form stereotypes of their low-income and foreign-born peers as academically inferior. Through this process, many students from low-income families and ethnic minority groups are prevented from gaining the skills and knowledge necessary to enter college or an apprentice trade.

You can take a number of steps to keep your prejudices from hurting students. A first step is to be conscious of your interactions with students in all school and non-school settings. If you are interacting with some students differently, analyze why. The differences may be appropriate, but you want to make sure you are not giving some students more attention and advantages than others. Also, consider asking a colleague to periodically observe your interactions with students and parents to provide a more objective review of your treatment of students from diverse groups. If you find that a group of students is not learning at the same level or is always having discipline problems, you should examine your own behaviors in the classroom to make adjustments to provide equality across groups.

Discrimination

Many of your students or their family members may have experienced **discrimination** through practices that excluded them from equal access to housing, jobs, and educational opportunities. Discrimination is different from prejudice in that it is more than an attitude against the member of a specific group. It is a process that prevents members of a specific group from participating equally in society. Most students of color, females, low-income students, students with disabilities, and gay students have already experienced discrimination in some aspect of their lives. For example, discriminatory practices lead to African Americans receiving more severe sentences in the judicial system than members of some other groups. They lead to women not being paid at the same rate as men for the same type of work. Individuals and groups that have been discriminated against may have not acknowledged it, or they may be angry or frustrated by it.

If we do not experience discrimination in our everyday experiences, we may have a difficult time acknowledging that it exists. Many white students do not see themselves as advantaged

otherness Assigning characteristics and behaviors to members of groups different from one's own to distinguish oneself from the group.

prejudice A preconceived negative attitude toward the members of a group.

socialization The process of learning the social norms of one's culture.

discrimination The process that prevents members of a specific group from participating equally in society. These include legislation, policies, and practices that treat persons differently in the judicial, educational, and social systems based on their group memberships.

or privileged in society. They do not think they receive any more benefits from society than anyone else. These students may have a difficult time fighting social injustices because they have neither experienced them nor become aware of their existence. As a result, rights based on group membership versus those of individuals are debated on college campuses, in board meetings of corporations, by politicians, and in many formal and informal neighborhood meetings. These discussions focus on programs that are perceived to favor one group over another, such as affirmative action, bilingual education, or equal funding for male and female athletes.

Laws and systems that promote and support members of one group maintain the superiority and power of its members. "English only" laws that prevent official documents and communications from being printed or spoken in any language other than English represent one example of these efforts. Such practices have become so ingrained in state and federal laws, the judicial system, schools, and other societal institutions that it is difficult to recognize them unless we are directly affected by the discriminatory policies.

GO TO ···→
Legal issues on discrimination are discussed in Chapter 10.

Racism

An assumption of superiority is at the center of **racism**. It is not a topic easily discussed in most classrooms. It is intertwined with the lived experiences of many people and evokes emotions of anger, guilt, shame, and despair. Most students have learned that the United States is a just and democratic society. They find it difficult to confront the societal contradictions that support racism. Educators must acknowledge how racism has benefited some groups because it gave them advantages over others for receiving an interview for a job or access to a home in some neighborhoods.

Families with a history of discrimination in society and schools may worry about how their children will be treated at school. They may distrust educators who are unable to acknowledge the role that racism has played in their lives. They may be very confrontational in their approaches to teachers or they may be very guarded and afraid to question a teacher. They may accuse teachers of being racist. These parents are standing up for their children and doing all they can to ensure that their children are treated equitably and have the same opportunities to be academically successful as other students. However, the behavior of these parents is usually incongruent with the school's view of positive and supportive parents. Teachers and school officials should avoid reinforcing the parents' perception of the school as racist and not caring about the success of their children. You will need to monitor your own interactions with students and families of color to ensure that you acknowledge and confront school policies and practices that appear racist. When parents believe that you care about their children and their academic and social achievement, you are beginning to develop a partnership with the parents with the students at the center of it.

JOURNAL FOR REFLECTION 8.2
- How have you personally experienced racism?
- What racism have you observed in your community?
- How could you become involved in combating racism, especially in the classroom?

Sexism and Other "Isms"

Women of all racial and ethnic groups, people with disabilities, gays, lesbians, persons with low incomes, the elderly, and the young suffer from discrimination and their lack of power in society. Individuals are members of multiple groups and may be victims of prejudice or discrimination based on one or more of the groups. For example, a low-income Latina may be triply harmed as a result of racism, classism, and **sexism**—the cultural attitudes and practices that devalue women.

Some persons with disabilities and their advocates argue that **ableism** greatly disadvantages people with disabilities and their ability to live a full and productive life. Ableism not only leads to viewing persons with disabilities as inferior to others but also results in treatments and accommodations designed to help them become more like persons without disabilities. These efforts are not necessarily in the best interests of individuals with disabilities. For example, activists with a hearing disability may reject the view that they should become hearing through surgery and other aids. Being deaf is their normality, even though it does not seem normal to those who hear. In other instances, teachers and aides without disabilities sometimes provide assistance or do things for persons with disabilities rather than encouraging them to do these tasks themselves.

racism The conscious or unconscious belief that racial differences make one group superior to others.

sexism The conscious or unconscious belief that men are superior to women and the subsequent behaviors and actions that maintain the superior, powerful position of males.

ableism The conscious or unconscious belief that persons with disabilities are inferior to persons without disabilities.

For educators, the strategy of overhelpfulness may be easier and less time consuming. Allowing individuals with disabilities to make the effort themselves may require a great deal of patience, but the long-term payoff for the student could be self-sufficiency.

ENGAGEMENT IN SCHOOL

Another challenge faced by some teenagers is staying engaged in the academic work at school. Some do not see the value of finishing their education. When students in grades 5 through 12 were asked how they were feeling about school, half of them said that they were engaged, but one in five were "actively disengaged." One in three students were struggling in schools ("Poll Adds," 2009). Others do not see themselves as academically able students and find no reason to participate actively in their own learning.

Sometimes they are not meeting the minimal standards as determined by standardized tests, resulting in grade retention, which will prevent them from graduating with peers of the same age. They believe they can learn the lessons for survival more effectively outside school. As a result, they drop out of high school and college for different reasons, without realizing the harm it is likely to cause them in the long term. The issue of retention or social promotion is debated from two perspectives in this chapter's "Who Is Right?" feature.

Leaving School Early

When we examine the data on how many students receive a regular standards-based diploma on time with the class with which they began high school, we find that only three in four students who enter ninth grade graduate with a regular diploma at the end of the twelfth grade (Aud et al., 2012). The problem is particularly critical in large, urban, segregated schools where African American, Native American, and Hispanic students have only about a fifty–fifty chance of completing high school (Swanson, 2009), placing them at great risk of not earning sustainable wages or being employed as adults. School districts with low graduation rates are more often in central cities with disproportionally high numbers of low-income and immigrant families. Of the 15,500 U.S. high schools with at least ten seniors, 10 percent of these schools have been labeled **dropout factories** in which less than 60 percent of their students graduate on time (Balfanz, Bridgeland, Bruce, & Fox, 2012).

Graduation rates vary across ethnic and racial groups, as shown in Figure 8.8. African American students have the lowest graduation rate, with Native American and Hispanic students not far ahead of them. The largest proportion of Hispanic dropouts was born outside the United States and may have not attended U.S. schools nor have completed more than elementary school in their countries of birth. First and later generation Hispanics graduate at higher rates than immigrants (Aud et al., 2012).

Students from low-income families drop out of high school at higher rates than students from middle- and high-income families. A greater percentage of females finish high school than

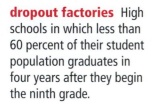

dropout factories High schools in which less than 60 percent of their student population graduates in four years after they begin the ninth grade.

FIGURE 8.8 On-time high school graduation rates by racial and ethnic group.

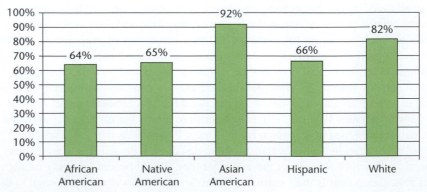

Source: National Center for Education Statistics.

WHO IS RIGHT?

IS RETENTION BETTER THAN SOCIAL PROMOTION FOR STUDENTS?

Today's emphasis on academic achievement may lead to students not meeting state standards as measured by standardized tests. As a result, they may not be able to graduate on time or even be pushed out of school because they fail the required tests. What are the appropriate strategies for ensuring that students meet standards? These two educators debate the effectiveness of retention in helping students learn at an acceptable level before being promoted to the next grade.

YES

John Mohl teaches German and social studies at Cedarbrook Middle School in Wyncote, Pennsylvania.

When I first called on "Brendan," a recent transfer to the district, to read, he refused. His homework was copied from a friend if done at all and he failed to comprehend a passage after fumbling over words when I finally got him to read aloud. Despite his third-grade reading level, Brendan was allowed into eighth grade. He was a product of social promotion.

Social promotion has three detrimental effects on the educational system. It taxes both teachers and students. Promoting a student into a higher level of English when he lacks basic reading skills, as was the case with Brendan, places undue burden on future teachers and students. Socially promoted students monopolize teacher attention, and other students' learning opportunities are limited as a result.

Second, it sends a message to students that they can move on to the next level even if they lack the required knowledge or effort. I once taught a summer school class with two particularly unruly students who were unfazed by the threat of being held back for failing. They knew they'd be eighth graders regardless of their performance. They were right, and became burdens to their new teachers (that oversight, fortunately, was later rectified).

Social promotion also distances schools from their goals of fulfilling the No Child Left Behind standards. How can anybody expect a student with elementary math skills to perform proficiently on an eighth-grade standardized math exam?

Some argue that social promotion maintains the self-esteem of low-achieving students. I agree that humanism should be an important component in our teaching. But the "real world" has neither time nor regard for making sure every person feels worthwhile. Teachers have the responsibility to introduce, to some degree, the benefits of making the mark and the consequences of not doing so. Truth be told, I'd rather see Brendan held back in eighth than held back in life.

NO

Jennifer Slifer teaches sixth-grade language arts at Thomas Edison Magnet Middle School in Meriden, Connecticut.

Each year, we all have a "Brendan" or two and we are frustrated and angry that he advances with such evident skill deficiencies. But would Brendan be helped by retention, the traditional solution for struggling students?

Social promotion by itself is not a good practice. Retention does not, however, solve the problems of low-achieving students. Research shows that retained students do not improve their academic performance compared with similar counterparts who were promoted, and retained students struggle with self-esteem.

Social promotion isn't the answer if it means we send students on to the next grade ill prepared for the workload. "Brendan" is failing, but so are we as educators if we don't provide the help he needs to keep up with his peers. So let's provide that help.

Is it time to review our centuries-old system of grouping students by age? Perhaps all students should be placed in multi-age classrooms. This arrangement would assist students who struggle to learn as quickly as their peers of the same age and would eliminate self-esteem issues caused by retention.

Another approach: Instead of retaining a student, why don't we promote struggling students with an individualized education plan (as we do for our special education students) to help them catch up to their peers? Most struggling students who are promoted do not meet the requirements for special education but they do need assistance that, unfortunately, we are not mandated to provide.

Maybe it's time to get serious about early intervention and provide funding for programs for struggling students *before* they reach middle and high school.

Our choices should not be just promoting students versus retaining them.

Passing struggling students to the next grade is a failure of the system if we don't have a plan to help them catch up. But retention isn't the answer, either.

WHAT IS YOUR PERSPECTIVE ON THIS ISSUE?

Source: "Is Retention Better Than Social Promotion for Students?" (2005, March). *NEA Today*, p. 48. Reprinted by permission of the National Education Association.

males, leading to concerns about fewer young men attending and completing college. Only 57 percent of students with disabilities complete high school (Planty et al., 2008); only 22 percent of persons with disabilities who are sixteen years old and older are in the workforce (U.S. Census Bureau, 2011). As one might expect, students who complete high school are more likely than dropouts to be employed. By age twenty-five, 62 percent of high school graduates without a college degree are in the labor force as compared to 46 percent of the population who did not complete high school by age twenty-five. More education does make a difference; 77 percent of college graduates are working and earning double the income of high school graduates who did not attend college (U.S. Census Bureau, 2011).

The ninth grade is a critical period in which students decide to leave school (Swanson, 2009). Middle school and the beginning of high school are key times in which we need to be engaging students in their education. The emphasis on the reform of high schools is to change these statistics by identifying effective ways of involving students in their education. While we maintain high expectations for student achievement, we must make the curriculum relevant to the real lives of students. They need to be engaged with the subject they are studying, not by listening to a lecture, but by being involved with each other in projects and problem solving to develop a deeper understanding. A number of urban high schools are particularly ineffective in engaging their students in learning, as shown in the "Perspectives on Diversity" feature.

One national initiative to dramatically decrease the dropout rate by 2020 is the Grad Nation Campaign, which is a centerpiece of General Colin Powell and Alma J. Powell's America's Promise Alliance. Other organizations and corporations have joined the Alliance to develop a "Civic Marshall Plan" with two goals: (1) a 90 percent high school graduation rate by the Class of 2020, and (2) the highest college attainment rates in the world by 2020 (Balfanz et al., 2012). If the state

PERSPECTIVES on DIVERSITY

Why Bother?

Carlos's mother just received another call from Roosevelt High School. Carlos was not in school again today. She called his cell phone, asking where he was. "In school," he responded.

"I know better Carlos. The school just called, and you have not been there for the past three days. If you miss another day, you won't be able to graduate. What is wrong with you? Get yourself back to school now."

Carlos turned back to his friends. "It was just my mom. The damn truant officer called her again. What's she want from me? I don't learn anything there anyway. I'm gonna get a job."

Carlos actually has been at school most of the past three days. He just can't find a reason to go to class. He's failing anyway, and it is much more interesting to hang with his friends in the halls. At least they talk about what is real. His teachers are boring, and they don't seem to care about his learning. They never want to talk about issues that are critical in his neighborhood—finding jobs and the dilemma of unauthorized families. School just does not seem connected to his life and future.

Even Carlos wonders what has happened to him. He used to go to his classes. Before he got to high school, he earned As and Bs and liked school. Something happened in the ninth grade when

he lost interest in doing his homework and being involved in school activities. None of the counselors or teachers seemed to care when he didn't make it to class. Was it his ethnicity or economic status that allowed adults in the school to let him stop participating?

His teachers are also stumped. Carlos does not usually cause trouble. He is a joker and spends most of his time talking to other students rather than engaging with the content. The school counselor says that his mother is a good parent and has been pushing him to go to college. She knows that he has the ability to make it, but is at a loss about how to keep him in school.

WHAT IS YOUR PERSPECTIVE?

1. What are some of the reasons that Carlos has given up on school?

2. If you were one of his teachers, what would you do to try to engage him in your class?

3. The Obama administration is telling school administrators that high school graduation rates must improve. What responsibility does a school have to ensure that all students both learn at high levels and graduate from high school?

or school district in which you are working is participating in this initiative, you are likely to be involved no matter what level or subject you are teaching. Among the benchmarks set to meet these goals are substantially increasing the number of students reading at proficiency by fourth grade, reducing chronic absenteeism, and providing sustained and quality adult and peer support for students who need it. In addition, the plan calls for states to raise compulsory attendance to age eighteen, which over thirty states have already done.

Resiliency

Many young people have the resiliency to overcome disastrous childhood and adolescent experiences and go on to become successful workers, professionals, and community leaders. The challenges discussed earlier in this chapter along with growing up in poverty can place children and youth at risk for developmental delays, behavior problems, and poor academic performance. The students who are most at risk live in dangerous environments that lead to health risks and threats to their safety. They may be attending schools in which students are not expected to perform at high levels and are not being pushed to do so. Their own parents may be so busy coping with several jobs or their own problems that they cannot support their children.

With all of these challenges, some students are still able to perform well, even at high levels, in school. Their personal attributes give them strength and fortitude and help them confront overwhelming obstacles that seem designed to prevent them from reaching their potential. Children who are resilient are able to cope effectively with stress. They believe in their own **self-efficacy**, can handle change, and have good social skills.

Higher family SES contributes positively to resiliency, but is not required. Other positive factors are family members who are involved with their children, provide caring environments, help their children with homework, attend to grades, and participate in school activities. Resilient students have positive relationships with teachers and have less exposure to violence or trauma. They are also helped by quality educational and recreational opportunities in school and their neighborhoods. Regardless of the challenges they face, they are usually social, optimistic, energetic, cooperative, inquisitive, attentive, helpful, punctual, and on task.

Access to Technology

One strategy for keeping students engaged in schools is to relate the content to the real life experiences of students and their families. When students are involved in hands-on projects that help them understand the subject and develop critical thinking skills, they are usually more engaged in the learning process. Technology provides valuable tools for helping students learn by drawing on resources with which they are generally familiar.

The problem is that not all families are able to provide the latest technology to support their children's learning, and these are the students who are most at risk for not completing high school on time. Seven of ten households have Internet access at home, and another 10 percent use the Internet in other settings. The higher the education and income of a family, the more likely they are to have access at home. White and Asian American families are more likely than other families to have access to the Internet at home (U.S. Census Bureau, 2011).

Do similar disparities exist in schools? Almost all schools in the country have Internet access. However, one in three teachers reports that educational technology at their school is not being kept up-to-date (MetLife, 2012). Not all classrooms have LCD or DLP projectors,

 Watch this **video** to listen to a superintendent at a large, urban school talk about how teacher expectations and behavior can affect the resiliency of students at risk for failure.

self-efficacy The belief that one can control one's life.

Some schools are integrating multiple technologies such as whiteboards, laptops, iPads, and iPhones to engage students in their own learning with real world tools that can help them expand their knowledge and skills.

interactive whiteboards, or digital cameras (Gray, Thomas, & Lewis, 2010). Teachers in low-poverty schools are more likely to have students use technology to prepare written text and develop multimedia presentations while teachers in high-poverty schools are more likely to use it to help students learn or practice basic skills. Teachers in low-poverty schools are almost twice as likely to use technology to communicate with parents (Gray et al., 2010).

Classroom computers may have graphics capabilities that allow students to design interesting presentations with audio and video clips. Math teachers have graphic calculators. Students can edit their own videotapes to produce a movie instead of a traditional written paper for a class project. School districts may offer professional development courses on the use of handheld devices and podcasting for instruction. Teachers are being encouraged to communicate with parents and guardians via e-mail and postings on the school's website. Students generally appreciate the opportunity to work on the computers. They like the interactivity of many of the software packages. The challenge for teachers is to figure out how best to use the technology for learning, not just for entertainment and fun.

One of the values of the Internet is the user's ability to search for information about almost any subject. Search engines identify resources from many different sources and multiple perspectives. One of the skills that students should develop is how to sort through multiple sources for the information they need and how to test its accuracy. Students could use the Internet to explore topics and concepts being presented in a unit. Class time can be spent for such research activities, but it may be difficult for all students to spend the time needed, especially if a classroom has a limited number of computers. Thus, a teacher may be tempted to assign homework that requires using the Internet. A problem with assigning homework on the Internet, however, is that not all students have computers at home. Even if an assignment does not require the use of the Internet, those students who have access to it at home have an advantage in completing school projects.

PARENT INVOLVEMENT

Parents report receiving most of their information about school from their child, but they view teachers as their second source of information (MetLife, 2012). Thus, teachers are critical to the development of good communications with parents. Communications are fairly easy when the school has a history of positive and supportive parent engagement, and parents know that they are expected to work with teachers to support their child's learning. In other schools without such a history, you may have to be more proactive in engaging parents in the school. The PTA (2008) reports that thrity years of research has identified the following advantages of teachers, schools, families, and communities working together:

- Improvement of student achievement
- Higher teacher morale
- Increased communication among parents, teachers, and administrators
- Increased connections among families, school, and communities

In this section we will explore how you can communicate with parents and engage them in the school and their child's learning.

Communicating with Families

 To see how one teacher effectively interacts with a parent during a parent-teacher conference, click on the video *Working with Parents: A Parent-Teacher Conference.*

Regular and consistent communication with families has long been considered vital to the success of students. The focus of communications between you and your students' families should be on their children's learning. You should help them understand the academic expectations for the class and how they can help their children at home. Family members should be equal partners in conversations with you and other school officials. You should not do all of the talking; you should ask questions and listen to the answers. A translator can be very helpful in conversations with family members who do not speak English or have limited proficiency in English. Ask your teacher leader or principal for assistance in identifying a translator. Remember to tell families about the positive as well as negative behaviors of their children.

You should follow up with families after report cards and progress reports are released to them, especially if a child is not performing up to expectations. A recent national survey of parents, teachers, and students by MetLife (2012) found that parents want to be contacted if their child is having academic, health, or social problems. They also want teachers and the school to be responsive to their requests for information. They want to know homework policies and school procedures, and they want guidance on how to help their children be successful in school. Parents, especially in urban areas, would like teachers to be flexible about times to meet to discuss their child's progress.

In the past, teachers were dependent on mail, phone, and students to facilitate this communication. Today, Internet technologies are augmenting these standard tools in some exciting ways. Most schools have websites that can provide valuable information for families and students. Contact information and a staff directory can be very helpful. In addition, schools find that providing significant information on their website reduces the number of phone calls to school staff for frequently asked questions (FAQs). Some school districts make homework assignments available via the Web and utilize the Internet to share students' grades with parents. Even with these technologies, most parents in a recent national survey rated written communications from school as essential or very important (MetLife, 2012).

You might also use e-mail messages, short newsletters, and written notes to maintain regular communications with families. Internet services, such as *Parent Connect,* provide families password-protected access to their children's attendance records, schedules, grades, health records, and assignments. Evening activities for families provide additional opportunities for you to interact with family members in workshop settings, student performances, and athletic events. Teachers in some schools organize workshops with families in the evening to assist them in helping their children with homework.

JOURNAL FOR REFLECTION 8.3

- In what ways do you envision using technology to communicate with the families of your students?
- How might your choices be affected by the economic level of the community in which you are teaching?

Engaging Families

Families from socioeconomic and racial backgrounds similar to those of the teachers seem to have more successful interactions with educators. Upper-middle-class families are more likely to volunteer to assist teachers and support school activities at a higher rate than other families. In turn, teachers see these parents as supportive, caring families who monitor the academic progress of their children. Family members at lower income levels may want to volunteer for work at the school, but their employers will not allow them the time off from work. Other families may feel uncomfortable because the school culture is unfamiliar or they speak little or no English.

Parents are more likely to be engaged in schools when they think the teachers and school officials know the community (MetLife, 2012). This expectation could be challenging for you if you are teaching in a community where you did not grow up. You could begin to learn the community and meet parents and grandparents by participating in community events. Some school districts encourage home visits to interact with families on their home territory. In addition, home visits could be used to help strengthen struggling families (Yaffe, 2011). If your classroom includes a number of students who speak Spanish, you might learn Spanish. You might become involved in community activities for improving the quality of life for families and students. Students and parents also appreciate being involved with school activities that provide them the opportunity to be engaged in community service (MetLife, 2012).

Teachers also have expectations for how parents should assist them in improving their children's learning. Teachers hold parents responsible for ensuring that their children get sufficient rest and nutritious meals. They would like parents to emphasize the importance of education to their children and to support the school rules for behavior. They would like parents to contact them about problems their child may be having, be available to meet with teachers about their child's progress and needs, and ensure that homework is completed.

Researchers working with MetLife (2012) on its national survey identified six types of parent involvement with schools:

1. Parenting in which educators work with parents to help them improve their parenting skills and establish conditions at home to support their children's learning.
2. Communicating about school programs and their student's academic and social progress.
3. Volunteering in which the school provides a wide range of opportunities for parents and community members to support students and the school.
4. Encouraging parents and guardians to help their children with their homework and other academic goals.
5. Decision making by involving parents in school decisions.
6. Collaborating with the community by coordinating resources and services from and to the community.[1]

Parents in the survey rated schools highest on communications and lowest on assisting them with parenting. More than half of the teachers and parents in the survey also thought there is room for improvement.

Parents appear to be more engaged in schools than in the past (MetLife, 2012). Nine in ten parents report that they have attended a general school or PTA/PTO meeting, and eight in ten have attended a parent-teacher conference. Almost half have volunteered or served on a school committee, and over half have participated in school fundraising (U.S. Census Bureau, 2011). Nearly half of the students in the MetLife (2012) survey reported that their parents visit school at least once a month.

Overall four in five parents rate their child's teacher as successful in engaging them in their child's education (MetLife, 2012). However, high school parents, low-income parents, and parents in rural areas don't rate their teachers as highly. Elementary school teachers rate parent support higher than middle school or high school teachers. Teachers in high-needs schools are less likely to rate parental support and support from other teachers highly. Parents in high needs schools—those in urban areas, with greater poverty, or with more than two-thirds students of color—are less engaged than parents in other schools (MetLife, 2012).

Effectively engaging families in the school has to be a two-way exchange. Parents may volunteer to work in a classroom periodically or help with a school event or fundraising. The school, in turn, could support families by offering after-school programs, ESL programs for parents, summer programs, and resources for helping their children learn at home. Some schools have created a comfortable room with computers and other resources for use by parents.

Teachers appear to be more satisfied with their jobs when parents are more engaged with the school. They also are more optimistic about improving student learning. Likewise, parents in schools with high parental engagement rate schools higher and are more optimistic about the improvement of their child's achievement.

---

[1]Based on "MetLife". (2012, March). MetLife survey of the American teacher: Teachers, parents and the economy.

SUMMARY

TODAY'S FAMILIES

- Students in schools today come from diverse family structures. Although a majority of children live with their mother and father, many live with single parents, grandparents, adoptive parents, foster parents, gay or lesbian parents, or relatives.
- Students from low-income families face food insecurity and sometimes find themselves homeless when their families can no longer pay their rent or mortgage with the wages they earn.

DANGERS CHILDREN AND YOUTH FACE

- One in 109 children is abused by a family member or caretaker, with children under age four being the most vulnerable.
- Nearly half of middle school and high school students report being sexually harassed at some time during their school career, with female and LGBT students most often being the victims of the attacks.

- Violence in the school setting is often the result of bullying in the hallways or school grounds but also includes electronic bullying through the Internet and cell phones.

CHALLENGES OF THE TEEN YEARS

- Adolescents struggle with economic and social realities that can affect their lives in negative ways when they make inappropriate decisions related to sexuality and the use of drugs and alcohol.
- As young people worry about what today's economic realities mean for their future, the majority are making positive decisions about postsecondary education.

PREJUDICE AND DISCRIMINATION

- Being white, high income, and English speaking provides benefits over people who are not.
- The prejudice that young people learn at home and in school can lead to discriminatory practices that harm people who are different from themselves.

ENGAGEMENT IN SCHOOL

- Less than 70 percent of African American, Hispanic, and American Indian students complete high school in four years. In many urban areas, the percentage drops to less than 50 percent for these students.
- Many young people exhibit amazing resiliency, allowing them to overcome economic and social hardships to finish school and become productive adults.
- Developing digital equity among students who have access to computers and the Internet and those who do not is one of the challenges in keeping students engaged in school.

PARENT INVOLVEMENT

- Achievement is improved when educators and families work together to support the academic and social growth of children.
- Engaging families in schools is facilitated by knowing the community and being involved in community events and projects.

DISCUSSION STARTERS

1. Families face a number of social and economic challenges that affect the well-being of their children. Which factors do you think are most damaging to children? What should teachers and schools do to help students develop resiliency and be able to achieve academically under adverse circumstances?

2. What signs might teachers see to make them wonder whether a child or adolescent is being abused? What steps should you take if you suspect abuse or other risk-taking behaviors?

3. Children and teenagers need adult support as they cope with the challenges of adolescence. Who do you think should be providing this support? What should be the role of teachers in providing the support?

4. Prejudice and discrimination can influence the academic performance of students. How can an educator's prejudice impact positively or negatively on student learning? What discriminatory practices in a school make learning at high levels difficult for a disproportionate number of students who are at the greatest risk of poor academic achievement? How will you ensure that your own prejudices will not negatively impact students in your classroom?

5. Some researchers are suggesting that the testing requirements supported by federal legislation are pushing students out of school. Some school districts have been accused of underrepresenting the number of dropouts. Why might a school system want to underreport the number of dropouts? Why would a skeptic suggest that the federal and state requirements are pushing some students out of school?

6. Teaching in a community in which you did not grow up or with which you have limited familiarity can be a challenge, especially for a new teacher. How could you learn about a community that was new to you? How could you become engaged in that community?

SCHOOL-BASED OBSERVATIONS

1. As you observe classrooms, pay attention to how teachers are interacting with students from different racial and socioeconomic groups. What, if any, differences do you observe? Are the differences appropriate? Why or why not? What adjustments in the interactions would you make if you were the teacher?

2. Technology can be used in a wide variety of ways in classrooms and within lessons. In classrooms that you are observing this semester, how is technology being used? What innovative practices have you observed? How is technology being used to promote student learning? How would you rate the use of technology to engage students in learning?

PORTFOLIO DEVELOPMENT

1. Prepare a paper on the educational opportunities for homeless students in your community or another area of the state with larger numbers of homeless families. What services are provided to these students by the school district? What is the school district doing to ensure that homeless students will be able to keep up with their academic work? Conclude your paper by reflecting on how you will work with homeless children when you become a teacher.

2. Compare the high school graduation rates in a suburban and urban school district in your area or state. To access graduation rates for a school district, visit the website of the National Center for Education Statistics at **www.nces .ed.gov** and prepare graphs and a summary of the most recent data available.

WEB SOLUTIONS

A number of schools are expecting teachers to visit with parents on their home turf to learn more about students and their cultures. However, many teachers are reluctant to conduct home visits. The following websites may assist you in preparing for this challenge:

www.pthvp.org The website of Parent Teacher Home Visit Project was initiated in Sacramento, California, to build trust and respect between teachers and families. The goal of the project is to instill cultural competency and increase personal and professional capacity for all involved. You will be able to download information about the project and the description of the Sacramento model for conducting home visits.

MyEducationLab™   Go to the topics **Student Diversity** and **Schools and Society** in the MyEducationLab (**www.myeducationlab.com**) for *Foundations of American Education: Becoming Effective Teachers in Challenging Times, 16e*, where you can:

- Find learning outcomes for **Student Diversity** and **Schools and Society**, along with the national standards that connect to these outcomes.
- Complete Assignments and Activities that can help you more deeply understand the chapter content.
- Apply and practice your understanding of the core teaching skills identified in the chapter with the Building Teaching Skills and Dispositions learning units.
- Access video clips of CCSSO National Teachers of the Year award winners responding to the question, "Why Do I Teach?" in the Teacher Talk section.
- Create, update, and share quality lesson plans with the Lesson Plan Builder.

- Access state licensure test requirements, overviews of what tests cover, and sample test items in the Certification and Licensure section.
- Access current state and national standards in the Licensure and Standards section.
- Learn how to create a high-quality teaching portfolio in the Preparing a Portfolio section.
- Access tips, advice, and other information on resume writing and interviewing, your first year of teaching, and law and public policies in the Beginning Your Career section.
- Check your comprehension of the content covered in the chapter with the Study Plan. Here you will be able to take a chapter pretest, receive feedback on your answers, and then access personalized Review, Practice, and Enrichment exercises to enhance your understanding of chapter content. After you complete the exercises, take a posttest to confirm your comprehension.

Organizing and Paying for Education

LEARNING OUTCOMES

After reading and studying this chapter, you should be able to:

1. Describe the organizational structure of schools, school districts, states, and the federal government. (InTASC 10: Leadership and Collaboration)

2. Explain the organizational relationship of teachers to their principal and how the responsibilities of the principal relate to those of the school district superintendent and the school board. (InTASC 10: Leadership and Collaboration)

3. Summarize the key sources of funding for public education and issues related to overreliance on any one of these sources. (InTASC 10: Leadership and Collaboration)

4. Identify key issues related to equity and equality in the financing of public education. (InTASC 3: Learning Environments)

5. Understand that politics are an inherent part of education, schools, and teaching and that it is important for you to see how teachers can be effective in this arena. (InTASC 9: Professional Learning and Ethical Practice)

6. Articulate themes related to expectations for school accountability. (InTASC 9: Professional Learning and Ethical Practice)

EDUCATION in the NEWS

BANGOR SCHOOL DEPARTMENT MAKES MORE BUDGET CUTS

By ANDREW NEFF

Bangor Daily News, Posted April 05, 2012

BANGOR, Maine – The Bangor School Department's proposed 2013 overall budget has gone from a 0.54 percent increase over last year to a 0.34 percent decrease, thanks to more cuts school officials were able to make.

The total proposed budget figure goes from $41,606,064 to $41,238,725.

That's the good news for Bangor residents. The bad news is the budget still represents an overall 1.86 percent increase in the amount Bangor taxpayers will have to fund.

The increase—$391,616—results primarily from decreases in both federal and state funding. The original proposed budget's local taxpayers' share was $946,794, meaning school officials have trimmed that total taxpayer increase from 4.5 to 1.9 percent.

"That's about 15 cents per person on the mill rate," said Alan Kochis, Bangor School Department business office director. "This budget is actually $200,000 less than our 2009 budget."

The cuts came through use of an additional $250,000 from the department's undesignated fund balance, a lowered estimate on health insurance ($140,239 less), and a $27,000 cut in the United Technologies Center budget for vocational education.

Kochis said another big help was the $2.8 million federal Qualified School Construction Bond approved by the City Council that allows the department to trim $200,000 in minor capital improvements from the budget.

"This allows us to get a whole bunch of projects done over the next two years that would normally take about six budget cycles to do," Kochis said.

"And with the other new cuts, we're now a negative budget without impacting programs."

Bangor Councilor Cary Weston was encouraged by the latest budget news, but still struck a cautious note.

"It's encouraging to see the school department and superintendent whittle down their budget to find all possible savings and priorities," Weston said.

"Though the budget shows a minimal change from last year to this year due to funding differences, it's still asking for $400,000 new dollars from Bangor taxpayers.

"We'll continue to look at all areas before approving any budgets as there are major shortages and fiscal challenges throughout the city."

The proposed budget will be initially presented to the Bangor Council on Monday, April 11. The final budget will be presented for approval on Wednesday, May 9.

QUESTIONS FOR REFLECTION

1. What are the different sources of funding for schools that are identified in this article?

2. As a teacher, how would you explain to Bangor citizens what the impact of the reduced budget will be on their schools and on you as a teacher? What will local citizens think about after reading this article?

3. In some cities the school district budget is connected to the city budget. How does this both complicate and simplify establishing the final school district budget?

Source: Andrew Neff, *Bangor Daily News*, April 5, 2012. Reprinted by permission.

MyEducationLab™

Visit the MyEducationLab for *Foundations of American Education* to enhance your understanding of chapter concepts with a personalized *Study Plan*. You'll also have the opportunity to hone your teaching skills through video- and case-based *Assignments and Activities* and *Building Teaching Skills* and *Dispositions* lessons.

Have you ever thought about the size of the public education system? It is large! For example, in the fall of 2011 more than 49 million students entered 99,000 public elementary and secondary schools. More than $525 billion would be spent across the 2011–2012 school year. These are big numbers.

A major challenge is how best to organize the very large system of education so that it is efficient and effective. In addition, the necessary funds have to be found, and they must be spent wisely. As a result, the organization of schools, taxes, spending, school efficiencies, and accountability are continuing hot topics. Examining each of these topics and making decisions about them entails complex processes that are addressed through politics.

Funding has been a nationwide problem especially since the beginning of the great recession in the fall of 2008. As is reflected in the "Education in the News" article, those engaged in deciding on school budgets have to keep in mind that obtaining sufficient funds from the various sources to support schools has to be accomplished without simultaneously causing a taxpayer revolt.

Teachers are just one part of the very large and complex education system that includes all levels of government. Historically, since the U.S. Constitution does not address education directly, the primary authority and responsibility for schools has been assigned to the states. However, in the past sixty years the federal government has become directly involved. The No Child Left Behind statute passed in 2001 is a clear example of this increasing federalism. It is likely that the role of the federal government will continue to increase.

Also, as is described later in this chapter, politics and accountability are closely linked. One consequence is that from here on teachers are not likely to receive pay increases by simply having one more year of teaching experience. Public and political pressures are setting community expectations that any increases in salaries are to be tied to increases in performance. Student test scores, qualifications of teachers and principals, and other indicators of increasing performance are now important aspects of accountability.

SCHOOL DISTRICTS: ORGANIZATION AND FINANCES

All families and communities in the United States have access to a public school. The school may be located around the corner or a very long bus ride away. Unless a community is very small and remote, it will have more than one school organized as a school district or **local education agency (LEA)**. During the 2009–2010 school year, 13,629 districts were operating. These districts have many common features and also some different features. For example, some districts only have elementary schools and others only secondary schools. One of the significant differences is their size. The one hundred largest school districts each have more than 45,000 students, while some two-thirds of all school districts have fewer than 2,500 students. Another way to think about these statistics is that the many more smaller school districts serve fewer (17 percent) students, while the fewer in number larger districts serve the most (83 percent) students. (*Note*: All data reported in this chapter, unless otherwise noted, are from the U.S. Department of Education, National Center for Education Statistics, 2012.)

School District Organization

The school district is governed by a school board, and its day-to-day operations are led by a **superintendent**. In most districts, your official hiring as a teacher will be done by the superintendent

local education agency The local formal organization for a set of schools, most commonly a school district.

superintendent The administrator with overall responsibility for school district operations.

making a recommendation to the school board. Each district has its own district office, which houses an array of administrative, instructional, financial, and clerical support staff. As the state and federal levels of government have become increasingly active in setting educational agendas, a concomitant response has occurred at the district level in the form of an ever-increasing list of tasks that must be accomplished. The typical school district **organization chart** presented in Figure 9.1 reflects the additional functions and personnel that are part of the district office.

LOCAL BOARD OF EDUCATION. Legal authority for operating local school systems is given to local boards of education through state statutes. The statutes prescribe specifically how school board members are to be chosen and what duties and responsibilities they have in office. The statutes also specify the terms of board members, procedures for selecting officers of the board, duties of the officers, and procedures for filling any vacancies. Local citizens serving as school board members, also called *trustees,* are official agents of the state.

Most school boards in the United States are elected by popular vote in special **nonpartisan** elections, in which candidates are not associated with a particular political party. In some cities the mayor will appoint board members. The percentage of appointed school boards is higher in school districts enrolling more than 25,000 pupils; yet even in three-fourths of these larger districts, the board members are elected.

Usually, teachers cannot be board members in the districts where they teach; however, they can be board members in districts where they live if they teach in different districts. The trend toward more teachers becoming board members most likely results from the goal of professional associations to secure seats on school boards.

organization chart
A graphic representation of the line and staff relationships of personnel in a school, school district, or other type of organization.

nonpartisan Candidates and elections that are not associated with a particular political party.

FIGURE 9.1 Typical school district line and staff organization chart.

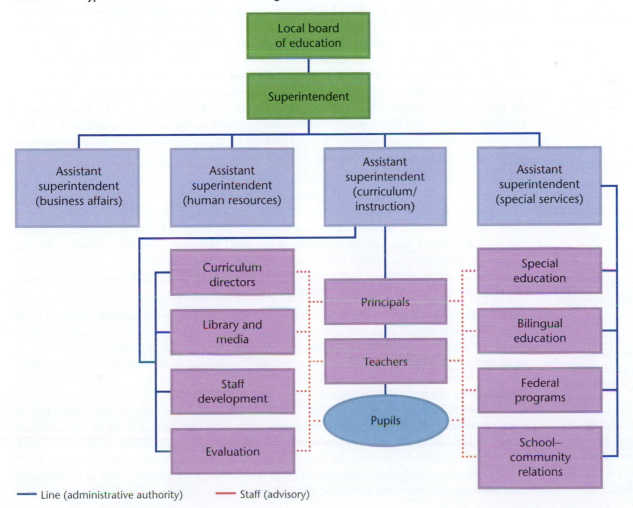

More than 90 percent of school boards are elected by popular vote; the rest are appointed.

 To hear one school superintendent describe the different challenges facing other superintendents, click on the video *Challenges Facing Superintendents: One Superintendent's Perspective.*

mandatory Duties and responsibilities that must be accomplished.

discretionary Duties and responsibilities that may be done by the designated body or may be delegated to another.

line relationship An organizational arrangement in which a subordinate is directly responsible to a supervisor.

staff relationship An organizational arrangement in which one party is not under the direct control or authority of another.

Powers and Duties of School Boards. The powers and duties of school boards vary from state to state; the school codes of the respective states spell them out in detail. A school board's major function is the development of policy for the local school district—policy that must be in harmony with both federal and state laws. Boards have only those powers granted or implied by statute that are necessary to carry out their responsibilities. These powers usually include the power to act as follows:

- Obtain revenue.
- Maintain schools.
- Purchase sites and build buildings.
- Purchase materials and supplies.
- Organize and provide programs of study.
- Employ necessary workers and regulate their services.
- Admit and assign pupils to schools and control their conduct.

Some duties of school boards are **mandatory**, whereas others are **discretionary**. Some duties cannot be delegated. If, for example, the state has given boards the power to employ teachers, they must do this; the power cannot be delegated—even to a school superintendent. Boards can delegate much of the hiring *process* to administrators, however, and then act officially on administrative recommendations for employment. An illustration of a discretionary power left to the local board is the decision whether to participate in a nonrequired school program—for example, a program of competitive athletics. Another illustration of discretionary power is the decision to employ only teachers who exceed minimum state certification standards.

SUPERINTENDENT OF SCHOOLS. One of the primary duties of the local board is to select its chief executive officer, the superintendent. There is one notable exception to the general practice of selection of the superintendent by school boards. In a few states, especially in the Southeast, some school district superintendents are elected by the voters. In these situations, school superintendent selection is a political process just like that used for the election of mayors, county commissioners, some judges, and others. In either case, whether named by the board or elected by the people, the superintendent is responsible for the day-to-day operations of the school district, responding to the interests of school board members, planning the district's budget, and defining the district's long-term aspirations. The superintendent is expected to be visible in the community and to provide overall leadership for the district.

THE CRITICAL IMPORTANCE OF LEADERSHIP. The importance of leadership by the superintendent and board members cannot be overemphasized. The quality of the educational program of a school district is influenced strongly by the leadership that the board of education and the superintendent provide. Without the communication and support of high expectations by boards and superintendents, high-quality education is not likely to be achieved. For example, offering curriculum programs that exceed state-required minimums is discretionary. For a school district to excel, the local authorities, board members, and superintendent must convince their communities that specified school programs are both needed and desirable.

LINE AND STAFF RELATIONSHIPS. Another important organizational concept to keep in mind is the difference between line and staff relationships. In any organization, some people will have the job of being executives, bosses, managers, or directors. Other people will be supervised by these persons. The supervisor typically has the authority, at least to some degree, to direct, monitor, and evaluate the work of the subordinate. When one person has this type of authority over another, there is a **line relationship**.

When there is no formal supervisory authority of one person over the other, they have a **staff relationship**. This distinction becomes especially important in education because in many instances it is not clear or absolute who has the authority or responsibility to direct the work of others. For example, teachers, as professionals, can legitimately claim more independence than can employees of other organizations. But teachers are not completely free to do whatever they want. If they were, the system of education would break down, at least in the experience of the students who must move through it, who would most likely not receive a coherent K–12 curriculum.

CENTRAL OFFICE STAFF. The superintendent of schools works with a staff to carry out the district's program of education. Although the size of the staff varies with the school district, some kind of formal organization is necessary. Each school district will have an organization chart similar to the one shown earlier in Figure 9.1.

In an organization chart, line officers hold the administrative power as it flows from the local board of education down to the pupils. Superintendents, assistant superintendents, and principals are line officers vested with authority over the people below them on the chart. Each person is directly responsible to the official above and must work through that person in dealing with a higher official. This arrangement is frequently referred to as the *chain of command*.

Administrative staff positions are shown in Figure 9.1 as branching out from the direct flow of authority. Staff includes librarians, curriculum coordinators, staff developers, guidance officers, transportation officers, and others. They are responsible to their respective superiors but have no line authority over teachers. They assist and advise others using their special knowledge and abilities. Teachers are generally referred to as staff even though they are in the direct flow of authority. However, their line authority in this arrangement prevails only over pupils.

School District Expenditures

One important task of school districts is to obtain and spend the money required for schooling. The amount of money involved is significant. For example, it is estimated that in the 2012 school year more than $571 billion will be spent on schooling. This will be an average of nearly $10,300 per pupil. All of this money has to come from somewhere (including your taxes) and must be allocated in ways that are equitable.

Major expenditure categories are presented in Figure 9.2. As you would expect, the largest percentage, approximately two-thirds of the total amount, is direct spending on instruction. However, more than one-third is spent on other components. School buses must be purchased and have drivers; district staff and administrators must report to the state and federal governments about activities and how funds are spent; school buildings have to be constructed and maintained. All of the funds cannot go directly to instruction.

INTERMEDIATE UNITS. One other type of organization that you as a teacher should know about is the **intermediate unit**. These organizations function between the state department of education and the local school districts. They may be organized by county or represent a consortium of several districts. These units have different names in different states. For example, in some states, such as New York and Colorado, they are called BOCES (boards of cooperative educational services); in Texas they are called regional service centers; in California, county education offices, and in Georgia, regional education service agencies (RESAs).

A fundamental purpose of the intermediate unit is to provide services that an individual district cannot efficiently or economically provide. Cooperative provisions for special education and vocational–technical education have been very successful. Other services that intermediate units can provide include audiovisual libraries, centralized purchasing, in-service training for teachers and principals as well as other school workers, health services, instructional materials, laboratories, legal services, and special consultant services. Stimulated by educational reform, the in-service dimension of the intermediate units has escalated in some states in recent years.

THE ORGANIZATION OF SCHOOLS

The basic building block of the U.S. education system is the school. There are nearly 99,000 public schools across the nation. To an amazing extent, schools are organized in the same way in each state. In fact, schools are organized pretty much the same in other countries too.

The all-too-typical school building consists of a set of classrooms, with corridors for the movement of students, and a central office. It has one or more large spaces for a cafeteria and gymnasium/auditorium. Schools also have staff lounges where teachers can make preparations, relax, and exchange ideas. School campuses have outside spaces for a playground, athletics,

intermediate unit An education organization located between local districts and the state that delivers support services to one or more school districts.

FIGURE 9.2   Percentage distribution of total current expenditures[1] for public elementary and secondary education in the United States, by function: 2008–09.

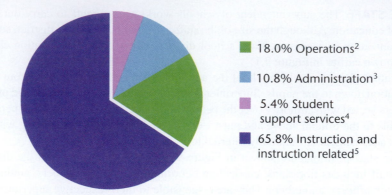

- 18.0% Operations[2]
- 10.8% Administration[3]
- 5.4% Student support services[4]
- 65.8% Instruction and instruction related[5]

NOTE: Values were affected by redistribution of reported values to correct for missing data items, and/or to distribute state direct support expenditures.

[1] Include instruction, instruction-related, support services, and other elementary/secondary current expenditures, but exclude expenditures on capital outlay, other programs, and interest on long-term debt.

[2] Include operations and maintenance, student transportation, food services, and enterprise operations.

[3] Include general administration, school administration, and other support services.

[4] Include attendance and social work, guidance, health, psychological services, speech pathology, audiology, and other student support services.

[5] Include current expenditures for classroom instruction (including teachers and teaching assistants), libraries, in-service teacher training, curriculum development, student assessment, and instruction technology.

Source: U.S. Department of Education, National Center for Education Statistics, Common Core of Data (CCD), "National Public Education Financial Survey (NPEFS)," fiscal year 2009, Version 1a.

parking (staff and students), and a driveway for dropping off and picking up students. Wherever you go, you will find this basic architecture.

This typical design of schools is frequently criticized for resembling an egg crate. If you viewed a school building with the roof off, you would see that it resembled an egg carton: a series of cells or pockets with routes running between them. Some educational critics see this architecture as interfering with the need to introduce new educational practices. For example, the walls restrict communication between teachers and channel the flow of student traffic. Teachers have to make an effort to see what goes on in any other classrooms.

Even when a school is built with modest attempts to change the interior space, teachers and students still seem to want to preserve the egg-crate concept. For example, you may have visited an elementary school that had an open-space design. Instead of self-contained classrooms, there might be an open floor plan equivalent in size to three or four classrooms. However, if you observed the arrangement of furniture, bookshelves, and screens, you probably noted that teachers and students had constructed zones and areas that were equivalent to three or four self-contained classrooms.

This is not meant to criticize teachers for how they have adapted to new school architectures; rather, it is meant to point out how the organization of the space parallels the activities of the people who use it. There are many good reasons for organizing schools around self-contained classrooms. And in the case of the open-space concept, the noise from three or four teachers and 90 to 120 students can be so disruptive that little learning can occur. One key to the successful use of open-space plans, then, is to be sure the building is designed in ways that control and dampen noise.

The physical arrangement of a school into individual classrooms has organizational as well as instructional implications. For example, it is easy for teachers to be isolated in their

FIGURE 9.3 A school organization chart.

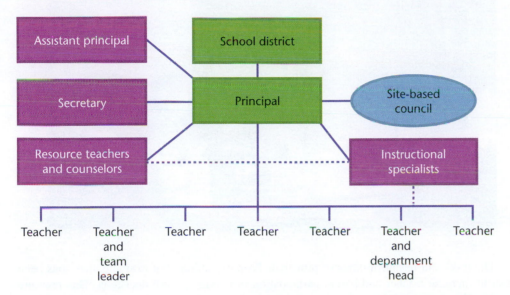

classrooms. This geographic isolation contributes to their not knowing about or becoming engaged with issues that affect the whole school. Geographic isolation can affect the school as a whole too. The school staff might not be aware of community concerns or of what is going on in other schools across the district. Teachers and administrators must make deliberate efforts to learn about other parts of the education system.

The School Organization Chart

All of the people within a school have to be organized in some way. Their formal working relationships can be pictured in the organization chart shown in Figure 9.3. The principal is the single line authority for all of these adults *and* for all of the students! Interestingly, most experts on organizations advocate that no more than five to seven people should be directly supervised by one administrator. Yet in nearly all schools, the principal is responsible for a minimum of thirty adults and several hundred students. In very large schools, the principal may have two hundred people to supervise. As you can see, the simple picture of "top-down" leadership breaks apart when one considers the wide array of tasks and the sheer number of people at work in each school. As a result, a number of formal roles and structures exist for arranging the relationships among the varied role groups and for facilitating coordination and communication.

JOURNAL FOR REFLECTION 9.1

Think about principals you knew when you were a student. How would you feel about having one of them as your principal when you are a teacher? What do you think each of those principals would expect of you as a teacher?

PRINCIPALS. As in school districts, schools also have line and staff relationships. At the top of the school organization chart is the principal. By law, the principal is the final authority at the school. The principal's responsibilities include instructional leadership, community relationships, supervision of staff (including teachers, secretaries, and custodians), teacher selection and evaluation, students, building and grounds, provisions of contracts, administration of the attendance office, and all budgets. The principal is in a line relationship with the school district superintendent. In larger school districts, the principal may have an intermediate supervisor, such as an assistant superintendent or a director of elementary or secondary education.

 To hear a superintendent describe characteristics of effective principals, click on the video *Effective Principals: A Superintendent's Perspective.*

The principal is responsible for the actions of all school personnel and must work closely with the superintendent and the school community.

The tasks and responsibilities of principals keep expanding. For example, there has been a push to increase teacher and parent participation in making school decisions. This pressure has led to the creation of special committees of teachers and parents to work with the principal. In addition to the traditional parent–teacher organization, most schools now have a **School Improvement Process (SIP)** and an SIP committee that includes teachers and perhaps a parent.

ASSISTANT PRINCIPALS. Larger elementary schools and most junior high schools, middle schools, and high schools have one or more additional administrators. Normally, they are called assistant principals, although sometimes in high schools they are titled vice principals. Large high schools will have several assistant or vice principals and other administrators that have "director" or "dean" titles, such as director of athletics and dean of students. These administrators share the tasks of the principal and provide additional avenues of communication between teachers, students, staff, parents, the community, and the district office.

In elementary schools, the job differentiation between the assistant principal and the principal is less clear, and both administrators will be a part of most operations. In the high school setting, specific roles and tasks will frequently be assigned to the different administrator roles. For example, in most districts, each teacher must be formally observed each year. This activity takes more time than the principal has available, so the assistant/vice principal(s) observes and evaluates some teachers. Usually, the principal concentrates on observing the new teachers because he or she makes the recommendation on whether (or not) they will be rehired.

DEPARTMENT HEADS AND TEAM LEADERS. Elementary schools normally have another, less formal level of leadership: grade-level or team leaders. These are full-time teachers who assume a communication and coordination role for their grade level(s) or team. Junior high schools and high schools have department chairs. Normally, departments are organized around the major subject areas (mathematics, science, English, and social studies) and the cocurricula (athletics and music). Teachers are members of one of the departments, which will have regular meetings to review data about student performance, plan curriculum, and facilitate communication. In middle schools the leaders of interdisciplinary teams serve in the same way. Department heads and team leaders also meet with the principal from time to time and bring information back to their departments. In most districts department chairs and team leaders are considered to be teachers, not administrators. One implication of this organizational arrangement is that they will not be a part of the formal teacher evaluation process.

School Improvement Process (SIP) The process whereby a school staff develop a plan and implement action steps to improve student test scores..

TEACHERS. The single largest group of adults in the school are the teachers. A typical elementary school has from fifteen to more than forty teachers, while a large high school will have more than one hundred. Teachers are busy in their classrooms working with their students, and this is where the egg-crate architecture of schools can be a problem. Unless special mechanisms are used, such as regular department/grade-level meetings, individual teachers can easily become isolated from the school as a whole. The self-contained classroom architecture and the work of attending to twenty to forty students in the classroom at any one time means that teachers have little time or opportunity to communicate with other adults. As a consequence, the principal and all of the teachers need to work hard with the other members of the school staff to facilitate communication. All must make an effort to work together to continually improve the school.

SCHOOL SUPPORT STAFF. A school has other personnel who support the administrators and teachers. One of the most important of these supporting roles is filled by the school secretary. Every experienced teacher and principal will advise you to be sure to develop a good working relationship with the school secretary, who is at the nerve center of the running of the school. When a student has a problem, when a teacher needs some materials, when the principal wants a piece of information from the files, or when a student teacher wants to know about parking a car, the first person to contact is the school secretary.

The cleanliness of your classroom as well as the whole school depends on the efforts of the custodians. They also can be helpful to teachers in locating supplies and moving furniture. Keep in mind that they observe and talk with students. Frequently, custodians and other support staff will know about something that is going on before the teachers do. Cafeteria workers are another group of adult workers in the school who can make a positive difference in how the school feels and functions. Make an effort to come to know each of these staff members. They can be a help to you, and you need to be a help to them.

INSTRUCTIONAL SPECIALISTS. An increasingly important group of education professionals in schools are the master teachers who are specialists in literacy, mathematics, and technology. These instructional specialists lead school-based professional development sessions, coach all teachers, and facilitate using data about student learning to plan instruction. Most schools will also have "resource" teachers who work with children who have special needs. They also may co-teach with the general education teachers.

Innovations in School Organization

There are several interesting and innovative approaches to school organization including on-line and hybrid programs as well as the alternative school models such as charter and magnet schools. Other organizational innovations include changing the school calendar and the daily schedule.

YEAR-ROUND SCHOOLS. The normal school year of nine to ten months with vacation all summer is often criticized. One concern is that students will forget too much over the summer. Critics point out that the current school year was instituted back in the 1800s, when most people lived on farms and the children were counted on to perform summer chores.

One interesting solution is the **year-round school**. This is not an extended school year in that students attend school for more days. Rather, year-round schools spread the time in school across twelve months. One way a school might do this is by having multiple "tracks" of six to eight weeks. During any one cycle, one-fourth to one-third of the students will be on vacation and the others will be attending classes. In this way, students have more frequent but shorter times away from school. An additional advantage is that the school site can handle more students on an annual basis. Curiously, much of the resistance to year-round schools comes from parents who are concerned about being able to schedule family vacations; however, once the schedule is implemented, most discover that being able to schedule vacations throughout the year has advantages.

FOUR-DAY WEEK. Some rural districts that have school buses traveling long distances have implemented four-day school weeks. Each of the four days is longer, but on the fifth day there is no school. Although there has been no research on this approach, the prevailing impression is that students accomplish just as much. One of the complicating factors in this structure is scheduling athletic and cocurricula activities.

STAGGERED START TIMES. A very effective solution to having several thousand kids arrive at school at the same time is have different start times. For example, ninth and tenth graders arrive for the beginning of the first period, while eleventh and twelfth graders don't arrive until the beginning of the second period.

GO TO ···>
Among the innovative instructive approaches to school organization are charter schools and vouchers, which were described in Chapter 6.

year-round school
School that is open all year, with only a proportion of the students attending at any one time.

LATER START TIME FOR HIGH SCHOOLERS. The research findings are clear, and we expect that your experience is consistent with the research. Adolescents' biological clocks have them not wanting to get up early in the morning, while elementary school students are more likely to wake up early (Mayo Clinic staff, n.d.). A few school districts are reversing the start times. Elementary schools have an earlier start time, with secondary schools starting later in the morning. There are even suggestions that student learning increases when this relatively simple schedule change is made. Of course the frequently heard objection is the bus schedule, which is perceived as too difficult to run in reverse. Another structure for increasing time for teaching and learning is to lengthen the school day, which is the topic in the "Who is Right?" feature.

FEEDER SCHOOL ALIGNMENT. In the majority of school districts, communication and co-ordination across levels of schooling are quite limited. A few school districts have created an organization arrangement that places a high school and the junior high/middle schools and el-ementary schools whose students "feed" into it in one unit. In this alignment there can be vertical communication and coordination that result in continuity around curriculum and more communi-cation among administrators and teachers. An additional strength is the possibility of all admin-istrators and teachers attending to the transition of students from one school to the next.

ORGANIZATION OF EDUCATION AT THE STATE LEVEL

In certain countries, such as Taiwan, the national constitution specifies responsibility for educa-tion, but the U.S. Constitution does not say anything about education. The Tenth Amendment has been interpreted as granting this power to the states. As a consequence, the states are the govern-mental units in the United States charged with the responsibility for education. Local school dis-tricts, then, receive through state law the power to administer and operate the school system for

WHO IS RIGHT?

SHOULD THE SCHOOL DAY BE LENGTHENED?

An important school organizational structure is the length of the school day. As many school districts are forced to cut budgets, some are push-ing for a longer school day. For example, in the fall of 2011 Chicago Mayor Rahm Emanuel announced an initiative to add ninety minutes to the school day. In other districts a seventh or eighth period is being added to the high school schedule. In some districts an additional week is being added to the school calendar. What do you think—is adding an hour or more to the school day a good idea, or a bad one?

YES

Extending the school day provides expanded learning time (ELT). There is more time for instruction and therefore more opportunity to increase student learning. ELT, when an extra period is added in secondary schools, provides added opportunities for electives, field trips and credit retrieval. ELT can be applied in more innovative ways too, such as having staggered start times, students having more time to do academic assignments, and teachers having more time to meet with students.

Adding to the school day has benefits for families too. In many families where both parents are working there will be less need to find after-school child care. ELT also can provide more flexibility in arranging parent conferences.

NO

This is just another simple solution to what really is a complex prob-lem. Simply adding more time doesn't mean that it will be used effectively. Many schools already have after-school programs. Ex-tending the day will mean later start times for after-school athletics and other extracurricula activities. More time in school means less time for children to play before it gets dark outside.

There also is the very serious question of how ELT will be paid for. The additions to teacher salaries, facilities costs, and supervisory costs must come from somewhere. ELT presumes that teachers do not have work to do other than being in the classroom. Teacher col-laboration, grading papers, and preparing for tomorrow's lessons have to be done sometime. Also, where is the research that supports ELT leading to increases in student learning?

WHAT IS YOUR PERSPECTIVE ON THIS ISSUE?

FIGURE 9.4 State organization chart.

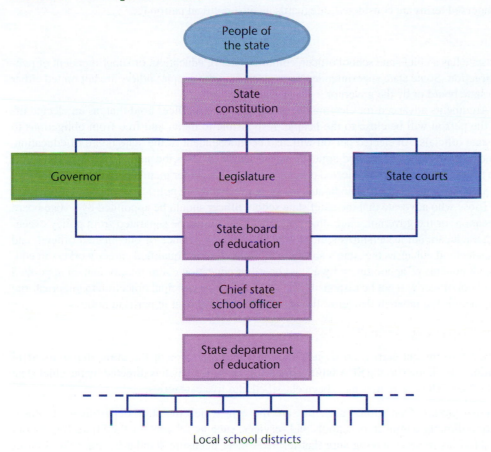

their communities. State legislatures, within the limits expressed by the federal Constitution and their own state's constitutions, are the chief policy makers for education. State legislatures grant powers to state boards of education, state departments of education, chief state school officers, and local boards of education. Figure 9.4 shows a typical state organization chart for education.

State Board of Education

State boards of education are both **regulatory** and **advisory**. Regulatory functions include the establishment of standards for issuing and revoking teaching licenses, the establishment of standards for approving and accrediting schools, and the development and enforcement of a uniform system for gathering and reporting educational data. Advisory functions include considering the educational needs of the state, both long and short range, and recommending to the governor and the legislature ways of meeting these needs. State boards of education, in studying school problems and in suggesting and analyzing proposals, can be invaluable to the legislature, especially because the legislature is under pressure to decide so many issues. A state board can provide continuity over time for an educational program that annual or biannual legislative procedures do not accommodate. A state board can also coordinate, supplement, and establish study commissions. These commissions examine questions and issues related to such topics as the impact of setting different levels of cut-scores on tests, textbook adoptions, school finance, licensure, student learning standards, school building standards, and teacher education.

STATE BOARD MEMBERSHIP. Members of state boards of education get their positions in various ways. Some are appointed by the governor, with confirmation by the senate. In other states they may be elected by the people, the legislature, or the local school board members in a regional convention, also with confirmation by the senate. The terms of members of state boards of education are usually staggered to avoid a complete changeover at any one time. Board

GO TO ···>
Chapter 10 analyzes how the U.S. Constitution cedes responsibility for education to the states.

regulatory Functions for which the state board has the authority to establish rules and regulations that limit and permit action.

advisory Functions and areas in which the state board can only offer suggestions and indicate preference for action.

members usually serve without pay but are reimbursed for expenses. The policies of nonpayment and staggered terms are considered safeguards against political patronage.

Chief State School Officer

Every state has a chief state school officer, commissioner of education, or superintendent of public instruction. Some state superintendents are elected by the people; others are appointed either by the state board or by the governor.

Arguments advanced for electing the chief state school officer hold that, as an elected official, the person will be close to the people, responsible to them, and free from obligations to other state officials. An elected person will also be independent of the state board of education. Opponents of the election method argue that this method exposes the state department of education to partisan politics, that an elected official is obligated to other members of the same political party, and that many excellent candidates prefer not to engage in political contests.

Those who advocate that the chief state school officer should be appointed by a state board of education, or the governor, claim that policy making should be separated from policy execution, that educational leadership should not rest on the competence of one elected official, and that this method enhances the state's ability to recruit and retain qualified career workers in education. Opponents of appointment by a state board of education claim mainly that an appointed chief school officer will not be responsible to the people. The principal objection to gubernatorial appointment is the inherent danger of the appointee's involvement in partisan politics.

State Department of Education

The state government carries on its activities in education through the **state department of education**, also known as the **SEA (state education agency)**, which is directed by the chief state school officer. These activities have been classified into five categories:

1. *Operational:* Operational activities are those in which the state department of education directly administers schools and services, such as schools for the blind. Regulatory activities include making sure that teachers meet licensure standards, that school buses are safe, and that curricular requirements are fulfilled. Service activities include advising and consulting, disseminating research, and preparing materials (on state financial aid, for example).

2. *Regulatory:* SEA personnel now regularly audit school performance on state tests, review school improvement plans, and force restructuring of low-performing schools and school districts.

3. *Developmental:* Developmental activities are directed at improving performance across all schools and districts; they include planning, staffing, and research into better performance for the operational and regulatory as well as the service functions.

4. *Public support:* Public support and cooperation activities involve public relations, political activities with the legislature and governor, and relations with various other governmental and nongovernmental agencies.

5. *Monitoring:* The monitoring function has become increasingly important as the federal government has pressed for more accountability.

State Legislature

state department of education The state office that has day-to-day oversight responsibility for K-12 education.

state education agency (SEA) The general term for the state department of education, or state department of public instruction.

State legislatures are generally responsible for creating, operating, managing, and maintaining state school systems. The legislators are the state policy makers for education. State legislatures create state departments of education to execute state policy. State legislatures, though powerful, also operate under controls.

In these difficult economic times, the most important actions of state legislatures involve making decisions about the financing of schools. The sources of funds, including tax structures, and the distribution of funds for education are determined by state legislatures. Legislatures also can become involved in other education issues such as licensure standards, tenure rights of teachers, programs of study, building construction standards for health and safety, and compulsory attendance laws.

State legislatures, in their legislative deliberations about the schools, are continually importuned by special-interest groups. These groups, realizing that the legislature is the focus of legal control of education, and how the funds are allocated, can exert considerable influence on individual legislators. Some of the representative influential groups are illustrated in Figure 9.8, which will be described later in this chapter.

It is not uncommon for more than a thousand bills to be introduced each year in a state legislative session. Many of these bills originate with special-interest groups. In recent years, state legislatures have dealt with education bills on a wide range of topics, including accountability, finance, textbooks, adult basic education, length of the school year, legal holidays, lotteries, teacher and student testing, no pass/no play policies, and school standards of various sorts.

Governor

The top executive in each state is the governor. Many governors have emphasized the importance of education in their states. Beginning in 2011, several Republican governors reversed the traditional perspective by supporting legislation that would reduce the influence and rights of teachers and other public employees. For example, governors in Wisconsin, Ohio, and Arizona supported legislation to eliminate the collective bargaining rights of teachers and selected other categories of public employees. Don't forget that governors can also veto school legislation. When there is a dispute over the interpretation of legislation or a challenge to its constitutionality, the attorney general and the state judiciary system will become involved.

PAYING FOR SCHOOLS

School systems nationwide receive their funds from federal, state, and local sources. In recent years the proportion of dollars from each source has remained quite constant. On average the state provides around 46 percent of the funding, local sources provide around 44 percent, and federal sources provide a little over 9 percent. However, as you can see in Figure 9.5, there are state-by-state differences in the amount of federal dollars received. Still, contrary to what you might have thought, public education is primarily funded by local and state sources of revenue. This means that the governor and legislature in each state will have the most say in how well their schools will be funded and where the majority of funds will come from.

Key Finance Questions

When the financing of education is considered, the first questions asked by the taxpayers are "How much do I have to pay?" and "How much will my school(s) receive?" In the last thirty years, two other questions have sharpened the discussions about education finance: "Does each school across the state have the same amount of funding?" This is the **equity** question. "Is there enough funding so that students can achieve?" This is the **adequacy** or **sufficiency** question. The equity question was at the center of many school funding lawsuits in the 1980s and 1990s. In 1989 a decision of the Kentucky Supreme Court brought the adequacy question to the forefront. That court decision held that every child in the state had the right to an "adequate" education. The direct consequence of that decision was the state legislature passing the Kentucky Education Reform Act (KERA) in 1990. The significance of KERA is that it did not deal solely with equalizing spending by each school district—that is, equity. KERA went further by specifically connecting funding with implementation of school and curriculum reforms, specifying student outcomes and development of a statewide strategy for assessing academic achievement.

Any discussion related to the financing of education now has to deal with all three questions: "How much will each source pay?" This question is the key theme in the "Education in the News" feature at the beginning of this chapter. The other two questions also have to be addressed: "Is there equity in the distribution?" and "Are the resources adequate so that all students can achieve the identified outcomes?"

System of Taxation and Support for Schools

The "Education in the News" article clearly illustrates how support for education is dependent on a variety of taxes paid to local, state, and federal governments. Each of these government sources distributes some of the tax dollars it takes in to local school districts.

equity Provision of the same amount of funding to all schools or students.

adequacy The provision of sufficient funds so that all students can achieve.

sufficiency The provision of adequate funding so that all students can achieve.

FIGURE 9.5 Federal revenues as a percentage of total revenues for public elementary and secondary education in the United States: 2008–09.

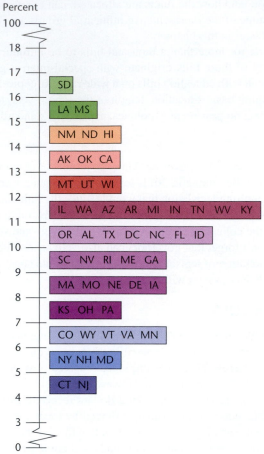

Note: Classification is based on the unrounded amount.

Source: U.S. Department of Education, National Center for Education Statistics, Common Core of Data (CCD), "National Public Education Financial Survey (NPEFS)," fiscal year 2009, Version 1a.

The three principal kinds of taxes that provide revenue for schools are property taxes, sales or use taxes, and income taxes. The property tax is generally a local tax, whereas the sales tax generally is a state and local mix, while income taxes are collected at the city, state, and federal levels. As mentioned earlier, more than $525 billion in revenues were raised by local, state, and federal governments to fund public education for the 2011–2012 fiscal year. Each type of tax has advantages and disadvantages, yet it is unlikely that any one of these taxes, used by itself for education, would be sufficient.

In evaluating a system of taxes, one should consider the varying ability of citizens to pay, the economic effects of the taxes on the taxpayer, the benefits that various taxpayers receive, the total yield of the tax, the economy of collection, the degree of acceptance, the convenience of paying, the problems of tax evasion, the stability of the tax, and the general adaptability of the system. Clearly, systems of taxation are complicated; each system is an intricately interdependent network.

PROPERTY TAXES AND LOCAL REVENUE. Until recently, the **property tax** was the primary source of revenue for schools. It is based on the value of property, both real estate and personal. Real estate includes land holdings and buildings such as homes, commercial buildings, and factories. Personal property consists of automobiles, machinery, furniture, livestock, and intangibles such as stocks and bonds. The property tax has both advantages and limitations.

Property Taxes: Advantages and Limitations. An advantage of taxing property is that it is not easily moved to escape taxation, as income might be. Also, because the owners of property pay

property tax A tax based on the value of property, both real estate and personal.

the tax, it is easy to identify them. Historically, the main advantage of the property tax was its stability. Although the tax tends to lag behind changes in market values, it provides a steady, regular income for the taxing agency. However, since the beginning of the 2008 recession there has been significant decline in property values. This has led to reduction in taxes being paid with a consequence being fewer dollars for schools.

The property tax has numerous limitations. It can have a negative impact on the value of housing: It tends to discourage rehabilitation and upkeep because both of these tend to raise the value of the property and therefore its taxes. The tax is often a deciding factor in locating a business or industry, and it is likely not to be applied equally on all properties.

The funding of schools is closely tied to the assessed value of property, especially real estate.

Determining the Value of Property. One problem with the property tax lies in the potential unfairness of inconsistent property assessments. In some areas, assessors are local people, usually elected, with no special training in evaluating property. Their duty involves inspecting their neighbors' properties and placing values on them. In other areas, sophisticated techniques involving expertly trained personnel are used for property appraisal. In either circumstance, assessors are likely to be subject to political and informal pressures to keep values low in order to keep tax rates low.

The assessed value of property is usually only a percentage of its market value. This percentage varies from county to county and from state to state. Attempts are made within states to equalize assessments or to make certain that the same percentage of full cash value is used in assessing property throughout the state. In recent years, attempts have been made to institute full cash value for the assessed value. For the property tax to be a fair tax, equalized assessment is a necessity.

Property Tax: Progressive or Regressive? Property tax is most generally thought of as a **progressive tax**—that is, one that taxes according to ability to pay; the more wealth one has in property, the more one pays. But because assessments can be unequal and because frequently the greatest wealth is no longer related to real estate, the property tax can be regressive. **Regressive taxes**, such as sales and use taxes, are those that affect low-income groups disproportionately. Some evidence supports the contention that people in the lowest income groups pay a much higher proportion of their income in property taxes than persons in the highest income groups.

Inequities of the Property Tax. Significant support for schools across the nation has been provided by the property tax. However, as described previously, because of schools' heavy dependence on property taxes for financing, enormous discrepancies in resources and quality have built up between schools located in rich and in poor communities.

Property taxes are calculated on the basis of assessed valuations, so a district with a high assessed valuation per pupil is in a better position to provide quality education than is one with a low assessed valuation per pupil. To illustrate the school finance consequences of differences in local wealth, let's look at a simple example. If school district A has an assessed valuation of $90 million and one thousand pupils, for example, and school district B has an assessed valuation of $30 million and one thousand pupils, a tax rate of $2 per $100 of assessed valuation would produce $1.8 million for education in district A and only $600,000 in district B. School district A could therefore spend $1,800 per pupil, compared with $600 per pupil in school district B, with the same local tax effort.

progressive tax A tax that is scaled to the ability of the taxpayer to pay.

THE PERSPECTIVE OF THE COURTS ON TAXATION AND EDUCATION. Can the property tax continue to be the primary base for financing schools? This question was asked of the U.S. Supreme Court in *San Antonio (Texas) Independent School District v. Rodriguez* (1979).

regressive tax A tax that affects low-income groups disproportionately.

Keep in mind that the U.S. Constitution does not mention education, so any litigation has to be based on indirect connections. In the *Rodriguez* case, the challenge was initiated under the equal protection clause of the Fourteenth Amendment. This clause prohibits state action that would deny citizens equal protection. The U.S. Supreme Court, in a five-to-four decision, reversed the lower court decision in *Rodriguez* and thus reaffirmed the local property tax as a basis for school financing. Justice Potter Stewart, voting with the majority, admitted that "the method of financing public schools … can be fairly described as chaotic and unjust." He did not, though, find it unconstitutional. The majority opinion, written by Justice Lewis F. Powell, Jr., stated, "We cannot say that such disparities are the product of a system that is so irrational as to be invidiously discriminatory." Justice Thurgood Marshall, in the dissenting opinion, charged that the ruling "is a retreat from our historic commitment to equality of education opportunity." Another part of the opinion in *Rodriguez* addressed the role of the states in supporting public education:

> The consideration and initiation of fundamental reforms with respect to state taxation and education are matters reserved for legislative processes of the various States, and we do no violence to the values of federalism and separation of powers by staying our hand. We hardly need add that this Court's action today is not to be viewed as placing its judicial imprimatur on the status quo. The need is apparent for reform in tax systems which may well have relied too long and too heavily on the local property tax. And certainly innovative thinking as to public education, its methods, and its funding is necessary to assure both a higher level of quality and greater uniformity of opportunity. These matters merit the continued attention of the scholars who already have contributed much by their challenges. But the ultimate solutions must come from the lawmakers and from the democratic pressures of those who elect them.[1]

These comments in *Rodriguez* foreshadowed the continuing string of school finance suits that have been filed in most states.

State Sources of Revenue

Clearly, states are the major source of funding for schools. In the most recent year for which statistics are available, the states provided 48.3 percent of the fiscal resources for local schools. This money is referred to as **state aid**, and within most states all or a major portion of this money is used to help achieve equality of opportunity.

The main sources of tax revenue for states have been classified by the Department of Commerce into four groups: sales and gross receipt taxes, income taxes, licenses, and miscellaneous. Sales and gross receipt taxes include taxes on general sales, motor fuels, alcohol, insurance, and amusements; income taxes include both individual and corporate; licenses include those on motor vehicles, corporations, occupations, vehicle operators, hunting, and fishing. The miscellaneous classification includes property taxes, taxes on severance or extraction of minerals, and death and gift taxes. The two largest sources of state revenues are sales and income taxes.

SALES AND INCOME TAXES. Sales and income taxes are lucrative sources of revenue for most states. Also, it is relatively easy to administer both. The sales tax is collected bit by bit, in a relatively painless way, by the vendor, who is responsible for keeping records. The state income tax can be withheld from wages; hence, collection is eased. Income taxes are considered progressive taxes because they frequently are scaled to the ability of the taxpayer to pay. Sales taxes are regressive; they affect low-income groups disproportionately. All people pay the sales tax at the same rate, so people in low-income groups pay as much tax as people in high-income groups. Part of the advantage of sales taxes and income taxes is that they can be regulated by the legislature.

GAMBLING: AN INCREASING SOURCE OF REVENUE. In 1964, New Hampshire implemented a lottery. Since then, legalized gambling in its many forms, from casinos and riverboats to horse racing, has become an important source of state and local revenues. By 2012 forty-three states and the District of Columbia were operating lotteries. Every state, except Hawaii and Utah, collect revenue from one or more forms of gambling. Further, in every year between 1998 and 2010 (with the exception of 2009), gambling revenues went up.

Gambling is an indirect source of revenue in the sense that it is not seen as a direct tax on citizens; instead, the revenues come through taxes on the games. Income for states from lotteries

state aid The money that states provide for the fiscal resources of local schools.

---

[1]U.S. Supreme Court, San Antonio (Texas) Independent School District v. Rodriguez (1979).

grew from $978 million in 1980 to nearly $18 billion in 2010. In total nearly $24 billion was collected by state and local governments. On average across all fifty states, gambling represents 2.4 percent of state revenue (Dadayan & Ward, 2011).

In most states, such as California and Florida, the original intent was for these funds to be used for educational enhancements. But within three years of the California lottery's implementation, in a tight budget year, the California legislature incorporated the lottery funds into the base education budget. Other states have had similar experiences. In general the revenues from gambling are but another source of funds for the state.

State Differences in the Funding of Education

A very useful statistic for evaluating differences in school funding is the **per-pupil expenditure**. This is a standardized statistic compiled by the National Center for Education Statistics that takes into account local, state, and federal funds invested in K–12 education state by state. The most recently available data are presented in Figure 9.6.

JOURNAL FOR REFLECTION 9.2

In comparison to other states (see Figure 9.6), how well is education funded in your state? Do you think the level of per-pupil expenditure for your state is sufficient?

Recent Challenges to School Finance Within the States

The number of court cases related to school finance has increased in recent years. Some states have had new suits initiated, while others are continuing to struggle to respond to earlier court decisions and directives. In all, forty-five of the states have experienced and/or are experiencing court cases that deal with school finance.

The different forms of legal gambling have become another source of funds for education.

THE STATE PERSPECTIVE ON TAXATION AND EDUCATION. The earliest court suits, those brought before 1989, were based in equal protection challenges and questions about unequal resource allocations. As LaMorte (2012) has observed, "plaintiffs were unsuccessful in about two-thirds of these cases" (p. 303). In some of these cases the plaintiffs emphasized a claim of equal protection; in others the focus was on specific language in the state's constitution.

For example, in *Serrano v. Priest* (1971), the California Supreme Court was called on to determine whether the California public school financing system, with its substantial dependence on local property taxes, violated the Fourteenth Amendment. In its six-to-one decision, the California court held that heavy reliance on unequal local property taxes "makes the quality of a child's education a function of the wealth of his parents and neighbors." Furthermore, the court declared, "Districts with small tax bases simply cannot levy taxes at a rate sufficient to produce the revenue that more affluent districts produce with a minimum effort." Officially, the California Supreme Court ruled that the system of school financing in California was unconstitutional, but it did not forbid the use of property taxes as long as the system of finance was neutral in the distribution of resources. Within a year of *Serrano v. Priest*, five other courts—in Minnesota, Texas, New Jersey, Wyoming, and Arizona—ruled similarly.

Since 1989 the plaintiffs have changed their argument from questions about equity to questions about adequacy. The question has become one of asking whether or not the state is meeting established standards. Using this new argument plaintiffs have been winning two-thirds of the cases. However, states have countered by claiming that they do not have the funds to comply. Even while acknowledging the difficulty, the courts have continued to insist that financial limitations are not an excuse to not do what the state's constitution sets out. For example, in *Claremont School District v. Governor*, 794 A.2d 744 (N.H. 2002) the court stated: "[w]e hold, therefore, that to the extent the minimum standards for school approval excuse compliance solely based on

per-pupil expenditure Average dollars spent per student.

FIGURE 9.6 Per-pupil expenditures for public elementary and secondary education in the United States: 2008–2009.

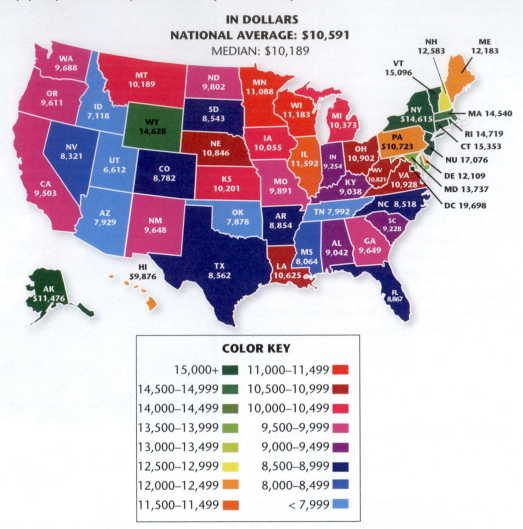

IN DOLLARS
NATIONAL AVERAGE: $10,591
MEDIAN: $10,189

WA 9,688	MT 10,189	ND 9,802	MN 11,088	WI 11,183	MI 10,373		NH 12,583	ME 12,183

NH 12,583
ME 12,183
VT 15,096
WA 9,688
MT 10,189
ND 9,802
MN 11,088
OR 9,611
ID 7,118
WY 14,628
SD 8,543
WI 11,183
MI 10,373
NY $14,615
MA 14,540
NV 8,321
UT 6,612
NE 10,846
IA 10,055
IL 11,592
IN 9,254
OH 10,902
PA $10,723
RI 14,719
CT 15,353
NU 17,076
CA 9,503
CO 8,782
KS 10,201
MO 9,891
KY 9,038
WV 10,821
VA 10,928
DE 12,109
MD 13,737
DC 19,698
AZ 7,929
NM 9,648
OK 7,878
AR 8,854
TN 7,992
NC 8,518
SC 9,228
MS 8,064
AL 9,042
GA 9,649
HI $9,876
TX 8,562
LA 10,625
FL 8,867
AK $11,476

COLOR KEY

15,000+	■	11,000–11,499	■
14,500–14,999	■	10,500–10,999	■
14,000–14,499	■	10,000–10,499	■
13,500–13,999	■	9,500–9,999	■
13,000–13,499	■	9,000–9,499	■
12,500–12,999	■	8,500–8,999	■
12,000–12,499	■	8,000–8,499	■
11,500–11,499	■	< 7,999	■

Note: The prekindergarten student membership was imputed for some states, affecting the total student count and per pupil expenditures calculation. Some values were affected by redistribution of reported expenditure values to correct for missing data items, and/or to distribute state direct support expenditures.

Source: U.S. Department of Education, National Center for Education Statistics, Common Core of Data (CCD), "National Public Education Financial Survey (NPEFS)," fiscal year 2009, Version 1a.

financial conditions, it is facially insufficient because it is in clear conflict with the State's duty to provide a constitutionally adequate education."[2]

STATES' RESPONSIBILITY TO GUARANTEE EQUAL EDUCATIONAL OPPORTUNITY. The signal year for the shift in direction of school finance suits was 1989, with several state supreme courts making significant decisions in the direction of requiring more funding of schools. Since then, in a number of states, the education finance systems were knocked down by the courts, and the state legislatures were directed to remedy the wrongs.

In Montana, in *Helena Elementary School District v. State* (1989), the Montana Supreme Court ruled that the state's school finance system violated the state constitution's guarantee of equal educational opportunity. The state's constitution article mandates that the state establish an educational system that will develop the full educational potential of each person. In 1990 the court delayed the effects of its decision to allow the legislature time to enact a new finance system.

The Kentucky Supreme Court also ruled that the state's entire system of school governance and finance violated the state constitution's mandate for the provision of an efficient system of

---
[2]Claremont School District v. Governor, 794 A.2d 744 (N.H. 2002).

common schools throughout the state (*Rose v. The Council for Better Education Inc.*, 1989). The Kentucky Supreme Court's opinion stated:

> The system of common schools must be adequately funded to achieve its goals. The system of common schools must be substantially uniform throughout the state. Each child, *every child,* in this commonwealth must be provided with an equal opportunity to have an adequate education. Equality is the key word here. The children of the poor and the children of the rich, the children who live in poor districts and the children who live in the rich districts must be given the same opportunity and access to an adequate education. This obligation cannot be shifted to local counties and local school districts.[3]

The court directed the state legislature to develop a new educational system, which was adopted as the Kentucky Education Reform Act (KERA) in 1990.

Throughout the 1990s, there continued to be suits, court actions, and legislative initiatives regarding how best to address funding inequities for public schools. Earlier court decisions were also revisited. For example, in a turnaround of earlier decisions, in 1994 the State Supreme Court of Arizona ruled that the state's property tax–based school financing system was unconstitutional because it created wide disparities between rich and poor school districts. As has been true in other states, the court left it up to the legislature to rectify the problem.

As each of these cases illustrates, changes are occurring in the state provisions for financial support for education. As you will see in the "Perspectives on Diversity" feature, many will argue that in comparison to other countries the U.S. costs of education are too high.

Entrepreneurial Efforts to Fund Education

The combination of reduced revenues, budgets cuts, increasing enrollments, and demands for better educational services is pressuring schools, school districts, and state officials to search for new funding sources. Some sources that were highly controversial in the past, such as the lottery, have now become a regular part of the main revenue stream. Other potential new sources of funds are now being considered, debated, and utilized.

ADVERTISING: A NEW SOURCE OF REVENUE. School districts are increasingly being approached to sell advertising space. Billboards around athletic fields and in gymnasiums have become common. Soft drinks and fast foods are advertised on the sides of school buses. Placing advertisements at the bottom of the school district's home page and placing ads on high school cafeteria tables are being considered. Many schools now receive significant "profits" from restricting the brands of soft drinks and snacks in dispensing machines. Other school districts are seeking corporate sponsorships to support music and sports programs. One school district near the Dallas–Fort Worth International Airport sold space for advertising on the rooftops of district buildings to catch the eye of travelers on incoming flights.

---

[3]Kentucky Supreme Court, Rose v. The Council for Better Education Inc., 1989.

PERSPECTIVES on DIVERSITY

International Comparisons: Expenditures per Student as an Indicator

Many indicators are used to demonstrate how the United States compares to other countries in education. Frequently the data are chosen to show that the United States is underperforming. One useful resource for international comparisons is the Organization for Economic Cooperation and Development (OECD) website at www.oecd .org. OECD is a partnership of the most developed nations, including those of Western Europe, the United States, Japan, and Australia.

To find financial data that shows expenditures per student, refer to the Institute of Education Sciences of the U.S. Department of Education. The data for eight countries, along with the average for OECD countries, are presented in Figure 9.7.

WHAT IS YOUR PERSPECTIVE?

1. Given the intense concerns about international competitiveness, how would you explain the fact that the United States is spending well above other countries yet our students perform below other countries on many of the tests?

2. How could you use these data to make a case for more or less spending for schools in the United States? Also, how would you allocate these funds?

FIGURE 9.7 Annual education expenditure per student, by education level and country 2006.

Expenditure per Student ($)

Country	Elementary	Secondary
Australia	6,311	8,700
Finland(2)	5,899	7,533
France	5,482	9,303
Germany	5,362	7,548
Japan(1)	6,989	8,305
Mexico	2,003	2,165
United States	9,709	10,821
OECD average(1)	6,875	8,560

■ Elementary ■ Secondary

(1) Mean for all reporting OECD countries
(2) Includes post-secondary non-higher-education

Profits from the sale of food and beverages can be an important source of funds for schools.

MORE STUDENT FEES. Expanded use of student fees, especially for noncore subjects and extracurricular activities, has become common practice. Fees for enrollment, gym clothes, yearbooks, and lab equipment have become standard. Fees for student parking are becoming routine as well. For parents with more than one child in a secondary school, these fees can quickly total more than $500 a year. Through various fees, a large high school can increase its revenues by $50,000 to more than $300,000 annually, which can add up to $1 million in four years. Participation in an athletic program means yet more fees.

MORE FUND-RAISING SCHEMES. The entrepreneurial spirit seems to have no bounds once school and school district administrators jump on the capitalist bandwagon. Bake sales and parent booster groups are *passé* compared to some of the more innovative approaches being tried these days. Recently in several school districts in California, students took home a form that their parents could sign to switch their long-distance telephone carrier. The school's parent–teacher association would receive 10 percent of the long-distance payment from each family. If the students signed up friends, neighbors, and relatives, the school would gain more revenue. Projections were that through this mechanism a large school could gain as much as half a million dollars a year. One step further is being implemented in some school districts with the installation of cell phone towers on school grounds. This represents another source of revenue, but also raises concerns about the possibility of the electronic waves damaging children's health.

One entrepreneurial activity was initiated at Del Oro High School in Loomis, California. At one fall football game, three cows were turned loose on the football field for "cow-chip bingo." The field was marked off in one-yard squares and chances were sold. The owners of squares where the cows made a "deposit" were the winners. The remaining funds were then available to support the school's athletic programs.

Questions About Fund-Raising Efforts. Given the special place and role of schools in society, important questions are being raised about the appropriateness of many of these newer fund-raising efforts. How to achieve equity is one important question. Schools in wealthy communities can raise more money than schools located in poor communities. If an important goal is to provide equal educational opportunity for all students, then the unequal distribution of funds and equipment is once again an issue.

A second important question has to do with children being exposed to advertising in schools. Students are a captive audience for those products that are being advertised. Many educators are concerned that students are impressionable, unsophisticated consumers and are easily influenced. In the school context, many students will have difficulty distinguishing advertising from lesson messages. Because of budget pressures, however, schools and school districts will likely continue to develop their commercial bent.

WHAT ABOUT TAXING MARIJUANA? As state policy makers and municipalities face the need to find more dollars—without raising income and real estate taxes—there is a pattern of casting the net ever wider. Thirty years ago the various forms of gambling were seen as inappropriate. Today all but three states have made one or more forms of gambling legal and are gaining tax revenue as a result. What could be future sources of revenue that were off-limits in the past?

One such source of revenue is the production and sale of marijuana. As of 2012, marijuana dispensaries had become legal in sixteen states and the District of Columbia. In Colorado in 2011, Denver collected more than $3.4 million and the state collected $5 million through sales taxes. Some have estimated that with legalization marijuana could be worth $40 to $100 billion in added revenue. As good as these dollar amounts sound, there are considerable risks associated with becoming reliant on this funding source, just as there are now for tobacco, alcohol, and gambling.

State Aid

State aid for education exists largely for three reasons: (1) The state has the primary responsibility for educating its citizens, (2) the financial ability of local school districts to support education varies widely, and (3) personal wealth is now less related to real property than it once was. State aid can be classified as having general or categorical use. *General aid* can be used by the recipient school district as it desires; *categorical aid* is earmarked for specific purposes. General aid is often administered through a program that funds each school district up to a foundation level of education required per pupil. Categorical aid may include, for example, money for transportation, vocational education, driver education, or programs for children with disabilities. Frequently, categorical aid is given to encourage specific education programs; in some states, these aid programs are referred to as *incentive programs.* Categorical aid funds may be granted on a matching basis; thus, for each dollar of local effort, the state contributes a specific amount.

GENERAL STATE AID: EQUALITY OF OPPORTUNITY. Historically, general aid was based on the idea that each child, regardless of place of residence or the wealth of the local district, is entitled to receive a basic education. General state aid was established on the principle of equality of opportunity and is usually administered through a foundation program. Creating a *foundation program* involves determining the dollar value of the basic education opportunities desired in a state, referred to as the foundation level, and determining a minimum standard of local effort, considering local wealth. The foundation concept implies equity for taxpayers as well as equality of opportunity for students.

How State Foundation Programs Work. Figure 9.8 shows how a foundation program operates. The total length of each bar represents the foundation level of education required per pupil, expressed in dollars. Each school district must put forth the same minimum local effort to finance its schools; this effort could be, for example, a qualifying tax rate that produces the local share of the foundation level. This tax rate will produce more revenue in a wealthy district than it will in a poor district; therefore, the poor district will receive more state aid than the wealthy district. Local school districts do not receive general state aid beyond that amount established as the foundation, but they are permitted in most instances to exceed foundation levels at their own expense.

State Foundation Programs: Limited Effectiveness. The effectiveness of using various state foundation programs to bring about fiscal equalization has been limited. A major limitation is

FIGURE 9.8   Equalization and the foundation principle.

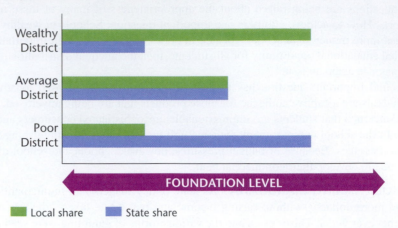

that the foundation established is frequently far below the actual expenditure or far below the level needed to provide adequate educational opportunity. For example, if a state established a per-pupil foundation level of $1,500 and the average actual per-pupil expenditure was $3,000, equalization would not have occurred.

A second limitation is that most general state aid programs do not provide for different expenditure levels for different pupil needs. Special education and vocational education, for example, both require more money to operate than the usual per-pupil expenditure for the typical elementary or secondary school pupil.

TAXPAYER REVOLT. In the past forty plus years, there have been a number of political initiatives by taxpayers to reduce their tax burden, especially the amount they pay in property taxes. In the past the anti-tax movement was called a **taxpayer revolt**. A most dramatic instance of taxpayer revolt occurred in California in June 1978 with the passage of a citizens' ballot initiative called Proposition 13, which limited by constitutional amendment the property tax as a source of revenue. Subsequent and similar propositions have been added in other states. Many of the more recent initiatives have included the demand for a "tax payer's bill of rights," or TABOR. All of these initiatives have been aimed at tax limitation, which reduces funds available for education. These efforts, along with a low success rate of local school bond referenda and the closing of school districts for periods of time because of insufficient operating funds, indicate more—and more serious—problems ahead for the funding of public schools.

THE FEDERAL GOVERNMENT'S ROLE IN EDUCATION

As mentioned earlier, under the Tenth Amendment to the U.S. Constitution, education is seen as a function of the states. Although the states have the primary responsibility for education and historically the schools were operated at the local level, during the past sixty years the federal government has assumed an ever-increasing involvement in education. In the 1960s and 1970s, the rationale for this interest and involvement was linked to national security and solving social problems. In the early 1990s, the rationale was based on economic competitiveness. In the late 1990s, the focus shifted to standards and testing, as well as concerns about funding of the infrastructure of schools.

The arrival of No Child Left Behind (NCLB) in 2002 accelerated the involvement of the federal government in education. This increasing centralization of power is called **federalism**. One consequence of federalism has been the establishment of more federal agencies, programs, and laws that address the performance of schools, teachers, and students at the local level.

Leadership

The federal government has historically provided leadership in education in specific situations, usually in times of need or in crises that could not be fully addressed individually by each state or local school district. In the 1980s, policy maker concerns over the quality of schools led to more active leadership on the part of the federal government, such as moves to establish national

taxpayer revolt The point at which taxpayers openly object to paying more.

federalism The process of centralizing more power and control over education at the federal level.

In the past sixty years, the federal government has increased its involvement in education, taking a bigger role in determining the direction education should be heading.

priorities in education and to raise major issues. For example, *A Nation at Risk,* the report prepared by the National Commission on Excellence in Education, was published in 1983.

That report was not a mandate, nor was funding recommended, but it did sound an alarm and provided recommendations for reform to be considered by states and local school districts. Identifying national educational issues and encouraging forums on these issues at the state and local levels, along with soliciting responses, have been appropriate federal activities. Other activities include research on significant national educational issues and dissemination of exemplary practices. During the past sixty years, the federal government has insinuated itself more and more by tying school district access to federal funds to education mandates. If states, and schools, accept federal dollars, then they also must accept the mandates that come with the funds.

JOURNAL FOR REFLECTION 9.3

What is your view about education federalism? Is it a good thing to have strong directions set nationally, or should states and local districts have more say?

The U.S. Department of Education

The first-ever agency of education in the federal government, established in 1867 through the diligent efforts of Henry Barnard, was called the Department of Education. Later, it was called the Office of Education (1869); at another time, it was the Bureau of Education within the Department of the Interior. In 1939 the Office of Education became a part of the Federal Security Agency, which in 1953 became the Department of Health, Education, and Welfare, wherein the U.S. Office of Education was assigned. In October 1979, President Jimmy Carter signed legislation creating a cabinet-level federal agency, the Department of Education. The latest version of the Department of Education, in contrast with the first in 1867, has become a powerful agency.

The U.S. Department of Education has some 4,400 employees and its 2012 budget was $68.1 billion. The department includes many offices and resources, including the National Center for Education Statistics, which compiles a wide range of statistics about education; the Office of Special Education and Rehabilitative Services; and the Office of Civil Rights. Information about grants, teacher resources, and statistics is available through the various Department of Education offices and programs or online at www.ed.gov.

There is no question that offering aid and awarding grants are effective ways to influence the goals of education nationally. However, debate continues about whether the offices of the federal government should have a stronger or weaker influence on education. Some people maintain that the socioeconomic forces of society are not contained within local school districts or state boundaries and therefore that direct federal intervention is needed. Others advocate dissolution of the department, insisting that education is a state responsibility. As is easy to see, over the last fifty years the clear trend in terms of acts of Congress and presidential leadership is toward a greater federal role in education.

Educational Programs Operated by the Federal Government

The federal government directly operates some school programs. For example, the public school system of the District of Columbia depends on Congress for funds. The Department of the Interior has the educational responsibility for children of national park employees; for Samoa (classified as an outlying possession); and for the trust territories of the Pacific, such as the Caroline and Marshall Islands. Many of the schools on Native American reservations are financed and managed through the Bureau of Indian Affairs (BIA) of the Department of the Interior. Twenty-five of these schools have become what are called contract schools, in which the tribe determines the program and staff but the BIA supports the schools financially. The Department of Defense (DOD) is responsible for the Military Academy at West Point, the Naval Academy at Annapolis, the Coast Guard Academy at New London, and the Air Force Academy at Colorado Springs. The DOD also operates a school system (Department of Defense Education Activity, or DoDEA) for the children of military staff wherever members are stationed. The instruction supplied by the vocational and technical training programs of the military services has made a big contribution nationally to education as well.

The federal government also funds education research by individual university faculty and a set of ten regional education laboratories, which provide curriculum development, technical assistance, and evaluation services to school districts and states. Other important resources for teachers are the various clearinghouses, including the Educational Resources Information Center (ERIC). This center maintains digital archives of research reports and curriculum materials. Teachers can request specific information and literature searches from the ERIC databases.

No Child Left Behind (NCLB)

The widest, most sweeping effort by the federal government to improve student learning and increase accountability for states and schools across the nation was the 2002 reauthorization of the Elementary and Secondary Education Act (ESEA), commonly known as No Child Left Behind or NCLB. This was not the first major education statute passed by Congress and signed by the President. The first ESEA was passed by Congress in 1965 as one of President Lyndon Johnson's Great Society initiatives. Since then, the ESEA has been reauthorized every four or five years. Each time the scope of the bill has expanded. Although a major intent of the ESEA was to increase the success of poor and minority students, the results during the past fifty years have not been dramatic.

With the leadership of President George W. Bush, the 2002 ESEA reauthorization represented a major rethinking based on the theme of No Child Left Behind. Two major purposes of NCLB were to raise student achievement across the board and to eliminate the **achievement gap** among students from different backgrounds. The nearly 2,100 pages of this bill contained many directives and initiatives for states and school districts. Two of these are particularly important for future teachers to understand: AYP (adequate yearly progress) and SINOI (schools in need of improvement).

ADEQUATE YEARLY PROGRESS (AYP). This has become the basis for determining whether schools, districts, and states are in compliance with the law. The primary criterion is student performance on standardized tests. In addition, instead of the average test score for all students being used to evaluate a school, student test scores had to be **disaggregated** by the subgroups of:

- Economically disadvantaged students
- Major racial or ethnic groups
- Students with disabilities
- English-language learners (ELL).

SCHOOLS IN NEED OF IMPROVEMENT (SINOI). NCLB set timelines and established consequences for states, school districts, and schools that did not show year-to-year increases in test scores. Schools that did not demonstrate progress have been labeled as "low performing" or "failing" schools. These schools received a label such as "N3" or "N4," which indicates the number of years during which the students in one or more subcategories did not meet AYP.

OTHER NCLB REQUIREMENTS. Many more elements, mandates, and expectations were part of the 2002 version of the NCLB Act, such as annual testing of students in grades 3 through 8 in math and reading/language arts, as well as testing them three times in science by grade 12.

achievement gap The systematic difference in learning between majority and minority, or rich and poor, students.

disaggregated The process of grouping test scores based on student characteristics such as gender, ethnicity, and socioeconomic status.

Annual state report cards were required, in which, among other things, SINOI schools must be listed. Also, school districts must make available to parents, on request, the following information about their child's classroom teacher:

- Whether the teacher has met state qualification and licensing criteria for the grade levels and subject areas taught
- Whether the teacher is teaching under emergency or other provisional status
- The baccalaureate degree of the teacher and any other graduate certification or degree held by the teacher and the subject area of the certification or degree
- Whether the child is provided service by paraprofessionals and, if so, the paraprofessional's qualifications.

The movement toward making more information about individual teachers available to the public keeps increasing. As you will read in the "Teaching in Challenging Times" feature, the pressure to link student performance to individual teachers has become another hot topic.

IMPACT OF NCLB. The NCLB legislation has placed heavy demands on teachers, schools, school districts, and states. There have been many positive outcomes as well as many criticisms. One important outcome of the requirement to disaggregate test scores has been that schools now strive to increase test scores for students. No longer can expectations for achievement by minority, special needs, or ELL students be lower than for other, more "mainstream" students.

Another impact has been the reality that more and more schools have failed to achieve AYP in all student categories and therefore have been labeled as "needing improvement."

A number of tactics are being used to increase test scores:

- "Bubble kids" are those who scored a few points below the proficient level. By targeting them it is hoped that at the next testing they will score higher.

Cost of Living Adjustment (COLA)
A procedure for increasing salaries based on the rate of inflation.

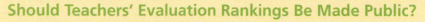

TEACHING IN CHALLENGING TIMES

Should Teachers' Evaluation Rankings Be Made Public?

In the past, information about teachers' salaries and their evaluations were considered personnel matters and kept confidential. There would be a published pay schedule that usually was based on years of teaching experience. With each increasing year of teaching experience there would be a "step" increase in a teacher's salary. Most pay schedules also added to salary when a teacher received a master's degree.

Teachers also receive supplemental pay for activities outside of their regular classroom assignment such as tutoring after school and leading extracurricular activities such as coaching and directing some of the performing arts. Another source of annual increases has been **COLA (Cost of Living Adjustments)**, which are adjustments in salary due to inflation.

In most states and districts, until now, individual teacher's salaries were kept confidential. Teacher evaluations were kept confidential too. Now, there is increasing pressure to make individual teacher salary and performance information public. The source of pressure is the federal government (e.g., NCLB Waivers and the reauthorization of ESEA), as well as many governors and state legislators. Two agendas are coming together resulting in the push for this significant change.

One of the initiatives is to implement value-added teacher evaluation systems. Instead of teacher salaries being based on years of experience, they are to be based in the growth in test scores of each teacher's students. The second initiative is to rank each teacher in comparison to other teachers and make this information available to the public. Some believe that basing teacher evaluation on student performance will lead to increases in teacher effectiveness. On the other hand, others are concerned that making this information public will result in parents shopping for the "best" teachers. Those opposing this initiative point out that test scores are not always accurate and there are more learning outcomes than what gets measured on the tests.

WHAT ARE MY CHALLENGES?

1. Describe your comfort level with having your evaluations as a teacher being based in large part on the test scores of your students?
2. What are your thoughts about being ranked in comparison to the growth in test scores of other teachers? Do you see this as a motivator or a detractor? Would it affect your teaching?
3. How comfortable are you with having your ranking published in the newspaper and probably reported on the local television news?
4. If a ranking system were implemented in one school district and not in another, all other things being equal, would that impact your decision on which district to choose?
5. As a parent, which district would you choose for your own children?

- "Safe harbor" is the status of a school that was in need of improvement and has made progress in reducing the number of students scoring below proficient, but has not reached the AYP target.
- "District in need of improvement" is the label applied when there is a district-wide pattern of schools not making AYP.
- "Corrective actions" are the steps that the state must take if a school/district fails to achieve AYP over time.
- "Supplemental services" are being provided, such as consultants to analyze data and provide training, as well as the addition of after-school programs.

NCLB WAIVERS. The NCLB mandated that student performance in the 2001–2002 school year was to serve as the baseline. In each subsequent year there was to be improvement in the test scores so that by the school year 2013–2014, all students would be "proficient." States then had twelve years to have all students meet the 2013–2014 proficiency level, which means that students within each subgroup who had test scores in 2001–2002 below the proficient level need to, on average, improve by one-twelfth each year. This goal was not achieved. As more and more schools were being placed on the "watch list" and all states were having more schools identified as failing, something had to be done. There also was a failure of Congress to pass the next reauthorization of ESEA. So in the fall of 2011, President Obama initiated a process by which states could apply for a waiver. States that received waivers had to address several elements:

- Adopt standards for college and career readiness (which for most states has meant adopting the Common Core Standards)
- Establish a new accountability system (which has meant moving to "growth scores")
- Implement purposeful ways of improving learning for ELL and SE students
- Develop an evaluation system based on measures to improve teacher effectiveness.

These are the same major themes that are being built into the new reauthorization of ESEA.

REFLECTIONS ACROSS THE MANY AUTHORIZATIONS OF ESEA. Thoughtful critics and historians have offered some interesting comparisons between the original 1965 ESEA and the 2002 NCLB reauthorization. Some critics of the original ESEA say that it failed because it provided money without accountability, and the NCLB Act would succeed because it had strict accountability. The ESEA of 1965 may have offered money without much educational accountability, but the NCLB Act demanded heavy accountability without much greater federal financial and technical assistance—an approach no more likely to succeed.

In 1965, extensive federal mandates like those of NCLB would never have made it through Congress. At that time, the federal role in education was marginal, and most state education agencies had limited authority and capabilities. Local people were extremely wary that more federal aid would bring federal control. Since then the federal and state roles in education have grown, and states and school districts recognize that accepting federal requirements goes along with receiving federal funding.

In summary, the No Child Left Behind Act has had far-reaching effects in terms of ratcheting up the accountability criteria and defining success in terms of student performance on standardized tests. What it has lacked are results showing clear patterns of success for all students, a system of positive awards, and sufficient funding to do all that was required.

Federal Aid

As illustrated earlier in Figure 9.5, the federal government provides the smallest proportion (9.1 percent) of revenue for public education. Still, the United States has a history of federal aid to education, but it has been categorical and not general aid; it generally has been related to the needs of the nation at the time. Federal aid actually started before the U.S. Constitution was adopted, with the Northwest Ordinance of 1785, which provided land for public schools in "western territories." Such specialized federal aid has continued in a steady progression to the present. Almost 200 federal aid-to-education laws have been passed since the Northwest Ordinance.

LOCAL CONTROL VERSUS FEDERALISM. In the past, an important and unique feature of education in the United States was **local control**, the belief that educational decisions should be made at the local level rather than at the state or national level. The rationale has been that people at the local level, including teachers and parents, know what is best for the students in their community. As has been described in this chapter, the trend during the past sixty years has been toward more federalism. The No Child Left Behind Act was the latest and heaviest centralization initiative by the federal government and includes many mandates to states, school districts, schools, and teachers.

Those who advocate for more federal and state involvement argue that education is a responsibility of all society. Some also argue that national survival requires centralized policies and programs, including a national curriculum. The underlying questions are not just about what is best for students and the nation; they are about power, authority, and who gets to decide.

Technology for School Administration

In schools today an important application of technology is in planning class schedules for students and teachers. In the "old" days school principals used entire chalk boards to sketch out, arrange, and rearrange teacher assignments and student schedules. Now there are computer programs to do this task.

A more significant use of technology—one that teachers experience weekly, if not daily—is for compiling, analyzing, and displaying student data. Many schools have a **school improvement team (SIT)** that meets once a week. The team has representatives from each grade level and/or content area. The special education resource teacher and literacy specialists are often members of the SIT. In each meeting the progress of all students who have been identified as in need of extra help is reviewed. Technology has been used to score and store the various tests and assessments for each student. During the meeting the data for each student is displayed on a screen. The student's progress is reviewed and agreement is reached on what instructional interventions should be done next. Due to the use of technology, the records of several hundred students can be compiled and retrieved as needed for these weekly reviews.

Technology for School District Administration

Technology is also important at the district level. One of the most obvious uses is for computing and managing budgets. Technology also will be used to manage heating and cooling, develop school bus schedules, keep personnel records, and prepare payrolls.

Nearly all districts now have a **student information system (SIS)**, which allows all test scores to be compiled and analyzed at the district office. District administrators can review how students are performing across the district, for each school, and even for each type of students. For example, the performance of students who receive free or reduced lunches can be compared to those who come from more wealthy neighborhoods. In the best SIS, teacher-friendly, up-to-the-day data displays are available for each student through the computer on the teacher's desk.

POLITICS AND ACCOUNTABILITY IN EDUCATION

So far this chapter has provided information about the formal organization and structures of public education. We also have introduced some aspects of the sources of revenue and expenditures for public education at the local, state, and federal levels. Although these organizational structures illustrate the line and staff relationships, another set of relationships is important to consider and understand. Each of these levels is involved in politics—the politics of education. Reread the "Education in the News" story at the beginning of this chapter. In this one article you can identify several of the interest groups—and conflicting agendas—that are engaged in influencing the development of the Bangor, Maine, School Department's annual budget.

Local school districts and professional associations follow closely what is happening in their state legislature. Their purpose is to influence representatives' understanding of local needs and the direction that will be taken within relevant legislation. These groups do not hesitate to let members in the legislature and their governor know how they should vote. It is not unusual for local school superintendents and board members, as well as teacher association members, to meet with their legislators, congressional representatives, and their governor in person. These contacts

local control Educational decision making by citizens at the local level rather than at the state or national level.

school improvement team (SIT) A team representing all subject areas or grade levels that reviews student progress on a weekly basis.

student information system (SIS) A computer-based data management system that is designed to compile and analyze test scores so that district administrators can review the performance of all students and each school.

FIGURE 9.9 Influencers on the politics of education decision making.

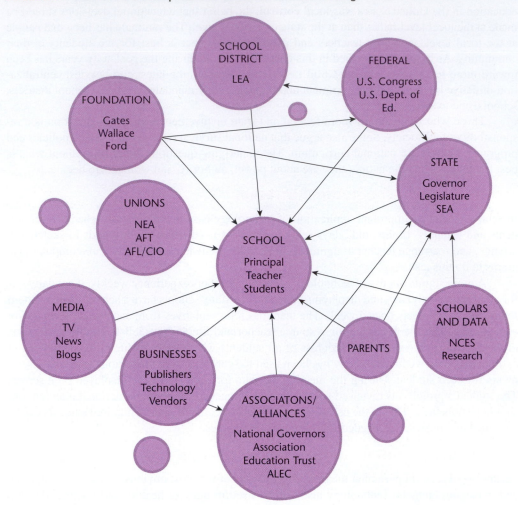

with federal and state agencies are examples of **political action**. You—today as a teacher education candidate, and in the future as a teacher—cannot escape politics. So learn all you can now and begin developing your political knowledge and skills.

Regardless of how education is defined in statute and how it is organized, the actual decision-making takes place in a political arena. Politics are always a factor. Stability, continuity, and leadership for education are influenced by many interest groups and coalitions. As diagrammed in Figure 9.9, many individuals and groups attempt to influence education decisions as they are being made by each governing body. In the end, the schools have to implement what is decided.

For example, some associations such as teacher unions and Chambers of Commerce have established records of heavy influence on the direction of education. Through their initiatives, new laws may affect any and all parts of the education system. In terms of the political arena, there are many other sources of influence. National foundations can have a major influence on the direction of education reform. Scholars and agencies that have data related to a particular issue may also influence the final decision. There are many other influences such as textbook publishers and little-known associations such as the American Legislative Exchange Council (ALEC) that can have a major influence on education policy. Suffice it to say, numerous participants, agencies, and interest groups strive to influence the shape and direction of the U.S. education system.

Politics: Neither Positive nor Negative

political action Becoming involved to influence decision making.

Politics are ongoing inside all organizations, including schools. People have varying interests and agendas. In many cases there are basic differences in points of view that need to be resolved for the organization to move ahead.

Advocating for one's point of view and interests is what politics is about. This is where knowledge and political skill become a special strength for teachers and school administrators. Policy makers, the media, and parents are very interested in the positions and views of educators. Another important political skill is being open to talking with all parties and negotiating areas of agreement. Rather than judging "politics" as bad, successful teachers learn how politics work and develop their skills to contribute to and influence the political process. Learn more about organizations and political processes and you will see politics as fascinating and, yes, even fun.

Politics Across the Education System

There is no escaping politics as a basic force within organizations and across society. Graphic examples in recent times include the desperate attempts in each state to balance budgets. Legislators, governors, school board members, superintendents, and mayors hear from different interest groups, all wanting more money for themselves. In each case if one side receives more, another side will receive less. As is well illustrated in the "Education in the News" feature, if the school district is to receive higher funding, then taxpayers will have to pay more. The wide-ranging, sharply stated, and often opposing views at the national level about what should be done in the reauthorization of the NCLB legislation illustrates how complex the issues are and how difficult coming to a decision can be. Politics can be just as intense and conflicted at the local level.

SCHOOL BOARD POLITICS. Most school districts have "at-large" elections to select board members. In at-large elections every voter in a community is able to vote for a candidate for each seat on the board. The alternative is to have each board seat represent a particular region of the district. Either way, there will be strong interest on the part of each voter in having a board member that will represent his or her interests. Nearly every decision a board makes has a political component. Issues such as approving the superintendent's salary, changing the boundaries of a school, raising taxes, reducing staff or extracurricular programs, busing students, and tolerating a losing athletic season bring out strong voices, often with competing points of view.

SUPERINTENDENT POLITICS. As the chief executive officer, the superintendent has to listen to the opinions of all board members and strive to maintain a majority of the board's support to be retained. The superintendent also has to work with and listen to teachers, principals, central office staff, and various members of the community. All will have suggestions for the superintendent and for what the school district should be doing.

School Politics

Schools are not devoid of politics, nor are you free from politics in your teacher education program. Principals, other teachers, parents, students, and teacher education faculty have certain things they would like to see accomplished. There also are likely to be conflicting views about how to accomplish those ends. Resolving these issues requires political leadership and skill.

JOURNAL FOR REFLECTION 9.4

How do you feel about the suggestion that education is political and that you should develop your political knowledge and skill? In what ways do you see this being important to you, your teaching, your students, and your school? Or, do you think that you can avoid politics as a teacher?

TEACHERS AS POLITICIANS. Teachers often state that they do not wish to become involved in politics—as if they have a choice. Teachers lobby the principal for preferred teaching assignments, parents want particular teachers for their children, and teachers join together to advocate for a particular instructional approach. Decisions about what committees and tasks (e.g., lunch duty) each teacher will do entail some political elements.

CLASSROOM POLITICS. Yes, there are politics in classrooms. When students approach the teacher to request clarification about an assignment or lobby to have a test rescheduled, they are engaging in politics. So are the parents who talk with the teacher about how their child is progressing. These are not bad actions—they are instead key to success in organizations and social systems.

WHEN TO TALK TO WHOM. When teachers have an idea about the school, want to try something different, or see a problem, it is important for them to talk with others to see what they think. Others may share an interest in the idea or may know about related thoughts of others. However, if you are aware of a serious problem, such as safety or a potentially illegal incident, then it is important to report this immediately to your direct supervisor. If department heads or team leaders are in place, then the first discussions should be with them. In any organization, including schools, if there is a serious problem, the normal protocol is to talk first with the person at the next level up the "chain of command." For teachers this means informing the principal. Depending on the issue, a beginning teacher, or one who is new to the system, might seek advice from an experienced colleague before taking further action. In terms of politics one must know how the system works; colleagues and principals can be helpful in this regard.

SOURCES OF POWER. Often when thinking about politics the idea of power comes to mind. Some people are seen as having more power than others. What may not be understood is that there are different sources of power. The early sections of this chapter introduced you to one important source, **position power**. For example, administrators in line positions have authority over the people under them in the organization chart.

There are other forms of power that at times can be more influential than position power. For example, **expertise** can be important. A teacher who has expert knowledge about teaching ELL students and a reputation for their excelling in his or her classroom has power. Being a member of certain **networks** or associations such as teacher unions and professional associations is another source of power.

Another important source of power is to form an **interest group** or **coalition**. Suppose several teachers are interested in using a certain computer program that the school does not have. By working together the group may be able to influence the principal, or a parent association, to purchase the program. Each teacher individually could not get the support, but by forming a coalition, together they have more power.

Accountability

Besides paying for schools, the most enduring theme in politics at this time is **accountability**. Accountability has its roots in two fundamental modern problems: the continuous escalation of educational costs and, closely related, the loss of faith in educational results. The failure of the U.S. educational system, particularly in the cities and in some remote rural areas, has been accurately documented. All too often the expectations of citizens for their children have not been met. The concerns are supported when the media report that certain schools have not made AYP and when test scores are compared with those of other countries.

Teacher Accountability

The president, congress, governors, legislators, school boards, and district administrators all want schools (and teachers) to be accountable. The elements of accountability vary from close monitoring of school finances to publication of school report cards and to new forms of teacher evaluation. Teachers are the primary contact with students, and they are directly responsible for instruction and student achievement. Therefore, they are expected to do their utmost to motivate students to learn and achieve. The idea of **value added** is now being tied to teacher evaluation. The key accountability question has become: To what extent did the school and each teacher add value as seen through increases in test scores? School districts and states are now implementing formulas for determing each teacher's pay that include analysis of growth in student test scores. One consequence is even more pressure on students to do well on the tests.

REWARDS FOR BEING ACCOUNTABLE. The other side of the accountability coin is determining the rewards for success and the sanctions for failure. In the 1980s, many reward programs consisted of bestowing special designations and plaques on schools. In the 1990s, there was a shift to the use of money as a reward or sanction. Under NCLB there were few rewards. Instead,

---

position power Power derived from holding a certain office, title, or job.

expertise Having a higher level of knowledge about a certain topic or skill than most people.

networks Personal connections gained through membership in an organization, club, or association.

interest group Group of people who have a shared agenda.

coalition Two or more interest groups that join in an effort to advance a shared agenda.

accountability Establishing expectations and consequences for achieving or failing to achieve certain levels of performance.

value added Linking increases in outcomes with the amount of teacher effort.

different forms of threats and sanctions hung over states, school districts, and schools, especially those that were "failing."

REWARDING TEACHERS AND PRINCIPALS. In some states and districts teachers and principals are rewarded for earning an advanced degree or achieving National Board Certification. There can be recognition and celebrations within a school, at the district level, and through state-wide awards for outstanding teachers. Each year national winners are recognized at the White House.

SCHOOL AND SCHOOL DISTRICT REPORT CARDS. In the past, report cards were used only to evaluate students. A new element in the accountability movement is the use of new forms of report cards to "grade" schools, school districts, and states. Advocates of school report cards argue that parents and voters need to know how well their school or school district is doing in comparison to others. They also point out that evaluating schools is complex; many factors need to be considered. A report card can incorporate many factors and present a clear picture. Opponents express concern that report cards still are overly simplistic representations. They argue that report cards increase competition, which is not supposed to be a part of public education. Proponents argue back that competition will make low-performing schools improve and/or inform parents so that they can make the choice of sending their children to another school.

SUMMARY

SCHOOL DISTRICTS: ORGANIZATION AND FINANCES

- In fiscal year 2012 the average expenditure per student was nearly $10,300.
- School boards have the authority to hire teachers and principals.
- Superintendents are the chief executive officer of the school district.
- Curriculum coordinators in the district office have staff authority.

THE ORGANIZATION OF SCHOOLS

- Department heads and team leaders are important communication sources.
- Don't forget to work well with school secretaries, custodians, and cafeteria workers.

ORGANIZATION OF EDUCATION AT THE STATE LEVEL

- The U.S. Constitution passes authority for education to the states.
- Each state has a superintendent of public instruction, also called the chief state school officer.
- The state department of education licenses teachers and administrators.

PAYING FOR SCHOOLS

- On average 46+ percent of the expenditures for education comes from the state.

- Until recently, the property tax has been the primary source of revenue for schools.
- The property tax is progressive, whereas the sales tax is regressive.
- Adequacy, equity, and equal opportunity are key themes that must be addressed in the financing of education.
- Foundation programs are one way in which states adjust funding to achieve equity.

THE FEDERAL GOVERNMENT'S ROLE IN EDUCATION

- The federal government has increased its influence by offering the carrot of extra funds along with the stick of mandates.
- No Child Left Behind was the name given to the 2001 reauthorization of ESEA.
- Adequate yearly progress (AYP) is the key to evaluating school performance.
- Teacher evaluations are increasingly being based on data about value added.

POLITICS AND ACCOUNTABILITY IN EDUCATION

- Politics are neither positive nor negative.
- Teachers need to be political too.
- Accountability is important at all levels, from states to school districts to schools to teachers.

DISCUSSION STARTERS

1. Do you think the federal government should be assuming such a strong role over states, school districts, and schools? What are some likely consequences of this increasing federalism?

2. What are the advantages of using sales and income taxes to fund elementary and secondary education instead of relying on the property tax?

3. What situations have you encountered that illustrate the tension between state and local education interests? Is local control an issue in your state?

4. When is it appropriate for teachers to engage in politics? How can teachers influence what goes on in their schools? How can they influence decisions at the district and board levels?

5. What forms or types of accountability do you believe should be used to evaluate schools and teachers? What are your thoughts about the increasing use of test scores to evaluate teachers?

6. Many states have turned to gaming (lotteries, riverboat casinos, and slot machines) as a source of revenue for schools. What are the arguments in support of this funding mechanism? What do you see as possible downsides?-

SCHOOL-BASED OBSERVATIONS

1. When you have the opportunity to visit a school or interview a teacher or the principal, ask the teacher or principal to draw an organization chart and place himself or herself in it. Did the person just draw line relationships or did he or she also consider staff relationships? If the person did not consider staff relationships, ask about organization relationships with the district office (e.g., relationships with curriculum coordinators and staff developers). Does the person see these relationships as line or staff?

2. Seek an opportunity to study a school budget. Determine the different sources of revenue (e.g., local, state, federal, grants, activity fees). What are the biggest line-item expenditures? Are some monies discretionary for teachers? Note that in most schools, especially high schools, a surprising number of activities generate cash. Inquire about the implications of having cash on hand, and ask how these amounts are secured and what policies guide their uses.

PORTFOLIO DEVELOPMENT

1. Develop an organizational chart for a school you are familiar with. Use solid lines to represent line relationships and dotted lines to signify staff relationships. Draw the arrangement of personnel in regard to each of the following decisions: (a) determining a child's grade on his or her report card; (b) expelling a student (hint—don't forget that the school is part of a school district); (c) deciding on the topic for a staff development day; and (d) determining whether a particular teaching activity will be used. After considering these different decisions, explain your thoughts and feelings about the authority and accountability of teachers within the school as an organization.

2. One important component of accountability is the role of standards. Most states have adopted the Common Core State Standards. Check your state's department of education website for information about the standards your state is using. What are the expectations? Can districts and schools opt out, or is there a mandate to use certain standards? For future use, be sure to make a record of the related Websites and information you find.

3. The funding of education and levels of taxation will continue to be hot topics for school districts, state legislatures, and taxpayers. Start a file of articles from newspapers and blogs as well as notes from television and radio news reports that deal with school finance and spending. As your file grows review the items. Do certain topics and themes, such as concern about high taxes and teacher pay, keep coming up? When you are ready to apply for a position, having knowledge about finance and spending issues will make you better informed and prepared.

WEB SOLUTIONS

Learning about a school district: Now is the time for you to get a head start in having information about the school district(s) where you would like to be employed as a teacher. What do you know already? Do you know the name of the superintendent? What do you know about the district's school board? Have you studied the job application process? What is the average Student/Teacher ratio? And, how does this district compare to other districts where you might want to teach, or the district(s) where you went to school? All of this information is available on the Web, if you know where to look.

The way to begin learning more is to study the website for the school district(s) that you are interested in learning about. That website will have information about the organization of the school district as well as tabs that lead to the human resource office, the school board, and information on how to contact each school.

School district websites do not provide comparative information. To find out more you should check with the state education department website. Also, have you checked out the website for the National Center for Education Statistics at **http://nces.ed.gov**? Within the NCES website you can find additional information about any school district and school. Begin by opening "School Search." Then click on "Public School District." Enter the name of your school district. The district page will provide information about the number of teachers and, of particular importance for you to consider, the Student/Teacher ratio. If you go deeper by clicking on the list of schools, you can even see the Student/Teacher ratio for each school.

Develop a table for comparing the contact information and key descriptive statistics, such as Student/Teacher ratios, for different schools and districts where you would like to be employed. You will be glad to have this information at hand when you start applying for that teaching position.

MyEducationLab™

Go to the topics **Governance and Finance** and **School Organization** in the MyEducationLab (**www.myeducationlab.com**) for *Foundations of American Education: Becoming Effective Teachers in Challenging Times, 16e*, where you can:

- Find learning outcomes for **Governance and Finance** and **School Organization,** along with the national standards that connect to these outcomes.
- Complete Assignments and Activities that can help you more deeply understand the chapter content.
- Apply and practice your understanding of the core teaching skills identified in the chapter with the Building Teaching Skills and Dispositions learning units.
- Access video clips of CCSSO National Teachers of the Year award winners responding to the question, "Why Do I Teach?" in the Teacher Talk section.
- Create, update, and share quality lesson plans with the Lesson Plan Builder.

- Access state licensure test requirements, overviews of what tests cover, and sample test items in the Certification and Licensure section.
- Access current state and national standards in the Licensure and Standards section.
- Learn how to create a high-quality teaching portfolio in the Preparing a Portfolio section.
- Access tips, advice, and other information on resume writing and interviewing, your first year of teaching, and law and public policies in the Beginning Your Career section.
- Check your comprehension of the content covered in the chapter with the Study Plan. Here you will be able to take a chapter pretest, receive feedback on your answers, and then access personalized Review, Practice, and Enrichment exercises to enhance your understanding of chapter content. After you complete the exercises, take a posttest to confirm your comprehension.

10

Legal Perspectives on Education

LEARNING OUTCOMES

After reading and studying this chapter, you should be able to:

1. Explain the relationships between the U.S. Constitution and the role and responsibilities of the states in ensuring the availability of public schools for all children. (InTASC 5: Application of Content)

2. Summarize key components of the rights and responsibilities of teachers as determined by key U.S. Supreme Court decisions (InTASC 3: Learning Environments; InTASC 7: Planning for Instruction)

3. Reflect about the legal implications of teacher and student potential misuses of social media. (InTASC 1: Learner Development, InTASC 9: Professional Learning and Ethical Practice)

4. Distinguish between students' rights and responsibilities as citizens and their rights and responsibilities as students. (InTASC 7: Planning for Instruction; InTASC 9: Professional Learning and Ethical Practice)

EDUCATION in the NEWS

THE RECORD: NORTHJERSEY.COM

By LESLIE BRODY

Staff Writer *Tuesday, November 8, 2011   Last updated: Monday November 14, 2011, 10:56 AM*

Paterson Teacher Suspended for Facebook Post Should Be Fired, Judge Rules

THE RECORD

The Paterson teacher who called her first-grade students "future criminals" in a Facebook post should lose her tenured job, an administrative law judge has ruled.

In a decision made public Tuesday, Judge Ellen Bass said Jennifer O'Brien's conduct would be "inexcusable" in any district, but especially in a city burdened by poverty and violence.

"O'Brien has demonstrated a complete lack of sensitivity to the world in which her students live," the judge wrote. "The sentiment that a 6-year-old will not rise above the criminal element that surrounds him cuts right to the bone."

Bass also noted that O'Brien, who lives in Elmwood Park, did not express genuine remorse at an August hearing in Newark.

"I came away with the impression that O'Brien remained somewhat befuddled by the commotion she had created," the judge wrote.

Bass said that with sensitivity training, O'Brien—a Paterson teacher since 1998—could return to a public school classroom, but not in Paterson, due to her damaged relationship with the community.

The judge also found that the district's need to efficiently operate its schools outweighed O'Brien's right to free speech.

"In a public education setting, thoughtless words can destroy the partnership between home and school that is essential to the mission of the schools," she wrote.

The state education commissioner has forty-five days to accept, reject or modify the judge's recommendations.

O'Brien's lawyer, Nancy Oxfeld, said she would appeal to the commissioner to let O'Brien keep her job. Oxfeld said O'Brien's words had been misinterpreted and that she never thought her students would become criminals. The teacher was concerned about a few students' behavior and believed they needed help, the lawyer said.

QUESTIONS FOR REFLECTION

1. What do you think—was the judge right or wrong to fire Jennifer O'Brien?

2. Do you think that a teacher's constitutional right to free speech should have protected her from dismissal?

3. Do you have any material on your Facebook, Twitter, e-mail, or other social media account that might become a problem during your student teaching or first years as a teacher?

Source: The Record (Bergen, County)/northjersey.com, November 8, 2011. Reprinted by permission.

MyEducationLab™

Visit the MyEducationLab for *Foundations of American Education* to enhance your understanding of chapter concepts with a personalized *Study Plan.* You'll also have the opportunity to hone your teaching skills through video- and case-based *Assignments and Activities* and *Building Teaching Skills and Dispositions* lessons.

enabling laws Laws that make it possible for educators to do certain things.

administrative law Rules and regulations that the executive branches of government create.

LEGAL ASPECTS OF EDUCATION

A critical component of becoming a teacher is to develop basic familiarity with the legal perspective. Teachers not only need to understand the law as it relates to their rights and responsibilities, they must also be knowledgeable about the rights of their students. As is readily apparent in the "Education in the News" story, a newly emerging area of legal disputes is inappropriate uses of social media by teachers *and* students. As students and teachers increase their use of these technologies, there are a growing number of challenges in the courts and policy makers are grappling with what rules of use need to be established.

Learning about the legal aspects of education begins with developing an understanding of the importance of the U.S. Constitution and the Bill of Rights. All else evolves from interpretations of the Constitution. Within the boundaries of U.S. law, each state is guided by its own constitution. Several additional sources of laws exist at the federal, state, and local levels, and a number of processes are in place for addressing disputes. As illustrated in Figure 10.1, in many ways the teacher is the implementer at the intersection between those who enact laws, those who administer laws, and those who interpret them.

Some laws are developed out of the legislative process. These are referred to as **enabling laws**, or those that provide opportunity or make it possible for educators to do certain things. Also, laws can impose restrictions or prohibitions. Another form of law, **administrative law**, is made up of the rules and regulations that the executive branches of government create. Once the legislative branch of government has established a new statute or policy, a government office, such as the U.S. Department of Education and/or the state education department, will develop

FIGURE 10.1   Sources of legal control in U.S. education as they affect the classroom teacher.

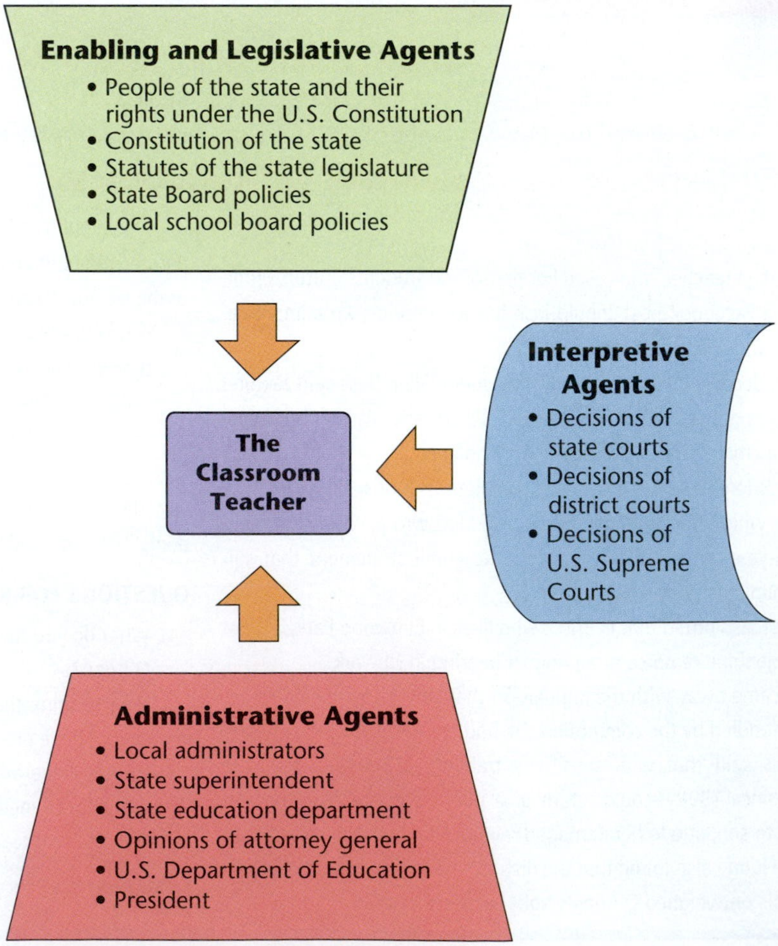

Enabling and Legislative Agents
- People of the state and their rights under the U.S. Constitution
- Constitution of the state
- Statutes of the state legislature
- State Board policies
- Local school board policies

The Classroom Teacher

Interpretive Agents
- Decisions of state courts
- Decisions of district courts
- Decisions of U.S. Supreme Courts

Administrative Agents
- Local administrators
- State superintendent
- State education department
- Opinions of attorney general
- U.S. Department of Education
- President

rules and procedures related to implementing the new policy. These rules and procedures can have the force of law too.

Once legislation is enacted into law and the rules and procedures are in place, if a question of interpretation is raised, then the **judicial interpretive process** is engaged. The judicial process also is used when it appears that a law has been violated. The interpretations of the state and federal court systems' decisions form a body of **case law**. The sampling of legal topics presented in this chapter includes examples from constitutional law, state and federal statutes, and case law based on court interpretations. All apply directly to schools, teachers, and students.

Legal Provisions for Education: The U.S. Constitution

The U.S. Constitution is the fundamental law for the nation. When Congress develops a new statute it must be in accordance with the U.S. Constitution. When a state legislature develops a new law it must be in accordance with the U.S. Constitution and that state's constitution.

Three of the amendments to the U.S. Constitution are particularly significant to the governance of education, both public and private. Interpretations by the courts of each of these amendments—the Tenth, First, and Fourteenth—have had profound impacts on the role and purpose of schools, the opportunities of all students to have access to an education, and the responsibilities and rights of teachers, students, and school administrators (see Figure 10.2).

TENTH AMENDMENT. *The powers not delegated to the United States by the Constitution, nor prohibited by it to the States, are reserved to the States respectively, or to the people.*

The U.S. Constitution does not specifically provide for public education; however, the Tenth Amendment has been interpreted as granting this power to the states. Therefore, education in the United States is not nationalized as it is in many other nations of the world. Each state has provided for education either in its constitution or in its basic statutory law. For example, Part 6, Section 2, of the Ohio Constitution reads:

> The General Assembly shall make such provisions, by taxation, or otherwise, as, with the income arising from the school trust fund, will secure a thorough and efficient system of common schools throughout the state; but no religious or other sect, or sects, shall ever have any exclusive right to, or control of, any part of the school funds of this state.

Through such statements, the people of the various states commit themselves to a responsibility for education. The state legislatures are obliged to fulfill this commitment.

FIRST AMENDMENT. *Congress shall make no law respecting an establishment of religion, or prohibiting the free exercise thereof; or abridging the freedom of speech, or of the press; or the right of the people peaceably to assemble, and to petition the Government for redress of grievances.*

As illustrated in the cases presented later in this chapter, two important clauses in the First Amendment have been applied repeatedly to issues confronting public education: (1) the *establishment clause,* "Congress shall make no law respecting an establishment of religion," and (2) the *free speech clause,* which has direct implications for teacher and student rights.

FOURTEENTH AMENDMENT. *No state shall make or enforce any law which shall abridge the privileges or immunities of citizens of the United States; nor shall any State deprive any person of life, liberty, or property without due process of law; nor deny to any person within its jurisdiction the equal protection of the laws.*

judicial interpretive process The judicial process of drawing conclusions about the intent of the wording in the Constitution and statutes.

case law Decisions of state and federal courts.

FIGURE 10.2	Key Elements of the U.S. Constitution That Are Significant to the Governance of Education

Not Provided for: Responsibility for education.
Tenth Amendment: Grants responsibility for education to each state.

First Amendment: Ensures freedom of speech, of religion, and of the press.
Fourteenth Amendment: Ensures equal educational opportunity.

The application of the Fourteenth Amendment to public education as considered in this chapter deals primarily with the equal protection clause: "nor shall any State . . . deny to any person within its jurisdiction the equal protection of the laws." Equal educational opportunity is protected under the Fourteenth Amendment. In effect, the rights of citizens of the United States are ensured by the Constitution and cannot be violated by state laws or action.

JOURNAL FOR REFLECTION 10.1

Before reading this chapter, did you know that the state has the responsibility for education, or did you think it was the role of the federal government? What do you see as the ideal balance between the state, the federal government, and local control?

Some of the enduring issues related to education are summarized in the next several sections of this chapter. You will become familiar with each topic. Herein we will be illustrating the legal reasoning and pointing out key decisions that have direct implications for you as a teacher. Later in the chapter we will return to the increasing challenges related to uses of social media.

Church and State

Our nation has a strong religious heritage. For example, in colonial times, education was primarily a religious matter and many of those who attended school were destined for the ministry. Now, with everyone attending school there are serious questions about the place of religion. Many private schools today are under religious sponsorship. But debate about the rightful role of religion in public education continues. Should public funds be used to support students in religious schools? Can prayer be said at high school commencement services or in classrooms? Does the teaching of creationism amount to public support for religion, or is it merely the presentation of an alternative scientific view? Agreements have not been reached through the debate process, so proponents of differing viewpoints have turned to the courts.

Court cases concerned with separation of church and state most frequently involve both the First and Fourteenth Amendments of the U.S. Constitution. The First Amendment is interpreted as being applicable to the states by the Fourteenth Amendment. For example, a state law requiring a daily prayer to be read in classrooms throughout the state could be interpreted as "depriving persons of liberty" (see the Fourteenth Amendment's due process clause) and as the state establishing a religion, or at least "prohibiting the free exercise thereof" (see the First Amendment's establishment clause). States are not permitted to make laws that abridge the privileges of citizens, and the right to the free practice of religion must be ensured.

Court cases related to the separation of church and state can be classified in three categories: (1) those dealing with the use of public funds to support religious education, (2) those dealing with the practice of religion in public schools, and (3) those dealing with the rights of parents to provide private education for their children. Key cases related to each of these categories are presented and summarized in Table 10.1.

PUBLIC FUNDS AND RELIGIOUS EDUCATION. In 2009, the most recent year for which statistics have been compiled, of the students who attend nonpublic schools, 39 percent were enrolled in parochial (Catholic) schools.[1] In states with relatively large enrollments in parochial schools, ongoing efforts have been made to obtain public financial assistance of one form or another for nonpublic school students. These attempts have often been challenged in the courts. We present a sampling of these cases and issues here to illustrate the reasoning and to assess trends in this difficult area. A summary of cases related to the use of public funds for private education is presented in Table 10.1.

Transportation for Students of Church Schools. The landmark case on the use of public funds to provide transportation for students to church schools was *Everson v. Board of Education*, ruled on by the U.S. Supreme Court in 1947. The Court held that in using tax-raised funds to reimburse parents for bus fares expended to transport their children to church schools, a New Jersey

---

[1]All data reported in this chapter, unless otherwise noted, are from the U.S. Department of Education, National Center for Education Statistics.

TABLE 10.1

Selected U.S. Supreme Court Cases Related to the Use of Public Funds for Private Education

CASE	ISSUE	DECISION
Everson v. Board of Education (1947)	Use of tax-raised funds to reimburse parents for transportation of students to church schools	Court ruled that reimbursement did not violate the First Amendment.
Lemon v. Kurtzman (1971)	Legislation to provide direct aid for secular services to nonpublic schools, including teacher salaries, textbooks, and instructional materials	Court ruled the legislation unconstitutional because of the excessive entanglement between government and religion.
Wolman v. Walter (1977)	Provision of books, standardized testing and scoring, diagnostic services, and therapeutic and remedial services to nonpublic school pupils	Court ruled that providing such materials and services to nonpublic school pupils was constitutional.
	Provision of instructional materials and field trips to nonpublic school pupils	Court ruled that providing such materials and services to nonpublic school pupils was unconstitutional.
Grand Rapids School District v. Ball (1985), and *Aguilar v. Felton* (1985)	Instruction of nonpublic school students in supplementary education by public school teachers	Court ruled that the action violated the establishment clause in that it promoted religion.
Zobrest v. Catalina Foothills School District (1993)	Provision of a school district interpreter for a deaf student attending a Catholic high school	Court ruled that government programs that neutrally provide benefits to a broad class of citizens without reference to religion are not readily subject to an establishment clause challenge.
Board of Education of Kiryas Joel Village School District v. Grumet (1994)	Creation and support of a public school district for Hasidic Jews by New York State	Court ruled that the district violated the establishment clause in that it was a form of "religious favoritism."
Agostini v. Felton (1997)	School districts' provision of Title I teachers to serve disadvantaged students in religious schools	Court overturned ban provided the district assigns teachers without regard to religious affiliation, all religious symbols are removed from classrooms, teachers have limited contact with religious personnel, and public school supervisors make monthly unannounced inspections.

school district did not violate the establishment clause of the First Amendment. The majority of the members of the Court viewed the New Jersey statute permitting free bus transportation to parochial school children as "public welfare legislation" to help get the children to and from school safely and expeditiously. Since the *Everson* decision, the highest courts in several states, under provisions in their own constitutions, have struck down enactments authorizing expenditures of public funds to bus children attending denominational schools; others have upheld such enactments.

The Lemon Test: Excessive Entanglement. A useful rubric emerged from the U.S. Supreme Court decision in *Lemon v. Kurtzman* (1971). This case dealt with an attempt by the Rhode Island legislature to provide a 15 percent salary supplement to teachers who taught secular subjects in nonpublic schools and a statute in Pennsylvania that provided reimbursement for the cost of teachers' salaries and instructional materials in relation to specified secular subjects in nonpublic schools. The Court concluded that the "cumulative impact of the entire relationship arising under the statutes in each

In *Zobrest v. Catalina* the Supreme Court ruled that no establishment clause was violated in the case of providing an interpreter for a student who was deaf who attended a Catholic school.

state involves excessive entanglement between government and religion." The Court pointed out another defect of the Pennsylvania statute: It provided for the aid to be given directly to the school. In the *Everson* case, the aid was provided to the students' parents, not to the church-related school. The Court posed three questions that have since become known as the *Lemon* test: (1) Does the act have a secular purpose? (2) Does the primary effect of the act either advance or inhibit religion? and (3) Does the act excessively entangle government and religion? Most subsequent cases dealing with the use of public funds in nonpublic school settings have referred to this test.

Special Situations. The U.S. Supreme Court seems to have wavered from a strict application of the *Lemon* test in two more cases: *Kiryas Joel v. Grumet* and *Zobrest v. Catalina.*

In a 1994 case, *Board of Education of Kiryas Joel Village School District v. Grumet*, the U.S. Supreme Court ruled that a New York State law that created a public school to serve children with disabilities in a village of Hasidic Jews was a form of "religious favoritism" that violated the First Amendment. Interestingly, in this case, as in some others recently, the justices ignored the *Lemon* test in making the decision. Instead, the focus was on the legislature's creation of a special school district; the justices noted the risk that "the next similarly situated group seeking a school district of its own will receive one." Another implication of this decision was the indication that the court was willing to revisit *Aguilar v. Felton* (1985) and *Grand Rapids School District v. Ball* (1985), which invalidated sending public school teachers to private religious schools to provide supplemental instruction.

Whether a public school district could provide an interpreter for a student who was deaf who attended a Catholic high school was the central question in *Zobrest v. Catalina Foothills School District* (1993). Under a federal statute, the Individuals with Disabilities Education Act (IDEA), students who are deaf are entitled to have a sign language interpreter in all regular classes. In *Zobrest v. Catalina,* the Court concluded that no establishment clause violation occurred because the provision of the interpreter was a "private decision of individual parents." In terms of the federal statute, the Court determined that this was a situation in which "government programs that neutrally provide benefits to a broad class of citizens defined without reference to religion are not readily subject to an establishment clause challenge just because sectarian institutions may also receive an attenuated benefit."

child benefit theory A criterion used by the U.S. Supreme Court to determine whether services provided to nonpublic school students benefit children and not a particular school or religion.

Child Benefit Theory. The use of public funds to provide secular services has led to a concept referred to as **child benefit theory**. More recent decisions supporting the use of public funds for transportation and textbooks for students in private schools have generally been based

FIGURE 10.3	Summary Statements on Church and State Related to Public Funds and Religious Education

- Laws and policies that have the effect of establishing religion in the schools will not be upheld by the courts.
- Use of public tax funds to pay for secular textbooks for loan to students and transportation of religious school children has been upheld by the courts.
- Use of public tax funds to pay for salaries of teachers in religious schools has not been upheld by the courts.
- Use of public funds to pay tuition of religious school children has not been upheld; in Minnesota, a tax deduction has been upheld for parents of children in public *and* private schools.

- Special support services such as speech and hearing teachers may be provided to students in religious schools.
- Religious schools may be reimbursed for administrative costs of standardized tests, test scoring, and record keeping required by the state.
- Public tax funds may not be used in support of public school teachers offering remedial or enriched instruction in religious schools.

on child benefit theory; this theory emerged out of commentary about the *Everson v. Board of Education* case. The reasoning was that transportation and books provide benefits to the children and not to the school or to a religion. Those opposed to the child benefit theory argue that aid to children receiving sectarian education instruction is effectively aiding the institution providing instruction.

The child benefit theory, as supported by the U.S. Supreme Court, has penetrated federal legislation. For example, the original Elementary and Secondary Education Act of 1965 (ESEA) and its subsequent reauthorizations, including No Child Left Behind, provide assistance to both public and nonpublic schoolchildren. For example, Title I of ESEA, which deals with assistance for the education of children from low-income families, states that children from families attending private schools must be provided services in proportion to their numbers.

Title I Teachers in Religious Schools. In *Agostini v. Felton* (1997), the U.S. Supreme Court seemed to be providing increased flexibility and easing the tensions created by *Aguilar v. Felton* (1985). In *Aguilar* the court struck down the use of Title I funds to pay public school teachers who taught in programs to help low-income students in parochial schools. But in *Agostini,* the court decided that, under specific safeguards, Title I teachers can be sent to serve disadvantaged students in religious schools.

The issue of public aid to church-related schools seems to have been settled. It is clear that aid for certain secular services (such as transportation; textbooks; and—under prescribed circumstances—testing, diagnostic, therapeutic, and remedial services) can be provided. Still, this is a difficult problem area. In fact, the whole body of law in this area continues to be somewhat confused and contradictory. Figure 10.3 summarizes our current understanding related to public funds and religious education.

A continuing topic of debate and judicial action is the place of prayer in public schools as determined by the First Amendment.

RELIGIOUS ACTIVITIES IN PUBLIC SCHOOLS. The limits and boundaries of the First Amendment in relation to public schools have been and will continue to be tested in the courts, especially in relation to what might be seen as support of religion. Many cases have dealt with prayer in school, the teaching of creationism and evolution, and the religious use of public facilities. Each case has contributed to a gradual process of clarification of what can be done and what should not be done to ensure the separation of church and state. Table 10.2 summarizes selected U.S. Supreme Court judgments in some of these cases.

Prayer in School. A number of attempts have been and continue to be initiated by school districts to incorporate some form of prayer into public school classrooms and activities. One such case began when the school district for Santa Fe High School, in Texas, adopted a series of policies that permitted prayer initiated and led by a student at all home athletic games. In June 2000, the

TABLE 10.2

Selected U.S. Supreme Court Cases Related to the Practice of Religion in Public Schools

CASE	ISSUE	DECISION
CREATIONISM		
Edwards v. Aguillard (1987)	Balanced treatment of biblical and scientific explanations of the development of life	A state cannot require that schools teach the biblical version of creation.
PRACTICE OF RELIGION		
Wallace v. Jaffree (1985)	Legislation authorizing prayer in public schools, led by teachers, and a period of silence for meditation or voluntary prayer	Court held that state legislation authorizing a minute of silence for prayer led by teachers was unconstitutional.
Mozert v. Hawkins County Public Schools (1987)	Request that fundamentalist children not be exposed to basal reading series in the public schools of Tennessee	Rejected by the Court of Appeals for the Sixth Court, which reasoned that the readers did not burden the students' exercise of their religious beliefs.
Board of Education of the Westside Community Schools v. Mergens (1990)	The right of a student religious club to hold meetings at a public school	Court ruled that based on the Equal Access Act (EAA) of 1984, if only one non-curriculum-related student group meets, then the school may not deny other clubs.
Lee v. Weisman (1992)	Inclusion of a religious exercise in a graduation ceremony where young graduates who object are induced to conform	Prayers as an official part of graduation exercises are unconstitutional.
USE OF FACILITIES		
Police Department of the City of Chicago v. Mosley (1972)	Government's refusal of use of a public forum to people whose views it finds unacceptable	"There is an equality of status in the field of ideas," and "government must afford all points of view an equal opportunity to be heard."
Lamb's Chapel v. Center Moriches Union Free School District (1993)	A church's screening of a family-oriented movie on public school premises after school hours	The district property had been used by a wide variety of audiences, so there was no danger of the district's being perceived as endorsing any given religion.
Santa Fe Independent School District, Petitioner v. Jane Doe (2000)	School district policy supporting student-led prayer before football games	"The policy is invalid on its face because it establishes an improper majoritarian election on religion, and unquestionably has the purpose and creates the perception of encouraging the delivery of prayer at a series of important school events."

U.S. Supreme Court ruled in *Santa Fe Independent School District, Petitioner v. Jane Doe* that the clear intent of the district policies was in violation of the establishment clause. The six-to-three majority observed, "the District, nevertheless, asks us to pretend that we do not recognize what every Santa Fe High School student understands clearly—that this policy is about prayer." Later in the decision, the Court noted, "This policy likewise does not survive a facial challenge because it impermissibly imposes upon the student body a majoritarian election on the issue of prayer." In other words, the district would be imposing a particular religious activity of the majority on all, a clear violation of the establishment clause. "It further empowers the student body majority with the authority to subject students of minority views to constitutionally improper messages. The award of that power alone, regardless of the students' ultimate use of it, is not acceptable." In concluding, the Court stated, "the policy is invalid on its face because it establishes an improper majoritarian election on religion, and unquestionably has the purpose and creates the perception of encouraging the delivery of prayer at a series of important school events." Figure 10.4 summarizes findings related to the practice of religion in public schools.

Evolution versus Intelligent Design. Education has been placed at the center of what seems to be a never-ending debate between science and certain religious perspectives. The beginning of this debate is traced to the publication of *The Origin of Species* by Charles Darwin in 1859. Following years of careful observation and documentation of the characteristics of plants and animals, Darwin theorized that today's animals and plants were the results of natural selection over thousands of years—in other words, evolution. In the approximately 150 years since that publication, the scientific base for evolution has become well established through study of the geologic record and, more recently, analysis of the genetic history of plants and animals.

Some religious perspectives and a large proportion of the population view evolution as an unproven "theory." The critics have used various strategies to challenge its teaching, or to require an alternative view based on religion to be taught as well.

One of the most famous trials involving religion and a teacher occurred in Tennessee in 1925, when a science teacher, John Scopes, was found guilty of teaching evolution. Although the decision was later reversed on a technicality, the "Scopes Monkey Trial" has been kept alive in the theater and through the more recent efforts of certain religious groups advocating for the teaching in science classes of alternative views based on the Bible. In the 1970s the alternative view was to advocate for a biblical account as scientific theory; this was called *creationism*. As the courts failed to support this theory, a new one, called *intelligent design,* has been advanced. Each of these views has argued that life is too complicated to have developed without there being a higher power involved. As summarized in Table 10.3, the courts have tended to view each of these efforts as attempts to advance religion.

GO TO ⋯➤
See Chapter 6 for an informative discussion on the place of religion in the culture of families and school.

TABLE 10.3

Selected Court Cases Related to the Teaching of Evolution in Science Classes

CASE	ISSUE	DECISION
The State of Tennessee v. John Thomas Scopes (1925), the "Scopes Monkey Trial"	The teaching of evolution in science classes	The teacher was guilty. The decision was later overturned on a technicality.
Epperson v. Arkansas (1968)	Can the state ban the teaching of evolution?	The "anti-evolution" statute violated the establishment clause.
Edwards v. Aguillard (1987)	Can the state require that the teaching of creationism be given equal time with the teaching of evolution?	The Court ruled that the Arkansas legislature violated the establishment clause.
Kitzmiller v. Dover Area School District (2005)	Can a school board require its science teachers to discuss intelligent design?	The district judge ruled that "intelligent design cannot uncouple itself from its creationist, and thus religious, antecedents."

FIGURE 10.4	Summary Statements on Church and State and the Practice of Religion in Public Schools

- To teach the Bible as a religion course in the public schools is illegal; to teach about the Bible as part of the history of literature is legal.
- To dismiss children from public schools for one hour once a week for religious instruction at religious centers is legal.
- Reading of scripture and reciting prayers as religious exercises are in violation of the establishment clause.

- Public schools can teach the scientific theory of evolution as a theory; a state cannot require that the biblical version of evolution be taught.
- If school facilities are made available to one group, then they must be made available to all other groups of the same general type.

Regardless of past Supreme Court decisions, some topics, such as the posting of the Ten Commandments in classrooms and Bible reading in public schools, continue to be challenged by legislatures, individuals, and various groups. One of the outcomes of these ongoing challenges is an accumulating series of judicial interpretations that can serve as guidelines about what can and cannot be done. The summary statements presented in Figure 10.4 outline the overall pattern of the many judicial decisions related to religion and the public schools.

Segregation and Desegregation

segregation Legal and/or social separation of people on the basis of their race.

A troublesome problem for U.S. society has been the history of legal and social separation of people based on their race—in other words, **segregation**. Up until the middle of the twentieth century, the public school systems in many states contributed to this problem through the operation of two separate sets of schools, one for Caucasians and one for African Americans ("Negroes"). Segregated schools were supported by the courts, state laws, and by the official actions of state and local government administrators. This kind of segregation, based in legal and official actions, is called *de jure* **segregation**.

de jure **segregation** The segregation of students on the basis of law, school policy, or a practice designed to accomplish such separation.

Since 1954 the courts and communities have made intensive efforts to abolish the racial segregation of school students, a process that has been called **desegregation**. A major instrument the courts have used to accomplish this end has been **integration**, the busing of students to achieve a balanced number of students, in terms of race, in each school within a school district. A second instrument has been the use of magnet schools, which are schools that emphasize particular curriculum areas, disciplines, or themes. The hope has been that these schools will attract a diverse set of students. These efforts to integrate the schools have had mixed success, and now there is increasing concern over the **resegregation** of schools based on where people live. Segregation—or resegregation—caused by housing patterns and other nonlegal factors is called *de facto* **segregation**.

desegregation The process of correcting illegal segregation.

integration The process of mixing students of different races in school.

resegregation A situation in which formerly integrated schools become segregated again because of changes in neighborhood population patterns.

"SEPARATE BUT EQUAL": NO LONGER EQUAL. Before 1954 many states had laws either requiring or permitting racial segregation in public schools (*de jure* segregation). Until 1954 lower courts adhered to the doctrine of "separate but equal" as announced by the Supreme Court in *Plessy v. Ferguson* (1896). In *Plessy v. Ferguson,* the Court upheld a Louisiana law that required railway companies to provide separate but equal accommodations for the black and the white races. The Court's reasoning at that time was that the Fourteenth Amendment implied political, not social, equality.

de facto **segregation** The segregation of students resulting from circumstances such as housing patterns rather than law or school policy.

The Failure of the Separate-but-Equal Doctrine. This separate-but-equal doctrine appeared to be the rule until May 17, 1954, when the Supreme Court repudiated it in *Brown v. Board of Education of Topeka.* The Court said that the separate-but-equal doctrine has no place in education and that separate facilities are inherently unequal. In 1955 the Court rendered the second *Brown v. Board of Education of Topeka* decision, requiring that the principles of the first decision be carried out with all deliberate speed.

From 1954, the time of the *Brown* decision, to 1964, little progress was made in eliminating segregated schools. On May 25, 1964, referring to a situation in Prince Edward County, Virginia,

TABLE 10.4

Selected U.S. Supreme Court Cases Related to School Desegregation and Integration

CASE	ISSUE	DECISION
Plessy v. Ferguson (1896)	Whether a railway company should be required to provide equal accommodations for the African American and white races	The Court indicated in its decision that the Fourteenth Amendment implied political, not social, equality. Thus the doctrine of "separate but equal" was established.
Brown v. Board of Education of Topeka (1954)	Legality of separate school facilities	The separate-but-equal doctrine has no place in education, and dual school systems (*de jure* segregation) are inherently unequal.
Griffin v. County School Board of Prince Edward County (1964)	Whether a county may close its schools and provide assistance to private schools for whites only	The Court instructed the local district court to require the authorities to levy taxes to reopen and operate a nondiscriminatory public school system.
Board of Education of Oklahoma City Public Schools v. Dowell (1991)	The conditions under which a school district may be relieved of court supervision	Court supervision was to continue until segregation was removed from every facet of school operations.
Freeman v. Pitts (1992)	Whether court supervision may be withdrawn incrementally, and whether a school district is responsible for segregation based on demographic changes (*de facto* segregation)	A district court is permitted to withdraw supervision in discrete categories in which the district has achieved compliance; also "the school district is under no duty to remedy imbalance that is caused by demographic factors."

the Supreme Court said, "There has been entirely too much deliberation and not enough speed in enforcing the constitutional rights which we held in *Brown v. Board of Education.*" The Civil Rights Act of 1964 added legislative power to the 1954 judicial pronouncement. The act not only authorized the federal government to initiate court suits against school districts that were laggard in desegregating schools, but also denied federal funds for programs that discriminated by race, color, or national origin.

Subsequently, many efforts have been made to meet the expectations of the Court decisions and legislation. The objective of these initiatives has been to promote integration, that is, to achieve a representative mix of students of different races in schools. In the sixty-plus years since *Brown,* there have been many efforts by school districts and communities and many additional lawsuits. Table 10.4 summarizes some key Supreme Court decisions on school desegregation and integration.

Release from Court Orders. As years of court directions and school district efforts related to integration unfolded a new question was raised: What conditions must be in place for a school district to be released from federal court supervision? Three cases in the 1990s offered instances of conditions under which the courts would back away. *Board of Education of Oklahoma City Public Schools v. Dowell* (1991) is important for at least three reasons: First, the U.S. Supreme Court made it clear that "federal supervision of local school systems was intended as a temporary measure to remedy past discrimination." Second, the Court stated that in relation to desegregation, "the District Court should look not only at student assignments, but to every facet of school operations—faculty, staff, transportation, extracurricular activities and facilities." Third, for the first time the Court defined what full compliance with a desegregation order would mean.

One of the positive long-term effects of desegregation can be seen in today's highly diverse schools and classrooms.

Two other cases added additional clarity to what the Court expects in order to release a school district from supervision. In *Freeman v. Pitts* (1992), the U.S. Supreme Court ruled that districts do not have to remedy racial imbalances caused by demographic changes, but the districts still have the burden of proving that their actions do not contribute to the imbalances. The third case was a return to *Brown*. The Court had ordered the Court of Appeals for the Tenth Circuit to reexamine its 1989 finding that the Topeka district remained segregated. In 1992 the appellate court refused to declare Topeka successful. The court concluded that the district had done little to fulfill the duty to desegregate that was first imposed on it in 1954. The judges wrote that to expect the vestiges of segregation to "magically dissolve" with so little effort "is to expect too much."

These three cases in combination made it clear that it is possible for school districts to be released from court orders. The decisions also made it clear that school districts have to make concerted efforts across time to address any and all remnants of *de jure* segregation. Further, it now appears that school districts are not expected to resolve those aspects of *de facto* segregation that are clearly beyond their control.

ACHIEVING INTEGRATION IN TODAY'S DIVERSE SOCIETY. At present more than 500 school districts have experienced some form of federal court oversight to address segregation. At the same time, instead of schools and communities becoming fully integrated, there is a clear trend toward resegregation, especially in urban areas. As well intentioned as the efforts have been to erase *de jure* segregation, *de facto* segregation is increasing. There also is increasing diversity in the number of other racial and ethnic groups in most communities. Schools continue to be challenged to ensure that all students have equal access to a quality education. The current strategy for achieving this end is some form of **race-conscious assignment** of students. Strategies such as magnet schools, including consideration of diversity in admissions, and giving priority to siblings in school assignment are being tried. As well intentioned as these efforts may be, some people perceive inequities and each strategy is being challenged in the courts.

Equal Opportunity

The equal protection clause of the Fourteenth Amendment has been instrumental in shaping many court cases and federal statutes that are directed toward preventing discrimination in schools. A judgment of **discrimination** can be defined as a determination that an individual or a group of individuals—for example, African Americans, women, or people with disabilities—has been

race-conscious assignment
The strategy of taking race into account for placement of students without making it the primary or single consideration.

discrimination Denial of constitutional rights to an individual or group.

denied constitutional rights. In common usage, the term applies to various minorities or to individual members of a minority who lack rights typically accorded the majority. The principle that discrimination violates the equal protection clause was reinforced in statutes such as Titles VI and VII of the Civil Rights Act of 1964 and Title IX of the Education Amendments Act of 1972. Title VI of the Civil Rights Act states:

> No person in the United States shall, on the ground of race, color, or national origin, be excluded from participation in, be denied the benefits of, or be subjected to discrimination under any program or activity receiving federal financial assistance.

Title VII states:

> It shall be an unlawful employment practice for an employer (1) to fail or refuse to hire or to discharge any individual, or otherwise to discriminate against any individual with respect to his compensation, terms, conditions, or privileges of employment, because of such individual's race, color, religion, sex, or national origin; or (2) to limit, segregate, or classify his employees or applicants for employment in any way which would deprive or tend to deprive any individual of employment opportunities or otherwise adversely affect his status as an employee, because of such individual's race, color, religion, sex, or national origin.

Title IX of the Education Amendments Act of 1972 states:

> No person in the United States shall, on the basis of sex, be excluded from participation in, be denied the benefits of, or be subjected to discrimination under any education program or activity receiving federal financial assistance.

AFFIRMATIVE ACTION. In the years since the 1964 Civil Rights Act, numerous statutes and court cases have encouraged steps designed to ensure that underrepresented populations have equal opportunity. These **affirmative action** initiatives have included such actions as formalizing and publicizing nondiscriminatory hiring procedures and setting aside a certain number of slots in hiring or college admissions programs. Over time, concern has increased about the possibility of **reverse discrimination**—situations in which a majority or an individual member of a majority is not accorded equal rights because of different or preferential treatment provided to a minority or an individual member of a minority. This concern has resulted in a new set of court cases, each of which is attempting to redress what is perceived as a new imbalance. A summary of the events, policies, and court cases related to affirmative action is presented in Figure 10.5.

As mentioned, the legal basis for affirmative action is found in Titles VI and VII of the Civil Rights Act of 1964 and in Title IX of the Education Amendments Act of 1972. However, affirmative action procedures and methods continue to be clarified and increasingly questioned. As of 2012, six states (California, Michigan, Arizona, Nebraska, Oklahoma, and Washington) have established

affirmative action
Policies and procedures designed to compensate for past discrimination against women and members of minority groups (for example, assertive recruiting and admissions practices).

reverse discrimination
A situation in which a majority or an individual of a majority is denied certain rights because of preferential treatment provided to a minority or an individual of a minority.

FIGURE 10.5	Events in the History of Affirmative Action

1941	President Roosevelt issues an executive order prohibiting discrimination by government contractors.	1978	In *University of California v. Bakke,* the Supreme Court rules that colleges can consider race as one factor in admissions.
1961	President Kennedy makes the first reference to affirmative action in an order mandating that federal contractors make employment practices free of racial bias.	1995	The Supreme Court limits racial preferences in federal highway contracts.
1964	Congress passes the Civil Rights Act.	2003	In *Grutter v. Bollinger* and *Gratz v. Bollinger* the Supreme Court rules that race can be considered by colleges in their efforts to have a diverse student body, but it cannot be done through a set formula or quota.
1965	President Johnson outlines specific steps federal contractors must take to ensure hiring equality.		
1970	The Nixon administration orders federal contractors to set "goals and timetables" for hiring minorities.		
1972	Congress passes Title IX of the Education Amendments Act that states that no person can be excluded from participation based on his or her sex.		

bans against using racial and gender preferences in hiring, contracting, and college admissions. The U.S. Supreme Court has once again been called upon to define the boundaries of affirmative action.

In this **video**, two educators discuss early legal breakthroughs for students with disabilities.

Opportunities for Students with Disabilities

The judicial basis for current approaches to the education of students with disabilities is also closely linked to the civil rights and equal opportunity initiatives. In addition, several specifically targeted statutes address the education of people with disabilities. Three particularly important statutes are Section 504 of the Rehabilitation Act; Public Law 94-142, the Education for All Handicapped Children Act (EAHCA); and the Individuals with Disabilities Education Act (IDEA).

These statutes encourage the education of individuals with disabilities by making grants to states and local education agencies for children ages three to five, require the federal government to be responsive to the increasing ethnic diversity of society and to those with limited English proficiency, and fund programs to provide education to all children with disabilities.

SECTION 504 OF THE REHABILITATION ACT. Under this civil rights act established in 1973, recipients of federal funds are prohibited from discriminating against "otherwise qualified individuals." Note that Section 504 is a federal statute and related regulations, not a court decision. Three important themes addressed in Section 504 are equal treatment, appropriate education, and people with disabilities. Equal treatment, as in other civil rights contexts, must be addressed. However, this does not necessarily mean the *same* treatment. For example, giving the same assessment procedure to students with disabilities and other students may not be equal treatment. Educational judgments in relation to students with disabilities require a "heightened standard." The measures must fit the students' circumstances, and procedural safeguards must be employed. Appropriate education means that the school system and related parties must address the individual needs of students with disabilities as adequately as the educational approaches for other students do. In Section 504, a "handicapped person" is defined as follows:

> Any person who (i) has a physical or mental impairment which substantially limits one or more major life activities, (ii) has a record of such an impairment, or (iii) is regarded as having such an impairment. (34 CFR 104.3)

PUBLIC LAW 94-142 (EAHCA). First passed by Congress in 1975, Public Law 94-142 has been amended several times since. This law ensures "a free appropriate public education" to all children with disabilities between the ages of three and twenty-one. Children with exceptional needs cannot be excluded from education because of their needs. The law is very specific in describing the kind and quality of education and in stating that each child with a disability is to have an individually planned education. Details of this plan must be spelled out in a written **Individualized Education Plan (IEP)**, formulated by general and special education teachers, and subject to the parents' approval. Originally, the law provided for substantial increases in funding; in subsequent years, however, the funding authorizations have been lower than the original commitment. Two priorities for funding were identified: (1) the child who currently receives no education and (2) the child who is not receiving all the services he or she needs to succeed. These priorities place the emphasis on need rather than on the specific disability.

Individualized Education Plan (IEP) A program designed to meet the needs of a child eligible for special education services. The plan helps educators understand the child's disability and provides directions for the services to be provided by teachers and other school professionals.

THE INDIVIDUALS WITH DISABILITIES EDUCATION ACT (IDEA). Since its original inception in 1975, PL 94-142 has been amended and reauthorized several times; it is now called *IDEA*. This statute addresses how states and schools, and other public agencies, provide services to children with disabilities. The purpose of IDEA is to make available to all children with disabilities a free appropriate public education. Federal funds are made available through various grants to support services for children from birth to twenty-six years of age.

Increased Quality and Rigor. Significant updates and changes were made in the 2004 reauthorization of IDEA. There was a need to align IDEA with NCLB, including making consistent such definitions as "highly qualified" teachers and "limited English proficient." Another important element was the heavy emphasis placed on "scientifically based research." Teachers and schools are expected to use classroom practices that are based on rigorous research.

Response to Intervention (RTI). As you become a teacher, *RTI* is an acronym that you will need to understand. A key IDEA theme now for teachers, schools, and school districts is to not just say "This kid needs to be in special education." Rather, there needs to be a systematic approach to assessing what the student already knows and determining identifiable needs. Secondly, documented efforts must be made to improve the students' learning by providing student need-specific (and research-based) interventions. More than likely, these interventions will be purposeful instruction, but they could be related to student behavior or other needs.

TEACHERS' RIGHTS AND RESPONSIBILITIES

Teachers have the same rights as other citizens; however, as teachers there are some limits. The Fourteenth Amendment gives every citizen the right to **due process** of law: both *substantive due process* (protection against the deprivation of constitutional rights such as freedom of expression) and *procedural due process* (procedural protection against unjustified deprivation of substantive rights). Most court cases related to teachers evolve from either liberty or property interests. Liberty interests are created by the Constitution itself; property interests are found in forms of legal entitlement such as tenure or certification.

Teachers also have the same responsibilities as other citizens. They must abide by federal, state, and local laws and by the provisions of contracts. As professionals they must also assume the heavy responsibility of educating young people. We discuss specific court cases briefly here to illustrate some of the issues and court decisions related to aspects of teacher rights and responsibilities. Note that the cases selected do not necessarily constitute the last word regarding teacher rights but rather provide an overview of some of the issues that have been decided in the courts. Table 10.5 summarizes the issues and decisions in selected cases involving teacher rights and responsibilities. This summary table is not intended to provide a complete understanding of the court decisions cited. Note also that most of the court cases were decided in the 1970s and 1980s; more recently, new federal statutes have been the defining force.

Conditions of Employment

Many conditions must be met for you to be hired as a teacher. These include your successful completion of a professional preparation program, being credentialed or licensed by the state, and receiving a contract from the hiring school district. In each of these instances, you have rights established in law and statute, as well as responsibilities.

TEACHER CERTIFICATION AND LICENSURE. The primary purpose of each state's **teacher certification and licensure** requirements is to make sure that the teachers in public schools are qualified and competent. Certification laws usually require satisfactory completion of a preparation program, citizenship, no criminal record, and increasingly evidence of instructional effectiveness. Establishing rules and procedures for obtaining a teaching license will be the responsibility of the state education department and/or a professional standards board. The certifying agency may not arbitrarily refuse to issue a certificate to a qualified candidate. The courts have ruled that local boards of education may prescribe additional or higher qualifications beyond the state requirements, provided that such requirements are not irrelevant, unreasonable, or arbitrary.

A teaching certificate or license is a privilege that enables a person to practice a profession—it is not a right. Teacher certification, however, is a property interest that cannot be revoked without constitutional due process.

TEACHER EMPLOYMENT CONTRACTS. Usually, boards of education have the statutory authority to employ teachers. This authority includes the power to enter into contracts and to fix terms of employment and compensation. In some states, only specific members of the school board can sign teacher contracts. When statutes confer the

due process The legal procedures that must be followed to safeguard individuals from arbitrary, capricious, or unreasonable policies, practices, or actions.

teacher certification and licensure The process whereby each state determines the requirements for certification and for obtaining a license to teach.

A big moment: Signing a contract to teach is a professional commitment by the teacher and a legal one for the school district.

TABLE 10.5

Selected U.S. Supreme Court Cases Related to Teachers' Rights and Responsibilities

CASE	ISSUE	DECISION
DISCRIMINATION		
North Haven Board of Education v. Bell (1982)	Allegation by former women faculty members of sex discrimination in employment	Court ruled that school employees as well as students are protected under Title IX.
Cleveland Board of Education v. LeFleur (1974)	Rights of pregnant teachers	Court struck down the board policy forcing all pregnant teachers to take mandatory maternity leave.
Burkey v. Marshall County Board of Education (1981)	Paying female coaches half the salary of male coaches	Court ruled that the policy violated the Equal Pay Act, Title VII of the Civil Rights Act of 1964.
CONTRACT RIGHTS		
Board of Regents of State Colleges v. Roth (1972)	Rights of nontenured teachers	Teacher had been hired under a one-year contract. Court concluded that he did not have a property interest that would entitle him to procedural rights under the Fourteenth Amendment.
Perry v. Sindermann (1972)	Rights of nontenured teachers	Court ruled that a state employee may acquire the property interest if officially fostered customs, rules, understandings, and practices imply a contract promise to grant continuing contract status and thus establish a *de facto* tenure system.
BARGAINING		
Hortonville Joint School District No. 1 v. Hortonville Education Association (1976)	Rights of boards of education to dismiss teachers who are striking illegally	Court said the law gave the board power to employ and dismiss teachers as a part of the municipal labor relations balance.
ACADEMIC FREEDOM		
Pickering v. Board of Education (1968)	Dismissal of an Illinois teacher for criticizing a school board and superintendent in a letter published by a local newspaper	Court upheld teacher's claim that his First and Fourteenth Amendment rights were denied.

employing authority to boards of education, the authority cannot be delegated. It is usually the responsibility of the superintendent to screen and nominate candidates to the board. The board, meeting in official session, then acts as a group to enter into contractual agreements.

A typical teacher contract will contain the following elements: the identification of the teacher and the board of education, a statement of the legal capacity of each party to enter into the contract, a definition of the assignment specified, a statement of the salary and how it is to be paid, and a provision for signature by the teacher and by the legally authorized agents of the board. The contract is not official until it has the signatures of all parties.

Teachers are responsible for making certain that they are legally qualified to enter into contractual agreements. For example, a teacher may not enter into a legal contract without having a valid teaching certificate issued by the state. Furthermore, teachers are responsible for carrying out the terms of the contract and abiding by them. In turn, under the contract they can legally expect proper treatment from an employer.

TEACHER TENURE. Tenure laws are intended to provide security for teachers in their positions and to prevent removal of capable teachers by capricious action or political motive. However, currently in many states there are serious challenges to teachers having tenure. Many perceive public employees as having too many benefits such as paid health insurance and participation in public-funded retirement programs. There also is a perception of it not being easy to terminate a poorly performing teacher. In the last few years these views have been used in several states by Republican governors and legislators to change tenure and teacher evaluation laws.

Teachers have had to work together to obtain and then to protect continuation of many of their rights as public employees.

Becoming Tenured and Tenure Rights. Beginning teachers are not automatically tenured. Instead, a teacher becomes tenured by serving satisfactorily for a stated time. This period is referred to as the **probationary period** and typically is two to three years. The actual process of acquiring tenure after serving the probationary period depends on the applicable statute. In some states, the process is automatic at the satisfactory completion of the probationary period; in other states, official action by the school board is necessary.

Even with tenure, teachers may be dismissed for any one of numerous reasons, including "nonperformance of duty, incompetency, insubordination, conviction of crimes involving moral turpitude, failure to comply with reasonable orders, violation of contract provisions or local rules or regulations, persistent failure or refusal to maintain orderly discipline of students, and revocation of the teaching certificate" (LaMorte, 2012).

A school board in Tennessee dismissed Jane Turk from her tenured teaching position after she was arrested for driving under the influence of alcohol (DUI) (*Turk v. Franklin,* 1982). Turk's appeal was upheld by the lower court judge because there was no evidence of an adverse effect on her capacity and fitness as a teacher. The school board appealed to the Tennessee Supreme Court, which rejected the board's appeal, finding that the school board "acted in flagrant disregard of the statutory requirement and fundamental fairness in considering matters that should have been specifically charged in writing." Tennessee law requires that before a tenured teacher can be dismissed, "the charges shall be made in writing specifically stating the offenses which are charged." Nevertheless, teacher tenure may be affected by teacher conduct outside school as well as inside. This issue, in a sense, deals with the personal freedom of teachers: freedom to behave as other citizens do, freedom to engage in political activities, and academic freedom in the classroom.

Tenure laws are frequently attacked by those who claim that the laws protect incompetent teachers. There is undoubtedly some truth in the assertion, but it must be stated clearly and unequivocally that these laws also protect the competent and most able teachers. Teachers who accept the challenge of their profession and dare to use new methods, who inspire curiosity in their students, and who discuss controversial issues in their classrooms need protection from politically motivated or capricious dismissal. Incompetent teachers, whether tenured or not, can be dismissed under the law by capable administrators and careful school boards that allow due process while evaluating teacher performance.

Rights of Nontenured Teachers. Although due process has been applicable for years to tenured teachers, nontenured teachers do not, for the most part, enjoy the same rights. As an example, reread the "Education in the News" feature at the beginning of this chapter. In the end, the judge ruled that the nontenured teacher should be "fired" for her actions.

tenure A system of school employment in which educators retain their positions indefinitely unless they are dismissed for legally specified reasons through clearly established procedures.

probationary period The required time, typically one to three years, during which a beginning teacher must demonstrate satisfactory performance as a basis for seeking tenure.

In general, tenured teachers enjoy two key rights: protection from dismissal except for cause as provided in state statutes, and the right to prescribed procedures. Nontenured teachers may also have due process rights if these are spelled out in state statutes or the teacher's contract; however, in most districts and states nontenured teachers may be nonrenewed without any reasons being given. If a nontenured teacher is dismissed (as distinguished from nonrenewed) before the expiration of the contract, the teacher is entitled to due process.

Cases in Massachusetts (*Lucia v. Duggan,* 1969) and Wisconsin (*Gouge v. Joint School District No. 1,* 1970) point to the necessity of following due process in dismissing nontenured teachers. In the Massachusetts case, the court said: "the particular circumstances of a dismissal of a public school teacher provide compelling reasons for application of a doctrine of procedural due process."

In the Wisconsin case, the court said:

A teacher in a public elementary or secondary school is protected by the due process clause of the Fourteenth Amendment against a nonrenewal decision which is wholly without basis in fact and also against a decision which is wholly unreasoned, as well as a decision which is impermissibly based. (*Gouge,* 1970)

In 1972 the Supreme Court helped to clarify the difference between the rights of tenured and nontenured teachers. In one case (*Board of Regents v. Roth,* 1972), it held that nontenured teachers were assured of no rights that were not specified in state statutes. In this instance, the only right that probationary teachers had was the one to be notified of nonrenewal by a specified date. In a second case (*Perry v. Sindermann,* 1972), the Court ruled that a nontenured teacher in the Texas system of community colleges was entitled to due process because the language of the institution's policy manual was such that an unofficial tenure system was in effect. Guidelines in the policy manual provided that a faculty member with seven years of employment in the system acquired tenure and could be dismissed only for cause.

Whether or not a teacher is tenured, that person cannot be dismissed for exercise of a right guaranteed by the U.S. Constitution. A school board cannot dismiss a teacher, for example, for engaging in civil rights activities outside school, speaking on matters of public concern, belonging to a given church, or running for public office. These rights are guaranteed to all citizens, including teachers. However, as in the "Education in the News" case, if a teacher's behavior is judged to be disruptive or dishonest, a school board can dismiss the person without violating the right to freedom of speech. Figure 10.6 provides a summary of teacher rights and responsibilities. Be sure to check how well you match with these requirements.

FIGURE 10.6 **Summary Statements on Teachers' Rights and Responsibilities**

- Prospective teachers must fulfill the requirements of laws and policies regarding certification before being employed as teachers.
- Boards of education have the authority to employ teachers, including authority to enter into contracts and to fix terms of employment and compensation.
- School districts are prohibited from use of discriminatory practices; discrimination in employment and salary of teachers on the basis of sex is in violation of Title IX of the Education Amendments Act.
- Most states have tenure laws that provide teachers with protection against arbitrary dismissal; rights of nontenured teachers are found in state laws.
- Teachers may speak out on matters of public concern, even in criticism of their school board, as long as their speech is not disruptive or a lie.

- Boards of education may remove books from library shelves under their authority to select materials for schools; however, the removal of a book merely because someone disagrees with its content was not upheld by the U.S. Supreme Court.
- Many states provide for school boards and teacher unions to bargain collectively on wages, hours, and terms and conditions of employment.
- Teacher strikes are unlawful when a statute is violated; in some states, it is legal for teachers to strike.
- Teachers are expected to exercise due care in foreseeing possible accidents and in working to prevent their occurrence; teachers may be sued for their negligence that led to pupil injury.

Right to Bargain Collectively

In the distant past, teacher groups met informally with boards of education to discuss salaries and other teacher welfare provisions. Sometimes the superintendent was even the spokesperson for such teacher groups. In more recent years formal **collective bargaining** procedures have been established. Instead of a more informal group of teachers meeting with the superintendent or school board to negotiate salaries and working conditions, formalized procedures have been established. Now a bargaining unit, such as a teachers' union, meets with a representative of the district, such as the assistant superintendent for human resources. Through bargaining an agreement is reached that applies to all teachers. The procedures must comply with the National Labor Relations Act (NLRA), and the collective agreement is enforceable under state law.

A contract arrived at by a teachers' union means that salaries, working conditions, and other matters within the scope of the collective bargaining agreement can no longer be decided unilaterally by the school administration and board of education. Instead, the contract outlines how the teachers' union and its members will participate in formulating the school policies and programs under which they work.

THE FIRST COLLECTIVE BARGAINING AGREEMENTS. The first teachers' group to bargain collectively with its local board of education was the Maywood, Illinois, Proviso Council of West Suburban Teachers, Union Local 571, in 1938. In 1957 a second local, the East St. Louis, Illinois, Federation of Teachers was successful in negotiating a written contract. The breakthrough, however, came in December 1961, when the United Federation of Teachers, Local 2 of the American Federation of Teachers (AFT), won the right to bargain for New York City's teachers. Since then, collective bargaining agreements between boards of education and teacher groups have grown phenomenally. Both the AFT and the National Education Association (NEA) have been active in promoting collective bargaining.

COLLECTIVE BARGAINING IS NOW BEING CHALLENGED. Beginning in 2011 in several states including Ohio, Florida, Pennsylvania, and Arizona, the right of teachers to bargain collectively came under major attack. The most visible example unfolded in Wisconsin where the Republican Governor, Scott Walker, and the Republican-controlled legislature passed a law eliminating teacher collective bargaining. The stated rationale was a need to balance the budget. However, collective bargaining agreements with other groups of public employees, such as police and fire, were not treated in the same way. Ironically, in 1962 Wisconsin was the first state to pass collective bargaining language similar to that found in NLRA.

JOURNAL FOR REFLECTION 10.2

You may be living in a state where teachers have or had collective bargaining rights, or maybe you live in a "right to work" state. Either way, what is your position about paying union dues? Do you see belonging to a teachers' union as an important benefit, or a waste of your money?

Academic Freedom

A sensitive and vital concern to the educator is **academic freedom**—freedom to control what one will teach and to teach the truth as one discovers it without fear of penalty. Academic freedom is thus essentially a principle of pedagogical philosophy that has been applied to a variety of professional activities. A philosophical position, however, is *not necessarily* a legal right. Federal judges have generally recognized certain academic protections in the college classroom while exhibiting reluctance to recognize such rights for elementary and secondary school teachers. For example, the contract of a history teacher at the University of Arkansas–Little Rock was not renewed after he announced that he taught his classes from a Marxist point of view. The court ordered that the teacher be reinstated in light of the university's failure to advance convincing reasons related to the academic freedom issue to warrant his nonrenewal (*Cooper v. Ross*, 1979). In another case, a university instructor claimed that he was denied tenure because he refused to change a student's grade. He argued that awarding a course grade was the instructor's right of academic freedom. Because the university had given several valid reasons for the nonrenewal of the instructor's contract, however, the court did not order a reinstatement (*Hillis v. Stephen F. Austin University*, 1982).

collective bargaining
A process through which teachers are represented as a unit to negotiate with a school board's terms and conditions of employment.

academic freedom The opportunity for a teacher to teach without coercion, censorship, or other restrictive interference.

ACADEMIC FREEDOM FOR ELEMENTARY AND SECONDARY TEACHERS. Although federal courts generally have not recognized academic freedom for elementary and secondary school teachers, the most supportive ruling was made in 1980 (*Kingsville IDS v. Cooper,* 1980). In a case that involved a high school history teacher whose contract was not renewed after she used a simulation game to introduce her students to the characteristics of rural life during the post–Civil War Reconstruction era. Although the role-playing evoked controversy in the school and the community, there was no evidence that the teacher's usefulness had been impaired. Therefore, the school erred in not renewing the teacher's contract, and she was ordered reinstated.

In *Pickering v. Board of Education* (1968), the U.S. Supreme Court dealt with academic freedom at the public school level. Marvin L. Pickering was a teacher in Illinois who, in a letter published by a local newspaper, criticized the school board and the superintendent for the way they had handled past proposals to raise and use new revenues for the schools. After a full hearing, the board of education terminated Pickering's employment, whereupon he brought suit under the First and Fourteenth Amendments. The Illinois courts rejected his claim. The U.S. Supreme Court, however, upheld Pickering's claim and, in its opinion, stated:

> To the extent that the Illinois Supreme Court's opinion may be read to suggest that teachers may constitutionally be compelled to relinquish the First Amendment rights they would otherwise enjoy as citizens to comment on matters of public interest in connection with the operation of the public schools in which they work, it proceeds on a premise that has been unequivocally rejected in numerous prior decisions of this Court. (*Pickering*, 1968)

It is difficult to define precisely the limits of academic freedom. In general, the courts strongly support it yet recognize that teachers must be professionally responsible when interacting with pupils. In most instances, teachers are not free to disregard a school board's decision about which textbook to use, but they are able to participate more when it comes to their choice of supplementary methods. Teachers have usually been supported in their rights to criticize the policies of their local school boards, wear symbols representing stated causes, participate in unpopular movements, and live unconventional lifestyles. But when the exercise of these rights can be shown to have a direct bearing on a teacher's effectiveness, respect, or discipline, these rights may have to be curtailed. For example, a teacher may have the right to wear a gothic costume to class, but if wearing the outfit leads to disruption and an inability to manage students, the teacher can be ordered to wear more conventional clothes.

In summary, academic freedom for elementary and secondary teachers is more limited than it is for higher education faculty. First Amendment protection of free speech is increasingly limited to a teacher's actions outside of the classroom and school. Before arguing for academic freedom and free speech in the classroom, a teacher must show that she or he did not defy legitimate state and local curriculum directives, followed accepted professional norms, and acted in good faith when there was no precedent or policy.

GO TO ···>
See Chapter 12 for information about how curriculum and instruction can be offered in ways that allow for teacher creativity.

BOOK BANNING AND CENSORSHIP. Ever since the United States has had public schools, some people have taken issue with what has been taught, how it has been taught, and the materials used. The number of people challenging these issues and the intensity of feelings have escalated since the mid-1970s. Well-organized and well-financed pressure groups have opposed the teaching of numerous topics, including political, economic, scientific, and religious theories; the teaching of values grounded in religion, morality, or ethnicity; and the portrayal of stereotypes based on gender, race, or ethnicity. Some complaints have involved differences of opinion over the central role of the school—whether the school's job is to transmit traditional values, indoctrinate students, or teach students to do their own thinking.

Several court cases since the 1970s have involved the legality of removing books from the school curriculum and school libraries. The courts have given some guidance but have not fully resolved the issue. In 1972 a court of appeals held that a book does not acquire tenure, so a school board was upheld in its removal of *Down These Mean Streets.* The Court of Appeals for the Seventh Circuit in 1980 upheld the removal of the book *Values Clarification,* ruling that local boards have considerable authority in selecting materials for schools. Removal of books on the basis of vulgar language has also been upheld.

FIGURE 10.7	Important Elements for Teachers to Know about the Family Educational Rights and Privacy Act

Family Educational Rights and Privacy Act (FERPA)
Protects the privacy of student's education records and gives parents access to education records.

Schools must:

- Allow for the inspection and review of all the student's education records.
- Inform all parents of what rights they have.
- Provide copies to a parent or eligible student if she/he is otherwise not able to inspect the records.
- Set reasonable fees for copies.
- Comply within a reasonable time but no later than forty-five days after the request is made.

Parents or eligible students have rights to:

- Seek to amend information within the student's educational records that is believed to be inaccurate or misleading.
- Provide permission before others than teachers and administrators can access information from the student's educational record.

Definitions:

Education record—information directly related to a student that is maintained by the school or school district.

Eligible student—a student becomes an eligible student when he/she turns eighteen years old or attends a postsecondary school.

Parent—natural parent, guardian, or person acting as a parent in the absence of a parent or guardian.

The U.S. Supreme Court treated this issue in 1982 (*Board of Education, Island Trees v. Pico,* 1982). The decision disappointed people who had hoped that the justices would issue a definitive ruling on the banning of books. Instead, Justice William Brennan ruled that students may sue school boards on the grounds of denial of their rights, including the right to receive information. The Court also indicated that removal of a book because one disagrees with its content cannot be upheld. The net effect of this decision was that the school board decided to return the questionable books to the library.

The latest censorship battleground has to do with limiting access to the World Wide Web and various social media. Many school districts and states are establishing policies that restrict access to particular types of websites and limit teacher and student uses of social media. New questions related to defining what is meant by "responsible use" and who decides—teachers, principals, school districts, or the state—are now occupying governing bodies and the courts.

FAMILY EDUCATIONAL RIGHTS AND PRIVACY ACT (FERPA). In 1974, Congress passed the **Family Educational Rights and Privacy Act (FERPA)**, which also is called the **Buckley Amendment**. This statute addresses the maintenance of confidentiality of student records. This statute does not prohibit teachers, principals, and other education professionals from making student information available for educational purposes as long as they take steps to maintain privacy of the information.

Even today many school administrators and teachers—and most parents—do not realize that parents now have the right to view their children's educational records. Many teachers are not aware that their written comments, which they submit as part of a student's record, must be shown at a parent's request, or in response to a student's request if the student is eighteen or older. Key points teachers should know about FERPA are presented in Figure 10.7.

Students Grading One Another's Papers. A common instructional practice for teachers is to have students grade one another's work. As common as the practice is, it resulted in a suit that went all the way to the U.S. Supreme Court. In *Owasso Independent School District v. Falvo,* the plaintiff alleged violations of FERPA in regard to "peer review." The suit was funded by the Rutherford Institute, a national conservative organization. The Court of Appeals for the Tenth Circuit agreed with an Oklahoma parent that students should not grade other students' work. In 2002 the Supreme Court was unanimous in overturning the circuit court and said that the privacy law was directed at records "kept in a filing cabinet in a records room or on a permanent secure database," not the grades on a classroom paper. The Court observed:

Family Educational Rights and Privacy Act (FERPA), 1974. Also referred to as the Buckley Amendment Schools and teachers must maintain confidentiality of student records, and parents must be able to review and challenge the records for their children.

Teachers are responsible for student safety in school and during all other school related activities.

Correcting a classmate's work can be as much a part of the assignment as taking the test itself. It is a way to teach material again in a new context, and it helps show students how to assist and respect fellow pupils. By explaining the answers to the class as the students correct the papers, the teacher not only reinforces the lesson but also discovers whether the students have understood the material and are ready to move on. We do not think FERPA prohibits these educational techniques. (*Owasso*, 2002)

Teacher Responsibilities and Liabilities

With more than 55 million students enrolled in elementary and secondary schools, it is almost inevitable that some will be injured in educational activities. Each year, some injuries will occasion lawsuits in which plaintiffs seek damages. Such suits are often brought against both the school districts and their employees. Legal actions seeking monetary damages for injuries are referred to as *actions in tort*. Technically, a **tort** is a legal wrong—an act (or the omission of an act) that violates the private rights of an individual. Actions in tort are generally based on alleged negligence; the basis of tort liability or legal responsibility is negligence. Understanding the concept of negligence is essential to understanding liability.

Legally, *negligence* is a failure to exercise or practice due care. It includes a factor of foreseeability of harm. Court cases on record involving negligence are numerous and varied. The negligence of teacher supervision of pupils is an important topic that includes supervision of the regular classroom, departure of the teacher from the classroom, supervision of the playground, and supervision of extracurricular activities. **Liability** is the responsibility for negligence—responsibility for the failure to use reasonable care when such failure results in injury to another.

EDUCATIONAL MALPRACTICE. Culpable neglect by a teacher in the performance of his or her duties is called **educational malpractice**. As you will see in the sample of cases described next, the courts have addressed many cases where it has appeared that teachers have been negligent. During your teaching career there are likely to be more tests of the educational malpractice question.

Negligent Chemistry Teacher. In a California high school chemistry class, pupils were injured while experimenting with the manufacture of gunpowder (*Mastrangelo v. West Side Union High School District*, 1935). The teacher was in the room and had supplemented the laboratory manual instructions with his own directions. Nevertheless, an explosion occurred, allegedly caused by the failure of pupils to follow directions. A court held the teacher and the board of education liable. Negligence in this case meant the lack of supervision of laboratory work, a potentially dangerous activity requiring a high level of "due care."

Field Trip Negligence. In Oregon a child was injured while on a field trip (*Morris v. Douglas County School District*, 1966). Children were playing on a large log in a relatively dry area on a beach. A large wave surged up onto the beach, dislodging the log, which began to roll. One of the children fell seaward off the log, and the receding wave pulled the log over the child, injuring him. In the subsequent court action, the teacher was declared negligent for not having foreseen the possibility of such an occurrence. The court said:

> The first proposition asks this court to hold, as a matter of fact, that unusual wave action on the shore of the Pacific Ocean is a hazard so unforeseeable that there is no duty to guard against it. On the contrary, we agree with the trial judge, who observed that it is common knowledge that accidents substantially like the one that occurred in this case have occurred at beaches along the Oregon coast. Foreseeability of such harm is not so remote as to be ruled out as a matter of law. (*Morris*, 1966)

Although liability for negligence is a vague concept involving due care and foreseeability, it is defined more specifically each time a court decides such a case.

tort An act (or the omission of an act) that violates the private rights of an individual.

liability Responsibility for the failure to use reasonable care when such failure results in injury to another.

educational malpractice Culpable neglect by a teacher in the performance of his or her duties.

Liability Insurance. Many states authorize school districts to purchase insurance to protect teachers, school districts, administrators, and school board members against suits. It is important that school districts and their employees and board members be thus protected, either through school district insurance or through their own personal policies. The costs of school district liability insurance have increased so dramatically in recent years that many school districts are contemplating the elimination of extracurricular activities. Consequently, state legislatures are being pressured to fix liability insurance rates for school districts; they are also being asked to pass laws to limit maximum liability amounts for school-related cases. For teachers, membership in the state affiliates of the National Education Association or membership in the American Federation of Teachers include the option of liability insurance programs sponsored by those organizations.

Figure 10.6, shown earlier, summarizes statements related to the rights and responsibilities of teachers.

USES OF SOCIAL MEDIA AND THE LAW

The ever-increasing variety of forms and uses of technology are sources of promising practices for teaching and learning. They also are potential sources of problems for teachers and students, and are increasingly playing a part in disciplinary and legal actions.

E-mail

One of the most ubiquitous forms of technology is e-mail. It has become the basic form of communication between administrators and teachers, and between teachers and other teachers. Teachers may use e-mail to communicate with students and parents. Problems can arise when the "Send" key is hit before the message is carefully composed, or by sending the e-mail to "All" instead of only replying to the original sender. These mistakes can create embarrassing moments. But some can have more serious consequences.

EMPLOYER MONITORING OF E-MAILS. You may wonder whether it is legal for a school district to monitor the e-mails of its teachers or for the college where you are studying teacher education to read your e-mails. If you use the college or school district's e-mail system, then the answer is yes. The courts view the e-mail system, and its content, as owned by the district or college. You can have a problem if inappropriate content is discovered in your e-mails or on your computer. For example, all too frequently school officials are finding pornography on a teacher's at-school computer.

Social Networking Risks

Using cell phones to take and share photos, as well as the extensive social networking through Facebook and Twitter, are causing concern and serious problems. Content that is of a personal or sexual nature will become the basis for dismissal, as you read in this chapter's "Education in the News" feature. Even the accidental discovery of inappropriate content can lead to the employee being fired. Keep the tips in Figure 10.8 in mind so that you do not become another case of inappropriate social networking.

The innocent acts of youth can lead to legal proceedings, as teenagers in several states have discovered with "**sexting**." In several cases officials have threatened, or are charging, girls who

sexting The use of social media to send sexually explicit photos and information.

FIGURE 10.8	Think Before You Send

- Remember: once sent, always available.
- Keep them separate: What is work related and what is personal?
- Acknowledge: What you have sent is yours.
- Be careful: Could this embarrass you at some future time?
- Does it add value? Will this improve teaching and learning?

- Reply to Sender or to All? Be sure your message is going only to whom you intend.
- Your personal website is not confidential. Nonwork systems can be found and reviewed by your employer.
- Wait! Take another minute to review these tips before hitting the Send key.

Inappropriate uses of social media, such as bullying and sexting, by teachers or students can result in criminal prosecution.

allegedly sent nude photos of themselves with lewd exhibition, and the boys who received the photos, with possession of child pornography. These are very serious charges that, if convicted, would affect each student's future for a lifetime. See the "Who Is Right?" feature.

The misuses of social networking by students may be viewed as happening through the innocence of youth. Similar behaviors by teachers are inexcusable and they are being prosecuted. For example, the number of incidents of teachers using technology with students in inappropriate and illegal ways is increasing. The recent case in a Los Angeles elementary school of a teacher taking bondage-style pictures of children is a case in point. The teacher had been teaching for more than thirty years. He now is charged with twenty-three counts of committing lewd acts on children.

An unfortunate part of the Los Angeles case, as well as many others, is that nothing was done when one or more of the children reported the teacher's behavior to other teachers and/or school administration. Adults have a legal responsibility to not only report but to make sure that possible misdeeds by teachers and students are investigated. Not doing so will make you legally responsible and potentially liable.

Cheating with Technology

Another increasing challenge for teachers is to determine when students are using technology to cheat. Instances of using a cell phone while taking a test to snap pictures of test items and having an outsider call in the correct answers are more common than teachers want to believe. Plagiarism on term papers is another problem. Fortunately, several websites and services are available that can be used to catch those who copy from published text. Teachers must be vigilant in the classroom and, unfortunately, suspicious of how their students are using social media and other forms of technology.

JOURNAL FOR REFLECTION 10.3

Today's teachers have responsibilities never imagined in earlier times. School districts specify expectations and evaluate teachers—especially probationary teachers—clearly and closely. Teachers need to know about curriculum standards and be sure that their students have learned the material that will be on the tests. Always present is the possibility of legal action. Take a few minutes to summarize the key points you have learned from reading about teachers' rights and responsibilities. Which of these points had you not anticipated? Which will you need to be sure to learn more about?

STUDENTS' RIGHTS AND RESPONSIBILITIES

The rights of students have changed since the late 1960s. Before 1969, school authorities clearly had the final say as long as what they decided was seen as reasonable. A key U.S. Supreme Court decision in 1969 changed the balance by concluding that students do not "shed their constitutional rights to freedom of speech or expression at the schoolhouse gate." Going further on behalf of student rights, in 1975 the Court decided that the principle of due process applied to students. These decisions led to several successful student challenges of school policies and procedures. However, since the late 1980s Court decisions have moved back toward increasing the authority of public school officials. Along the way, student life has become more complex, not only because of such threats as the increased use of drugs and the presence of weapons and gangs, but also because a diverse multicultural and shifting political context has made it more difficult to determine what is and what is not appropriate to do and say within a school environment.

To illustrate some of the issues and decisions related to student rights and responsibilities, we present specific court cases here. Note that the cases do not necessarily constitute the last

WHO IS RIGHT?

SHOULD STUDENTS BE PROSECUTED AS SEX OFFENDERS FOR SEXTING?

Across the United States, school districts are being confronted with information and cases of one or more students having inappropriate pictures on their Facebook or MySpace pages or texting them to others. In one recent case two high school students in Colorado faced felony charges for having and sharing a sexually explicit video. On a dare a girl did "things" with a guy in a car, which was recorded and then texted to friends and beyond. If found guilty, the charges could lead to many years in prison and the students being labeled as sex offenders. However, since the students are minors their punishment might be limited to two years in juvenile detention. Another possibility is that the charges will be reduced or dropped with a requirement that the students participate in some form of education program. What do you think? Should incidents of students' sexting require criminal prosecution, or should there be consideration of their being minors with less severe punishment? What is your position and what are your reasons?

YES

This most certainly has been the veiw of many in law enforcement. One of the first such cases developed in a Pennsylvania high school. School officials discovered that several boys were trading photos of female students in various states of undress. Several students' phones were confiscated and searched. Three boys and thirteen girls were identfed as either appearing in the photos or found to be in possesion of them. The then–district attorney threatened the students with child porn charges unless they agreed to participate in a "diversion program," which consisted of six months of probation, submitting to drug testing, and attending a five-week education program.

In the end, even though the charges were dropped, the photos are still part of the government record. On behalf of the girl in the photos, the ACLU has sued the district attorney, the school district, and the county for violating their constitutional rights to privacy and freedom of expression. The plantiff is seeking to have the photos destroyed and modest reimbursement for the cost of the course ($100) and lost wages ($71).

NO

Threatening children with child porn charges is too far a reach. The related laws were established to prosecute adult production and distribution of child pornography. Applying these laws literally to children is failing to understand the new situations brought about by the widespread use of social media. The sensible alternative is to see most cases of student sexting as something to be handled outside of the courts. School officials and parents should work out what should be done. Such acts are likely due to immaturity and youth not understanding the potential negative ramifications. Students are not likely to think ahead or understand that such photos could be spread widely on the Internet or end up in the hands of a sexual predator.

There also are questions of constitutional rights. What is probable cause? When can school officials legally take student cell phones? When can they search the content within cell phones and other social media? In the Pennsylvania case three other students who refused to participate in the mandated education program sued to bar prosecutors from charging them with a crime. They have won a permanent injunction.

WHAT IS YOUR PERSPECTIVE ON THIS ISSUE?

word regarding student rights, but rather provide an overview of some of the issues that have been decided by the courts. Table 10.6 is a summary of key cases; however, it is not intended to provide a complete understanding of the court decisions. You should read the following subsections to learn more about these and other student rights issues.

Students' Rights as Citizens

Through a series of court decisions, all children in the United States have been granted the opportunity for a public school education. Further, although school officials have a great deal of authority, children as students maintain many of the constitutional rights that adult citizens enjoy all the time. As obvious as each of these points might seem, each has been the subject of debate and court decisions.

STUDENTS' RIGHT TO AN EDUCATION. Children in the United States have a right to an education; this right is ensured in many state constitutions. It has been further defined by court decisions and is now interpreted to mean that each child has an equal opportunity to pursue education.

The right to an education, however, is not without certain prerequisites. Citizenship alone does not guarantee a free education. Statutes that establish public school systems also generally

TABLE 10.6

Selected U.S. Supreme Court Cases Related to Students' Rights and Responsibilities

CASE	ISSUE	DECISION
Plyler v. Doe (1982)	Rights to education of illegal aliens	Court struck down Texas law that denied a free public education to children of illegal aliens.
Goss v. Lopez (1975)	Suspension of high school students without a hearing	Court ruled that only in an emergency can a student be suspended without a hearing.
Wood v. Strickland (1975)	Question of whether school board members can be sued for depriving students of their constitutional rights (through suspension)	Students can seek damages from individual school board members but not from the school district.
Tinker v. Des Moines Independent Community School District (1969)	Free speech rights of students to wear black armbands to protest U.S. involvement in Vietnam	Court ruled against school district—recognizing to an extent constitutional rights of pupils.
Board of Education, Island Trees Union Free District No. 26 v. Pico (1982)	School board's decision to remove books from the school library	Court issued decision that under certain circumstances, children may challenge board's decision to remove books.
Ingraham v. Wright (1977)	Power of states to authorize corporal punishment without consent of the student's parent	Court ruled that states may constitutionally authorize corporal punishment.
Bethel School District No. 403 v. Fraser (1986)	Power of school officials to restrain student speech	School officials may discipline a student for making lewd and indecent speech in a school assembly attended by other students.
Hazelwood School District v. Kuhlmeier (1988)	School district control of student expression in school newspapers, theatrical productions, and other forums	School administrators have broad authority to control student expression in the official student newspaper, which is not a public forum but is seen as part of the curriculum.
Honig v. Doe (1988)	Violation of the Education for All Handicapped Children Act (P.L. 94-142); school indefinitely suspended and attempted to expel two emotionally disturbed students	P.L. 94-142 authorizes officials to suspend dangerous children for a maximum of ten days. Justice Brennan said, "Congress very much meant to strip schools of unilateral authority to exclude disturbed students."
New Jersey v. T.L.O. (1985)	Search and seizure	School officials must have a reasonable cause when engaged in searches.

establish how operating costs will be met. As was previously described in Chapter 9, real estate taxes are the usual source of funds, so proof of residence is necessary for school attendance without tuition. *Residence* does not mean that the student, parent, or guardian must pay real estate taxes; it means that the student must live in the school district in which he or she wants to attend school. Residence, then, is a prerequisite to the right of a free public education within a specific school district. The "Perspectives on Diversity" feature illustrates one teacher's dilemma in striving to involve an undocumented parent.

PERSPECTIVES on DIVERSITY

What If Your Student's Mother Is Undocumented?

Bill, a second year teacher of science, was in a reflective mood. He had found that his weekend bike rides were a good time to reflect on how his classes were going this year ("A lot better than last year") and to think about how much his students were learning ("Most of them seem to be getting it"). One of the challenges was the continual arrival of new students, especially those whose first language was not English.

For example, one of the girls, Neide, had recently arrived from Brazil. It was amazing how fast she was learning English in social situations. However, her academic vocabulary most definitely needed help. One of the strategies for improving vocabulary in the content areas is to have a parent go over a vocabulary list with the student in the evenings. Bill had checked about the possibility of his meeting with Neide and her mother to work out a vocabulary homework plan. But Neide avoided answering and seemed somehow reluctant. As he reflected further, a light bulb went on: "What if her mother is an illegal alien?" "Now, what do I do?"

WHAT IS YOUR PERSPECTIVE?

1. Should Bill pursue this problem?
2. If Neide's mother is an illegal alien, will Neide be removed from school? (Hint: For part of the answer take a look at Table 10.6.)
3. What would you do, or not do, in this situation?

ALIEN AND HOMELESS CHILDREN HAVE THE RIGHT TO GO TO SCHOOL. In 1982, the Supreme Court ruled in *Plyler v. Doe* that the children of illegal aliens had a right to a free public education. Although today some continue to question this right, the courts have been consistent in holding that the Equal Protection Clause applies to all. In addition, the Court considered the impact on society of the failure to educate all students.

> Education has a fundamental role in maintaining the fabric of society. We cannot ignore the significant social costs borne by our Nation when select groups are denied the means to absorb the values and skills upon which our social order rests. (*Plyler*, 1982)

A related problem is the more than 500,000 homeless children in the United States. Because access to public school usually requires a residence address and a parent or guardian, as well as transportation, homeless children in the past were squeezed out of the system. Congress addressed this growing problem in 1987 with passage of the Stewart B. McKinney Homeless Assistance Act, which requires that "each State educational agency shall assure that each child of a homeless individual and each homeless youth have access to a free, appropriate public education." The law was amended in 1990 to require each school district to provide services to the homeless that are comparable to the services offered other students in the schools. These services include allowing homeless children to finish the school year in the school they were in before they lost their housing, providing transportation to school, tutoring to help catch students up, and giving homeless children the opportunity to take part in school programs offered to other children.

STUDENTS' RIGHT TO SUE. The U.S. Supreme Court has affirmed that students may sue school board members who are guilty of intentionally depriving students of their constitutional rights. In *Wood v. Strickland* (1975), the Supreme Court held that school officials who discipline students unfairly cannot defend themselves against civil rights suits by claiming ignorance of pupils' basic constitutional rights. As a result of this decision, Judge Paul Williams, a federal judge in Arkansas, ordered that certain students who had been suspended could seek damages from individual school board members—though not from the school district as a corporate body. The judge also ruled that the school records of these pupils must be cleared of the suspension incident. From these decisions, it is apparent that the U.S. Supreme Court is taking into account the rights of students.

STUDENTS' RIGHT TO DUE PROCESS. Much of the recent involvement of the courts with student rights has concerned due process of law for pupils. Due process is guaranteed by the Fourteenth Amendment. The equal protection clause states, "nor shall any state . . . deny to any person within its jurisdiction the equal protection of the laws." Due process of law means following those rules and principles that have been established for enforcing and protecting the rights of the accused. As explained earlier, due process falls under two headings—procedural and substantive. *Procedural due process* has to do with whether the procedures used in disciplinary cases are fair; *substantive due process* is concerned with whether the school authorities have deprived a student of basic substantive constitutional rights such as personal liberty, property, or privacy (LaMorte, 2012, pp. 5–8).

The application of due process to issues in schools is a recent phenomenon. Historically, schools functioned under the doctrine of ***in loco parentis*** ("in the place of a parent"). This doctrine meant that schools could exercise almost complete control over students because they were acting as parent substitutes. Under the doctrine of *in loco parentis*, the courts have usually upheld the rules and regulations of local boards of education, particularly about pupil conduct. However, the courts have not supported rules that are unconstitutionally "vague" and/or "overboard." The cases discussed next illustrate the difficult balance between protecting students' right to due process and giving schools sufficient authority to pursue their mission.

PROCEDURAL DUE PROCESS IN CASES OF SUSPENSION AND EXPULSION. Zero tolerance policies have complicated the local schools' ability to balance students' right to due process and serving students' educational needs. Procedural due process is scrutinized especially in cases of suspension and expulsion. These cases most often result from disciplinary action taken by the school, which may or may not have violated a pupil's substantive constitutional rights. For example, in *Goss v. Lopez* (1975) the U.S. Supreme Court dealt with the suspension of high school students in Columbus, Ohio. In that case, the named plaintiffs claimed that they had been suspended from public high school for up to ten days without a hearing. The action alleged deprivation of constitutional rights. Two students who were suspended for a semester brought suit charging that their due process rights were denied—because they were not present at the board meeting when the suspensions were handed out.

In ruling that students cannot be suspended without some kind of hearing, the Court said:

> The prospect of imposing elaborate hearing requirements in every suspension case is viewed with great concern, and many school authorities may well prefer the untrammeled power to act unilaterally, unhampered by rules about notice and hearing. But it would be a strange disciplinary system in an educational institution if no communication was sought by the disciplinarian with the student in an effort to inform him of his defalcation and to let him tell his side of the story in order to make sure that an injustice is not done. Fairness can rarely be obtained by secret, one-sided determination of the facts decisive of rights. . . . Secrecy is not congenial to truth-seeking and self-righteousness gives too slender an assurance of rightness. No better instrument has been devised for arriving at truth than to give a person in jeopardy of serious loss notice of the case against him and opportunity to meet it. (*Goss*, 1975)

Procedural due process cases usually involve alleged violations of the Fourteenth Amendment, which provides for the protection of specified privileges of citizens, including notice to the student, impartiality of the hearing process, and the right of representation. These cases might also involve alleged violations of state constitutions or statutory law that call for specific procedures. For example, many states have procedures for expulsion or suspension. Expulsion usually involves notifying parents or guardians in a specific way, perhaps by registered mail, and giving students the opportunity for a hearing before the board of education or a designated hearing officer. Suspension procedures are usually detailed as well, designating who has the authority to suspend and the length of time for suspension. Teachers and administrators should know due process regulations, including the specific regulations of the state where they are employed.

SUBSTANTIVE DUE PROCESS AND STUDENTS' RIGHTS TO FREE SPEECH. Substantive due process frequently addresses questions of students' constitutional rights to free speech versus the schools' authority to maintain order in support of education. The *Tinker* case (*Tinker v. Des Moines Independent Community School District,* 1969) was significant. It involved a school board's attempt to keep students from wearing black armbands in a protest against U.S. military activities in Vietnam. In 1969, the U.S. Supreme Court ruled against the Des Moines school board. The majority opinion of the Court was that

> [T]he wearing of armbands in the circumstances of this case was entirely divorced from actually or potentially disruptive conduct by those participating in it. It was closely akin to "pure speech" which, we have repeatedly held, is entitled to comprehensive protection, under the First Amendment. . . . First Amendment rights, applied in the light of the special characteristics of the school environment, are available to teachers and students. It can hardly be argued that either students or teachers shed their constitutional rights to freedom of speech or expression at the schoolhouse gate. (*Tinker*, 1969)

in loco parentis Meaning "in the place of a parent," this term describes the implied power and responsibilities of schools.

In the *Tinker* opinion, the Court clearly designated that the decision "does not concern aggressive, disruptive action or even group demonstrations." The decision did make it clear that whatever their age, students have constitutional rights, and the decision has had a widespread effect on the operation of schools in the United States. Schools have had to pay attention to U.S. law. Educators as well as lawyers have been guided by the principles set forth in the decision regarding the constitutional relationship between public school students and school officials.

A more recent U.S. Supreme Court decision appears to have at least narrowed the breadth of application of the *Tinker* ruling. The case involved Matthew Fraser, a high school senior in a school outside Tacoma, Washington. In the spring of 1983, Fraser was suspended from school for two days after he gave a short speech at a school assembly nominating a friend for a position in student government. School officials argued that Fraser's speech contained sexual innuendos that provoked other students to engage in disruptive behaviors unfavorable to the school setting. The U.S. District Court for the Western District of Washington held that Fraser's punishment violated his rights to free speech under the First Amendment and awarded him damages. The U.S. Court of Appeals for the Ninth Circuit affirmed the decision, holding that Fraser's speech was not disruptive under the standards of *Tinker*. However, the Supreme Court reversed the decision. In the majority opinion in *Bethel School District No. 403 v. Fraser* (1986), Chief Justice Warren Burger wrote, "The determination of what manner of speech in the classroom or in school assembly is inappropriate properly rests with the school board."

Students' Rights and Responsibilities in School

The right, or privilege, of children to attend school also depends on their compliance with the rules and regulations of the school. To ensure the day-to-day orderly operation of schools, boards of education have the right to establish reasonable rules and regulations controlling pupils and their conduct. Boards' actions have been challenged in numerous instances, however. Challenges have concerned questions such as dress codes and grooming, corporal punishment, the rights of married students, abuse and neglect, student publications' freedom of expression, disabilities, and searches.

DRESS CODES AND GROOMING. Lower court cases dealing with grooming have been decided in some instances in favor of the board of education—in support of their rules and regulations—and in other instances in favor of the student. A general principle seems to be that if the dress and grooming do not incite or cause disruptive behavior or pose a health or safety problem, the court ruling is likely to support the student. Dress codes, once very much in vogue, are less evident today. Although the U.S. Supreme Court has yet to consider a so-called "long hair" case, federal courts in every circuit have issued rulings in such cases; half of them found regulations on hair length unconstitutional, and half upheld them. In all, over a two-decade period, federal and state courts decided more than 300 cases on this subject. If there is a trend, it is that students have won most of the cases that dealt with hairstyle. The courts have usually refused to uphold dress and hair length regulations for athletic teams or extracurricular groups unless the school proves that the hair or dress interfered with a student's ability to play the sport or perform the extracurricular activity (*Long v. Zopp*, 1973).

In the late 1970s and continuing through the 1980s, courts entertained fewer challenges to grooming regulations. The later decisions, however, continued to be consistent with earlier court rulings. Courts have supported school officials who attempted to regulate student appearance if the regulation could be based on concerns about disruption, health, or safety. Presumably, controversy over the length of students' hair or grooming in general is no longer critical because officials and students have a more common ground of agreement about what is acceptable. However, as the new century begins, new questions could be raised in relation to school efforts to control the clothing and other grooming symbols of gangs.

CORPORAL PUNISHMENT. In 1977 the U.S. Supreme Court ruled on and finally resolved many of the issues related to corporal punishment (*Ingraham v. Wright*, 1977). The opinion established that states may *constitutionally* authorize corporal punishment without prior hearing or notice and without consent by the student's parents, or may as a matter of policy elect to prohibit or limit the use of corporal punishment. It also held that corporal punishment is not in violation of the Eighth Amendment (which prohibits "cruel and unusual punishments").

GO TO ⋯›
As is described in Chapters 4 and 5, a teacher's philosophy of education will influence what is seen as important student rights.

In response to the greater sensitivity to student rights, many school districts have adopted administrative rules and regulations to restrict the occasions, nature, and manner of administering corporal punishment. Some school districts specify that corporal punishment can be administered only under the direction of the principal and in the presence of another adult.

SEX DISCRIMINATION. Until relatively recently, educational institutions could discriminate against females—whether they were students, staff, or faculty. In 1972 the Ninety-Second Congress enacted Title IX of the Education Amendments Act to remove sex discrimination against students and employees in federally assisted programs. The key provision in Title IX states, "No person in the United States shall, on the basis of sex, be excluded from participation in, be denied the benefits of, or be subjected to discrimination under any education program or activity receiving federal financial assistance." Title IX is enforced by the Department of Education's Office of Civil Rights. An individual or organization can allege that any policy or practice is discriminatory by writing a letter of complaint to the secretary of education. An administrative hearing is the next step in the process. Further steps include suing for monetary damages under Title IX, which the U.S. Supreme Court affirmed in *Franklin v. Gwinnett County Schools* (1992).

MARRIAGE AND PREGNANCY. In the past, it was not unusual for school officials to expel students who married. Some educators reasoned that marriage brought on additional responsibilities, such as the establishment of a household, and therefore that married students could not perform well in school. They also believed that exclusion would help deter other teenagers from marrying. Courts tended to uphold school officials in these positions. Both courts and school officials acted consistently in not rigidly enforcing compulsory attendance statutes for underage students who married.

School officials today cannot prohibit a student from attending school merely because he or she is married. This position is based on the above-mentioned Title IX and on the notion that every child has a right to attend school. Public policy today encourages students to acquire as much education as they can. Not only are married students encouraged to remain in school, but they are also entitled to the same rights and privileges as unmarried students. Thus, they have the right to take any course the school offers and to participate in extracurricular activities open to other students. That is, participation in extracurricular activities cannot be denied a student solely on the basis of marital status. However, a student's attendance and participation rights can be removed if his or her behavior is deleterious to other students.

Today's schools enroll pregnant students without hesitation. Title IX prohibits their exclusion from school or from participation in extracurricular activities. Many school systems have reorganized their school programs so that courses can be offered during after-school hours or in the evenings to accommodate married and pregnant students. This arrangement makes it easier for students to work during the day and complete their education at a time that is convenient for them. Such programs often include courses and topics aimed at the specific audience, as well as counseling programs to assist students with their adjustment to marriage and family life.

CHILD ABUSE AND NEGLECT. Government bodies in the United States have the right to exercise police power, which means that the government is entrusted with the responsibility of looking after the health, safety, and welfare of all of its citizens. In effect, each state acts as a guardian over all of its people, exercising that role specifically over individuals who are not able to look after themselves. This guardianship extends to care for children who have been either abused or neglected by their parents. All fifty states have statutes dealing with this issue. These statutes generally protect children under the age of eighteen, but the scope of protection and definitions of abuse and neglect vary considerably among the states. In 1974, Congress passed the Child Abuse Prevention and Treatment Act, which provides financial assistance to states that have developed and implemented programs for identifying, preventing, and treating instances of child abuse and neglect.

The severity of this problem has been highlighted by the requirement of mandatory reporting of suspected abuse and neglect to social service agencies. Formerly, this reporting was limited mainly to physicians, but today educators are also required to report instances of suspected abuse and neglect. Some teachers are reluctant to do so because they fear a breakdown in student–teacher–parent relationships and the possibility of lawsuits alleging invasion of privacy, assault, or slander. Their fear should be diminished, however, by statutes that grant them immunity for acting in good faith.

STUDENT PUBLICATIONS. A significant decision relative to "underground" student newspapers was made in Illinois in 1970 (*Scoville v. Board of Education*, 1970). Students were expelled for distributing a newspaper named *Grass High,* which the students produced at home and which criticized school officials and used vulgar language. The students were expelled under an Illinois statute that empowered boards of education to expel pupils guilty of gross disobedience or misconduct. A federal court in Illinois supported the board of education, but on appeal the Court of Appeals for the Seventh Circuit reversed the decision. The school board was not able to validate student disruption and interference as required by *Tinker.* The expelled students were entitled to collect damages. An implication is that the rights of students regarding newspapers they print at home are stronger than their rights of free expression in official school publications.

Early in 1988, in a landmark decision (*Hazelwood School District v. Kuhlmeier*), the U.S. Supreme Court ruled that administrators have broad authority to control student expression in official school newspapers, theatrical productions, and other forums that are part of the curriculum. In reaching that decision, the Court determined that the *Spectrum,* the school newspaper of the Hazelwood District, was not a public forum. A school policy of the Hazelwood District required that the principal review each proposed issue of the *Spectrum.* The principal objected to two articles scheduled to appear in one issue. One of the articles was about girls at the school who had become pregnant; the other discussed the effects of divorce on students. Neither article used real names. The principal deleted two pages of the *Spectrum* rather than delete only the offending articles or require that they be modified. He stated that there was no time to make any changes in the articles and that the newspaper had to be printed immediately or not at all.

Three student journalists sued, contending that their freedom of speech had been violated. The Supreme Court upheld the principal's action. Justice Byron White decided that the *Spectrum* was not a public forum, but rather a supervised learning experience for journalism students. In effect, the censorship of a student press was upheld by the Supreme Court. In Justice White's words:

> [S]chools must be able to set high standards for the student speech that is disseminated under [their] auspices—standards that may be higher than those demanded by some newspaper publishers and theatrical producers in the "real" world—and may refuse to disseminate student speech that does not meet those standards.
>
> Accordingly, we hold that the standard articulated in Tinker for determining when a school may punish student expression need not also be the standard for determining when a school may refuse to lend its name and resources to the dissemination of student expression. (*Hazelwood*, 1988)

The issue of institutional control over publications has not yet been fully resolved. In response to questions about student publications and their distribution, school boards have endeavored to write rules and regulations that will withstand judicial scrutiny. A prompt review and reasonably fast appeal procedures are vital. Students should also be advised of distribution rules and abide by them.

RIGHTS OF STUDENTS WITH DISABILITIES. Before the early 1970s, the access to education of students with disabilities was left to the discretion of different levels of government. In the early 1970s, court decisions established the position that students with disabilities were entitled to an "appropriate" education and to procedural protections against arbitrary treatment. As was described earlier, Congress subsequently specified a broad set of substantive and procedural rights via Section 504 of the Rehabilitation Act and Public Law 94-142, the Education for All Handicapped Children Act (EAHCA). Since that time there has been a continuing series of legislative and legal refinements and extensions of the intents to see that students with special needs have appropriate educational opportunities. The problem has been to define what is meant by "appropriate." This examination and clarification process continues to unfold.

One early test case regarding student rights dealt with a violation of P.L. 94-142. That law requires public school officials to keep disruptive or violent students with disabilities in their current classrooms pending hearings on their behavior. In the decision made in *Honig v. Doe* (1988), the U.S. Supreme Court upheld lower court rulings that San Francisco school district officials violated the act in 1980 when they indefinitely suspended and then attempted to expel two students who were, as officials claimed, emotionally disturbed and dangerous.

The act authorizes officials to suspend dangerous children with disabilities for a maximum of ten days. Longer suspensions or expulsions are permissible only if the child's parents consent

Where reasonable suspicion exists, school authorities do not need a warrant to search a student's locker or a student's vehicle on campus.

to the action taken or if the officials can convince a federal district judge that the child poses a danger to himself or herself or to others. The rules under which school officials must operate are also more limiting if the misbehavior is a manifestation of the student's disability.

It is clear that Congress meant to restrain the authority that schools had traditionally used to exclude students with disabilities, particularly students who are emotionally disturbed, from school. But P.L. 94-142 did not leave school administrators powerless to deal with dangerous students.

STUDENT AND LOCKER SEARCHES. Most courts have refused to subject public school searches to strict Fourth Amendment standards. In general, the Fourth Amendment protects individuals from search without a warrant (court order). Many lower courts, however, have decided in favor of a more lenient interpretation of the Fourth Amendment in school searches. The rationale is that school authorities are obligated to maintain discipline and a sound educational environment and that that responsibility, along with their *in loco parentis* powers, gives them the right to conduct searches and seize contraband on reasonable suspicion without a warrant. First, however, school officials may only search for evidence that a student has violated a school rule or a law. Also, there must be a valid rule or law in place.

School authorities do not need a warrant to search a student's locker or a student vehicle on campus. For searches of a student's person, however, courts apply a higher standard. Where reasonable suspicion exists, a school official's actions will likely be upheld. Reasonable suspicion exists when one has information that a student is in possession of something harmful or dangerous or when there is evidence of illegal activities such as drug dealing (money, a list of customers, or rolling papers). The second consideration is the way in which the search of a student's person is conducted. School officials are advised to have students remove contents from their clothing rather than having a teacher or administrator do it.

A further caution is not to force students to remove all their clothing or undress to their underwear. In a nearly unanimous eight-to-one decision in 2009, the Supreme Court put school districts on clear notice that strip searches are "categorically distinct" from other efforts to combat illegal drugs. In *Safford Unified School District #1 v. Redding*, the court concluded that an intrusive search of a thirteen-year-old girl for suspicion of hiding ibuprofen was an overreaction. In writing for the majority, Justice Souter said that what was missing "was any indication of danger to the students from the power of the drugs or the quantity, and any reason to suppose that Savana was carrying pills in her underwear." Concern about strip searches being degrading has led a number of states and school districts to ban strip searches.

PEER SEXUAL HARASSMENT. Title IX prohibits sex discrimination, and this includes students' harassing other students. Teasing, snapping bra straps, requesting sexual favors, making lewd comments about one's appearance or body parts, telling sexual jokes, engaging in physical abuse, and touching inappropriately are examples of peer sexual harassment. It is important for teachers to make it clear that sexual harassment will not be tolerated. School districts are supposed to have in place a grievance procedure for sex discrimination complaints. Students and/or their parents can also file a complaint with the Office of Civil Rights. All allegations must be investigated promptly, and schools must take immediate action in cases in which harassment behaviors have been confirmed. Keep in mind that sexual harassment is not limited to high school students; middle school and in some cases elementary schoolchildren are also sexually harassed. To summarize the topics covered in this section, Figure 10.9 lists brief statements related to the rights and responsibilities of students.

FIGURE 10.9	Summary Statements on Students' Rights and Responsibilities

- State constitutions provide that a child has the right to an education; to date, students have been unsuccessful in suing school board members on the ground that they have not learned anything.
- The due process clause provides that a child is entitled to notice of charges and the opportunity for a hearing prior to being suspended from school for misbehavior.
- Students enjoy freedom of speech at school unless that speech is indecent or leads to disruption; courts are in agreement that school officials can regulate the content of student newspapers. Underground newspapers are not subject to this oversight.
- Students may be awarded damages from school board members for a violation of their constitutional rights if they can establish that they were injured by the deprivation and that the school official deliberately violated those rights.
- The use of corporal punishment is not prohibited by the U.S. Constitution, but excessive punishment may be barred by the Fourteenth Amendment.

- Students may be restricted in their dress when there are problems of disruption, health, or safety.
- Assignments of students to activities or classes in general on the basis of sex is not consistent with Title IX. These assignments may be made in such areas as sex education classes or when sports are available for both sexes.
- Restricting a student's activities on the basis of marriage or pregnancy is inconsistent with the equal protection clause and Title IX.
- Teachers are required to report to proper authorities suspected instances of child abuse and neglect.
- Parents have the right to examine their children's educational records. Students age eighteen or older have the right to examine their records.
- School officials may search students, lockers, and student property without a search warrant, but they must have reasonable grounds for believing that a student is in possession of evidence of a violation of a law or school rule.

EMERGING CHALLENGES

Teachers, students, and administrators must continually be aware of their responsibilities and the legal safeguards that protect students as well as educators. There are likely to be new cases related to drug testing, searches, weapons, and assaults. There most certainly will be new policies, administrative directives, and court cases related to appropriate and inappropriate social networking. Be sure that you, today as a teacher education candidate and in the future as a teacher, are fully cognizant of your responsibilities under the law. As the saying goes, ignorance of the law is no excuse.

JOURNAL FOR REFLECTION 10.4

Now, it should be clear to you that students have rights and that teachers need to be aware of them. Teachers should always be sure that another teacher or administrator is present when disciplinary action is taken. When taking any such action, teachers must be sure that the principal or other administrators are informed. As a way of making these rights and responsibilities real for you, think back across your years as a student. Compare some of the things that you experienced or witnessed with what you have just read about the legal rights and responsibilities of students.

SUMMARY

LEGAL ASPECTS OF EDUCATION

- The U.S. Constitution is the starting point for viewing schools from the legal perspective.
- Education is not mentioned directly in the U.S. Constitution.
- The Tenth Amendment has been interpreted as assigning responsibility to each state for education of its citizens.
- How education is addressed in each state's constitution is of paramount importance.

- Interpretations of law and the resolution of disputes, whether they are about separation of church and state, desegregation, or teachers' rights, ultimately are decided by the U.S. and state supreme courts.
- Public funds can be used to support some kinds of education services offered by church schools.

TEACHERS' RIGHTS AND RESPONSIBILITIES

- Teachers' rights as citizens and employees, including procedural and substantive due process, are protected.
- However, teachers do not have absolute academic freedom.
- FERPA protects the privacy of student records.
- Teachers must be vigilant in guarding against placing students in risky situations.
- Teachers can be sued for negligence and malpractice.

USES OF SOCIAL MEDIA AND THE LAW

- Teacher and student use of school district e-mail systems can be monitored.
- Teachers and teacher education candidates can be dismissed based on what is discovered on their social networking sites.

- Teachers must be vigilant in monitoring the use of technology to cheat.

STUDENTS' RIGHTS AND RESPONSIBILITIES

- Students, too, have rights as citizens, including the right to an education.
- They have due process rights; protection from discrimination; and, within limits, freedom of expression.
- However, schools have the authority to determine when student conduct is disruptive.

EMERGING CHALLENGES

- Teachers must always be aware of their and their students' legal rights and responsibilities.

DISCUSSION STARTERS

1. How do you view the use of public funds to support certain activities in church schools? Do you see a trend toward "excessive entanglement"? Where do you see the line needing to be drawn so as not to conflict with the establishment clause?

2. In *Ingraham v. Wright* (1977), the U.S. Supreme Court ruled that states may authorize the use of corporal punishment as school policy. The U.S. military has not allowed corporal punishment for more than one hundred years. Why should it

be disallowed in the military but be permissible in schools? Is it ever appropriate in schools?

3. As a teacher, in your classroom, where will you draw the line between what are appropriate and inappropriate uses of social media?

4. What are your thoughts about balancing student rights against school officials' need to maintain an environment conducive to learning? Should school officials have more authority? Should students have greater freedom?

SCHOOL-BASED OBSERVATIONS

1. Beginning teachers do not have the same rights as tenured teachers, but they do have rights. With a partner, compare and contrast the rights of beginning teachers as stated in the employment contracts of two school districts. Some of the items to check are length of the probationary period, the basis for a tenure decision, how the tenure decision-making process works, and the due process rights of probationary teachers.

2. Interview an experienced teacher about students' rights. Ask him or her to provide examples of situations in which it was important for the teacher to be aware of student rights. What were the critical points to be considered? What were the related responsibilities of the teacher? What advice would this teacher have for today's beginning teachers?

PORTFOLIO DEVELOPMENT

1. Pick a school district where you think you would like to work as a teacher. Obtain a copy of the teacher employment contract from the district human resources/personnel office and study it. What does the contract say about your

rights as a district employee and as a teacher? What does it say about your responsibilities? There may be references to other legal documents such as an employee handbook and board policies; if so, become familiar with those documents too. Together, these documents set the parameters for what you can, should, and should not do as a teacher. Place these documents and your notes in a folio file folder and save them for later use.

2. From time to time, newspapers and weekly news magazines carry reports about disagreements between students and school officials. Collect several of these reports, paying

special attention to the legal interpretations drawn by each side, and consider the implications for you. In all instances, keep in mind that both teachers and students have legal responsibilities as well as rights. These clippings and notes may be a useful resource for you someday, when as a teacher you are confronted with a question about student and teacher rights.

WEB SOLUTIONS

A continuing dilemma for teachers is deciding what they and their students should place on their Facebook and MySpace pages. It should be clear that neither teachers nor students have absolute First Amendment rights to say and display whatever they like. Even the media are doing "investigative" reports of what teachers have on their social media pages. Search the following websites for examples of teachers and students being disciplined for content on their personal social media pages. Based on your review, develop three to five guidelines that you see as being important for you and your students to follow in order to not be exposed in the media, disciplined at school, or lose your teaching position.

A good place to start your analysis would be to read the article "Social Networking Nightmares" by Mike Simpson, which can be found within the NEA website **www.nea.org**

Other websites to check out for related information include:

www.dirksencongressionalcenter.org The Dirksen Congressional Center offers a newsletter, curriculum resources, and links for educators to aid in improved understanding of Congress.

www.lawschool.cornell.edu The Cornell Law School's Legal Information Institute (LII) website provides access to court decisions, news related to court cases, directories, and current awareness items.

www.cnn.com/law CNN operates a number of useful websites including the Law Center, which reports on state, national, and international court proceedings.

MyEducationLab™ Go to the topic **Ethical and Legal Issues** in the MyEducationLab (**www.myeducationlab.com**) for *Foundations of American Education: Becoming Effective Teachers in Challenging Times, 16e,* where you can:

- Find learning outcomes for **Ethical and Legal Issues**, along with the national standards that connect to these outcomes.
- Complete Assignments and Activities that can help you more deeply understand the chapter content.
- Apply and practice your understanding of the core teaching skills identified in the chapter with the Building Teaching Skills and Dispositions learning units.
- Access video clips of CCSSO National Teachers of the Year award winners responding to the question, "Why Do I Teach?" in the Teacher Talk section.
- Create, update, and share quality lesson plans with the Lesson Plan Builder.

- Access state licensure test requirements, overviews of what tests cover, and sample test items in the Certification and Licensure section.
- Access current state and national standards in the Licensure and Standards section.
- Learn how to create a high-quality teaching portfolio in the Preparing a Portfolio section.
- Access tips, advice, and other information on resume writing and interviewing, your first year of teaching, and law and public policies in the Beginning Your Career section.
- Check your comprehension of the content covered in the chapter with the Study Plan. Here you will be able to take a chapter pretest, receive feedback on your answers, and then access personalized Review, Practice, and Enrichment exercises to enhance your understanding of chapter content. After you complete the exercises, take a posttest to confirm your comprehension.

Standards, Assessment, and Accountability

LEARNING OUTCOMES

After reading and studying this chapter, you should be able to:

1. Analyze the importance of standards and list different types of standards and the expected ways they are to improve our educational system. (InTASC 7: Planning for Instruction; InTASC 9: Professional Learning and Ethical Practice)

2. Understand and apply formal and informal assessments to determine what students know and are able to do. (InTASC 6: Assessment)

3. Discuss ways that teachers, schools, school districts, and states are being held accountable for student achievement. (InTASC 6: Assessment)

EDUCATION in the NEWS

COLORADO TEACHER-EVALUATION BILL SIGNED INTO LAW

POSTED: 02/16/2012 01:00:00 AM MST

By YESENIA ROBLES

The Denver Post denverpost.com

Rules that change how teachers and principals will be evaluated—and how they will earn or lose tenure—were signed into law this morning by Gov. John Hickenlooper.

The rules were passed on Tuesday as House Bill1001, with ninety-nine of one hundred possible votes in the general assembly.

"The work the council did initially plus the input from the state board was truly collaborative," said Kerri Dallman, a member of the council who drafted the rules. "That's one of the reasons I think it sailed through without changes."

The signing this morning was the culmination of the work behind the controversial Senate Bill 191, passed in 2010. That bill created a council that after more than a year of meetings developed evaluation rubrics and definitions of effective teachers and educators.

The definition of an effective teacher includes six quality standards, including the need to demonstrate content knowledge, leadership, and taking responsibility for student growth.

Those rules were approved by the state board of education before they were presented to the legislature.

A few pieces of the rules still are not finalized. One that is now making its way through the state board of education is the development of an appeals process for teachers who receive two consecutive ineffective ratings, which triggers a loss of nonprobationary status, known as tenure.

The law also now requires 50 percent of teacher evaluations to be based on student test scores, but 70 percent of licensed teachers do not have standardized assessments for their grade level or the content they teach.

Colorado is working on developing guides and assessments for those untested subjects, so that districts have tests to pick from that can provide reliable data.

Dallman, who is also the president of the Jefferson County Education Association, said now it's up to school districts to work with their communities to find ways to implement the rules.

"Our district is looking at a cost of $4.2 million or $4.8 million for the first year. In a district where we just cut $37.5 million last year, that's really going to be a struggle," Dallman said. "To ensure educators have the proper training and administrators have enough time, I don't know that we will come up with that $4.8 million."

The Colorado Department of Education is currently piloting the model evaluation system in select districts.

Jefferson County School District is one of the pilot districts, but Dallman said the district decided to only pilot the half of the system evaluating principals, and is not currently testing teacher evaluations.

Every school district will be expected to either adopt the state system or create their own similar system by the 2014–2015 school year, although the evaluations will not have consequences for teachers until about 2016. *Yesenia Robles: 303-954-1372 or* yrobles@denverpost.com

QUESTIONS FOR REFLECTION

1. In what ways do you see this new Colorado statute increasing teacher and principal accountability?

2. Do you think the three identified areas for teacher evaluation are appropriate?

3. Teachers will no longer have tenure—they will have instead "nonprobationary" status. What do you think this change of words means?

Source: "Colorado teacher-evaluation bill signed into law" by Yesenia Robles, *The Denver Post*, February 16, 2012. Reprinted by permission.

MyEducationLab™

Visit the MyEducationLab for *Foundations of American Education* to enhance your understanding of chapter concepts with a personalized *Study Plan.* You'll also have the opportunity to hone your teaching skills through video- and case-based *Assignments and Activities* and *Building Teaching Skills* and *Dispositions* lessons.

 One principal discusses the impact of standards on education in her district and in the country in this **video.**

standards A statement of a desired outcome, which in education is usually a description of student learning.

high-stakes tests Tests that have major consequences or implications.

standards-based education The use of explicit outcomes of what students should know and be able to do, which are outlined in standards, to develop instruction and assessments.

The "Education in the News" story brings home the three major topics to be addressed in this chapter. Each of these topics—standards, assessments, and accountability—represents an area of significant challenges for current and future teachers. As never before, teachers are being held accountable for making a difference in student learning. The only way to accomplish this is to have clear understanding about what students are to learn, responsible ways for measuring learning, and a fair process for evaluating teachers. Keep the news article in mind as you learn more about each of these major areas of challenge in the following pages.

EDUCATION STANDARDS

Standards are a popular topic in both the business and education worlds. Standards are a description of the expected output from some sort of endeavor. In manufacturing there will be standards related to the quality of the product. In education, standards are descriptions of desired student learning. State and federal policy makers expect students to meet standards. In addition, achievement of the standards is increasingly linked to a student being promoted or receiving a diploma. As you read in the "Education in the News" story, student results on standardized tests are now being used in determining whether teachers and principals retain their jobs. The challenge for educators now and in the future is to figure out how they will ensure that their students meet those standards.

Standards have different meanings to different users. Some people view them as synonymous with rigor and the setting of high expectations for schools, teachers, and students. Others focus on learner outcomes or what students or teachers should know when they finish a grade or college. Still others equate standards with **high-stakes tests** such as annual state tests, or teacher licensure tests, which must be passed to receive a license to teach. As an instructional approach, **standards-based education** places student learning at the center.

Standards as a concept set specifications. These could be about school construction, school accreditation, licensure of doctors and lawyers, or the criteria for performance of a new aircraft. In education today, standards are specifications for student learning. They can range in scope from being extremely global and ambitious to very narrow and specific. They can be a mix of expectations too. For example, accreditation standards for your teacher education program expect that you know the standards for the subject/grade you will teach. The program accreditation standards also set expectations related to your development of the necessary knowledge, skills, and professional dispositions to be an effective teacher. At their simplest, standards are statements that describe what we should know and be able to do.

Conceptions of Standards for Student Learning

Diverse conceptions of standards stem from differing expectations. Business leaders tend to want high school graduates who are ready for work. They should be able to read, write, and compute as well as have the dispositions that will make them desirable workers. They are willing to provide specific job training, but they do not want to teach what they consider the basic skills that all students should have before entering the world of work.

Policy makers think about the larger, long-term needs of society. They are concerned about graduates having the knowledge and skills that will help the United States maintain its competitive edge in the global economy. Therefore, they promote rigorous academic standards that will ensure that students perform at high levels on international comparisons. They want students to know more science, history, mathematics, literature, and geography than students in other countries.

Parents choose standards based on their own personal goals and family histories. Some parents want their children to go to prestigious colleges. Others want their children to obtain a job immediately after high school. Still others want their offspring to prepare for a professional career such as a medical doctor, lawyer, or engineer. These expectations influence the type of learning outcomes that parents support.

Developing and adapting a clearly articulated, coordinated set of standards is not easy. Not all members of a community agree on what standards are appropriate. Despite these difficulties, the development of clear standards enables different constituencies within the school community to clarify their needs and aspirations. The process of selecting and adapting standards also provides a forum, not only for conducting dialogues and negotiating what schools should do, but also for what schools, teachers, and students should be held accountable. At this time there is a developing national consensus around what are called Common Core State Standards.

In order to graduate in most states students must pass high-stakes tests that are based in standards.

 To hear how one teacher integrates standards into the curriculum, click on the video *Standards and Accountability: Using Standards to Guide Instruction.*

COMMON CORE STATE STANDARDS (CCSS). Beginning in the 1980s many professional associations, curriculum groups, and state-wide education committees began developing standards related to student learning for the major subject areas. The first set of standards to receive widespread attention was published by the National Council for the Teaching of Mathematics (NCTM) in 1989. Mathematicians, teachers, and mathematics educators joined together to develop this statement of student learning outcomes *and* related standards about instructional approaches that were deemed effective. Over the next ten to twenty years, many sets of standards were published. So many, in fact, that it became impossible for all of them to be addressed.

In 2009 the National Governors Association and the Council of Chief State School Officers (CCSSO) announced an initiative to develop one set of standards around which there would be widespread consensus. The first two curriculum areas to be addressed were English language arts and mathematics. Development of science standards has been underway but has taken more time. These are now known as the **Common Core State Standards**. As of 2012, all but four states (Alaska, Nebraska, Texas, and Virginia) had signed on to adopt these standards and implement them by 2014.

The intent has been to develop standards that focus on what is most essential. Other learning outcomes can be added, but the consensus is that all students should learn what is identified in the CCSS. Also, the standards are **learning-centered**, not **teaching-centered**. Rather than describing what teachers should do and the design of instruction, which would be teaching-centered, the standards focus explicitly on the expectations for student learning.

The development of each set of CCSS has involved a broad range of experts including teachers, scholars, and some policy makers. Careful consideration has been given to what students should learn in each year of schooling and what high school graduates should know in order to be successful in postsecondary education and/or in obtaining and keeping a job. The foundational design considerations for the English language arts CCSS are presented in Table 11.1. As you review these considerations, think about what instruction will need to be like in your classroom. Regardless of the grade level and subject you will be teaching, there is an expectation

Common Core State Standards A set of standards that describe knowledge and skills that students need for success in college and careers.

learning-centered Focusing directly on student learning, rather than on what teachers do.

teaching-centered Standards that focus on what teachers do and the design of instruction.

TABLE 11.1

Key Considerations in the Design Statement for the English Language Arts Common Core State Standards

Excerpts from page 4 of *Common Core State Standards for English Language Arts & Literacy in History/Social Studies, Science, and Technical Subjects.* Common Core State Standard Initiative: Preparing America's Students for College & Career.

KEY CONSIDERATIONS IN THE ELA CCSS	EXPLANATION OF KEY CONSIDERATIONS
Grade-Specific	End-of-year learning expectations are defined and there is a cumulative progression.
Grade Levels and Bands	K–8 expectations are defined by grade while two-year bands are used for 9–12.
Focus on Results	What teachers are to do and the design of instruction are not prescribed.
Integrated Model	The processes of communicating (reading, writing, speaking, and listening) are closely connected.
Research and Media Skills Are Blended	Use of these skills is embedded throughout.
Shared Responsibility	Development of literacy skills is interdisciplinary and needs to be addressed across subjects.

Source: Common Core State Standards: © Copyright 2010. National Governors Association Center for Best Practices and Council of Chief State School Officers. All Rights Reserved.

of a "shared responsibility for students' literacy development." In other words, all teachers are expected to help their students learn to read and communicate.

Now take a look at Table 11.2, which highlights the "standards of mathematical practice" that should be developed in all students. These standards are derived from two sources: (1) the earlier NCTM process standards for problem solving, reasoning and proof communication, representation, and connections; and (2) the strands of mathematical proficiency—adaptive reasoning, strategic competence, conceptual understanding, procedural fluency, and productive dispositions—that are specified in the National Research Council's report, *Adding It Up.* Notice that in both the ELA considerations and the Math CCSS practices, the traditional content of standards, such as literature and calculations, are not directly mentioned. Instead, the CCSS are organized around the major intellectual processes and strategies that are foundational to each subject.

JOURNAL FOR REFLECTION 11.1

As you consider the design specifications (Table 11.1) for the ELA CCS Standards and the Standards for Mathematical Practice (Table 11.2) what thoughts do you have about how to teach to these standards? Jot down some notes about questions you have and key topics where you know you need to learn more about how to be a learning-centered teacher.

THE CCSS HAVE NOT BEEN WITHOUT DEBATE. One aim in their development was that the CCSS would be available to all states, but their adoption would be voluntary. However, in the fall of 2011 President Obama tied receiving a waiver from the mandates of the 2002 NCLB to states implementing "college and career-ready standards." States had the option to develop their own standards, but the step taken by most has been to adopt the CCSS. This direction has angered conservatives who see the president's move as an overreach by the federal government and leading to less state control of education.

As this debate began to take shape, the governor of South Carolina, Nikki Haley, pressed lawmakers to abandon the state's commitment to adopt the CCSS. Some academics have argued that there is not a research base to support the standards. Where some see a conspiracy, others see the collaborative effort of the National Governors Association and the Council of Chief State

TABLE 11.2

Standards for Mathematical Practice

Excerpts from *Mathematics introduction: How to read the grade level standards.* Retrieved on 19 June 2012 from http://www.corestandards.org

MATHEMATICALLY PROFICIENT STUDENTS	HOW THEY DO IT
Make sense of problems and persevere in solving them	Start by explaining to themselves the meaning of a problem and looking for entry points to its solution. They analyze givens, ... consider analogous problems, ... monitor and evaluate their progress... (and) "change their viewing window."
Reason abstractly and quantitatively	Make sense of quantities and their relationships in problem situations.
Construct viable arguments and critique the reasoning of others.	Understand and use stated assumptions, definitions, and previously established results in constructing arguments.
Model with mathematics.	Apply the mathematics they know to solve problems arising in everyday life, society, and the workplace.
Use appropriate tools strategically	Consider the available tools when solving a mathematical problem.
Attend to precision	Try to communicate precisely to others.
Look for and make use of structure.	Look closely to discern a pattern or structure.
Look for and express regularity in repeated reasoning.	Notice if calculations are repeated, and look both for general methods and for shortcuts.

Source: Common Core State Standards: © Copyright 2010. National Governors Association Center for Best Practices and Council of Chief State School Officers. All Rights Reserved.

School Officers to develop a shared set of expectations for student learning that in the end would contribute to the nation's global competitiveness. This debate is likely to be long lasting.

THERE ARE OTHER LISTS OF STANDARDS. As was previously mentioned, there now is a rich history of groups and associations that have developed standards. The development of the CCSS was based in and learned from these earlier efforts. The following sections introduce a sampling of related initiatives and alternative ways of framing standards.

World-Class Standards. At the beginning of the twenty-first century there was great concern that the United States retain its competitiveness and prosperity in the global economy. Countries around the world have learned that education plays a major role in being competitive. Also, completion of schooling and college help individuals develop higher level skills that translate into higher incomes over their lifetimes. The National Governors Association, the Council of Chief State School Officers, and Achieve, Inc., reported in 2008 that "If the United States raised students' math and science skills to globally competitive levels over the next two decades, its GDP [i.e., gross domestic product] would be an additional 36 percent higher 75 years from now." Proponents then called for the development of world-class standards that would become national standards. (Do you see the connection between the advocates of world-class standards and what are now the CCSS?)

Real-World Standards. Another segment of the public believes that standards should be real-world goals. This conception of standards places primary emphasis on the necessary knowledge and skills that will make students employable and enable them to live independent lives. In contrast to world-class standards, real-world standards are seen as being achievable in schools. Real-world standards set the expectation that students learn the basic skills of reading, writing, and computing that allow them to balance checkbooks, prepare for job interviews, manage their daily lives, and maintain employment. (How does this view contrast with the views in Tables 11.1 and 11.2?)

Opportunity to learn standards address the sufficiency, quantity and quality of instructional resources.

Opportunity-to-Learn Standards. At the beginning of the standards movement in the 1980s, standards were generally *input* standards that indicated resources and other areas of a school's organization that should be in place for quality educational programs. They required specific topics to be addressed in the curricula. They also addressed conditions such as setting a maximum student-to-teacher ratio in the classroom and requiring that teachers have a bachelor's degree and be certified to teach the courses they were teaching. School resources were addressed through standards about adequate budgets, numbers of library books, and adequate technology. Standards that address the adequacy and appropriateness of instructional resources and the structures that provide the proper conditions for teaching and learning are called **opportunity-to-learn standards**. Their intent is to ensure that all students have an equal chance to achieve the "output" (i.e., the learning standards). Opportunity-to-learn standards also mean that students with disabilities and English-language learners have to be provided with appropriate accommodations to support their learning as outlined in the standards. (Attention to these standards disappeared following the 2008 recession.)

Content Standards. Standards that describe what students should know and be able to do in various subject areas such as science, mathematics, language arts, history, geography, social studies, physical education, and the arts are called **content standards**. They are often accompanied by content standards for what teachers should know about the subjects they teach, as well as their knowledge about instruction.

Content standards establish the knowledge and skills that should be learned in various subject areas. They are often linked to big ideas, themes, or conceptual strands that should be nurtured throughout a student's education. For example, in the earlier science standards, there are explicit descriptions of the big ideas of evolution and equilibrium, form and function, systems, and the nature of science, along with specific grade-level expectations (National Committee on Science Education Standards and Assessment, 1996). The same was true for the earlier social studies standards; ten themes—including, among others, culture; civic ideals and practices; and people, places, and environments—provide a framework for the social studies curriculum in the early grades, middle grades, and high schools. The standards of the National Council for the Social Studies (NCSS, 2009) also included learning expectations and snapshots of classroom practices for each theme.

Furthermore, the earlier National Council of Teachers of Mathematics (NCTM) standards stated that students should be able to understand and use numbers and operations; specifically, they should:

- *Understand numbers,* ways of representing numbers, relationships among numbers, and number systems;
- *Understand meanings* of operations and how they relate one to another;
- *Compute fluently* and make reasonable estimates (NCTM, 2000).

In addition to knowledge acquisition statements, content standards often specify what thinking and process skills and strategies students and/or teachers should acquire. These skills and strategies might include developing a plan and hypothesis; interpreting, extrapolating, and drawing conclusions; and communicating results. Standards may also include statements about the habits or dispositions that should be nurtured in students. These habits or dispositions include curiosity, perseverance, tenacity, caring, and open-mindedness.

opportunity-to-learn standards Standards that identify the instructional resources, assessments, and system structures required to create the proper conditions for students to achieve content and performance standards.

content standards Standards that specify learning outcomes in a subject or discipline (for example, mathematics or social studies).

TWENTY-FIRST CENTURY KNOWLEDGE AND SKILLS FRAMEWORK. Since standardized tests became an integral part of the educational landscape following the passage of the No Child Left Behind Act, educators have been concerned that important areas such as critical thinking and problem solving have been ignored. A number of business leaders and policy makers agree. They called for attention to be paid to "twenty-first-century skills" that would be needed in a global economy and rapidly changing world.

The Partnership for 21st Century Skills took the lead in writing about standards for twenty-first-century knowledge and skills. The partnership included more than thirty member organizations representing technology companies such as Adobe Systems, Dell, Apple, and Microsoft; companies that produce educational technology such as Blackboard, LeapFrog SchoolHouse, and Discovery Education; testing and publishing companies such as Educational Testing Service (ETS) and Pearson Education; communications companies such as AT&T, Corporation for Public Broadcasting, and Verizon; and foundations. Two associations were involved: the National Education Association and the American Association of School Librarians. The partnership developed a framework for teaching and learning that stretches from preschool through graduate school. It identified the knowledge, skills, and expertise that they believe students should master to be successful in this century. The four broad outcomes and support systems required to support the development of these outcomes are shown in Figure 11.1.

JOURNAL FOR REFLECTION 11.2

What skills do you think you and your students will need to develop that your parents and grandparents never needed? What is so different about the world today than when they grew up that requires different skills? What impact is technology having on the skills needed to live and work today?

The Core Subjects are the ones addressed in the content standards of what students should know and be able to do, which were described earlier in the chapter. Some of the 21st Century Themes can be found in specific content standards such as social studies. These themes are meant to be interdisciplinary and promote higher level understanding. One theme is global awareness, which includes "learning from and working collaboratively with individuals representing diverse

FIGURE 11.1 Twenty-first-century student outcomes and support systems.

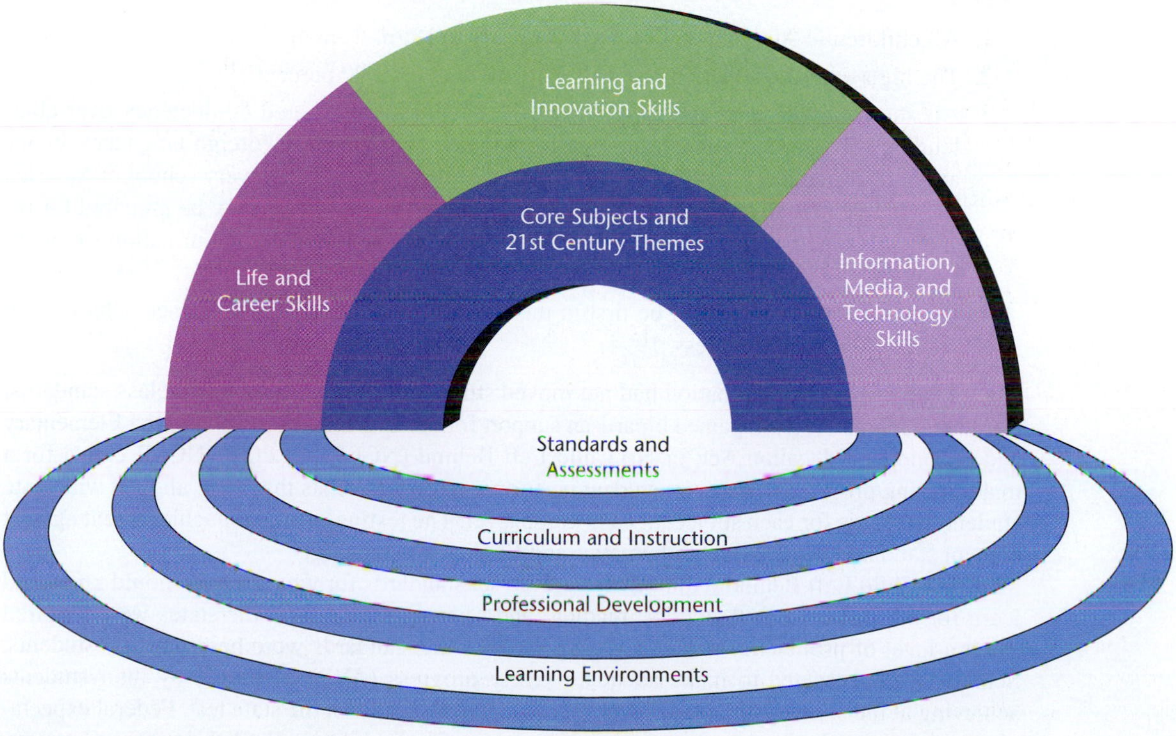

Source: "Framework for 21st Century Learning" *Partnership for 21st Century Skills.* Revised 03/2011. www.P21.org/overview/skills-framework. Reprinted by permission.

cultures, religions and lifestyles in a spirit of mutual respect and open dialogue in personal, work and community contexts" as well as "understanding other nations and cultures, including the use of non-English languages" (Partnership for 21st Century Skills, 2011). The other themes are financial, economic, business, and entrepreneurial literacy; civic literacy; and health literacy.

The other four outcomes demonstrate an even more dramatic change from the traditional curriculum. The Learning and Innovation Skills prepare students for the increasingly complex life and work environments they will face in the future. They include creativity and innovation, critical thinking and problem solving, and communication and collaboration. Having skills related to information, media, and technology will be important in a world where the Internet and other technologies provide access to an abundance of information. As we see every day, technology tools are rapidly changing, and technology makes it possible to communicate with people around the globe. The Information, Media, and Technology Skills that the partnership has identified include information literacy; media literacy; and information, communications, and technology literacy. The fourth set of outcomes are Life and Career Skills for working and living in a "globally competitive information age." They include flexibility and adaptability, initiative and self-direction, and social and cross-cultural skills.

The Federal Role in Standards: A Historical Review

At a meeting of governors in 1989, President George Bush called for the development of content standards to ensure that the nation's students would be first in international academic competitions. The first set of student standards was released in 1989 by the National Council of Teachers of Mathematics (NCTM). With federal support, standards for P–12 students were developed in subsequent years by professional associations and other groups such as the National Research Council. The standards developed by these associations sometimes had great support from Congress, but not always. For example, the standards for social studies, which promoted the multicultural contributions to the nation, were defeated in 1995 by Congress with a 99-to-1 vote (Symcox, 2002).

President Bill Clinton followed up by signing the Goals 2000: Educate America Act in 1994, which established a framework for moving students to world-class standards by the year 2000. The lofty goals called for the following results before the beginning of the twenty-first century:

1. All children in America will start school ready to learn.
2. The high school graduation rate will increase to at least 90 percent.
3. All students will leave grades 4, 8, and 12 having demonstrated competency over challenging subject matter including English, mathematics, science, foreign languages, civics and government, economics, the arts, history, and geography, and every school in America will ensure that all students learn to use their minds well, so they may be prepared for responsible citizenship, further learning, and productive employment in our nation's modern economy.
4. United States students will be first in the world in mathematics and science achievement (H.R. 1804, U.S. Congress, 1994).

Recognizing that the nation had not moved student performance to world-class standards, President George W. Bush gained bipartisan support for the new reauthorization of the Elementary and Secondary Education Act, or No Child Left Behind (NCLB), in 2001. NCLB called for a major testing program to measure student performance on state tests that were aligned with state student standards for each subject at each grade level. The testing of student achievement against content standards began with mathematics and English language arts.

No Child Left Behind required all states to set standards for what a child should know and learn for all grades in mathematics, reading, and science. In addition, the states were required to set a level of proficiency for determining whether the standards were being met by students. Schools were expected to make adequate yearly progress (AYP) as shown by their students achieving at the state's proficiency level at grade level or above on the state test. Federal expectations were stated that low-income students, students with disabilities, English-language learners, and students from different racial and ethnic backgrounds also were to meet state proficiencies for their grade level. If AYP is not achieved by one or more of these groups for more than two years, the school would be identified as "needing improvement." NCLB also required that by 2013 all students would be at the proficiency level for their grade level.

By 2011 it was clear that all children would not be proficient by 2013. In addition, it was becoming clear that the majority of schools in each state were not meeting their AYP targets, which would likely lead to the majority of schools in each state being labeled as failing. There also were the onerous pressures on schools to have test scores continually rising. Due to the failure of Congress to pass the next reauthorization of ESEA, in the fall of 2011 President Obama announced a waiver process through which states could move out from under the unachievable NCLB mandates. As part of the waiver application states had to adopt "college and career-ready standards," move to growth scores for interpreting the results of annual testing, and develop an educator evaluation system that included student test scores.

The President and Congress have become major forces in determining the directions and priorities for education.

The Future of Standards-Based Education

There is no escaping standards in schools today. They are not abstract statements of ideals that teachers can simply ignore. They are now driving what teachers teach and are increasingly an underlying base for teacher evaluation. Standards-based education is a complex and sophisticated approach to teaching and learning. It is a professional challenge for beginning teachers, as well as experienced teachers, to learn to teach this way. The teacher's role shifts from conveyor of knowledge and dispenser of grades to coach and facilitator of students as they engage in learning. The expectations and checkpoints are stated and known by the teacher *and* need to be known by their students before instruction begins. Students not only know beforehand what is to be learned, but they also know what the assessment tasks will be like—that is, the types of performances described in the expectations.

Many questions influence the future of standards. How will school organization, use of time, graduation requirements, and power relationships change because of the standards movement? Will the Common Core State Standards really become the basis for determining a national curriculum? If the standards movement is to be worth the upheaval it has generated, such questions must be answered by thoughtful, knowledgeable participants who are engaged in the process of changing instruction in ways that not only address what students learn but also how they learn. One important outcome of the standards movement is the intense focus on and use of data. There is now a universal expectation that all decisions about instruction, student learning, and teacher and school quality will be based in data. One important consequence is that from now on, teachers need to pay significant attention to ways of assessing student learning and to using the information to design and adjust instruction.

ASSESSING STUDENT LEARNING

Standards are not an end unto themselves. Simply listing standards in a school brochure will make little difference in the way students learn and achieve. If standards are to have any real effect on schools and on student achievement, they need to be supported by other elements in a school's structure: an articulated curriculum, professional development sessions focused on improving student achievement, instruction that is based in the standards, and a well-thought-out array of assessments that align with the standards.

When assessments are linked to standards, there must be consideration about the types of measures used, the kinds of data collected, and the ways the results are used to adjust instruction in ways that will enhance student learning. These changes in the assessment process can be quite dramatic for teachers and their students. In the past, assessing often meant little more to teachers than using the results of tests to produce grades. For students the main question was "What do I have to do to get an 'A'?"

The standards movement requires teachers and students to ask different questions. For teachers, the question now is "How do I need to adjust my teaching so that all of my students are learning?" For students the questions now become "What is it I am to learn?" And, "How will I know that I have learned it?" Answering each of these questions requires data. Answering each of these questions also requires thinking about the meaning of the data. Related implications with a standards-based framework are that there need to be many forms of assessments and that assessing needs to be ongoing. One important consequence of efforts to answer the teacher and student questions is that the data are varied and meaningful to teachers and students alike. In this section, we examine the assessments of student learning and the ways in which assessing can enhance the teaching and learning process.

What Is Assessment?

Assessment in education implies many things: evaluation, grades, tests, performances, reflection, criteria, **rubrics**, and more. To encompass adequately its many dimensions, we will examine assessment in a broader sense by analyzing its root meanings. The term *assessment* is derived from the Latin word *assessio,* which means "to sit beside." This image provides an excellent metaphor. Ultimately, assessment can be thought of as the act of sitting beside ourselves and analyzing what we observe. In a sense, all assessment is based on this image: the examination of ourselves through the perception of an examiner who sits beside us and provides feedback. Some theorists contend that all true assessment is ultimately self-assessment. Assessors can provide information, but in the end it is the person being assessed who accepts the information or rejects it, either using the information to further his or her development or setting aside the information as unimportant.

The image of an assessor sitting beside a learner also implies the use of tools or measuring devices that enable the assessor to gather different types of information. Observations, paper-and-pencil tests, performance tasks, portfolios, journals, and media productions are some of the many possible assessment measures. Often these tools are labeled assessments, but in fact they are merely sources of data that assessors can use to provide feedback to the teacher *and* to students. Keep in mind that **assessing** is the larger process of gathering information, interpreting the information, providing feedback, and ultimately adjusting teaching (and learning) strategies so that more learning can take place.

Purposes of Assessment

The ultimate reason for assessment in the classroom is to help students learn. However, assessments of students and teachers today are being used for a number of other purposes as well. It is important for you to understand these different purposes. Otherwise you, your students, school administrators, and others—without knowing it—may be interpreting the same data with different ends in mind. Put simply, for teachers and students, assessing in classrooms is done for two purposes:

1. **Formative assessment** is done to determine what students have learned and provide feedback to them so that both you and the students can understand where to next focus your efforts.
2. **Summative assessment** is to make a final judgment about whether the desired level of accomplishment has been attained, such as passing a course.

In the past most of the assessment measures would have been developed by the teacher. Now teacher-developed assessments will be used in combination with school, district, and state measures. In standards-based education, every teacher, school administration, and school district will be checking throughout the year for evidence that all students are making progress toward meeting the standards. The checking done within the school year is mainly formative, and the information is used to make adjustments in instruction and learning. The end-of-term and end-of-year tests are summative. These are the basis for decisions about final grades, passing a course, moving to the next grade, and graduation. Ideally the results from most summative

---

assessments The use of a variety of methods, including tests, to evaluate the current level of student learning; used in planning future steps in instruction.

rubric Scoring guides that describe what learners should know and be able to do at different levels of competence, such as developing, proficient, and advanced.

assessing The use of assessment information to review learning progress and to plan next steps in instruction.

formative assessment Is done to provide feedback to students and teachers about what has been learned so far and to be used by the teacher and students to plan next steps in instruction.

summative assessment Data about student performance that are used to make a concluding judgment about a grade, promotion to the next grade, graduation, college entrance, etc.

assessments will also be used to improve student learning. These two assessment purposes can be translated into either assessment *for* learning or assessment *of* learning.

ASSESSMENT OF LEARNING. State achievement tests are designed as summative assessments that tell school officials, parents, and the public whether students are meeting required benchmarks. They are assessments *of* learning. Educators should review the results to gauge how well their students have learned and to consider what changes in instructional strategies could be made to ensure that students in the future do better in meeting the standards. However, summative assessments of learning often create high-stakes situations for students, teachers, and their schools. The data help principals know which teachers are more successful

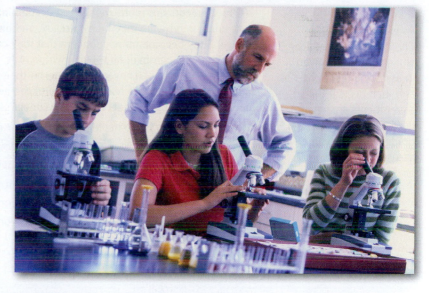

at improving test scores, which is not necessarily the same as which teachers have the students who learned the most. The data help school districts and the state and federal governments rank schools from highest to lowest.

Formative assessment is ongoing and includes checking for understanding as well as careful observation of students at work.

A major use of summative assessments is acting as gatekeepers to determine who moves to the next grade, who is qualified to graduate, or who is admitted to a profession. For example, college admissions offices have a long history of using students' performance on standardized tests such as the ACT and SAT to determine who can be admitted. Professions such as law, medicine, nursing, physical therapy, certified public accountancy, and architecture require persons to pass a standardized test before they are admitted to the profession and allowed to work in a specific state. Most state departments of education require new teachers to pass a standardized test to be eligible for a license to teach. The use of test results for gatekeeping purposes has also become a way of life at the P–12 level. One of the first steps for children entering some of the prestigious preschools in a number of metropolitan areas is passing a test. A growing number of states require students to pass a test before a diploma of graduation is granted. In many states students have to score sufficiently well to be eligible for certain academic programs and to participate in extracurricular activities. These states are using assessments of learning to decide what will—and will not—be happening next.

ASSESSMENT FOR LEARNING. Student essays, projects, and portfolios are valuable resources for knowing how deeply students understand the content of a subject. Observing students as they conduct experiments, demonstrate how to solve a mathematics problem, and interact with other students on a group project provide assessment information about students as learners and about their learning. More and more teachers are recording their observations of student learning throughout the school year. They also maintain records about how well lessons went, what adaptations they made, and what they will do the same and different next time. Recorded notes and evidence about student work also can be an important part of teacher journals. An additional element should include notes about growth over time.

When used for the purpose of helping students learn at higher levels, assessments can help you identify the current levels of student understanding of the concept or skill you are trying to teach. The analysis of the data on student learning can help you clarify what you want to do next to move them to the next level. Assessments that are conducted formally and informally on a regular basis can help you find out which students are struggling with specific lessons. When teachers collaborate on assessment activities, they are not only helping students, but also informing and improving their own instructional practice (Popham, 2010). All of these activities are elements of formative assessment.

Do not think of assessment as something that only teachers do. Students of any age can be involved in the assessments of their learning. Research finds that academic achievement improves when teachers and students become partners in the assessment process (Stiggins & Chappuis,

GO TO ···>
As was pointed out in Chapter 10, it is legal for students to be involved in assessing themselves and their peers if the assessments are being used for learning, not a grade or other summative assessment.

2011). Students are more engaged in academic work when they understand the lesson's objective, understand what they know already, and have strategies in mind to help them learn the next pieces. They become more confident that they can succeed.

Students can maintain their own records, or perhaps a portfolio, that shows how they are achieving over time. They can learn to do their own self-assessments to know where they need help and when they are ready to move to the next level. Stiggins (2009) suggests the following steps for involving students in the assessment process:

- Let students know the learning target for instruction in student-friendly language.
- Provide samples of student work that show success along a continuum.
- Give students descriptive feedback that will help them improve their performance.
- Teach students how to conduct their own self-assessments of their progress.
- Help students improve pieces of their work as they pull it together for a final product.
- Help students learn to reflect on their work as they become more academically competent and confident.[1]

Types of Assessment Measures

Educators use different types of measures depending on the purpose of the assessment. The types described next are among the most common. Many are manifested in paper-and-pencil formats; others take the form of the demonstration of skills. Increasingly measures are based in some form of technology such as handheld calculators and video cameras. Educators and parents should know the basics about the type of measure being administered to their students and children. One important check is to determine whether the measure is designed to compare students across the state or nation or whether it is designed to determine if students have developed the core knowledge and skills expected in standards. The first is usually summative in nature; the second is formative. Let's take a look at four types of measures and their related assessment purposes.

DIAGNOSTIC MEASURES. One important purpose of testing is to determine at what level a student is functioning compared to the level at which he or she should be able to function developmentally. The feedback from these sources should help teachers design new or different instructional strategies that will assist a student who is having difficulty. For example, the teacher in the "Perspectives on Diversity" feature is using performance assessments to help determine what a new student knows and whether he might need special services.

These types of assessments provide an array of questions and tasks for a student to perform in a specific area such as reading, writing, mathematics, or motor skills. In such assessments, the questions and tasks might be organized by difficulty. As the student performs each task successfully, she or he is given another, more difficult question.

Diagnostic assessments are also used to determine the need for special services or accommodations. When a student is not performing at the level of other students, there may be sufficient concern to want to refer them for consideration for special education services. When such a referral is made the diagnostic assessment will usually be conducted by a special education teacher, school psychologist, speech/language pathologist, occupational therapist, or another professional who is trained to administer specific tests. Most students who take these tests have been referred by teachers or parents for special education or gifted and talented services.

GO TO ···>
RTI, which was discussed in Chapter 7, is an example of an assessment process for determining whether students need special services.

NORM-REFERENCED MEASURES. Norm-referenced assessments are used to demonstrate who is best in some area. With norm-referenced assessment, the individual's performance is compared with that of a norm group of similar individuals. Often these are referred to as "standardized tests." Development of these tests is rigorous and expensive. Also, once they are developed, they are carefully revised on a regular basis to ensure that the measure continues to yield varied test scores from low to high. These types of assessments do not reveal all that an individual child knows or is able to do. They are not the appropriate measure to use to determine whether

---

[1]From Assessment for learning in upper elementary grades. *Phi Delta Kappan, 90*(6), February 2009: 419–421. Reprinted by permission of the author.

PERSPECTIVES on DIVERSITY

Using Assessments for Learning

When Jason arrived in Ms. Ehrenberg's multicultural third-grade class for the first time about halfway through the school year, he took an open seat next to the wall, saying nothing after he was introduced to the class. He looked out the window most of the first week, making no attempt to participate in class activities. Ms. Ehrenberg soon learned from the principal that he had already been expelled from one school because he threw a chair at the teacher.

During his second week in the classroom, Jason moped around and never appeared on task. He began snapping back at his classmates when they tried to involve him in conversations or at play during recesses. He certainly seemed unhappy at school and was becoming Ms. Ehrenberg's greatest challenge. Based on Jason's address, she guessed that his single mother was struggling financially. She was puzzled about how to engage him in the schoolwork. She knew that if she did not get him engaged this year, he was likely to become more disenchanted with school year by year, leading him to drop out or be a low-performing participant for the rest of his school career. She had to take some action.

Ms. Ehrenberg wondered if she could conduct some assessments that would help her determine what Jason already knew (that is, his prior experience) and what interested him. Maybe he had special needs that had not been detected before. She had already noticed that Jason was more disruptive when students were involved in English language arts. She decided to systematically record when the disruptions occurred. Were they at a specific time of the day or when a specific subject was being taught? She also could look for signs that would suggest she should recommend him for special testing by the school psychologist.

After a few weeks of observation and note taking, Ms. Ehrenberg found that Jason was much more engaged when he was working on a project that required him to be actively involved in problem solving or figuring out an answer. He was not comfortable talking in front of the class and never responded when asked a direct question in a whole-group lesson. He appeared to like to draw and had signs of some creative talent. He would much rather be doodling than reading a story that she had assigned.

WHAT IS YOUR PERSPECTIVE?

1. How is Ms. Ehrenberg using her knowledge of performance assessment to learn more about Jason to figure out instructional strategies that will encourage him to become more involved in his schoolwork?

2. Now that Ms. Ehrenberg has some sense of Jason's interests and areas in which he might excel, what should she do?

3. What tactic would you take if Jason arrived in your class?

students meet proficiencies outlined in standards. In some ways, norm-referenced measures are like a contest; it is expected that some students will excel and others fail.

Norm-referenced measures are misused more often than most other assessments. Teachers must be cautious in concluding that individual students who score low are not doing well. Norm-referenced tests typically sample only a portion of what students in a particular class are expected to know and do. Therefore, the student may not be performing well in those areas measured by the test but may be doing better in other areas that were not included on the test.

Sometimes state authorities penalize a school district or school whose students as a group perform below a specific level on a norm-referenced test. This is a flawed practice because norm-referenced tests are designed such that 50 percent will score below the fiftieth percentile. In fact, when schools begin to score regularly above this percentile, the test is made more difficult. A related problem is that the nature of the test prevents the inclusion of questions on some of the core, most important concepts in content standards. Too many students select the correct answer because their teachers focused on this key concept in their teaching to ensure that students learned it. If a large number of students select the correct answer, the test question is revised. As a result, many of the items on the test address peripheral areas of the standards, avoiding the important knowledge and skills at the heart of the standards. The goal is not to determine if most students meet standards but to make sure there is an appropriate distribution of scores.

CRITERION-REFERENCED MEASURES. Instead of comparing a student's performance with that of a comparison group of students, criterion-referenced assessments compare a student's performance with a specific type of accomplishment or criterion. For instance, you can assess whether students can add two-digit numbers without regrouping. To measure this skill, a student could be asked to answer ten different questions. If a child successfully answers all ten, or nine or even eight of the ten questions, a teacher can state with some degree of confidence that the child knows how to add two-digit numbers without regrouping.

Most classroom tests should measure students' knowledge in a criterion-referenced manner. The test items should be drawn directly from the subject and grade level standard. The student's performance should be evaluated relative to the standard (i.e., did she or he achieve the standard or not?). Comparing one student's level of learning to another's moves you back to the norm-referenced assessment model. Also, students can be asked to answer more than one question that measures the same learning. Then, instead of scoring the test by using some sort of A through F range, the teacher sets an acceptable score that indicates that the student understands a learning outcome at an acceptable level.

CAPSTONE/SUMMATIVE ASSESSMENTS. Capstone or summative assessments can be developed to celebrate a milestone accomplishment or to demonstrate how well a person has mastered something. These types of assessments are used near the end of major accomplishments such as completion of a course, a recital, or graduation. For instance, after completing courses in education, a teacher candidate student teaches. One of the major assignments could be to accomplish a work sample. The candidate is to prepare and teach a unit of instruction. The assignment also entails collecting preunit and postunit student assessments in order to document what the students have learned. Hence, within the capstone experience of student teaching there is a major assignment that will be a key part of the candidate's summative evaluation. This whole capstone experience is evaluated by a master teacher who notes all of the accomplishments that are shown by the student teacher throughout the performance. In such a capstone assessment, deficiencies also can be identified, but the major focus is to evaluate all that a teacher candidate has learned throughout a program of study.

In schools, most capstone assessments come at the end of a school year. Students can be asked to apply all they have learned in science by completing a science project, or in English by writing a short story, or in history by creating a media presentation. Some schools require a comprehensive test, presentation of student work in a portfolio, an essay, or perhaps a PowerPoint presentation as the capstone experience for graduation.

Performance Measurement

In this **video,** educator John Van de Walle talks about the importance of performance assessment.

What assessment is about has changed a lot during the past decade. For years, educators have called for better standardized testing, but the response was the proliferation of a number of different kinds of tests with different emphases. Tests of achievement, basic skills tests, criterion-referenced tests related to the many sets of standards, tests of cognitive ability, tests of flexibility, and tests of critical thinking were developed. Although worthy attempts, these tests provide a limited view of what students are learning. Many educators viewed these paper-and-pencil instruments as an intrusion and not directly related to what was really happening in the classroom and real world.

Parents and educators want assessments that allow students to demonstrate in a number of ways that they have met the standards in real-world or **authentic** settings—in other words, **performance**. The best performance measures are designed to promote student understanding, learning, and engagement rather than simply having them recall facts. The development of performance measures is discussed in the "Teaching in Challenging Times" feature.

Performance assessments can be used to demonstrate a specific proficiency. For example, if students have been taught a specific method for using a piece of science equipment, such as a gram balance, a performance assessment would include having the student weigh several objects on a balance. The teacher would typically observe the student to see whether all the specific techniques in accurately weighing a sample were used. Assessments of specific proficiencies in schools include many teacher-made tasks that focus on the specific things a student has studied. An example of a performance-based assessment outside the classroom is the road test employed in most states as a prerequisite to receiving a driver's license. The critical characteristic of such an assessment is that the activity is directly related to what the successful learner is to do. Hence, in the road test, a person drives a car in situations that the driver will typically experience: turning left or right, backing up, parking, and so forth. The person is usually scored

authentic Assessment tasks that are grounded in real-world settings and applications of what has been learned.

performance Demonstration of learning through doing.

TEACHING IN CHALLENGING TIMES

Leading the Development of Performance Assessments

"Common assessments—those created collaboratively by teams of teachers who teach the same course or grade level—also represent a powerful tool in effective assessment in professional learning communities," reported Stiggins and DuFour (2009), who work with school districts and teachers on the development of formative assessments.

Your principal, Mr. Jennings, wants to try this approach. He has asked the middle school teachers to work together to identify key performance assessments that all of you would use at critical junctures of the program. The principal has made it clear that these assessments cannot be multiple-choice tests and that student performance on them must be analyzed and used by the teachers to help students develop more in-depth understanding of the key concepts and skills for the subject they are learning. He has said that improvement in state test scores would be a wonderful result, but not his bottom line. He wants students to be learning to think critically about important issues in the subject. They should be able to problem solve about real issues in their community.

Mr. Jennings asked you to cochair this project with another teacher. He wants an initial report on your plans within a month and wants you to begin testing the new assessments next semester.

WHAT ARE MY CHALLENGES?

1. Where do you begin? What will be some of the issues on the agenda for your first meeting?
2. Why does Mr. Jennings appear not to be concerned about students' performance on the state tests this year?
3. How will you and your colleagues go about developing assessments that do not include tests? What assessments might you develop?
4. How could this collaborative effort lead to gains in student learning?

---

through an observation checklist that the assessor uses, and then the summative judgment is made.

AUTHENTIC ASSESSMENTS. Performance assessments that are authentic represent another important characteristic of good measures. When the tasks are realistic in terms of being as close as possible to how the learning would be applied in a real-world setting, they are considered to be authentic. Too often, test items and activities are extremely remote from what a learner would need to do in life. When assessments are authentic, the tasks are based on problems and contexts that are clearly seen as relevant and real. Some possibilities for authentic performance tasks are presented in Table 11.3.

There are three major areas to consider in developing authentic assessments for standards. First, a rich context needs to be designed, one that permits inquiry to occur. Second, it is important to fill the context with a wide variety of questions so that different types of thinking can occur. Finally, the critical indicators for learning need to be identified.

Developing a performance assessment task begins by considering the learning standards, **benchmarks**, and objectives that are the intended outcomes of instruction. It is critical that students be assessed on the intended outcomes as described in the district/state standards and benchmarks.

An important step in developing authentic assessments is to structure the tasks so that they are complex enough to permit students to show important learning, motivating enough to encourage students to think, rich enough to offer multiple opportunities to show how and what students have shaped into an understanding, and relevant enough that students can use their own experience. Some writers call the structure of the task the **context**, by which they mean the various activities, hands-on experiences, and questions that encourage learners to think and show how they can apply what they know.

Once a context has been selected, it needs to be structured and filled with opportunities to show how and what students have learned. Asking students to display their cognitive abilities in as many ways as possible enhances the teacher's understanding of students' unique ways of knowing. This is where assessment tools are helpful. Observing students in action and recording these observations in a variety of ways are critical.

benchmarks A level of performance at which a standard is met. Examples of levels include "proficient" and "correct response on 80 percent of questions or performances."

context The various elements of the experience, questions asked, and setting.

TABLE 11.3

Types of Performance Assessment Tasks

TYPE	WHAT IT IS	USES	TIPS FOR THE TEACHER FOR EFFECTIVE USE
Learning logs and journals	Notes, drawings, data, charts, artwork, and other notes written by the student	• Encourages reflection as one is learning • Provides a record of questions and thoughts	• Generate questions for students to ponder and respond to • Make the questions as varied as possible
Folios and portfolios	Folio is the storage bin, box, or file. Portfolio is the organization and presentation of selected folio artifacts for a particular purpose.	• Documents learning and growth over time • Encourages self-assessment • Shows student's best work	• Ask students to explain why they have included the various items • Require entries to be tied to standards • Provide feedback • Discuss the portfolio with students and their parents
Interviews	Peers and/or the teacher asking a set of questions	• Helps determine what has been learned	• Use a variety of question types to obtain a range of responses
Observation with anecdotal record	Observing and note taking during day-to-day activities	• Provides documentation of performance and learning over time	• Conduct observations on a regular basis • Write notes clearly and include specific descriptions of what was observed • Review notes • Distinguish carefully between facts and interpretations
Student products and projects	Specific products such as lab reports, presentations, and digital productions	• Provides cumulative evidence about the extent of learning	• Display student work

JOURNAL FOR REFLECTION 11.3

Consider the types of assessments that have been used throughout your college studies. Select one assessment experience that you have found to be especially helpful in displaying what you believe you really know and can do. Most likely this was an authentic task. What were the characteristics of the assessment that made it so relevant to you?

Too often teachers assess one way but teach another. For example, assessing by using paper-and-pencil tests or using single-answer questions when instruction has been emphasizing inquiry is inappropriate. The reverse is also true. Assessing students in a hands-on inquiry mode when all instruction was lecture and reading/writing is equally incorrect.

Teachers have long been aware that questioning is an important way to cue students to display their understanding. Research indicates that the types of questions students are asked determine the academic culture of a classroom. Questions that focus on a single aspect of knowing (knowledge or skills) limit the opportunities for showing understanding (the interactions of knowledge, skills, and habits of mind). Having a clearer picture of the multidimensionality of understanding (ways of knowing) directs teachers to ask a wide variety of questions. This is especially true during an assessment experience. Students should be asked many different types of questions within a rich, hands-on context. Table 11.4 presents examples of the variety of question types that allow students multiple opportunities to show their various ways of knowing.

Once students are engaged in a motivating inquiry, they will be better able to exhibit learning development. It is important that teachers focus on all aspects of learning when they examine

TABLE 11.4

Examples of the Types of Questions That Encourage Students to Show Different Ways of Knowing

TYPE OF QUESTION	EXAMPLES
Analysis questions	What are the key parts? Which parts are essential and why?
Comparison questions	How are these alike? What specific characteristics are similar? How are these different? In what way(s) are they different?
Classification questions	Into what groups could you organize these things? What are the rules for membership in each group? What are the defining characteristics of each group?
Connections/clarification questions	What does this remind you of in another context? To what is this connected?
Constructing support questions	What data can you cite that support this conclusion? What is an argument that would support this claim?
Deduction questions	On the basis of this rule, what would you deduce? What are the conditions that make this inevitable?
Inferring and concluding questions	On the basis of these data, what would you conclude? How likely is it that this will occur?
Abstracting questions	What pattern underlies all of these situations? What are the essential characteristics of this thing?
Error analysis	How is this conclusion misleading? What does not match?

student performance and not simply focus on those aspects that are easy to assess. If a context is truly authentic, students will have ample opportunities to display what they know and can do across a variety of different standards:

- Knowledge and comprehension of concepts, application of concepts, and connection of concepts to real-world contexts
- Ability to solve problems and exercise thinking skills
- Ability to perform and apply process skills
- Ability to structure thinking
- Collaboration and other dispositions
- Communication and ability to modify ideas on the basis of new evidence.

A rich assessment context allows students to display many of these components of understanding and skill. The art of assessing well includes identifying indicators—things that can be observed that relate to different aspects of some important standard. Identifying indicators in a performance task is much like acting as an X-ray: You need to notice what behaviors count and what successful ways of doing and knowing look like. To do this, teachers need to step back from the performance, much like a physician, and identify those actions that are meaningful and, more important, the learning that those actions indicate. Once teachers develop lists of indicators, they can easily assess what a child knows and does not know. These lists can form the basis for assigning grades, discussing student progress, and making decisions about student needs.

Authentic assessment is both an art and a science. As an art, assessment is like the world of a play. Placing students in the proper context is like situating characters to play a particular role; once in this context, students cannot help but display the knowledge, thinking, and habits of mind they have developed. On the other hand, authentic assessment is also like a science in that the educator needs to meticulously identify and examine the questions and other types of learning indicators that are important to the task.

FIGURE 11.2   Examples of rubric levels.

Absolutely	Kind of	Not Sure	No Way
4	3	2	1

Advanced	Proficient	Developing	Beginning
4	3	2	1

Target	Acceptable	Unacceptable
3	2	1

As can be seen, authentic assessment is an attempt to make testing both in and out of the classroom more closely grounded in the context of student learning and less narrowly focused on a few aspects of what has been learned. Its very name implies trying to better determine what children have really learned.

RUBRICS. In its simplest and most basic sense, a rubric is a scoring guide. It is a way of describing different levels of accomplishment or degrees of being proficient. A rubric is not the measurement itself; it is a way of interpreting, scoring, and summarizing how well a student has performed. Figure 11.2 represents three different ways of thinking about labels for the levels of a rubric. Rubrics are a tool for focusing on the important elements in an assessment and combining these elements into a single score. They also provide guidance to ensure that different assessors rate students in the same manner and that students know what is expected for each level.

Rubrics can be analytic or holistic measures. *Analytic* refers to looking at each dimension of the performance and scoring each. *Holistic* refers to considering all criteria simultaneously and making one overall evaluation. You might sum all the analytic scores for a total score, or you might have one holistic dimension within an analytic rubric to provide an overall impression score. By doing this, assessors can access the benefits of both analytic and holistic scoring procedures. Analytic scoring, of course, provides the most specific data for use as a diagnostic assessment; it also limits flexibility because the dimensions are prescribed ahead of time. Holistic scoring does not require specific dimensions to be assessed; as such, it provides more flexibility and allows an assessor to give credit for unexpected dimensions that may contribute to the overall success of a performance. However, holistic scoring provides less direction for students than analytic scoring does. Tables 11.5 and 11.6 provide examples of analytic and holistic scoring rubrics.

Note that in Tables 11.5 and 11.6 two other important aspects of assessment are included: Depth of Knowledge (DOK) and examples of assessment tasks. Bloom's Taxonomy has been introduced at several points in this book. Bloom's six levels have become the traditional way of describing different levels of knowledge use and understanding. At the Wisconsin Center for Education Research, Webb (2002) has proposed a DOK model that has only four levels: (1) Recall and Reproduction: using simple facts; (2) Skills and Concepts: using facts and processing in simple ways; (3) Short-term Thinking and Reasoning: going beyond what is given and being able to explain or connect ideas; and (4) Extended Thinking: higher order thinking and more complex analyses. Webb's DOK model is being applied in several states—for example, Tennessee and Kentucky—as well as in many school districts. Webb's four levels also are built into the example rubrics presented in Tables 11.5 and 11.6.

BASING ASSESSMENTS IN THE WORK OF A DISCIPLINE. You will need to consider how the learning goals and standards relate to the lives and actions of scientists, writers, historians, and mathematicians. Consider what professionals do and how they use their different ways of knowing. Together, these considerations will often suggest ideas for the performance context.

To illustrate this way of determining a context, consider a curriculum that is filled with learning experiences focused on food chains, prey and predator relationships, and the balance of nature. How does this translate into a real-world context? Having students dissect owl pellets and analyze findings in light of the previous concepts provides one such context that is closely tied to the real world and to environmental issues. Like practicing scientists, students could be asked to

TABLE 11.5

Analytic Rubrics for Mathematics

The rubric below uses a scale of one to four to analyze a student's level of understanding. Level 1 is a beginning or low level of performance; Level 4 is a high level of performance.

LEVEL OF PERFORMANCE	POSSIBLE ASSESSMENT ACTIVITIES
4—Develops a rule for explaining the pattern in the data and can apply it to a different data set.	Applying rule to new data set and providing explanation; creating charts and explaining reasoning to another.
3—Explains how the product will change when the value of one of the elements is changed.	Graph with explaining text. Oral or written report/presentation.
2—Organizes data and constructs a display.	Illustration, interview, demonstration.
1—Multiplies two- and three-digit numbers; doing simple calculations.	Quiz, worksheet, Show and Tell.

TABLE 11.6

Holistic Presentation Rubric

5—Expert Performance	The presentation has a smooth flow from beginning to end. The topic is addressed in text and visuals that are interesting and keep up the attention of the audience. There are no verbal tics or distracting motions. Questions are answered accurately and with elaboration.
4—Proficient Performance	The presentation is organized with introduction, clear flow of ideas, and a conclusion. Visuals are connected to the flow and the topic is addressed in full. Questions are answered accurately and directly. If any, there are only a few "ah's" or other verbal tics, or distracting motions. Most of the time the audience is engaged.
3—Basic Performance	The presentation is organized with an introduction and conclusion. Sufficient information is included and related to the topic. There are a few "ah's" and/or other verbal tics, and/or distracting motions. Questions are answered simply, but without elaboration. Along the way most of the audience lost interest.
2—Limited Performance	In general the presentation addresses the question and there is basic organization and sequencing. However, there is no new information in the text and/or the visuals. There are errors at several points. Answers to questions are vague. There are several verbal tics and/or distracting motions. Those in the audience who attempted to attend are now confused.
1—Partial Performance	Presentation does not have a clear opening, sequencing, or conclusion. Little or no creativity in the visuals. There are errors of omission and inaccuracies. Answers to questions are nonspecific. The audience dropped out early.

investigate a set of owl pellets that have been collected from a specific area of the country. Students can apply what they know and use skills and thinking processes throughout the investigation. The assessment should provide students with opportunities to take measurements and make and record observations about the owl pellets. Students can be asked to create data tables that summarize the types of prey that were consumed, make inferences and draw conclusions about food availability, and finally even answer direct questions about food chains.

Professional Aspects of Good Assessments

Thus far, we have examined the purposes and described a variety of the methods being applied to performance assessment. However, assessing student learning has more to it than the mechanics of constructing authentic tasks. Assessing student learning is an activity that influences and affects many people. Therefore, the professional and ethical aspects of assessment must be considered. A number of very technical issues are also related to whether each assessment task is fair and truly assesses what was intended.

PRINCIPLES FOR HIGH-QUALITY ASSESSMENTS. Like other professionals who have knowledge that their clients do not have and whose actions and judgments affect their clients, classroom teachers are responsible for conducting themselves in an ethical manner. This responsibility is particularly important in education because, unlike other professions, students have no choice about whether they will or will not attend school. The following principles are keys to developing and using powerful and responsible assessments:

- Base assessments on standards for learning.
- Represent performances of understanding in authentic ways.
- Embed assessments in curriculum and instruction.
- Provide multiple forms of evidence about student learning.
- Evaluate standards without unnecessary standardization.
- Involve local educators in designing and scoring assessments (Darling-Hammond & Falk, 1997).

ACCOMMODATIONS. Issues of assessment become even more glaring for students who are English-language learners and those with special needs and learning disabilities. State and national assessments usually allow appropriate accommodations for these groups as outlined in Table 11.7. The purpose of an accommodation is to allow these students access to the test content without changing the accuracy of the test so that results are comparable to students who did not need accommodations. Determining the accommodation depends on a number of factors including the student's disability, age, the nature of the assessment, and the skill or subject being assessed. An inappropriate accommodation could compromise the validity of the scores, leading to inaccurate information about students' academic achievement. Often, simply changing the way in which learning is assessed can provide significant new opportunities for these students to demonstrate their knowledge and skills against a set of standards.

FAIRNESS. Some of the attractions of state tests are that they are standardized, perceived as objective, and inexpensive in comparison to performance assessments. One of the problems is that they ignore the lived experiences of many test takers, resulting in biases that give students from

---

TABLE 11.7

Testing Accommodations for English-Language Learners and Students with Disabilities

ENGLISH-LANGUAGE LEARNERS

- Use of a dictionary or glossary that defines words specific to the content areas
- Use of plain or simplified English on the test
- Use of a bilingual dictionary that provides equivalent meanings of terms
- Dual-language or side-by-side presentation of test items
- Native-language versions of the test
- Small-group administrations
- Allowing extra testing time

STUDENTS WITH DISABILITIES

- Reading questions aloud for reading comprehension and math problem-solving tests
- Use of dictation services or software programs for writing portions
- Allowing extra time to complete the test
- Small-group administration of the test
- Individual administration of the test

Source: From Addressing achievement gaps: The language acquisition and educational achievement of English-language learners. *Policy Notes, 16*(2): 10 Copyright © 2012 Educational Testing Service. www.ets.org. Reprinted by permission.

Source: Jablonski, G., Potts, E., & Wiley, A. (n.d.). *Providing access to assessment: How should IEP teams make decisions about accommodations? CEC Today.* Council for Exceptional Children.

one group an advantage over another. Analyses of test items show that many of them are biased against students from low-income families. Basing assessments on a set of standards provides appropriate standardization. Performance assessments, unlike standardized tests, can take into account the variations in students' learning contexts while still holding to the levels of achievement expected to meet standards (Darling-Hammond & Falk, 1997).

RELIABILITY AND VALIDITY. Two critical aspects of any effort to assess student learning, whether the assessment items have been developed by an individual teacher or a national testing company, are reliability and validity. Each of these terms is regularly used in professional discussions; however, their meaning and implications might not be appreciated. The only way in which any assessment of student learning can be counted on to be fair is if each and every item is both valid and reliable.

It is appropriate to make accommodations for students with special needs. For example, an adult may read the test items aloud to a student with limited vision.

Validity refers to whether the assessment items measure what they are intended to measure. All too frequently, test items do not measure what the test maker had in mind. For example, a history teacher could have a learning objective related to students being able to describe key social, economic, and political causes of the Civil War. If the teacher then uses a test item that asks students to describe the results of key battles during the Civil War, the test item would not be valid. It did not ask students to demonstrate what they had learned in relation to the stated learning objective. This is a simple and obvious example of an assessment item that is not valid. Problems related to validity are many and can be extremely complex. Still, it is essential that teachers make every effort in the construction of assessment items to make sure that what students are being asked to do is closely aligned with the statement of standards and learning objectives.

Reliability is an equally important technical aspect of high-quality assessments. Reliability has to do with the consistency of information about student learning that results from repeated use of each assessment item or task. If two students who have learned the same amount complete the same assessment, do they receive identical scores? If they do, then the item has high reliability. If two students with the same level of learning receive discrepant scores, then the item is not consistent or reliable. Test makers often check the reliability of their items by using an approach called test–retest. In this approach to checking reliability, the same student responds to the same test item after a carefully selected time interval, typically a week or two. Here, too, the reliability question is "How consistent are the results from both administrations of the assessment?" If both assessments yield similar results, then the assessment is considered to be reliable.

Assessing the Performance of Teachers

Before leaving the assessment topic, you likely will be interested in some of the new approaches to assessing the performance of teacher education candidates. There are some interesting and promising directions in this area as well. In this section, we review two approaches that a growing number of teacher education programs are using to help candidates develop their assessment skills. You should begin now to practice developing performance assessments that you can use when you begin to teach.

validity An indication of whether assessment items measure what they are intended to measure.

PERFORMANCE ASSESSMENT FOR CALIFORNIA TEACHERS (PACT). The PACT project is a consortium of more than twenty colleges and universities in California that are using this particular performance assessment with teacher candidates to determine if they are ready to teach. Institutions in a number of other states will be testing PACT over the next few years. You may be required to use this assessment or the Teacher Work Sample, which is described in the next section.

reliability An indication that the information about student learning is consistent across repeated use of each assessment item or task.

The assessment package includes a "Teaching Event," which is modeled after the portfolio that experienced teachers complete for National Board Certification, which was discussed in Chapter 1. Teacher candidates complete the assessment near the end of their teacher education program. During student teaching, they "plan and teach a unit of instruction, including development of an assessment plan, and to analyze their students' learning in relation to their teaching" (Shepard et al., 2007). They identify two students in their class with different instructional challenges; one of them must be an English-language learner. As part of the assessment, they include three samples of each student's work to show their learning. With the samples of student work, they respond to the following issues and questions:

1. Describe the student as a person and learner. What are the student's strengths and approaches to learning, levels of knowledge and skills, academic needs, individual learning goals, and other relevant characteristics?

2. Discuss what each work sample illustrates about the student's developing skills and understandings. What was the student able to do? In what areas did the student have difficulty?

3. Describe what learning progress you can see across the samples. Are there aspects of the student's learning you have observed that are not well represented in these particular assessments?

4. Describe how you assess each response. What feedback did you give to the student?

5. Discuss what you believe supported or impeded the student's progress. Were there particular modifications you made to support the student's success?

6. Finally, discuss what you have done or you will do as a teacher to build on what the student has already accomplished and to support the student's ongoing learning (Shepard et al., 2007).[2]

This assessment helps future teachers understand how student learning evolves and pushes them to think about their teaching in terms of what students are or are not learning.

In addition to the "Teaching Event," the PACT portfolio requires a more summative assignment in which student teachers present the data from an assessment of the whole class around lessons that they taught. The student artifacts might include homework assignments, papers, tests, and journals. The assignment requires teacher candidates to summarize the data for the full class and provide samples of the responses from three students to show what they understood and in what areas they were still struggling. In an accompanying commentary, they describe what they learned about the students' achievements related to the learning objectives and what their next instructional choices will be.

TEACHER WORK SAMPLE. The Teacher Work Sample (TWS) methodology was developed by Del Shalock at Western Oregon University to help teacher candidates develop the skills for assessing student learning. The process has been refined during the past twenty years and is used by many programs across the country. Even though your teacher education program may not require you to use the TWS, you may find it another helpful tool for thinking about what students are learning as you teach.

Similar to PACT, the TWS requires teacher candidates to demonstrate their ability to assess, plan, and instruct in a standards-based educational system and impact positively on student learning. The standards that candidates must show they can meet through the TWS at Western Oregon University require them to do the following:

• Analyze contextual information to determine relevant factors that influence curriculum instruction, learning goals, and management decisions.

• Set developmentally appropriate, challenging, and varied learning goals and objectives that are derived from the district, state, or national content standards and/or common curriculum goals.

• Demonstrate the ability to plan a unit that connects learning goals and objectives, methods of teaching and assessment, and the knowledge of students and their prior knowledge.

---

[2]From Shepard, et. al. "Assessment" in Darling-Hammond and Bransford (Eds.), *Preparing teachers for a changing world: What teachers should learn and be able to do.* Copyright © 2005 by John Wiley & Sons. Reprinted by permission.

- Develop lessons for a unit that includes activities using a variety of instruction and assessment strategies that help students meet learning outcomes.
- Demonstrate the ability to design valid assessments and analyze assessment data to determine student learning relative to expected outcomes.
- Reflect thoughtfully about the relationship between their own teaching and student learning.

For the TWS, student teachers identify the context of their classroom, including the characteristics of students such as English-language learners and students with disabilities. They test students' knowledge of the unit to be taught. They plan the lessons and discuss why they chose certain instructional strategies instead of others. After the unit is taught, they assess what students learned, compile the data, and analyze them to determine what additional teaching is needed. Their reflections on their teaching and the data of student learning help the teacher candidates determine if their teaching made a difference. They also consider what worked well and what they would do differently the next time.

In both PACT and the Teacher Work Sample, you would learn how to develop good assessments, collect data on what students are learning, and analyze the assessment data to promote student learning. Both systems include reflection in which you think about whether your teaching has actually helped students learn and the next steps needed to ensure that students are learning—which should be the goal of all teaching. These truly are examples of authentic performance assessments.

ACCOUNTABILITY

As illustrated in the news story at the beginning of the chapter, policy makers in many areas of the country are starting to hold teachers directly accountable for student learning as never before. All that we have just introduced about the importance of assessment and the design of measures has new meaning with the results being applied to evaluation of teachers. State and national policy makers are demanding more accountability. The pressure is not diminishing, it is increasing.

Sources and Uses of Data for Accountability

New accountability models for methods for measuring performance and outcomes are being developed. There also are important new approaches to analyzing and interpreting test data. It is important for you to become conversant with what these newer approaches entail as well as some of the questions and issues related to their being used to judge students, schools, states, and teachers.

GROWTH MODEL. A major criticism of the way that test scores were analyzed under NCLB was that there was no comparability from one school year to the next. The test scores for each year were for all the students in the school for that year. Under NCLB the test scores for Year 1 would be compared to the school's total scores for Year 2. Remember, the law mandated negative consequences for the school if the Year 2 scores did not increase by a specified amount, for example 10 percent. At first, simply looking for an increase over the previous year might make sense to you. However, what happens to a school that has a high transiency rate? In other words, schools where one-third or—in some schools—more than half of the students move each year. For these schools it is not reasonable to simply compare test scores from Year 1 to those for Year 2. The school doesn't have the same students and surely can't have made any cumulative difference in learning, especially when each year the teachers are starting over with so many students that are new to the school.

The new approach is to use a **growth model**. With this model the analysis of year-to-year test scores includes only those students that attended the school for that time period. The accountability question then becomes something like: Did those students who were in the school for a year gain more or less than similar students in other schools? This question is asking about growth and is also building a database for comparing one school to others.

Another way to ask the question in the growth model is "By how much, on average, did math scores of the students attending this school improve over the course of a year?" (Jennings & Corcoran, 2009). These data help school districts and states know more about the academic

growth model A statistical model that compares change in test scores of the same students over time.

growth of students in their schools, which should lead to more appropriate interventions for improved learning than those that occurred under NCLB by labeling a school as "low performing."

VALUE-ADDED MODEL. Another evaluation model that is in increasing favor is called **value-added**. Like the growth model, the value-added model begins by looking at measures of student growth over a period of time. There is a comparison of student performance on the last examination with performance on the current examination. The difference in this approach from the growth model comes in the perspective for interpreting the findings. Keep in mind that both models, growth and value-added, use technically sophisticated procedures to account for student characteristics, such as poverty, that can affect test scores. The procedures are so precise that they are able to isolate individual student performance so that it can be matched with a specific teacher or school.

In the value-added model, as the name implies, the interpretation focuses on whether a particular school, class, or student made more—or less—gains than the average. When the students of a teacher or school score at a higher level than predicted, the inference is that that school added extra value. There was an extra benefit/gain for students. In some states and districts these school are given a special designation such as "high-performing" or "five star." In some districts these schools are being given more autonomy over curriculum, instruction, scheduling, and even staffing arrangements. Some states and districts are using these data to determine which teachers deserve a bonus or higher pay raises. In several states these data systems are now using the test scores of the students of past teacher education graduates as evidence to judge the effectiveness of your own teacher education program.

JOURNAL FOR REFLECTION 11.4

Policy makers are increasingly demanding that teacher accountabilty be judged using a value-added model. The result is procedures for teacher evaluation that include student test scores. In many states there now is a requirerment that as much as half of the weight in teacher evaluations be based in test scores. What are your thoughts about this? What other elements will you want to be incuded in your teacher evaluations?

MULTIPLE MEASURES. An important concern related to the making of evaluative judgments about students, schools, and teachers is that most of the time the summative decision is being made based on the score from a single measure. For example, a particular standardized test is selected. A policy board such as the state board of education or a committee of the legislature decides on the **cut score** (i.e., the test score that is high enough to be judged as a pass). Then the fate of all the test takers depends on whether they score above or below that score.

A significantly more responsible way is to use **multiple measures**. Any gate-keeping type of decision should be based on several measures and different types of measures, not a single test score. Policy makers at all levels should require multiple measures. This should also be a self-imposed requirement of you as a teacher. Any time you are making a summative judgment you should be basing it on multiple sources of data. Multiple measures should be used in evaluating schools and districts too. To determine how well a program is doing, it is important to use multiple assessments. For example, evaluators at an elementary school program should look beyond test scores and teacher qualifications. They could look more broadly, such as by gathering information about how well the students are performing in middle school. A parallel approach for a high school would be to examine how well their graduates do in the real world. Information about how many students successfully graduate without being retained could be another useful indicator. Having a broad array of types of data can enable teachers, schools, and even school districts to take stock and redirect efforts by using such strategies as changing the types of instruction being used and the types of learning being emphasized.

TWO MULTI-STATE TEST-DEVELOPING CONSORTIUMS. The first major topic introduced in this chapter was about standards for learning and especially the arrival of the Common Core State Standards. The next section addressed assessing and assessments. This section has been describing different aspects of accountability. Now we introduce one way that standards, assessment, and accountability are intersecting, which has major implications for schools, states, students, and for you as a teacher.

---

value-added model A statistical model that measures student growth over a period of time and evaluates the extent to which student performance is above or below what is expected.

cut score The score on a test that is the demarcation between passing and failing.

multiple measures Using more than one test or type of evidence for making a decision.

In 2011 the federal government, along with foundations such as the Gates Foundation, awarded $360 million to two consortia to develop new annual state tests for grades 3 through 8 and grade 11. The tests are to measure students' progress on a path toward college and/or career readiness. The tests are to have common scaling and cut points so that it will be possible to do cross-state comparisons. The tests will be administered using computers and both will include assessments of higher order thinking and problem solving.

States have a choice of joining both consortia as an observer or joining one with decision-making authority. More western and New England states have joined the *SMARTER Balanced Assessment Consortium*, while more eastern states are members of the other consortium, *Partnership for the Assessment of Readiness for College and Careers (PARCC)*. There are interesting differences in the approach each is taking to testing. For example, SMARTER Balanced is aiming to use "computer-adaptive" testing. In this approach the computer chooses the next test item based on the student's response to the last item. This approach is better for measuring individual student knowledge and skills. PARCC's plan is to have "through-course" tests and an end-of-year test. PARCC's system design emphasizes college and career preparation, along with considerations of participation in a global economy.

ARE WE MOVING TOWARD A NATIONAL CURRICULUM? A growing concern of some people is that the practice of many states using the same standardized test is just one step away from a national exam. This concern parallels the questioning of so many states adopting the Common Core State Standards. All of this could be leading to a national curriculum. Others believe that a national curriculum already exists and that national requirements are appropriate. Some point out that certain other countries, such as China and Japan, that have had national exams and national curricula are concerned about students in these systems not being creative problem solvers. These countries and other places such as Hong Kong are attempting to move toward curriculum and assessments that are more open-ended.

There already is one national test in the United States, the **National Assessment of Educational Progress (NAEP)**. This exam is administered each year to samples of fourth, eighth, and twelfth graders in a sample of schools in each state. The NAEP assesses student proficiencies in mathematics, reading, science, writing, the arts, civics, economics, geography, and U.S. history. One of its purposes is to make it possible for policy makers and educators to view the achievement of students nationally. Comparisons are made with student achievement in other countries, and most assuredly comparisons are also made from state to state in this country.

The NAEP is also designed to make inferences about student achievement within states. However, it is not designed to make judgments about individual students or schools. Until recently, although the NAEP has existed for several decades and its findings are very useful, states, school districts, and schools have been unwilling to participate in this testing program because of the mounting pressure and time demands of the many other required tests. Some states are now considering adopting NAEP instead of the traditional vendor-provided standardized tests.

Using Technology to Track Student Learning

A critical and often missing component of an effective lesson is addressing the individual needs of students. Inevitably, teachers are faced with a very diverse class of students in terms of their understanding of any particular concept. Now there are very user-friendly technology systems for tracking assessment information at all levels. Most schools and districts now have database systems that collect and report student assessment results in a format that is easy to access. For example, teachers can easily view up-to-the-minute records of their students' performance on assessment items specific to a standard, as well as their scores on recent district interim assessments and the state-mandated tests. The same system will have references to grade level and course-specific standards. There also will be templates for lessons that match the record of current levels of student performance. All of this information can then be used by the teacher to develop the next days' lessons and have added ideas for guiding discussions as well as examples of assessment items that are standards-based.

National Assessment of Educational Progress (NAEP) The national test system that samples students and schools within each state.

Technology tools now provide teachers, principals and others with immediate access to assessment information, which can be used to plan next steps in instruction.

Companies such as Northwest Evaluation Association (NWEA), Plato Learning, and Tungsten Learning have systems that allow teachers to regularly assess students against state and district standards. Some schools test their students monthly, using systems that make performance data available immediately to teachers. Sophisticated systems are able to track student growth from year to year (Borja, 2006). These assessments and their instantaneous feedback are helping teachers use data as the basis for intervening in the learning process in ways that assist students in improving their academic learning. These systems can also help in designing tests of other knowledge and skills such as critical thinking and problem solving that in the past were measured on the state tests only.

International Comparisons

When newspapers release the latest results on students' performance on international exams, educators and policy makers hold their breath. At best, U.S. students are usually around average, not in the top tier where we think we belong. Policy makers declare that our poor performance indicates that schools and teachers are not doing their job well. Educators wonder why students aren't performing at a competitive level. They want to know how other countries are doing so much better, deploying academicians to study their curricula, instructional strategies, and teachers with the goal of improving student performance in the next round of tests. Secretary of Education Arne Duncan has indicated that states should benchmark their test scores against international standards, which is one of the steps in the national standards project that most states have adopted.

Critics of testing and the use of test scores caution us against simplistic interpretations of the international test results. Some of them also worry that the average performance on test scores has become an excuse for companies moving jobs to other countries. This perspective was reflected in a commentary in *Education Week*. Iris C. Rotberg asks: "Is there a shortage of U.S. scientists, as some firms have reported, or is there a shortage at the wages the firms would prefer to pay? Are companies outsourcing jobs to China and India because Americans are not qualified for them, or because the firms can pay much lower wages to workers in these countries? . . . Is the underrepresentation of native-born U.S. students in some science, mathematics, and engineering Ph.D. programs the result of a failure of our education system, or of personal decisions made by students to select other fields—perhaps more lucrative fields like investment banking, law, or business?" (Rotberg, 2008).[3]

Not all U.S. students score at the average level. A sizable number are among the top tier of test performers in this international competition. There is an achievement gap in all countries based on the family's socioeconomic status, but it is especially severe in the United States. The problem is that vast numbers of U.S. students are performing at low levels (Cavanagh & Manzo, 2009). The president of Educational Testing Service, which produces assessment tests for elementary and secondary students as well as professional licensure tests, stated at a recent meeting that "Policymakers and reformers on both the right and left agree that achievement gaps based on race, ethnicity and class must close if the United States is to maintain its economic pre-eminence and live up to its founding principles" (Educational Testing Service, 2009).

In the next section, we review the most common international tests that are tracked by policy makers and education officials. They are often the subject of discussions in social settings as well as among your education colleagues. As you will see, performance of U.S. students varies by the test being used.

TRENDS IN INTERNATIONAL MATHEMATICS AND SCIENCE STUDY (TIMSS). TIMSS tests the math and science skills of students at the fourth and eighth grades. It is designed to measure students' knowledge of the math and science curriculum that they should be learning in

---

[3]Excerpt from "Quick Fixes, Test Scores, and the Global Economy," by Iris Rotberg, which first appeared in Education Week, June 11, 2008. Reprinted with permission from the author.

school. Both developing countries with fewer economic resources and industrialized countries such as the United States participate in this program.

One current effort is to link the state scores on NAEP with the TIMSS results. This will make possible several additional international comparisons. U.S. students did fairly well on the 2007 TIMSS, scoring above the average at both grade levels. Our fourth graders scored higher, on the average, than students in twenty-three countries and lower than those in eight countries on the mathematics exam and higher, on the average, than students in twenty-five countries and lower than those in four countries on the science exams. A similar pattern existed at the eighth-grade level, as shown in Figure 11.3. The top-performing countries at both grade levels are in Asia: Singapore, Chinese Taipei, Japan, Hong Kong, and Korea.

PROGRAMS IN INTERNATIONAL STUDENT ASSESSMENT (PISA). Every three years, the PISA tests math, science, or reading skills that students learn in and out of schools with more of a focus on the application of what they have learned to real-life situations. The test is taken by students who are fifteen years old in industrialized countries and other jurisdictions. The program is administered by the Organisation for Economic Co-operation and Development (PISA–OECD,

FIGURE 11.3   2007 TIMSS: Average science scale scores of eighth-grade students by country.

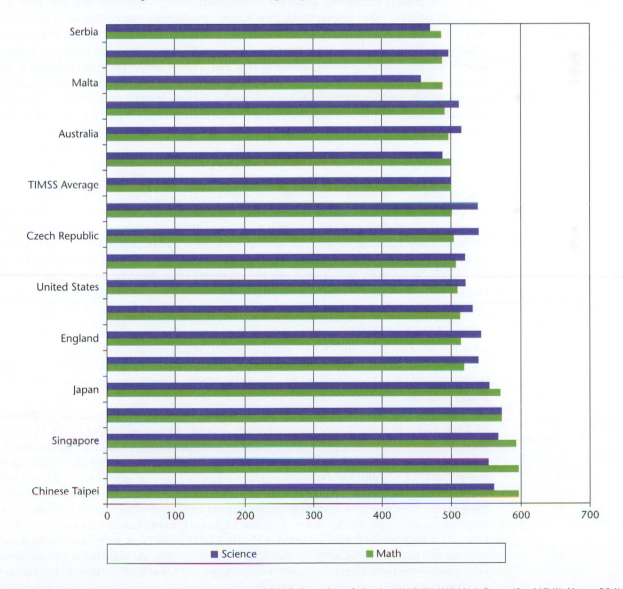

Source: Planty, M., Hussar, W., Snyder, T., Kena, G., KewalRamani, A., Kemp, J., et al. (2009). *The condition of education 2009* (NCES 2009-081, Indicators 15 and 16). Washington, DC: National Center for Education Statistics, Institute of Education Sciences, U.S. Department of Education.

n.d.), which facilitates discussions and projects of the "governments of countries committed to democracy and the market economy from around the world."

The analysis of PISA data indicates that gender, origin, language, and socioeconomic status are related to top performance on the test. However, some countries have a much lower percentage of students performing at low levels regardless of the students' gender, origin, language, or socioeconomic status, which suggests that all students can achieve at high levels. Across countries, girls outperform boys in reading; boys perform somewhat better than girls in mathematics; and both genders perform about the same in science (OECD, 2008). U.S. students do not perform well on the PISA, being below the average of students in the thirty-two industrialized countries that participated. On the science assessment, U.S. students were ranked twenty-one of thirty-two participating countries. Students from Finland, Canada, and Japan were the top performers in science. In mathematics, U.S. students ranked twenty-six of thirty-two countries, with students from Finland, Korea, and the Netherlands scoring the highest (OECD, 2008).

PROGRESS IN INTERNATIONAL READING STUDY (PIRLS). The PIRLS tests the literary and informational skills of fourth graders on a five-year cycle. Forty-eight countries are participating in the 2011 cycle, up from forty countries that participated in the 2006 administration. In 2006 the Russian Federation, Hong Kong, and Singapore were the top-performing countries, but U.S. fourth graders scored well above the international average, with only nine countries scoring better. As on most other reading tests, girls scored significantly higher than boys in all but two countries. Other findings included the confirmation of a positive relationship between reading achievement and parents engaging their children in early literacy activities before they started to school, including reading books, telling stories, and singing songs. Other contributors to higher scores were the presence of children's books in the home, parents who were frequent readers, and parents who had a favorable attitude toward reading. Across countries, 40 percent of the students reported reading for fun on a daily basis; another 28 percent read for fun at least weekly (Mullis, Martin, Kennedy, & Foy, 2007).

Testing Challenges

The nationwide movement toward standards, performance, and a variety of assessment strategies is a good one, especially for teachers and their students. The goals of teaching and learning are made clear, which then makes it easier for teachers to know what to teach and how. Having standards certainly aids students in understanding what is most important to learn. And having standards helps teachers, schools, school districts, and states in determining the learning outcomes that should be assessed. Still, as with any education initiative, the standards movement has had a number of unintended consequences that have provided challenges for schools and teachers. You are likely to face some of these challenges when you begin to teach.

HIGH-STAKES TESTING. As the pressure for accountability has intensified, the federal government has mandated that students be tested annually. At a minimum student test results for each school are compiled by each state and reported to the public. Schools are named and ranked in the newspaper, and sharp questions are asked about those schools that are not meeting adequate yearly progress.

Testing becomes high stakes when the assignment of rewards and sanctions are determined by a test score. In a few states, high-performing schools receive additional funds. In some districts, teachers and/or principals receive salary bonuses if test scores improve. Some states provide rewards to high-performing schools, but much more likely is some sort of sanctioning of the low-performing schools. On the positive side, some states provide assistance to schools that are "in need of improvement" by assigning an experienced master teacher or principal to work with the schools. In other cases, principals are reassigned and entire school staffs replaced. In some states an entire school district that is designated low performing can be taken over by the state. Criteria for high-stakes testing are listed in Figure 11.4. As you know, tests can be high stakes for students and their future as well. For example, most states now use standardized exams to determine graduation from high school, and most colleges used standardized tests to help determine admission. Further examination about the pros and cons of high-stakes testing are debated in the "Who Is Right?" feature.

FIGURE 11.4	Criteria for High-Stakes Testing Practices

The American Education Research Association's (AERA) *Public Policy Statement on High-Stakes Testing in PreK–12 Education,* adopted in July 2000, provides twelve criteria, based on solid research, that state education leaders, local school leaders, parents, and others can used to assess the assessments. AERA states that every high-stakes testing program should ensure:

- Protection against high-stakes decisions based on a single test
- Adequate resources and opportunity to learn
- Validation for each separate intended use
- Full disclosure of likely negative consequences of high-stakes testing programs
- Alignment between the test and the curriculum
- Validity of passing scores and achievement levels
- Opportunities for meaningful remediation for examinees who fail high-stakes tests
- Appropriate attention to language differences among examinees
- Appropriate attention to students with disabilities
- Careful adherence to explicit rules for determining which students are to be tested
- Sufficient reliability for each intended use
- Ongoing evaluation of intended and unintended effects of high-stakes testing.

For more information, visit AERA's website at www.aera.net.

PRESSURES TO CHEAT. In high-stakes conditions, teachers and principals invest concerted effort in helping their students do well on the tests. In nearly every school and classroom, teachers stop their regular instruction for weeks or more to help students prepare for the test. These preparations can be as practical as practicing how to bubble-in answers to multiple-choice questions and reviewing what has been taught during the year. The problem arises when teachers—and in some cases principals—help their students cheat. Cheating ranges from telling students how to answer specific test items to teachers, principals, and school district administrators actually changing students' responses on individual tests, as happened several years back in Atlanta, Georgia. In other instances, schools have encouraged some students, such as those with learning disabilities, to stay at home on the day of testing.

TEACHING TO THE TEST. Any single test is bound to sample a very limited part of what students learn. Also, state tests might have little overlap with the various sets of content standards and the emphasis in district curriculum materials. Time spent on preparing for high-stakes tests reduces the time available to teach related material and other subjects, such as the performing arts, that are not being tested or for which the stakes are not as high. Teaching to the test also often means that the development of critical thinking and higher order thinking skills is neglected. If the entire district curriculum is aligned with state standards, then those students whose instruction covers more of the standards should perform better on the tests.

A related issue has to do with balancing the time teachers spend on topics that are likely to be on the test versus instructional time spent on the rest of the curriculum. About two-thirds of teachers indicate that their instruction is too focused on content that will be tested, to the detriment of covering other material. An immediate impact from implementation of NCLB was pressure on teachers to teach to the test. One survey at the time (Olson, 2001) found almost 80 percent of teachers reporting that they were teaching test-taking skills to students. Two experienced teachers provide their views about teaching to the test in the "Who Is Right?" feature.

Other data refute the claim that teachers spend less time teaching content than in the past, at least at the elementary school level. Lorin W. Anderson at the University of South Carolina reviewed this claim by teachers by comparing their concerns with conditions in the 1970s and

WHO IS RIGHT?

DOES PREPPING FOR HIGH-STAKES TESTS INTERFERE WITH TEACHING?

States require students to pass a test in order to graduate or to receive a diploma. Some states offer different types of diplomas based on how well a student performs on a test. This type of testing is called high-stakes testing and it poses many questions. What does it mean to be "educated" in a high-stakes testing environment? How reasonable is it to be making gate-keeping decisions based on a single test? What student and teacher behaviors do high-stakes testing encourage? The following debate raises these types of questions.

YES

Nancy Buell teaches fourth grade at the Lincoln School in Brookline, Massachusetts. She has taught for thirty-two years and serves on the state Board of Education's Advisory Council for Mathematics and Science.

As I watch my students debate how much taller fourth graders are than first graders, I am struck by their intuitive use of significant features of the data. As in:

> Lee: Fourth graders are 10 inches taller because the tallest fourth grader is 64 inches and the tallest first grader is 54 inches.
>
> Tamara: A first grader is about 5 inches shorter. I found the middle height for each and just subtracted. The middle for the fourth graders is 57 inches and the middle for the first graders is between 51 inches and 52 inches.
>
> Dana: 5 inches or 4 inches, because the most common height for first graders is 53 inches and the most common height for fourth graders is 58 inches or 57 inches.

These students are exploring ideas involving maximum, median, and mode. They are considering what features to use to tell what is typical of the two groups so they can be compared. Students support their ideas with information in the data itself. They are developing ways to think about data that will lead to a deep understanding of more formal statistics.

The rich mathematical discussions in my class are an outgrowth of my participation in professional development that focused on inquiry-based teaching and the big ideas we should be teaching.

But since high-stakes testing arrived, professional development meetings often focus on how to improve test scores, not on how to improve learning.

Teaching that concentrates on improving test scores is very limited—by the nature of both testing and teaching. Testing involves sampling student knowledge. It is fragmented and only examines learning outcomes. It seldom looks at how well a student understands complex ideas.

A typical test item might give students a set of data and ask for the median. Students would not be asked to select the appropriate statistic to address a question and justify their choice. Yet knowing how to find the median, without knowing when to use it, is useless, except on tests.

If we teach facts and procedures likely to be on the test, without the deeper understanding behind them, we shortchange our students. We must not limit what we teach to what will be tested.

Many teachers feel pressured to choose teaching techniques that help with testing more than learning. They're urged to spend more time on information that mimics test items.

Students should, of course, know how to answer multiple choice, short answer, and open response questions, but teaching these test-taking skills should not be confused with teaching a subject. Some teachers spend a day a week using test-like items, not to sample what children know, but to try to teach the content.

Teaching should build on what students already know and help them develop a rich web of interconnected ideas. Real learning involves inquiry, hypothesis testing, exploration, and reflection.

Teaching to the test will not help my students think about how to use features of data sets to answer real questions. Teaching to the test is not teaching.

NO

Charlotte Crawford teaches fourth grade at Coteau-Bayou Blue School in Houma, Louisiana. A twenty-seven-year teaching veteran, she helped set the cut scores for her state's high-stakes fourth-grade test and now serves on a state panel for staff development.

Preparing students to take high-stakes tests does not interfere with teaching. It enhances teaching. When used properly, high-stakes tests can focus attention on weaknesses in the curriculum and in the teaching of it, as well as furnish an assessment of student progress. Once identified, student weak areas can be strengthened.

When the new high-stakes tests and revised curriculum were introduced in Louisiana, along with new accountability standards, many teachers were bewildered at the prospect of being held accountable for teaching a new curriculum without being told how to teach it.

Yet many of these teachers were also open to the new ideas and began working to find ways to implement them. They were aided by funding from the state for additional reading materials and in-service training.

(continued)

(continued)

Teachers often feel overwhelmed by the changes involved in our state's rigorous new standards, but many Louisiana educators are beginning to take ownership of their new curriculum. They're growing confident when making scope and sequence decisions. They're consistently reevaluating what they have taught, and how they have taught it, so they can do better next time.

These educators are revamping their classroom activities and their teacher-made tests to match them more closely to the format and tone of the state-mandated tests.

Helping students become familiar with the state-mandated test formats, by using them in the classroom, prevents having to spend valuable class time to "practice" for the high-stakes tests.

Learners, meanwhile, are reaping the benefits of having teachers who are determined that their students will be as prepared as possible to relate the skills they learn in school to real-life situations. They're becoming lifelong learners, besides performing well on standardized tests.

Some educators complain that they must "teach to the test."

But others consider this to be a weak objection since the state tests focus on information and skills students are expected to know at certain points in their schooling.

These educators say the curriculum objectives covered by the state tests should be taught before the tests are given, with the remaining objectives covered afterwards. This is a very workable arrangement when high-stakes tests are given early in the spring.

To be sure, some Louisiana educators are still resisting the changes that come with the state tests.

But most realize this is an idea whose time has come.

In 1998, my school helped pilot the fourth-grade language arts test. I was nervous about how my students would fare. When they finished, I asked for reactions.

Much to my surprise, students calmly informed me that the state test was "kind of hard, kind of easy, kind of fun."

That day, my students unwittingly reassured me that learners who are prepared for high-stakes tests need not fear them.

WHAT IS YOUR PERSPECTIVE ON THIS ISSUE?

Source: "Does Prepping for High-Stakes Tests Interfere with Teaching?" *NEA Today* (January 2001), p. 11. Reprinted by permission of the National Education Association. Also search www.neatoday.org for more high stakes stories.

1980s before testing became so prevalent. He found that elementary school teachers have always spent much more time teaching English language arts than any other subject. The amount of time teaching mathematics has remained constant; attention to science and social studies has always been limited (Anderson, 2009).

ONE-SIZE-FITS-ALL. Another critical issue related to the heavy focus on testing is the assumption that the same test is appropriate for all students, schools, and states. Historically, heavy emphasis has been placed on the importance of addressing individual differences and emphasizing that all students do not develop at the same rate. Now policy makers are mandating that one test be given to all students at a certain grade level at a specified time—in other words, "one-size-fits-all." No matter how unique individuals might be, all are to take the same relatively narrow test, and major decisions about individual students and/or schools are based on the test results. Students who are economically advantaged in suburban schools take the same test that low-income urban students take. This practice undermines the credibility of the test and its results clearly disadvantage some students and schools.

INCREASED TEACHER BURDEN. As exciting and important as the new approaches to assessment are, one of the downsides is the increased work for teachers. Developing more authentic tasks takes more time than does constructing multiple-choice and true/false test items. Deriving scoring devices for authentic tasks is added work too. Holistic scoring entails first developing a scoring rubric and then examining each student's response in sufficient detail to determine a total score.

The load on teachers becomes even heavier in secondary schools because each teacher has contact with more students. One of the important solutions to the risk of an increased burden is for teachers within a school or school district to collaborate in the development of assessment tasks. There also is national sharing of assessment items through discipline-based professional associations and various chat rooms on the Web. A related key for individual teachers is to keep in mind that many of the traditional activities that teachers have been doing to assess student learning, such as noting their performance in laboratories and in the field, have become more legitimate with the move to authentic assessment.

Equity Within Accountability

One positive outcome of NCLB was the mandate to disaggregate the data. Schools, districts, and states could no longer ignore the various "subgroups" in schools. Schools, teachers, districts, and states have to break out the performance of students by socioeconomic status, ethnicity, race, first language, disability, migrant status, and gender. In fact, performance by students from each of these groups must be reported on school and district annual report cards. Thus, teachers and school administrators are held responsible for helping all students learn as reflected on the single assessment—the state content test. Meeting this goal is more difficult in some settings than others, especially when resources are limited or nonexistent, both for providing students with the facilities and support necessary to promote learning at a high level and for providing teachers the necessary professional development. Nevertheless, it is a goal worth achieving.

A continuing point of criticism about these traditional tests is that they do not address or accommodate the diversity of students in today's classrooms. Each student brings a unique set of background experiences, prior knowledge, and cultural perspectives to learning. Asking all students to show what they know on a narrow standardized test is a very real problem.

The gap between the test scores of white students and most students of color remains wide, as does the gap between students from low-income and higher income families. NAEP data on achievement levels for mathematics show an achievement gap between white and African American, Hispanic, and American Indian students of more than 21 percentage points at the fourth grade and more than 27 percentage points by the eighth grade (see Figure 11.5). The gap grows even wider by the twelfth grade. Ironically, many researchers have found that state tests are much better determiners of the family's socioeconomic level or parents' education than of academic ability. Students who perform at low levels on these tests are disproportionately from low-income families.

FIGURE 11.5 Performance on NAEP mathematics tests by race and ethnicity.

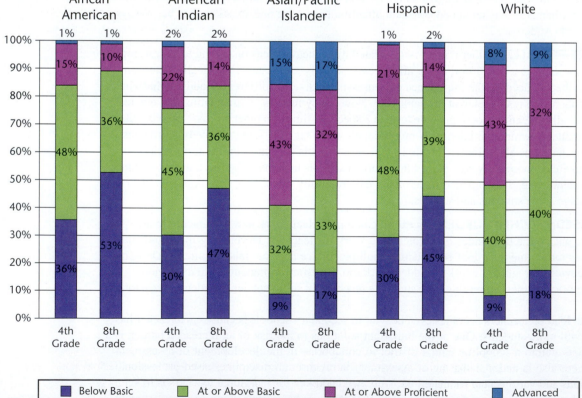

Source: National Assessment of Educational Progress of the National Center for Education Statistics of the U.S. Department of Education, Washington, DC.

Supporters of NCLB argue that African American and Hispanic students will perform at a more equal level over time because schools will be able to raise their test scores by hiring only **highly qualified teachers**, teaching reading more effectively, basing instruction on what is known to work from "scientifically based research," and allowing parents to remove their children from low-performing schools and place them in higher performing schools. Critics also believe that all students can learn and that highly qualified teachers are essential. They also question the ability of schools, especially in high-poverty areas, to raise test scores without intensive professional development of teachers, reduction of student-to-teacher ratios, greater involvement of parents, and more stimulating curriculum and instruction—all areas that require financial resources that are not usually available in communities with the greatest need.

Researchers are finding that multiple assessments demonstrate that students from different cultural groups perform at higher levels on different assessments. Some students who do poorly on standardized tests effectively demonstrate their knowledge and skills on other assessments based on their interests or real-life settings. The teacher's assessment of prior knowledge and development of instruction with those data in mind are particularly helpful in improving the academic achievement of low-income students and students of color (Shepard et al., 2007).

highly qualified teachers Teachers who are licensed without a provision and have passed a standardized content test in the subject they teach or for the grades they teach.

SUMMARY

EDUCATION STANDARDS

- The focus of standards today is on what students know and are able to do.
- Most states have adopted and are now engaged in implementing the Common Core State Standards (CCSS).

ASSESSING STUDENT LEARNING

- Once the standards of learning have been set, teachers, as well as curriculum developers and policy makers, want to know how well students are doing.
- Assessing is more than testing. It entails developing and using good measures along with making interpretations and judgments about what has been accomplished and what needs to be done next.
- Formative evaluation for teachers means using data about student learning to plan for and adjust instruction.
- Summative evaluation entails making concluding decisions about whether or not students have learned the standard.

- Using multiple measures to make judgments about the amount of student learning is very important for teachers when making high-stakes decisions.
- The Performance Assessment for California Teachers (PACT) and Teacher Work Sample (TWS) are examples of authentic performance assessments that allow teacher candidates to demonstrate their ability to develop and implement instruction that is based on effective assessments.

ACCOUNTABILITY

- The pressures on states, school districts, schools, and teachers have never been higher. Everyone wants to see higher levels of student learning.
- Two tools are being used to hold educators accountable: standards and testing.
- The stakes of testing can be high for states, school districts, schools, teachers, and students.
- Every effort must be taken to ensure that the tests are of high quality and that high-stakes decisions are based on multiple sources of evidence.

DISCUSSION STARTERS

1. Standards-based education is now the paradigm that teachers are expected to use. Thinking about your own education at school and college, how would you describe the integration of standards in the curriculum and instruction? Were you made aware of the standards that you were supposed to be meeting? Did the standards support higher order thinking or were they more factual in nature?

2. Assessing has been described as being more than testing. In adopting this perspective, what do you see as the major challenges for you as a teacher? How will you know if

your students are engaged in assessing, rather than simply testing?

3. Standards-based education calls for the use of performance assessments in determining whether students meet standards. How could student portfolios be used to show what students have learned? What problems might such assessments cause?

4. In the name of accountability students, regardless of their ability or socioeconomic status, are expected to master a specific set of learning standards, such as the Common Core State Standards, before obtaining a diploma. In what cases, if any, do you think students should be exempt from testing requirements for graduation?

SCHOOL-BASED OBSERVATIONS

1. Talk with teachers in the schools that you are observing and review the school district's website to identify the standards that teachers are supposed to use. During your observations, record the evidence that convinces you that standards are (or are not) integrated into classroom instruction. What evidence indicates that the students understand the standards and how they will be assessed?

2. Ask several teachers about what they do to help students prepare for the state testing. Ask specifically about their role during the administration of the tests. Develop a list of strategies you may use to help students in preparing for testing. Develop a second list of the procedures teacher can, and cannot, use during testing.

3. One of the distinguishing characteristics of standards-based education is that students, regardless of grade level, are supposed to be able to describe the expectations for learning (standards and benchmarks). Interview some students and see how they describe what they are doing in a particular lesson. Do they tend to describe the instructional activity ("We are studying the Civil War"), or do they describe what they are supposed to be learning ("We are learning about the economic factors that led to the Civil War")? Can they describe how much they have learned?

PORTFOLIO DEVELOPMENT

1. Authentic assessments attempt to provide students with opportunities to show what they know and can do within a real-world setting. Go to the website for the Common Core State Standards, www.corestandards.org. Go to the standards for English Language Arts & Literacy in History/ Social Studies, Science, and Technical Subjects. Within these standards find the grade level you plan to teach, select one of the standards, and develop an authentic assessment you could use with your students. Keep in mind that the CCSS expect *all* teachers, regardless of grade level or subject, to "integrate" ELA into their instruction and assessments.

2. Rubrics are used to assess performance in many classrooms. To gain practice in developing and using a rubric, design one that could be used to assess the level at which you have learned and are able to demonstrate an important component of the information presented in this chapter. Ask several of your classmates to self-assess their learning extent using your rubric. Note the questions and suggestions they offer that would help you refine your rubric.

WEB SOLUTIONS

Today's classrooms will have a wide range of students. They bring to class different abilities to learn. They represent different ethnicities, family social-economic situations, and current capabilities to communicate using the English language arts (ELA). Some students will have IEPs and others will be identified as LEPs (limited English proficiency) or ELL (English-language

learners). Teachers need to understand the types of accommodations that can, and cannot, be provided to this diverse set of students. Conduct a Web search related to making accommodations in your classroom. Instead of doing this activity from the point of view of finding out what is legal, take a standards-based approach: What can I find out about accommodations that will help all my students learn? A hint: Start the search at your state's education department's website.

www.ccsso.org The website of the Council of Chief State School Officers, which is the professional association for state superintendents of education, provides links to each state, where it is possible to explore that state's standards and information about test results.

www2.edtrust.org/edtrust The Education Trust's website provides data, policies, and recommendations related to academic achievement with an emphasis on students who have not been served well in the educational system.

www.nces.ed.gov/nationsreportcard The National Assessment of Educational Progress website provides information about the national testing programs and national report card.

www.relearning.org This site for Relearning by Design provides information on standards and authentic assessment and is hosted by the Coalition for Curriculum and Assessment (CCA).

www.nctm.org Information about the National Council of Teachers of Mathematics and its standards can be found at this website.

MyEducationLab™

Go to the topic **Assessment, Standards, and Accountability** in the MyEducationLab (**www.myeducationlab.com**) for *Foundations of American Education: Becoming Effective Teachers in Challenging Times, 16e,* where you can:

- Find learning outcomes for **Assessment, Standards, and Accountability**, along with the national standards that connect to these outcomes.
- Complete Assignments and Activities that can help you more deeply understand the chapter content.
- Apply and practice your understanding of the core teaching skills identified in the chapter with the Building Teaching Skills and Dispositions learning units.
- Access video clips of CCSSO National Teachers of the Year award winners responding to the question, "Why Do I Teach?" in the Teacher Talk section.
- Create, update, and share quality lesson plans with the Lesson Plan Builder.

- Access state licensure test requirements, overviews of what tests cover, and sample test items in the Certification and Licensure section.
- Access current state and national standards in the Licensure and Standards section.
- Learn how to create a high-quality teaching portfolio in the Preparing a Portfolio section.
- Access tips, advice, and other information on resume writing and interviewing, your first year of teaching, and law and public policies in the Beginning Your Career section.
- Check your comprehension of the content covered in the chapter with the Study Plan. Here you will be able to take a chapter pretest, receive feedback on your answers, and then access personalized Review, Practice, and Enrichment exercises to enhance your understanding of chapter content. After you complete the exercises, take a posttest to confirm your comprehension.

Designing Programs for Learners in Challenging Times: Curriculum and Instruction

LEARNING OUTCOMES

After reading and studying this chapter, you should be able to:

1. Analyze the effects of different influences on the selection and design of curricula in your state. (InTASC 10: Leadership and Collaboration)

2. Describe and compare different curriculum designs. (InTASC 4: Content Knowledge; InTASC 6: Assessment; InTASC 7: Planning for Instruction; InTASC 8: Instructional Strategies)

3. Identify different curriculum evaluation approaches and studies across multiple levels including classrooms, schools, districts, nations, and globally. (InTASC 9: Professional Learning and Ethical Practice)

4. Identify and apply different types and forms of learning objectives to instruction. (InTASC 7: Planning for Instruction; InTASC 8: Instructional Strategies)

5. Describe and analyze characteristics of direct and indirect teaching strategies. (InTASC 8: Instructional Strategies)

6. Compare the learning needs of different types of learners and the relative effectiveness of different teaching strategies. (InTASC 1: Learner Development; InTASC 2: Learning Differences)

EDUCATION in the NEWS

BIPARTISAN GROUP BACKS COMMON SCHOOL CURRICULUM

By SAM DILLON

A bipartisan group of educators and business and labor leaders announced on Monday their support for a common curriculum that states could adopt for public schools across the nation.

The proposal, if it gains traction, would go beyond the common academic standards in English and mathematics that about forty states adopted last year, by providing specific guidelines for schools and teachers about what should be taught in each grade.

For decades, similar calls for common academic standards, curricular materials, and tests for use nationwide—the educational model used by many countries in Europe and Asia—have been beaten back by believers in America's tradition of local control of schools.

But last year's successful standards-writing movement was a departure, leaving the outlook for this proposal uncertain.

"We are well aware that this will require a sea change in the way that education in America is structured," says a statement the group published on Monday. But, it adds, attaining the goals laid out in the new common core standards "requires a clear road map in the form of rich, common curriculum content."

"By 'curriculum' we mean a coherent, sequential set of guidelines in the core academic disciplines, specifying the content knowledge and skills that all students are expected to learn," the statement said. "We do not mean performance standards, textbook offerings, daily lesson plans or rigid pedagogical prescriptions."

The curricular guides "would account for about 50 to 60 percent of a school's available academic time," the statement says, with the rest added by local communities, districts, and states.

The three-page statement was published on the website of the Albert Shanker Institute, a research group associated with the American Federation of Teachers.

Signers include Randi Weingarten, president of the federation, and prominent Democrats, including Richard W. Riley, secretary of education under President Bill Clinton.

Several Republicans also signed, including former Gov. Tom Kean of New Jersey; Chester E. Finn Jr., an assistant secretary of education under President Ronald Reagan; and Susan B. Neuman, an assistant secretary of education under President George W. Bush.

Ms. Weingarten, Dr. Neuman, and several other signatories announced the initiative in a conference call on Monday.

"The new standards are good, but standards are merely a guidepost," Dr. Neuman said. A common curriculum would serve as a resource that teachers could use as they build their daily lessons, she said. "This doesn't mean all teachers will be teaching the same thing. It means that there will be a shared background of knowledge that teachers could draw on."

Last year's common-standards effort began as an initiative of the National Governors Association. The Obama administration endorsed it, and many states adopted the standards quickly because doing so conferred an advantage in the White House's $4 billion Race to the Top grant competition. The administration is now financing the development of tests aligned with the common standards.

A number of prominent Republicans, including Representative John Kline of Minnesota, chairman of the House Education Committee, believe in local control, are suspicious of the standards movement, and seem likely to oppose the common-curriculum proposal.

"The administration went from encouraging states to carry out common standards to funding the creation of the tests," Mr. Kline said in a recent interview. "I and my colleagues object vehemently. We do not want to politicize the curriculum."

On the other hand, many corporate executives concerned about the nation's competitiveness endorsed the standards movement and are likely to support a common curriculum, several signers of the new statement said.

"There were a number of Republicans who agreed to the common standards," Mr. Kean said, "and this is the next logical step beyond that."

Deborah Wince-Smith, who was an assistant commerce secretary under the first President George Bush and is the president of the private, nonpartisan Council on Competitiveness, said, "Our K–12 system is not up to snuff."

"As a nation, we need the human capital to compete," she said, "so there's a consensus that setting a high standard and pushing a curriculum that prepares our children for a world of complexity is very important."

QUESTIONS FOR REFLECTION

1. A school curriculum specifies what students will learn across different grade levels. Even though there are now national and state standards that guide decisions about what students should know and be able to do, these standards can be interpreted very differently. This common curriculum proposal calls for the development of "a coherent, sequential set of guidelines in the core academic disciplines, specifying the content knowledge and skills that all students are expected to learn." As a future teacher, would you support the development of a common curriculum across all school districts? Or, do you think that providing such specificity limits your professional judgment? Provide reasons for your answer.

2. Think about your own school experiences in reading and mathematics. Did teachers across the different grade levels teach the same content or did the content vary? In what ways do you think a common school curriculum might help students learn, and in what ways might a common school curriculum fall short of meeting the individual needs of students?

Source: *New York Times*, March 7, 2011. Reprinted with permission.

GO TO ⇢
More information about school curriculum throughout history can be found in Chapters 2 and 3.

curriculum An environment created by the interaction of all of the elements that support learning: the content taught, the materials selected, the teaching strategies used, the learning activities in which children engage, and the way a school is organized.

WHAT IS CURRICULUM AND HOW DOES IT DEVELOP?

Curriculum relates to anything and everything that supports learning. As such, it is a general term that is used in many different ways depending on the circumstances in which it is used. For example, in textbook selection committees, curriculum implies the scope of learning content and the grade-level sequence in which that content will be taught. In a school improvement meeting, curriculum might imply the types of competencies that students should be able to master at a certain grade level. At a daily teacher planning session, curriculum can mean that type of teaching that teachers use to help students learn.

Curriculum also includes the informal and less obvious parts of the school day such as mottos or slogans on school walls, the types of student work displayed in classrooms, and even the way desks are arranged in classrooms. Ultimately, **curriculum** is the total environment that is created by the interaction of all of the elements that support learning: the learning standards, the content taught, the materials selected, the teaching strategies used, the learning activities in which children engage, and the way a school is organized.

You might be wondering how a curriculum environment develops. Clearly, the curriculum of a school comes together over time and results from many different influences and decisions made by state officials, school administrators, teachers, and the community.

FIGURE 12.1   **The many influences on curriculum.**

Religious
beliefs

Mass
media

Textbook
publishers

Political
climate

Local test
results

Educational
research

School
policies

Teachers'
strengths and
interests

School–community
harmony or discord

Values

Traditions

Beliefs

Court
decisions

Community
pressures

Assumptions

**THE
CURRICULUM**

School culture

Resources
and
materials

Teacher
organizations

Teachers' role
with staff

Teachers' role
in school

Learners'
social status

National
reports

Enrollment
shifts

Students'
needs and
interests

National
test norms

Students' personal and
academic background

Accreditation
agencies

Legislation

Curriculum theorists
and researchers

Source: Parkay, Forrest W.; Stanford, Beverly Hardcastle, *Becoming a teacher*, 8th Ed., © 2010. Reprinted and Electronically reproduced by permission of Pearson Education, Inc., Upper Saddle River, New Jersey.

The Many Influences on Curriculum

As befits our democracy, many people and groups have a say in selecting the curriculum for public schools. Figure 12.1 illustrates the many different actors and forces involved in determining the curriculum. Around the outer circle is the array of forces and interest groups that represent the macro view. The middle ring summarizes many of the local factors and conditions that influence curriculum decisions. The inner ring shows the school context and influences. The product of this array of forces and interests is the curriculum that is selected and implemented in each classroom.

LARGE-SCALE INFLUENCES ON CURRICULUM. The primary effect of the various elements that form the outer ring in Figure 12.1 is to influence what will be common for curriculum in all states and school districts. Court cases, state and federal legislation, teaching and content standards developed by national professional organizations, common core standards and national assessments, and educational research, as well as textbook publishers, determine much of what will be taught and learned in all schools and classrooms. In fact, this set of influences works against local control of schools. Instead of local control, there is a growing movement toward the establishment of a statewide and even national curriculum.

Another macro-level influence on the curriculum is the various interest groups, such as teacher and administrator organizations, political parties, and religious advocacy groups. **Interest groups** are informal and formal organizations of individuals who hold a common interest and shared agenda in regard to a particular topic or policy. These groups pay close attention to the work of committees charged with developing standards, curriculum guides, and test items. Each group is likely to have its own unique perspective and agenda. For example, teacher associations tend to resist any accountability moves that would link student performance on tests with the identity of the teachers who taught them. Many religious groups advocate that their positions, such as intelligent design, be included and that contrary positions, such as evolution, receive less emphasis.

MyEducationLab™

Visit the MyEducationLab for *Foundations of American Education* to enhance your understanding of chapter concepts with a personalized *Study Plan.* You'll also have the opportunity to hone your teaching skills through video- and case-based *Assignments and Activities and Building Teaching Skills and Dispositions* lessons.

 Two educators talk about the influence of student motivation and state standards on their curriculum decisions in this **video.**

interest groups Informal and formal organizations of individuals who hold a common interest and shared agenda in regard to a particular topic or policy.

Student participation in the cocurriculum and extra-curriculum such as involvement with school plays, as shown here, can provide important opportunities for learning, as well as encouragement for staying in school.

The various accrediting bodies, such as the Southern Association of Colleges and Schools (SACS) and the New England Association of Schools and Colleges (NEASC), influence the curriculum through the standards they apply to all schools they accredit. These standards in some ways set a common curriculum for all schools. For example, school accrediting bodies require each school to have a **school improvement process (SIP)**. A SIP usually is written by a school committee and the principal during the spring of the year. The plans include analyses of data about student learning, reports about the year's efforts to improve the school, and specific plans for the next year. Key expectations for these plans include analyses of student success on state tests such as those in mathematics, literacy, and, in some states, writing. The accrediting body expects improved student performance on state tests; a direct consequence of this expectation is that each school and teacher is expected to provide curriculum and instruction designed to enhance student achievement on the prescribed test. In ways such as this, a common curriculum is defined and implemented for all accredited schools.

COMMUNITY INFLUENCES ON CURRICULUM. At the local school district level, many additional factors influence the curriculum. Clearly, community interests and priorities are an influence. If the community values high school football and marching band, these two program areas will be an integral part of the cocurriculum. The personal background of students also influences the curriculum. For example, in many school districts a significant proportion of the students are English-language learners. English-language learners (ELLs) are students whose first language is not English and who therefore are learning English at the same time they are learning the content specified in the curriculum standards.

The curriculum influences of this ELL population are many. This population creates demand for teachers who speak their native languages. ELL students also need more assistance in learning academic subjects because they are learning English at the same time. One likely consequence is that ELL students do less well on high-stakes tests, especially if they are expected to read and respond in English. The overall result is that the curriculum in the classroom needs to be adjusted in response to these influences.

SCHOOL INFLUENCES ON CURRICULUM.. The inner circle of Figure 12.1 summarizes influences that an individual school can have on the curriculum. Assumptions about learning, for example, make a significant difference in which subjects are emphasized, what is taught, and how. For example, if teachers in a particular school truly believe that all students can learn, then the curriculum is organized and delivered in ways that support all students learning: Students are grouped according to their needs; regular classrooms include students with special needs; and most group activities are organized to take advantage of the diverse talents and interests of students rather than having like students grouped together. In comparison, if teachers in a particular school believe that some of the children cannot learn, then "those" children are given less opportunity and more limited access to the curriculum. The result confirms the teacher's beliefs: Those students do less well.

In addition to teachers' beliefs about students' learning, available resources can also influence curriculum. If a school has a great deal of instructional technology resources teachers will tend to integrate technology in their teaching. Students benefit from the sophistication that is available when having easy access to national and international resources. If a school has limited technology, students will tend to rely on textbooks as their primary source of knowledge.

In spite of the many influences on curriculum selection, its development, and its implementation, it is clear that in the end the curriculum is delivered in classrooms. This has two important implications. The first is that the role of the teacher in implementing today's curriculum is enormous. Although teachers have relatively little say in curriculum selection, they have the primary responsibility for helping students learn and achieve the desired outcomes. The second

school improvement process (SIP) A plan for future action that results from a school leadership team review of current successes and needs.

implication is that teachers have a plethora of curriculum resources to work with: curriculum guides, teacher-training sessions, and textbooks as well as standards and benchmarks. All of these curriculum resources assist teachers in understanding what they should be teaching, and help them see what came before and what will happen next year with the students they teach this year.

Developing Curriculum

Those who are engaged in developing curriculum bring their own views and beliefs to the effort. For example, people who believe that students can be trusted will press for activities that allow for student initiative and open-ended explorations, whereas curriculum developers who believe that students will make a mess and break manipulative materials will develop activities that rely more on the teacher and are more structured for the students.

Beliefs about student learning and effective teaching come into play as well. Some theorists believe that what is to be learned should be broken down into subparts and each of these taught separately and sequentially, whereas others advocate for presenting the whole and letting the students "figure it out." Consider how these different perspectives can influence the teaching of addition. Should students be taught a single way to do addition and be expected to always do it that way, or should they be encouraged to do addition in different ways, as long as they can explain how they obtained the correct answer? There is not a single correct answer to any of these questions; the best answer is a matter of perspective. Depending on the perspectives of the developers, the curricula they produce can be quite different. Three key questions must be addressed for each curriculum development initiative:

1. What should be taught?
2. Who should decide?
3. How will it be taught?

Think about each of these questions. Determining what will be taught has serious implications for the learner, the teacher, and society. Should the content prepare students for the world of work? Should it contribute to the development of "good" citizens? To what extent should the selected content prepare the student to learn advanced content?

Who should make these decisions—teachers, experts, politicians, or citizens? Should we ask community members for their input? Should we bring in experts from different disciplines to help decide the content? Should we include principals and teachers? The more people involved in the decision, the more differences that will arise and this leads to another difficulty—reaching agreement.

Question 3 brings up another new set of challenges: How will the curriculum be taught? Each teacher will have her or his own views about which way is best. What is to be done when the curriculum developers and teachers have different views? Answering each of these three overriding questions begins with philosophical assumptions and beliefs about what is important for society and individuals, as well as understanding the discipline. What should happen during instruction also requires careful deliberation.

STEPS IN THE CURRICULUM DEVELOPMENT PROCESS. A good place to start understanding how the curriculum of a school develops is to consider some general steps in which the design of a curriculum is made explicit in the form of outcomes, learning objectives, teaching strategies, and assessment. Over the next several pages, we describe these steps in the curriculum development process along with implications for classrooms, teachers, and their students.

Curriculum theorists of the past identified a logical sequence of steps when developing new curriculum, as shown in Table 12.1 (Taba, 1962; Tyler, 1950). The steps may seem overly simple, logical, and sequential; however, they continue to be as essential as they were in the past. The development of any curriculum should incorporate each of these steps. When one or more of these steps is neglected, teachers and their students struggle to fill in the missing pieces.

The seven steps to curriculum development outlined in Table 12.1 make the work look easy. However, the reality is that developing curriculum is hard work and involves answering a number of very important value-laden questions that will be addressed either explicitly or implicitly. As each step is completed, theses value-laden questions must be reasked and reanswered:

1. To what extent should the learning outcomes support preserving a democratic society?

TABLE 12.1

Basic Steps of the Curriculum Development Process

STEP	PURPOSE	EXAMPLE ACTIVITY
1	Determine what needs to be learned and why.	Survey parents or business leaders about what future citizens/workers will need to know; or identify the big ideas in a discipline.
2	Describe the desired learning outcome(s).	Use standards and benchmarks to write learning objectives for each grade level.
3	Select the specific content.	Relate what is expected in the standards with the important topics in the discipline.
4	Organize the content.	Design a topic and objectives sequence so that what is learned first builds toward what will be learned later.
5	Select the learning activities.	Identify specific lesson activities, tasks, and materials that will engage the learner and be congruent with the core ideas of the discipline.
6	Sequence the learning activities into a whole.	Sequence the learning from the early grades through high school and organize the topics within each year so that they are coherent and rigorous, with objectives that can be learned.
7	Evaluate the effectiveness of the materials, instruction, and student learning.	Collect evidence from teachers about instruction and from students about learning outcomes.

Source: Basked on Taba, 1962; Tyler, 1950.

2. Which outcomes are important for the individual learner's self-worth?
3. Is the curriculum biased in some way against certain individuals or groups?
4. Will the curriculum be available to all? Or is it too expensive, too hard to teach, or does it have components that are inaccessible to some?
5. Is it built around the essential center of the discipline or is it composed of peripheral and isolated elements?

You will likely be asked to participate in one or more steps in the curriculum process. When you do, keep in mind these challenging, value-laden questions and carefully determine your personal point of view. This will help you, as a curriculum committee member, recognize how the ideas of other committee members resemble or contradict your own. This clarity will assist you and others in the process of coming to a consensus. For, as challenging as these questions are, coming to a consensus about their answers is both critical and at the core of the curriculum development process.

Curriculum Designs

Over time, a number of curriculum designs have been identified by comparing the way curricula are structured. Each curriculum design has particular strengths and weaknesses, and each has different implications for teachers. Some designs are typically found in U.S. schools, whereas others are more apt to be seen in schools in other countries. Each design is based on assumptions about what is important for students to learn as well as particular philosophies about teaching and how students learn best. Summaries of common designs are presented in Table 12.2.

TYPES OF CURRICULUM. The earliest curriculum design in American schools was the *subject-centered curriculum*, which focused on content disciplines. There were only three subjects or disciplines: religion, Latin, and Greek. The only teaching style was lecture. Students were expected to learn—in other words, memorize—the content. Surprisingly, the subject-centered curriculum is still the most common curriculum design in the United States, albeit the subject areas have changed as has the number of subject areas taught. Schools now include mathematics, reading, literature, social studies, science, physical education, and so forth.

TABLE 12.2

Varied Curriculum Designs and Implications for Teachers and Students

CURRICULUM DESIGN NAME	DESIGN	ROLE OF THE TEACHER	ROLE OF THE STUDENT	RELATIONSHIP TO STANDARDS
Subject centered	Selected subjects are identified. Organization of content is tight and narrow, and the sequence is specified.	Primary strategy is lecture. Teachers are expected to teach subject matter according to the prescribed sequence and use the prescribed materials.	Students learn the content. The narrow focus allows students to learn more content in less time.	Standards for each subject are specified and taught across grade levels
Theme or big idea centered	A number of subjects are integrated into a theme; themes are examined for big ideas drawn from each subject area and these big ideas are emphasized.	Teachers may lecture. Focus is on the broad generalizations instead of depth in a particular content.	Students are expected to develop a broad understanding across a number of content areas. Students may not understand the broad themes and may instead simply memorize them.	Standards are selected from different subject areas and linked to the big ideas.
Spiral	The curriculum is viewed across the P–12 continuum, key content is taught more than once. In an early grade, a particular topic is introduced in a general way. Several years later, the topic is taught with more depth.	Teachers use a variety of teaching strategies and must have sufficient depth of knowledge to offer more content depth with each cycle in the spiral. Teachers make a concerted effort to add depth to student understanding with each subsequent pass.	Students are expected to learn the content at the depth taught over time. The risk is that they will not retain the knowledge and understanding developed in the previous cycle.	Standards from varied subject areas are linked to the different topics.
Common Core	Focuses on key concepts and skills all students should know.	Rather than discrete disciplines, integrated blocks of content may be offered. Core content is taught in relation to daily life and topics. Typically, teachers teach as interdisciplinary teams.	Students learn through the study of interdisciplinary topics and daily life examples. Accompanying this learning is learning ideas in related subjects.	Core standards are identified and emphasized.
Mastery	Levels of learning that all students are to reach are identified. Students are given as much time as they need and a variety of activities to aid their reaching mastery.	Teachers provide a variety of activities and ways for students to reach mastery. Teachers also must be skilled at assessing what students do and do not know.	Once students have met the criterion for a particular learning objective, they move on to addressing the next learning target.	Benchmarks for standards are identified and emphasized.
Problem based	Students work in groups and are presented with a problem. Solving the problem requires that they learn new content.	The teacher is a guide and coach rather than a dispenser of content. Only when the need arises does the teacher present content.	Students are expected to be able to work cooperatively as members of problem-solving teams. They must be self-starters and motivated to study the problem.	Standards drawn from varied subject areas are linked to the different problems.
Standards based	The standards of learning become the content.	Student learning is placed at the center rather than the topic or problem. Teachers use a wide variety of instructional and assessment strategies, all of which are aimed at assisting students in constructing their own understanding.	Students know the standards and specific benchmarks they are studying. They self-assess in relation to these.	The standards of learning become the focus, content, and organization for the topic curriculum.

GO TO ⋯➔

More information about subject-centered curriculum in the past can be found in Chapter 2.

Because of the explosion in the number of subject areas taught, there has been a move toward integrating subjects into themes or big ideas. *Themed curriculum* design focuses on teaching generalizations or big ideas that underlie various subjects. **Big ideas** such as change, cause and effect, symmetry, and interaction are studied through the perspectives of different disciplines. So, students might study change as it looks in chemistry and change as it looks in social science. Students might study symmetry through the lens of mathematics and through the lens of biology. A *spiral curriculum* is closely related to a themed curriculum in that it also focuses on big ideas. The main difference is that in a spiral curriculum the big ideas or cross-disciplinary concepts are taught over and over again across grade levels. Over time, the ideas are taught in an increasingly more abstract manner and students' understandings about these big ideas deepen.

Another curriculum design that has developed in response to the explosion of subjects that need to be taught is the core curriculum. A *common core curriculum* focuses on key concepts and skills that are extremely important to learning and further understanding. So, key ideas and concepts are selected that must be mastered by all students. Once students show mastery of the core, they are permitted to investigate other related ideas and deepen their understanding. A *mastery curriculum* is closely related to the core curriculum design, but a mastery curriculum focuses more on very specific content and skills that must be mastered a certain way. For example, students in a mastery curriculum setting would be required to answer very specific mathematics questions (like adding two-digit numbers with no regrouping) on a test.

Curriculum designs must also take into account the importance of motivating students and making them more interested in their learning. Instead of focusing only on abstract content, newer curriculum designs focus on current problems and issues. As teacher lecture decreases in popularity, the increased use of learning activities is one example of ways to increase student motivation. The problem-based curriculum design emphasizes the importance of students' motivation. A *problem-based curriculum* focuses more on authentic, contemporary problems, rather than abstract ideas or skills that are under investigation in the world of work. Students are invited to tackle a problem with the intent of helping society find a solution. Ideas and skills are learned as students investigate the problem.

Although all of today's curricula are in some way standards based, some school districts have adopted a total *standards-based curriculum* design. By total standards based, we mean that the standards themselves are the key components of the curriculum design. The standards statements are used directly with no intervening organizational overlay. In some ways this makes the standards more prominent, but it also can chop up curricular content in artificial ways.

COLLEGE-READY OR CAREER-READY CURRICULUM. The overall goal of a curriculum also influences the structure and components of that curriculum. Currently, there is a national debate about the proper overall goal of a public school curriculum. Should elementary and secondary schools prepare students for a career, should they emphasize preparation for college, or should they provide separate tracks for either college or a career and allow students and parent to choose? Today, U.S. schools focus heavily on a wide array of important outcomes drawn from many different areas: academic subject matter content, social education, physical education, vocational education, art, music, and theater—and the list goes on. Some question that this list of goals is too broad and propose that public schools should provide families and students alternatives that are more focused and could be selected earlier (Achieve, Inc., 2012).

One example of this call to provide a more focused alternative comes from the Association for Career and Technical Education (ACTE). The ACTE has called for a clearer distinction between college-ready and career-ready curriculum (ACTE, 2010). The ACTE contends that career readiness involves three major skill areas:

1. Core academic skills and the ability to apply those skills to concrete situations in order to function in the workplace and in routine daily activities;
2. Employable skills (such as critical thinking and responsibility) that are essential in any career area; and
3. Technical, job-specific skills related to a specific career pathway.[1]

big ideas The organization of content around major themes and principles.

---

[1]*What is career ready?* (2010) Reprinted by permission of Association for Career and Technical Education (ACTE).

Examining curricula in other countries can broaden our perspective about determining the proper goal for curriculum in the United States. Germany provides a curriculum that distinguishes a career-ready and college-ready curriculum much earlier. Up until the sixth grade, the German curriculum focuses on the three Rs, special education, and socialization. Extracurricular activities, from music to sports, are the responsibility of the communities, churches, and amateur athletic associations. Vocational education is the primary responsibility of business and industry. Health and safety are the responsibility of health maintenance organizations, government, churches, private institutions, and the home.

After the sixth grade, German students elect, by choice and examination, their main school: *Hauptschule* (about a third of the students), the *Realschule* (about one-fourth of the students), or the *Gymnasium* (about one-third of the students). Whereas the *Hauptschule* and *Realschule* prepare students for vocational education and apprenticeship programs, the *Gymnasium* is the academic school for the development of the mind and preparation for college attendance for professional careers.

Currently, the U.S. debate about college ready versus career ready continues. Most schools tend to offer one general curriculum for all students and aspire to have all students college ready. There is some movement toward providing an alternative career-ready curriculum in magnet schools and in charter schools.

COCURRICULUM AND EXTRA-CURRICULUM. When most teachers, parents, and the public think about curriculum, they think about the core academic subjects of language arts, science, mathematics, and social studies. However, school includes other subjects, such as world languages, physical education, and—especially in secondary schools—athletics, band, drama, choir, and many clubs. These other subjects, after-school activities, and clubs make up the **co-curriculum**, which sometimes is called the **extra-curriculum**. In many ways, it can be argued that the cocurriculum is of equal importance to the basic subject areas. The cocurriculum is especially important in high schools. Unfortunately, during times of budget cuts, various pieces of the cocurriculum are targeted. For example, driver education used to be a free component of the cocurriculum in most public high schools. Now, if it is offered through the school at all, a fee is required. This is unfortunate because for many students participation in the cocurriculum is a prime reason for staying in school. Cocurriculum teachers are excited about their programs and spend long hours after school, at night, and on weekends working with students to publish the student newspaper or yearbook or to prepare the team or band for the next competition. These highly dedicated teachers and their programs provide students with experiences and skills they will carry with them throughout their adult lives.

THE HIDDEN CURRICULUM. As the name implies, the hidden curriculum is not readily seen. In fact, it is invisible! At the same time it is a very critical and significant component of teaching and schools. The hidden curriculum is experienced through the messages that are sent to students about expectations and about what is important to succeeding with each teacher and across the school. The hidden curriculum can be detected through examining the meaning behind the rules of the classroom and school, noting what is celebrated, what is deemed to be important, and what is rewarded, punished, and ignored. For example, are academic accomplishments celebrated as well as athletic? Are students with special needs included or isolated? Do all students have equal access to algebra and advanced placement classes or just certain groups of students?

When a teacher emphasizes neatness, or speaking one at a time, or is open to divergent student talk, messages are made clear about what is important for students to do and not do. Social behavior, dress codes, and rules about how to behave in the corridors become important ways that students learn about expectations. Whatever teachers value about learning, the subject matter, and the uniqueness of their students become elements of the hidden curriculum. Students learn what is important or not important through this invisible curriculum.

cocurriculum/ extra-curriculum School activities and programs, before, during, and after regular school class hours, that enrich the curriculum and provide extended opportunities for student participation.

Special interest groups are a powerful influence on the selection of curriculum.

Curriculum Resources

The curriculum delivered in each classroom has a rich and complex foundation. The tangible items for the teacher and the students include curriculum guides, textbooks, student workbooks, available technologies, and manipulative materials and lab supplies. However, the curriculum is more than simply printed documents and hands-on manipulatives. It also encompasses schoolwide resources and special-purpose facilities such as the media/resource center, playground and athletic facilities, cafeteria, auditorium, band practice hall, and arts and crafts classroom. Each of these curriculum resources is important for teachers to understand, carefully examine, and use wisely.

STANDARDS. Of all the curriculum resources available to teachers, the most important are the learning standards. The reason learning standards are so important is that they drive the focus for learning outcomes. These learning outcomes then drive instruction and assessment. For most subjects there are at least three sources of standards: (1) those published by the professional associations such as the National Council of Teachers of English or the National Council of Teachers of Mathematics, (2) those developed within each state and available through each state's department of education website, and recently (3) **common core standards** for English/language arts and mathematics developed by a consortium of professional groups and adopted by most states. These common core state standards contain benchmarks for each standard across grade levels K–12. Common core state standards for science have also been collaboratively developed by the National Science Teachers Association, the National Research Council, the American Association for the Advancement of Science, and the school standards group ACHIEVE. Many states adopted these science standards when they were in their draft form. Common core standards are currently under development for social studies, and it is likely that most states will adopt these as well. Although learning standards determine learning outcomes, they do not describe how to teach to the standard; teachers will need to turn to the other curriculum materials and resources to plan instruction.

ASSESSMENTS. As a student, how often have you thought about asking or heard someone else ask the teacher, "Will this be on the test?" An important indicator of which elements of the curriculum are seen as most important is what is actually tested. With the continuing emphasis on high-stakes testing, teachers and their students must be knowledgeable about what is tested. A core assumption in some school districts and states—such as Texas or Florida, both of which have "no pass/no play" rules—is that students will work harder to learn the material if they are tested and experience the direct consequences of the results.

For you as a teacher, understanding what is on the high-stakes test is important for at least two reasons: (1) Your students will be highly motivated to learn what will be on the test, and (2) you will quickly discover that for your grade level or subject, some critical topics are not covered on the high-stakes test. Both of these reasons illustrate an important aspect of the curriculum: The curriculum is not just what is in the textbook, nor just what is in the classroom lessons; it also is embedded in the expectations for learning and related assessments.

TEXTBOOKS. For teachers, one of the primary sources of information about the curriculum is the commercially published textbook. Textbook publishers employ expert author teams and invest large sums of money to provide students and teachers with up-to-date and well-designed materials. In U.S. schools, for most subjects, textbook packages provide the bulk of the content, lesson objectives, and audiovisual resources, as well as student assignments. Most textbooks have an accompanying instructor's guide that provides the teacher with additional background subject information, lesson plans, suggestions for extensions and special assignments, and test items. A number of additional resources exist for teachers who use textbooks in the major subject areas such as science, mathematics, and English. These additional resources include training workshops, access to supporting websites, and perhaps videos of classroom lessons in which the textbook is used.

CURRICULUM GUIDES AND COURSE SYLLABI. Another important curriculum resource consists of support materials for the teacher prepared by the school district and state. These district-developed support materials might include syllabi and curriculum guides for each subject area and grade level. Syllabi and curriculum guides draw the connections between what is to be taught at each grade level and the expectations for student learning in state and district standards. These guides also provide a vertical view of how the subject is to be covered from grade level

common core standards A set of standards in mathematics and English/language arts that have been developed across a number of states in an effort to have a shared learning focus for the nation.

to grade level. This is important because students experience school one year at a time, but their learning needs to be cumulative across the years. Teachers need to see how what they are teaching this year relates to what students learned last year and what they will be expected to learn next year. District and state curriculum guides are very useful for teachers as they plan daily lessons, especially when information is provided about the specific benchmarks for student learning that must be addressed and assessed at each grade level and for each subject.

CURRICULUM FRAMEWORKS. In some states such as California and Massachusetts, instead of having curriculum guides, the state curriculum is organized around the big ideas for each subject area and published as *curriculum frameworks*. For example, in describing the nature of science in California's Curriculum Framework, three broad assumptions are stated:

1. Change occurs in observable patterns that can be extended by logic to predict what will happen next.
2. Anyone can observe something and apply logic.
3. Scientific discoveries are replicable.[2]

The Pennsylvania Curriculum Framework differs from the California Currriculum Framework in that it specifies what is to be taught for each subject in the curriculum and it includes Big Ideas, Concepts, Competencies, Essential Questions, Vocabulary, and Exemplars aligned to Standards and Assessments. Each of these components of the framework are defined as follows:

- **Big Ideas:** Declarative statements that describe concepts that cut across grade levels. Big Ideas provide a focus for teaching specific content for all students.
- **Concepts:** Describe what students should know and understand (key knowledge) specific to each grade level.
- **Competencies:** Describe what students should be able to do (key skills) specific to each grade level.
- **Essential Questions:** Questions that are specifically linked to the Big Ideas. These questions guide student inquiry, promote critical thinking, and assist in learning transfer.
- **Vocabulary:** Key words, terms, and definitons that relate to the big ideas and concepts specific to each subject area and grade level.
- **Examplars**: Performance assessments and examples of student work that meet the criteria for a specific task. Exemplars can be thought of as concrete examples of students' understanding of the Big Ideas, concepts and competencies (Pennsylvania Department of Education, 2012).

CURRICULUM PACKAGES. Some school districts develop their own set of materials that should be used to deliver the district curriculum and place these materials into a total package. The materials provided in these district-developed curriculum packages differ greatly. Some districts simply provide a set of core standards and grade-level benchmarks for learning organized by grade level. Other districts include specific lessons and teaching materials. In Prince George's County teachers are provided a curriculum package that includes a progress guide, related lessons to be taught each day, the corresponding lessons in the student and teacher books, and the focus objective(s) from the state curriculum. In theory, the Prince George's County curriculum package is only a guide for instruction and teachers can choose between specific activities to meet the needs of the students. The important thing to remember about curriculum packages is that you as a future teacher may be provided a great deal of detail about the way your school district wishes to implement its curriculum.

JOURNAL FOR REFLECTION 12.1

Use Table 12.2 to think about a subject area that you plan to teach. Which curriculum design(s) did you experience when you were in school learning this subject? What do you see as the strengths and weaknesses of that design(s)?

[2]California Department of Education. (2009). Curriculum Framework and Evaluation Criteria Committee Guidelines for the Science Framework for California Public Schools, Kindergarten through Grade Twelve. Reprinted by permission.

SELECTION AND MANAGEMENT OF CURRICULUM

Clearly, many levels of interest and many perspectives directly influence the selection of a curriculum. This large and diverse set of influences also affects the processes for designing curricula. Without some sort of control mechanisms or an organized authority, it would be impossible for each teacher to choose what to teach and how to teach it in ways that satisfy a majority of the influences. Without some sort of overall authority, there would be no continuity in the curriculum from teacher to teacher, grade level to grade level, or school to school.

In the United States, the legal responsibility for schools and, therefore, for the curriculum, lies with each state. In large part, state legislatures and state boards of education determine the curriculum. Additional structures exist to set and support the curriculum at the school district level. However, even with the centralizing roles of the state and district, schools and teachers retain a number of important roles and responsibilities.

The State's Role in Managing Curriculum

Because each state has the primary responsibility for setting the curriculum for schools within that state, teachers need to know how this is done and what they can do to contribute to the process. The states have assumed two major areas of responsibility for curricula. The first is establishing what students are expected to learn, and the second is determining the instructional materials that can be used.

THE STATE SETS STANDARDS. The statements of expectation for student learning are determined at the state level. The typical process is to establish a statewide committee comprising teachers, school administrators, higher education faculty, and state policy makers, such as a representative state board of education member or a legislator, such as chair of the House Education Committee. Standards committees with similar composition are established for each content area. Each committee reviews the national curriculum standards for its content area. These committees hold public hearings around their state so that the various interest groups (remember the different circles in Figure 12.1) can present their positions. When each of these committees completes its work, members recommend a set of state standards to the state board of education. Once the state board approves them, all districts, schools, and classrooms in the state are required to teach to those standards.

THE STATE MAY CHOOSE CURRICULUM MATERIALS. There is some variation from state to state in the extent of state-level involvement in selecting curriculum materials. The main area of involvement is in selecting textbooks. States have either open adoption or state adoption policies. An **open adoption policy** permits local school districts to select curriculum materials and textbooks based on their own specific needs. A **state adoption policy** requires school districts to purchase curriculum materials and textbooks based on a list approved by the state. Some states (e.g., Texas and California) have formal state-level processes for adopting textbooks; these are state adoptions. In these states, a committee is charged with reviewing the various available textbooks and establishing an adoption list. School districts and schools then select the textbooks they will use from this list of approved materials. If schools wish to select curriculum materials from the adoption list, they receive state funding to support the purchase. If a district or school decides to select materials not on the state's adoption list, it will have to pay the full cost of those materials. In open states (e.g., Illinois and Nevada) the adoption of textbooks is a matter of local choice; that is, the state leaves responsibility for the selection of curriculum materials to each school district, even when there is state funding for their purchase.

The District's Role in Managing Curriculum

Regardless of whether a school district is subject to a state adoption or open adoption policy, major curriculum-related tasks and responsibilities are assumed by each school district. These often include textbook selection or review of a list of state-adopted texts as well as provision of curriculum specialists.

DISTRICT TEXTBOOK SELECTION. One obvious district task is to select the textbooks and related curriculum materials to be purchased and used within the district. A curriculum committee

---

open adoption policy
A state textbook adoption policy that allows each school district the autonomy to review and select whichever textbooks it chooses.

state adoption policy
A state textbook adoption policy that limits financial support and selections to those that are included on a state-approved list.

is established that includes teachers, principals, parents, and perhaps higher education faculty. The committee reviews the current status of the subject area, including how well students are doing on tests. The committee examines available text and materials options, and then recommends to the district superintendent and school board which materials should be purchased. Teacher participation on these committees is important since they are the ones required to use these textbooks and other curriculum materials.

DISTRICT OFFICE CURRICULUM SPECIALISTS. School districts also employ a number of professional specialists whose responsibility is to see that each curriculum area is supported and that teachers are prepared to teach the chosen curriculum. One important role is that of curriculum coordinator/liaison/specialist. Typically, earlier in their careers these individuals were master teachers. Now their role is to guide and support teachers and champion their subject areas. In smaller districts, an individual might have responsibility for a number of content areas, such as language arts and social studies. Larger school districts have curriculum specialists assigned for at least each of the "big four" areas: reading, mathematics, science, and social studies. There are also specialists for special education, bilingual/ELL education, compensatory education, and other need areas.

In addition to the subject-specific specialists, most school district office staffs include **generalists**. Instead of being experts in a particular content area, these individuals are experts in helping teachers learn and apply different teaching strategies, assessment procedures, and use of technology. District office generalists include:

- Experts in general teaching strategies, such as cooperative grouping and assessment methods, that can be used in most content areas
- Induction specialists, who are responsible for offering workshops, mentoring, and other support for beginning teachers
- Staff developers, who coordinate and present teacher in-service workshops, including those offered district-wide at the beginning of each school year
- **Teachers on special assignment (TOSAs)**, expert teachers who leave the classroom for one to three years to participate in a curriculum review, including selection of new materials, and to support teachers during the implementation phase.

Local Schools' Role in Managing the Curriculum

Even with all of the activities done at the national, state, and district levels, each school has major tasks and responsibilities for managing the curriculum. It still is up to each school and teacher to bring the curriculum alive in each and every classroom. Each teacher must do her or his part by being informed about the state standards and the benchmarks for his or her students' grade level. Teachers must also use the materials and strategies that will help all students learn. In middle and secondary schools, an important curriculum management structure is the department. When teachers for one subject are organized as a department, they can easily seek ideas from colleagues who know the content, and they can coordinate across grade levels to determine what is taught in each course. The same ends are obtained in elementary schools by having grade-level teams and in larger schools by establishing content-specific curriculum committees.

EVALUATING CURRICULA

How do we know if the selected and implemented curriculum is making any difference? The obvious answer is that without systematic and well-organized evaluation studies, we cannot know. Evaluation of the curriculum has to be done carefully and at all levels, from teachers in classrooms, to school- and district-level evaluation, to statewide evaluation. In addition, national and international curriculum evaluation studies are conducted.

Curriculum evaluation is primarily based on what occurs in the classroom. Until the curriculum is implemented and student learning is assessed, direct evidence of effectiveness cannot be obtained. The first evaluation step is done by each teacher who implements the curriculum. Teachers' informal assessments of how easy it is to teach, the effectiveness of textbooks and materials, and the amount of student interest and motivation are early indicators of how effective any

generalists Professional educators housed in the district office who provide classroom support across a number of content areas.

teachers on special assignment (TOSAs) Teachers who are assigned to the district office for a limited time in order to accomplish a specified curriculum support task.

curriculum will be. Another early indicator is teacher assessments of the extent of student learning. Through informal teacher assessments and the formal testing done in the classroom, teachers and curriculum specialists can obtain early evidence of how well a curriculum is working.

Researchers and curriculum evaluators also focus on classrooms to determine curriculum effectiveness. Whereas the teacher examines only her or his classroom, researchers systematically document use of the curriculum and related student learning in a large number of classrooms. For example, in a study of teaching and learning mathematics, researchers conducted ongoing observations of classrooms and examined the achievement of 2,533 students in ten middle schools taught by thirty-three teachers over a two-year period. Rural, small community, suburban, and urban schools were chosen to reflect the diversity of the U.S. school population. For this study, researchers focused on classrooms that exhibited a standards-based learning environment, which was defined as an environment in which students make conjectures about mathematical ideas and explain their responses or strategies. Results indicated that when NCTM content is supported by a standards-based learning environment there was a significant impact on students' achievement. Specifically, this study provides evidence that a standards-based learning environment has a positive impact on students' achievement on performance assessments that measure mathematical reasoning, problem solving, and communications skills, but only when such an environment is coupled with best practices outlined in NCTM curriculum (Tarr et. al., 2008).

National Curriculum Evaluation Studies

Two important national approaches to curriculum evaluation are the National Assessment of Educational Progress (NAEP) and the testing at most grade levels mandated in NCLB. These approaches reflect two very different philosophies about curriculum evaluation. In NAEP a random sample of students is selected from across each state. The sample is drawn from all students in the state, but does not include all of the students in one school or from one classroom. Therefore, the findings from NAEP indicate how well students are doing in reading, science, or mathematics by state. NAEP cannot make judgments about the effectiveness of particular schools or school districts.

In NCLB, Congress has mandated that all public school students be tested each year in grades 3 through 8 and in one year of high school. Each state can select the test, but the major content areas must be tested. These data will allow the labeling of schools and districts, even ranking each in terms of student performance on the selected tests.

District and State Curriculum Evaluation Practices

In today's high-stakes testing environment, school districts and states are focusing on student performance on standardized tests. Schools and school districts are often judged and labeled based on overall test score results. The No Child Left Behind (NCLB) Act mandates that the test scores for each school be published in the local newspaper. In extreme situations, when test scores are at the bottom year in and year out (such as in Hartford, Connecticut; Compton and Oakland, California; Lawrence, Massachusetts; and Trenton, New Jersey) the state may "take over" operation of the school district. The results of these state takeovers are mixed, at best. In some districts, such as Hartford Public Schools, student test scores have gone up. In other districts, they have remained low.

Looking at Data from Local Assessments

Ultimately, curriculum evaluation starts and ends with local schools. Even though it is important to evaluate curriculum by making comparisons across districts and across states, the bottom line to knowing if a curriculum makes a difference belongs to teachers and administrators who examine data from individual schools and classrooms. It is the teachers who are on the front line of the curriculum because they personally deliver instruction and see the effects of curricular materials on a daily basis.

That is why the practice of teachers and administrators regularly examining assessment results is so important. By so doing, trends can be determined concerning what aspects of the curriculum are working and what aspects of the curriculum are not working. The following are some examples of the types of reflective practices that teachers can employ to keep the curriculum current:

- Regularly examine your students' performance on tests and classroom assessments. Note and record any trends that you see in the performance of your students. Use this information to determine if there is something in the curriculum materials that is not working.
- Meet with other teachers in your grade level or subject area. Share your notes and reflections about your students' performance. Ask other teachers to do the same and then identify the strengths and weaknesses in the curriculum practices that you are using. Some schools provide time for such meetings but even if your school does not, try to initiate this practice on your own.
- Provide summaries of your meetings to your principal or assistant principal and make suggestions based on your local assessments.
- Actively participate in setting school improvement goals each year by showing strengths and weaknesses drawn from your own examination of classroom tests and assessments.

INSTRUCTION: THE TEACHING SIDE OF CURRICULUM

Once the influences and committees have converged and a curriculum has been designed, teachers have the responsibility to bring it to life in classrooms. This is extremely important work. If teachers fail in the delivery of the curriculum, students cannot learn material required in the stated benchmarks and standards. One dire consequence of students not learning is failure—failure for the students and the teacher as well as failure for the school and community that had supported development of the curriculum.

Just like curriculum development, instruction begins with what students need to learn. Teachers need to think about student learning in relation to the outcomes for each lesson and how these lessons will unfold across days and weeks. Based on the expectations for learning and the characteristics and interests of the students, particular teaching strategies are selected. Another important influence on instruction is the school-wide effort to improve learning that includes components that are expected to be implemented in all classrooms. For example, all elementary teachers in a school or school district may be expected to use the same instructional approach when teaching reading.

Instructional Objectives for Student Learning

Standards and benchmarks are descriptions of expected student learning that represent relatively long-term steps. Teachers and their students need more focused and short-term statements in order to focus on individual lessons. The instructional tools for creating this focus are called **objectives**; these are the statements of expected student learning for each lesson. The difference between objectives and standards is the size and scope of learning described. Standards represent the broad learning outcomes that students are expected to achieve across several years. Benchmarks address parts of standards, but they still are quite broad and can describe learning accomplishments that can take months. Instructional objectives address the daily learning expectations for students; they help both teachers and students identify the focus for the day's learning. Daily lessons, classroom activities, and quizzes need to be clearly tied to the important expectations for learning stated in the standards and benchmarks. Contrary to what some teachers practice, objectives for instruction should be known and understood by both the teacher and the students.

One of the important elements of writing objectives is having an understanding of their purpose. When teacher education candidates first write objectives, they frequently write them as input statements, which describe what the teacher will do and what will happen in the lesson. The following objective is one example: "The students will be assigned to groups and they will read the chapter in the text." Such an input objective is no longer acceptable because it fails to clarify what students need to learn.

Objectives should be written as output statements, which describe what students are to learn as a result of experiencing the lesson or lessons. For example, "As a result of this lesson, students will be able to compare the reasoning behind the economic and political arguments for and against withdrawing troops from Afghanistan."

 Watch this **video** to listen to a teacher discuss her philosophy of teaching and how it influences her curricular decisions in preschool.

objectives Statements of learning outcomes for a lesson or several weeks of lessons.

FIGURE 12.2   Two emphases to teacher thinking: which should be first?

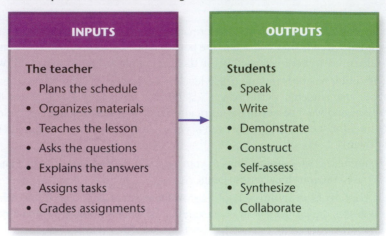

INPUTS	OUTPUTS
The teacher	**Students**
• Plans the schedule	• Speak
• Organizes materials	• Write
• Teaches the lesson	• Demonstrate
• Asks the questions	• Construct
• Explains the answers	• Self-assess
• Assigns tasks	• Synthesize
• Grades assignments	• Collaborate

behavioral objectives Expectations for student learning that are stated in terms of observable behaviors.

task analysis The process of systematically identifying and sequencing the small learnings that must be accomplished in order for students to demonstrate mastery of a particular task or benchmark.

Analysis of the various skills that students are to learn is an important early step in planning instruction.

The difference between thinking in terms of inputs and outputs is crucial to becoming a successful teacher (see Figure 12.2). The natural tendency of teachers and professors is to think in terms of "what I am teaching." They may even say things such as "I teach English." In the past, this way of thinking about instruction was acceptable; however, in today's schools teachers need to be thinking and talking in terms of what their students are learning. "My students have been learning about the Civil War and the terrible cost of life that occurred." Fortunately, the use of instructional objectives can help teachers make this important shift in thinking.

Types of Instructional Objectives

As an additional support for teachers, scholars have identified different ways of writing learning outcomes. The development and refinement of these typologies has occurred during the last thirty to forty years. Each type of instructional objective addresses a different kind of learning, and assessing student learning requires different methods, depending on the type of objective. For most lessons, teachers will likely have at least two kinds of learning objectives, which means that careful thought has to be given to how the learning outcomes will be assessed.

BEHAVIORAL OBJECTIVES. As the name implies, **behavioral objectives** focus on an observable performance or task. In fact, the proponents of behavioral objectives advocate that if the learning cannot be described in terms of observable behaviors, then there is no way to tell if learning took place. From this point of view, student learning is to be described in terms of behaviors. This means that in behavioral objectives, the verb, or *action word*, is key. The objective needs to focus on a behavior that can be perceived, such as to *observe, classify, name, list,* or *interpret,* and not on words, such as *appreciate* and *understand*.

Behavioral objectives are a useful instructional tool for teachers in planning, teaching, and assessing student learning. A useful approach to identifying student behaviors is to perform a **task analysis**, which is the systematic identification of the key skills that someone needs to be able to do to complete a task or satisfy a benchmark. The typical steps for a task analysis include the following:

- Examine the related standards and benchmarks in order to identify the observable skills that students must demonstrate.
- Identify the small learning steps that in combination would result in students being able to do the whole task.
- Describe each step in terms of behaviors that can be observed.
- Determine the sequence in which students will need to learn the behaviors.

- Write behavioral objectives for the most central and important of these behaviors.
- Be attentive as the lesson unfolds to facilitating students' acquisition of those behaviors.
- Create an end-of-lesson, or end-of-unit, test that focuses on whether the students can exhibit the behaviors described in the behavioral objectives.

This approach to thinking about learning and teaching has been criticized as too linear and rational. Still, it is a useful way for teachers and students to maintain a focus on the key elements of a lesson. The real risk with behavioral objectives is in having too many objectives and/or having objectives that are so specific and narrow that they are trivial. It is one thing to write a behavioral objective that describes what both hands are doing when a person is touch typing, but it's another thing—and on a much more micro level of task analysis—to have an individual objective for the placement of each finger on the keyboard.

LEARNING OBJECTIVES FOR THE COGNITIVE DOMAIN. In 1956 a significant book was published titled *Taxonomy of Educational Objectives: The Classification of Educational Goals Handbook 1: Cognitive Domain*. The lead author of this book was a scholar named Benjamin Bloom (1956). He and his coauthors had developed a typology of different types of learning objectives in the area of knowledge. The basic premise was that educational objectives should be classified according to the type of knowledge the learner was acquiring. This book and the classification system it introduced have become cornerstones of curriculum and instruction; the classification system is known as **Bloom's taxonomy**. Rather than treating all knowledge that is learned as being the same, Bloom and his colleagues identified six different levels of learning and therefore educational objectives. Over time, Bloom's colleagues revised his original list slightly. The revised version of Bloom's taxonomy includes six levels of learning and is summarized in Table 12.3 (Anderson & Krathwohl, 2001).

Bloom's taxonomy
A system for classifying knowledge learning outcomes in terms of the complexity of mental activity required.

TABLE 12.3

The Six Levels of Bloom's Revised Taxonomy of the Cognitive Domain

1 Remember	Knowledge and behaviors that emphasize remembering and recall. This could be relatively simple memorization such as facts, word spelling, and the multiplication tables. This domain also includes knowledge of criteria, rules, principles, methods, and theories.
2 Understand	Students are able to communicate the key components of an idea and can use the idea. The communication may be oral, written, or an equation or some other symbolic form. Three types of comprehension are translation, interpretation, and extrapolation. Translation entails the ability to understand an idea presented in one form, such as a graph, and be able to describe its meaning in another form, such as a written paragraph. Interpretation moves beyond translation to being able to weigh the different parts of a communication and to identify and understand the major ideas as well as the interrelationships. Extrapolation is extending beyond the presented communication by predicting consequences or likely next steps.
3 Apply	The student is able to apply learning to a new situation. Furthermore, the student is able to select the correct application without coaching by the teacher or other students. Using a principle to predict what will happen when a certain factor is changed is application.
4 Analyze	Analysis addresses the ability to break something down into its parts or pieces. Analysis also deals with detection of the relationships between the parts and how the whole is organized. Analysis begins with identifying the elements and then the relationships and interactions between the elements. Analysis goes beyond the stated and also includes recognition of the implicit.
5 Evaluate	Evaluation is about making judgments about the value or worth of ideas, products, or problem solutions. Although evaluation is presented as the fifth level, Bloom emphasizes that some effort at evaluation is a component of most of the other levels as well. At this level, evaluation is seen as a considered process based on criteria. It is not a simplistic rush to opinion. Instead, there is a reasoned analysis of all facts and weighing of alternatives and the consequences of each.
6 Create	To create is the process of putting together the parts to make a whole. Bloom points out that this is the level of the taxonomy that addresses creative behavior. This does not mean completely free creative effort, because there are likely lesson and problem contexts that set outside limits. At this level, the learner is working with a given situation. The product of this type of thinking might be an original idea.

Source: Based on Anderson, L. W., & Krathwohl, D. R. (Eds.) *A taxonomy for learning, teaching and assessing: A revision of Bloom's taxonomy of educational objectives.* Allyn & Bacon, 2001. pp 67–68.

In Bloom's taxonomy, each of the six levels of the cognitive domain represents different stages of complexity of knowledge and different extents to which knowledge is used. Teachers require different types of learning of students, depending on which level of the taxonomy is being addressed. In addition, teachers must keep in mind that this taxonomy is also a learning hierarchy. Students cannot perform at the higher levels unless they have already learned the necessary knowledge at the lower levels. The level of learning must be reflected in the way the learning objective is written. Simple memory and recall is a very different level of learning than is application or analysis.

LEARNING OBJECTIVES FOR THE AFFECTIVE DOMAIN. The **affective domain** of student learning also is important for teachers to consider as they plan instruction, teach lessons, and assess student learning. The affective domain addresses human reactions and responses to the content and subject matter. Student attitudes, feelings, and dispositions are a key component of instruction. Shortly after the development of the cognitive domain taxonomy, a parallel effort was under way to develop a taxonomy of educational objectives in the affective domain (Krathwohl, Bloom, & Masia, 1964).

An unavoidable part of instruction is consideration of students' attitudes and beliefs because these affective elements are related to classroom behaviors. Krathwohl's affective domain taxonomy provides an analytical tool for planning instruction and an aid for teachers to think about different levels of student learning in terms of values and beliefs (see Table 12.4).

In planning instruction and during teaching, the affective domain can be used to assess the openness to and interest of students in learning about a particular topic. If certain students are at level 1, Receiving (Attending), the lesson will need to be aimed at having students become more engaged with the topic and opening a willingness to move toward level 2, Responding, and level 3, Valuing. If students are already at level 4, Organization, then the learning objectives can

affective domain
A system for classifying learning outcomes in the area of human reactions and responses.

TABLE 12.4

The Five Levels of Krathwohl's Taxonomy of Affective Domain

1 Receiving (Attending)	The learner is sensitized to the condition, phenomenon, or stimulus that is the aim of the lesson or topic of study. At the most basic level, the learner is *aware* of the object or phenomenon. For example, in music students are aware of differences in mood or rhythm. Another component of this level is the *willingness to receive* or to attend to the topic of study. If there is not openness to learning more, then higher levels of the affective domain cannot be reached.
2 Responding	At this level, the learner is motivated beyond simply attending and is actively attending. At the lowest level of responding, there is *acquiescence in responding;* in other words, the learner is willing to go along. Slightly higher is the *willingness to respond,* in which the student looks for additional information or experience. A higher level of responding is indicated when the student shows *satisfaction in response*.
3 Valuing	At this level, the student is behaving in ways that reflect a sense of belief or attitude. Within this level, there is the range of behavior from *testing for acceptance of a value* to *commitment*. Actions of reaching out to learn more about a new topic, such as asking questions or searching out the topic on the Web, are indicative of acceptance. With commitment there is a conviction and loyalty to the topic, position, or group.
4 Organization	As more than one value becomes relevant, there is a need to develop an internal system of organization of values. Organization begins with *conceptualization* of particular values and beliefs. This does not necessarily require verbal expression, but the learner is able to compare one value or belief to another. This process leads to *organization of a value system*, which brings together a number of values and their relationships.
5 Characterization by a Value or Value Complex	At this level, the learner has a set of values in place, the values are organized into some kind of internal system, and behaviors are consistent over time in relation to these values. The values represent a *generalized set*, and there is a *characterization* of the person in terms of the internal consistency of thought and an external consistency of action that is characteristic of the person.

Source: Based on Krathwohl, D. R., Bloom, B. S., & Masia, B. B. *Taxonomy of educational objectives: The classification of educational goals handbook II: Affective domain.* David McKay, 1964.

ask students to weigh, compare, and form judgments. Values and beliefs, as well as motivation and interests, are a core component of learning. Students of teachers who continually attend to the affective domain will have greater learning success in the cognitive domain. When students are interested in learning and see the value of learning certain content, they will more intensely engage with the curriculum, which makes instruction more interesting and successful.

LEARNING OBJECTIVES FOR THE PSYCHOMOTOR DOMAIN. Another domain for learning objectives relates to learning physical skills, which require the mind and body to work together. Music, art, drama, industrial arts, and other vocational courses require students to perform tasks physically. The corresponding taxonomy, the **psychomotor domain**, has received attention from curriculum theorists and was developed by E. J. Simpson (1972). The first two levels are *Perception* and *Set*, which address the learner becoming aware of a particular stimulus and becoming ready to act. For example, the band director raises the baton and all members prepare to play the first note. Levels 3 and 4 of Simpson's psychomotor domain taxonomy address *Guided Response* and *Mechanisms*. When trying something for the first time, it helps to have suggestions and directions as a guide. With time the steps become automatic. At Level 5, *Complex Overt Response*, the learner can accomplish more complex tasks and movements independently. At the still higher level, *Adaptation*, the learner is able to adjust her or his behavior and accommodate its application in different settings or under different conditions. At the highest level, *Origination*, creativity is demonstrated. For example, the trumpet student moves beyond playing the written music to improvisation.

TEACHING STRATEGIES

Once the curriculum has been established and instructional objectives have been written, it is time to plan for and teach lessons that will help students learn the knowledge, dispositions, and skills identified in the objectives, benchmarks, and standards. For many decades, there was only one teaching strategy—lecture and recitation; the teacher talked and the students memorized and recited. Today this "stand and deliver" strategy is but one of many teaching methods. Students are not willing to sit through continuous lectures and a variety of teaching strategies have been demonstrated to be significantly more effective in engaging students and having students achieve at higher levels.

Direct Instruction

Although the lecture/recitation method continues to receive criticism, there is an appropriate time for teachers to impart information directly. **Direct instruction** is a teaching approach in which the teacher clearly and succinctly provides precise information about a specific topic, concept, or skill. During the last thirty years, extensive research has been done on the behaviors of the teacher and the effectiveness of direct instruction. When direct instruction is done well and with appropriate learning objectives, students learn. Two basic, underlying assumptions of this teaching strategy are that the teacher knows the content and that the easiest way for students to learn it is for the teacher to directly communicate it to them.

Although with direct instruction information is passed from teacher to students, additional ways to communicate information exist besides teacher lecture. Reading the textbook, asking questions that require answers, and using different technologies such as videos, television programs, computer-assisted learning programs, interactive computer simulations, and information searches on the Web are all ways to impart information and to make direct instruction more interesting and motivating for students.

To be most effective in using direct instruction, the teacher must manage a number of important steps (see Figure 12.3). With direct instruction, the teacher is at the center and maintains full control of the lesson. The teacher must control the flow and keep all talk focused. Sidebars and off-topic discussion are discouraged. A primary purpose of direct instruction is to maintain a high amount of on-task learning time, or **active learning time (ALT)**. Higher proportions of class time in which students are engaged will yield higher levels of student learning.

One debate that flows from the need to maintain a learning focus is the role of homework. Teachers recognize that focused learning is important and one way to maintain that focus outside of school is homework. Given what we know about differences in students' home lives, homework assignments can pose problems. The "Who Is Right?" feature explores this issue.

 To see a teacher using direct instruction in an elementary language arts lesson, click on the video *Applying Cognitive Motivation Theory: Writing Paragraphs.*

psychomotor domain
A system for classifying learning outcomes that require physical activity and performance.

direct instruction
A teaching approach in which the teacher clearly and succinctly provides clear, precise information about a specific topic, concept, or skill.

active learning time (ALT) The proportion of time within a lesson that students are actively engaged with the task of learning the objectives.

FIGURE 12.3	Key Characteristics of Effective Direct Instruction

1. Direct instruction works best when the learning objectives are clear and narrow in scope.
2. Information and/or tasks should be presented in sequence and one step at a time.
3. The teacher should check carefully for student understanding as the presentation unfolds.
4. Build in student practice with corrective feedback.
5. Avoid negative criticism.
6. Include review at key points.
7. Tasks and assignments should be clearly structured.

WHO IS RIGHT?

SHOULD WE ABOLISH HOMEWORK?

The value of homework remains a controversial topic. Although some research confirms the value of homework, other studies question the wisdom of assigning homework to students who have limited resources at home.

YES

Mike Burman teaches high school English and journalism at Horace Mann High School in North Fond du Lac, Wisconsin.

If students are in school seven hours a day, what right do I have to interfere with their family time? One of my fellow teachers had a son in middle school who would come home from basketball practice, then go to the basement to do, on average, three hours of homework a night. Does this sound healthy?

At the younger grades, it is almost criminal to assign homework. I spoke to a mother of a first-grader who was getting 30 minutes a night. She is very frustrated that instead of quality time with her son, she has to go through homework that at times is frustrating for him.

In my own classroom, I have actually noticed an increase in achievement, thanks to my reduction in homework. I used to assign a big project at the end of a novel or unit, and then give students a week or so to do it on their own. Later, I tried giving students time in class to work on these projects. Two positive things happened as a result: a higher percentage of students turned in a project and there was an increase in the quality of the projects.

Educators have about seven hours a day to create meaningful learning experiences. If they cannot then they are not using time efficiently. Children are not machines. They need "downtime" just like any adult.

NO

Henry Adeoye is a special education teacher at Moorhead Junior High School in Conroe, Texas.

Abolishing homework will negatively impact students' learning in no small measure. First, it would be detrimental to continuity. Homework allows students to practice the skills they learned earlier in the day, so that when they return to school the next day, those skills aren't lost. I don't know of many students who willingly study the next chapter without being asked. There are exceptions, but most students do not study on their own. They need direction; homework is just one tool to keep them on track.

Also, when students have assignments that are to be completed at home, it often encourages parents to become more involved with their children's education. When reviewing homework assignments, parents are able to see firsthand what their children are learning in school, which fosters communication between teachers and parents. This has been an invaluable tool in my classroom to foster the home/school relationship.

Teachers should not relent in using homework to enhance students' performance, but it should not be assigned to the extent that students become inundated or overwhelmed, and it should never be assigned as punishment.

Although homework is an essential ingredient to a quality education, breaks from homework can certainly be given from time to time—students sometimes need breaks just as we need breaks from our work.

WHAT IS YOUR PERSPECTIVE ON THIS ISSUE?

Source: "Should We Abolish Homework?" *NEA Today* (March 2007), p. 51. Reprinted by permission of the National Education Association.

FIGURE 12.4	Key Characteristics of Effective Indirect Instruction			

1. The teacher or students pose a problem or puzzle.
2. The problem or puzzle is one that stimulates student interest and inquisitiveness.
3. The teacher does not provide the answer or problem solution.
4. Students initiate activities and investigations to analyze the problem or puzzle.
5. The teacher serves as a guide or coach only when students are stymied.
6. All possible solutions/answers are given open consideration.
7. Students articulate orally, in writing, and/or through presenting the reasoning behind their answer/solution.

Indirect Instruction

The opposite approach to direct instruction is **indirect instruction**, which covers a large number of teaching strategies in which students have greater responsibility for structuring tasks and managing their own learning. The teacher still has overall responsibility, but students have to initiate more, have to organize more of their tasks and their thinking, and in the end must be able to construct their own product or way of demonstrating what they have learned. Key characteristics of indirect instruction are presented in Figure 12.4.

GUIDED DISCOVERY. Guided Discovery lessons are carefully designed learning activities that require students to investigate a specific question. The procedures for the investigation are carefully designed by the teacher so that students eventually arrive at an understanding that is the desired learning outcome. Students are allowed to work through the investigation at their own pace but the instructions designed by the teacher guide them in a preferred direction. Gradually students discover the learning concept.

INQUIRY AND PROBLEM-BASED LEARNING. Inquiry lessons begin with a problem or puzzle being posed by either the teacher or students. Then, the students initiate investigations or problem-solving strategies in an effort to construct an answer. *Problem solving* is another name for this general approach. Students assume major responsibility for their learning with this approach.

In an inquiry lesson, the first phase is to define the problem. The teacher might pose a dilemma, or in a science lesson do a demonstration, for which the answer is not obvious. The students then have to define the specific question or problem. The second major phase in inquiry lessons is discovery of the solution. The discovery phase might include conducting an experiment; seeking out information from reading or on the Web; or, in a mathematics lesson, using manipulative materials. In the end, the students will have constructed new understanding and will have learned new concepts and principles.

One innovative adaptation of the inquiry approach, which was first used in medical education, is **problem-based learning (PBL)**. In this approach, a real or simulated problem is posed, and students work in groups to develop a solution. The problem does not have a quick or obvious answer, nor is it one about which the students will already have sufficient knowledge. The purpose of PBL is to engage a team of four to six students in systematic inquiry, decision making, and problem solving. The result is deeper understanding of the subject as well as the development of skills in inquiry and collaborative work. Using inquiry approaches such as problem-based learning tends to engage students because they

indirect instruction
A set of teaching approaches in which students have greater responsibility for structuring and managing their own learning.

Guided Discovery
Carefully designed learning activities that require students to investigate a specific question.

inquiry An instructional approach that begins with a problem or puzzle posed by either the teacher or students.

problem-based learning An inquiry learning approach in which an authentic, contemporary, or simulated problem is posed and students work in groups to develop a solution.

When using an inquiry approach to instruction, the teacher acts more like a coach than a lecturer.

have a voice in the way that they approach new ideas. Instead of following specific directions by the teacher, the students take charge of their learning and the teacher becomes more of a coach.

PBL units tend to include multidisciplinary objectives. Science, mathematics, language arts, and even social studies objectives can be taught in a single problem-based learning unit. For example, an interdisciplinary PBL unit could focus on improving the nutritional value of the school lunch menu. The unit might begin with a letter sent by the principal to a class of students asking them to help her improve the school lunch menu by developing proposals that both describe problems within the current menu and also present a revamped menu that is both tasty and nutritional. Learners would then be assigned to small groups and the teacher would help the groups clarify problems with the current menu, investigate ways that the problems could be solved, study foods with high nutrition values, investigate costs, and ultimately design a new menu. The unit might end by having students write letters to the principal concerning their proposal and explaining why their new menu should be selected. To make the inquiry authentic, the principal could select one or more of the menus and implement them.

Throughout the unit, the teacher would provide instruction in a variety of areas including nutrition, digestion, cost analysis, organic farming, survey development, interviewing, and proposal and letter writing. Generally such units extend for several weeks, so it is important that the content and skills that are required by the curriculum are embedded in the problem focus.

Self-Regulated Learning Strategies

Although there are two distinct types of instruction, there are learning strategies that need to be included in all instruction because they focus on teaching students to learn on their own. These strategies focus on self-regulated learning and enable students to learn on their own, make better decisions about where to get information, recognize and correct misunderstandings, and expand their understanding. There is considerable evidence that explicitly teaching students a variety of self-regulating learning strategies enhances their understanding (Fisher, Frey, & Williams, 2002; Neufeld, 2005; Schmocker, 2006). Three specific types of self-regulated learning strategies have been identified: cognitive learning strategies, metacognitive strategies, and social/affective strategies.

COGNITIVE LEARNING STRATEGIES. Cognitive learning strategies are skills that relate to a specific learning task and are used by students when they need to organize information, mentally or physically manipulate material, or apply a specific technique to a learning task. Previewing a story prior to reading, establishing a purpose for reading, consciously making connections to personal experiences, taking notes during a lecture, and completing a graphic organizer are examples of cognitive strategies. Making certain that you directly teach these strategies is an important component to any instructional practice.

METACOGNITIVE STRATEGIES. The process of purposefully monitoring our thinking is referred to as metacognition. Metacognition is characterized by clarifying the purposes for learning, monitoring one's own comprehension through self-questioning, and taking corrective action if understanding fails. The use of these skills requires awareness, reflection, and interaction with others. Studies have found that when metacognitive strategies are taught explicitly, comprehension improves (Hacker, Dunlosky, & Graesser, 2009; Snow, Griffin, & Burns, 2005).

SOCIAL AFFECTIVE STRATEGIES. These are learning strategies that enable students to interact with others to clarify a confusing point, to participate in a group discussion, or to work with a cooperative learning group to solve a problem. When designing an instructional unit, it is important to provide experiences for students to interact with other students with a focus on learning something new or solving a problem. Explicitly helping students to practice listening skills, restate what others have said, design probing questions, and determine how their talents can complement the talents of others are important features to any instructional approach.

SCAFFOLDING STRATEGIES. Scaffolding is a term associated with Vygotsky's (1978) notion of zones of proximal development. A zone of proximal development is the difference between what a child can do alone and what a child can accomplish with the help of a more experienced individual. Scaffolding instruction means that teachers create a substantial amount of support and assistance in the beginning stages of teaching a new concept or strategy. Then, teachers gradually decrease the amount of support they provide as learners acquire experience through multiple practice opportunities (Vacca, 2002).

Organizing Students to Maximize Learning

Another important component of all teaching strategies has to do with how students are grouped. Should students be taught as a whole class? When should students be divided into groups? What should be the size of the groups? Should the groups be kept the same? What should be done about the different ability levels and skills of students? All of these questions must be answered to determine the best organizational model for learning.

HOMOGENEOUS OR HETEROGENEOUS GROUPING. Grouping together students who have similar levels of achievement and abilities is called **homogeneous grouping**. Grouping together students with different levels of achievement and different abilities is called **heterogeneous grouping**. The best way to group depends to some extent on the task. Deciding on which way to group students is philosophical too. Proponents of heterogeneous grouping point out that high-achieving students help the lower achieving ones and that everyone learns. On the other hand, the proponents of homogeneous grouping believe that mixed-ability grouping slows down the fast learners. The unstated assumption in this debate is that the only learning that counts is that of each student individually; however, the accomplishment of the group also should be considered. The "Teaching in Challenging Times" feature presents a scenario to help you determine which type of grouping you might prefer.

COOPERATIVE LEARNING. A widely used approach to grouping is **cooperative learning**, in which students are expected to work together to accomplish tasks and are held accountable for both individual and group achievement. In this approach, the general plan is to have a mix of students, so that each group will include students with high, middle, and lower abilities. An alternative is to group students together according to interests and assign them activities according to those interests. Typically, cooperative learning groups work together for several weeks or longer. Each group member has an assigned role, including group leader, monitor, resource manager,

homogeneous grouping Grouping students who are alike in terms of their ability to learn or interests.

heterogeneous grouping Grouping students who are diverse in their interests and ability to learn.

cooperative learning A strategy for grouping that provides specific roles and responsibilities for each member.

TEACHING IN CHALLENGING TIMES

Should I Use Homogeneous or Heterogeneous Ability Grouping?

The issue of how to group students for instruction can be very controversial. Some propose homogeneous grouping and others argue for heterogeneous grouping. Homogeneous ability grouping is a practice that seems to have merit. Permitting students who require the same level of instruction to be clustered in a single setting makes planning and resource allocation much easier. Such grouping patterns permit students to receive instruction that is tied to their specific needs, because they are with others who need the same information or skill development.

Those who oppose homogeneous ability grouping contend that labeling students and placing them in similar ability groups based on their academic skill sets up structures that often inhibit future growth and development. Both teachers and parents begin to view students according to these labels; once tracked by ability, students seldom break out of the initial labels assigned at an early age. These critics call for multiability or heterogeneous grouping. They believe that having students from a variety of backgrounds and ability levels work together is more in keeping with a democratic society. Furthermore, such multiability grouping

permits students to help one another, fostering cooperativeness and caring among those from different backgrounds. Indeed, opponents of tracking programs have pointed to the disproportionate number of minority and low-income students who seem to make up the lower level groups.

WHAT ARE MY CHALLENGES?

1. List other pros and cons of homogeneous ability grouping. List other pros and cons of heterogeneous ability grouping. Using these pro and con lists, what educational philosophies are compatible with homogeneous ability grouping and what educational philosophies are compatible with heterogeneous ability grouping?

2. Should one type of grouping be used in all instructional settings or circumstances, or should the types of grouping be varied according to task and context?

3. What type of grouping would you choose to use most of the time and why?

recorder, and reporter. In this way, leadership and task responsibilities are shared. Extensive research has been done on this approach to grouping. Some of the outcomes are improvement in understanding of content, development, and support of using acceptable social skills; opportunities for student decision-making; and encouragement of student responsibility (Johnson & Johnson, 1999). Criticisms of cooperative learning include the arguments against homogeneous grouping cited previously. Other critics, including many parents, object to grading students based on group accomplishments.

USE OF TECHNOLOGY TO ENHANCE INSTRUCTION

When technology is used to actively engage students in learning, applying, and analyzing important concepts, achievement gains result. For example, researchers have found that in classrooms in which computer simulations are used to support higher level cognitive tasks, subsequent achievement gains can result (Wenglinsky, 2005). Other studies indicate that when using technology, the following instructional features make a positive difference: (1) students who worked in small groups learned more than those who worked alone; (2) students achieved across a variety of learning outcomes including cognitive, process or skill, and affective growth; (3) students needed to have prior experience in working in groups; (4) students needed instruction in specific cooperative learning strategies; and (5) the content needed to include tutorials, practice software, an opportunity to learn computer skills, and an interdisciplinary subject matter such as social science (Abramovich & Ehrlich, 2007; Bebell & O'Dwyer , 2010; Houssart & Sams, 2008; Li & Ma, 2010; Norris et al., 2010).

The current challenge for using technology effectively in the classroom is to develop an *integrated approach* to instruction rather than to simply use a computer-assisted learning program here and there. Effectively integrating technology requires that you always keep the instructional goal in mind rather than simply focusing on the technology. This may seem obvious, but you can easily get lost in the many new and exciting technologies that are emerging. Keep this important focus in mind (the instructional goal comes first) as you review the many technology tools available to you. The following sections provide an overview of the many aspects of computer-based technology that teachers need to consider as they integrate technology into an effective teaching approach that matches their instructional objectives and teaching approaches.

Software Tools

One way to consider using technology in instruction is to view it as a set of tools. Word processing, spreadsheet, presentation programs, and adaptive assessment software are four basic tools that have been used for decades. *Word processing* is often used to support English/language arts and foreign language learning activities, and to report development assignments. *Spreadsheets* are often used in mathematics, science, and business education areas to support instructional activities that require data storage and analysis. *Presentation* software is used across all subject areas and assists teachers in the development of lectures as well as students in the development of oral reports. *Test generators* enable teachers to input test items into an item pool, randomly generate the questions, and automatically score student responses. *Adaptive assessment* software allows students to show what they know and do not know through the use of carefully paced assessment programs that adjust questions to match the ability of the student. These assessment programs provide increasingly more difficult questions to students based on their responses to easier questions. The assessment automatically terminates when students can no longer answer questions at a certain difficulty level. These types of assessments provide excellent information for teachers to use as they plan instruction.

Drill-and-Practice Technology

Drill-and-practice software provides exercises in which students work example items, usually one at a time, and receive feedback on their correctness. Programs vary considerably on the type of feedback they provide; some programs simply display "Ok" or "Try again" while others restate the answer a student selected and explain why it is incorrect. The key to using a good drill- and -practice program is to offer each student meaningful feedback in a form that he or she can easily understand and make progress in learning. Generally, feedback that is visual as well as textual is best in that students who read well will understand the text responses and students who have difficulty with text may benefit from the visuals. A drill-and-practice exercise can be presented in the form of a type of flash card activity, a fill-in chart or graphic organizer activity, or a branching drill activity. In branching drills the software moves students on to advanced questions after they get a number of questions correct at a predetermined mastery level.

Benefits to using drill-and-practice software are that they provide students immediate feedback, motivate them to practice, and save teacher time. Limitations to using drill-and-practice software are that teachers sometimes misuse drills as a way to introduce a concept rather than as a way to practice and reinforce concepts that have already been taught. Also, critics are concerned that simply introducing isolated skills and directing students to practice them does not adequately allow students the opportunity to connect these skills to daily life or to make connections to other concepts. For example, just having students practice how to hit or catch a ball does not necessarily enable them to exercise these skills in a game of baseball.

Tutorial Software Technology

Tutorial software is an entire instructional sequence on a topic and is similar to a teacher's classroom instruction. This instruction usually is expected to offer a self-contained instructional unit rather than offering a supplement to other instruction. Tutorials are often categorized as linear or branching. A linear tutorial gives the same instructional sequence of explanation, practice, and feedback to all learners regardless of their abilities. Branching tutorials offer more options as they direct learners down different paths depending on their response to questions.

Selecting good drill-and-practice technology requires that teachers consider the following characteristics: extensive interactivity, thorough user control, appropriate teaching approach, adequate answer and feedback capabilities, appropriate graphics, and adequate record keeping. Using tutorial software in the classroom does not replace designing and presenting instruction by the teacher. Rather, tutorial software enables teachers to provide self-paced reviews of prior instruction, alternative learning for students who prefer structured learning, and self-paced instruction for advanced students who wish to glean additional information about a concept.

Simulation and Virtual Reality Technology

Recent developments in the area of gaming software have resulted in many rich learning simulations and virtual reality scenarios. Simulations provide interdisciplinary learning opportunities often focused on science and social studies scenarios. Interactive simulations allow students to enter into different eras and scenarios and experience events based on their own response to the simulated realities. Mathematics and language are integrated into these experiences so that students begin to understand how the abstract concepts of mathematics or the skills of language are part of everyday life and experience. Many simulations are available free online while others are often provided by publishers who provide them with the purchase of textbooks.

Related to simulations are *real-time technology data banks*. Teachers and students can now access and track daily weather conditions, stock-market performance, daily star charts, and so on. These are helpful when teaching long-term trends that require the collection of data over time. Now that students can use real data, not just data from the past, they can better understand how these trends relate to their own lives.

Interactive Whiteboard Technology

An interactive whiteboard consists of a regular whiteboard glossy surface that uses erasable markers and is connected to a computer and digital projector that allows information projected on the screen to be manipulated with hands and special pens. Interactivity software allows learners and teachers to highlight information, create charts, play games, view videos, and search the Internet as needed. Information from the Internet can be instantly displayed on a whiteboard and interactive lessons can be designed and tailored to specific learning objectives.

Web-Based Collaboration and Social Networking Learning Tools

Currently one of the most powerful uses of Internet tools is for collaboration and social networking. Powerful tools that make collaboration quite rich include avatar spaces, wikis, podcasts, e-portfolios, blogs, video and photo sharing, and social networking websites. The key to using these different tools is to integrate them into specific instructional units as needed. For example, e-portfolios allow students to showcase their work and to organize, revise, and store digital learning products that they have created inside and outside the classroom. Blogs allow students to show their thinking as they compose or share reflections on classwork. Duffy (2008) notes that wikis can be used to document research projects, build collaborative bibliographies, and provide a reflective tool for teachers and students during any learning experience. Social networking sites allow students to design and upload content, meet and connect with others from around the world, and share media and interests online. This type of sharing encourages students to reflect upon their work and lives in the context of a broad community of connected individuals. The current challenge teachers and parents face when using these powerful collaboration tools is keeping the focus on learning and sharing ideas.

Assistive Technology for Special Needs Learners

Physical disabilities can affect a person's agility. Assistive technology for individuals with severe physical disabilities may take the form of a power wheelchair operated by a joystick, a control device with a handle that moves in all directions. To provide access to a computer, it is often necessary to offer an alternative to the keyboard. Switches are commonly used for controlling and receiving input as well as activating environmental control systems. Assessing the need for assistive technology involves a team of specialists including occupational and physical therapists, rehabilitation engineers, and assistive technology specialists. There are increasingly more and more sophisticated technologies such as canes with sensor technology, tools to convert printed information for the blind, optical character recognition software, screen readers, amplification systems, and assistive hearing devices. Technology for students with mild cognitive disabilities includes talking story books, voice recognitions software for students who cannot easily write with their hands, talking calculators, and so on. Teachers working with special needs students must be familiar with their assistive technologies and vigilant in keeping current with the many technologies now available as well as developing technologies as they become available.

MATCHING INSTRUCTION TO LEARNERS' NEEDS

A central consideration in designing instructional strategies is how well they match up with the learning needs of diverse students. In many ways, each student in a classroom is unique. Effective teachers use strategies that take advantage of each student's strengths and that accommodate areas of need. Students will vary in their ability to read and calculate. They will vary in their ability to use English and in how well they can communicate orally and through writing. Some will be exceptionally fast at learning, and others will be slow. It is critical to employ different types of instructional approaches based on the unique needs of students.

Differentiated Instruction

Differentiated instruction is the regular practice of employing a variety of instructional methods and learning activities to match the different ways that students learn and to accommodate the different levels of learning that students require. Regardless of the type of instructional approach used, students will respond differently to the intended learning outcomes. Some students may immediately show mastery of the outcome, others may exhibit misconceptions, while other students may end up confused. This type of outcome is typical when students are taught in a classroom setting. The key to success is to immediately design follow-up learning activities based on the different needs of students. The group of students who showed immediate mastery could be provided with an inquiry lesson in an effort to allow them to deepen their understanding. The group of students with specific misconceptions could receive direct instruction focused on the misconceptions. The group of students who are confused might benefit from exposure to a totally different instructional method to reteach the content. This process is ongoing and is at the heart of differentiated instruction.

Differentiation can be based on several different areas: academic ability, learning style differences, subject matter misconceptions, career interests, second language learner needs, special education learner needs, and so on. Obviously, all of these differences cannot easily be identified, but an ongoing attempt to examine the results of instruction based on these different areas of need can provide insights about the adequacy of the curriculum.

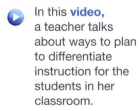

In this **video,** a teacher talks about ways to plan to differentiate instruction for the students in her classroom.

differentiated instruction The regular practice of employing a variety of instructional methods and learning activities to match the different ways that students learn and to accommodate the different levels of learning that students require.

DIFFERENTIATION BASED ON ABILITY AND PRIOR EXPERIENCE. The most common approach to differentiating instruction is based on different levels of ability. Some students learn quickly through a simple definition, explanation, or example. Other students need many different examples, repeated practice, and hands-on activities. Learning is much more enjoyable and efficient when students are provided learning approaches that match their specific needs. Clearly, designing a single lesson that fits all needs is a thing of the past. Teachers now regularly design lessons that are differentiated according to students' prior understandings about the target concepts and skills.

One common outcome for this approach is that teachers group students according to the different approaches that have been designed for a single lesson and each group receives unique explanations and assignments. One result is that students often collaborate with each other in an effort to learn the concept or skill.

DIFFERENTIATION BASED ON LEARNING STYLES. Research about learning styles has shown that students process information differently and hence might benefit from different ways of presenting concepts and new ideas. A **learning style** is a student's consistent way of responding to and using stimuli in the context of learning. There are many different learning styles and to date no one theory has received general acceptance. For example, you can look at children based on *sensory input,* meaning in light of their ability to learn through visual, aural, or kinesthetic methods. To differentiate instruction based on these sensory inputs implies that you would develop a lesson using as many different sensory inputs as possible. For example, when teaching about the concept of adaptation, you could state the definition of adaptation and provide some examples. You might then show pictures of birds with different beaks and ask students to predict the type of food each bird might eat based on the shape of the beak. You could then distribute models of birds with different beaks and ask students to measure the length and width of the different beaks and discuss their answers about the types of food each bird probably eats. Finally, a video of different types of birds in their natural environment could be viewed while students took notes about different bird species. By providing different types of sensory experiences, the concept of adaptation is made clearer to students.

Another way of thinking about learning styles is based *on the way students process information* when ideas are presented. Felder, Silverman, and Spurlin (1988, 2002, 2005, 2010) collaboratively developed an information-processing learning-style model based on their work in engineering education. According to this model there are four dimensions. Think of these dimensions as a continuum, with one learning preference on the far left and the other on the far right. The dimensions are:

1. **Sensory ⟷ Intuitive**

    Provide both hard facts and general concepts.
2. **Visual ⟷ Verbal**

    Incorporate both visual and verbal cues.
3. **Active ⟷ Reflective**

    Allow both experiential learning and time for evaluation and analysis.
4. **Sequential ⟷ Global**

    Provide detail in a structured way as well as the big picture.

There are other ways of thinking about student learning styles (Kolb, 2007). The key for teachers is to be aware that there are different types of learning styles and to strive to tailor instruction that matches the unique needs of learners.

DIFFERENTIATION BASED ON CONCEPTUAL MISCONCEPTIONS. The recent work on national standards development by subject matter has given rise to increased research concerning common misconceptions about reading, mathematics, and science concepts (AAAS, 1993; Bamberger & Oberdoft, 2010). A *conceptual misconception* is an incorrect understanding about a concept that students often display. These misconceptions are incorrect ideas that one could reasonably conclude based on limited experience and understanding. One of the difficulties caused by these misconceptions is that once they are formed, they can be difficult to change. So, the earlier they are uncovered and corrected, the better.

learning style A student's consistent way of responding to and using stimuli in the context of learning.

These misconceptions are often described in national standards documents and provide insight into how students develop misunderstandings about different concepts. Monitoring students' understandings and developing assessments that check for these common misconceptions gives rise to opportunities to use them to differentiate instruction. Examples of common misconceptions in science include thinking that gravity causes surface tension or that the seasons relate to the rotation of the earth around the sun. Examples of misconceptions in mathematics are that 0.8 equals 1/8, or that you can add fractions by simply adding the numerators and denominators.

As teachers develop experience looking for misconceptions, they are better able to check for them through formative classroom assessments. Then, based on the results of these assessments, teachers can differentiate instruction to match the specific misconceptions that learners exhibit.

Teaching Strategies for English-Language Learners and Students with Disabilities

Another way of thinking about differentiation is based on the specific needs that relate to designated learner populations such as second language learners and special education learners. The following section explores the ways that instruction can be tailored to meet the needs of specific learner populations.

One important component of instruction that teachers must examine and understand is how best to address the array of students with special needs and those who are English-language learners. For example, students with learning disabilities are apt to have difficulty with direct instruction strategies, especially lecture. However, they benefit from having clear and concrete teacher directions and activities that are well structured and sequenced. ELL students can be very successful with strategies that facilitate their interaction with other students and that provide ample time for processing what is happening. ELLs also benefit from indirect instruction strategies, because in these approaches learning is less dependent on understanding everything the teacher says. ELL students in secondary school classes in particular do not benefit from direct instruction. Fortunately, a number of well-developed instructional practices exist for accommodating the needs of diverse learners. Consider some of the challenges related to providing opportunities for students to help each other learn as you read the following "Perspectives on Diversity" feature.

INSTRUCTIONAL PRACTICES FOR ENGLISH-LANGUAGE LEARNERS. In practice, teachers of ELL students should include two kinds of objectives for every lesson: language and content. Content objectives are established for all students. For the ELL students, adding a language objective helps with their language development. For example, a language objective could be that the ELL students will be able to identify and say vocabulary words when shown a picture. The picture would relate to the content objective and the vocabulary words relate to the language objective.

During an elementary school lesson, the teacher could speak key words while pointing to them in a *Big Book* or writing them on the whiteboard. In a secondary classroom, the teacher could use a worksheet that has sentences with blanks where the key vocabulary words should go. This task will help the ELL student focus on the key words and concepts. Another useful technique in both elementary and secondary classrooms is to have one or two of the students model the task before the whole class begins individual or group work. ELLs, as well as all the other students, are then able to see what is expected of them. Figure 12.5 presents another useful set of tips for assisting ELL students.

Among the many resources for teachers who work with ELL students are several federally funded centers. One of these is the National Clearinghouse for English Language Acquisition (NCELA). The NCELA is a repository for best practices, research, and related information for teachers who work with ELL, dual-language, and migrant education. Another instructional resource is the National Association for Bilingual Education (NABE), which is devoted to representing bilingual learners and bilingual education professionals. NABE publishes a bilingual research journal, updates instructional resources, and provides news updates on changes in bilingual education policy.

The following best practices assist second language learners as they attempt to develop competence in both content acquisition and language proficiency (Gass & Selinker, 2008; Lessow-Hurley, 2003; Quindlen, 2002):

- **Create a predictable classroom environment.** Establish classroom routines, mark transitions between activities, and use clear signals to assist second language learners in understanding expectations. These routines provide a way to reinforce language learning.

PERSPECTIVES on DIVERSITY

This Is Science Class, Not Language Arts

Joanna Wilenski has taught sixth-grade science in the same middle school for more than ten years. Over time, Joanna noticed a gradual but significant change in the composition of the student body. The number of Spanish- and Vietnamese-speaking children had increased to such a degree that her school had adopted and now implemented a language immersion program. She, along with other experienced teachers, attended a variety of language immersion workshops. Thanks to this effort, Joanna was certain that more of her language-diverse students would succeed.

As she has always done, Joanna started the new school year with an introduction to cooperative learning in science. She knew, from experience, that it is important to teach students how to cooperate in a learning environment. Joanna explained that in science it is helpful to investigate the world together and learn from different perspectives.

After several class sessions practicing different cooperative learning techniques, Joanna created small science groups to work on a science investigation. Students were asked to determine how many drops of water would fit on a penny before spilling over. She asked students to assume different roles as they investigated this question together, including materials handler, recorder, and observer. Students seemed eager and ready to explore this question about surface tension.

After several minutes, however, Joanna noticed that some groups were not working well. She walked over to one of the groups and noticed that only two of the four students were working and the other two were sitting quietly and uninvolved. Concerned, she asked the students if they needed help. Immediately, one of the participating students said: "Yes, tell Juanita and Chou to learn English or go to another group. We don't have time to teach them ourselves."

WHAT IS YOUR PERSPECTIVE?

1. Why do you think that the student felt it was a burden to have students who were not versed in English in the group?
2. What could Joanna say to the student that might help her work with language diverse students in the classroom?
3. Would it have been better to group students according to their different languages? Why or why not?

- **Provide second language learners many nonverbal ways to demonstrate knowledge and comprehension**. For example, ask learners to indicate a response on a map, a chart, or a graph. Have students point to a hands-up picture or a hands-down picture to express agreement or disagreement. Use as many visuals as possible and connect these visuals to text and vocabulary.
- **Develop subject-matter content around themes**. Providing a context for learning activities lends itself to using visuals and hands-on activities and this enhances comprehension. This approach also allows for repetition of vocabulary, allows learners to hear the same ideas presented in different contexts, and permits a variety of different learning activities that overlap.

FIGURE 12.5 | Entrees to English: Tips for Assisting Language Learners

- **Engage cooperative groups of English-language learners (ELLs) and English speakers in common tasks.** This gives students a meaningful context for using English.
- **Develop content around a theme.** The repetition of vocabulary and concepts reinforces language and ideas and gives ELLs better access to content.
- **Allow students nonverbal ways to demonstrate knowledge and comprehension.** For example, one teacher has early primary students hold up cardboard "lollipops" (green or red side forward) to indicate "Yes" or "No" to questions.
- **Don't constantly correct students' departure from standard English.** It's better to get students talking; they acquire accepted forms through regular use and practice. A teacher can always paraphrase a student's answer to model standard English.
- **Consider using visual aids and hands-on activities to deliver content.** Information is better retained when a variety of senses are called upon.
- **Use routines as a way to reinforce language.** This practice increases the comfort level of second language learners; they then know what to expect and associate the routine with language.

- **Use questions effectively.** Leave enough time for a response because second language learners may need more time than native speakers to answer a question. Listen for meaning in their answers, rather than correctness of speech, and acknowledge correct content.

- **Facilitate understanding.** Check your own understanding of what a learner says. If necessary, repeat and rephrase questions and answers. Listen for comprehension, not correctness. When understanding and communications are emphasized, learners will feel comfortable, generate language, and receive language input.

- **Engage cooperative learning groups of second language learners and English speakers in a common learning task.** Make certain that students are assigned different roles that they can reasonably complete and that allow each member to make a unique contribution. This approach permits second language learners to contribute in a meaningful way and shows that they have knowledge to share.

- **Create a warm, welcoming classroom atmosphere that encourages students to communicate in a variety of ways.** Use strategies such as buddies, "pair shares," and creating and sharing family shields.

DEVELOPING A COLLABORATIVE CLASSROOM. There is a wide range of variability in student needs and the resources that teachers have to address them. In the past, most students with special needs were isolated and placed in "special education" classrooms. This self-contained model came under heavy criticism for a number of reasons, including the absence of contact with general education student role models as well as special education students losing out on many school activities and events. One consequence of P.L. 94-142 was establishment of the resource room and a major change in philosophy. Today there is an expectation that students with special needs are members of the general education classroom and will go to the resource room only for special instruction.

The first step in addressing teaching and learning for students with special needs is to help them develop appropriate attitudes. There is a strong tendency on the part of all students to look for differences and to prefer to interact with peers who are like themselves. Rather than accepting and valuing diversity (here there is a hint of the need for affective learning objectives), students may have a predisposition to reject and isolate peers who are different in gender, race, socioeconomic class, or ability to learn. The expectations that students in any classroom hold and act on in regard to learners with special needs begin with the attitudes and behaviors of the teacher. There is no escaping the fact that students' respect for diversity is in large part related to the values and behaviors of the teacher. This is true for each school as a whole. In schools where the principal and teachers share the belief that all students can learn and where there is a shared responsibility for helping all students learn, all students do learn more. This is a matter of dispositions and it begins with the adults in the school. **Dispositions** are habits of mind or ways of acting that develop over time (e.g., respect for others, perseverance, open-mindedness). A useful set of questions for assessing how well students are doing to promote a sense of community and social acceptance is as follows:

- Do learners without disabilities display interest in and listen to the ideas and opinions of learners with disabilities?

- Do learners actively seek to converse with learners with and without disabilities?

- Do learners with disabilities show enthusiasm and interest in learning activities that include other learners?

- Do all learners show concern for each other and offer assistance to those in need without being asked to do so?

- Do learners without disabilities disproportionately tease learners with disabilities?

INSTRUCTIONAL PRACTICES FOR LEARNERS WITH SPECIAL NEEDS. Designing instruction for learners with special needs is a collaborative process between the classroom teacher and the special education teacher. Students with special needs have instructional educational progress plans that are specifically developed for them. These plans provide instructional objectives and suggested teaching approaches and modifications. Carefully reviewing a special needs child's IEP and discussing it with the special education teacher is a critical first step to designing instruction. One of the biggest changes for educators is in deciding to share the role that has traditionally

dispositions Habits of mind or ways of acting that develop over time (e.g., respect for others, perseverance, open-mindedness).

belonged to the individual teacher: to share the goals, decisions, classroom instruction, responsibility for students, assessment of student learning, problem solving, and classroom management. The teachers must begin to think of it as "our" class.

Developing a general list of instructional strategies for learners with special needs is problematic because their needs differ considerably. Students with learning disabilities, visual and aural impairments, physical impairments, emotional difficulties, and attention deficits require different instructional modifications. The best approach to designing these modifications is to develop an awareness of each child's unique characteristics, examine the many teaching resources that are available, share ideas and questions with other teachers, note learner responses to the instruction, and make additional modifications. The following sections provide an overview of instructional strategies that have been identified as worthy based on the learners' unique special needs characteristics. Like any general overview, the instructional suggestions are merely the beginning of a process that must be revised and tailored over and over again.

Teaching Students with Learning Disabilities. Students with learning disabilities differ greatly in that some learners have difficulty conceptualizing, others have difficulty processing information, others have difficulty making connections, and so on. It is critical that the specific learning disability is taken into account when designing instruction. It is also important to remember that students with learning disabilities are not students who are incapacitated or unable to learn; rather, they need differentiated instruction tailored to their distinctive learning abilities. Here are some appropriate strategies that relate to the needs of students with learning disabilities:

- Provide students with learning disabilities with frequent progress checks and offer positive feedback concerning their progress toward an individual or class goal.
- Give immediate feedback to students with learning disabilities. They need to quickly see the relationship between what was taught and what was learned.
- Provide oral instruction for students with reading disabilities. Allow these students to take written assessments orally.
- Make activities concise and short, whenever possible. Long, drawn-out projects are particularly frustrating for a child with a learning disability.
- Provide concrete examples, objects, and events to learners who have difficulty with abstract ideas. These learners benefit from hands-on learning experiences.
- Do not hesitate to repeat instructions or offer information in both written and verbal formats. Allow children who have learning disabilities to employ as many of their sensory modalities as possible.
- Encourage collaborative learning and invite students of varying abilities to work together on a specific project or toward a common goal.

Teaching Students with Hearing Impairments. Hearing impairment ranges from mildly impaired to total deafness. It is unlikely that you will have deaf students in your classroom; however, it is possible one or more learners will need to wear hearing aids. It is also likely that some students will not be identified as hearing impaired but may have less than perfect hearing. The following are some strategies that relate to students with impaired hearing:

- Seat a child with a hearing impairment in the front of the classroom and in a place where he or she has a good field of vision of both you and the chalkboard.
- Provide written or pictorial directions. Physically act out the steps for any learning activity. Allow other students in the class to do this.
- Clearly enunciate your words and discretely look in the direction of the student with a hearing impairment regularly.
- Provide a variety of multisensory experiences for students. Use lots of concrete objects such as models, pictures, and diagrams. Try to demonstrate what you are saying by using touchable items.
- Wait longer than usual for a response from a hearing impaired student. Model patience and proactively include students with hearing impairments in discussions.

Teaching Students with Visual Impairments. All students exhibit different levels of visual acuity. Often learners need to wear special glasses and require the use of special equipment. Although it is unlikely that you will have a student who is blind in your classroom, it is conceivable that you will need to provide a modified instructional plan for students with visual limitations. The following are some instructional modifications that may be helpful for these students:

- As with learners with hearing impairments, it is important to seat the student with a visual impairment close to the main instructional area.
- Tape-record portions of textbooks, trade books, and other printed materials so students can listen (with earphones) to an oral presentation of written material.
- Provide clear oral instructions. Probe students with questions to make certain they understand what you have said.
- Be aware of terminology that demands visual acuity. Phrases such as "right here" and "like this one" are inappropriate.
- Partner the student with other students who can assist or help.

Teaching Students with Physical Impairments. Learners who are physically challenged include those who require the aid of a wheelchair, walker, braces, or other physical aids for getting around. They may have difficulty speaking, breathing, or swallowing. Despite these physical impairments, these students do not differ intellectually from other students. The following are some helpful instructional techniques:

- Provide adequate access to all parts of the classroom. Keep aisles between desks clear, and provide sufficient space around demonstration tables and other apparatus for students with physical disabilities to maneuver.
- When designing a learning activity or constructing necessary equipment, be on the lookout for alternative methods of display, manipulation, or presentation.
- Allow students who are physically able to assist students with physical disabilities in moving about the room. Students enjoy the opportunity to assist others.
- Students with physical disabilities can become frustrated because they cannot respond quickly. Take time to help them express their feelings and/or frustrations out in the open. Remind these learners that their feelings are natural.

Teaching Learners with Emotional Difficulties. Students with emotional difficulties suffer from many diverse problems. They may have difficulty developing interpersonal relationships, or they may develop physical symptoms or fears associated with personal or school problems. Some learners may be quite passive and silent or they may act out and exhibit inappropriate types of behavior even under normal circumstances. Although it is not always possible to solve the underlying problems that such learners experience, it is possible to have a positive impact on such learners' ability to seek solutions and work in concert with those trying to help them. The following are some guidelines for helping learners with emotional difficulties:

- Seat the child with an emotional impairment away from any distractions (highly verbal students, equipment, tools, etc.).
- Provide opportunities for the student to self-select a learning activity that he or she would like to pursue independently. Invite the student to share his or her findings or discoveries with the rest of the class.
- Get the student involved in activities with other students—particularly those students who can serve as good role models for the child. It is important that the child with emotional disabilities have opportunities to interact with fellow students who can provide appropriate behavioral guidelines through their actions.
- Students with emotional disabilities generally benefit from a highly structured program— one in which the sequence of activities and procedures is consistent and clear. Whenever possible, keep the activities short and quick. Provide immediate feedback, reinforcement, and a sufficient amount of praise.

You are not alone when you are working with students with special needs. Often specialists, clinicians, and other experts are available in the school as part of an educational team. Included on the team may be special education teachers, diagnosticians, parents, social workers, representatives

Often, determining students' dispositions is as easy as looking at each student individually.

from community agencies, administrators, and other teachers. By working in concert and sharing ideas, you can provide a purposeful education plan for each student with special needs.

JOURNAL FOR REFLECTION 12.2

An important part of teacher success is related to how well teachers implement the learning standards of the school district. Select one standard from your state standards and list a differentiated set of learning activities that relate to the target standard but also meet the diverse learning needs of students in a typical classroom. Consider specific learning activities for learners with different abilities, learning styles, and misconceptions as well as for ELL and special education learners. Once you have listed these different learning activities, consider how you might have students collaborate.

MONITORING PROGRESS THROUGH DATA-DRIVEN INSTRUCTION

We have examined the many pieces that make up the curriculum and how the delivery of the curriculum through teaching adds another dimension. A third component of the curriculum relates to the ongoing monitoring of progress. Monitoring student achievement has always been embedded in the act of teaching, but recently "Monitoring Progress" is often noted as a separate piece to the curriculum puzzle. The process of monitoring students' progress is much more than simply examining tests and assessments or giving grades. It is equally important to design new instruction in light of daily assessments.

Classroom-based assessments are invaluable tools toward achieving differentiated instruction that meets the unique needs of different types of learners. Assessments can range from short quizzes that relate to the specific learning outcomes of the day to performance and summative assessments that relate to multiple outcomes. However, it is not enough merely to provide these assessments, it is equally important to take time to examine them and connect the results to new instructional approaches. In her book *Data Driven Instruction*, Rebecca J. Blink (2007) suggests that teachers break down data-driven instruction into six steps:

Data Collection—determine which pieces of data you will need to make a good instructional decision about a student. For example, you might want to know if a student understands that to multiply 2-digit numbers by 2-digit numbers implies that the first number (the multiplicand) is really added to itself over and over again as many times as the second number (multiplier). Simply asking students to multiply 2-digit numbers and show their answers is NOT a good data collection approach. What is really needed is to observe and collect students' work as they try to multiply the 2-digit numbers. Examining the approach that students use is more important than simply collecting their answers. You might even interview some students as they are working on their answers; you would then take notes on what they tell you.

Data Reflection—plan some time every day to look at and analyze information you have on your students to help you determine what they need from you.

Data Translation—what BIG things need to change based on the information you have (curriculum, course offerings, scope and sequence, etc.)

Data-Driven Instructional Design—plan your lessons based on the data you have for each student. This requires instructional differentiation to meet the needs of all learners in your classroom.

Design Feedback—watch and see if your data-driven lesson has been effective. If not, what can you change? If so, celebrate that success!

Summative/Formative Assessment—use the information you have to evaluate student progress (formative assessment) and the success of programs or processes (summative assessment).[3]

No matter what method you use, the key here is that an effective teacher is one who constantly rethinks and redesigns instruction based on an on-going data collection processes. By so doing, not only do students learn, but they also benefit from instruction that is differentiated according to their needs.

MODELS FOR SCHOOL CURRICULUM REFORM

During the past three decades, there has been continuing and ever-increasing frustration with U.S. schools. National, state, and local policy makers frequently use criticism of schools in their campaigns for political office. Education researchers and leading educators also regularly express concern about the quality of schools and the readiness of high school graduates to enter the workforce. In response, educators have developed a number of school reform models. **School reform** models are comprehensive schoolwide efforts to change curriculum and instruction with the expressed intent of increasing student test scores. School reforms are systematic, multiyear, involve all school staff and all subject areas, and are organized to focus all efforts on curriculum and instruction in order to increase student learning.

Each of these reform models is led by a university scholar, and the participating schools will often belong to a regional or national network of schools engaged in the same approach. Teachers receive special training and are expected to use certain instructional approaches. Each approach involves a number of schoolwide elements including acceptance of certain beliefs about students and learning, use of specified curriculum and teaching strategies, and a special vocabulary that draws attention to the core philosophy and principles of the reform model. A sampling of these reform models are described briefly in the following paragraphs.

Professional Learning Communities

A widespread approach for gradual improvement of school curricula is the school improvement process (SIP), discussed earlier. The typical SIP requires a number of steps, including principal leadership, and the establishment of a school SIP team composed of teachers, department chairs or grade-level team leaders, and parents. School improvement processes have an annual rhythm to them. During spring the SIP team will hold meetings and examine test scores and other data about how well students are performing. The SIP team produces a school improvement plan that identifies specific targets that everyone in the school will work on during the next year.

Many school districts realize that to achieve ongoing improvement, teachers need to work together and understand what each other is doing in their respective classrooms. Professional learning communities (PLC) are often established as a mechanism for enabling teachers to work on the school improvement plan by collaboratively determining unique approaches that they will use in an effort to meet the targets for that year. **Professional learning communities** are teams of teachers who work together to improve student learning by developing common goals, determining ways to meet these goals, implementing different approaches, and collecting data to determine if the approaches have met their goals.

GO TO ···›
More information about school improvement can be found in Chapter 9.

school reform The use of comprehensive programs that are intended to bring about schoolwide changes in curriculum and instruction and thereby increase learning outcomes for all students.

professional learning communities Teams of teachers who work together to improve student learning by developing common goals, determining ways to meet these goals, implementing different approaches, and collecting data to determine if the approaches have met their goals.

---

[3]From Data-Driven Instructional Leadership by Rebecca J. Blink. Reprinted by permission of Eye on Education.

Success for All (SFA)

The Success for All (SFA) school reform model was developed by Robert Slavin (1996) of Johns Hopkins University. The foundations for SFA demonstrate another important feature of school reform models—they are based on findings from classroom research. In the case of SFA, much of the research was done in inner-city schools with children who were truly at risk of failure and in schools with track records of failure. As a result, SFA was developed around the core assumption that every child can read. Implementation of SFA begins with a structured approach to the curriculum and support for children as they learn to read. For example, the first step is the use of strategies designed to get children ready for school, including strong preschool and kindergarten reading-readiness programs. Curriculum instruction and classroom management are addressed through training for all teachers.

The approach includes specific reading books, the use of reading tutors, and eight-week reading assessments. All reading teachers employ a prescribed strategy. For example, reading time begins with the teacher reading children's literature to the students and engaging them in a discussion of the story. Another component is Story Telling and Retelling (STaR), which engages the students in listening, retelling, and dramatizing literature. Each of these components has been derived from earlier research studies, and SFA is regularly evaluated to assess how well it is working in terms of increasing student achievement.

School Development Program (SDP)

Developed by child psychologist James Comer and his colleagues at the Yale Center for the Study of Children, the School Development Program (SDP) is a research-based, comprehensive K–12 education reform program grounded in the principles of child, adolescent, and adult development (Comer, 2009; Comer, Joyner & Ben-Avie, 2004). The Comer Process is a way of managing, organizing, coordinating, and integrating programs and activities. Three teams—the School Planning and Management Team (SPMT), the Student and Staff Support Team (SSST), and the Parent Team—work together to create a Comprehensive School Plan (CSP). This involves designing and conducting staff development aligned with the goals of the Comprehensive School Plan and assessing and modifying the plan as necessary using a wide range of student and school-level data to ensure that the school is continuously improving. The teams are guided by three principles: decision making by consensus, no-fault problem solving, and collaboration. The process also facilitates the creation of an environment that promotes the adult–student interactions necessary for good student development and academic learning in school, even when such an environment was not adequately provided prior to school.

Increased Emphasis on Science, Technology, Engineering, and Mathematics (STEM)

Given that school districts often require annual testing in reading and mathematics, there is now an increased emphasis on teaching these subjects. One unexpected outcome from this emphasis is that other subjects (such as social studies and science) have been somewhat neglected. For example, teachers have begun to emphasize reading skills rather than science and social studies concepts. Science classrooms, which at one time had students investigating various science phenomena, now have students reading from textbooks while using some new reading strategy. The reasoning behind this is that by embedding reading strategies that relate to technical content students learn science content while also mastering a specific reading skill needed in science.

In 2011–2012, researchers from Interactive Educational Systems Design (2012) conducted an online survey of 1,079 K–12 educators that showed serious challenges facing STEM education: insufficient K–12 funding specifically designated for STEM education, inadequate K–8 STEM education, and insufficient professional development for STEM teachers . Such concerns about the quality of science and social science education have led to the development of a number of coalitions focused on supporting science, technology, engineering, and mathematics (STEM) education. The STEM Education Coalition is dedicated to ensuing quality STEM education at all grade levels and is comprised of different sectors of the technological workforce—from knowledge workers, to educators, to scientists, engineers, and technicians.

GO TO ···>
More information about professional learning communities can be found in Chapter 13.

Growing awareness of the importance of improving STEM education has led to a variety of opportunities for school curriculum improvement. School districts have begun to develop elementary, middle, and high school magnet **STEM schools** that focus on developing science, technology, engineering, and mathematics curriculum. Other school districts have taken advantage of developing STEM grant proposals available through private foundations and the National Science Foundation. Clearly, these initiatives have the potential to change the current curriculum and instruction landscape.

STEM schools Schools that focus on developing science, technology, engineering, and mathematics.

JOURNAL FOR REFLECTION 12.3

Think about the curriculum reforms that were presented. Which of these would you personally endorse and why?

SUMMARY

WHAT IS CURRICULUM AND HOW DOES IT DEVELOP?

- Curriculum is the environment that is created by the interaction of all of the elements that support learning.

- As befits our democracy, many people and groups have a say in selecting the curriculum for public schools. The most important beginning step in developing a curriculum is gaining consensus about desired learning outcomes.

- Large-scale influences on curriculum include court cases, state and federal legislation, national reports, common standards, and educational research, as well as textbook publishers. Another macro-level influence on the curriculum is the various interest groups, such as teacher and administrator organizations, political parties, and religious advocacy groups.

- The local community's unique population and characteristics also influence the design of a curriculum. Ultimately, however, curriculum is delivered in classrooms and the role of the teacher in implementing today's curriculum is critical.

- Establishing the curriculum is a complex and dynamic process that takes place well before teachers plan for instruction.

- The various curriculum designs include subject-centered, themed, spiral, core, mastery, and problem- or standards-based approaches.

- Two other significant components of the curriculum are the co-curriculum and the hidden curriculum. For many students these are their reasons for staying in or dropping out of school.

SELECTION AND MANAGEMENT OF CURRICULUM

- In the United States, the legal responsibility for schools and for the curriculum lies with each state. In general, states establish what students are expected to learn and what instructional materials can be used.

- School districts assist in the management of curriculum by setting up textbook selection committees and hiring professional specialists whose responsibility it is to see that each curriculum area is supported and that teachers are prepared.

- On the local level, teachers must do their part by keeping informed about the state standards and the benchmarks for their students' grade-level while teaching with the materials and strategies that help all students learn.

EVALUATING CURRICULUM

- Two important national approaches to curriculum evaluation are the National Assessment of Educational Progress and the testing at most grade levels mandated in the No Child Left Behind Act.

- In today's high-stakes testing environment, school districts and states are focused on student performance on standardized tests as an evaluation of the curriculum.

- Curriculum evaluation is primarily based on what occurs in the classroom. Until the curriculum is implemented and student learning is assessed, direct evidence of curriculum effectiveness cannot be obtained. Teachers are on the front line of the curriculum because they personally deliver instruction and see the effects of curricular materials on a daily basis.

- It is important for teachers to collect and examine student achievement data regularly. Sharing insights drawn from classrooms with other teachers and administrators keeps the curriculum current.

INSTRUCTION: THE TEACHING SIDE OF CURRICULUM

- Teachers have primary responsibility for translating the standards for learning and the curriculum into minute-to-minute and day-to-day learning experiences for students—in other words, instruction.

- Following analysis of the standards and benchmarks, teachers must develop instructional objectives for each lesson and employ teaching strategies that will engage the students.

- Teaching involves the development of cognition, skills, and dispositions.

TEACHING STRATEGIES

- Direct instruction provided by lecture and recitation is one of the oldest forms of instruction and still has a place in contemporary teaching.
- Indirect instruction strategies are those that cover a large number of teaching strategies in which students have greater responsibility for structuring tasks and managing their own learning.
- Indirect instruction strategies include guided discovery, inquiry, and problem-based approaches.
- Self-regulated learning strategies are important for all types of instruction. These include cognitive learning strategies, metacognitive strategies, social and affective strategies, and scaffolding strategies.
- Organizing students in groups is an important component of instruction. Three common types of grouping are homogeneous, heterogeneous, and cooperative.

USE OF TECHNOLOGY TO ENHANCE INSTRUCTION

- The current challenge for using technology effectively in the classroom is to develop an *integrated approach* to instruction rather than to simply use a computer-assisted learning program here and there.
- One way to consider using technology in instruction is to view it as a set of tools. Four basic tools that have been used for decades are word processing, spreadsheet, presentation programs, and adaptive assessment software.
- Drill-and-practice software provides exercises in which students work example items, usually one at a time, and receive feedback on their correctness. Programs vary considerably on the type of feedback they provide; some programs simply display "Ok" or "Try again" while others restate the answer a student selected and explain why it is incorrect.
- Tutorial software is an entire instructional sequence on a topic similar to a teacher's classroom instruction. This instruction usually is expected to offer a self-contained instructional unit rather than offering a supplement to other instruction.
- Simulations provide interdisciplinary learning opportunities often focused on science and social studies scenarios. Interactive simulations allow students to enter into different eras and scenarios and experience events based on their own response to the simulated realities.
- An interactive whiteboard consists of a regular whiteboard glossy surface that uses erasable markers and is connected to a computer and digital projector that allows information projected on the screen to be manipulated with hands and special pens.
- Currently one of the most powerful uses of Internet tools is for collaboration and social networking. Powerful tools that make collaboration quite rich include avatar spaces, wikis, podcasts, e-portfolios, blogs, video and photo sharing, and social networking websites. The key to using these different tools is to integrate them into specific instructional units as needed.
- Assistive technology for individuals with severe physical disabilities may take the form of a power wheelchair operated by a joystick, a control device with a handle that moves in all directions. To provide access to a computer, it is often necessary to offer an alternative to the keyboard. Switches are commonly used for controlling and getting input as well as activating environmental control systems. Assessing the need for assistive technology involves a team of specialists including occupational and physical therapists, rehabilitation engineers, and assistive technology specialists.

MATCHING INSTRUCTION TO LEARNERS' NEEDS

- Differentiation can be based on several different areas: academic ability, learning-style differences, subject matter misconceptions, career interests, second language learner needs, special education learner needs, and so on.
- Teachers must make sure that all students, including ELLs and students with special needs, are able to participate and develop understanding.
- In practice, teachers of ELL students should include two kinds of objectives for every lesson: language and content. Content objectives are established for all students. For the ELL students, adding a language objective helps with their language development.
- In schools where the principal and teachers share the belief that all students can learn and where there is a shared responsibility for helping all students learn, all students do learn more.
- Developing a general list of instructional strategies for learners with special needs is problematic because their needs differ considerably. Students with learning disabilities, visual and aural impairments, physical impairments, emotional difficulties, and attention deficits require different instructional modifications.
- The best approach to designing these modifications is to develop an awareness of each child's unique characteristics, examine the many teaching resources that are available, share ideas and questions with other teachers, note learner responses to the instruction, and make additional modifications.

MONITORING PROGRESS THROUGH DATA-DRIVEN INSTRUCTION

- Monitoring students' progress means that teachers, schools, districts, and states examine ways to differentiate and look at all sorts of data on a regular basis.
- Data Driven Instruction includes six steps: data collection, data reflection, data translation, data-driven instructional design, design feedback, and summative/formative assessment.

MODELS FOR SCHOOL CURRICULUM REFORM

- Many schools are implementing a curriculum reform model that provides teachers with additional curriculum resources and instructional strategies.

- School improvement programs are the most general type of school reform in that they propose setting target achievement levels and making changes to the curriculum based on annual evaluations. Professional learning communities provide a collaborative way of developing the curriculum and keeping it current.

- Success for All (SFA) reform implements a structured approach to the curriculum and support for inner-city children to read. Curriculum instruction and classroom management are addressed through training for all teachers. The approach includes specific reading books, the use of reading tutors, and eight-week reading assessments. All reading teachers employ a prescribed strategy.

- School Development Program (SDP) reform is a way of managing, organizing, coordinating, and integrating programs and activities. Three teams—the School Planning and Management Team (SPMT), the Student and Staff Support Team (SSST), and the Parent Team—work together to create a Comprehensive School Plan (CSP) to design and conduct staff development aligned with the goals of the Comprehensive School Plan and to assess and modify the plan as necessary, using a wide range of student and school-level data to ensure that the school is continuously improving.

- There is a concerted effort to place greater emphasis on science, technology, engineering and mathematics (STEM).

DISCUSSION STARTERS

1. The curriculum comprises not only the formal statement of standards, materials, and teacher guides, but also the cocurriculum and the hidden curriculum. For a particular subject such as literacy, mathematics, or science, how have you seen these three types of curriculum affect you and other students? What roles did your teachers play with each type of curriculum?

2. Today's teachers have the major responsibility for instruction. For the most part the curriculum is set. What do you see as the keys to providing effective instruction? What can you do to be sure that the instructional objectives you set for a given lesson engage all your students?

3. Integrating technology is the best way to use technology in today's classrooms. Share a specific example of using an integrated approach to technology while teaching a single lesson.

4. Select two or three instructional practices that meet the needs of English-language and special needs learners. Explain why you think these practices are especially worthy.

5. Describe ways that one of your teachers monitored progress in an effort to determine if students were learning well. What would you as a teacher do differently?

6. Which model for school reform do you think really will make a difference to today's schools? Explain why.

SCHOOL-BASED OBSERVATIONS

1. During practicum and other classroom observation experiences, be sure to examine the curriculum materials provided for the teacher. Which elements of the curriculum designs can you trace back to the various sources and influences on curriculum development?

2. Examine a teacher's lesson plans in order to see the connections to state and district standards, to yearly benchmarks, and to the learning objectives for the lesson(s) you are observing. What are the clear themes in terms of expectations for student learning? In what ways does the lesson facilitate students learning the stated objectives?

3. When observing classrooms, look for the students who have limited English-language skills. What special steps does the teacher take to facilitate these students' learning? What are these students doing to learn the content of the lesson as well as the English language?

4. Technology can be used in a wide variety of ways in classrooms and within lessons. In classrooms where you are observing, how is technology used? Which types of technology are supports for the teacher? Which types are used directly by the students? What types of integrated technology are used?

PORTFOLIO DEVELOPMENT

1. Find a copy of a curriculum guide for a subject that you plan to teach. As you study the guide, make notes about the topics you already know well enough. Also identify those topics where you will need to learn more before you can be an effective teacher. Make a table for these two lists that has a "Comments" column so that in the future you can make notes about what you have learned as you continue with your teacher education program.

2. At the library or when visiting a school curriculum resource room, examine the curriculum materials for a subject that you plan to teach. For one lesson, use Bloom's taxonomy as a guide and write a set of learning objectives. This task will provide you with experience and a sample product that you can use as you are planning lessons in the future.

WEB SOLUTIONS

There is a growing concern about the lack of emphasis in science and social studies within elementary schools. If your school asked you to participate in a curriculum committee charged with the task of strengthening its science and social studies curriculum, the following websites might help you determine recommendations for change.

www.ascd.org Founded in 1943, the Association for Supervision and Curriculum Development is dedicated to advancing best practices and policies for the success of each learner. The professional organization of more than 175,000 members in 119 countries includes professional educators from all levels and subject areas: superintendents, supervisors, principals, teachers, professors of education, and school board members. The site has a wealth of resources about curriculum improvement.

http://nces.ed.gov/timss/ The Trends in International Mathematics and Science Study (TIMSS) provides reliable and timely data on the mathematics and science achievement of U.S. fourth- and eighth-grade students compared to that of students in other countries. TIMSS data have been collected in 1995, 1999, 2003, 2007, and 2011.

www.stemedcoalition.org/ The Science, Technology, Engineering, and Mathematics (STEM) Education Coalition works to support STEM programs for teachers and students in the United States. Its website provides research reports about STEM programs across the nation as well as resources that can help teachers integrate science, social studies, mathematics, and language.

MyEducationLab™

Go to the topic **Curriculum and Instruction** in the MyEducationLab (www.myeducationlab.com) for *Foundations of American Education: Becoming Effective Teachers in Challenging Times, 16e,* where you can:

- Find learning outcomes for **Curriculum and Instruction**, along with the national standards that connect to these outcomes.
- Complete Assignments and Activities that can help you more deeply understand the chapter content.
- Apply and practice your understanding of the core teaching skills identified in the chapter with the Building Teaching Skills and Dispositions learning units.
- Access video clips of CCSSO National Teachers of the Year award winners responding to the question, "Why Do I Teach?" in the Teacher Talk section.
- Create, update, and share quality lesson plans with the Lesson Plan Builder.

- Access state licensure test requirements, overviews of what tests cover, and sample test items in the Certification and Licensure section.
- Access current state and national standards in the Licensure and Standards section.
- Learn how to create a high-quality teaching portfolio in the Preparing a Portfolio section.
- Access tips, advice, and other information on resume writing and interviewing, your first year of teaching, and law and public policies in the Beginning Your Career section.
- Check your comprehension of the content covered in the chapter with the Study Plan. Here you will be able to take a chapter pretest, receive feedback on your answers, and then access personalized Review, Practice, and Enrichment exercises to enhance your understanding of chapter content. After you complete the exercises, take a posttest to confirm your comprehension.

Becoming an Effective Teacher in a Challenging World

LEARNING OUTCOMES

After reading and studying this chapter, you should be able to:

1. Present an overview of the continuing national pressures to reform schools. (InTASC Standard 10: Leadership and Collaboration)

2. Describe key characteristics of effective schools. (InTASC Standard 9: Professional Learning and Ethical Practice)

3. Present the case for why and how high-quality teachers use evidence. (InTASC Standard 6: Assessment) and clarify your philosophy of what high-quality teaching and high-quality schools are like. (InTASC Standard 7: Planning for Instruction)

4. List several ways that you, as an educator, may effectively deal with challenging changes in the future. (InTASC Standard 10: Leadership and Collaboration)

5. Summarize key sources of support that you will have access to as a first-year teacher. (InTASC Standard 7: Planning for Instruction)

6. List and discuss several professional organizations that you may wish to join and in which you may wish to participate. (InTASC Standards 9 and 10: Professional Responsibility)

EDUCATION in the NEWS

NEWMARKET TEACHER EARNS "ED" AWARD

By JOSHUA CLARK

Seacoastonline.com

In her five years as a teacher at the Newmarket Junior/Senior High School, Venera Gattonini has endeavored to inspire and instill within her students the same passion and understanding for the industrial arts that she has.

On Saturday, she was rewarded for her work with a 2009 New Hampshire Excellence in Education Award for Program Excellence in Technology Education. In a ceremony held at the Radisson Hotel in Manchester, the 16th Annual "ED"ies, hosted by the New Hampshire Excellence in Education Award Program organization, gave out forty awards to outstanding public schools, programs, and educators.

Gattonini said she was both excited and encouraged to be honored with the award.

"It makes me feel encouraged to keep moving forward and continue to get students excited about what I feel passionately about," she said.

Chris Andriski, principal of the Newmarket Junior/Senior High School, said the school is truly excited to see one of its teachers recognized for her hard work in such a manner.

"An award like this is long overdue for the amount of time and work she puts in both inside and outside the classroom creating high-quality work that makes us all proud," Andriski said.

Through her work Gattonini teaches students in grades 6 to 12. She instructs them to understand and properly use each of the tools in the wood shop. She also introduces them to each of the disciplines within the industrial arts program, including manufacturing, construction, architecture, and design.

"I want them to understand and experience each of the different facets [of industrial arts]," she said.

Gattonini has made it a point to make it clear to her students that "they have a voice they can imbue within whatever they make." This point was evidenced by her work with grades 6 to 8 students that showcased each of their aesthetic sensibilities.

Students are asked to infuse personal experiences and tastes into their work whether it be a fork, spoon, cutting board, clock, or coat rack.

The goal is to design and ultimately create what Gattonini hopes will be "something completely different from what they're used to seeing."

"I want the students to know they have the ability to accomplish anything they set out to do," she said.

One of the most important aspects of the program, said Gattonini, is providing students with practical, hands-on experience that enables them to leave school with viable tools and skills that can be utilized in a number of areas.

Providing them with real-world skills aside, Gattonini said the greatest part of working with the students comes from being able to see them "light up at seeing what they've created," after confronting any fears they may have had about using the tools.

"Hopefully, the skills they learn here can be something they carry with them throughout life, whether in their career, as a hobby or being able to fix something around the house," she said.

"It truly delights me to see the reactions in students when they become confident in their abilities," she said.

QUESTIONS FOR REFLECTION

1. What are some of the qualities of Ms. Gattonini that make her a high-quality teacher?
2. Ms. Gattonini teaches industrial arts. To what extent are you aware of the dramatic changes in this program area in recent years?
3. What are some ways in which this program area can help all students succeed?
4. If you were a teacher in this school, how would you collaborate with Ms. Gattonini so that the students you share will benefit?

Source: "Newmarket Teacher Earns 'ED' Award" by Joshua Clark. Seacoastonline.com June 16, 2009. Reprinted by permission of Seacoast Media Group.

MyEducationLab™

Visit the MyEducationLab for *Foundations of American Education* to enhance your understanding of chapter concepts with a personalized *Study Plan.* You'll also have the opportunity to hone your teaching skills through video- and case-based *Assignments and Activities* and *Building Teaching Skills and Dispositions* lessons.

DIFFERENT PERSPECTIVES FOR VIEWING EDUCATION AND TEACHING

This text has been organized around the major theme: perspectives on education in a changing and challenging world. As you already know there are many different viewpoints (or perspectives) regarding education. Some viewpoints are similar and others are diametrically opposed, such as idealism versus realism or local control versus direction from central governments. The world will continue to change rapidly—perhaps even at an accelerated rate. For example, as society becomes more diverse, so do schools. Different philosophical perspectives lead to different expectations for the curriculum and for the teacher's role.

In spite of these many challenges and rapid changes, this is an exciting and very important time to be a teacher. The United States has a three hundred plus–year history of development of education policies, sixty plus years of findings from systematic research, and continuing development of innovative practices that offer a rich foundation for teachers to use in making a difference. From here forward, the most critical factor for you to keep in mind is that high-quality teachers are continually focused on doing those things that make a positive difference in student learning. Your every effort as an educator must first and foremost be aimed at improving the learning of all students.

Recent Trends in Attempts to Improve Education

GO TO ⋯>

Chapters 2 and 3 provide rich descriptions of the historical background, events, and actions that have led to the shape of education today.

As we have seen in recent years, as economic conditions have declined schools have suffered the consequence of lower funding. Table 13.1 shows a number of other trends that have emerged and that have significant implications for schools, teachers, and students. Each of these trends has an additional implication for you and your teaching career. There will be change! Much of what teachers did well in the past will not work in the future. Much of what you see as effective teaching today will likely not be what you will be doing a decade from now.

Continuing Pressures to Reform Schools

school reform Major school-wide initiatives to change curriculum, instruction, and/or within-school organizational arrangements.

In many ways, the concerns about and expectations for education and for teachers have always been based on the contemporary problems and concerns of American society. When there has been a problem in society, policy makers have typically turned to the schools as a source of the problem and/or as a resource for solving the problem. This pattern of moving from crisis to **school reform** has happened repeatedly, as discussed in the following section.

TABLE 13.1

Key Trends with Implications for Schools, Teachers, and Students

TRENDS	IMPLICATIONS FOR SCHOOLS, TEACHERS, AND STUDENTS
Economic recession, mortgage defaults, bankruptcies, and increased unemployment	• Reduced taxes lead to reductions in school budgets • Loss of extra-curriculum activities • Increases in class size • Fewer teachers being hired
Increased expectations for accountability	• Annual testing as required by NCLB • Increased criteria for teacher licensure • School reform • School improvement plans • Evaluation of schools based on student performance • Teacher pay based on student and school performance
Availability of research and evaluation findings	• Required use of evidence-based curriculum • Expectation that schools will use data in planning improvement efforts • Expectations that teachers will use data in planning instruction
Increasing student diversity	• Use of multicultural curriculum • Teaching students with limited English proficiency • Reducing the achievement gap • Ensuring appropriate assessment, placement, and instruction for students with special needs
Rapid technology developments	• More tools and resources to support classroom instruction • More tools for administration of budgets, schedules, and communication • Social networking

REFLECTING ON THE OVERALL PATTERN OF FEDERAL REFORM STRATEGIES. One of the challenges for you as a teacher education candidate, both now and in your future as a teacher, is to be able to see overall patterns and themes. It is all too easy to become fully occupied with details of the moment. Each day, each class period, and each week will be filled with tasks and demands. Be sure to regularly take time to pull back and view the big picture of what is happening. Otherwise, you run the risk of not seeing professional growth in yourself and each student's growth in learning. This is an important reason for taking time to reflect, instead of quickly acting. The metaphor of not only seeing the details of a tree but also being able to see the forest is appropriate. High-quality teachers do both. They see the details of how each of their students is doing within each lesson, and they also can see patterns of student growth across lessons, days, weeks, and months.

DIFFERENT LEVERS FOR "FIXING" SCHOOLS. Federal education policy has changed and evolved over time. These policy changes suggest that the following four different levers have been used by the federal government as ways of reforming education:

1. *Fix the parts:* This perspective is reflective of the massive curriculum development projects of the 1960s.

2. *Fix the people:* Some see teacher training and professional development as the key to improving education.

3. *Fix the school:* Implementing one of the various whole-school reform models and reorganizing schools are seen as ways to change whole schools.

4. *Fix the system:* We now are in a time when the whole system of education is seen as needing change. This requires consideration of all perspectives discussed in this text.

As a teacher you will be part of many efforts to change and improve education. To help you in being reflective, you can use these four "fixes" as a way of considering the intent of future change approaches.

During the last fifty years, federal involvement in educational policy has continued to increase.

Each New President Has a New Agenda for Education

The arrival of each new president spurs new initiatives to improve education. Education is often seen as a key lever for solving state and national problems such as, for instance, an economic crisis. As an example, a policy response in 2009 by Congress was to pass the American Recovery and Reinvestment Act. This act included heavy investments in education. Under this act $5 billion was provided for early learning programs; $77 billion for reforms to strengthen K–12 education; and $8.5 billion was to be used to encourage states to make improvements in teacher effectiveness, make progress toward college and career-ready standards, and improve achievement in low-performing schools. A key rationale was to link improving the nation's economic competitiveness with every child receiving an education "that will enable them to succeed in a global economy that is predicated on knowledge and innovation" (*Issues: Education*, 2009).

All economic crises make the future financial support of education very uncertain, as do changes by policy makers. It is likely that our schools will have less financial support in the future and will need to find new, more creative, and more economical ways to help students learn.

Findings from Education Research and Development: Another Pressure for Changes in Teaching and Schools

Beginning with President Johnson's Great Society initiatives some years ago, education research—like education itself—also came under the direction of the federal government. Both the 1965 and 1966 ESEA statutes included major multiyear funding for education research and development (R&D). This was unprecedented for education. Results from these efforts include many studies of what teachers do, identification of school characteristics that are correlated with student test scores, the role of principals, and the importance of teacher training and professional development. In all cases the criterion for quality and effectiveness is whether there are improvements in student learning.

LENGTH OF SCHOOL YEAR. Some people believe that there is evidence, and it also seems logical, that a longer school year would help students learn more. Others seem to believe that students and teachers need our current school vacations to "recharge their batteries." Some schools have already lengthened their school year.

EFFECTIVE TEACHING AND CLASSROOM MANAGEMENT. In the 1970s researchers funded through ESEA grants identified strong correlations between student test scores and teacher behaviors. Across school years some teachers' students always scored higher, whereas the students of other teachers always scored lower (Brophy & Good, 1974). This research has resulted in the formulation of a model called the "effective teaching" model. The first principle in this model is for teachers to create a classroom climate that is supportive and where students feel comfortable making mistakes.

Other researchers and educators have identified other important characteristics of effective classrooms (Emmer, Evertson, & Anderson, 1980). For example, effective teachers have a middle-range number of classroom rules. Fewer than five rules means the rules are too broad, and more than ten means they are too specific. Food for thought?

EFFECTIVE SCHOOLS. In the 1980s researchers examined the characteristics of schools where students had higher test scores. This research led to the formulation of an "effective schools" model. Characteristics of these schools included a shared vision and goals, concern about teaching and learning, purposeful teaching, high expectations, and home–school partnerships. One concern to keep in mind about both the effective teaching and effective schools models is that the criterion for effectiveness is student academic achievement. Much less is known about social and affective outcomes.

"VALUE ADDED" FOR SMALL CLASS SIZE. In the 1990s, another approach to identification of the relationships between teachers and student learning emerged out of Tennessee. In this project, the Student/Teacher Achievement Ratio (STAR) study, students entering kindergarten were assigned at random to "small classes" (thirteen to seventeen students), a "regular class" (twenty-two to twenty-six students), or a "regular class with a full-time teacher aide" within each participating school. A total of 329 classrooms in seventy-nine schools in forty-six districts participated. The study followed the students throughout the 1990s. Findings include the following: (1) Students in small classes had superior academic performance. (2) No differences were found between teacher-aide classes and regular classes. (3) Small classes were advantageous for boys and girls, there were greater benefits for minority students and students attending inner-city schools, the small-class advantages were found for all subjects, and students in small classes had higher engagement behaviors (Finn & Achilles, 1999).

In the 1990s these types of benefits became known as **value-added** benefits. In other words, making an investment in a particular change, such as small class size, resulted in gains above what would normally be observed. Through research, an improvement in outcomes from making a particular change or an additional investment was documented.

Today's corollary of value-added benefits is **evidence-based practice**. The first question that is likely to be asked whenever a new practice, an innovative approach, or a change in instruction is proposed is, "What evidence is there that this makes a positive difference in student outcomes?" If the initiator of the change cannot provide data related to this question, there is not much likelihood that it will be adopted.

JOURNAL FOR REFLECTION 13.1

As you can see, across the last sixty years, having evidence that documents the effectiveness of classroom practices has become increasingly important. As you become a teacher, what types of evidence will you want to be able to provide about the quality of your teaching? Record your thoughts in your journal.

How to Recognize an Effective School

One important outcome of the accountability movement and the pressures to reform schools is that many indicators are now available that can be used to judge the quality of schools. Effective schools are different in a number of identifiable ways. The characteristics presented in the following sections have been selected because knowing about them is important to your success as a teacher education candidate. Chances are good that the schools where you have clinical experiences and conduct your student teaching will be attending to each of these indicators. When the time comes for you to seek a teaching position, these indicators may be good predictors of what being a teacher in the school would be like.

Data-Driven Decision Making

High-quality schools and their teachers use data continually, especially in relation to student achievement. Data are used to make instructional decisions, as well as budgetary ones. These schools do not rely heavily on the annual federal- and state-mandated testing because they do

value added A product or process for which there is evidence of greater gain than if the approach was not used.

evidence-based practice A curriculum or instructional approach for which there is research and/or evaluation studies of its effectiveness.

not delay making decisions until these results are made available. Instead, they continually study, refer to, and use three levels or *tiers* of data:

- *Tier 1:* standardized tests typically administered once a year by the state and/or the district.
- *Tier 2:* interim assessments that may have been developed for district-wide use or developed specifically by a school. These assessments are typically administered one to four times a year. They are both diagnostic and predictive. They are designed to measure the same learning outcomes as the Tier 1 tests and are scored quickly. The results are used as an early predictor of how well students will do on the Tier 1 tests. The scores from Tier 2 assessments are also diagnostic. Areas where students do not do as well can then be targeted for further instruction.
- *Tier 3:* teacher-developed measures, teacher judgment, and examples of student work. This information is used by the teacher to plan instruction daily and weekly. It also can be of use to other teachers who work with a particular student and for grade-level and department meetings.

In combination, these three tiers of evidence provide each teacher, each grade level or department, and the whole school with information to guide the next steps in instruction. Obviously, these data also provide indicators of how well the school is doing in terms of having all students succeed. Another indicator of the quality of a school is how it uses data in the development and implementation of its school improvement plan and process.

School Improvement Process

An important annual effort for all schools is a **school improvement process (SIP)**. The process begins with the school reviewing data and developing a set of **action steps** that address areas of student learning that are deficient. The data, the action steps, and a timeline for implementation are placed in a major document, the **school improvement plan**. In some schools principals write the plan and, unfortunately, teachers may not even see it. In high-quality schools a committee of teachers and administrators will lead the SIP work and at times all staff will be engaged with studying data and proposing action steps. In high-quality schools the plan will not be left on a shelf; it will be a guide for what happens across the school year, including staff development and how school resources will be allocated.

Professional Learning Communities

Effective schools have a special organizational culture that is known as a **professional learning community (PLC)**. When you visit a PLC school you will see teachers working collaboratively. They visit each other's classrooms and openly share plans, resources, and ideas. They also have a shared vision for the school and what teaching and learning should be like. There is mutual respect, high levels of trust, and regular introduction of innovative solutions to problems. An additional critical feature is that of **collegial learning**. In a PLC school there is an expectation that the adults are continually learning along with the students (Hord, 2004). A caution to note with this indicator of a high-quality school is that a PLC is not something that happens at a scheduled time: "We have PLC every Friday at 9:30." Rather, a true PLC is an indicator of the organizational culture of the school: "This is how things are done around here."

Parent and Community Involvement

Unfortunately, some schools seem to structure rules and activities in ways that limit parent involvement. Visits to classrooms are restricted, parent conferences are scheduled at times when most parents are still at work, and school office staff are not welcoming. In contrast to this, high-quality school staff members understand the importance of parent involvement.

High-quality schools use many strategies to involve parents in addition to the traditional PTA and parent volunteer programs. Strategies include sending home frequent newsletters, having class web pages, using voice mail, calling to homes to inform parents about student homework assignments, and holding early morning activities such as "Donuts with Dads" and "Muffins with Moms." They hold parent meetings on different nights for different languages and sponsor school fairs and student performances specifically designed to draw in parents and community members.

school improvement process (SIP) The annual activities that school staff members engage in to identify and resolve shortcomings in student learning.

action steps The procedures such as teacher training and use of new assessments that are implemented to address deficiencies identified in the school improvement plan.

school improvement plan The document produced each year that summarizes the data analyses and specifies action steps that will be taken.

professional learning community (PLC) A school organization culture that emphasizes collaboration and all members continuing to learn.

collegial learning Teachers learning from teachers.

Parent involvement is particularly important and challenging to achieve with immigrant families, minorities, and families with cultural differences. Parent and community involvement is also challenging in communities with a high percentage of poor families and where many of the adults have limited or no English. To address these factors, many schools employ a parent/community liaison to visit parents and facilitate communications.

Some communities have organizers who help develop parent advocacy groups. For example, in Los Angeles, a grassroots parent advocacy group called Parent U-Turn conducts surveys of parents and youth and then develops proposals for urban school reforms.

School personnel, including the principal and teachers, meet regularly to review how well all students are succeeding.

High-Quality Teachers Who Communicate Effectively with Parents

Teachers are, or should be, required to communicate frequently, skillfully, and effectively with their students' parents/caregivers. Like many new teachers, you may find this task daunting during the first few years of teaching. But like many aspects of the profession, you will likely find talking with parents very enjoyable as the years go by. The following "Perspectives on Diversity" feature provides one possible scenario of parent–teacher conferencing.

PERSPECTIVES on DIVERSITY

Parent–Teacher Conference

As the holiday season approaches, it is time for Bill to schedule his second round of parent–teacher conferences. The Red Rock school district mandates that teachers schedule a conference at the end of each report marking term. Bill's students are diverse, with the majority being Latino, and the parents are recent immigrants many of whom cannot speak English. Before the first round of conferences, he had asked other teachers how they conducted parent–teacher conferences with parents who did not speak English. Most teachers had used their students who were proficient in English to serve as translators.

Bill had done this and found that the parents were not very talkative. This was discouraging since he believed that developing parent support for education was a key to preventing so many of these kids from dropping out. His first thought was that both he and the parents had self-concerns. He sure knew that he was uncertain about how the conferences would go. It also made sense that the parents would have self-concerns about meeting with this teacher and hearing evaluations of their child. Also, in checking his class notes

from his Foundations of Education class he remembered reading that for Latino parents, placing children in a position of equal status can upset the traditional family relationships. So this time Bill decided to form small-group parent conferences for Latino parents who could not speak English. He scheduled parents based on their children's academic progress and hoped that this way there would be more parent talk and dialogue. He planned to start each conference by having the students walk their parents around the classroom and show their individual work.

WHAT IS YOUR PERSPECTIVE?

1. What do you think would be the advantages and disadvantages of having small-group parent conferences?
2. In what ways might this approach be culturally sensitive?
3. What problems/challenges would you anticipate in having several sets of parents and students meeting at the same time?
4. What do you think Bill should do about issues of student confidentiality?

In addition to the traditional PTA and parent volunteer programs, high-quality schools use many strategies to involve parents in school life.

Effective Principals

Regardless of whether the students come from poor families or middle class families, and whatever the mix of ethnic groups, how the principal and teachers lead the school makes a major difference in the quality of the education students receive. A key responsibility of the school principal is to be an effective facilitator. Each school principal is unique and each has her/his own facilitator style. Table 13.2 shows several examples of principal facilitator styles.

VISIONARY AND SUPPORTIVE PRINCIPAL LEADERSHIP. Effective schools have principals that have a vision for what the school should be like and what will make a difference in student success. They also have high expectations for their teachers. However, not all principals are like this. Recent research can be used to illustrate some of the differences in principals and their leadership. For example, one set of researchers has identified three different leadership styles of principals. They are called *initiators, managers,* and *responders* (Hall & Hord, 2011).

If you were to interview for a teaching position with each of these types of principals, they would ask you some very different questions. Study the descriptions in Table 13.2 and then think about how you would respond to their interview questions.

Initiator-Style Principal Interview Question: What evidence do you have that you can make a difference in student learning?

You should be ready to pull from your portfolio examples of lessons you have taught and the assessments you used with the lessons. You should also be ready to explain what went well, what you would do next for any students who did not do well, and how you would do the lesson differently next time.

Manager-Style Principal Interview Question: Tell me about how you would organize your classroom and schedule for a typical day.

Be ready to draw from your portfolio—which should be well organized with tabs and nothing falling out—examples of schedules you have used in your field experiences. If you have a PDA or other form of technology, be ready to show how you have used this as an organizer. Be ready to show a well-organized and clearly written plan.

Responder-Style Principal Interview Question: We have a wonderful school. I want everyone to enjoy working here. Now tell me, how would you fit in?

TABLE 13.2

Three Principal Facilitator Styles

INITIATORS: Have clear and strongly held images for what the school should be like. They focus on what will be best for students, have a passion for the school, and support their teachers. They use data, expect teachers to be involved beyond their classrooms, and champion the school to parents, the community, and the district.

MANAGERS: Are very knowledgeable about policies, rules, and procedures. They also are skilled at obtaining and managing resources including dollars and materials. They expect teachers to follow the procedures, get lesson plans and reports in on time, and maintain a focus on instruction.

RESPONDERS: Respect their teachers and assume that they know what needs to be done. They trust teachers and others to take the lead and don't believe principals need to monitor each classroom closely. They are friendly and always ready to chat about what is happening with teachers beyond their classrooms.

Yes, you will have to take more of a lead in this interview. Be ready to describe how you are prepared to teach and that you can manage your classroom well. Do not count on a lot of direct supervision or support; you will be more on your own. You also will want to indicate that you are social and friendly in your contact with colleagues.

JOURNAL FOR REFLECTION 13.2

How do the descriptions of the three principal styles compare with your experience? When you were a student and now in your field experiences, which style of principal have you found to be most effective? What did the more effective principals do that the less effective principals did not do?

LEADERSHIP STYLES. In addition to identifying these different principal styles, researchers also have found that teachers have more success with change when their principal leads with the initiator or manager style. Also, students have higher test scores in schools with principals who have a vision for what teaching and learning should be like (initiators) and those who are well organized (managers). A complicating factor for teachers is that initiator-style principals press teachers, students, and parents to do more and to work together, whereas responder-style principals leave teachers alone to do the teaching in their classrooms (Hall, Negroni, & George, 2008). You will discover that each principal you work with will make a major difference in the quality of the school and your quality as a teacher.

Checking a School for Indicators of High Quality

Any given school is likely to have some of the characteristics of a high-quality school, but probably not all. Table 13.3 is a sample checklist that could be used to assess the extent to which some of these characteristics are found in a school. This checklist is not intended to be used to evaluate a school. Instead the checklist is provided as one way to summarize some of the characteristics of a high-quality school.

EVIDENCE OF STUDENT LEARNING

In the end, the goals of having all students learning and graduating and having schools of high quality require that you become a high-quality/effective teacher. As described at the beginning of this chapter in the "Education in the News" feature about Venera Gattonini, high-quality teachers like to teach and they do everything possible to have all their students learn and succeed. These factors will increasingly be the basis for judging your quality as a teacher.

Evidence of Effective Teaching

As your career unfolds, a key term for documenting accountability will be *evidence-based practice*. Your teaching and the quality of your school will be judged based on data about student performance. In the past schools were most likely to be judged in terms of the quality of facilities and the quantity of resources such as the number of books and computers. Now schools and teachers are evaluated in terms of test scores and other indicators of student success such as graduation rates. This is what evidence-based practice is about: collecting and compiling data and providing documentation related to how well students are performing. Schools as a whole must do this, and so must individual teachers. Be sure to collect evidence of how well students have performed and what they have learned as a part of every lesson you teach.

High-quality teachers plan their lessons, manage instruction, and assess student progress.

TABLE 13.3

Checklist of Characteristics of a High-Quality School

HIGH-QUALITY CHARACTERISTICS	INDICATORS OF HIGH-QUALITY SCHOOL CHARACTERISTICS	QUESTION TO THINK ABOUT OR OBSERVATION TO MAKE
Data-Driven Decision Making	• Data about student learning are readily available. • Data are used by teachers, the principal, and other leaders. • Instructional decisions are data based. • Professional development strategies are data based.	• What types of data (Tier 1, 2, or 3) do teachers talk about? • What data are analyzed within the school improvement plan? • How easy is it for teachers to access evidence of student learning? • How often does the principal refer to data?
Visionary Leadership	• The principal has a strongly held vision for the school. • The learning needs of students come first. • The principal supports teachers. • The principal is visible in classrooms.	• What's most important to the principal? • What leadership style does the principal use? • What leadership styles do the assistant principal(s), team leaders, and department chairs use? • Do the teachers talk with the principal about instruction?
Professional Learning Community	• Teachers are collegial. • Teachers share ideas about teaching. • Teachers own all of the students in the school (not just those in their classroom). • Adults are also expected to be learners.	• What do teachers talk about in the staff lounge? • Are opportunities to attend workshops valued? • Do teachers observe in other teachers' classrooms? • Do teachers discuss what they see in other teachers' classrooms?
Parent and Community Involvement	• Parents are participating members of the school community. • One or more businesses support the school.	• Are parents regularly in classrooms? • Are parents involved in a variety of activities? • Does the school have one or more business partners?
Continuous Refinement and Testing of New Approaches	• Evidenced-based curricula are used. • Emerging new approaches are tested.	• Are there changes in curriculum and instruction approaches each year? • Are staff informed about current research and best practices?

High-Quality Teachers Are Reflective and Have a Stated Educational Philosophy About Teaching and Learning

Throughout this text one of the emphases has been on your becoming reflective. Reflection is an important characteristic of high-quality teachers. They reflect *before* teaching on what each student now knows, what they need to learn next, and what can be done in terms of instruction. High-quality teachers also are reflective *during* the act of teaching. They are thinking about how the lesson is going, continually checking for student understanding, and refining what they will do next. Of course, teachers are also reflective *after* instruction. They examine assessments for each student and think through how the lesson unfolded, what they should do next, and what they will do the next time they teach that lesson.

All of this reflection is based on a personal framework or philosophy of education. As your study of the foundations of education comes to a close, you should take a half hour to update your philosophy statement. Reflect on how far you have come in your thinking about what high-quality teaching entails. This is important to do for several reasons. For instance, you will be asked about what's important to you as a teacher when you interview for that first teaching position. Key topics and questions for you to think about in refining your statement are provided in Figure 13.1.

GO TO ⋯›
Chapter 5 provides guidance for developing an educational philosophy and rich examples of elements to be considered.

| FIGURE 13.1 | Refining Your Philosophy of Education Statement | | | | |

From time to time it is important for teachers to take a half hour or so to revisit their personal framework or philosophy of education. As you engage in reflecting on and refining your philosophy of education statement, consider the following questions:

1. What elements of schools and teaching from the past do you see as being important to continue using today?
2. Which philosophy do you think best matches your approach to teaching?

3. What role do you think schools should have in a diverse society?
4. Don't forget that there are legal, financial, and organizational aspects of schools. How do these perspectives play out in your philosophy?
5. What are your views of the standards movement, curriculum, and the current focus on student learning?
6. Given your views, what does it mean for you to be an ethical teacher?

ETHICS IS AN IMPORTANT COMPONENT OF AN EFFECTIVE TEACHER'S PHILOSOPHY. Not only should you continue to reflect on which philosophies will ground your point of view as a teacher, you also should be considering what is ethical. Much of what teachers should, can, and cannot do is specified by law. Statutes, case law, policies, and procedure manuals all specify what teachers can and cannot do. Ethics, however, is a more principled view of what it means to be a high-quality teacher. As you continue to reflect on your philosophy, be sure to consider the ethical component.

GO TO ··>
Review Chapter 10 as a reminder of how law affects the ethics of teachers.

High-Quality Teachers Have Three General Types of Knowledge

Teacher education researchers have identified three domains of professional knowledge and skill that expert teachers possess: *content knowledge, pedagogical knowledge,* and *pedagogical content knowledge* (Berliner, 2001). Each is important and each is essential. You might want to think about your current level of understanding within each of these domains. Becoming a high-quality teacher requires continuing to develop knowledge and skill within each of these domains.

CONTENT KNOWLEDGE: HOW WELL DO YOU KNOW THE SUBJECT(S) YOU WILL TEACH? Needing to have knowledge about and an understanding of the subject one teaches is obvious, but difficult to achieve. This is especially challenging for elementary school teachers who may have to teach as many as six different subjects. Having sufficient content knowledge also is a challenge for secondary school teachers because they need depth of understanding. At the secondary school level, if teachers do not have in-depth knowledge about a subject, they might teach inaccuracies and misconceptions.

PEDAGOGICAL KNOWLEDGE: HOW MUCH DO YOU KNOW ABOUT HOW STUDENTS LEARN AND DIFFERENT TEACHING STRATEGIES? Knowing about curriculum, instruction, and multiple ways to assess learning and understanding how students learn are other domains that expert teachers have mastered. Nearly all of the opportunities to learn in these areas will be found in the professional education courses that are part of your teacher education program. Also important within this domain is developing the actual skill of teaching, which is why clinical, field, and student teaching experiences are so important. How often have you heard a student say, "He really knows his subject, but he can't teach it so that I can understand it"?

PEDAGOGICAL CONTENT KNOWLEDGE: ARE YOU ABLE TO CONNECT WHAT YOU ARE TEACHING WITH THE EXPERIENCES AND BACKGROUNDS THAT YOUR STUDENTS BRING TO EACH LESSON? This domain of professional knowledge has a curious name, which also can be confusing. However, this domain is probably the most important for you to develop. This is where the teacher's content knowledge and pedagogical knowledge intersect with real students. This set of knowledge relationships is pictured in Figure 13.2. Students bring their personal level of understanding of the subject to the lesson. They also arrive in your classroom with a rich array of past experiences, cultural and social backgrounds, and attitudes toward learning.

Teachers with pedagogical content knowledge understand the knowledge that their students bring to the lesson and know how to build on that uniqueness. High-quality teachers also can anticipate the misconceptions that their students are likely to have when learning something new. These

FIGURE 13.2   Intersection of three domains of expert teacher knowledge.

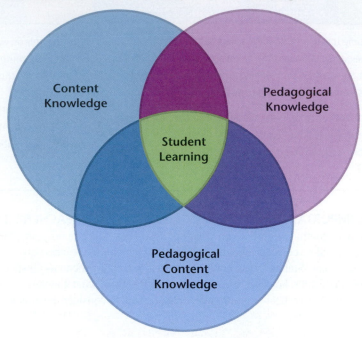

teachers are able to choose examples and metaphors that their students will understand. For example, using snow as an example with students who have always lived in the desert may not make the most sense. This is why the authors of this text have placed so much emphasis on the importance of your developing an understanding of the cultural and social, as well as academic, backgrounds of your students. With this knowledge, you can be much more successful in helping them to learn.

HIGH-QUALITY TEACHERS CONSTANTLY CHANGE AND IMPROVE

The reality of all the pressures, expectations, needs, and the many innovations that teachers are expected to implement means that change will be a regular part of your career—as we have reminded you throughout this book. Frequently, teachers have just become comfortable with an approach when they are asked to start doing something differently. There is no escaping the fact that educators are living in a time of rapid change. As ready as you may be to accept the new, each innovation brings with it challenges and uncertainties. Will the new way really work better? Will you be able to make the change successfully? These and other questions face teachers every time something new is proposed.

Teachers must work together to implement the changes that will always be a part of their careers.

Teachers Have Different Kinds of Concerns About Change

As you have read through this chapter you can see that teachers are being asked to make many changes. Some of these will make sense to you and reinforce things you already are doing. Some will seem foreign and will cause you concern. Some will likely be very challenging to understand and to use in your classroom. And, for many of these you will have no alternative but to implement the new way. You will have mixed feelings and perceptions about each of these change efforts.

Think some more about Venera Gattonini, the teacher in this chapter's "Education in the News" feature. Clearly, Ms. Gattonini loves teaching. She is doing all that she can think of to provide her students with "practical, hands-on experiences." She wants her students to leave school with skills they can use for the rest of their lives. She is delighted when her students gain confidence. She also is pressing them to do "something completely different." It appears that Ms. Gattonini is excited about change and thinking mainly about what will benefit her students.

There is a personal side to change that is reflected in the different perceptions and feelings people have. Teachers, their students, principals—in fact, everyone—have mixed feelings about their experiences with change. There are perceptions about what the change will mean. Some will be excited, while others will dread the whole idea. Having these feelings, attitudes, and perceptions is a natural component of the change process. In fact, forty plus years of research have been conducted related to understanding people's concerns about change (Hall & Hord, 2011).

What Are Your Concerns About Becoming a Teacher?

To illustrate what researchers have learned, let's think about your concerns right now. Before reading any further, write a paragraph in Figure 13.3 about your concerns.

Use the following subsections and Table 13.4 to assess what you have written.

DIFFERENT CONCERNS AS A CHANGE PROCESS UNFOLDS. People's concerns about change vary as they experience the process. Researchers have identified four phases or groupings of **concerns**: *Unconcerned, Self, Task,* and *Impact* concerns (Hall & Hord, 2011). The basic description for each of these concerns is presented in Table 13.4. Keep in mind that each of these categories of concerns is neither good nor bad. Instead they are characteristic of what all of us feel as we experience change.

Concerns Before the Beginning of a Change Process. In addition to identifying the four types of concerns, researchers have found that as a change process unfolds some concerns will be most intense at different times. Before the change initiative begins, teachers are most likely to be *Unconcerned.* "I am so busy with ———— that I don't even want to think about it right now." Thoughts and preoccupations will be on all of the other things that they are doing already.

Concerns at the Beginning of a Change Process. As the time to actually learn about and begin using the innovation gets closer, *Self* concerns become most intense. Questions about one's ability to be successful with the new approach will be raised: "I don't know if I can do this." Concerns may also arise about whether there will be support from supervisors to do things the new way. "What if my principal doesn't agree?" This is a time of high uncertainty during the change process.

concerns The composite of mental thoughts, attitudes, worries, and enthusiasms about teaching or an innovation.

Concerns as Implementation of the Change Gets Under Way. When implementation of the innovation begins, *Task* concerns become very intense. "It is taking me hours to prepare for the next

FIGURE 13.3	What Are Your Concerns About Becoming a Teacher?					

Open-ended concerns statement about becoming a teacher:

When you think about becoming a teacher, what are your concerns? Do not think about the concerns of others, but about what concerns you have right now. Please be frank and write your response using complete sentences (not a list of topics).

TABLE 13.4

Four Types of Concerns That Teachers Can Have as They Experience Change

IMPACT: The most intense focus is on how use of the change/innovation is affecting student learning. Thoughts are on how to be sure all students are "getting it," what can be done to further improve student learning, and possibly collaborating with one or more colleagues so that together the outcomes are even better.

TASK: Time, scheduling, organizing tasks and materials, and fitting everything into the available time are of utmost concern. Attention related to implementing the innovation/change is heavily focused on time, logistics, and coordination of tasks.

SELF: Uncertainty about what is being demanded, whether you can do it well, and whether you will be supported are key concerns. There is a need to have more information about the change, what it entails, and how it will work.

UNCONCERNED: The teacher is concerned about things other than the current innovation. This does not mean that the teacher is opposed to the change. However, for some reason, other efforts, some other initiative, or perhaps something outside of school is of more concern.

day, and still everything doesn't go smoothly." Concerns about time, logistics, and organizing materials can go on for months or even several years if the change is big and complex.

Concerns When Use of the Innovation Is Mastered. Ultimately, if the change process unfolds successfully and principal support for it is strong, then teachers' Self and Task concerns will be resolved, and *Impact* concerns will become the most intense. "By collaborating and working together we are seeing big improvements in what our students are learning." Impact concerns are the ideal end for a change process. However, to successfully complete a change process and experience all four areas of concern normally takes three to five years.

REFLECTING ON YOUR CONCERNS. Now, let's check back on what you wrote in response to the question in Figure 13.3. Read what you wrote and compare it to each of the four categories of concerns using Table 13.4 as a scoring guide. Which phase(s) of concern is most intense for you at this time? Are you Unconcerned about becoming a teacher and more concerned about something else? ("I have to get a different roommate.") Do you have more intense Self concerns? ("When I am student teaching, I hope I will know enough and can control the students.") What about Task concerns? ("I have so much to do just to finish this course/semester.")

What about Impact concerns? Did you write down anything related to student success? ("I want each of my students to learn all they can.") Or, did you write anything about what you want to do to improve your effectiveness as a teacher? ("I think I will take that other methods course because it will help me work with ELL students.")

It is likely that your Impact concerns are much lower in intensity at this time. It would not be unusual for you, at this point in your teacher education program, to not have written anything related to student learning. Impact concerns do not normally become intense until the end of student teaching and after several years of teaching full time. So, don't be worried about not having intense Impact concerns at this time. You are very early in the change process of becoming a teacher. Keep in mind that having intense Impact concerns is a positive indicator that you are becoming a high-quality teacher. High-quality teachers are first and foremost concerned about their students learning rather than themselves or the tasks of teaching. The "Teaching in Challenging Times" feature illustrates one of the challenges that all teachers face.

EFFECTIVE TEACHERS SEEK SUPPORTIVE RESOURCES

You are probably now near the end of a semester in which you have probably taken your first professional education course(s). Becoming a high-quality teacher is up to you. It will take time, study, and practice to transition from novice to expert. Still, as you know from your own experiences in schools, high-quality teachers do exist. They know more and teach in different ways than do those who are less effective. Fortunately, many resources and supports are available to help you succeed. A sampling of these resources follows.

TEACHING IN CHALLENGING TIMES

Keeping Up with Constant Change

Teachers are extremely busy and are confronted with countless professional expectations. For instance, as a teacher, you will be expected to: help each student learn at an advanced level, work effectively with other teachers and administrators, communicate frequently with parents, participate in a variety of professional improvement activities, find and understand reliable research results to incorporate in your teaching, evaluate educational activities, help plan and institute school improvement projects, participate in countless professional meetings, etc., etc., etc.

You will also be expected to keep up on the many important changes constantly taking place in the world, in the United States, in your state, in your community, in your school district, in the education field, in the lives of your students, etc., etc., etc.

And on top of all of these expectations, you will have a very important personal life with changes and problems that will require serious attention and also take up much of your time. And don't forget that you will need exercise and relaxation to maintain your mental health. You will indeed be very busy, like all good educators.

WHAT ARE MY CHALLENGES?

1. What will be my priorities when confronted with competition for my time?
2. What proportion of my time will I be willing to devote to my teaching responsibilities? And what proportion to my personal life?
3. How will I find time to relax?

Induction of New Teachers

During the past twenty years, the thinking about and approaches to induction of beginning teachers have changed dramatically. In earlier times little or no accommodations were made for new teachers. They were assigned to a classroom, given a key, and expected to be up and functioning just as well as the veteran teachers. Now, most school districts offer a number of programs and resources to support novice teachers.

NEW TEACHER ORIENTATIONS. Larger school districts usually offer one or more meetings for all new teachers that will address many of your teaching-related questions. In smaller districts the new teacher orientation may be more informal and school based. These sessions often review classroom management techniques, the school year calendar, report cards, and the schedule for testing. If you will be teaching in a district that has teacher-friendly computer systems for scoring tests and monitoring student progress, these topics will be introduced as well.

NEW EMPLOYEE WORKSHOPS. In early August, after you have signed your contract, you and the other newly hired teachers will be invited to a new employee workshop. These sessions are usually conducted by the district's human resource department. Typically these sessions will not address your concerns about teaching students or organizing your classroom. Instead, likely topics will include your rights and responsibilities as an employee of the district, how to sign up for health insurance, sick leave policies, how you get paid, and reminders about legal protections and responsibilities.

TEACHER MENTORS. Mentors are a very important resource for new teachers. Mentors are experienced teachers from whom the novice teacher can seek advice. They are not evaluators—that is the job of the principal. In many states and in most larger districts, someone will be assigned to be your mentor for at least the first year. Mentors are master teachers who can help you with the design of lessons. They can sit in your classroom when you are teaching and follow up with suggestions to help you reflect.

Sometimes beginning teachers discover an experienced teacher who can serve as an informal mentor. This person might be another teacher at your grade level or within your department. As the school year unfolds, you will likely find yourself turning to one of these colleagues more and more often.

SCHOOL-BASED SPECIALISTS AS NEW TEACHER RESOURCES. Another source of support will be the various specialist teachers within the school. The special education resource teacher can be of great help to you in teaching the students with special needs in your classroom. Other specialists that might be in your school include a technology coordinator, library/media coordinator, literacy specialist, mathematics specialist, ELL coordinator, and possibly a home–school community liaison person.

 To hear a first-year teacher describe her experiences in her first year, including the value of mentor teachers, click on the video *Succeeding in Your First Year of Teaching.*

 Principals can be a valuable resource to new teachers. To hear advice from two veteran principals on preparing to teach, click on the video *Preparing to Teach: Advice from Two Professionals.*

The Future of Technology for Teaching and Student Learning

Each of the preceding chapters in this text addressed one or more forms of technology and explored connections to teaching and student learning. These descriptions have been based on what is available today. The one certainty for the future is that new forms of technology will be created and innovative applications of current forms will be developed. Any of these might be used in classrooms and schools.

The "Who Is Right?" feature outlines the dilemma for teachers. How much of and which applications should teachers be using? There is no doubt that as a teacher you will be confronted with opportunities and questions about whether or not to use various new technologies in your classroom. The following paragraphs use a sampling of some emerging technologies and applications to illustrate the dilemma. Each technology has potential benefits for teaching and learning, and each also has potential risks.

WHO IS RIGHT?

SHOULD TECHNOLOGY BE USED IN EVERY CLASSROOM?

The various forms and possible uses of technology in schools seem to be never ending. Whiteboards, the Web, personal computing, cell phones, and more recently various social networking applications can be made available for use by teachers and/or students in classrooms. But should they be made available? How much technology and which types do you want to use in your classroom? Two teachers offer opposing views below.

YES

Keith Parker *is a history education student at Austin Peay State University in Clarksville, Tennessee.*

When I begin teaching history and social studies in the fall of 2007, I'll require students to use as much technology as I have the resources for. They'll learn how important technology is for conducting research and how best to leverage it for that purpose. However, the students who aren't as interested in history will still learn skills that will help them when they enter the workforce. In almost every field of work, some type of technology is used. Students must be prepared.

If we complement and reinforce our lessons with technology—from Microsoft PowerPoint to streaming media, and computer spreadsheets to podcasts—we'll help students to be more receptive of the material and to become more familiar with the sorts of technology that have become a part of everyday life at home and in the workplace.

Finally, while students might not be familiar with workplace technologies and software, they are whizzes when it comes to Internet and telecommunications technology. By using more technology in the classroom, we're speaking their language and teaching them in a way that they might learn. Ignacio "Nacho" Estrada once said, "If a child can't learn the way we teach, maybe we should teach the way they learn."

NO

Timothy Kubinak *teaches algebra and geography at King's Fork Middle School in Suffolk, Virginia.*

Overuse of technology has inadvertently provided students with a deck of "get out of work free" cards. As a math teacher, I've seen that the use of technology, such as graphing calculators, has some positive effects—students can check their work, create graphs, and work together to solve problems. But too often I see students using technology to perform basic operations that should have been mastered in elementary school.

Some of my colleagues in the English department attribute their students' writing skills, or lack thereof, to the heavy use of instant messaging and spell check. These technologies, though useful when used as directed, can lead to a decrease in proficiency. The need for core skills development must be the first priority of the student and teacher.

Our generation learned how to read, write, and do arithmetic by learning from our teacher's example—with pencils, paper, and our minds. True, educators have learned that our students' needs are unique from past generations, but we remember what is truly important in our children's education. The need to learn how to organize, apply, analyze—in essence, we're teaching them how to learn. Yes, technology is an integral part of this process, but that does not mean it is a required component of every classroom setting.

WHAT IS YOUR PERSPECTIVE ON THIS ISSUE?

Source: "Should Technology Be Used in Every Classroom?" *NEA Today* (September 2006), p. 43. Reprinted by permission of the National Education Association.

RAPID DEVELOPMENT OF NEW FORMS OF TECHNOLOGY. Older adults will reminisce about the "days before we had the Web and e-mail," while today's students have no memory of life without cell phones. In terms of history both of these forms of technology are recent developments. They also are indicators of how fast new forms of technology are created. An additional unique characteristic of technology is that, once created, never-ending adaptations and refinements follow. For example, when watching a movie that was made ten years ago, note what cell phones were like then compared to now. They were larger and were capable only of making phone calls. Now they are multifunction devices. As another indicator of rapidly changing technology, you merely have to chart the annual evolution and increasing capacity of electronic devices.

This rapid creation of new forms and applications of technology has important implications for teachers:

1. Tech-savvy teachers will see interesting and useful ways to incorporate some of the new forms, yet will be uncertain about the usefulness of others.
2. Students will be early to adopt and creative in using the new forms of technology.
3. The establishment of school and district policies related to appropriate and inappropriate uses of new forms of technology will lag behind the technologies' introduction in the classroom.

These three implications pose a dilemma for teachers in the future. Which forms and applications will you encourage, and what are your guiding principles for what will not be allowed? This is the underlying theme of the "Who Is Right?" feature. It is likely that you will be confronted with the need to make decisions about technology uses in your classroom before your school or district has a rule or policy in place. You will need to be thoughtful about your reasoning and understand the legal, ethical, and instructional elements related to your decision.

SOCIAL NETWORKING TECHNOLOGY. The rapid growth of websites such as Facebook, digital photos, text messaging, and many other unique applications creates a dilemma and challenge for teachers and school officials. Each of these applications can be used in ways that enhance teaching and student learning, yet they also can be a diversion for students and can even be used to cheat. Some districts have decided to suspend students who bring cell phones or iPods to school. Others have decided that students may carry them as long as they are turned off. These policies still mean, however, that teachers must monitor the availability and uses of each. And some schools have even elected not only to allow, but also to require, students to use various electronic devices in the classroom.

Unfortunately, teachers also must be continually attentive to the possibility of students using technology to cheat. One indicator of the extent of the problem is found in a survey of nearly 30,000 high school students conducted by the Josephson Institute for Ethics (2008) in Los Angeles: 64 percent reported cheating on a test with 38 percent indicating they did so two or more times. As sad as it may be, teachers need to view each new form and application of technology as possibly providing a new way for students to cheat.

PROMISING NEW APPLICATIONS. Often forms and applications of technology that have been around for some time are merged into new systems of classroom support. This will most certainly happen in the future. A current example that is just now showing up in classrooms is based on integrating several technologies that have been around for a long time. Microphones, speakers, and amplifiers have been around for more than one hundred years. In the early days each microphone had to have its own wire and if two were turned on at the same time, a very loud screeching noise would be heard. Now, with the addition of computer software and advances in technology, many wireless microphones can be on at the same time. What do you suppose could be done in classrooms by combining these "old" technologies?

Several vendors have created **classroom audio technology** systems. One of the stresses for teachers and students is having to talk loud enough to be heard. This effort is tiring for teachers and usually means that some students will not have heard everything. For a relatively small investment, technology systems are now available that can fix this problem. In these classrooms speakers are located strategically so that all can hear. The teacher has a wireless microphone and others are available for students. Everybody can talk in normal voices and all can hear what is being said.

GO TO ···>
Chapter 10 addresses the legal aspects and implications of the uses and misuses of social networking and other forms of technology.

classroom audio technology The use of wireless microphones and speakers in the classroom.

INCREASING INTEGRATION OF TECHNOLOGY USES. Teachers in the future will have even more forms and applications of technology to learn about and use. Three keys to taking advantage of this future are flexibility, imagination, and innovation.

1. Teachers need to be flexible and open to considering whether some new technology really is better.
2. They must be creative in thinking up new ways to use technology.
3. They must devise strategies to integrate the uses of technology into their lesson plans.

As just described with classroom audio technology, each technology and application can be used by itself, but the high-quality classroom will integrate these uses. For example, technology makes possible differentiation according to student needs. A variety of ways should be available for each student to achieve each objective. Students in the same classroom with different needs should be able to use books on tape, writing templates, charts, and instruction in different languages to learn the same material. Connecting to the Internet to retrieve content or to communicate with students in another state or country can be another integrated practice. Teachers in the future need to think about how all of the individual technology resources can be integrated to form a whole system that supports teaching and learning.

School-Based Administrators Can Be Important Supports for New Teachers

As a teacher, you will need to work closely and effectively with your principal(s) and other school personnel. This is an especially important relationship because one of the principal's responsibilities is to evaluate first-year teachers. However, do not permit the evaluation role to block out any possibility of the principal being a resource. Nearly all principals have been teachers earlier in their careers. They also know what is available around the school that can be of help.

GO TO ···>
Review Chapter 9 if you are not clear about teacher organizational relationships with the principal.

Assistant principals also can be a resource, and in schools that have deans and department chairs they too can be important resources. An important theme cutting across all of these people resources is that beginning teachers should not become isolated in their classroom. When you need help, or just need an opportunity to ask someone else what they think, get out of your classroom and seek out one or more of these resources. They will be pleased that you asked.

EFFECTIVE TEACHERS ACTIVELY PARTICIPATE IN THE PROFESSION

One of the rewarding aspects of becoming a teacher is the opportunity to work with other well-educated and highly dedicated professionals. There are many types of professional organizations and associations that teachers can join. In most school districts, teachers are represented by a teachers' organization or union that is responsible for negotiating contracts and setting working conditions. These organizations and associations have had a major influence on the development of national education policy; on the determination of state policies, laws, rules, and regulations related to schooling; and (at the local level) on curriculum decisions and labor contract negotiations. At all of these levels, teachers are actively involved and are responsible participants who will eventually work with the resultant policy decisions and curriculum products.

Teachers have opportunities to become involved in professional or specialty associations as well. These associations deal directly with issues such as the development of student and teacher standards, the design of curriculum, innovations in teaching, and improving instructional processes. They provide teachers with the opportunity to collaborate with other teachers who have like concerns and interests; they also enable teachers to participate in various professional leadership activities. Some specialty associations focus on teaching specific subjects, such as science, math, literature, and reading, or specific grade levels, such as middle school and early childhood education. These associations usually have national, state, and local chapters. Clearly, teachers can profit from membership and participation in both professional organizations and professional or specialty associations.

Teacher Unions

Teacher unions were organized to improve working conditions. The National Education Association (NEA) and the American Federation of Teachers (AFT) are the two major unions for teachers in the United States. Some teachers have chosen to join other state or local organizations that are not affiliated with the NEA or the AFT but operate similarly to a union. The unions provide a number of services for their members; leadership on a number of professional issues; and a political presence at the local, state, and national levels.

National Education Association

The National Education Association is by far the largest teachers' organization, with 2.5 million members, including teachers, administrators, clerical and custodial employees, higher education faculty, and other school personnel. Teacher education candidates can join the NEA's Student Program. More than a million teacher education candidates have joined the student group since it was formed in 1937. You might wish to explore the advantages of joining this organization on your campus.

The NEA is committed to advancing public education. The organization was founded in 1857 as the National Teachers' Association (NTA). In 1870 the NTA united with the National Association of School Superintendents, organized in 1865, and the American Normal School Association, organized in 1858, to form the National Education Association. The organization was incorporated in 1886 in the District of Columbia as the National Education Association and was chartered in 1906 by an act of Congress. The charter was officially adopted at the association's annual meeting of 1907, with the name National Education Association of the United States.

The Representative Assembly (RA) is the primary legislative and policy-making body of the NEA. NEA members of state and local affiliates elect the 9,000 RA delegates who meet annually in early July to debate issues and set policies. The president, vice president, and secretary-treasurer are elected at the annual RA. The top decision-making bodies are the board of directors and the executive committee. An executive director has the primary responsibility for implementing the policies of the association, and standing committees and ad hoc committees carry out much of the work.

Given its long history of advocacy of teaching as a profession, it should not be surprising to learn that the NEA sponsors many professional initiatives designed to disseminate best practices, facilitate teacher leadership, and empower teachers to reform schools. The NEA has organized to provide professional help in student assessment and accountability; professional preparation, state licensure, and national certification; and governance and member activities. The NEA also initiated in 1954, along with four other associations, the accrediting body for teacher education, NCATE, and continues today to provide leadership through appointments to NCATE's governance board and board of examiners. The examiners are practitioners who visit college campuses to apply the standards. These and other program areas offer an array of activities and initiatives to further advance teacher professionalism.

Members of the NEA receive its newsletter, *NEA Today*, and have access to numerous other publications and products, including publications that are available online through its professional library. Recent reports from the association address diversity, portfolios, student assessment, school safety, cooperative learning, discipline, gender, inclusion, reading and writing, and parent involvement. Handbooks published by the NEA and written by experienced teachers are helpful resources for new teachers.

American Federation of Teachers

The second largest teachers' union is the American Federation of Teachers, with national headquarters in Washington, D.C. It was organized in 1916 by teachers in Winnetka, Illinois, to establish an organization to meet their needs and to create a strong union affiliation. The Chicago Teachers' Federation preceded the AFT, having been established in 1897 and affiliating with the American Federation of Labor (AFL) in 1902. Since 1916, AFT membership has grown steadily. The late Albert Shanker, who was AFT president from 1974 until his death in 1997, is given much of the credit for the growth and success of the AFT, including its national involvement in political discussions related to education. In 1965, membership was at 110,500; by 2000, membership exceeded one million. The organization of the AFT includes a president, numerous vice presidents, a secretary-treasurer, and administrative staff. The membership serves on standing committees and council committees.

Since its inception, the AFT has boasted of its affiliation with the AFL, and later the AFL-CIO. AFT has stressed that organized labor was an important force in establishing our system of free public schools and that it has actively supported school improvement programs. Affiliation with organized labor gives the AFT the support of the roughly fifteen million members of the AFL-CIO. Support from local labor unions has often worked to the advantage of local AFT unions in their efforts to gain better salaries and improved benefits from local boards of education.

The AFT has diverse resources available to its members. Its lobbying and political action activities support a number of professional issues, in addition to bargaining issues at the local, state, and national levels. Its publications include the journal *American Educator.* Jointly with the NEA, the AFT conducts the annual QUEST conference to convene the leadership of both organizations to discuss professional issues. The AFT's Educational Research and Dissemination Program helps make selected findings from recent research on classroom management and effective teaching available to teachers.

POLITICAL ACTION. Both the NEA and AFT have political action committees and government relations departments. Political action committees are engaged in actions to elect political candidates who are sympathetic to education and teachers' issues. They monitor elected officials' voting records on education bills and analyze the platforms of new candidates. They actively participate in the election campaigns of the president, governors, and key legislators. The state and national political action committees of the NEA and AFT have a common aim: to promote education by encouraging teachers to participate in the political life of their local, state, and national communities. These committees throughout the states are responsible for recommending political endorsements to their respective boards of directors.

Professional Associations

Teachers can join, participate in, and provide leadership for many professional associations that focus on their chosen professional interests. These associations are organized around academic disciplines and specific job assignments, such as science teaching, mathematics teaching, special education, school psychology, reading, cooperative learning, and multicultural education.

PHI DELTA KAPPA INTERNATIONAL. The professional association Phi Delta Kappa International (PDK) is one of the largest and most highly regarded organizations for educators in the world. Today it is open to all educators, although in its earlier years women were not allowed to join. It publishes excellent professional material, including the journal *Phi Delta Kappan,* a newsletter, *Fastback* booklets on timely educational topics, research reports, books, and various instructional materials. The organization also sponsors many surveys, research projects, grants, awards, conferences, training programs, and trips. Local PDK chapters bring together teacher candidates, higher education faculty, and local teachers and administrators. You might want to consider a student membership and become involved in your local chapter.

SPECIALTY PROFESSIONAL ASSOCIATIONS. There are more than five hundred specialty associations in education based on different academic disciplines, different types of students, and different instructional approaches. Over time, you will find those specialties that apply to your unique role in education. Participation in these associations will enable you to network with others who have similar interests and focus.

Of the specialty associations that could be described, the Association for Supervision and Curriculum Development (ASCD) is profiled here because it provides an international forum focused on all aspects of effective teaching and learning. Founded in 1943, ASCD is a nonprofit, nonpartisan organization representing over 175,000 educators from more than 135 countries and more than sixty affiliates. Members span the entire profession of education—superintendents, supervisors, principals, teachers, professors of education, and school board members. ASCD offers broad, multiple perspectives in reporting key policies and practices. The association focuses on professional practice within the context of public and private schools and cites as its primary goal the building of an engaged diverse community to improve learning and teaching for each student.

BE THE BEST YOU CAN BE

Now that you have studied the different perspectives that comprise the foundation of education, you should be ready to reflect on their implications for your career as a teacher. As you have seen, our profession is rich in history and expertise and diverse in thoughts and perspectives. No matter which perspective is selected, which chapter(s) you found most interesting, or the contexts you considered, one theme stands out: Education and the profession of teaching will continue to change and be challenging. The pressures to continuously find better ways to teach and to improve student learning will not cease.

FIGURE 13.4	A Great Teacher			

- Has the ability to be flexible, optimistic, self-reflective, progressive, and innovative;
- Must possess the ability to build relationships with students and teachers and have a passion for teaching;
- Excites a passion for learning in his or her students through skillful facilitation, using 21st-century tools;
- Goes beyond the classroom as a collaborator with colleagues;
- Wants to improve himself or herself by learning good instructional skills;
- Is someone who knows the curriculum and works well as part of a team;
- Builds relationships and facilitates lifelong learning;

- Collaborates with families, peers, and the community;
- Shows appreciation and enthusiasm for cultural differences;
- Inspires others to achieve their potential;
- Understands the complexities of the teaching and learning environment;
- Has consistently high expectations for all students;
- Recognizes and adapts when he or she isn't getting through to students;
- Addresses the needs of the whole child;
- Uses assessment to inform instructional decision making; and
- Gives back through mentoring.

Source: Erin Young, "What Makes a Great Teacher?" *Phi Delta Kappan* (February 2009), p. 439. Reprinted by permission of *Phi Delta Kappan*.

The theme of continuous efforts to improve and change will be with you throughout the remainder of your teacher education program and throughout your career as a teacher. You have the responsibility of trying new approaches and providing evidence about the difference each makes in your teaching, your students, and your school.

We would like to remind you, at this point, of some of the qualities of a great teacher that appeared in Chapter 1. They are relisted in Figure 13.4. They can remind you of the skills you should now be developing, and can serve as challenging goals throughout your career.

The authors of this text represent very different perspectives and personal histories. Interestingly, regardless of their academic discipline and teaching experiences, the authors frequently observe that this is an exciting time to become a teacher. In your developing career you will continue to learn, and all along you will have opportunities to make a difference in student learning and in the learning of your colleagues. We hope you, your students, and your colleagues benefit as much from the American education system as we have.

JOURNAL FOR REFLECTION 13.3

The authors of this text believe that this is an exciting time to become a teacher. Do you agree? What excites you about becoming a teacher? Enter your reactions in your journal.

A Final Word

We, the authors, wish you the very best in your developing career. We need many more high-quality teachers. As you now know from reading this text, there is a long and rich legacy of efforts, people, and ideas to help you grow. You will likely have moments of doubt (those Self concerns again), and you most certainly will have days where you have too much to do (Task concerns). We hope, though, that you will also move on to truly experiencing the excitement and wonderment that comes from having your students "get it." As you know firsthand, high-quality teachers make a lasting difference in the lives of their students. High-quality teachers will have Self and Task concerns too, but what really drives them are their Impact concerns. As reported in the "Education in the News" feature about Venera Gattonini earlier in this chapter, high-quality teachers are always striving to be the best they can be and to do everything they can think of to help all of their students learn. We sincerely wish you much success and enjoyment in your career as a "great" educator.

SUMMARY

DIFFERENT PERSPECTIVES FOR VIEWING EDUCATION AND TEACHING

- Different perspectives can be applied to our understanding of education and teaching: sociological, historical, philosophical, organizational, economic, legal, and multicultural.
- The United States has a three hundred–year history of trying to improve its educational system.
- In recent decades the federal government has been increasingly pressuring schools to change.
- Crises in society are a catalyst for school change.
- Findings from research can lead to change.
- Evidence about student learning unveils areas of needed change.

HOW TO RECOGNIZE AN EFFECTIVE SCHOOL

- Today's expectations for students and for teachers are higher than in the past.
- Data are used to make instructional and budgetary decisions.
- School improvement is a process, not just a plan.
- High-quality schools have a special organizational culture called a professional learning community.
- Many strategies are employed to involve parents and community members in student learning.
- The principal has a vision for the school and provides supportive leadership.
- Accountability is centered on student learning.

EVIDENCE OF STUDENT LEARNING

- High-quality teachers use evidence to determine if they are making a difference in student learning.
- High-quality teachers are reflective and have a stated philosophy.
- Ethics is an important component of a high-quality teacher's philosophy.

- High-quality teachers have depth in three types of knowledge: content knowledge, pedagogical knowledge, and pedagogical content knowledge.

HIGH-QUALITY TEACHERS CONSTANTLY CHANGE AND IMPROVE

- Four categories of concerns are Unconcerned, Self, Task, and Impact concerns.
- Teacher concerns change as the teacher becomes more expert.
- Beginning teachers will have more Self concerns than other types of concerns.
- High-quality teachers have more Impact concerns than other types of concerns.
- Reflecting on your concerns can be helpful.

EFFECTIVE TEACHERS SEEK SUPPORTIVE RESOURCES

- Induction is the first one-to-three years of teaching.
- Beginning teachers have many resources available to them: workshops and orientations, mentors, and professional associations.

EFFECTIVE TEACHERS ACTIVELY PARTICIPATE IN THE PROFESSION

- Associations provide opportunities for teachers to work together.
- The NEA and AFT advocate for teachers' rights.
- Professional associations provide opportunities for teachers to specialize in activities related to a particular professional interest or curriculum subject.

BE THE BEST YOU CAN BE

- High-quality teachers strive to have all of their students learn.
- High-quality teachers are always looking for ways to improve their teaching and increase student learning.

DISCUSSION STARTERS

1. What changes have you seen in your lifetime that have affected what today's schools are like?

2. Which indicators of accountability for schools do you think are most important?

3. Do you think that the trend toward increased federal direction of public education has gone too far, or should the federal government take even more control?

4. What characteristics of high-quality schools do you agree with? Are there other characteristics that you think should be added or deleted?

5. How have your concerns about becoming a teacher changed since this academic term started? In what ways have they stayed the same?

6. For which domain of high-quality, or expert, teacher knowledge do you have the most to learn?

SCHOOL-BASED OBSERVATIONS

1. Ask a teacher about the various changes that she or he has made during her or his teaching career. Which of the changes turned out to be most beneficial? Which were the biggest challenges?

2. Obtain a copy of a school's school improvement plan and see which tiers of data were used. Did the school rely solely on Tier 1 data (standardized test scores) or were other tiers also considered? (If you don't have access to a school's plan, check the district and state websites. The school's plan should be there.)

PORTFOLIO DEVELOPMENT

1. Keep a copy of the open-ended concerns statement that you wrote while reading this chapter. (If you didn't do it then, go back to Figure 13.3 and do the task now.) Every six weeks or so as you move on in becoming a teacher, take time to write out your concerns. You can score them using the general definitions provided in Table 13.4. As you continue to do this you should see a developing pattern and several trends in relation to your becoming a teacher.

2. Now would be a good time for you to use the student learning–centered teaching model to sketch out a lesson plan for a topic you would like to eventually teach. Be sure to think about what your students might know already and what you would do to incorporate their background and past experiences into the lesson. This is what pedagogical content knowledge is about.

WEB SOLUTIONS

You will be challenged often during your teaching career to find information that you need. For instance, you will need to keep up on federal laws and regulations that effect what you do in your classroom. One such example may require you to find the most recent information on NCLB. The following website may help you find this information.

www.ed.gov/policy/elsec/leg/esea02/index.html This is the official U.S. Department of Education website for P. L. 107–110, which is better known as the No Child Left Behind Act of 2001. The site describes the various parts of the statute and provides links to related government documents and departments.

MyEducationLab™ Go to the topic **Professional Development** in the MyEducationLab (www.myeducationlab.com) for *Foundations of American Education: Becoming Effective Teachers in Challenging Times, 16e,* where you can:

- Find learning outcomes for **Professional Development**, along with the national standards that connect to these outcomes.
- Complete Assignments and Activities that can help you more deeply understand the chapter content.
- Apply and practice your understanding of the core teaching skills identified in the chapter with the Building Teaching Skills and Dispositions learning units.
- Access video clips of CCSSO National Teachers of the Year award winners responding to the question, "Why Do I Teach?" in the Teacher Talk section.
- Create, update, and share quality lesson plans with the Lesson Plan Builder.

- Access state licensure test requirements, overviews of what tests cover, and sample test items in the Certification and Licensure section.
- Access current state and national standards in the Licensure and Standards section.
- Learn how to create a high-quality teaching portfolio in the Preparing a Portfolio section.
- Access tips, advice, and other information on resume writing and interviewing, your first year of teaching, and law and public policies in the Beginning Your Career section.
- Check your comprehension of the content covered in the chapter with the Study Plan. Here you will be able to take a chapter pretest, receive feedback on your answers, and then access personalized Review, Practice, and Enrichment exercises to enhance your understanding of chapter content. After you complete the exercises, take a posttest to confirm your comprehension.

REFERENCES

CHAPTER 1

Darling-Hammond, L. (2000). Teaching for America's future: National commissions and vested interests in an almost profession. *Educational Policy, 14*(1), 162–183.

U.S. Department of Education. (1999–2011). Data gleaned and summarized from U.S. Department of Education, National Center for Education Statistics, Schools and Staffing Survey (SASS), "Public School Teacher and Private School Teacher Data Files," 1999–2000 and 2007–2008 and "Charter School Teacher Data File, 1999–2000," other Department of Education Data Files, and the "Condition of Education 2011."

CHAPTER 2

Compayré, G. (1888). *History of pedagogy* (W. H. Payne, Trans.). Boston: Heath.

Monroe, P. (1905). *History of education*. New York: Macmillan.

Quintilian. (1905). *The institutes of oratory* (W. Guthrie, Trans.). London: Dewick and Clark.

Shurtleff, N. B. (Ed.). (1853–1854). *Records of the Governor and Company of the Massachusetts Bay in New England* (Vol. II, 1642–1649). Boston: William White, p. 203.

Shurtleff, N. B. (Ed.). (1853–1854). *Records of the Governor and Company of the Massachusetts Bay in New England* (Vol. II, 1642–1649). Boston: William White, pp. 6–7.

Smith, L. G., & Smith, J. K. (1984). *Lives in education*. Ames, IA: Educational Studies Press.

Willard, E. (1893). A plan for the improvement of female education. In A. C. Brackett (Ed.), *Women and the higher education* (pp. 12–14). New York: Harper & Brothers.

CHAPTER 3

Armytage, W. H. G. (1951). William Byngham: A medieval protagonist of the training of teachers. *History of Education Journal, 2,* 108.

Educational Policies Commission. (1938). *The purposes of education in American democracy*. Washington, DC: National Education Association.

Educational Policies Commission. (1944). *Education for all American youth*. Washington, DC: National Education Association.

Educational Policies Commission. (1952). *Imperative needs of youth*. Washington, DC: National Education Association.

Havighurst, R. J., & Neugarten, B. L. (1962). *Society and education* (2nd ed.). Boston: Allyn & Bacon, Inc.

U.S. Department of Commerce, Bureau of the Census. (1982). *Digest of education statistics, 1982*. Washington, DC: Government Printing Office.

CHAPTER 4

Alexander, H. G. (1987). *The language and logic of philosophy*. Lanham, MD: University Press of America.

Bransford, J. D., Brown, A., & Cocking, R. R. (Eds.). (2000). *How people learn: Brain, mind, experience and school* (expanded ed.). Washington, DC: National Academies Press.

Dewey, J. (1897). My pedagogic creed. *The School Journal, 54*(3), 77–80.

Donovan, M. S., & Bransford, J. D. (Eds.). (2005). *How students learn: History, mathematics, and science in the classroom*. Washington, DC: National Academies Press.

Greene, M. (1988). *The dialectic of freedom*. New York, NY: Teachers College Press.

Heidegger, M. (1993). The question concerning technology. In D. Krell (Ed.), *Basic writings* (p. 21). New York: HarperCollins Publishers. (Original work published 1954.)

Kohlberg, L. (1981). *Essays on moral development, Volume I: The philosophy of moral development: Moral stages and the idea of justice*. San Francisco: Harper & Row.

Kor, A.-L., Self, J., & Tait, K. (2001). *Pictorial Socratic dialogue and conceptual change*. Paper presented at 2001 International Conference on Computers in Education (ICCE 2001), Seoul, Korea, November 2001.

Locke, J. (1812). Some thoughts concerning education. In *The works of John Locke, Volume X*. London: Printed for W. Otridge [and others].

Martin, J. R. (1985). *Reclaiming a conversation: The ideal of the educated woman*. New Haven, CT: Yale University Press.

Nietzsche, F. (1986). The wanderer and his shadow. In R. J. Hollingdale (Trans.), *Human, all too human* (p. 6). Cambridge: Cambridge University Press. (Original work published 1880.)

Noddings, N. (1993). *The challenge to care in schools*. New York, NY: Teachers College Press.

Noddings, N. (2005). *The challenge to care in schools: An alternative approach to education* (2nd ed.). New York: Teachers College Press.

Noguchi, S. (2012). Among many teens, cheating is part of school. *San Diego Mercury News*, March 31, 2012.

Ozman, H. A., & Craver, S. M. (2008). *Philosophical foundations of education*. Columbus, OH: Merrill.

Sassone, L. (2002). *The process of becoming: A democratic Nietzschean philosophical pedagogy for individualization*. Chicago: Discovery Association.

West, C. (1993). *Prophetic thought in postmodern times*. Monroe, ME: Common Courage Press.

Whitehead, A. F. (1929). *The aims of education*. New York, NY: Free Press.

Wilson, T. P. (1994a). *Navajo: Walking in beauty*. San Francisco, CA: Chronicle Books.

Wilson, T. P. (1994b). *Lakota: Seeking the great spirit*. San Francisco, CA: Chronicle Books.

Wilson, T. P. (1994c). *Hopi: Following the path of peace*. San Francisco, CA: Chronicle Books.

CHAPTER 5

Bowles, S., & Gintis, H. (1975). *Schooling in capitalistic America* (pp. 18–20). New York: Basic Books.

Bowles, S., Gintis, H., & Fehr, E. (Eds.). (2006). *Moral sentiments and material interests: The foundation of cooperation in economic life*. New York: Basic Books.

Buber, M. (1958). *I and Thou*. Trans. Ronald G. Smith. New York: Charles Scribner.

Campbell, T. (2012, May 26). Girl who fought bullies now labeled one by school. *The Daily Commercial*.

Canter, L. (2010). *Assertive discipline: Positive behavior management for today's classrooms*. Bloomington, IN: Solution Tree Press.

Dewey, J. (1916). *Democracy and education* (pp. 1–9). New York: Macmillan.

Dewey, J. (1937). Education and social change. In *The School Frontier III* (pp. 235–238).

Duck, L. (1981). *Instructor's manual for teaching with charisma* (Item 4, p. 40, Item C, pp. 50–51). Boston, MA: Allyn & Bacon.

Giroux, H. A. (1981). *Ideology, culture and the process of schooling*. Philadelphia: Temple University Press.

Giroux, H. A. (1985). Teachers as transformative intellectuals. *Social Education, 4,* 376–379.

Giroux, H. A. (2001). *Theory and resistance in education: Towards a pedagogy for the opposition*. Westpoint, CT: Bergin and Garvey.

Glasser, W. (2000). *Counseling with choice theory: The new reality therapy*. New York: Harper Collins.

Glickman, C. D., & Wolfgang, C. H. (1978). Conflict in the classroom: an eclectic model of teacher–child interaction. *Elementary School Guidance and Counseling, 13,* 82–87.

Goodlad, J. (1984). *A place called school: Prospects for the future*. New York: McGraw-Hill.

Goodlad, J. (2004). *A place called school, Twentieth anniversary edition*. New York: McGraw Hill.

Greene, M. (1975). Curriculum and consciousness. In W. Pinar (Ed.), *Curriculum theorizing: The reconceptualists* (p. 12). Berkeley, CA: McCutchan.

Greene, M. (2000). *Releasing the imagination: Essays on education, the arts, and social change*. New York: Jossey Bass.

Johnson, S. M. (1990). *Teachers at work: Achieving success in our schools* (pp. xvii–xix). New York: Basic Books.

Kandel, I. L. (1938). *Conflicting theories of education* (pp. 77–88). New York: Macmillan.

Noddings, N. (2005). *The challenge to care in schools: An alternative approach to education* (2nd ed.). (Advances in contemporary educational thought.) New York: Teachers College Press.

Noddings, N. (2010). *The maternal factor: Two paths to morality*. Berkeley, CA: The Regents of the University of California.

Peirce, C. S. (1955). The fixation of belief. In J. Buchler (Ed.), *Philosophical writings of Peirce* (pp. 5–22). New York: Dover.

Perrone, V. (Ed.). (1991). *Expanded student assessment for supervision and curriculum development*. Alexandria, VA: Association for Supervision and Curriculum Development.

Ravitch, D. (2001). *A century of battles over school reform*. New York: Simon and Schuster.

Rousseau, J-J. (1782). *Émile*. Alan Bloom, trans. (1979). New York: Basic Books.

Schmuck, R., & Schmuck, P. A. (1983). *Group processes in the classrooms*. Dubuque, IA: Wm. C. Brown.

Sheive, L. T., & Schoenheit, M. B. (1987). Vision and the worklife of educational leaders. In *Leadership: Examining the elusive* (p. 99). Alexandria, VA: Association for Supervision and Curriculum Development.

Sizer, T. (2004). *The red pencil: Convictions from experience in education*. New Haven, CT: Yale University Press.

Sizer, T., Sizer, N., Benitez, M., Davidson, J., & Flaxman, N. (2009). *Small schools, big ideas: The essential guide to successful school transformation*. San Francisco, CA: John Wiley and Sons.

CHAPTER 6

Agus, J. (2010, December). *High schools in the United States*. Washington, DC: National High School Center, American Institutes for Research. Retrieved on April 12, 2012, from http://www.betterhighschools.org/pubs/documents/HSInTheUS_1210.pdf

Alliance for Excellent Education. (2010, September). *High school dropouts in America* (Fact Sheet). Washington, DC: Author. Retrieved on April 12, 2012, from http://www.all4ed.org/files/GraduationRates_FactSheet.pdf

Alliance for Excellent Education. (2011, June). *Caught in the crisis: Students with disabilities in U.S. high schools*. Washington, DC: Author. Retrieved on April 12, 2012, from http://www.all4ed.org/files/CaughtCrisisSWD.pdf

Alliance for Excellent Education. (2012, January). *Caught in the crisis: Students of color and native students in U.S. high schools*. Washington, DC: Author. Retrieved on April 12, 2012, from http://www.all4ed.org/files/CaughtCrisisSOC.pdf

Annie E. Casey Foundation. (2010). *Learning to read: Early warning! Why reading by the end of third grade matters*. Baltimore, MD: Author.

Aud, S., Hussar, W., Kena, G., Bianco, K., Frohlich, L., Kemp, J., & Tahan, K. (2011). *The condition of education 2011* (NCES 2011-033). Washington, DC: U.S. Department of Education, National Center for Education Statistics.

Aud, S., Hussar, W., Planty, M., Snyder, T., Bianco, K., Fox, M., … Drake, L. (2010). *The condition of education 2010* (NCES 2010-028). Washington, DC: National Center for Education Statistics, Institute of Education Sciences, U.S. Department of Education.

Bellah, R. N., Madsen, R., Sullivan, W. M., Swidler, A., & Tipton, S. M. (2008). *Habits of the heart: Individualism and commitment in American life*. Berkeley: University of California Press.

Bloom, H. S., & Unterman, R. (2012, January). *Sustained positive effects on graduation rates produced by New York City's small public high schools of choice*. New York City: MDRC. Retrieved on April 12, 2012, from http://www.mdrc.org/publications/614/policybrief.pdf

Bransford, J., Darling-Hammond, L., & LePage, P. (2005). Introduction. In L. Darling-Hammond & J. Bransford (Eds.), *Preparing teachers for a changing world: What teachers should learn and be able to do* (pp. 1–39). San Francisco: Jossey-Bass.

Broughman, S. P., Swaim, N. L., & Hryczaniuk, C. A. (2011). *Characteristics of private schools in the United States: Results from the 2009–2010 private school universe survey* (NCES 2011-339). Washington, DC: National Center for Education Statistics, Institute of Education Sciences, U.S. Department of Education.

Broughman, S. P., Swaim, N. L., & Keaton, P. W. (2008). *Characteristics of private schools in the United States: Results from the 2005–2006 private school universe survey* (NCES 2008-315). Washington, DC: National Center for Education Statistics, Institute of Education Sciences, U.S. Department of Education.

Carnevale, A., Smith, N., & Strohl, J. (2010, June). *Help wanted: Projections of jobs and education requirements through 2018*. Washington, DC: Center on Education and the Workforce, Georgetown University.

Center on Education Policy. (2011, July). *Keeping informed about school vouchers: A review of major developments and research*. Washington, DC: Author.

Character Education Partnership. (2010, May). *Developing and assessing school culture: A new level of accountability for schools*. Washington, DC: Author. Retrieved on April 2, 2012, from http://www.character.org/uploads/PDFs/White_Papers/DevelopingandAssessingSchoolCulture.pdf

Cuban, L. (2011, May 27). Locating the coordinates of school reform in 2011. Retrieved on April 11, 2012, from http://larrycuban.wordpress.com/2011/05/27/locating-the-coordinates-of-school-reform-in-2011/

Darling-Hammond, L. (2010). *The flat world and education: How America's commitment equity will determine our future*. New York: Teachers College Press.

Florida Virtual School. (2011, June 30). *Quick facts*. Orlando, FL: Author. Retrieved on April 17, 2012, from http://www.flvs.net/areas/aboutus/Pages/QuickFactsaboutFLVS.aspx

Foundation for Excellence in Education. (2010, December 1). *Digital learning now!* Tallahassee, FL: Author. Retrieved on April 12, 2012, from http://digitallearningnow.com/wp-content/uploads/2011/11/Digital-Learning-Now-Report-FINAL.pdf

Frey, W. H., Berube, A., Singer, A., & Wilson, J. H. (2009). *Getting current: Recent demographic trends in metropolitan America*. Washington, DC: The Brookings Institution. Retrieved on April 12, 2012, from http://www.brookings.edu/~/media/Files/rc/reports/2009/03_metro_demographic_trends/03_metro_demographic_trends.pdf

Fry, R. (2009). *The rapid growth and changing complexion of suburban public schools*. Washington, DC: Pew Research Center. Retrieved on April 12, 2012, from http://pewhispanic.org/files/reports/105.pdf

Gay, G. (2010). *Culturally responsive teaching: Theory, research, & practice* (2nd ed.). New York: Teachers College Press.

Gould, J. (Ed.). (2011). *Guardian of democracy: The civic mission of schools*. Washington, DC: Campaign for the Civic Mission of Schools & Leonore Annenberg Institute for Civics, University of Pennsylvania.

Harvey, J. (2011 December/2012 January). Privatization: A drain on public schools. *Educational Leadership, 69*(4), 48–53.

High Tech High. (2012, March 21). *About High Tech High*. San Diego, CA: Author. Retrieved on April 12, 2012, from http://www.hightechhigh.org/about/

International Association for K–12 Online Learning (iNACOL). (2012, February). *Fast facts about online learning*. Vienna, VA: Author. Retrieved on April 12, 2012, from http://www.inacol.org/press/docs/nacol_fast_facts.pdf

Leithwood, K., & Jantzi, D. (2009). A review of empirical evidence about school size effects: A policy perspective. *Review of Educational Research, 79*(1), 464–490.

Lutz, R. A. (2004). *Response of selected middle schools to the accountability demands of No Child Left Behind within mathematics curriculum and instruction*. A dissertation to the University of Pittsburgh.

McEwin, C. K., & Greene, M. W. (2011). *The status of programs and practices in America's middle schools: Results from two national studies*. Westerville, OH: Association for Middle Level Education.

Miron, G., Urschel, J. L., Aguilar, M. A. Y., & Dailey, B. (2012, January). *Profiles of for-profit and nonprofit education management organizations*. Boulder, CO: National Education Policy Center.

National Center for Education Statistics. (2011, April). *Common core of data (CCD): Public elementary/secondary school universe survey* (2009–10, Version 1a). Washington, DC: Institute of Education Sciences, U.S. Department of Education.

National Council for the Social Studies. (2010). *The ten themes of social studies*. National Curriculum Standards for Social Studies: A Framework for Teaching, Learning, and Assessment. Silver Spring, MD: Author. Retrieved on April 8, 2012, from http://ncss.org/standards/strands

National Governors Association Center for Best Practices & Council of Chief State School Officers. (2010). *Common Core State Standards*. Washington, DC: Authors.

New Tech Network. (n.d.). *Our story*. Napa, CA: Author. Retrieved on April 12, 2012, from http://www.newtechnetwork.org/our-story

Partnership for 21st Century Skills. (2011). *P21 framework definitions document*. Tucson, AZ: Author. Retrieved on May 28, 2012, from http://www.p21.org/storage/documents/1.__p21_framework_2-pager.pdf

Planty, M., Hussar, W., Snyder, T., Kena, G., KewalRamani, A., Kemp, J., … Dinkes, R. (2009). *The condition of education 2009* (NCES 2009-081). Washington, DC: National Center for Education Statistics, Institute of Education Sciences, U.S. Department of Education.

Project Tomorrow. (2011). *The new 3 E's of education: Enabled, engaged, empowered. Speak up 2010 national findings*. Irvine, CA: Author. Retrieved on April 17, 2012, from http://www.tomorrow.org/speakup/pdfs/SU1 0_3EofEducation%28Students%29.pdf

Quillen, I. (2011, March 17). Policies seen to slow innovation. *Education Week, 30*(25), 42.

Ravitch, D. (2010). *The death and life of the great American school system: How testing and choice are undermining education.* New York: Basic Books.

Ray, B. D. (2011, June 8). *Research facts on homeschooling.* Salem, OR: National Home Education Research Institute. Retrieved on April 10, 2011, from http://www.nheri.org/research/research-facts-on-homeschooling.html

Sable, J., Plotts, C., & Mitchell, L. (2010). *Characteristics of the 100 largest public elementary and secondary school districts in the United States: 2008–09* (NCES 2011-301). Washington, DC: U.S. Department of Education, National Center for Education Statistics.

Sanders, W. I., & Rivers, J. C. (1996). *Cumulative and residual effects of teachers on future student academic achievement.* Knoxville, TN: University of Tennessee Value-Added Research and Assessment Center.

Spring, J. (2011). *The American school: A global context from the Puritans to the Obama era* (8th ed.). New York: McGraw-Hill.

Swanson, C. B. (2009). *Cities in crisis 2009: Closing the graduation gap.* Bethesda, MD: Editorial Projects in Education.

The Center for Education Reform. (2010). *Annual survey of America's charter schools.* Washington, DC: Author.

The Center for Education Reform. (2012a). *Charter school laws across the states: 2012.* Washington, DC: Author.

The Center for Education Reform. (2012b). *Facts.* Washington, DC: Author. Retrieved on April 9, 2012, from http://www.edreform.com/issues/choice-charter-schools/facts/.

The Center for Education Reform. (2012c). *Laws and legislation.* Washington, DC: Author. Retrieved on April 9, 2012, from http://www.edreform.com/issues/choice-charter-schools/laws-legislation/

The Conference Board, Partnership for 21st Century Skills, Corporate Voices for Working Families, & Society for Human Resource Management. (2006). *Are they really ready to work? Employers' perspectives on the basic knowledge and applied skills of new entrants to the 21st century U.S. workforce.* New York: The Conference Board.

Thomasian, J. (2011). *Building a science, technology, engineering, and math education agenda.* Washington, DC: National Governors Association Center for Best Practices.

U.S. Census Bureau. (2011). *Statistical Abstract of the United States: 2012* (131st Edition). Washington, DC: Author.

Watson, J., Murin, A., Vashaw, L., Gemin, B., & Rapp, C. (2011). *Keeping pace with K–12 online learning: An annual review of policy and practice.* Durango, CO: Evergreen Education Group.

CHAPTER 7

Addy, S., & Wight, V. R. (2012, February). Basic facts about low-income children, 2010: Children under age 18. New York City: National Center for Children in Poverty. Retrieved April 12, 2012, from http://nccp.org/publications/pdf/text_1049.pdf

American Psychological Association. (2008). Answers to your questions: For a better understanding of sexual orientation and homosexuality. Washington, DC: Author. Retrieved March 28, 2011, from http://www.apa.org/topics/sexuality/orientation.aspx

Anderson, S., Collins, C., Klinger, S., & Pizzigati, S. (2011). *Executive excess 2011: The massive CEO rewards for tax dodging.* Washington, DC: Institute for Policy Studies and United for a Fair Economy.

Aud, S., Hussar, W., Kena, G., Bianco, K., Frohlich, L., Kemp, J., & Tahan, K. (2011). *The Condition of Education 2011* (NCES 2011-033). Washington, DC: U.S. Department of Education, National Center for Education Statistics.

Barton, P. E., & Coley, R. J. (2010). *The blackwhite achievement gap: When progress stopped* (Policy Information Report). Princeton, NJ: Educational Testing Service.

Barton, P. E., & Coley, R. J. (2009). *Parsing the achievement gap II.* Princeton, NJ: Education Testing Service.

Brault, M. W. (2008, December). *Americans with disabilities: 2005.* Washington, DC: U.S. Census Bureau.

Bureau of Indian Affairs. (2011). What we do: Services overview. Retrieved October 11, 2011, at http://www.bia.gov/index.htm

Civil Rights Project, Harvard University. (2002). *What works for the children? What we know and don't know about bilingual education.* Cambridge, MA: Author.

Cleveland, K. P. (2011). *Teaching boys who struggle in school: Strategies that turn underachievers into successful learners.* Alexandria, VA: ASCD.

Council for Exceptional Children. (n.d.). *Response to intervention.* Arlington, VA: Author. Retrieved on April 30, 2012, from http://www.cec.sped.org/AM/Template.cfm?Section=Response_to_Intervention&Template=/TaggedPage/TaggedPageDisplay.cfm&TPLID=37&ContentID=8363

Eliot, L. (2009). *Pink brain, blue brain: How small differences grow into troublesome gaps—and what we can do about it.* Boston, MA: Mariner, Houghton Mifflin Harcourt.

Fass, S. (2009, April). Measuring poverty in the United States (Fact Sheet). New York City: National Center for Children in Poverty. Retrieved on April 23, 2012, from http://nccp.org/publications/pdf/text_876.pdf

Gollnick, D. M., & Chinn, P. C. (2013). *Multicultural education in a pluralistic society.* Upper Saddle River, NJ: Pearson.

Hacker, J. S., & Pierson, P. (2010). *Winnertake-all politics: How Washington made the rich richer—and turned its back on the middle class.* New York: Simon & Schuster.

Handwerk, P., Tognatta, N., Coley, R. J., & Gitomer, D. H. (2008). *Access to success: Patterns of advanced placement participation in U.S. high schools.* Princeton, NJ: Educational Testing Service.

Haynes, C. C. (2012, January). Getting religion right in public schools. *Phi Delta Kappan, 93*(4), 8–14.

Jordan-Young, R. M. (2010). *Brainstorm: The flaws in the science of sex differences.* Cambridge, MA: Harvard University Press.

Keen, L. (2011, April 8). LGBTs comprise 3.5 percent of U.S. adult population. *Keen News Service.* Retrieved on April 10, 2011, from http://www.keennewsservice.com/2011/04/08/lgbts-comprise-3-5-percent-of-u-s-adult-population/

Kelley, M. (2000, September 8). Indian affairs head makes apology. *The Free Press.*

Kosciw, J. G., Greytak, E. A., Diaz, E. M., & Bartkiewicz, M. J. (2010). *The 2009 National School Climate Survey: The experiences of lesbian, gay, bisexual and transgender youth in our nation's schools.* New York: Gay, Lesbian and Straight Education Network.

Lipsky, D. K., & Gartner, A. (1996). Inclusion, school restructuring, and the remaking of American society. *Harvard Educational Review 66*(4), 762–796.

Meyer, E. J. (2010). *Gender and sexual diversity in schools.* New York: Springer.

National Center for Education Statistics, Integrated Postsecondary Education Data System (IPEDS). (2011, November). Bachelor's degrees conferred by degree-granting institutions, by sex, race/ethnicity, and field of study: 2009–10 (Table 301). Washington, DC: U.S. Department of Education. Retrieved on April 30, 2012, from http://nces.ed.gov/programs/digest/d11/tables/dt11_301.asp

National Center for Education Statistics, U.S. Department of Education. (2009). *NAEP 2008 trends in academic progress.* Washington, DC: Author.

National Center for Education Statistics. (2007). *The condition of education 2007* (NCES 2007-064). Washington, DC: U.S. Department of Education.

National Clearinghouse for English Language Acquisition. (n.d.). Types of language instruction educational programs (LIEPs). Washington, DC: Author. Retrieved on April 29, 2012, from http://www.ncela.gwu.edu/files/uploads/5/Language_Instruction_Educational_Programs.pdf

National Federation of State High School Associations. (2011). *2010–11 high school athletics participation survey.* Indianapolis, IN: Author. Retrieved on April 30, 2012, from http://www.nfhs.org/content.aspx?id=3282

Newport, F. (2009). *Despite recession, no uptick in Americans' religiosity.* Princeton, NJ: Gallup Organization, March 23, 2009. Retrieved on May 14, 2009, from http://www.gallup.com/poll/117040/Despite-Recession-No-Uptick-Americans-Religiosity.aspx

Noguera, P. A. (2011, November). A broader and bolder approach uses education to break the cycle of poverty. *Phi Delta Kappan, 93*(3), 8–14.

Organisation for Economic Co-operation and Development. (2011). CO2.2: Child poverty. Paris, France: Author. Retrieved on April 23, 2012, from http://www.oecd.org/dataoecd/52/43/41929552.pdf

Ost, J., & Gates, G. J. (2004). *The gay & lesbian atlas.* Washington, DC: Urban Institute.

Page, B. I., & Jacobs, L. R. (2009). *Class war? What Americans really think about economic inequality.* Chicago: The University of Chicago Press.

Passel, J. S., & Cohn, D. (2011). *Unauthorized immigrant population: National and state trends, 2010.* Washington, DC: Pew Hispanic Center.

Passel, J. S., Cohn, D., & Lopez, M. H. (2011, March 24). *Hispanics account for more than half of nation's growth in past decade.* Washington, DC: Pew Hispanic Center.

Pew Forum on Religion & Public Life. (2010). *U.S. religious knowledge survey.* Washington, DC: Pew Research Center.

Planty, M., Hussar, W., Snyder, T., Provasnik, S., Kena, G., Dinkes, R., ... Kemp, J. (2008). *The condition of education 2008* (NCES 2008-031). Washington, DC: National Center for Education Statistics, U.S. Department of Education.

Sabo, D., & Veliz, P. (2008). *Go out and play: Youth sports in America.* East Meadow, NY: Women's Sports Foundation.

Sadker, D., Sadker, M., & Zittleman, K. R. (2009). *Still failing at fairness: How gender bias cheats girls and boys in school and what we can do about it.* New York: Scribner.

Savage, T. A., & Harley, D. A. (2009, Summer). A place at the blackboard: LGBTIQ. *Multicultural Education, 16*(4), 2–9.

Short, D. J., & Boyson, B. A. (2012). *Helping newcomer students succeed in secondary schools and beyond.* Washington, DC: Center for Applied Linguistics.

Staurowsky, E. J., Hogshead-Makar, N., Kane, M. J., Wughalter, E., Yiamouyiannis, A., & Lerner, P. K. (2007). Gender equity in physical education and athletics. In S. S. Klein, B. Richardson, D. A. Grayson, L. H. Fox, C. Kramarae, D. S. Pollard, & C. A. Dwyer (Eds.), *Handbook for achieving gender equity through education* (2nd ed., pp. 381–410). Mahwah, NJ: Lawrence Erlbaum.

Takaki, R. (1993). *A different mirror: A history of multicultural America.* Boston: Little, Brown.

Torff, B. (2011, November). *Phi Delta Kappan, 93*(3), 21–23.

U.S. Bureau of Labor Statistics. (2010, July 8). *Women's-to-men's earnings ratio by age, 2009.* Washington, DC: Author. Retrieved on May 7, 2012, from http://www.bls.gov/opub/ted/2010/ted_20100708.htm

U.S. Census Bureau, Population Division. (2008, August 14). Table 6. Percent of the projected population by race and Hispanic origin for the United States: 2010–2050 (NP2008-T6). Washington, DC: Author. Retrieved April 22, 2012, from http://www.census.gov/population/www/projections/summarytables.html

U.S. Census Bureau. (2008). *Statistical abstract of the United States: 2009* (128th ed.). Washington, DC: U.S. Government Printing Office.

U.S. Census Bureau. (2011). *Statistical abstract of the United States: 2012* (131st ed.). Washington, DC: Author.

U.S. Department of Health & Human Services (2012, February 9). *2012 HHS poverty guidelines.* Washington, DC: Author. Retrieved on April 23, 2012, from http://aspe.hhs.gov/poverty/12poverty.shtml

Viadero, D. (2009, January 8). Delving deep: Research hones focus on ELLs. *Education Week, 28*(17), 22–25.

Zgonc, E. (2010). *NCAA sports sponsorship and participation rates report: 1981–82—2009–10.* Indianapolis, IN: National Collegiate Athletic Association. Retrieved on April 30, 2012, from http://www.ncaapublications.com/productdownloads/PR2011.pdf

CHAPTER 8

American Association of Suicidology. (n.d.). *Know the warning signs.* Washington, DC: Author. Retrieved on June 3, 2012, from http://www.suicidology.org/stats-and-tools/suicide-warning-signs

Annie E. Casey Foundation. (2009, July). *Kids count indicator brief: Reducing the teen birth rate.* Baltimore, MD: Author. Retrieved on June 5, 2012, from http://www.aecf.org/~/media/Pubs/Initiatives/KIDS%20COUNT/K/KIDSCOUNTIndicatorBriefReducingtheTeenBirthRa/Corrected%20teen%20birth%20brief.pdf

Aud, S., Hussar, W., Johnson, F., Kena, G., Roth, E., Manning, E., ... Zhang, J. (2012). *The condition of education 2012* (NCES 2012-045). Washington, DC: U.S. Department of Education, National Center for Education Statistics.

Balfanz, R., Bridgeland, J. M., Bruce, M., & Fox, J. H. (2012). *Building a grad nation: Progress and challenge in ending the high school dropout epidemic.* Washington, DC: Alliance for Excellent Education, America's Promise Alliance, Civic Enterprises, and the Everyone Graduates Center at Johns Hopkins University.

Barton, P. E., & Coley, R. J. (2009). *Parsing the Achievement Gap II* (Policy Information Report). Princeton, NJ: Educational Testing Service.

Bushaw, W. J., & Lopez, S. J. (2011). Betting on teachers: The 43rd annual Phi Delta Kappa/Gallup poll of the public's attitudes toward the public schools. *Phi Delta Kappan, 93*(1), 9–26.

Centers for Disease Control and Prevention (CDC). (2009). *Suicide prevention: Youth suicide.* Atlanta: Author. Retrieved on June 3, 2012, from http://www.cdc.gov/violenceprevention/pub/youth_suicide.html

Centers for Disease Control and Prevention (CDC). (2010, June 4). Youth risk behavior surveillance – United States, 2009. *Morbidity and Mortality Weekly Report, 59*(SS-5).

Centers for Disease Control and Prevention (CDC). (2011a). *Teen pregnancy: The importance of prevention.* Atlanta: Author. Retrieved on June 4, 2012, from http://www.cdc.gov/Features/VitalSigns/TeenPregnancy/

Centers for Disease Control and Prevention (CDC). (2011b). *Understanding bullying.* Atlanta: Author. Retrieved on June 3, 2012, from http://www.cdc.gov/ViolencePrevention/pdf/Bullying_Factsheet-a.pdf

Centers for Disease Control and Prevention (CDC). (2012). *Child maltreatment prevention.* Retrieved on June 4, 2012, from http://www.cdc.gov/ViolencePrevention/childmaltreatment/

Cunningham, M., Harwood, R., & Hall, S. (2010, May). *Residential instability and the McKinney-Vento homeless children and education program: What we know, plus gaps in research.* Washington, DC: Urban Institute. Retrieved on June 1, 2012, from http://www.aecf.org/~/media/Pubs/Topics/Education/Other/ResidentialInstabilityandMcKinneyVentoProgram/412115%20mckinney%20vento%20program.pdf

Diaz, E. M., & Kosciw, J. G. (2009). *Shared differences: The experiences of lesbian, gay, bisexual, and transgender students of color in our nation's schools.* New York: Gay, Lesbian and Straight Education Network.

Gay, Lesbian & Straight Education Network (GLSEN). (2011). *Talking about suicide and LGBT populations.* New York: Author. Retrieved on June 4, 2012, from http://www.glsen.org/binary-data/GLSEN_ATTACHMENTS/file/000/001/1800-2.pdf

Gray, L., Thomas, N., & Lewis, L. (2010). *Teachers' use of educational technology in U.S. public schools: 2009* (NCES 2010-040). Washington, DC: U.S. Department of Education, Institute of Education Sciences, National Center for Education Statistics.

Hamburger, M. E., Basile, K. C., & Vivolo, A. M. (2011). *Measuring bullying victimization, perpetration, and bystander experiences: A compendium of assessment tools.* Atlanta: Centers for Disease Control and Prevention, National Center for Injury Prevention and Control.

Hamilton, B. E., & Ventura, S. J. (2012, April). Birth rates for U.S. teenagers reach historic lows for all age and ethnic groups. *NCHS Data Brief, 89.* Retrieved on June 4, 2012, from http://www.cdc.gov/nchs/data/databriefs/db89.htm

Hertz, M. F., & David-Ferdon, C. (2008). *Electronic media and youth violence: A CDC issue brief for educators and caregivers.* Atlanta: Centers for Disease Control. Retrieved on May 2, 2009, from http://www.cdc.gov/ViolencePrevention/pdf/EA-brief-a.pdf

Hill, C., & Kearl, H. (2011, November). *Crossing the line: Sexual harassment at school.* Washington, DC: AAUW.

Johnston, L. D., O'Malley, P. M., Bachman, J. G., & Schulenberg, J. E. (2012). *Monitoring the future: National results on adolescent drug use: Overview of key findings, 2011.* Ann Arbor: Institute for Social Research, The University of Michigan.

Kosciw, J. G., Greytak, E. A., Diaz, E. M., & Bartkiewicz, M. J. (2010). *The 2009 national school climate survey: The experiences of lesbian, gay, bisexual and transgender youth in our nation's schools.* New York: GLSEN.

MetLife. (2012, March). *MetLife survey of the American teacher: Teachers, parents and the economy.* New York: Author.

National Association for the Education of Homeless Children and Youth. (2007–2011). *Facts about homeless education.* Minneapolis, MN: Author. Retrieved on June 2, 2012, from http://www.naehcy.org/facts.html#impact

National Campaign to Prevent Teen and Unplanned Pregnancy. (2009). *What works: Curriculum-based programs that prevent teen pregnancy.* Washington, DC: Author.

National Center for Education Statistics. (2011, August). *Student reports of bullying and cyber-bullying: Results from the 2009 school crime supplement to the national crime victimization survey.* Washington, DC: U.S. Department of Education, National Center for Education Statistics. Retrieved on June 4, 2012, from http://nces.ed.gov/pubs2011/2011336.pdf

National Center for Education Statistics. (2012). *Digest of education statistics: 2011.* Washington, DC: U.S. Department of Education, Institute of Education Sciences.

National Center on Family Homelessness (NCFH). (2011, December). *The characteristics and needs of families experiencing homelessness.* Needham, MA: Author. Retrieved on June 1, 2012, from http://www.familyhomelessness .org/media/306.pdf

National Coalition for the Homeless (NCH). (2008, June). *Homeless youth.* Washington, DC: Author. Retrieved on June 2, 2012, from http://www.nationalhomeless.org/factsheets/ youth.html

National Coalition for the Homeless (NCH). (2009, June). *LGBT homeless.* Washington, DC: Author. Retrieved on June 2, 2012, from http://www.nationalhomeless.org/factsheets/ lgbtq.html

National Law Center on Homelessness and Poverty (NLCHP). (2012). *Homelessness and poverty in America.* Washington, DC: Author. Retrieved on June 1, 2012, from http:// www.nlchp.org/hapia.cfm

Planty, M., Hussar, W., Snyder, T., Provasnik, S., Kena, G., Dinkes, R., ... Kemp, J. (2008). *The condition of education 2008* (NCES 2008-031). Washington, DC: National Center for Education Statistics, U.S. Department of Education.

Poll adds "youth voice" on schools. (2009, May 13). *Education Week, 28*(31), 4.

PTA. (2008). *Discover the power of partnerships.* Alexandria, VA: Author.

Sable, J., Plotts, C., & Mitchell, L. (2010). *Characteristics of the 100 largest public elementary and secondary school districts in the United States: 2008–09 (NCES 2011-301).* Washington, DC: U.S. Department of Education, National Center for Education Statistics.

Swanson, C. B. (2009). *Cities in crisis 2009: Closing the graduation gap.* Bethesda, MD: Editorial Projects in Education.

The U.S. Conference of Mayors. (2011, December). *Hunger and homelessness survey: A status report on hunger and homelessness in America's cities: A 29-city survey.* Washington, DC: Author. Retrieved on June 1, 2012, from http://usmayors.org/pressreleases/ uploads/2011-hhreport.pdf

U.S. Bureau of Labor Statistics. (2011, July). *School's out.* Washington, DC: Author. Retrieved on June 5, 2012, from http://www.bls .gov/spotlight/2011/schools_out/

U.S. Census Bureau. (2011). *Statistical abstract of the United States: 2012* (131st ed.). Washington, DC: Author.

U.S. Department of Agriculture. (2012, March 23). Income eligibility requirements. *Federal Register, 77*(57), 17006.

U.S. Department of Education. (2011, August 31). *Improving Basic Programs Operated by Local Educational Agencies (Title I, Part A).* Washington, DC: Author. Retrieved on June 2, 2012, from http://www2.ed.gov/programs/ titleiparta/index.html

U.S. Department of Health and Human Services, Administration for Children and Families, Administration on Children, Youth and Families, Children's Bureau. (2011). *Child maltreatment 2010.* Washington, DC: Author.

Yaffe, D. (2011, Winter). *Addressing achievement gaps: The family: America's smallest school.* Princeton, NJ: Educational Testing Service.

CHAPTER 9

Dadayan, L., & Ward, R. B. (2011, June 23). Back in the black: State's gambling revenues rose in 2010. *Fiscal Studies.* Albany, NY: The Nelson A. Rockefeller Institute of Government.

LaMorte, M. S. (2012). *School law: Cases and concepts* (10th ed.). Upper Saddle River, NJ: Pearson.

Mayo Clinic Staff. (n.d.). Teen sleep: Why is your teen so tired? *Tween and Teen Health.* Retrieved from http://www.mayoclinic.com/ health/teens-health/CC00019

National Center for Education Statistics. (2012). *Fast facts.* Washington DC: National Center for Education Statistics, U.S. Department of Education. http://nces.ed.gov/ fastfacts

CHAPTER 10

Goss v. Lopez, 419 U.S. 565 (1975).

Gouge v. Joint School District No. 1, 310 F.Supp. 984 (W.D.Wis.1970).

Hazelwood School District et al. v. Kuhlmeier et al., 484 U.S. 260 (1988).

LaMorte, M. W. (2012). *School law: Cases and concepts.* Upper Saddle River, NJ: Pearson.

Morris v. Douglas County School District, 403 P.2d 775, 776 (Or.1965).

Owasso Independent School District No. 1 v. Falvo, 534 U.S. 426 (2002).

Pickering v. Board of Education, 391 U.S. 563 (1968).

Tinker v. Des Moines Independent Community School District, 393 U.S. 503 (1969).

CHAPTER 11

Anderson, L. W. (2009). Upper elementary grades bear the brunt of accountability. *Phi Delta Kappan, 90*(6), 413–418.

Borja, R. R. (2006). Risk and reward. *Technology Counts 2006: The information edge: Using data to accelerate achievement (Education Week, 25*[35]). Bethesda, MD: Editorial Projects in Education.

Cavanagh, S., & Manzo, K. K. (2009). International exams yield less-than-clear lessons. *Education Week, 28*(29), 1, 16–17.

Darling-Hammond, L., & Falk, B. (1997). Supporting teaching and learning for all students: Policies for authentic assessment systems. In A. L. Goodwin (Ed.), *Assessment for equity and inclusion: Embracing all our children.* New York: Routledge.

Educational Testing Service. (2009). Addressing achievement gaps. *Policy Notes, 17*(1), 1.

H.R. 1804 (103d Congress). Goals 2000: Educate America Act. Washington, DC: 103d Congress, 1993–1994.

Jennings, J. L., & Corcoran, S. P. (2009). "Beware of geeks bearing formulas": Reflections on growth models for school accountability. *Phi Delta Kappan, 90*(9), 635–639.

Johnson, D.W. & Johnson, R. (1999). Learning together and alone: Cooperative, competitive and individualistic learning (5th edition). Boston, MA: Allyn & Bacon.

Mullis, I. V. S., Martin, M. O., Kennedy, A. M., & Foy, P. (2007). *PIRLS 2006 international report: IEA's progress in international reading literacy study in primary schools in 40 countries.* Chestnut Hill, MA: TIMSS & PIRLS International Study Center, Boston College.

National Committee on Science Education Standards and Assessment, National Research Council. (1996). *National science education standards.* Washington, DC: National Academies Press.

National Council for the Social Studies. (2009) *Expectations of excellence: Curriculum standards for the social studies.* Silver Spring, MD: Author.

National Council of Teachers of Mathematics. (2000). *Principles and standards for school mathematics.* Reston, VA: Author.

National Governors Association, Council of Chief State School Officers, and Achieve, Inc. (2008). *Benchmarking for success: Ensuring U.S. students receive a world-class education.* Washington, DC: National Governors Association.

OECD. (2008). *Growing unequal-income distribution and poverty in OECD countries* (CO8: Child Poverty). Paris: Author. Retrieved on May 11, 2009, from http://www.oecd.rog/ dataoecd/52/43/41929552.pdf

Olson, L. (2001). Overboard on testing? *Quality Counts 2001: A better balance (Education Week 20[7]).* Bethesda, MD: Editorial Projects in Education.

Partnership for 21st Century Skills. (2011). *A Framework for 21st century learning.* Washington, DC: Partnership for 21st Century Skills.

Pennsylvania Department of Education. (2012). *Standards aligned system.* Accessed December 29, 2012. http://www.pdesas.org/module/ sas/curriculumframework

Popham, W. J. (2010). *Classroom assessment: What teachers need to know* (6th ed.). Upper Saddle River, NJ: Pearson.

Programme for International Student Assessment (PISA). (n.d.). Washington, DC: Organization for Economic Co-operation and Development (OECD), Washington Center.

Progress in International Reading Literacy Study (PIRLS). (n.d.). Chestnut Hill, MA: TIMSS & PIRLS International Study Center, Boston College.

Rotberg, I. C. (2008). Quick fixes, test scores, and the global economy: Myths that continue to confound us. *Education Week, 27*(41) 27, 32.

Shepard, L., Hammerness, K., Darling-Hammond, L., Rust, F., Snowden, J. B., Gordon, E., Gutierrez, C., & Pacheco, A. (2007). Assessment. In L. Darling-Hammond & J. Bransford (Eds.), *Preparing teachers for a changing world: What teachers should learn and be able to do* (pp. 275–326). San Francisco: Jossey-Bass.

Stiggins, R. (2009). Assessment FOR learning in upper elementary grades. *Phi Delta Kappan, 90*(6), 419-421.

Stiggins, R. J., & Chappuis, J. (2011). *An introduction to student-involved assessment FOR learning* (6th ed.). Upper Saddle River, NJ: Pearson.

Stiggins, R., & DuFour, R. (2009). Maximizing the power of formative assessments. *Phi Delta Kappan, 90*(9), 640-644.

Symcox, L. (2002). *Whose history? The struggle for national standards in American classrooms.* New York: Teachers College Press.

Webb, N. L. (2002, March 28). *Depth-of-Knowledge Levels for Content Areas.* Madison, WI: Wisconsin Center for Education Research.

CHAPTER 12

AAAS. (1993). *Benchmarks for Science Literacy.* New York: Oxford University Press.

Abramovich, S., & Ehrlich, A. (2007). Computer as a medium for overcoming misconceptions in solving inequalities. *Journal of Computers in Mathematics and Science Teaching, 26*(3), 181–196.

Achieve, Inc. (2012). What is college- and career-ready? Retrieved on May 18, 2012, from http://www.achieve.org/what-college-and-career-ready

Anderson, L. W., & Krathwohl, D. R. (Eds.). (2001). *A taxonomy for learning, teaching and assessing: A revision of Bloom's taxonomy of educational objectives.* New York: Longman.

Association for Career and Technical Education. (2010). What is career ready? Retrieved on May 18, 2012, from https://www.acteonline.org/uploadedFiles/Publications_and_Online_Media/files/Career_Readiness_Paper.pdf

Bamberger, H., & Oberdoft, D. (2010). *Activities to undo math misconceptions, grades 3–5.* Portsmouth, NH: Heinemann.

Bebell, D., & O'Dwyer, L. (2010). Educational outcomes and research from 1:1 computing settings. *The Journal of Technology, Learning and Assessment, 9*(1), 5–15.

Blink, R. J. (2007). *Data driven instruction.* Larchmont, NY: Eye on Education.

Bloom, B. S. (Ed.). (1956). *Taxonomy of educational objectives: The classification of educational goals handbook I: Cognitive domain.* New York: David McKay.

California Department of Education. (2009). *Curriculum framework and evaluation criteria committee guidelines for the science framework for California public schools, kindergarten through grade twelve.* Sacramento, CA: Author.

Comer, J. P. (2009). *What I learned in school: Reflections on race, child development and school reform.* San Francisco: Jossey-Bass.

Comer, J. P., Joyner, E. T., & Ben-Avie, M. (Eds.). (2004). *The field guide to Comer schools in action.* California: Corwin Press.

Dillon, S. (2011, March 7). Bipartisan group backs common school curriculum. *New York Times.*

Duffy, P. (2008). Engaging the YouTube Google-eyed generation: Strategies for using Web 2.0 in teaching and learning. *The Electronic Journal of e-Learning, 6,* 119–130.

Felder, R. M. (2010, September 27). Are learning styles invalid? (Hint: No!). *On-Course Newsletter.*

Felder, R. M., & Silverman, L. K. (1988, revised in 2002). Learning and teaching styles in engineering education. *Engineering Education, 78*(7), 674–681.

Felder, R. M., & Spurlin, J. (2005). Reliability and validity of the index of learning styles: A meta-analysis. *International Journal of Engineering Education, 78*(7) 674–681.

Fisher, D., Frey, N., & Williams, D. (2002). Seven literacy strategies that work. *Educational Leadership, 60*(3), 70–73.

Gass, S., & Selinker, L. (2008). *Second language acquisition: An introductory course.* New York: Routledge.

Hacker, D., Dunlosky, J., & Graesser, A. (Eds.). (2009). *Handbook of metacognition in education.* New York: Taylor and Francis.

Houssart, J., & Sams, C. (2008). Developing mathematical reasoning through games of strategy played against the computer. *International Journal for Technology in Mathematics Education, 15*(2), 59–71.

Interactive Educational Systems Design in collaboration with Daylene Long and Scott Long of STEM Market Impact. (2012). *2012 National survey on STEM education.* New York: Author. Retrieved on May 18, 2012, from http://www.learning.com/stem/2012-stem-report/

Kolb, D. (2007). *Learning style inventory (Version 3.1).* New York: Hay Group.

Krathwohl, D. R., Bloom, B. S., & Masia, B. B. (1964). *Taxonomy of educational objectives: The classification of educational goals, Handbook II: Affective domain.* New York: David McKay.

Lessow-Hurley, J. (2003). *Meeting the needs of second language learners.* Alexandria, VA: Association for Supervision and Curriculum Development.

Li, Q., & Ma, X. (2010). A meta-analysis of the effects of computer technology on school students' mathematics learning. *Educational Psychology Review, 22,* 215–243.

Massachusetts Department of Elementary and Secondary Education. (2011). *Progress Report of the Mathematics Curriculum Framework Revision Panel.* Boston, MA: Author.

Neufeld, P. (2005). Comprehension instruction in content classes. *The Reading Teacher, 59*(4), 302–312.

Norris, C., Soloway, E., Menchhofer, K., Bauman, B., Dickerson, M., Schad, L., & Tomko, S. (2010). Innovative leaders take the phone and run: Profiles of four trailblazing programs. *District Administration, 46*(6), 35–38.

Quindlen, T. (2002, Fall). Entrees to English: Tips for assisting language learners. *Curriculum Update,* p. 2.

Schmocker, M. (2006). *Results now: How we can achieve unprecedented improvements in teaching and learning.* Alexandria, VA: Association for Supervision and Curriculum Development.

Simpson, E. J. (1972). *The classification of educational objectives in the psychomotor domain: The psychomotor domain (Vol. 3).* Washington, DC: Gryphon House.

Slavin, R. (1996). *Education for all.* Exton, PA: Swets & Zeitlinger.

Snow, C., Griffin, P., & Burns, S. (Eds.). (2005). *Knowledge to support the teaching of reading: Preparing teachers for a changing world.* San Francisco: Jossey-Bass.

Taba, H. (1962). *Curriculum development theory and practice.* New York: Harcout, Brace & World.

Tarr, J., Reys, R., Reys, B., Chávez, Oacute;., Shih, J., & Osterlind, S. (2008). The impact of middle-grades mathematics curricula and the classroom learning environment on student achievement. *Journal for Research in Mathematics Education, 39*(5), 247–280.

Tyler, R.W. (1950). *Basic principles of curriculum development.* Chicago, IL: University of Chicago Press.

Vacca, R. T. (2002). From efficient decoders to strategic readers. *Educational Leadership, 60*(3), 6–11.

Vygotsky, L. (1978). *Mind and society: The development of higher psychological processes* (M. Cole, V. John-Steiner, S. Scribner, & E. Soubermann, Eds. & Trans.). Cambridge, MA: Harvard University.

Wenglinsky, H. (2005). *Using technology wisely: The keys to success in schools.* New York: Teachers College Press.

CHAPTER 13

Berliner, D. C. (2001). Learning about and learning from expert teachers. *International Journal of Educational Research, 35*(5), 463–483.

Brophy, J. E., & Good, T. L. (1974). *Teacher-student relationships: Causes and consequences.* Retrieved from http://eric.ed.gov (ERIC Document Reproduction Service No. ED091495).

Emmer, E. T., Evertson, C. M., & Anderson, L. M. (1980), Effective classroom management at the beginning of the school year. *The Elementary School Journal 80*(5), 219-231.

Finn, J. D., & Achilles, C. M. (1999). Tennessee's class size study: Findings, implications, misconceptions. *Educational Evaluation and Policy Analysis, 21*(2), 97–109.

Hall, G. E., & Hord, S. M. (2011). *Implementing change: Patterns, principles and potholes* (3rd ed.). Upper Saddle River, NJ: Pearson.

Hall, G. E., Negroni, I. A., & George, A. A. (2008). *Examining relationships between urban principal leadership and student learning.* Paper presented at the annual meeting of the American Education Research Association, New York.

Hord, S. M. (Ed). (2004). *Learning together, leading together: Changing schools through professional learning communities.* New York: Teachers College Press.

Issues: Education. (2009). Retrieved from http://www.whitehouse.gov/issues/education/.

Josephson Institute for Ethics. (2008). *The ethics of American youth—2008 summary.* Los Angeles, CA: Author.

NAME INDEX

SUBJECT INDEX

poverty and, 172
at proficient level or above, 157
race, 167
student population, 170
test result discrepancies, 326
Race-conscious assignment of students, 270
Racism, 213
Rationalists, 33
Rational process, change as, 130–131
Ratio Studiorum, 32–33
Readers (McGuffey), 42
Reagan, Ronald, 331
Realism, 85–87, 88, 93, 103
Real-time technology data banks, 355
Real-world standards, 299
Reason, Age of, 33
Recesses, 154
Reclaiming a Conversation (Roland), 84–85
Reconstructionism, 192
Reduced-price lunch, 203
Reflection, 19–20, 380
Reform. *See* School reform
Reformation, Protestant, 31, 32–33
Reggio Emelia approach, 155
Regional accreditation, 14
Regional education service agencies
    (RESAs), 229
Regressive taxes, 239
Regulatory state boards of education, 235
Rehabilitation Act, Section 504, 53, 272, 289
Reinforcement, 107–108
Reliability, 315
Religion. *see also* Church/state separation
    in the classroom, 37
    diversity in, 185–187
Religion-affiliated schools, 47
Religious activities, in public schools, 265–268
Religious education, 262–265. *see also*
    Parochial schools
Renaissance, 31, 32
Renewal, license, 23
Report cards, school/school district, 255
Representative Assembly (RA), 389
Republic (Plato), 29
Research
    teachers keeping up with historical and
        contemporary, 48
    teachers using to conduct educational, 13
Research, educational, 13, 48, 374–375
Resegregation, 268
Residence, proof of, 284, 285
Resiliency, student, 202, 217
Resources, teachers seeking supportive, 384–388
Resource teachers, 155, 233
Responder facilitator style, 378
Response to Intervention (RTI) instructional
    model, 185, 273
Retention, student, 215
Retirement, 22
Revenue sources
    advertising, 243
    budget cuts, 225–226
    fund-raising efforts, 244–245
    key finance questions, 237
    property taxes, 238–239
    recent challenges within states, 241–243
    state aid, 245–246
    state differences in, 241, 242
    state sources, 240–241
    student fees, 244
    taxation and support for schools, 237–240
Reverse discrimination, 271
Revisionist historians, 28
Revival of learning, age of, 31

Rewards for accountability, 254–255
Rich, Brenda, 101–102
Rich, Stormy, 101–102
Rickover, Hyman, 66
The Right Method of Instruction (Erasmus), 32
Riley, Richard W., 331
Roman Catholic Church, 30, 32, 186
Roman Catholic parochial schools, 47, 58, 148
Roman schools, 29–30
Rorty, Richard, 89
Rose v. The Council for Better Education Inc.
    (1989), 243
Rousseau, Jean-Jacques, 34–35, 113–114
RTI (Response to Intervention) model, 185, 273
Rubrics, 304, 312
Rules, classroom, 124, 127, 128
Runaways, 201–202
Rural communities, schools in, 158
Rutherford Institute, 279
Ryans, D. G., 67

Sacramento, California, 197–198
Safe harbor, 250
Safford Unified School District #1 v. Redding
    (2009), 290
Salaries, teacher, 21–22
Salary schedule, 22–23
Sales taxes, 238, 239, 240
Sale taxes, 240
*San Antonio (Texas) Independent School District
    v. Rodriquez* (1979), 239–240
San Francisco school district, 289
*Santa Fe Independent School District, Petitioner
    v. Jane Doe* (2000), 266–267
Sartre, Jean-Paul, 90, 91
SAT (Scholastic Aptitude Test), 305
Scaffolding strategies, 352–353
Scholasticism, 31
School architecture, 230–231
School board politics, 253
School boards, 227–228
School Breakfast Program, 203
School budget. *See* Revenue sources; School
    funds/funding
School buildings, 229–230, 229–231
School choices, 148–153
School culture, 147
School day, lengthening, 234
School Development Program (SDP), 365
School districts
    consolidation of, 55
    curriculum evaluation, 344
    expenditures, 229
    location of, teacher demand and, 10
    organization, 226–229
    organization chart, 227
    report card, 255
    role in managing curriculum, 342–343
    statistics, 226
    technology for administration, 251
School financing. *See* Revenue sources
School funds/funding. *see also* Revenue sources
    colonial education, 38
    increase in, 55
    shortage of, 11–12
School improvement plan, 376
School improvement process (SIP), 232, 334,
    364, 376
School improvement team (SIT), 251
School levels, 153–158
    early childhood education, 153–155
    elementary school, 155
    high school, 156–158
    middle level, 156

School of Education, University of the District
    of Columbia, 43
School Planning and Management Team
    (SPMT), 365
School politics, 253–254
School prayer, 266–267
School reform
    continuing pressures for, 372–374
    curriculum reform models, 364–366
    defined, 364, 372
    Essentialist Schools movement, 106
    high school, 157
Schools. *see also* High schools; Public schools
    characteristics of effective, 375
    charter, 148, 149, 150
    common elementary (colonial), 38
    dame, 37
    effective, 375–379
    elementary, 155, 232
    high-quality, 375–376, 380
    influences on curriculum, 334–335
    Jesuit, 32–33
    Latin grammar, 30, 37, 39
    magnet, 148, 149, 160
    monitorial (colonial), 38
    Montessori, 154
    need for more, 54
    normal, 65, 66
    online, 139–140
    organization chart, 231–233
    organization of, 229–233
    parochial, 47, 151–152, 262–263
    private, 151–152
    public view of, 5–6, 7
    purposes of, 140–143
    Reggio Emelia, 155
    religion in, 186–187
    report cards, 255
    role in curriculum management, 343
    role of culture in, 143–146
    rural, 158
    secondary, 38–39
    single-sex, 152
    suburban, 158–159
    urban, 159–160
    virtual, 139–140, 148, 149–150
    year-round, 233
School/school district report cards, 255
School secretaries, 233
Schools in Need of Improvement (SINOI), 248
School vouchers, 148, 150
School year, length of, 374
Science class, 359
Science of Education (Herbart), 35
Science standards, 340
Science teachers, 10
Science, Technology, Engineering, and
    Mathematics (STEM), 365–366
Scopes, John, 267
Scopes Monkey Trial, 267
Scoville v. Board of Education (1970), 289
SEA (state education agency), 236
Searches, student, 284, 290
Secondary schools, 38–39
Second Morrill Act (1890), 53
Secretaries, school, 233
Section 504, Rehabilitation Act (1973), 53,
    272, 289
Secular, 186
Segregation, 267–270
Self-efficacy, 217
Self-esteem, 209
Self-regulated learning strategies, 352–353
Sensorimotor stage (Piaget), 68

CREDITS

Photo Credits

Monkey Business/Fotolia, pp. 2, 282; Triangle Images/Photodisc/Getty Images, pp. 7, 232; Alexander Raths/Fotolia, p. 8; Jake Johnson/ Dorling Kindersley, p. 10; Bob Daemmrich/PhotoEdit, pp. 17, 100; INTERFOTO/Alamy, p. 26; Lee Foster/Alamy, p. 29; North Wind/ North Wind Picture Archives, p. 35; Mary Evans Picture Library/Alamy, p. 40; North Wind Picture Archives/Alamy, p. 41 (top); Robert Martin/Alamy, p. 41 (bottom); Library of Congress Prints and Photographs Division Washington, p. 43; North Wind Picture Archives/The Image Works, p. 52; Courtesy of the Library of Congress, p. 55; Universal Images Group (Lake County Discovery Museum)/Alamy, p. 65; Bettmann/CORBIS, p. 68; Masterfile Royalty Free Division, p. 74; Ian Shaw/Alamy, p. 81; Paul Chesley/Getty Images, p. 96; Superstock/ Jupiter Images, p. 103; CandyBox Images/Shutterstock, p. 105; Thinkstock/Superstock, p. 109; Bob Nichols/USDA/NRCS/Natural Resources Conservation Service, p. 114; Banana Stock/Superstock, p. 121; Scott Cunningham/Merrill, pp. 129, 176, 300; Myrleen Pearson/ PhotoEdit, p. 131; Chris Schmidt/istockphoto, p. 138; ZUMA Wire Service/Alamy, p. 143; Michael Chamberlin/Fotolia, p. 147; Mark Medici/Silver Burdett Ginn/Pearson, p. 152; Margrit Hirsch/Fotolia, p. 158; Susan Law Cain/Shutterstock, p. 159; diego cervo/Fotolia, p. 164; Amy Myers/Fotolia, p. 180; Lon Diehl/PhotoEdit, p. 185; David Grossman/Alamy, p. 192; Yuri Arcurs/Fotolia, p. 196; Wavebreakmedia/ Shutterstock, p. 200 (top); Rob Crandall/The Image Works, p. 200 (bottom);Alexander Raths/Fotolia, p. 207; Radius Images/Alamy, p. 211; Annie Fuller/Pearson, p. 217; Jim West/Alamy, p. 224; Bob Daemmerich/The Image Works, p. 228; Lindasj22/Shutterstock, p. 239; siart/ Fotolia, p. 241; Karen Huntt/Alamy, p. 244; Jan Richter/istockphoto, p. 247; Imagesource/Glow Images, p. 258; Janine Wiedel Photoli- brary/Alamy, p. 264; Annie Griffiths Belt/Corbis, p. 265; © Myrleen Pearson/Alamy, p. 270; OJO Images Ltd/Alamy, p. 273; Mark Hirsch/ ZUMAPRESS/Newscom, p. 275; Steve Skjold/Alamy, p. 280; David Duprey/AP Images, p. 290; Anthony Magnacca/Merrill, pp. 294, 377, 379; Spencer Grant/PhotoEdit, p. 297; Chuck Kennedy/The White House/PSG/Newscom, p. 303; Corbis Bridge/Alamy, p. 305; Elena Rooraid/ PhotoEdit, p. 315; Rob Marmion/Shutterstock, p. 320; Hope Madden/Merrill, p. 330; Blend Images/Alamy, p. 334; AP Images, p. 339; Michelle D. Bridwell/PhotoEdit, p. 346; Image Source IS2/Fotolia, p. 351; Jeff Greenberg/PhotoEdit, p. 363; auremar/Shutterstock, p. 370; Mark Reinstein/The Image Works, p. 374; Michael Dwyer/Alamy, p. 378; Krista Greco/Merrill, p. 382.